Economic Engagements with Art

Economic Engagements with Art

Annual Supplement to Volume 31
History of Political Economy

Edited by Neil De Marchi and Craufurd D. W. Goodwin

Duke University Press
Durham and London 1999

Printed in the United States of America
on acid-free paper.
ISBN 0-8223-2632-9 (cloth)
ISBN 0-8223-2489-X (paper)
This is the 1999 supplement to
History of Political Economy, ISSN 0018-2702.

Contents

Part 2. Art and Economic Policy

Part 3. The Business of Art

Economic Engagements with Art

Introduction

Neil De Marchi

Engaging Art

There is a flourishing economics of the *arts*, while studies also abound of art *objects*, especially the production, rewards to their makers, and investment value thereof. All that, however, has arisen in the past four or five decades; historically, economists have not had much to say about art. Or so we were told by some colleagues who were sure we were mistaken in wanting to hold a conference on "Economists and Art, Historically Considered."

The Supposed Exceptionalism of Art

The warning had some warrant. The single most consistent interest displayed by economists across the centuries has been in pricing, and the valuation of art has generally been considered problematic for economic analysis. Why should this be? A painting—we shall be concerned mostly with paintings in this volume—is a durable good, and it yields services during its lifetime. The stream of yields, it is usually argued, can be compared with those from a riskless bond. It is true that the yield from owning and holding a painting is not registered in money terms. The benefits may reside in a painting's being regarded as valuable for aesthetic, instructional, or inspirational reasons; or it may be viewed as a means to distinction, or whatever else gives its owner pleasure (see Grampp 1989, 38). But for as long as it is held (neither sold nor discarded), the opportunity cost of its services has a lower bound set by the yield on the bond. As to the price it will fetch when it is again put on the market, in principle the same or a similar list of things that made its possession worthwhile are also relevant at resale. The weighted value put on all those factors by the market may differ from those that influenced its initial buyer and holder, and the "market's" view may have changed even if originally it coincided perfectly with the buyer's. Nonetheless, there will be a price at market, determined by the prevailing consensus among expert and interested parties (32). But if the prices of paintings are determinate, whence arises the widespread conviction that the pricing process itself is problematic?

We get some clues by looking at what economists and others have said over the years as to why art must be considered something out of the ordinary. At its clearest, the problem has been posed in this way: even if the prices of paintings are determinate, those prices do not obey the usual rules, or indeed any rule. First, then, what are the usual rules governing pricing? We may usefully begin with Ferdinando Galiani's views. All things, he insisted, are subject to order, and the general rule for valuation is that prices are due to scarcity and utility ([1751] 1923, 283). Even unique objects are no exception to this rule. Their prices, however, are determinate only to within a range. The lower bound is set by "the esteem of the seller" (in modern terminology, the seller's reserve price), and the upper bound by "the needs or desires of the buyers" (296). This rule holds, Galiani insisted, despite the fact that value will vary according to circumstances: "Values are varied, but not capricious" (294; see also 296).

Galiani nonetheless allowed one exception—fashion, which he judged "an affection of the brain," peculiar to Europeans (294). Although fashion does not affect objects universally agreed to be beautiful, such as gems and the precious metals, all others are subject to its influence. This set up a tension that Galiani himself did not resolve: for if fashion affects the esteem and desire for art objects, and fashion is understood in terms of disease, whimsicality, or irrationality, then the order in art prices may be difficult to discern, much less understand.

Adam Smith (1982, 358) made Galiani's account somewhat more precise. The expression of desire, he maintained, is conditional upon wealth, while the prices of unique objects are fixed by the selling method applied to such things, the auction. Consider a unique object that happens to take the fancy of two potential buyers equally. Its price will be determined by the relative power reflected in the buyers' respective means or "abilities." "The case is here the very same as at an auction": the highest bid will secure the object, and it will tend to go to the richest since "he is best able to bid high[e]st."

Michael White's chapter in this volume enables us to add nineteenth-century contributions to the discussion. As I interpret them, Nassau Senior, like Marshall much later in the century, took the grain market as the exemplar of a market where supply is temporarily fixed. Just as grain prices can be subject to speculative pressures because of the irregularity or uncertainty of supply, the prices of art objects, Senior suggested, "are subject to no definite rules"; they bear a "fancy price . . . a price depending principally on the caprice or fashion of the day."

Both Jevons and Marshall examined whether the two available theories of price—the cost of production theory, and the final degree of utility theory—can cope with unique objects. For the sake of brevity, I combine what are really two distinct lines of argument. If the prices of such objects are essentially "fancy prices," driven by desire, then the cost approach clearly fails. However, since unique objects (for which Marshall cites as example "old master paintings"), like labor, exhibit an all-or-nothing character on the supply side (supply is either one or zero), then there is no final degree of utility. No demand curve, therefore, can be drawn, and certainly not one undergirded by marginal utility thinking.

Jevons reluctantly acknowledged that art appeared to be an exception. Marshall also drew this inference, emphasizing, however, not uniqueness but the special character of art objects—that they "cannot be 'graded' at all" (cited by White, this volume). This caused fancy prices to be "a matter of accident," driven by the happenstance that a person of wealth attends an auction and is drawn to a particular object. Unique art objects certainly constitute an exception, Marshall concluded, but all art objects acquire their market values as a matter of accident; there is no theoretical rule that we can apply.

There is a single line to these observations. Galiani's strong hint of irrationality in art prices differs both from Senior's concern that speculation may control them and Marshall's ascription to them of a purely accidental character, but only in terms of where the emphasis is placed. Galiani was impressed by the power of fashion to render things valueless simply because they happen not to be new; Marshall was impressed by the fact that the price of the same object might differ in successive auctions. These views are still current. White refers to William J. Baumol's (1986, 10) well-known judgment that the prices of art objects are "inherently rudderless"; there are no "reliable forces pulling the actual prices" in the direction of an equilibrium determined, in the classical way, by responsiveness of supply. Investing in paintings therefore has the character of a "floating crap game."

What is truly curious about this story up through the nineteenth century is that the pricing of unique art objects lost its status as a valid subject of scientific investigation *because of* clarifications in economic theory. It was against the background of the most refined understandings of cost of production and marginal utility theories of pricing that the case of the unique object had to be deemed exceptional. But even in the eighteenth century, when strangeness and unaccountability rather than a clear set of analytical options defined exceptionality, art seemed not to fit.

Suspicion of Auctions

In part, this might be ascribed to the bad name carried by art auctions in England at the time, when they were quite unregulated. A government memorandum of 1741 complained that they were "a loss to the fair Trader," and were otherwise calculated "to take in the Ignorant or Unwary" (Pears 1988, 65). Much of the complaining may be ascribed to a widespread conviction that auctions were rigged—in particular, that the auctioneers made a practice of "puffing," or falsely bidding up prices with the assistance of henchmen in the audience. Auctioneers were also accused of promoting copies as originals.

This may have continued to Marshall's day. But that would not have stopped him from investigating auctions under ideal circumstances. A great deal has changed in art auctions (and antique auctions generally) over the past few decades, bringing the practice closer to ideal conditions. Problems of lack of information and of asymmetric information (about quality, for example) have been addressed in practical ways. Auction houses now stand behind what they offer.[1] This, as well as dis-

1. This refers to property that may turn out to be counterfeit and in general is meant to protect the buyer against fraud. Auction houses are careful to protect themselves against liability in matters of attribution.

closure (of the lower bound of reserve prices, and of experts' presale price estimates), has tended to widen participation and in the process probably has reduced the prevalence of blatant "rings" formed by members of the "trade."[2] In some locations, prices of art on sale must now be posted, and many are now available on the Internet, reducing the potential for unwarranted disparities;[3] moreover, on-line auctions have started, reducing those accidents of attendance that so troubled Marshall.

Analyzing Taste

Baumol's problem differs from Marshall's, though it is a natural extension of it. Baumol was interested in whether art might be considered a sound investment in strictly financial terms, but he was drawn to the conclusion that other factors appear to play the major role. What might those other factors be? In the eighteenth century they would have been bundled under the rubric "wants of the mind" or of the imagination—"capricious" or "unreasonable" demands in Smith's terminology. Imaginary needs are not subject to the same rules as strictly bodily needs, and for that reason they have always been a bit suspect. To describe them as rudderless is just a new way of saying they are at the mercy of whatever it is that moves "tastes" or "fancy."

But if the cost of production theory no longer anchors "market" prices—though it still did "natural" price, for Smith—then one needs a theory of taste. As Horace Walpole in 1779 explained to a friend, there is indeed an "imaginary" component to the prices of old paintings (quoted in Pears 1988, 103). It was Walpole's opinion, moreover, that

2. Legislation has not proved effective against buyers' rings, and gentlemen's agreements among insiders still operate, but wider participation outside the trade may have lessened their power to affect outcomes. The Uniform Commercial Code in the United States provides that sales will be with reserve unless explicitly announced otherwise, and Christie's, New York, actually advertises that the reserve will not be below the lower presale published estimate. Considerable research has been conducted into the "efficiency" of presale estimates. The evidence is mixed, but it seems fair to say that if predictions are not fully "rational," they often come close. Certainly there is not the total absence of order in pricing suspected by some of our nineteenth-century observers.

3. New York State law requires that dealers post the prices of art objects on sale, a requirement that encourages obfuscation as to what exactly is on sale. ArtNet, however, publicizes selling prices and enables potential buyers to inquire about differences that seem unwarranted. (Weisberg 1999 gives some casual evidence of price differences for the same print on offer being narrowed in this way, and one would expect the effect to become much stronger.)

the high prices he had observed in the mid-1770s were due to "opulence and rage for virtu" (103). This rage for virtue, meaning a taste for excellence, combined several strands. These included revivals of Greek notions of propriety and beauty, of classical rules governing poetic composition, and of the mid-seventeenth-century French view that the highest aim of a painter should be to represent poetic conceits, preferably in an elevating manner. Auctioneers and dealers could not control such movements of thought; at most, they could play along with them. So in this instance the forces affecting the market prices of paintings were outside the control even of the direct players in the art market. Galiani's suggestion about the role of fashion made thirty years earlier was a generic form of that diagnosis; and Baumol's use of the descriptor "rudderless" is just another way of saying that economists feel at a loss if prices reflect influences for which economic theory supplies no explanation.

But eighteenth-century "economists" did not all feel that way. Indeed, many among them—particularly Scottish, but many English thinkers, too—thought it both important and possible to investigate taste as part of moral philosophical inquiry. For writers and thinkers such as Richard Steele, analyzing taste was a matter of finding categories in terms of which criticism might proceed. Taste was part of rational discourse and was shaped by communication. "It is a very good service one man renders another," he wrote, "when he tells him the manner of his being pleased" (quoted by Bryce, editor's introduction to Smith 1985, 29). Hugh Blair, Adam Smith's student in Edinburgh in the late 1740s, and subsequently professor at the University of Edinburgh, added important nuances to this. Taste, Blair seemed to argue, in effect comprises the capability to criticize appropriately, while such just criticism depends on understanding the manner of manufacture of the object of one's criticism. In his own words: "Whatever enables genius to execute well, will enable taste to criticise justly" (quoted by Bryce, 29).

Taste, criticism, and the knowledge of how things are made were all related in Adam Smith's theory of preference. The "ground of preference," he suggested, is to be found in the pleasure we derive from four characteristics of objects: their form, color, rarity, and ingenuity of design and manufacture (their "imitation") (Smith 1982, 337, 488). Smith is here principally concerned with objects of "art," meaning goods contrived, rather than naturally available to us. Taste and criticism enter because the sensual and mental pleasures we enjoy from objects made are inevitably matters of degree, and this will vary with the nature and measure of form, ingenuity, and so on. We must try various forms and judge their effects. Thus, repeated simple forms, for example, quickly bore us; but forms so complex that they cannot be grasped at a glance merely confuse and decrease our pleasure. There is a range, then, from the simple and repetitious to highly elaborated figures, and in that range pleasure at first increases, then diminishes. Appropriate form, it follows, lies within the range and enables us to maximize our pleasure. Comparable stories can be told of two of the other characteristics of contrivances that yield us pleasure: color and ingenuity. Rarity, however, is prized for the distinction it brings an owner, and it is not clear that this pleasure has a maximum.

David Hartley (1749, quoted in Ashfield and de Bolla 1996, 103), Smith's contemporary, suggested that the problem of declining pleasure can sometimes be avoided altogether, or at least staved off for long periods. For example, a scene that gives us great pleasure can quickly become familiar, but if we allow intervals of time between viewings, we bring to each one a different state of mind, and we can attend to different elements of the scene at each viewing. Here our pleasure is renewed, the familiar is made novel again and again, and we are thereby enabled to sustain the maximum of pleasure.

Is this analysis really of importance? Smith (1982, 336–37) thought so, because it explains choice and division of labor. We desire novelty; moreover, we seem driven to make unceasing refinements upon things naturally available to us. These two drives, in turn, become the basis for our preferences among objects, turning them into "goods" for us. To gratify our preferences—our "frivolous distinctions and preference[s] in things otherwise equall"—almost all of the arts and sciences have been invented. It is preferences, then, that decide directions of specialization and invite division of labor, while division of labor is the main determinant of growth in income.

In short, taste for the eighteenth-century British man of letters was not obscure, unimportant to material concerns, or incapable of being analyzed. It was a natural focus for (a) characterizing objects, (b) understanding what it is about them that makes them goods to us, and (c) assessing how well they satisfy us in this or that configuration of their characteristics. In addition, and because of the links between preferences, choice, and specialization, it was a wholly natural preoccupation for economists.

Nonetheless, this interest in preferences and taste has been lost from economics, though it survived outside the economics discipline, in nineteenth- and some twentieth-century psychobiological research, in the work of Wilhelm Wundt and D. E. Berlyne (see De Marchi and Van Miegroet, this volume). In art criticism, however, a similar interest both preceded that shown in it by people like Smith and was refined in the late seventeenth century in ways that make it very accessible still. The initiator of this "modern" form was Roger de Piles (1635–1709), French art critic and adviser. De Piles saw clearly that taste or criticism involves two processes. First, we must develop categories that reveal the "art" of an object, or characterize it in terms that enable us to know it for the thing it is—a poem, a painting, a cloak. Second, we reveal our taste via just criticism: by evaluating in appropriate ways the measure in which any particular object displays the characteristics of its family sort. These evaluations may reflect our personal biases, or those of a whole group, but in either case to be just they may not be arbitrary.

De Piles (1708) constructed a famous table in which he evaluated the performance of fifty-six of the most prominent painters, on a scale of zero through twenty, in each of four characteristics: design, composition, coloring, and expression. These characteristics summed up the "art" of painting, while the evaluations expressed a particular taste.

Figure 1 is an adaptation of this table to diagrammatic form, with the four characteristics listed along the vertical axis and the scale of values along the horizontal. Individual paintings, as well as artists, can be diagrammed for comparative purposes in this two-dimensional space, though the categories will not be fixed for all time or be appropriate to all paintings. My two-dimensional construct compares two seventeenth-century painters, by way of illustration. One, Nicolas Poussin, worked in the classicized Italianate mode popular in official Paris during the second half of the seventeenth century. The other, David II Teniers, a Flemish court painter to Archduke Leopold Wilhelm, regent of the southern Netherlands, made works of many sorts, including peasant scenes. His peasant scenes, in particular, disobeyed many of the precepts followed by Poussin. I have used de Piles's numerical valuations in each case.

Without going into more detail, it should be evident that this adapted de Piles construct does several useful things. Each line defines the critical reception of painting of a specific sort, according to a par-

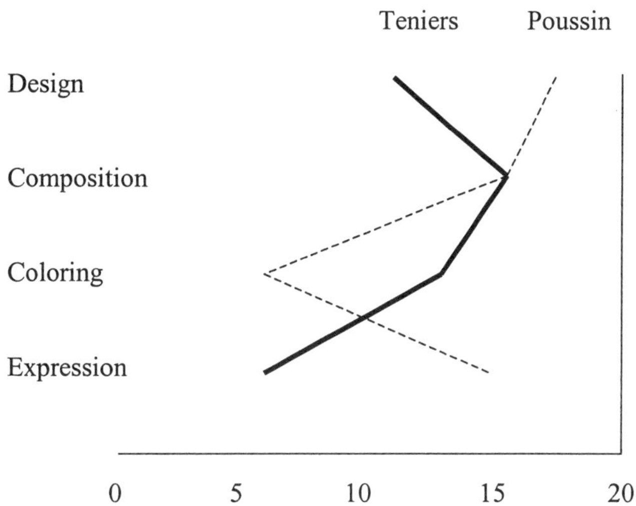

Figure 1 De Piles's critical characterization of the work of Poussin and Teniers.

ticular taste. This critical reception is defined in space relative to "perfection" (here shown by the right-hand vertical). First, then, we are able to depict both the familiar and the acceptable in terms of our two dimensions. The farther to the left the line describing performance in a particular painter or a specific work lies, the closer it is to being outside the range of the familiar, the recognizable, the acceptable. Second, it is because we possess analytical categories—the characteristics—that we can compare various individual instances of the art of painting. That is what a comparison of any two examples of painting involves, and such comparisons lie at the heart of criticism. Without the abstract categories, no criticism would be possible since no mechanism for comparing would exist. But such comparisons can also be stretched to include radically different versions of painting—the novel and truly innovative versus the conventional or the fashionable, for example. In other words, and third, the construct shows us just how much ground has to be covered, and in which directions, before the radically new can become the familiar and accepted. In these three ways the diagram becomes a flexible instrument embodying the notion of just criticism and expressing both familiarity and difference.[4]

Whether or not de Piles's prejudices were shared, his technique for comparison and criticism found immediate acceptance in Great Britain. Jeremy Bentham (1827, 81 n) observed that "copies after copies" of it, adaptations galore, had appeared over the course of the eighteenth century, including "a tabular sketch exhibiting some of the most eminent characters amongst the judges and lawyers of the day." Smith took direct from de Piles the categories he used in his own discussions of painting (and paintings) in his essay on the imitative arts. Hester Thrale, friend of Reynolds and of Samuel Johnson, in a more playful exercise not meant to see the light of day, applied the joint notion of categories and assessment to the various members of the Johnson literary circle. She compared them on such characteristics as their knowledge, wit, religious conviction, manner, humor, and so on (Balderston 1942, 1:329). Bentham himself, in his *Rationale of Judicial Evidence* (1827, 81 n), recommended de Piles's method for improving the way witness testimony can be weighed. He greatly admired it, as being "among the first" attempts at putting numbers to "psychological quantities."

The de Piles method has reentered economics in recent years, through the approach to choice of Kelvin Lancaster (1971, 1991). Lancaster has proposed that objects be analyzed into characteristics and that preferences be thought of as being formed over bundles of characteristics. In work based on his suggestions, characteristics are allowed to be present in varying degree. In turn, hedonic price indexes have rendered operational the idea of choice over characteristics, and hedonic regressions are now frequently used in attempts to account for variations in art prices. Nonetheless, this differs from the critical tradition in which price, far from being the variable to be explained, is just one characteristic of an object. Even if price is not considered to be an aspect of the "art" of painting, it may well be a defining characteristic for various specific types of painting. De Piles did not introduce price

4. On all these things, see the work of Bianchi (1998, 1999), who has done the most to develop and apply to the economics of goods this way of thinking, which she calls, following Kress and Van Leeuwen (1996), a "markers of modality" approach.

into his table, but in negotiations for securing paintings by Rubens for his client the duc de Richelieu, price certainly figured prominently in the assessment.[5] Focusing on choice over characteristics that are *given*, moreover, severely limits the role that can be played by novelty and also deflects the question why some objects, but not all, become goods to us.

This touches on a more general problem, allusions to which have been scattered throughout this account: we need to know *how* at least some of the objects available to us come to serve as goods in the sense that they meet our wishes and needs. Brian Loasby (1991, 28) reminds us that this was a concern of Carl Menger's, but he expresses it in his own words as the need to recognize that "goods are not basic; there are no goods without knowledge." Goods not only have to become goods but also can lose their goods status with us; to understand either process, we must possess knowledge of their characteristics and of the pleasures associated with each. The de Piles–Smith approach helps keep this in view.

In other words, there are still things of importance to be extracted from the critical approach. Not the least of these is the retrieval of the analysis of art preferences from the limbo into which economists are apt to cast them when intuitively reasonable explanatory variables fail to account for very much of the price variation of art objects. Certainly, the eighteenth-century experience suggests that tastes can be coherently addressed and need not be relegated to the realm of the irrational, the whimsical, the accidental, or the wholly incomprehensible.

Art and Economic Theory

The contributors to this volume did not go so far as to construct a framework for understanding taste. In fact, what most of them do is reinforce by example the impression that economists have long found art to be troublesome—not, in this case, that art prices know no rule; rather, that there is a gap between what the theory of price can *explain* and the sense that value is created by art. This is the gap of knowledge that Menger was hoping might be filled by economic analysis. In fact, the modern positivist movement in early-twentieth-century economics

5. So-called discrete choice models do allow price to enter utility functions, along with other characteristics. See Anderson, de Palma, and Thisse (1992, chap. 4).

altogether eschewed such exploration. The eighteenth-century practice of analyzing taste as a process of criticism and evaluation offers one way to narrow the divide, though it was not the solution chosen by any of the individuals studied in this section.

Zarinés Negrón's short note on Francisco Pacheco, teacher of Velasquez and artistic adviser to the Holy Inquisition in Seville, brings this out, though indirectly. She shows Pacheco probably borrowing from the School of Salamanca and formulating a sort of "just price" view of the pricing of necessaries. Painting, however, is not a necessary, and Pacheco finds it appropriate to stress that there are in paintings, and in the activity of painting, certain "intrinsic" qualities that require a modified formula for judging whether price is proper. What he looked for in addition to market factors, however, was not fashion, but "nobility"—that of the subject and of the artist's profession—and truth, which religion supplied as a complement to classical and humanistic ideals of beauty and human aspiration.

Bertil Fridén has Rousseau offering an account of the value of art, hence of paintings, that is similarly couched in terms remote from the language of the market. Rousseau's account is tempered by his awareness of ordinary human passions, but there are elements that bear directly on our inherited economic theory. For Rousseau, because paintings are non-necessaries, their *prices* turn out to be set quite arbitrarily. This is not because of fashion, but because fine paintings have envy value. Since quality (fineness) is judged by price, a high price invites envy and thus begets still higher prices. At the same time, art is at the core of the true riches of a nation. This is because to appreciate it requires the same imaginative (and projective) faculty as drives Smith's moral device, the impartial spectator. Art thus becomes an agent of morality and of what Rousseau calls the "social optimum."

Fridén concedes that Rousseau's economic views are more like flashes than worked-out theories, but a number of these flashes are tantalizing. One is Rousseau's notion that for art to become part of true riches it must be rendered exclusive. This is not a difficult requirement, since an ordering subject is required to personalize all possessions, paintings and other art objects included. Uniqueness, or active personalization, becomes Rousseau's paradigm for use. He therefore emphasizes what we might think of as the nonsatiation condition rather than the diminishing marginal utility aspect of consumption. Fridén refers in this context to Marina Bianchi's (1998) elucidation of the potential for increasing utility in consumption as consumers reorder and so in a sense re-create their goods.

The next three essays are all in varying degree concerned with Jevons. Jevons had trouble with art. I have referred already to Michael White's discussion, showing that Jevons could accept neither the cost of production account of the price of unique objects nor his own final degree of utility theory. Without marginal utility or, in Marshall's version, because art objects are not easily graded, there could also be no demand curve. Comparisons based on quality might be made, but then it is the ranking procedure used that accounts for the demand curve, not marginal utility theory. The upshot, Jevons ruefully concluded in his *Principles of Economics*, was that there could be "no approach to rule or congruity" in such cases. "No consideration of cost of production or utility can apply; the arbitrary fancy of some monarch or wealthy person is the only rule" (quoted in White, this volume, 72). We are back with arbitrariness.

Harro Maas extends White's analysis, suggesting that, had Jevons drawn a utility of labor diagram for the artist (or philosopher, or creative scientist), the result would have been equally disturbing to his utility theory, for these occupations can yield ever-increasing satisfaction. But then truly inventive capabilities, too, Jevons thought, are inexplicable, just like the prices of art. Perhaps as a way of salvaging something from inexplicability, he separated the creative few from the many and insisted that, for the latter, mental powers should be thought of as just as mechanical and routine as manual operations. Routine labor, moreover, was a necessary discipline, and therefore the factory system, despite its acknowledged social ills, was also valuable. The great social problem remaining was how to routinize in the same way the leisure time of workers—above all, to prevent the mental wastage caused by drinking and "riotous and vicious assemblages." Jevons's solution here was music—not the music of high art, but the music that conduces to absence of thought: literally, tranquilizing music. Maas sets Jevons's view alongside the view of routine labor held by John Ruskin. Ruskin deplored the crushing of the universal creative impulse that resulted whenever labor was required to perform like a machine: to be as accurate as tools, precise, and in every way perfect. He therefore wished to undo the factory system altogether. The contrast could not be greater.

Bert Mosselmans and Ernest Mathijs offer a rather different perspective on Jevons. Basing themselves on unpublished manuscript material by him, in particular fragments and a chapter on music from what they conclude was part of his project for a "science of man," they find evidence that Jevons considered music and some of the other arts to have an intellectual component. Although Jevons thought of much music as being just a temporary distraction from other preoccupations, a kind of tranquilizer, Mosselmans and Mathijs stress that he also insisted, even if in terms that remain somewhat obscure, that music pertains to the "essential" pleasures of humankind and that the higher sorts of music, like poetry and mental pictures of beauty, involve both "memory and understanding." The essential pleasures are those capable of elevating the human spirit. Jevons seems to have had in mind here the traditional hierarchy of genres of the connoisseur of painting. In this ranking, "history" paintings (biblical and mythological)—which represent some poetic conceit pertaining to the human condition, human aspirations, or achievements—stand highest; scenes of everyday life and still lifes are lowest, and portraits lie somewhere in between. Indeed, poetry stood very high in Jevons's estimation, as did music with words. Both convey emotion, and both approach, though they remain below, science and metaphysics, perhaps also religion, as supplying objects of contemplation.

Jevons appears to have been groping toward categories and distinctions that had been common in the eighteenth century. One of these is the distinction between surprise (or wonder) and admiration. He spoke of the pleasure and of "a sort of confident moral strength" that arises on encountering anything—music, poetry, scenery, perhaps an architectural or engineering work—that holds "a degree of fresh interest, beauty or grandeur." These feelings do not last, though Jevons also considered that a "sense" for music, once developed, becomes part of a person. Perhaps this was something like the "habitual" human capital of George J. Stigler and Gary S. Becker (1977, reprinted in Becker 1996). Jevons's notion of transience in pleasure may be compared with Adam Smith's suggestion that the pleasure of surprise we feel when we encounter objects of beauty or grandeur is probably at its maximum at the very first moment of encounter, after which it declines. But Smith also held, in language more focused than Jevons's vague suggestion about an appropriable "sense," that as mere wonder gives way to awe, respect, admiration—above all, to understanding—so pleasure increases again. For Smith (1985, 69), however, this pleasure also reaches a maximum, after which it declines. David Hartley, as we have seen, offered an alternative to this last and at the same time a different possible challenge to Jevons's notion that our pleasures are transient. This sort of insight has recently been incorporated—in this case by Becker alone (see 1996, 119)—into an expanded notion of preferences, in which what are short-term substitutes become, with time lags, "complementarities" of consumption. The latter can involve increasing marginal utility (78). Rousseau's hint about increasing satisfaction in consumption through personalization of goods and the ways we connect goods in use seems to lead in the same direction.

Should we read Jevons as having wanted to make concessions to the power of fancy without quite knowing how to knit an eighteenth-century analytical approach to taste with late-nineteenth-century price analysis? Mosselmans and Mathijs give us one clue that this may have been the case, but leave its interpretation open. They draw our attention to an unpublished note by Jevons in which he observed that, while it may be useless from a utilitarian point of view to produce objects of agreeable and beautiful shape yet, as we have become more and more refined, so "more and more *value*" (my emphasis) has come to depend on such characteristics.

Craufurd Goodwin's contribution explores a set of fascinating attempts to come to grips with just that sort of observation. Roger Fry, art critic, friend of Keynes, essayist on art and civilization, and a figure of some importance in the art market and art world of the first half of the twentieth century, simply accepted that art increases "value" and ran with the idea. So also did two somewhat younger men whom Fry influenced greatly, Clive Bell and Kenneth Clark. But they understood value in a sense that transcended the market. All three held that art is the great carrier of human progress, though each defined advance in the human condition in somewhat different terms. If it is fair to combine their views into a single proposition, they stood for the notion that civilization lies with the imaginative life. That is where one finds science, contemplation, and art, each pursued for its own sake. Applications of social value may not be obvious or forthcoming in the short run, but both independence of spirit and true creativity reside in the imaginary life. And there alone genuine aesthetic emotion is communicated between artists and the consumers of art. The tension that seems to have tormented Jevons (Fry, Bell, and Clark held) must be resolved in favor of what Walpole had called "imaginary," rather than utilitarian, value.

Though Fry might have disagreed, it seems plain that he (and the other two) stood in the same tradition with respect to the roots of civilizing progress as Mill, the tortured Jevons, their own friend Keynes, and Lionel Robbins (as Márcia Balisciano and Steven G. Medema show in their chapter in part 2 of this volume). But Fry did not experience their struggles in reconciling this conviction with costs and efficiency—the concomitants of scarcity. Fry simply relegated economics to the realm of survival and the struggle for basic goods, a solution Keynes also adopted, though he viewed the downgrading of economics as a realistic possibility only for the world that would be inhabited by "our grandchildren," *after* the problem of scarcity had been solved.

Like Keynes, Fry was at various times a serious player in the art market and knew better than to think that art could simply ignore the market. He had a great deal to say about the constraints and assistance the market gave to art and artists, and he dwelt at length on those aspects of the market that public and private initiatives needed to understand better and exploit, to the advantage of the imaginative life. Goodwin suggests that Fry would like to have found in psychology an account of the creative moment and of the transformation of artistic insight into product—a sort of psychology of art supply. Since none was developed, he turned to the demand side and gave us a detailed typology of consumers of art, which Bell applied to public policy toward the arts and Clark applied to the evolution of art and civilization. Fry's key category of consumer was the middle-class aesthete, a group whom he believed could be nurtured to perceive and to want genuine art. The implications for public policy toward the arts are not entirely clear, and there seem to have been differences of emphasis between Fry, Bell, and Clark on this end of things. But Fry's free use of a supply-and-demand framework, unhindered by the strictures applying to "deeper" explanations of price, makes refreshing reading.

Art and Economic Policy

Policy is the focus of the next group of five essays. Two of these address British concerns, two detail American concerns, and one offers us a political economy perspective of part of the Hilton hotel empire.

Helen Rees notes the conflicting pressures experienced by British landed families in the final decades of the nineteenth century and shows deftly how these shaped a debate over private responsibility in respect of property—pictures—that the nation had begun to regard as part of its patrimony. After centuries during which aristocratic virtues of stability and disinterestedness had been reinforced by legal constraints on the settlement of property, a sustained agricultural depression had strained the resources of many families. The Settled Lands Act of 1882 allowed for the first time, and under certain conditions, the sale of land and "hierloom" property. This brought much-needed relief, but it also "signaled a decline in both the usefulness and the authority of land, and by implication, in the aristocratic virtues." Then, and as part of a wholesale revision of inheritance taxation, the Finance Act of 1894 imposed graduated death duties, but in the process made available a pretext—fiscal pressure—"to justify the disposal of property that had been facilitated by the . . . Act."

In the twenty-five years to 1915 hundreds of "important pictures" left Great Britain, many sold by landed families under the new dual conditions of enablement-plus-incentive. Two much publicized examples, Rembrandt's *Mill*, which was lost, and Holbein's *Christina of Denmark*, saved at the last minute after a successful public appeal, concentrated attention on the "Old Masters problem." A committee to inquire into this question was appointed by the National Gallery, under Lord Curzon. This committee addressed the problem as one of bringing together a new coalition between owners (the declining landed interest), experts (the art business), and the nation (represented by the state-appointed keepers of the patrimony, the National Gallery Trustees). The committee recommended that property rights be respected by allowing the trade in paintings to be unfettered. But as a concomitant of this, the state should provide the means to buy paintings at risk of being exported, funds being supplied with the help of a new tax on sales at auction, and the earmarking of death duties payable on works of art. Fry was among the witnesses who appeared before the committee.

Two chapters by William Barber follow. The first recounts the history of U.S. tariffs on imported art, to 1913. Unimportant in the larger picture of protection against industrial imports, the U.S. tariff on imported art nonetheless came to be regarded by the arts community as "a litmus test of the government's posture toward the nation's cultural life." The tariff dated from the founding of the Republic, but it was investigated anew as part of a general tariff review in 1882, the year of the Settled

Lands Act in Great Britain. The coincidence is doubly striking since the outcome of the investigation also had implications for the "Old Master problem" in Great Britain. The tariff probably prevented some works from leaving for the United States. The committee to inquire into the tariff heard arguments of extraordinary variety, including a view to the effect that the then-prevailing duty, at 10 percent, was too low. The argument was that a low duty plays into the hands of those who think American art inferior. Dealers who, with a 10 percent duty, continue to flood the American market with cheap and inferior European imports, claiming these as significant works warranting a price that included the tariff, would be deterred by a 40 percent tariff, to the benefit of local artists.

The committee of experts recommended a general reduction in tariffs, but Congress saw fit to raise the tariff on imported art to 30 percent, and this position survived challenge until, in the mid-1890s, the duty was suddenly dropped to zero. This was reversed in 1896, and a duty was reinstated, at 20 percent, though with the traditional exemption for works by American artists abroad. The rate was reduced to 15 percent in 1909, but there was also an important new provision: works over twenty years old were added to the free list. This meant, however, that only contemporary art was penalized, and a further campaign, headed by canny and well-connected lawyer-collector of French avant-garde paintings, John Quinn, resulted in a new law exempting all "original" works of whatever age.

There are several nice aspects to this history. For a long time, as Barber notes, artists were advocating free trade in paintings, but the politicians, perhaps unaccustomed to an industry asking *not* to be protected, did not hear. Equally curious were the arguments that were unconsciously resurrecting older debates. One, already discussed in connection with the 1882 review, urged that a low duty merely encouraged unscrupulous dealers to import "bogus pictures" but pass them off on the ignorant as paintings worth paying the tariff to acquire. Here quality was ostensibly at issue, but the real point of the argument was that the low tariff was fostering the prejudice that modern American paintings were inferior to older European works. Local artists suffered unnecessarily from this prejudice, and the low tariff made their situation worse. Virtually the same scenario was played out in Amsterdam in 1608, when dealers from the southern Netherlands were said to be importing bogus paintings—"mostly copies," "poor student work," "mere trash"—and selling them (in this case illegally) "far above their worth" to those unable to judge quality (De Marchi 1995). In Amsterdam, prohibition rather than a higher tariff was the solution advocated. But this is a difference of degree only between the two situations; the circumstances, and the response, were the same. As in the American case, quality was ostensibly what bothered the Amsterdam artists; protecting their livelihoods was of greater importance.

Another twist is to be found in the argument that levying a duty only on contemporary work was a mistake since competitiveness in products required that a country be open to all currents in design. A similar argument, though in reverse, was employed in England several times during the first half of the eighteenth century. If prints facilitate the dissemination of industrial design, a group of British designers argued in 1735, then designers who publish their own prints should be protected against pirate printers. Such protection would help ensure that only the best versions of a design would be made public and that British luxury products would remain preeminent (Clayton 1997, 83). Circumstances here clearly differed, but there is also a common element: a real or supposed threat to national competitiveness. In the American case, this arose supposedly because the tariff on modern works needlessly hindered access to good, recent foreign design; in the British case, the threat allegedly emanated from a failure to protect the domestic inventor-publishers of original work.

Yet a third curious element in the American story is that, as Barber points out, when Congress agreed to eliminate the discrimination on recent works, not by making them free goods but by exempting all "original" art, it was in effect embarking on a form of quality control. Direct quality control was a medieval concern of guilds, but as the guilds declined in influence and as cost of materials became a less important component of price, quality came to be most conveniently measured simply by a work's having been made by an accredited master. Originality was reserved as the province of masters, an acknowledgment of the inventiveness they had acquired through long honing of taught skills. Claims on behalf of ingenuity became, in this way, part of an argument favoring "liberal" status for the art of painting and an implicit claim on behalf of preserving traditional master-journeyman payment differentials in a time of declining guild authority (De Marchi and Van Miegroet 1996). In modern America, the equivalent claim (even if only implicit) was for some sort of professional, or at least status, recognition. Congress's apparent intervention on behalf of quality, then, in fact amounted to acknowledging that there is a difference—all measurement difficulties aside—between the creative artist and the mere copyist, and that creativity should not be discouraged.

In all three instances singled out here, and allowing for differences of circumstance, there seems to have been something at work like spontaneous institutional regeneration. New rules for the market game are not tried once only, it seems, but reappear, perhaps in modified form, as conditions require. The regulations and institutions of the art market are no exception.

Barber's second contribution chronicles U.S. federal government patronage of the arts during the Great Depression. This account can also be used as a source for the spontaneous regeneration hypothesis, but Barber's own interpretation is that hidden in the history is a novel argument for state patronage. That case is usually made in terms of the "public good" character of art, an argument that many economists find not wholly convincing. But in the circumstances of the 1930s, Keynes urged the need for increased spending, even if this meant less saving in the short term. He also envisaged that redistributive taxation in favor of those who typically spent a larger share of their income would add permanently to the demand for goods and might help prevent the slump from acquiring a secular character. One downside to this, however, would be that the wealthy would be less able to act as patrons of the arts. Just as the state might be needed to centralize investment plans to avoid recurrent failures of nerve on the part of private investors, so, too, the state might reasonably be expected to pick up portions of this patronage function. Keynes used this rationale to support the Arts Council of Britain. The case for state support of the arts here is made in terms of trade-offs; it is not necessary to suppose that indirect social benefits flow from art. If sustained high employment is necessary for social stability, and this stability is incompatible with allowing the rich to keep the means to act as patrons, then state support of the arts may be part of the trade-off. This argument was not developed within the Roosevelt administration, which always saw public support for the arts as a temporary expedient; but whether it would have found broad support is doubtful.

An economist who at the time opposed Keynes on the nature of and responses appropriate to the Great Depression was Lionel Robbins. But Robbins also acquired a taste for the arts and urged that since the arts, like pure science, add quality and meaning to life, they are proper objects of state support. There are echoes of Fry and his followers here, though they opposed state funding as likely to be bad for quality. Moreover, Robbins imposed a double obligation on himself. First, he needed to find an economic basis for state funding, if one was to be discovered. Second, he needed to attend to the objections of those who, like Fry, feared that circumstances which are too cozy tend to be bad for the production of genuine art, and of those who asked why there should be any interference with the market. The theme of Balisciano and Medema's chapter is how Robbins found a point of balance for himself as economist and as citizen.

Robbins was not persuaded by the argument that attending to the aesthetic aspect of life will increase the national product. Indeed, though he appealed to Smith's third duty of the state—to erect and maintain certain public works and institutions not in the private interest—his defense of public support for the arts was made in terms of the need for "high excellence in culture." The case was equated with that for supporting basic research. Even if no claim can be made for immediate or material benefits, yet to insist that therefore basic research should be left to fend for itself simply made no social sense and suggested a poor grasp of the history of civilizations. Thus, although Robbins conceded that scientific economics might have little to say about whether art should or should not be financially encouraged, choices have to be made in society, and these cannot all be made using the insights of economics alone. Once having determined that state support is proper, however, Robbins urged that arts *policy* be conducted using all the insights that can be gleaned from economics.

In the final chapter of this section, Annabel Wharton invites us to consider particular aspects of the eastward expansion of the Hilton hotel chain in the Cold War 1950s. Certain politically and strategically sensitive countries were chosen: Greece, Egypt, and Turkey. As Conrad Hilton tells the story in his autobiography, the Hilton organization was encouraged by the U.S. State Department and the Department of Commerce to expand into "important world cities," as a contribution to the U.S. program of foreign aid. The exact intent, and the full extent of the encouragement, remain to be ascertained, though Marshall Plan funds heavily contributed to the Istanbul Hilton. In any case, powerful influences are suggested by the prime sites made available, the strikingly modernist Western designs used, and the extraordinary terms on which Hilton was able to build. He was able to select his own sites and architects and to control specifications, materials, and furnishings, while all costs were borne by the local owners; yet a third of the gross profits went to Hilton International with no capital investment. The Cairo, Istanbul, and Athens Hiltons were symbols of American culture and commercial prowess, beacons of these things to local observers, but also engines for meeting the needs of American business travelers and growing numbers of middle-class tourists. Thus Wharton refers to the hotels as architectural spectacles, which yet carried the message of a "modern aesthetics of quality" and of a "remarkably effective commoditization of space."

The Business of Art

The final group of contributors addresses how artists saw themselves and were regarded by others. Some also take up the matter of how the proper pricing of and spending on art has been considered historically, while several provide examples of making and consuming art, in both public and private ways, all with ties to economic thinking.

Toon Van Houdt asks why early humanists had relatively little to say about art and concludes that this had a lot to do with the way they viewed artists—as manual workers. This changed over the course of the sixteenth and seventeenth centuries, but a large gap remained. The distance meant that most men of letters were unable to discuss typical features of art or to capture at all adequately the multiple aspects of an artist such as Rubens, who was also businessman and diplomat, as well as something of a scholar in his own right. Nevertheless, Van Houdt focuses on a group of southern Netherlandish humanists from the late sixteenth and early seventeenth centuries, considering what they had to say about art under three heads: What was the social status and economic position of the artist? What did they say about the valuation of art objects? How was the consumption of art viewed, and along with it spending and virtuous princely conduct more generally?

In the early sixteenth century, artists were considered to occupy an intermediate position—between craftsmen on the lower side, and men of letters on the upper. This was because art involved manual labor, but also mind. Increasingly, however, the mental received more emphasis; and the humanist Beyerlinck, even as early as 1631, acknowledged that painting depends primarily on the mind. There is good and bad painting, and the good reflects both divine inspiration (*genius*) and talent (*ingenium*). However, it was also acknowledged that artists make art in order to sell with gain; hence, their reward comprises profit as well as wages, and, accordingly, they were regarded as businessmen or *negotiatores*.

This raised questions about how art products should be valued. Cost of materials was no longer the main component in price, while profits typically were the result of fluctuations in the market that could not be wholly foreseen. Nor were art objects like victuals, whose just price was established by a common estimate—the informed judgment of participants in the market, taking all circumstances into consideration. Lessius recognized that public auctions, like the Friday Market in Antwerp, were an increasingly important avenue of selling, and prices there would depend on who happened to be present and what the mood of participants happened to be—just as Marshall judged was the case almost three centuries later. However, Lessius did not consider the pricing at auction of near-unique objects; for this we must turn to the late scholastic theologian Antoninus Diana, who treated unique items under the general category of luxury goods. He judged these to be priced appropriately when there is free bargaining because the buyer of a luxury item wants the purchase for his pleasure or to increase his splendor and cannot be considered easily exploited. If such a buyer pays more than the just price, the difference must be considered a sort of gift, as it often was when friends exchanged, or even when an artist or dealer sold to a regular client. Under these considerations, art objects could display sizable variations in price, but without these being viewed as improper.

Propriety, or morality, continued for years to condition thinking about art. Nobles were expected to display virtue through "magnificence," but humanists were expected to celebrate this virtue in their noble patrons; and they, as well as artists, were meant to contribute to the elevation of spirit that could come from contemplating their forebears' deeds, whether celebrated in word or images. There was thus an essentially moral function to the liberal arts, and the art of painting became in principle a sort of "moral *exemplum*." But this was also part of an exchange relationship, for artists "deserved to be protected and supported by wealthy, powerful, and educated patrons" (Van Houdt, this volume, 325). The consumption of art too therefore fell under these considerations.

In concluding, Van Houdt shows how Rubens, as artist-businessman and man of letters, exemplified much of the teaching of the humanists in his personal approach to negotiations over the value of art objects.

Guido Guerzoni gives an in-depth history of both magnificence and liberality, the latter a more private virtue, and explores in detail how these two notions shaped models of noble behavior and thus directed spending to the ends of splendor and luxury in fifteenth-century Italy. How these ancient notions were redefined during the Renaissance is of great importance to understanding how a morally safe path of consumption could be chosen, one between avarice and profusion. But magnificence and liberality were also interpreted to establish correct social distances between noble and patrician classes and the ordinary citizen, and within the ranks of the aristocracy itself. Perfect matches were sought between the quality of men and the quality of the things on which they spent.

Since objects were meant to reflect the status of the buyer, while the quality of the buyer was measurable in terms of how much was spent and for what purposes, an elaborate system of accounting was required. Grades and amounts of goods, and what they cost, had to be meticulously recorded for every member of the household or court. But this system also took the place of a market. Art objects had to be graded for their appropriateness and the status that they confirmed in the buyer.

This became the basis for an aristocratic hierarchy of genres for paintings, in which historical subjects, along with portraits and family or individual allegories of apotheosis, took pride of place. The system also meant that artists could not be rewarded simply either for their labor time or for any purely artistic qualities in their work. Rather, these elements had to be combined in a complex process of valuation that reflected the importance of the patron and the degree to which an acquired work properly confirmed that person's status. The gift aspect in the pricing of luxury goods identified by Antoninus Diana was embedded in Renaissance Italian court acquisitions and exchanges and applied wherever that model was adopted. Thus Emperor Charles V paid Titian a substantial sum for two portraits of himself, one a copy of an existing portrait by a German court painter, but he also invested him with a knighthood (Humfrey 1995, 164). This last was a proper display of liberality by the emperor in exchange for confirmation of his own worth, and at the same time an appropriate recognition of the artist's stature, even if he employed Titian partly to reproduce another's work.

This system was so cumbersome, and so fraught with possibilities for receiving or giving offense, that it was vulnerable to being toppled by something simpler, more open. By early in the seventeenth century, dealers had begun to appear in Rome and Venice, and the beginnings of an art market were evident.

The chapter by De Marchi and Van Miegroet brings us back to the question of ingenuity, already mentioned briefly in connection with the payment differential between masters and journeymen artists. Here, however, the connection is with pricing. The price of a rare object may differ considerably from cost, including under cost materials, and labor measured at the conventional wage rate for the sort of work involved. Both Adam Smith and his contemporary the artist Joshua Reynolds perceived this distinction. An artist of special abilities such as Reynolds could create one-of-a-kind pictures and drive a wedge between price and cost (again measuring wage or labor cost in terms of a conventional wage). The wedge actually captures the difference between the conventional reward to the artist and the reward extractable for special talent, so there is not, strictly speaking, any difference between price and cost, only a distinction between conventional and exceptional rewards to the artist. But there has to be a mechanism for extracting exceptional rewards. Reynolds can be viewed as having aimed at seducing the senses of his buyers to enable him to enhance the price of his paintings and thereby capture something like the reward due to exceptional talent. In these efforts, he exploited aspects of the making of pictures, since the seduction occurred with the help of special design qualities and the surface effects Reynolds created with paint and various mediums. For Smith, ingenuity in their contrivance was a distinctive characteristic of works of "art" from which we take pleasure. He even separated the pleasure of ingenious contrivance from any real convenience or use these objects may have. Smith and Reynolds not only shared this interest in ingenuity but also explained its appeal in similar ways—as the pleasure we feel at understanding unexpected cause-effect relations.

Smith's theory of pleasure in contrivance was intuitively grasped by Reynolds and put into practice by him. Sara Zablotney, in her contribution, draws on other evidence to show that Reynolds had a fine if intuitive understanding of the economics of the business of making and selling images. In negotiations with the print-publisher and entrepreneur John Boydell, Reynolds revealed that he understood clearly that the value of a painting made to serve as model for an engraving derives from the stream of income expected from sales of the prints taken from the block. Zablotney finds plenty of examples in Boydell's own practice to confirm the economic sophistication of participants in the eighteenth-century print trade.

The roles of ingenious artificer or "artist" and imaginative man of business were also combined in James Cox, jeweler and toymaker extraordinary. Marcia Pointon sees in Cox's museum of elaborate and decorative mechanical clocks, which was the talk of London for a few years during the 1770s, "a unique resource for examining art in relation to economics." She extracts from it a whole series of interesting observations.

First, Cox also proceeded from the insight that ingenuity indeed pleases and thereby creates value. Second, this value may be subjective, but Cox effectively claimed that it is nonetheless very real and also objectively measurable. He argued that by importing escapement mechanisms and using them in clocks made for export, and sold at greatly enhanced prices, to Eastern potentates, he was contributing positively to England's balance of trade. He was not only adding value to the escapements but also helping to reduce the flow of silver to the East to sustain imports from that quarter. Third, the value in contrivances or in art objects may be ephemeral. Cox's museum was short-lived; Reynolds's visual effects often were unstable and fleeting—his techniques resulted in cracking, sometimes in flaking of the paint itself, and frequently in loss of color. We are apt to deplore this, yet there is also something inevitable about the short-lived character of pleasure in contrivance. Smith (and others) acknowledged that we crave novelty. A consequence, however, is that value must be constantly re-created. That is part of the contribution of ingenuity. But Pointon notes that this line of thought also challenges the traditional ideal of the museum as a place where private capital is turned into "transcendent worth." Fourth, the same tradition also privileges painting over other visual media, whereas Cox's and other late-eighteenth-century museums displayed objects, not images, and had a greater impact on metropolitan audiences than did exhibitions of paintings alone. Cox was aware of this and actually embellished portraits of the king and queen made especially for his display with mechanical niceties—a mechnical band, for example, that played "God Save the King"—as a way of suggesting the superiority of his "artists" to those of the Royal Academy of Arts. Finally, Cox's clocks showed that economic value may reside partly in visual illusion; he both excited and exploited to the full the "imaginary" wants of his visitors.

A critical rethinking of the role of art is also a theme of Robert Leonard's narrative of the use made of modern German graphic art by the Vienna Circle socialist thinker and activist Otto Neurath (1882–1945) in his efforts to create a new socialist sensibility among workers. Neurath considered imagery a way to convey pleasantly and effectively to those accustomed to the cinema and visual illustration key features of the economy. He viewed the economy itself not in terms of metaphysical and premodern entities—utility and money, respectively—but as a set of social engineering relations: "people, things, and their arrangement." He observed wartime planning and control in the Balkan states in 1912–13 and noted that during war (a) profit considerations took second place to production and efficiency and (b) barter could replace monetary exchange without apparent disruption being caused to allocative needs. The theme of the efficacy of central planning without prices informed Neurath's work as an organizer in southern Saxony after World War I, and at that time he also started using "statistical tables and models designed to show the mechanism of the economy in conditions of war."

Neurath's thinking also developed into a sharp critique of orthodox economics, along strict positivistic lines. He wished to avoid all nonempirical terms, such as utility or mind, and all pretense that we are able to supply deep explanations to surface phenomena. "Reality," therefore, was also a banished referent. So, too, was "optimum," though for the additional reason that it implied that there exists a single, determinate measure of well-being. Instead, Neurath insisted that economic means are plastic, possible futures many, and that the social engineer can capture in descriptive, visual statements people in circumstances of greater or less happiness, without our having to define this notion or pin it down in some abstract manner. His economic ideas brought him into conflict with the Von Mises circle and with Friedrich Hayek, whose *Road to Serfdom*, though ostensibly a corrective for well-meaning but misguided English socialists, was largely directed against Neurath (Uebel 1998).

The art Neurath adopted was meant to reflect his economic and epistemological convictions. It was to depict things, and people in relation to things, consistently with his new view of the economy, or what he liked to call "physicalist sociality." One symbol meant a given number, so that larger and smaller quantities could be seen at a glance, and the symbols should be chosen so as to fix an impression: rows of black coffins and white babies, for example, stand for deaths and live births. No interpretation should be needed, the imagery being its own explanation. This art obeyed different laws than those of creative painting. As Neurath's chief graphic designer after 1928, the German Gerd Arntz, put it: "The proportions are given through the reality of the quantity of things, and a harmonization is not possible on the surface of [a] chart, if the content is to be shown with all its contrasts."

This was didactic art in the service of political and social ends, and intended to both inform and energize its viewers. Its motivating force therefore was quite distinct from Jevons's music as distraction for the mind or Fry's "genuine" art as nurturing, civilizing force. But its import was clear, in the same way as the early postwar Hiltons were unmistakably emblematic of American culture and commerce or as Cox's ingenious contrivances signaled the superior British blend of design and mechanical prowess in luxury goods. Of course, Neurath's hoped-for effects moved in a quite different direction from these symbolic displays, but he knit together economic thinking and imagery quite as completely as did Reynolds, Cox, and Boydell.

Conclusion

We have seen in a variety of ways and contexts that writers on economics have consistently found themselves conflicted over art. On the one hand, art is acknowledged to possess and convey civilizing value. On the other, no place for it has been found in economic analysis. Economists are left with a choice. They can develop terminology such that the social, historical, aesthetic, symbolic, or other sorts of value added by art can be discussed and decisions affecting resources can be made in terms comparable to measured, market value. Or they must accept to exclude this whole realm, in the same way as an exclusive focus on known costs automatically limits any serious discussion of novelty.

References

Anderson, Simon P., André de Palma, and Jacques-François Thisse. 1992. *Discrete Choice Theory of Product Differentiation*. Cambridge, Mass.: MIT Press.

Ashfield, A., and P. de Bolla. 1996. *The Sublime*. Cambridge: Cambridge University Press.

Balderston, Katherine C., ed. 1942. *Thraliana. The Diary of Mrs. Hester Lynch Thrale*. 2 vols. Oxford: Clarendon Press.

Baumol, William J. 1986. Unnatural Value: Or Art Investment as Floating Crap Game. *American Economic Review* 76 (May): 10–14.

Becker, Gary S. 1996. *Accounting for Tastes*. Cambridge: Harvard University Press.

Bentham, Jeremy. 1827. *The Rationale of Judicial Evidence*. Edited by John Stuart Mill. 5 vols. London: Hunt and Clark.

Bianchi, Marina. 1998. *The Active Consumer: Novelty and Surprise in Consumer Choice*. London: Routledge.

———. 1999. Design and Efficiency: New Capabilities Embedded in New Products. In *Knowledge and Economic Organization: Essays in Honour of Brian Loasby*, edited by Sheila Dow and Peter Earle. Cheltenham, England: Edward Elgar.

Clayton, Timothy. 1997. *The English Print, 1688–1802*. New Haven, Conn.: Yale University Press.

De Marchi, Neil. 1995. The Role of Dutch Auctions and Lotteries in Shaping the Art Market(s) of Seventeenth-Century Holland. *Journal of Economic Behavior and Organization* 28:203–21.

De Marchi, Neil, and Hans J. Van Miegroet. 1996. Pricing Invention: "Originals," "Copies," and the Relative Value in Seventeenth-Century Netherlandish Art Markets. In *Economics of the Arts: Selected Essays*, edited by Victor A. Ginsburgh and Pierre-Michel Menger. Amsterdam: Elsevier.

De Piles, Roger. 1708. *Cours de peinture par principes*. Paris. English edition: *The Principles of Painting*. London, 1743.

Galiani, Ferdinando. [1751] 1923. *Early Economic Thought*, book 1. Translated and edited by Arthur Eli Monroe. Cambridge: Harvard University Press. Originally published as *Della Moneta*.

Grampp, William D. 1989. *Pricing the Priceless: Art, Artists, and Economics*. New York: Basic Books.

Humfrey, Peter. 1995. *Painting in Renaissance Venice*. New Haven, Conn.: Yale University Press.

Kress, Gunther, and Theo Van Leeuwen. 1996. *Reading Images: The Grammar of Visual Design*. London: Routledge.

Lancaster, Kelvin. 1971. *Consumer Demand: A New Approach*. New York: Columbia University Press.

———. 1991. *Modern Consumer Theory*. Aldershot, England: Edward Elgar.

Loasby, Brian. 1991. *Equilibrium and Evolution*. Manchester, England: Manchester University Press.

Pears, Iain. 1988. *The Discovery of Painting: The Growth of Interest in the Arts in England, 1680–1768*. New Haven, Conn.: Yale University Press.

Smith, Adam. 1985. *Lectures on Rhetoric and Belles Lettres*. Edited by J. C. Bryce. Glasgow edition of the *Works and Correspondence of Adam Smith*, vol. 4. Indianapolis: Liberty Press.

———. 1982. *Lectures on Jurisprudence*. Edited by R. L. Meek, D. D. Raphael, and P. G. Stein. Glasgow edition, vol. 5. Indianapolis: Liberty Press.

Stigler, George J., and Gary S. Becker. 1977. De gustibus non est disputandum. *American Economic Review* 67: 76–90. Reprinted in Becker 1996.

Uebel, Thomas E. 1998. Heterodox Neopositivism as a Response to the *Methodenstreit*? Philosophy of Social Science in the Long Shadow of an Old Debate. Mimeograph, University of Manchester.

Weisberg, Jacob. 1999. The Internet Breaks open the Art Market. *Slate Magazine* (Friday, February 5) [http://www.slate.com].

Part 1

Art and Economic Theory

Francisco Pacheco: Economist for the Art World

Zarinés Negrón

When Francisco Pacheco died in 1644 he left behind a treatise significant to the development of art theory in Spain. *Arte de la pintura*, published five years after his death, is a collection of art theories and practices proposed in his lifetime, including the ideas of his scholarly friends and synthesizing existing art theory for the Sevillian public. However, *Arte* is more than a simple collection of theories and discussions of technique; there are economic implications as well: The treatise is in part a market guide meant to educate *los afficcionados del arte* (the fans of art) about art production and valuation.

Throughout his career, Pacheco was an important and influential figure in the art world of Seville. In 1616 he was elected dean of the painters' guild, and two years later he was chosen as overseer of religious painting for the local Inquisition. He was involved with the intellectual elite of the city and oversaw an unofficial academy frequented by well-known poets, theologians, and art collectors. An artist by trade, an active participant in the art market, and a learned intellectual, Pacheco considered himself, and was considered by his academy, an expert on the product of art. In the prologue of *Arte* (1990, 68), he admits his intent to educate the ignorant through a treatise on the essential parts and practices of painting: "And in their language there should be written everything that needs to be known to liberate them

I would like to thank Craufurd Goodwin, Neil De Marchi, and Toon Van Houdt for their valuable comments and suggestions. I would also like to thank Craufurd Goodwin, Neil De Marchi, and the Ford Foundation for giving me the opportunity and the means to do this project, which has truly enriched my undergraduate experience.

from this common ignorance, since the books in their own language shall teach them."[1]

The treatise consists of three books and a lengthy appendix. Book 1 discusses the superiority of painting over sculpture, the aims of painting, and the three levels of painterly skill; book 2 includes the theory and parts of painting; book 3 describes the practice of painting; and the appendix addresses religious iconography. The contents of *Arte* are meant to educate the two sides of the art market, both suppliers and buyers. Suppliers benefit from the treatise because it serves as an instructional manual on good form and technique and high-quality production; buyers also benefit because after reading the treatise they are able to recognize the important qualities of a painting and thus make a fair purchase. This essay focuses on the education of buyers. Embedded in his reflections about art are Pacheco's economic commentaries. He specifies the products of painting, outlines the important elements in determining their value, and defines their necessary parts. Essentially, Pacheco creates for the buyer a model for the valuation of paintings. This valuation corresponds in certain respects to the just price.

To understand the model Pacheco proposes, it is helpful to review the literature of the moralists and juriconsultants at the University of Salamanca since Pacheco utilizes the same general economic principles as the Scholastics. During Pacheco's lifetime, the professors at the University of Salamanca, now referred to as the Salamantinos and the School of Salamanca, dominated economic thought in Spain. As moralists, they questioned the capacity of the market to function always in a just manner and sought ways of guarding buyers against exploitation. As the learned of the community in matters of morality, they saw it as their obligation to minimize injustice, and thus sin, by proposing a set of guidelines for market exchanges: "It is the obligation of those who have wisdom and understanding to serve the republic, teaching ways of business which will benefit many" (Mercado 1571, prologue). Our concern is with these Scholastics' views on the determination of price.

The Scholastics believed that a thing was worth as much as it ought to be sold for. They relied on a "common estimate" to approximate this just price: "There is a law cited by Falcidius which says: 'The price of goods is not determined by the wish or convenience of individuals but by the community.' That is, by common estimation" (de

1. Excerpts from Pacheco, Mercado, and de la Calle are translated by the author from the Spanish.

Soto 1553, 546).[2] If the market were functioning in a normal state, then the common estimate would correspond with the just price. Odd Langholm (1998, 85) describes the normal state of the Scholastic conception of the market as being the state in which market factors are in accordance with the moral universe such that the terms of exchange grant no advantage to either party. However, the market rarely, if ever, functioned in a normal state. It was affected by factors such as supply and demand, utility, and scarcity. In his *Instrucción de mercaderes*, Saravia de la Calle (1547, 26–27) wrote: "Excluding all deceit and malice, the just price of a thing is the cash price it commonly fetches at the time and place of the deal, bearing in mind the particular circumstances and manner of the sale, the abundance of goods and money, the number of buyers and sellers, the difficulty in procuring the good, and the benefit to be enjoyed by their use, according to the judgment of the honest man." All of these factors caused the common estimate to fluctuate around the just price. If the market was not in a normal state, then the common estimate served as a guideline for the just price (Langholm 1998, 86).

Another important element that affected the common estimate was whether the good was a necessity or a luxury. Unlike that of necessities, the determination of the price of luxury goods was left completely to the forces of the market. If the good was a luxury, then—once again excluding fraud and deceit—it could be sold justly and without sin for as much as the seller could get for it:

> Such things are least necessary to the republic and may be sold for whatever price a prudent well-informed purchaser may care to pay. Fine horses, jewels, and falcons fall into this class. We look to such things for the adornment, dignity, and splendor of the nobility: And it is for the magnificence of magnates to esteem them magnificently. But food, clothes, and other things of the sort are necessary to the republic. Let no fraud or malice creep into their pricing; which means, reader, that you are not to sell such things piecemeal for whatever price you can demand. (de Soto 1553, 549)

Paintings fell under the category of luxury goods, and thus their value was to be resolved by an educated purchaser in the manner described above.

2. Translations of de Soto's *De justitia et jure* are taken from Grice-Hutchinson 1952, text 2, pp. 83–88.

The principles of the just price that appear in the writings of the School of Salamanca also appear in *Arte de la pintura*. Pacheco accepts that a painting is a luxury good and that its estimated value depends on the highest price a seller can demand from a "prudent well-informed purchaser." This is why Pacheco feels the need to educate buyers of art. He is concerned with making the market estimate as close as possible to the true value of a painting. What allows the purchaser to assess the value is recognition of the nobility of a painting.

Pacheco (1990, 234–36) adopts the extrinsic-intrinsic distinction in connection with the nobility of a good painting, and he appears to use nobility as a way of determining the just price of the painting, even though nobility is a larger concept than value:

> The first group [the juriconsultants] says that the nobility of a thing should be considered two ways. The first is born from the approval of men and depends on someone else's judgment, which is called extrinsic nobility, or accidental. The other . . . consists of the nature and the perfection of the thing, and is called intrinsic nobility because it comes from itself and the philosophy it participates in or at least belongs to. . . . the first, coming from a clear knowledge about the quality of things, takes its dignity from the estimation and reputation in which it is held. And because this often varies (according to the place and its customs) they have called it accidental or civil nobility, and the juriconsultants resolved this matter by stating that an object can be noble if it is esteemed as such by the community. . . . And by combining one nobility with the other, we say that the price of a thing, the difficulty in making it, the utility it brings, the honor that is attributed to it by great persons, the inspiration of virtue, the discipline and teaching it gives to the community—all are the parts that make an art skill truly noble. There is no doubt that considering all things, it would be of great price, dignity, and splendor.

Pacheco's definitions of the extrinsic and intrinsic qualities of a painting are similar to the distinctions made by the Salmantinos. In Scholastic monetary theory, metal and tale together composed the intrinsic value, usually referred to as *valor*, and estimation determined the extrinsic value (Grice-Hutchinson 1952, 51). In Pacheco's terms, intrinsic nobility encompasses the "nature" and the quality of the product, whereas extrinsic nobility involves the "accidental" value, or estimated value, given to the painting dependent on market factors. It seems, then, that the recognition of the nobilities of a painting will help guide the purchaser in arriving at the just price.

Before we continue, we must address Pacheco's use of *nobleza* (nobility) as a guide for the estimation of the price of a painting. In sixteenth- and seventeenth-century Spain, *nobleza* signified grace, adornment, and ability. According to Pacheco, the nobility of a painting is determined by the approval of men (extrinsic nobility) and by the painting's nature and perfection (intrinsic nobility). Thus nobility and value are not synonymous, though Pacheco feels that both extrinsic and intrinsic nobility help the consumer of art arrive at a just price. By correctly estimating the nobility of a painting, we are assisted in estimating its true value.

Because the extrinsic nobility is determined by market factors, Pacheco is interested in educating the buyer to recognize the intrinsic nobility of a painting. He provides a set of criteria to help the purchaser in this endeavor. The criteria Pacheco mentions are *invención* (invention), *debuxo* (drawing), and *colorido* (coloring). Each of these criteria is further defined. Under *invención* lay *noticia* (knowledge of the humanistic and divine letters), *caudal* (a stock of images and techniques), and *decoro* (decorum). *Debuxo* includes *buena manera* (good form), *proporcíon* (proportion), and *anatonomía y perspectiva* (anatomy and perspective). Finally, *colorido* comprehends *hermosura* (beauty), *suavidad* (softness), and *relivio* (relief). These are the distinct characteristics of a painting that the reader must consider when estimating its worth. Books 2 and 3 of *Arte* describe each of these components in greater detail to educate and adequately prepare the reader for what he or she should be looking for in a painting.

The *grado* (level) of the painter also affects the intrinsic nobility. Pacheco (1990, 269) divides painters into three categories in the following passage:

> We will not speak here of those who know only how to copy and have to follow good or bad originals, be they prints, drawings, or paintings. They belong to the first level, as we have seen (Book 1, Chapter 12). Those of the second level can still make use of these sources, join them together at the end, and thus take better advantage of them. These painters, when the opportunity is offered to them to paint a figure or a history, can choose from among prints, drawings,

> or paintings—a head from one, a half-figure from another, another figure or two from someplace else, plus arms, legs, draperies, buildings, and landscapes—and join them all together. In this way they are at least responsible for the compositions and for the many other things that make a unified picture. Certainly, the ability to make sketches, drawings, and cartoons straight away belongs to those painters who occupy the third and final level of painting, because they are obliged to make new things, and thus when they are asked to do a figure or history, be it old or new, they try to discover how it should be painted, whether by asking scholars or reading books, and in their mind they construct unified ideas.

According to Pacheco, painters of the third level should be the most highly compensated because they utilize the most *ingenio* (genius). *Ingenio* is what separates the three levels—the first level requiring little or no *ingenio* in its production, and the third level requiring the most. A first-level painting would therefore have lesser intrinsic nobility than a third-level painting.

Pacheco includes examples of painters who he believes display a high quality in their works and exercise the practices and techniques he advocates. He extols painters such as Titian, Michelangelo, Rubens, El Greco, and his own former apprentice Diego Velázquez. Pacheco (1990, 149) also includes examples of the amount some of these painters were awarded for their works, mainly by the nobility: "But the one that has exceeded them all in the estimation of our craft was our invincible emperor Carlos V. He rewarded [Titian's] medium painting with 2,000 ducados, and liked to be painted often by him, each time giving him 1,000 ducados, and never allowed another painter to paint him. He esteemed him so highly that he knighted him and paid him 2,000 additional ducados in Naples." Here Pacheco illustrates the price a painting of high quality may command and implies that paintings of similar quality should be so valued.

Pacheco does not differ much from the juriconsultants when it comes to costs of production. Costs alone do not determine the just price. They are only meant to guide the buyer in finding the correct value of a good (Grice-Hutchinson 1952, 48). However, in painting, it is not the usual costs of production such as material costs or manual labor that should be considered. Rather, the costs of the production of a painting are genius and perfection of form:

> Sculpture is not ennobled by the precious materials it uses nor the difficulty of working with them. Materials, even though they may be precious, do not give praise to art. And the greater use of manual labor only makes it more servile. Clearly he who utilizes better form on his figure and makes it more natural is a greater sculptor, because form is more noble than materials. No painter who paints on bronze, gold, or silver, or uses ultramarine and other precious colors and metals, will be greater than he who works with fragile and poor materials such as panel, linen, and wall, with earth and cheaper colors. (Pacheco 1990, 104–6)

The utility of painting will also play a role in its estimation. According to our author, "painting is more disposed to the use of men and is more accommodating for the decoration of houses, therefore it is *apeticida* (desired) by many" (Pacheco 1990, 102). Painting embraces an infinite number of techniques and subjects, making it more flexible to meet the needs of those who demand it. Francisco García, who belonged to the School of Salamanca, wrote that the value of a good increased if the good had many more uses and served more purposes than another, if it rendered a greater service, or if it performed the service better (Grice-Hutchinson 1952, 104). Pacheco understood this and included this rationale in determining the value of a painting.

Pacheco is an artist who understands not only the product of painting but also the Scholastic paradigm of the market. He works within this moral framework to create a model for buyers to correctly value paintings. Although Pacheco uses the same economic principles of the just price as do the Salamantinos, it would be a mistake to place him entirely under their umbrella. Pacheco is an artist writing about the art market; the Salamantinos, by contrast, wrote about the business world even though they were not businessmen—they were moral philosophers whose aim was to protect buyers from exploitation. Pacheco protects buyers in a way other than elucidating moral obligation; he aims to instruct the buyer to understand the product. It is possible for an ignorant lover of art to pay an excessive amount for a painting of little true worth or too little for a painting of exceptional genius and form. By educating the buyer, Pacheco hoped to ensure that the offered price would be closer to the just price in any particular instance.

By comparing the literature of the Salamantinos with Pacheco's *Arte de la pintura*, we clearly see the economic ideas in Pacheco's writing.

Although he was not an economist by trade, the ideas found in his treatise were significant contributions to the understanding of the product of paintings and their valuation. He understood the art market in Scholastic terms and was able to construct a useful model (one that focused on the intrinsic qualities of paintings) for resolving the nobility and thus the true value of paintings.

References

de la Calle, Saravia. 1547. *Instrucción de mercaderes muy provechosa: En la qual se enseña cómo deben tratar.* Medina del Campo.

de Soto, Domingo. 1553. *De justitia et jure.* Salamanca.

Grice-Hutchinson, Marjorie. 1952. *The School of Salamanca.* Oxford: Clarendon Press.

Langholm, Odd. 1998. *The Legacy of Scholasticism in Economic Thought: Antecedents of Choice and Power.* Cambridge: Cambridge University Press.

Mercado, Tomas de. 1571. *Summa de tratos y contratos.* Seville.

Pacheco, Francisco. 1990. *Arte de la pintura.* Edited by Bonaventura Bassegoda i Huegas. Madrid: Catedra.

The Problem of Unique Goods as Factors of Production: Rousseau on Art and the Economy

Bertil Fridén

One of Jean-Jacques Rousseau's projects was to develop a philosophy for the economy of what he thought were the most important things in life for mature women and men. Within those economic structures this philosophy claims to treat, art appears in both destructive and constructive functions. Art is discussed in relation to the provision of three categories of goods: *luxury goods*, *physical necessities*, and "*true riches*." A kind of dual economy between luxury goods and necessities is presented. As part of luxury consumption, on the one hand, art makes it difficult for society to efficiently and securely provide people with physical necessities such as food. As a component of social morality, on the other hand, art may counter free-riding and other economically destructive behavior. Properly enjoyed, however, what we would call art belongs among those "true riches" which Rousseau's economic philosophy is all about.

This three-function conception of art may explain some apparent tensions in Rousseau's views on the value of art. One of them concerns prices. Like Adam Smith, Rousseau is struck by the high prices of the performances and works of artists. His explanation is totally different from Smith's, however. Smith finds the prices on artists' performances determined by, first, "the rarity and beauty of their talents" and, second, the "discredit" of their work. In the eyes of public opinion, the use of one's artistic talents "for the sake of gain" is, claims Smith ([1776]

This essay has benefited from the generous suggestions and references by Neil De Marchi and an anonymous referee.

1976, 124), "a kind of publick prostitution" for which the artist must be compensated by generous pay. To Rousseau, in contrast, the pay for artists' services is indecently liberal because the high prices per se increase the value of the services of the artists. In *Emile*, he writes: "Those self-important persons working exclusively for the idle and the rich, set an *arbitrary* price on their lapri, and as the merits of these futile works exist only in the opinion of people, and the price itself is part of their merit, one estimates them in proportion to their price" (*OC,* 4:457; italics added).[1]

Rousseau's opinion that art is overpriced may be expected, perhaps, considering his *Discours sur les sciences et les arts*, but it is still remarkable in view of his high appreciation of art in his personal life, as well as in many of his political proposals. He was an author of novels, drama, and music, and he participated with very elaborated arguments in the controversy with Jean-Philippe Rameau on music. The apparent paradox can be understood by explaining the various functions he gives to art within his economic philosophy.

Indeed, Rousseau presents an economic philosophy, though it is no grand conceptual system à la François Quesnay or David Ricardo. His use of concepts is consistent; his understanding of the economic problems that are of concern to him is stable; and he obviously had an audience, being the one asked to write the main article on political economy in the great *Encyclopédie* (*OC,* 3:239–78).[2] His writings confirm that he is well informed on the economic doctrines of his time. The importance he gives to uniqueness in his economic philosophy has radical implications not easily faced by modern economics (Fridén 1998).

Dual Economy of Physical Necessities and Luxuries

Luxury goods are discussed with a comparatively high degree of precision. They are contrasted to physical necessities—in Rousseau's view those endowments that are indispensable for one's survival. Although art is not explicitly included in this category but rather jux-

1. All translations are mine unless otherwise noted. *OC* refers to Rousseau's *Oeuvres complètes.*

2. Mirabeau, for example, approached Rousseau with his views, in a kind invitation letter. Within a year after the publication of *Theorie de l'impôt* (in 1760), Rousseau (*OC,* 3:1750) responded in a critical spirit.

taposed to it, beauty and aesthetic quality in general are certainly counted as necessary parts of a good life. Art in this sense appears as a quality of necessary and functional items of everyday life. I shall return to this aspect later in the article.

In Rousseau's opinion, everyone has an unquestionable right to the endowments necessary for physical survival. First among them is food. One of the first concerns of government should be to establish an economic policy that secures the supply of corn. Thus Rousseau approaches the discussion of what Frédéric-Melchior Grimm called the "maladie à la mode"—the problem of recurrent grain shortages (Fox-Genovese 1976, 24–25)—and rejects various policy proposals by mercantilists, physiocrats, étatists, and liberals.

In the dual market structure of food and luxury goods (Fridén 1998, chap. 6), the latter are understood to be goods used in people's strivings to appear in a certain way before others, particularly to appear attractive or powerful: this is what today may be called *conspicuous consumption*. Such goods are associated with a momentary excitation, a passing "dazzling," in contrast to the lasting joy of the "abundance in the necessary." In *Emile*, the difference is epitomized in the striking contrast between two meals. The first meal is an almost orgiastic "magnificent but tedious" dinner where "course follows course." It takes place in an "opulent house" where "all that apparatus of pleasure and feasting brings something *dazzling* which carries away the head as long as one is not accustomed" (*OC,* 4:463). The author suggests Emile should be asked by his teacher to compare this temporary excitement to a second meal composed exclusively of local produce, where the "white bread that you like so much" and the wine, "dark and crude but thirst-quenching and healthy," are made by wheat and grapes from the fields and vineyards of the estate (Starobinski 1988, 105; *OC,* 4:464).

Market prices of luxury goods behave differently from prices of necessities. While the usual low price elasticity of the demand for corn may be disastrous to the poor buyer in years of poor yields, a low elasticity price may be attractive to the buyer of luxury goods. This is the basis of Rousseau's argument. Since the users of luxury goods strive to use their luxury as a kind of hierarchical goods, a high price may increase their utility. For this reason, the price elasticity of the demand for such goods may be even lower than that of necessities. "The rich think so much of these things," Emile should learn, "not because they are useful, but because they are beyond the reach of the poor. *Nolo habere bona, nisi quibus populus inviderit* [I only want the goods as long as people envy them]" (*OC*, 4:457; see also the discussion in Smith [1759] 1976, 181–85, and notes).

As pointed out in the passage from *Emile* quoted in the beginning of this essay, art products can serve the desire to be envied: One estimates them in proportion to what they cost. This explains why the prices of art products become "arbitrary." Values are set by the general public on the various arts "in contradiction to their real utility" (*OC,* 4:457). The lower the price, Rousseau seems to claim, the higher the real social value of the good. "This might be expected," he claims, in one of the standard translations: "The most useful arts are the worst paid, for the number of workmen is regulated by the *demand*, and the work which everybody requires must necessarily be paid at a rate which puts it within the reach of the poor" (Rousseau 1984, 149; *OC,* 4:457; emphasis added).[3]

This formulation is far from clear. But in the French original Rousseau uses the word *besoins* for "demand." If the French noun is understood as "needs" rather than "demand," the formulation becomes reasonable. Prices of goods that are demanded as *needs* or necessities, Rousseau claims, are determined differently from those demanded, like art, as conspicuous consumption. His view is somewhat related to Ferdinando Galiani's ([1770] 1959, 222; see also Fridén 1998, chap. 6) interesting rejection of laissez-faire solutions of the "maladie à la mode," where Galiani in a similar spirit as Rousseau argued that nature is "too big a Lady to be given the responsibility for our small problems." Rousseau's view is here more precise than Smith's discussion about the value of water and diamonds, where Smith ([1776] 1976, 44–45) merely claims that the "value in exchange" of a good may be noncongruent with its "value in use."

The fact that the prices of necessities—unlike, for example, art—are not "arbitrary," makes it highly dangerous to be dependent on someone else for the provision of necessities, since such a dependence can, in bargaining, be exploited by that agent who does not need to buy and who therefore "can wait." Talking about international trade policy, Rousseau warns that other states can dictate the terms of trade for a nation which is not self-sufficient on food. The former nations "can

3. The same idea is already present in a note to the *Discours sur l'origine et les fondements de l'inégalité* (*OC,* 3:206).

wait," he claims, in a Quesnay-sounding formulation in the *Considérations sur le gouvernement de Pologne* on which he worked during the 1770s: "The bread which for you is necessary, has for you a price that you have no possibility to dispute, and in the entire species of commerce it is always the least pressed who reads the law for the other" (*OC*, 3:905).[4]

For reasons such as this, Rousseau consistently opposes provision by means of market exchange and advocates small-scale subsistence economies—family farms. But he has other reasons for advocating small-scale economies, too. In several texts he questions the efficiency of market exchange because of what today could count as various kinds of information costs. In a passage in the *Confessions* he portrays an information asymmetry problem in his personal life:

> One must bargain and purchase and often be cheated, paying dear for poor services. I want an article of quality; but my money is sure to obtain a poor one. I pay a lot for a new laid egg and it proves stale; for a ripe fruit, and it is green; for a girl, and she is debauched. I enjoy good wine, but where can I get it? At a wine merchant's? Notwithstanding all my precautions he will poison me. (Starobinski 1988, 106; *OC*, 1:36–37)

He describes how he again and again feels exploited by a seller who knows the quality of the good better than he and therefore can cheat him. This kind of information asymmetry is understood as a cost problem:

> Supposing I insist on getting what I want. What trouble and embarassment I must put myself to! I must use my friends and correspondents, give orders, write, go hither and thither, wait; and often I shall be cheated in the end. What a trouble my money is! I am not fond enough of good wine to disturb myself to that extent. (Rousseau 1984, 45; *OC*, 1:37)

The risk that the safe provision of necessities may be threatened by increasing "differences" in market power (implying a perverse overestimation of art relative to food) and various kinds of information costs are two reasons that Rousseau found the provision of necessities by

4. This very important theme in Rousseau's writings also has much of the flavor of Sir James Steuart's ([1767] 1966, 167) attempt to capture the power structure of the market as determined by the agents' "degree of eagerness."

means of a subsistence economy preferable to market provision. A subsistence economy of the kind portrayed in *Julie, ou La nouvelle Héloïse* also facilitates a more reasonable evaluation of art itself. Within the estate economy of Julie, he points out in his discussion of the aesthetic qualities of the household, "nothing is held in contempt because it is common" (*OC*, 2:550). And in several contexts he presents proposals for such a subsistence peasantry economy (see, e.g., *Considérations sur le gouvernement de Pologne* and *Discours sur l'économie politique*).

But there is a problem. Rousseau very clearly admits that such an economy is feasible only as long as the population is small enough. It is merely a temporary solution. The most explicit recognition of this can be found in the uncompleted *Projet de constitution pour la Corse* where he writes: "When the country is replete with inhabitants, one can no more allocate its surplus back to agriculture, but it is necessary to allocate it to industry, to commerce, to the arts, and this new system demands another administration" (*OC*, 3:907). Although Rousseau does not present anything near a clear or complete program for that "other administration," he does stubbornly discuss one part of it: how individual rationality is to be prevented from threatening the social optimum, and how those who are most dependent on others should be protected. Art is critical to that analysis.

Agent of Social Morality in a Dual Economy

The problem of specialization is that it may give rise to an *asymmetric* dependence that some may abuse. If some people, for example farmers or landlords, control the provision of food "which for you has a price that you have no possibility to dispute," and you can offer merely dispensable goods, then you may be forced to accept any conditions of exchange. The problem is not the fact per se—that you as a specialist worker are socially dependent, nor that the farmers are independent—but the *asymmetry*: the fact that some are dependent but others are not.

Rousseau's treatment of art is part of a peculiar dialectic of dependence. On the one hand, dependence is a prerequisite to serf bondage and other kinds of lasting, nonvoluntary obedience. This is made particularly clear in the *Discours sur l'origine et les fondements de l'inégalité*. A large-enough population, efficient property rights, and the possibility to exclude others from all land usable for cultivation are necessary preconditions to keep someone obedient. Without these conditions, sooner or later a person "tormented" at one place would soon exit, heading somewhere else—"Who would prevent me from moving elsewhere?" Rousseau (*OC*, 3:161) asks. And if a master would try to keep me as his slave, he would have to show a considerable activity, to "keep me" from escaping. He explains in a vivid passage, reminiscent of Defoe's Robinson Crusoe:

> He must resolve not to loose me out of sight for one single instant, to carefully keep me bound during his sleep, from fear that I escape or kill him: that is to say that he is obliged to expose himself voluntarily to a pain much worse than that which he wanted to avoid, and than that he gives to me.
>
> . . . I take five steps into the forest, my iron is broken, and he will never see me again in his whole life. (161)

On the other hand, in his dialectics, dependence is also a prerequisite for preventing individual rationality from threatening social rationality. That is, in fact, the main message of one of the most quoted and most misunderstood passages in Rousseau's work: the stag hunt presented in the same *Discours* (Fridén 1998). When he mentions the possibility that the hunter may desert his post (in game-theoretical terms, that the equilibrium choice may differ from the optimal),[5] he points out one significant precondition: It is "his absolute and naturally independent existence" that makes it attractive for him to exploit the gain motive to desert. It is that condition which makes him regard such goods that are due to the "common cause" as free, argues Rousseau (*OC*, 3:166–67).

It is therefore significant that the stag hunt dilemma is treated within the discussion of the (hypothetical) state of nature. People are assumed to take care of their provision on their own or with the help of family members. Other "trees" are available for sport or hunting: there is other game to subdue, there are other caves to make one's dwelling, and so on. In this situation, it would *only at times* be advantageous to cooperate. Man "found himself," the text goes, "able to distinguish a few cases, in which mutual interest might justify him in relying upon the assistance of his fellows" (Rousseau 1983, 78; *OC*, 3:166–67).

In these "few" cases, merely temporary associations would be

5. Often this tale is wrongly assumed to be an assurance game (a game with several equilibria, only one of which is optimal). As is shown in Fridén 1998, it is at least possible to understand it as a case of the prisoners' dilemma game with a unique but suboptimal equilibrium. Such an interpretation gives Rousseau's argument much more bite and consistency, which is why I believe it was intended in this way.

formed. They would last "no longer than the transitory occasion that formed them." But, as long as anyone could gain by not cooperating, there would be no certainty that agreements were kept; nothing in the world could stop that participant who could gain by leaving. Rousseau (*OC*, 3:166) writes in illustration, for example:

> If a deer was to be taken everyone could see that, in order to succeed, each hunter must abide faithfully by his post; but if a hare happened to come within the reach of any one of them, it is not to be doubted that he would pursue it without scruple, and, having seized his prey, care very little if by so doing he caused his companions to miss theirs.[6]

Cooperation, in the state of nature, would only be temporary, because nobody would be continually dependent on the assistance of others. The independence of people in the state of nature would *impede* cooperation. In the social state, on the contrary, the problem is that some are dependent, while others are not because they have power; most people are "subjected to a universal dependence, being obliged to get everything from those who are not obliged to give them anything" (153).

To solve this problem, Rousseau suggests, rather vaguely, (1) that economic systems should be constructed so that people become as mutually dependent as possible and (2) that art and education are to be used in this context to activate the citizen's compassion and implement a high social sense; empathy and imagination activated by art even appear to be substitutes for symmetric dependence. In Rousseau's view, the imaginative capability of man has the potential to increase the ability to "see the self common to the whole," which is another expression for the "general will," or the social optimum. "Pity" is a natural sentiment, present latent or active, regardless of the degree of civilization or socialization. But in the social state, it is brought into action by imagination; it is, perhaps, recovered from the very paralysis of this state. Rousseau claims pity lets us be placed "outside of ourselves":

> Pity, although natural, would rest eternally inactive in the heart of a man, unless imagination puts it into play. How could we let ourselves be moved to pity? By placing ourselves outside of ourselves; by identifying ourselves with the suffering one. We only suffer as long as we

6. The translation in this paragraph follows closely Hardin 1982, 167.

judge that he suffers; it is not within ourselves, but within him that we suffer. (Robinson 1984, 133)

Since art has the potential to activate this indispensable imaginative capability of pitying, it must not be wasted on mere "theatricality"—or momentary dazzlings. When Jean d'Alembert proposed that a theater should be set up in Geneva, Rousseau expected that precisely such theatricality would result. If the actors put imagination into action, without causing a lasting active response, only "entertaining" passive listeners or viewers, it would merely be a waste of time. It would become a kind of "ethical masturbation, a 'dangereux supplément' which spills the seed of our positive moral impulses on the ground, and renders them sterile" (Robinson's characterization; Robinson 1984, 140–42).

Music, to Rousseau, is another agent of social morality. In a quite sophisticated discussion, he dismisses, for several reasons, Rameau's claim that harmony is more essential to music than melody and rhythm (Wokler 1974). Melody, says Rousseau, is essential to import a moral effect to the listener. It is perhaps natural that melody and rhythm are essential in Rousseau's view, since he emphasizes the interactive and communicative power of music rather than its capacity to instill certain emotions in the listener in a planned, unidirectional process. He denies strongly, in opposition to Rameau, that there is a mechanical connection between certain harmonies and certain sentiments. The effects of music are always culturally mediated and thus communicative (*OC,* 5:342–43). All this, of course, does not imply that Rousseau denies the importance of harmony.

In summary, Rousseau calls for theater, dance, and music to instigate moral action and social responsibility (Fralin 1986, 145) and facilitate a sense of togetherness among the citizenry.

True Riches

It is obvious from Rousseau's examples that art is the very core of *true riches.* A rich society is one where people by their work can obtain "everything necessary for life," he writes in an unpublished answer to an award question formulated by the Société Economique de Berne in 1762 (*OC,* 3:524). And when in his different texts he states what is "necessary for life," he includes dance, music, poetry, paintings, architecture, gardening, and other forms of art. These appear, however, as expressions of the individual's personality rather than as celebrated and certified monuments or artifacts. The individual users' active striving to organize their lives in a way that is beautiful according to their own criteria is the true source of aesthetic value. Quite unambiguously and explicitly, Rousseau states that anything which is to be part of true richness *must*—Marina Bianchi's (1998a, 2, 10) terms—be deliberately "personalized" or "singularized."

The presence of a privatizing process—by an organizing or *ordering* subject—is, in fact, one of the criteria of the rich and authentic life. In *Julie, ou La nouvelle Héloïse* the "simple" and "modest" home of Julie and her husband is contrasted to the palace. The critical difference lies in the lack of personalized order in the one and its presence in the other. The inhabitant of the palace seeks her fortune and her happiness on the ruin of another, and in a general disorder." In contrast, the "magnificence" of Julie's home consists "less in the richness of things than in the good order of everything, which marks the concert of all the parts and the unity of intent of the ordering person [*ordonnateur*]."

> The well-regulated home is a unity and forms a whole that is agreeable to watch: In the palace one finds nothing but a confused assembly of diverse objects, of which the connection is hardly apparent. At first sight one thinks one sees a common end, but looking closer one is soon brought out of this illusion. (*OC,* 2:546)

On the other hand, it is Julie's active *coproduction* of true richness that gives value to the objects: "Taste loves to create, to be the one to give value to things" (*OC,* 2:550). Julie has created a home by making riches out of mere endowments: "It is by the use of wealth rather than by its acquisition that we really get it" (466). In another context (in the *Fragments politiques*), Rousseau (*OC,* 3:530) exclaims that one is rich from possessing a small lot of cultivable land, while others are poor "in the midst of heaps of gold." The user is a coproducer (Fuchs 1985) like the listener whose attention, sensibility, and pre-understanding influence the quality of the aesthetic experience of the musical performance.[7]

To become true riches, Julie's endowments have to be personalized in a second sense. In order to be authentically her own, they must be made "private," exclusive. This is made explicit when Rousseau describes the

7. This is also the sense in Becker and Stigler 1977.

crown jewel of Julie's home as the "elysium," the personal paradise. The elysium is a garden so evidently exclusive, so visibly impossible to use for display or for showing to others, that it cannot even physically be seen from the outside. Rousseau does not let it be available to anyone but Julie and her gardener: "Although the place is located very close to the house," Saint Preux, the observer in the novel, notices, "one cannot see it even at close quarter because it is hidden by the heavily shaded alley which separates it from the house. The tight foliage that surrounds it does not let the eye penetrate it, and the gate is always carefully locked" (*OC,* 2:466). Julie here truly lives "sufficient to herself," in "an order of things in which nothing is conceded to opinion and in which everything has real utility defined by true natural needs" (547).

Unique Goods as a Factor of Production

There are several problems in Rousseau's treatment of art. One has to do with the fact that personalization of goods is described as a singularization process, although Rousseau elsewhere testifies to its necessarily social character in the social state.

A good life must be lived nonrandomly, formed by deliberated choices in the sense of Aristotle's *Nicomachean Ethics*. Rousseau very clearly ascribes to what Isaiah Berlin calls a negative concept of freedom (Wokler 1979). The individual's own striving to find unique ways to perfect life is *part of* the happy life. But this striving after a nonrandom living (of which the singularization process is a part) must in a specialized and democratic society be a social process, a *social* choice. That is why the problem of social choice (the relation between general wills and particular wills) is treated so extensively in Rousseau's (*OC,* 3:239–78) *Encyclopédie* article on political economy, *Discours sur l'économie politique*. How does one live nonrandomly *when in a state of deep mutual dependence* (Cohen 1986, 287, 294)? Rousseau does not fully face this question in his illustrations of true richness. This dilemma, which is present again and again in his writings, was also there in his personal life. "As long as others were my brothers," he confesses in *Les rêveries du promeneur solitaire*, "I invented plans of earthly happiness for myself; these plans were always universal in scope, I could be happy only in the happiness of all and my heart was never touched by the idea of private happiness" (Rousseau 1984b, 111–12; *OC,* 1:1066).

Later, however, when he searched in vain for brothers (and sisters?) he encountered only people who acted toward him "like automata, entirely governed by external impulses, and I could only calculate their behaviour according to the laws of motion" (Rousseau 1984b, 127; *OC,* 1:1078). In the terms of *Les rêveries du promeneur solitaire*, they contented themselves with "living at random."

Rousseau's illustrations of a rich life do not portray social choice dilemmas at all; they are strictly individual choices. In *Julie, ou La nouvelle Héloïse*, for example, Julie's attempt to live an authentically human life is strictly individual. She is supported by others, by servants, but there is no discussion of how the terms between the "ordonnateur" and her helpers should be set without anybody becoming a soulless *automaton.*

This problem, like those of a dual economy and of information costs, obviously prompted Rousseau's aversion to market provision and support of small, self-sufficient family farms. But as already mentioned, he admits that subsistence economies can only be temporary solutions in social development and that specialization is unavoidable in the long run. Although he stresses the importance of a social sense in a specialized economy, he does not really discuss the long-term relations among subsistence agriculture, market exchange, and other complementary modes of provision.

To the modern reader, both the complementarities and the incompatibilities of different modes of provision are discussed by Rousseau at too low a level of specificity for the proposals to be fruitfully applied to the problems addressed. To be more specific, Rousseau would have had to face a number of new problems. His perceptive portrayal of "true riches" includes features that are perhaps insufficiently considered, not only by him but also by others, though intriguing thoughts were put forward by Roger Fry, Clive Bell, and Sir Kenneth Clark (see Goodwin, this volume). In conclusion, I want to indicate four such features.

It is not at all evident, first, that decreasing marginal utility is typical for the consumption pattern of the highest quality of life. On the contrary, Rousseau describes how the value of goods increases with learning, singularization, and collecting. Again and again, he describes close complementary relations among objects that make up what one may call finite sets (cf. Bianchi 1998c). When Rousseau in *Julie, ou La nouvelle Héloïse* describes the "abundance in the necessary" of the estate of Julie and her husband, he points out that although "one finds only necessary things" at the estate, it "is impossible to think of anything that might be added or subtracted." He lets Saint-Preux exclaim on seeing the dining room: "Add to it the golden luster of galon or tableaux and you will impoverish it" (*OC,* 2:548). Rousseau describes a case in which up to a certain maturity point there is no decreasing marginal utility. This is not what standard microeconomics asks us to expect. Of course, some implications of such situations have been explored in the literature (Bianchi 1998b), but they have been given marginal attention and their importance is still not analyzed.

Uniqueness, second, in Rousseau's perspective, is not a marginal quality of human richness. Being an aspect of singularization and nonrandom living, it is near its core and prompts specific care in economic theory. In many acts of consumption, the consumer is uncertain about the quality of the good on the market. But unlike the case with standardized goods, in the case of unique goods the only way for the consumer to diminish quality-uncertainty is to consider the trustworthiness and competence of the *producers* of those unique goods.

Third, Rousseau illustrates in *Julie, ou La nouvelle Héloïse* how the properties of a household acquire value to a visitor just because they have value to the "ordonnateur"—how upon entering a room, the trusted guest gets an "initiation to intimacy." What the visitor appreciates is not something known beforehand, not even what was expected, but the surprises, those qualities she or he cannot possibly have appreciated ex ante, but which are revealed by means of the ordering mind of the other, by the "ordonnateur." In this way, Rousseau describes a kind of "irreducibly social good" (Taylor 1990, 54–55), the values of which are dependent on and coproduced by the other users.

Producing, fourth, is often enjoyable in Julie's home. "Those cares," Julie explains, which you call burdensome are to us "simultaneously duties and pleasures" (*OC,* 2:549). One example is the elysium that Julie enjoys so much to tend. It is significant that it does not perish like food and other orthodox consumption goods, but remains as a factor of production. Its productivity, in terms of pleasure, may not even be decreasing but increasing under Julie's care—simultaneously duty and pleasure. The garden may become more and more productive to her, through her interventions, in the sense that it gives her more and more joy. By her consumption, the garden becomes singularized—personal and unique. Her productive consumption probably increases the value to the few others who are let into the garden, such as her children, her friends, and even future generations who can enjoy the "intimacy" as a result of her contingent productive singularization.

The idea that the value of a site or building may increase by something we could call *singularization* appears in the aesthetic literature. Just to pick one example, Frank Lloyd Wright already in 1894 wrote that "it is the individuality [not of the architect, but] of the occupants that should give character and color to the building and furnishings." While a conventional house soon grows "flat and stale," an individualized house may grow more valuable even in a monetary sense because it gets "character" (Wright 1992, 23; see also Guerzoni and Troilo 1998).

Thus, not only may the consumption of the elysium have increasing marginal utility to the user, but the demand for it may cause peculiar information costs, and enjoying it with someone else may increase its value (shared intimacy). The elysium may also refine the garden, causing a continuous growth in the garden's utility. In that way the garden is simultaneously a consumption good and a factor of production. By consuming, the user may spur accumulated increases in the garden's productivity and thereby defy the usual assumption about declining productivity. If such an accumulated productive consumption is properly taken into account, it may have crucial consequences for an aging factor of production like a garden or building. Obviously, such objects may have a nonlinear development of productivity. At least since Riegl (1982) it has caused concern that the utility of, for example, a monument may initially decrease (due to diminishing "newness") up to a certain point; then, however, its "value" starts to increase due to its "patina" or age. Consequently, there may *temporarily* be a critical period in the existence of such a factor of production when its utility net of costs is negative (even after the conventional present value calculations). Considering the presence of accumulated productive consumption in light of Rousseau's view of a rich life, such a period may look different, get shorter, and even disappear.

References

Becker, Gary, and George Stigler. 1977. De gustibus non est disputandem. *American Economic Review* 67.2:77–90.

Bianchi, Marina, ed. 1998a. *The Active Consumer: Novelty and Surprise in Consumer Choice*. London: Routledge.

———. 1998b. Design and Efficiency: New Capabilities Embedded in New Products. Cassino, Italy: University of Cassino. Unpublished manuscript.

———. 1998c. Taste for Novelty and Novel Tastes. In Bianchi 1998a.

Cohen, Joshua. 1986. Reflections on Rousseau: Autonomy and Democracy. *Philosophy and Public Affairs* 15.3:275–97.

Fox-Genovese, Elizabeth. 1976. *The Origins of Physiocracy: Economic Revolution and Social Order in Eighteenth-Century France*. Ithaca, N.Y.: Cornell University Press.

Fralin, Richard. 1986. Rousseau and Community: The Role of *Mœurs* in Social Change. *History of Political Thought* 7.1:131–50.

Fridén, Bertil. 1998. *Rousseau's Economic Philosophy: Beyond the Market of Innocents*. Dordrecht: Kluwer.

Fuchs, Victor R. 1985. An Agenda for Future Research on the Service Sector. In *Managing the Service Economy: Prospects and Problems*, edited by Robert Inman. Cambridge: Wharton School, University of Pennsylvania.

Galiani, Ferdinando. [1770] 1959. *Dialogues sur le commerce des bleds*. Milan: Richard Ricciardi Editore.

Guerzoni, Guido, and Gabriele Troilo. 1998. Silk Purses out of Sows' Ears. In Bianchi 1998a.

Hardin, Russel. 1982. *Collective Action*. Baltimore: Johns Hopkins University Press.

Riegl, Alois. 1982. The Modern Cult of Monuments: Its Character and Its Origin. *Oppositions* 25: 21–51.

Robinson, Philip E. J. 1984. *Jean-Jacques Rousseau's Doctrine of the Arts*. Bern: Peter Lang.

Rousseau, Jean-Jacques. 1983. *The Social Contract and Discourses*. Translated by G. D. H. Cole. London: Everyman.

———. 1984a. *Emile*. Translated by Barbara Foxley. London: Everyman.

———. 1984b. *Reveries of the Solitary Walker*. Translated by Peter France. Harmondsworth, England: Penguin.

———. 1959–95. *Oeuvres complètes de J.-J. Rousseau*. 5 vols. Paris: L'édition de la Bibliothèque de la Pléiade, Gallimard.

Smith, Adam. [1759] 1976. *The Theory of Moral Sentiments*. Oxford: Clarendon Press.

———. [1776] 1976. *An Inquiry into the Nature and Causes of the Wealth of Nations*. Oxford: Clarendon Press.

Starobinski, Jean. 1988. *Jean-Jacques Rousseau: Transparency and Obstruction*. Chicago: University of Chicago Press.

Steuart, Sir James. [1767] 1966. *An Inquiry into the Principles of Political Economy*. Edited and with an introduction by Andrew S. Skinner. Chicago: University of Chicago Press.

Taylor, Charles. 1990. Irreducibly Social Goods. In *Rationality, Individualism, and Public Policy*, edited by Geoffrey Brennan and Cliff Walsh. Canberra: ANUTECH.

Wokler, Robert. 1974. Rameau, Rousseau, and the *Essai sur l'origine des langues*. *Studies on Voltaire and the Eighteenth Century* 117:179–238.

———. 1979. Rousseau's Perfectibilian Libertarianism. In *The Idea of Freedom: Essays in Honour of Isaiah Berlin*, edited by Alan Ryan. Oxford: Oxford University Press.

Wright, Frank Lloyd. 1992. The Architect and the Machine. In *Frank Lloyd Wright, Collected Writings*, edited by Bruce Brooks Pfeiffer. New York: Rizzoli.

Obscure Objects of Desire? Nineteenth-Century British Economists and the Price(s) of "Rare Art"

Michael V. White

There is more similarity in a precious painting by Degas and a frosted mug of beer than you ever thought possible.
—A. F. Taubman, Chairman, Southeby's Holdings Inc.

In 1970, Penguin Books issued an edition of W. Stanley Jevons's *Theory of Political Economy* (hereafter, *Theory*) using, for the front cover, a detail from a painting by Edgar Degas, the title of which was translated as *Cotton Exchange of New Orleans*. In some respects, this appears to have been an inspired choice. Having read of the art collection of the Manchester cotton manufacturer William Cottrill, Degas specifically intended his painting of 1873 to be sold to the Mancunian.[1] Two years before, Jevons had written the *Theory* in Manchester, illustrating his exchange theory of market-period trading in chapter 4 by referring to wholesale markets such as those for cotton (Jevons [1871] 1970, 132). The *Theory* is often characterized as constituting the British leg of the 1870s "marginalist revolution" in economic theory. Although the Penguin series did not include an edition of the French leg, the *Elements of Political Economy* ([1874–77, 1926] 1954) by Leon Walras, if an edition had been published, a corresponding choice for its front cover would have been Degas's painting *Portraits, at the Stock Exchange* (Brown 1994, 128–30). For in his account of market-period trading in lesson 5

I would like to thank Neil De Marchi and Roy Weintraub for helpful comments and discussion, and Marilyn Brown and Simon Schaffer for information and suggestions.

1. For information on this and other aspects of Degas's painting considered here, see the remarkable study by Marilyn Brown (1994, esp. the introduction and chap. 1).

of the *Elements*, Walras illustrated his theory of exchange by referring to trading in "3 per cent French Rentes on the Paris Stock Exchange," where disequilibrium trades were disallowed. Hence, in that Walrasian model, "theoretically trading should come to a halt" until equilibrium prevailed (Walras [1874–77, 1926] 1954, 84, 85). Such halts to trading until an equilibrium price was attained had no place in Jevons's *Theory*. The huddling of the figures in Degas's *Bourse* could then be read, in this context, as a metaphorical representation of the different types of trading assumed by Walras when compared with Jevons.

Degas, however, missed the mark on both the topic and the timing of the *Cotton* painting. Cottrill, in common with other Manchester industrialists, was taken with "rural landscapes, sentimental domestic scenes, and morally edifying historical and religious pictures" (Brown 1994, 55). Moreover, in March 1873, again in common with other cotton manufacturers, Cottrill faced a severe recession, which appears to have forced the sale of his art collection. Those events suggest a link not with Jevons's *Theory* but with Jevons's work on "business fluctuations" (or "cycles"), which was discussed in a letter to a Manchester newspaper in the same month that Cottrill liquidated his collection (see Jevons 1873). Indeed, on closer examination, the appropriateness of Degas's *Cotton* painting for the cover of the *Theory* begins to slip. Although the painting has been exhibited under various titles, the translation of the title as *Cotton Exchange of New Orleans* is unsatisfactory. The New Orleans Cotton Exchange was in a different building from Degas's uncle's cotton factoring office, which features in the painting. (Thus, the title *A Cotton Office in New Orleans* seems more to the point).[2] Moreover, there is a marked difference between the painting and Jevons's picture of market trading. In chapter 4 of the *Theory*, markets are a hive of activity with prices continually changing. While a "quiescent" market was the exception in the *Theory* (Jevons [1871] 1970, 150), a comparative lack of activity, even indolence, marks Degas's office.[3] Perhaps the most ironic slippage, however, is that while both Jevons and Walras claimed to provide a more precise explanation of market-period trading than did their predecessors, they either did not (Walras) or could not (Jevons) provide a satisfactory theoretical expla-

2. The painting is now exhibited at Pau with the title *Un Bureau de coton à la Nouvelle-Orléans*.

3. Actually, at the time Degas was painting, the New Orleans firm failed. For discussion of this and the representation of apparent indolence, see Brown 1994, 31–33.

nation of the prices of irreproducible commodities, such as the originals of these two Degas paintings. After considering the work of British economists during the nineteenth century, this result is not so surprising. For both David Ricardo ([1819] 1951), writing near the opening, and Alfred Marshall ([1891] 1961), writing near the close of the century, argued that it was not possible to provide a systematic theoretical explanation for the prices of "rare art" and that such commodities could be ignored in a general account of value and prices. While the conclusions reached were similar, the reasons given were quite different, so that examination of the "rare art" question provides a means of illustrating the significant changes in economic theory that took place during the nineteenth century. It should be noted that rare art was one example of a group of commodities referred to here as "irreproducibles," because their quantity was, to a large extent, fixed. In this sense, Old Masters were regarded as no different from rare coins, so that the same arguments applied and the illustrations given were not restricted to "art."

This essay has three main sections. Section 1 examines Ricardo and some anti-Ricardian economists writing during the 1830s, showing that the principal problem they identified with explaining art prices was due to the irreproducibility of such commodities, rather than to any unpredictability of demand. The increasing resort to a "thin" representation of human behavior and a lack of theoretical attention paid to the process of market price formation meant that when Thomas De Quincey attempted to include such commodites in a general theory of value, he relied on little more than mechanical metaphors (section 2). Although J. S. Mill adopted part of De Quincey's perspective, thereby suggesting that the prices of rare art could be included in value theory, section 3 shows that possibility became problematic in the 1860s and 1870s—for in the new theories and representations of supply and demand, the prices of rare art were incapable of a "determinate" representation, once economic behavior was cast in functional terms.

1. The Problem of Irreproducibility

The analysis in Ricardo's *Principles* depended on one variant of what has since been described as the classical method of analysis,[4] which

4. See the recent discussion of the distinction between classical method and theory in Kurz and Salvadori 1995, chap. 1.

argued that it was possible to provide a systematic theoretical explanation of long-period prices, variously described as "natural," "ordinary," "normal," "average," or "prices of production." Under a system of "free competition," with capital mobility between sectors of the economy, prices of production would, subject to a set of given techniques, correspond to a cost-minimizing production system where there was a uniform profit rate and uniform rates of renumeration for each of the "primary" production inputs. In classical theory generally, long-period prices were "taken to be known independently of the interplay of 'demand and supply'" (Kurz and Salvadori 1995, 5). They acted as "centers of gravitation" or "attractors" for market or "actual" prices, which, in fluctuating around and tending toward the minimum costs of production, were explained in terms of demand and supply. Market prices were not capable of being analyzed in the same systematic way as prices of production because they were subject to "forces" of an accidental or temporary nature. Such prices were relevant in a market period where the quantity of potentially exchangeable commodities was given. Prices and outputs would thus fluctuate in a series of market periods as the economy tended toward a long-period position. Such fluctuations could be analyzed in a detailed descriptive manner, but that necessitated a different type of analysis from that for a long-period outcome.

For Ricardo ([1819] 1951, 12), the long-period or "natural" value in exchange of most commodities was explained by "the quantity of labour required to obtain them," although this was subject to a number of important qualifications. Those commodities were reproducible because they "can be increased in quantity by the exertion of human industry" and were subject to the "unrestrained competition" of capital. However, a different explanation of value was required for irreproducible or "scarcity" commodities, such as "rare statues and pictures," "scarce books and coins," or wines from a particular location (12). With the quantity fixed, their value was, in effect, a "monopoly" or "fancy" price and, with competition all on the "side" of the buyers, depended on the "tastes, the caprice, and the power [or wealth] of purchasers" (194, 240, 249, 250). Like market-period prices, such values were explained by the "proportion of supply to demand, or demand to supply," as Ricardo indicated when he cited a long passage from the Earl of Lauderdale's *Inquiry* in that regard (383–85). Irreproducible commodities were thus quite different from reproducibles because their value "is wholly independent of the quantity of labour originally necessary to produce them, and varies with the varying wealth and inclinations of those who are desirous to possess them" (12). The unpredictability or volatility of demand was not the principal reason for the lack of systematicity, however, for Ricardo used virtually the same language to refer to manufactured commodities in a market period. While demand for agricultural output was fairly "uniform" (volatility in market prices depended largely on harvest fluctuations), manufactures were subject to "varying demand" due to "the influence of fashion, prejudice or caprice" of the purchasers (89, 263). The problem with scarcity commodities was rather that, because the supply was given, the forces of competition, in the form of capital mobility, could not alter the level of production so that there was no long-period center of gravitation. With no systematic or determinate explanation possible for such commodities, they could be put to one side because "they form a very small part of the mass of commodities daily exchanged in the market" (12).

Ricardo's value theory was subject to a good deal of criticism in the 1820s and 1830s, and one of the most influential critiques appeared in Samuel Bailey's *Critical Dissertation on the Nature, Measure and Causes of Value* ([1825] 1967). Two moves in this critique were replicated in G. P. Scrope's *Principles of Political Economy* ([1833] 1965) and in Nassau W. Senior's "encyclopaedic" *Outline of the Science of Political Economy* ([1836] 1951). The first was to argue that *value* could only be defined as an exchange ratio in what Ricardo would have deemed a market period. Moreover, it should be specified in terms "of the esteem in which any object is held. It denotes, strictly speaking, an effect on the mind" (Bailey [1825] 1967, 1; see also 181). In Scrope's ([1833] 1965) formulation, which was followed by Senior and other economists, value depended on the "desirability," "scarcity," and "exchangeability" of commodities, which would be manifested in the "proportion" between the "*demand*" ("the quantity required") and the "*supply*" ("the quantity produced") (164, 165, 168).[5] The second move was to argue that the values of most commodities included "monopolistic" elements (Bailey [1825] 1967, 223, 227; Scrope [1833] 1965, 168–69; Senior [1836] 1951, 103–11). The effect of the first move was to claim, virtually by definition, that the value of commodities could not be explained by their labor embodied. The effect of the second was that Ricardo's distinction between scarcity (or monopolized) and repro-

5. All emphases in quotations appear in the original materials.

ducible commodities would not hold, since scarcity commodities were by no means "relatively unimportant." Ricardo did not "allow sufficient importance to that basis of value which he called scarcity . . . or, in other words, monopoly, or protection from competition." Scarcity commodities constituted "a most extensive source of value" (Bailey [1825] 1967, 227, 229).

These three accounts differed as to the possibility of systematicity in the explanation of value once the cost of production and the mobility of capital were taken into account. For Bailey ([1825] 1967, 231–32), there could be no systematicity, and all that could be done was to identify post hoc the possible causes of changes in value. Scrope ([1833] 1965, 162–63), however, attempted to maintain a clear distinction between a market- and a long-period analysis by arguing that, with cost of production defined to include monopolistic elements (such as land, machine patents, and skilled labor), market prices oscillated around the long-period position. Senior ([1836] 1951, 114) resurrected Bailey's position in part, by arguing that because monopolistic elements entered as elements of cost of production, many commodities "are but little governed by any general rules."

Despite the heat generated by the disputes over value and the criticism directed at Ricardo's treatment of "scarcity" commodities, the critics had surprisingly little to add to Ricardo's analysis of such commodities. Bailey, Senior, and Scrope argued that their prices were to be explained in terms of the proportion between supply and demand and that there could be no systematic explanation for their values. As noted, Bailey ruled out any systematicity, and Scrope's discussion of cost of production could not include irreproducibles. Indeed, after referring to commodities such as "superior works of art" having a "*monopoly* value" over and above their cost of production because of their "permanent scarcity, or *rarity*," Scrope ([1833] 1965, 168–69) suggested that a further cause for the volatility of their values came from the supply side:

> A person passing through the streets of a town is struck by a stained and dirtied piece of canvas at a broker's door. He buys it for a trifle, cleans it with a little labour and expence, and it proves to be a Claude or Raphael, worth a hundred times after this discovery what it was before. It is the rarity of fine pictures by such artists that confers a monopoly value on them. Objects which are *unique* of this sort are

> often of great value in consequence. When there are but two known copies of a scarce work, it has happened that the possessor of one has bought the other at an extravagent price, for the purpose of destroying it, his single copy being, in its unique state, of greater value in the market than the two were before.

In providing the most sophisticated account of purchasers' behavior, Senior ([1836] 1951, 24) repeated Bailey's criticism of Ricardo's treatment of scarcity commodities: "The articles of wealth which do not owe the principal part of their value to the labour which has been bestowed on their respective actual production, form, in fact, the bulk of wealth, instead of a small and unimportant portion of it." Nevertheless, when discussing what were, in effect, long-period prices, he observed:

> There are some commodities the results of agents no longer in existence, or acting at remote and uncertain periods, the supply of which cannot be increased, or cannot be reckoned upon. Antiques and relics belong to the first class, and all the very rare productions of Nature or Art, such as diamonds of extraordinary size, or pictures, or statues of extraordinary beauty, to the second. The values of such commodities are subject to no definite rules, and depend altogether on the wealth or taste of the community. In common language, they are said to bear a fancy price, that is, a price depending principally on the caprice or fashion of the day. The Boccaccio, which a few years ago sold for £2000, and after a year or two's interval for £700, may, perhaps, fifty years hence, be purchased for a shilling. . . . In the following discussion we shall altogether omit such commodities, and confine our attention to those of which the supply is capable of increase, either regular, or sufficiently approaching to regularity, to admit of calculation. (97)

Whatever Senior's abilities as a political economist, they were not to be found in predicting the future prices of Old Masters. Once again, however, the problem was not that the demand for such commodities was fundamentally different from that for reproducible commodities. In his discussion of price fluctuations in a market period, Senior referred to

> how the demand is affected not merely by the existing, or the anticipated obstacles to the supply, but often by a spirit of speculation as

> blind as that of a gambler ignorant of the odds and even of the principles of his game. . . . Those who are not practically conversant with commercial transactions, and who are probably accustomed to consider our merchants and capitalists as men of sobre minds, and cautious conduct, may perhaps think that we exaggerate the influence of imagination over judgement when we suppose that large fortunes are often risked on such reasoning as this. (20, 18)

Despite the marked differences regarding value theory, Senior thus agreed with Ricardo that the problem of irreproducible commodity prices was not due to the peculiar nature of their demand. The problem was rather that such commodities were not subject to competition in their production so that their prices had no long-period anchor. They could then be ignored in a general account of price systematicity.

Two characteristics of work during this period are relevant for the subsequent analysis here. First, because market-period prices could not be subject to a systematic theoretical explanation, little attention was paid to the actual processes of price formation in a market period. Detailed examination was left to those analysts providing a more detailed descriptive account of particular topics and markets. So, for example, Senior illustrated his discussion of "blind speculation" and fluctuations in supply and demand with a long quotation from Thomas Tooke's account of the 1825–26 crisis (18–19; see also Tooke [1826] 1996, 29–32).[6] Such analyses of market-period prices were able to provide broad quantitative estimates of how different groups of prices and patterns of expenditure would change, depending on substitution, with fluctuations in demand and/or supply.[7] Indeed, in 1871 Jevons's *Theory* drew on such accounts that dated from the 1820s (Jevons [1871] 1970, 176–78). Nevertheless, the actual process of price formation in market periods was not pursued.

The second characteristic was an increasingly "thin" representation of human behavior, which was depicted as driven by the desire for wealth. This was by comparision with the "thick" depiction of behavior that Adam Smith had used in *The Wealth of Nations*, although the full explanation can be found in texts such as *The Theory of Moral Sentiments* (Smith [1759] 1976, 4:1). This is not to suggest that economists

6. This is not to suggest that Tooke's account was uninformed by theory (see Matthew Smith's introduction in Tooke [1826] 1996).

7. See, for example, the cases cited in White 1987.

assumed that the pursuit of wealth per se was a sufficient motivating factor. As Senior and J. S. Mill (1909) both acknowledged, a complex set of motives could be assumed to drive behavior where wealth was the instrument to satisfy those motivations. (Wealth was thus the domain of political economy.) Nevertheless, the detailed discussion of consumption behavior, for example, which Senior gave in the *Outline*, drawing in large part on Smith, was unusual.[8] A more mechanical depiction of behavior became the norm. The effects of this characteristic, when coupled with the first regarding price formation, can be seen in the work of the one theorist who argued subsequently for a detailed treatment of irreproducible commodity prices.

2. De Quincey and Anomalous Values

Thomas De Quincey began writing in political economy as a staunch Ricardian with the *Dialogues of Three Templars* (1824), where irreproducible commodities were not even mentioned. By the early 1840s, however, he had shifted analytical tack and his *Logic of Political Economy* (1844) can be characterized as anti-Ricardian (Groenewegen 1982). There seem to have been two reasons for the shift. First, De Quincey was alarmed by what he regarded as the "political misuse of Ricardo's doctrines by anarchists, chartists, and so on" (Groenewegen 1982, 54). Second, the *Dialogues* had been singled out by Samuel Bailey (see above) for criticism because of its Ricardian treatment of value. In the *Logic*, De Quincey now argued that reproducible and irreproducible commodities could and should be treated as analytically symmetrical within a unified theory of value.

For De Quincey (1897), there were two causes (or forces) of value: utility and difficulty of attainment. Utility (*U*), the "attractive" basis of value, based on the "intrinsic serviceableness" of a commodity, was "*affirmative* value," constituting the "whole benefit . . . the whole power . . . for possession" (150). Difficulty of attainment (*D*), ostensi-

8. See the discussion of Senior in White 1992. Senior ([1836] 1951, 12) argued that consumption behavior was often driven by a lack of careful comparision of cost and benefits or "pleasure and pain." While this was a very Smithian point (Smith [1759] 1976, 181), it was also consistent with the "irrational" behavior that Senior ascribed to market trading. This seems difficult to square with the reported comment that "in Senior there is a real economic man and he is motivated all the time by rational choice. Nassau Senior was thus the true Lionel Robbins of the 19th century" (*History of Economic Thought Newsletter*, 7).

bly identified with the cost of production, was "*negative value*," constituting "a pure resistance to that desire" of possession or "the whole resistance to your possession" (151). While the presence of both *U* and *D* was required for a commodity to have exchange value, only one force could "take effect at one time," so that either *U* or *D* would dominate. In 99 percent of cases, the dominating force would be *D*; however, if there was a situation of scarcity, for example, *U* would dominate. The case of a complete monopoly, where the seller could "screw" the price up to the maximum and the purchaser would pay rather than not obtain the commodity, was a case of "affirmative value carried to extremity" (168). With *U* and *D* understood as "forces"—*U* as a "power" and *D* as "resistance" (166)—the monopoly case was illustrated by the (subsequently much-cited) "hypothetic" sale of a musical snuffbox on a steamboat on Lake Superior (138–40). This case, where *D*, though "not absent" was "unlimited" and hence "inoperative" (139), could be represented by figure 1 from the *Logic*, where *D* is 10 and the maximum *U* is 20.

The role of *U* in governing prices was illustrated with a number of cases of irreproducible commodities, instances of "anomalous values not considered in books of political economy" (173). De Quincey did provide some explanation of the motivations governing *U* in these cases. The price of a rhinocerous (in the 1680s) depended on its "power and strange conformation," which could be exhibited as a "public curiosity," while the contemporaneous price for Turkish horses depended on their "beauty and docility." The price of a rare book or manuscript depended on its "rarity," but as a "fancy price" it was highly "variable" because it was largely dependent on the "caprice" of purchasers (their "feelings" and "fortunes"), and some allowance had to be made for regret in purchases. That type of rarity could be contrasted with "Italian masterpieces" (Da Vinci or Michelangelo) whose prices did not fluctuate but rather rose consistently due their "pre-eminence." Here, *U* was based on an "enlightened sensibility to the finest effects of art" (163, 164, 168, 192). Keeping in mind that this was not an analysis couched in terms of the later marginal utility theory or supply and demand functions, De Quincey also provided instances of market prices where limits were set by the possibility of substitution (salmon), of the conditions when a monopolist would destroy part of the supply to increase total revenue (spices), and why the actual price would not cor-

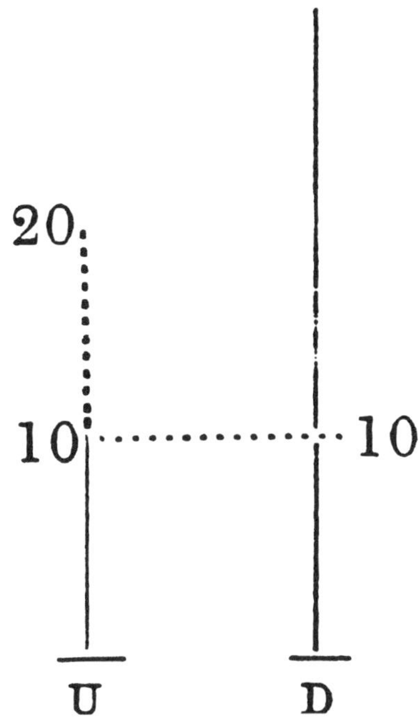

Figure 1 De Quincey's value/air pump diagram. From De Quincey 1897, 9:141.

respond to cost of production because of lags between demand and adjusting supply (coach-horses) (169–70, 158, 204–5).[9]

Nevertheless, the discussion of the examples indicated little about the processes by which prices were actually determined. The pertinence of the examples lay in their novelty rather than in a discussion of market processes. Moreover, there was no substantive theory of behavior deployed to explain the theory of value. Instead, De Quincey resorted to a series of mechanical metaphors, drawing on Robert Boyle's *Hydrostatical Paradoxes* (1664; in Boyle 1772). For example, to explain how it might appear paradoxical that only one force could be operative at any moment, De Quincey referred to specific gravity in "physics": "One gravity rises through another gravity. True, it is specifically

9. These examples were the same or similar to those found in the preceding literature discussing changes in market-period prices and their effects (see section 2).

lighter, but it still *has* a specific gravity . . . the same machinery serves for sinking objects and for raising them. By gravity they fall; by gravity they rise" (De Quincey 1897, 136). The analogue with *U* and *D* was that while both must be "uniformly present," only one could be "operative" at any time (137).[10] The *Paradoxes* was also used to explain how *U* could be operative, as in figure 1, where De Quincey relied on a pressure pump metaphor. In the musical snuffbox example, *D* is "inoperative. The inertness of D allowed U to put forth its total effect. The practical compression of D being withdrawn, U springs up like water in a pump when released from the pressure of air" (139). Since *D* could not exert "any positive force" (because it was "unlimited"), the "retirement of D from all agency whatever on the price . . . creates, as it were, a perfect vacuum, and through that vacuum U rushes up to its highest and ultimate graduation" (140). Given this, De Quincey's diagrams are reminiscent of some of those produced by Boyle (figure 2).[11]

These were not the only metaphors used to explain why the two forces were "equally indispensable" but only one "becomes operative in the price" (140).[12] De Quincey returned again to the specific gravity metaphor to criticize Adam Smith's reference to utility in *The Wealth of Nations*: "You might as well say that abstractedly, and without reference to *specific gravity*, pine timber is heavy or not heavy. . . . Specific

10. This appears to rely on Boyle's paradox 2: "That a lighter fluid may gravitate or weigh upon a heavier" (Boyle 1772, 754–59).

11. It has been suggested that the "basis for De Quincey's understanding of consumer psychology," as in the snuffbox analysis, can be found in his opium addiction (Henderson 1995, 107). Attractive though this may be, it is not convincing. De Quincey was an addict before he wrote the Ricardian *Templars*. A more secure explanation could draw on the following: (1) De Quincey's response to Bailey on scarcity commodities; (2) his familiarity with the *Hydrostatical Paradoxes*, which is mentioned in the *Templars* (but only regarding the definition of paradoxes); (3) Bailey's use, in a chapter where he criticized the *Templars*, of a "hydrostatics" metaphor to discuss the link between value and cost of production (Bailey [1825] 1967, 195); (4) De Quincey's interactions with "friends . . . drawn, chiefly, from the intellectual circles surrounding the universities" of Glasgow and Edinburgh after he moved to Scotland in 1830 (Lindop 1995, 9). In the early 1840s, De Quincey stayed, and maintained contact, with the astronomer J. P. Nichol. In 1846 that contact led to De Quincey's notorious article that discussed the "nebular hypothesis," Nichol's astronomical model that drew on hydrodynamic principles (Lindop 1995, 10; Schaffer 1989). For a contemporary Edinburgh University assessment of the role of Boyle and air pumps, see Wilson 1849.

12. For example, if *U* were pushed to its "ultimate value," it is as if "a screw were made to operate upon the purchaser's secret appreciation of its serviceable qualities." Or, *U* and *D* "must eternally form the two limits within which the tennis-ball of price flies backward and forward" (De Quincey 1897, 140, 191).

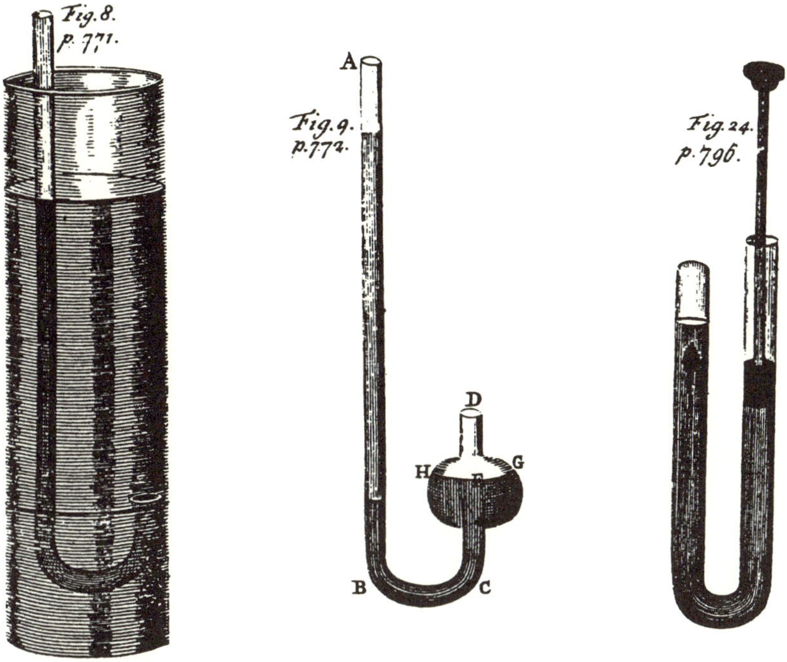

Figure 2 Diagrams of Boyle's hydrostatistical paradoxes. From Boyle 1772, 750, 772, 780.

gravity . . . always presupposes a past collation of weights, because it compares the weights under equal bulks; and then it becomes reasonable to say that lead is heavy, else the proposition is unmeaning. A little water, and in the wrong place, has no value: a great deal of water, and in the right place . . . has a very great value" (188). This criticism of Smith (and hence Ricardo) was not based on a careful critique of Smith's discussion of behavior and utility in *The Theory of Moral Sentiments*. Indeed, questions of moral philosophy were brusquely dismissed from the domain of political economy. Moreover, De Quincey basically repeated some earlier arguments of Jeremy Bentham by misrepresenting Smith's reference so as to dismiss it (White 1996a). What is striking, then, is that, with no theory of human behavior as such, the mechanical metaphors now comprised virtually the whole argument.

In this context, there were two significant departures from Ricardo's analysis. First, De Quincey effectively reduced difficulty of attainment to a subjective category to make it commensurate with *U*.[13] Second, the focus was on the *actual* price in a market. By arguing that most reproducible commodities would sell at their cost of production, which became the "actual price," and which could then be compared with the market prices of commodities not selling at their cost of production, De Quincey in effect collapsed the distinction between long-period and market prices that underpinned Ricardo's analysis.[14] In this way he claimed that the Ricardian distinction between scarcity and cost value was nonsense.[15]

De Quincey also attacked references to supply and demand as an explanation of value, basically on the ground that they could not explain the underlying value of transactions. Nevertheless, it was possible, as J. S. Mill noted, to read it as a type of supply and demand theory. In his *Principles*, Mill (1909, book 3, chap. 2) made extensive use of the *Logic*, particularly the musical snuffbox example, to fold it back into Mill's version of the classical method where the prices of irreproducibles and the market-period prices of irreproducibles were explained by reference to supply and demand. It is noteworthy, however, that while irreproducible commodities were no longer declared irrelevant, there was no systematic treatment of such commodities by Mill and the mechanical approach continued to dominate, neatly illustrated by Mill's discussion of how equilibrium would occur between supply and demand in a market period.

3. Problems with Functional Behavior

In the mid- to late 1860s, Mill's analysis of supply and demand was subject to a detailed critique by William Thornton (1869), who switched attention to the explanation of trading on a "day" within a market period. (See the discussion and references in White 1994.) Thornton's argument provided a focal point for three analysts to be considered in this section—W. Stanley Jevons, H. C. Fleeming Jenkin, and Alfred

13. Although difficulty of attainment was identified at one point with the labor and profit required to produce a commodity, it was defined as the "resistance to the reproduction of the article" and as "the whole resistance to your possession" (De Quincey 1897, 186, 157, 179, 151).

14. This was the principal reason for the savage criticism of Ricardo on "market" prices in the *Logic*: "A very short chapter, and a very bad one (the worst in the whole series)" (De Quincey 1897, 200).

15. For further discussion of the differences with Ricardo in the *Logic*, see Groenewegen 1982.

Marshall—all of whom attempted to defend and recast the meaning of supply and demand by representing economic behavior in functionalist terms. While their work marked a significant break in British political economy, Jevons and Jenkin maintained the method of distinguishing between a market and a long period, albeit paying more attention to trading on a market day.[16] It was in the latter context that the explanation of "rare art" prices was of particular relevance. Since these theorists argued that their functionalist approach could provide a more rigorous explanation and representation of both market-period and long-period outcomes, and given that the use of mechanical metaphors can often be found in their work, it might be thought that De Quincey would be accorded an honorable place as a forerunner of their approach. But Jevons singled out De Quincey's treatment of utility and the value of irreproducible commodities for scathing (and inaccurate) criticism (Black 1973–81, 7:79–80). It is thus more than ironical that his own approach could not provide a determinate explanation for the market price of such commodities. The same conclusion applies to the accounts of supply and demand given by Jenkin and Marshall. To show this, and because of the differences in the theories used, it will be useful to consider first Jevons and then Jenkin, since the points considered provide a necessary background for evaluating Marshall's comments on rare art in his *Principles*.

While Jevons provided a summary of the marginal utility theory in his "Brief Account" of 1862, the more detailed version was published in the *Theory* of 1871. In chapter 4 Jevons set out a theory of market-period prices couched in terms of equilibrium conditions or "equations of exchange."[17] The depiction of a market equilibrium by means of the calculus required the assumption that commodities were "divisible *ad infinitum*" (Jevons [1871] 1970, 158). A particular problem was thus represented by indivisible commodities, such as, Jevons ([1862] 1866, 285) noted in "Brief Account," "unique objects, like a statue, a rare book, or gem, which do not admit of the conception of more or less." Clearly, this could include pieces of rare art. With the exchange of an indivisible commodity for a divisible one (money), the decision of the purchaser was between "the whole, or none" and, instead of marginal

16. Marshall's market periodization went beyond the two mentioned here.

17. In a letter to J. E. Cairnes in 1872, Jevons made clear that chapter 4 dealt with a market period, while the following chapter contained his long-period analysis of cost of production (Black 1973–81, 3:246).

conditions, the analysis could only be conducted in terms of the total utilities of the two commodities for the two transactors. The exchange equations then "certainly fail . . . [and] the problem proves to be, within certain limits, indeterminate" (Jevons [1871] 1970, 157, 158), for the price could range between the highest offer that the purchaser was prepared to make and the reservation price of the seller.[18] Provided a sale did occur, the price would depend on the process of bargaining and hence on "the disposition and force of character of the parties, their comparative persistency, their adroitness and experience in business or it may be on feelings of justice and kindliness. . . . These are motives more or less extraneous to a theory of economics, and yet they appear necessary conditions in this problem. It may be that indeterminate bargains of this kind are best arranged by an arbitrator or third party" (159).[19] He noted subsequently that, for commodities that were "practically unique and incomparable with . . . another," there was "no approach to rule or congruity . . . no consideration of cost of production or utility can apply; the arbitrary fancy of some monarch or wealthy person is the only rule" (Jevons 1905, 149–50). Where there was indeterminacy, "the laws of supply and demand do not apply" (Jevons [1882] 1894, 157–58).

As far as Jevons was concerned, the ramifications of indeterminacy that accompanied indivisibility were profound. For the exchange equations would also "fail" when commodities such as wine, paper, and ink were divisible "but not to infinitesimally small quantities." In that case, a commodity would be purchased only if the total utility of the unit was greater than that of the money paid at the price set in the market (Jevons [1871] 1970, 160–61). This was the thin edge of a wedge that threatened the commodity domain and hence the applicability of the theory. Jevons's exchange theory was not meant to be a general account as he specifically restricted its commodity domain: "A very large part of the labour of any community is spent upon the production of the ordinary necessaries and conveniences of life, such as food, clothing,

18. Here, Jevons cited Thornton's *On Labour* regarding the possible price range. It was the only instance in which he was prepared to acknowledge that Thornton's analysis had any substantive validity.

19. For divisible commodities in the *Theory*, prices were assumed to be set by brokers so that, in general, market transactors were price-takers. In Jevons's (1878, 99–100) *Political Economy* primer, however, a small local market was discussed in which both buyers and sellers changed prices.

buildings, utensils, furniture, ornaments etc.; and the aggregate of these things, therefore, is the immediate object of our attention" (101).[20] Given this, the acknowledgment that indivisible commodities included not just those mentioned in the "Brief Account" but also "every house, mansion, estate, factory, shop and other complete whole which is sold for money" and that such (bargaining) sales were "exceedingly common" (158), it is evident that the representation of value and exchange in terms of marginal equilibrium conditions in the *Theory* was restricted to a confined group of reproducible commodities that were consumed by the mass of the population.

Jevons received no help from the first edition of Walras's *Elements* on this matter. Following his discussion of trading modeled on the "competitive conditions" of the bourse, Walras ([1874–77, 1926] 1954, 86) loftily observed:

> Economists, generally speaking, have fallen all too frequently into the error of studying value in exchange under unusual circumstances. They are always talking about diamonds, Raphael's paintings, and concert recitals given by famous singers. . . . Of course our theory should cover all such special cases. The general laws of the market . . . should even apply to a market like the one Mr. De Quincey imagines, in which there is a single buyer, a single seller, one commodity and only one minute in which to make the exchange. But logic demands that we consider general before special cases, and not the other way round. What physicist would deliberately pick cloudy weather for astronomical observations instead of taking advantage of a cloudless night?

Apart from De Quincey, just which economists were "always talking" about such commodities was not explained.[21] And, as was so often the case, an airy reference to physics obscured an absence. For Walras neglected to return to explain how his general equilibrium theory would deal with such cases.[22]

Jevons then queried sympathetic correspondents about the solution to the indivisibility problem but again received little help. Part of the

20. The limits of the commodity domain were consistent with Jevons's ([1871] 1970, 226, 239–40) subsequent definition of "capital" as a bundle of commodities.

21. It might be noted that De Quincey's analysis of *U* and *D* sounds similar to some work by Rau and Herman, dating from the 1820s and 1830s, as described by Erich Streissler (1990, 48).

reason for this was that his discussion in the *Theory* ran together several analytically distinct questions: indivisibility with homogeneous and heterogeneous commodities and indivisibility with large and small numbers of transactors. There was a tendency by his correspondents to treat the problem as simply one of small numbers of transactors, which was deemed to be of little practical importance. The only substantive aid came from F. Y. Edgeworth's (1881) *Mathematical Psychics*, which explained how an "exchange is indeterminate, if *either* (1) one of the trading bodies (*qua* individual or *qua* union) or (2) the commodity supplied by one of the dealers, be *indivisible or not perfectly divisible*" (29–30). But even this analysis was of limited help for the particular problem Jevons had posed. Edgeworth's theory of recontracting in exchange simply assumed "the indivisibility of each article of *contract*. . . . This species of imperfection will not be explicitly treated here; partly perhaps because it is of secondary practical importance; and partly because it has been sufficiently treated by Professor Jevons" (19, 109).[23] The threat to the commodity domain of the *Theory* remained. When he referred to Ricardo's discussion of the "value" of irreproducible commodities such as "rare pictures" in the *Theory*, Jevons ([1871] 1970, 186) resurrected an old criticism by claiming that Ricardo had himself provided a decisive objection to a labor theory of value: "The mere fact that there are many things, such as rare ancient books, coins, antiquities, etc., which have high values, and which are absolutely incapable of production now, disperses the notion that value depends on labour." Yet his own theory could not provide a determinate explanation for the values of such commodities.

Supply and demand functions or diagrams had no place in Jevons's analysis. This was in contrast to Jenkin's 1870 contribution to the reformulation of the laws of supply and demand, which followed the debate over Thornton's critique. Jenkin (1870, 151) claimed that he would show, "in a rigorous manner," how the laws "admit of being stated as

22. Walras ([1874–77, 1926] 1954, 400) did note subsequently that, for scarce books and wines, "the value of such products, as both Ricardo and Mill admit, is the result of the law of offer and demand alone."

23. After reviewing *Mathematical Psychics*, Jevons acknowledged Edgeworth's analysis in his *State in Relation to Labour* ([1882] 1894), when he discussed wage bargaining with a union "combination" of labor, referring to the analysis of indeterminacy in the *Theory* and to Edgeworth's "dead lock." In that case, "the laws of supply and demand do not apply" (157–58).

accurately, and defined in the same manner, as any mathematical laws affecting quantities of any description." The analysis depended heavily on the use of diagrams with a "minimalist" explanation of behavior represented by the geometry. Indeed, Jenkin subsequently made clear that he rejected Jevons's marginal utility theory and could see "little or no advantage" in representing the laws of supply and demand in equations.[24]

In his discussion of a market period where there was a given stock or "*whole supply*" from which trading could occur, Jenkin simply assumed a given "purchase fund," so that the quantity demanded would vary inversely with the price. (No clear explanation was given for the upward-sloping supply curve.) Here, the first law was that "*in a given market, at a given time, the market price will be that at which the supply and demand curves cut*" (153). If the curves applied to trading at a particular "moment" on a market day, Jenkin also noted it was highly unlikely they would remain fixed for even "five minutes." He further illustrated the effects of shifts in the curves by shifting the "whole supply" or "purchase fund," the effects of which were summarized in the second law: "*If the whole supply be increased, it will most frequently, but not always, happen that the supply at a price will throughout the scale, be increased; prices will then fall. . . . If the purchase fund is increased it will often happen that the demand at a price will rise throughout the whole scale; prices will then rise*" (157).

After discussing some of Thornton's criticisms by means of different shapes in supply and demand curves, Jenkin turned to the explanation of long-period or "long-run" prices, arguing that neither of the first two laws would provide much help in at least one case:

> If the supply be limited, as in the case of pictures by an old master, the desire for the article may rise or fall to any extent both on the part of buyers and sellers. The knowledge that only 200 pictures of a given artist exist helps us in no conceivable way to determine what their value will be, nor whether that value will rise or fall. In a given market, on a given day, the elements of demand and supply curves already exist in the minds of purchasers and sellers, and both laws

24. Jenkin and Jevons had corresponded on the marginal utility theory in 1868, following Jenkin's publication of a general equation for supply and demand functions (Jenkin 1868, 13 n–14 n, 17 n, 19 n; Black 1973–81, 3:166–78). For Jenkin's rejection of the marginal utility theory and equations, see Jenkin 1871, 618, 620.

> will apply, but neither law in the least helps us to determine the absolute height of either the supply or the demand curve at any one time (164).

Indeed, with such a "limited supply we are thrown back on the truism that the price of the article depends on the desire felt for that article relative to others," although the outcome would be subject to any reservation price set by the seller. Since the analytics of value in this case were "unapproachable," Jenkin turned to the long-run prices of manufactured commodities (164).[25] In one respect, this simply reproduced, albeit in a supply and demand format, the old conclusion that there could be no systematic explanation for the long-period prices of such commodities. At the same time, Jenkin's comment that both laws of supply and demand would "apply" in a market period, which entails the claim that a determinate solution could be represented by the diagrams, is unsatisfactory. In the case of an Old Master sold on a market day, it is not possible to draw Jenkin's usual supply and demand curves, as that would require depicting a series of prices offered or sought for different quantities of the same commodity. Since this is not possible for a single Old Master, a more appropriate diagram might be Jenkin's representation of the separate sales of two horses, *Sunshine* and *Fairy* (reproduced here as figure 3).[26] In the *Sunshine* example, there could be no sale because the seller's reservation price is above the demander's maximum. In the *Fairy* case, a sale was possible but there is no determinate outcome since there is a range of possible prices. As Jenkin put it, "the price is indeterminate, depending on the relative skills of the two people bargaining" (161). That outcome is analogous to Jevons's analysis of indeterminacy.[27] Although Jenkin's argument was restricted to the case of a single buyer and a single seller with an indivisible commodity, the possibility of a market demand curve for a series of Old Masters is also problematic. The shape of Jenkin's downward-sloping demand curves simply depended on a given purchase fund divided by

25. Even here, Jenkin's (1870, 165) analysis looks peculiar with regard to subsequent supply and demand theory: "*In the long run, the price of the manufactured article is chiefly determined by the cost of its production, and the quantity manufactured is chiefly determined by the demand at that price.*"

26. As with all Jenkin's diagrams, prices are indicated on the abscissa and quantities on the ordinate. It was Marshall who established the tradition of "inverting" the axes (Gordon 1982; White 1996b, 117).

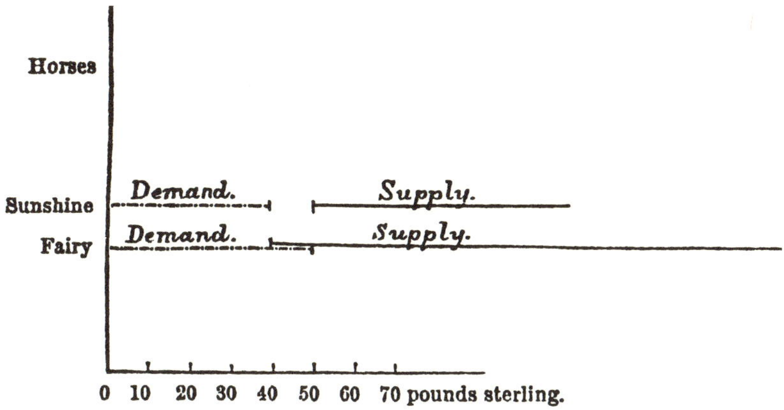

Figure 3 Jenkin's "Sunshine and Fairy" diagram. From Jenkin 1870, 161.

different quantities of the commodity. This seems to assume that the commodities are homogenous. If the commodities are heterogeneous, however, as would presumably be the case with works by one Old Master, it is not clear what shape the demand curve would have without some further specification of the behavior represented by the curve.

This point can be illustrated by considering some remarks by Alfred Marshall and Mary Paley Marshall in their *Economics of Industry* (1879). While Alfred had begun working with supply and demand diagrams before reading Jenkin or Jevons, he explained that a downward-sloping market demand curve was created by purchasers buying discrete units of the commodity and exiting the market as the price increased. This was not a marginal utility theory, and Marshall's use of that theory to explain a demand curve, for example, only became evident after he had reviewed Jevons's *Theory*. (See discussion and references in White 1996b.) The review rejected Jevons's argument that "*value depends solely on the final degree of utility*" (Jevons [1871] 1970, 187),[28] and the criticism was renewed in the *Economics of Industry* in part by arguing that Jevons's statement could only apply in the "exceptional" case

> of a commodity which is fixed in amount, as for instance Raphael's pictures. Their price depends on the desire that people have for such

27. Although Jevons referred to indivisibility in the "Brief Account," the terms of the discussion in the *Theory* suggest that he had drawn on Jenkin when constructing the analysis.

> pictures, and the means at their disposal for purchasing them. According to the Law of Demand, the price of a commodity "measures its final utility to each purchaser, that is, the value in use to him of that portion of it, which it is only just worth his while to buy." The greater the number of pictures, the less will be the competition among purchasers of them, the less will be the price which measures their value in use to those who are only just induced to purchase them. In this exceptional case in which the supply is fixed, the price is determined solely by the utility of the thing; Demand is the sole regulator of value. (Marshall and Marshall 1879, 92–93)[29]

This argument could be represented diagrammatically by (at least two) perfectly inelastic supply curves intersected by a downward-sloping demand curve, the shape of which is explained by Jevons's final degree of utility. It is, however, misleading or, at best, incomplete. Marshall appears to be discussing a market for a series of Raphaels. A smoothed or continuous demand curve simply ignores Jevons's discussion of the problem of indivisibility.[30] It is possible, as later work has shown, to represent the demand for a series of Old Masters by a "stair step" function, which would deal with indivisibility although there is no single "determinate" price for each sale.[31] That representation depends on the assumption that the buyers are indifferent between each Raphael, so that all units are effectively homogenous. Where the different units are heterogeneous, however, so that the buyers (or their agents) discriminate between them, the trade in each painting must be treated separately, and no downward-sloping demand function can be drawn.[32] Marshall had simply suppressed Jevons's problem with an indivisible "unique" commodity.[33]

28. Jevons's "final degree of utility" can be taken here as equivalent to the later "marginal utility."

29. See also Marshall and Marshall 1879, 69–70. The internal quotation in the passage cited here is from p. 71 of the Marshalls' text. The same argument was used in Marshall's ([1891] 1961) *Principles* to criticize Jevons's formulation of his argument in the now (in)famous "catena." Although the point will not be pursued here, Marshall's criticism rested on a misunderstanding of the meaning Jevons gave to *value*.

30. Moreover, assumptions should be specified regarding the marginal utility of money for different transactors; much of Marshall's criticism of Jevons turned on this matter (White 1996b).

31. Each price would be in the range between the bids of the two highest bidders, provided that these exceeded any reservation price of the seller. See Heilbrun and Gray 1993, 156; for a more detailed exposition, see Weintraub 1974, 69–72.

That Marshall recognized subsequently that *The Economics of Industry* ignored indivisibility and rested on a homogeneity assumption is suggested by the different argument that appeared in his *Principles*. In the second chapter of book 5, where he considered the explanation of market-day prices under the heading of the "temporary equilibrium of demand and supply," Marshall ([1891] 1961, 2:353) argued:

> We may put aside also as of very little practical importance, a class of dealings which has occupied a good deal of space in economic literature. They relate to such things as pictures by the old masters, rare coins and other things, which cannot be "graded" at all; for each of them is unique and has no direct equivalent or competitor. Anyone who offers to buy such a thing, without any thought of selling it again, has to assure himself only that the pleasure he will derive from its possession is as great as that which he could get by spending its price in any other way; the highest price to which he will go is governed by the utility or pleasure giving power to him of money on the one hand and the object of worth on the other. And therefore the price at which such a thing is sold will depend very much on whether any rich persons with a fancy for that particular thing happen to be present at its sale. If not, it will probably be bought by dealers who reckon on being able to sell it at a profit; and the variations in the price for which the same picture sells at successive auctions, great as they are, would be greater still if it were not for the steadying influence of professional and semi-professional purchasers. The "equilibrium price" for such sales is very much a matter of accident; but the curious might reap some reward from a minute study of it.[34]

32. For Marshallian-type diagrams that ignore this point, see Heilbrun and Gray 1993, 154, 157.

33. The problem with homogeneity is reminiscent of that raised by Wicksteed (1934, 789–95) regarding the erroneous use of heterogeneous (rather than homogenous) inputs for a marginal product function. For further consideration of this point, with regard to labor and "capital," see Sylos Labini 1988. It is relevant for Sylos Labini's analysis that much confusion has arisen in the reading of Keynes's *General Theory* because of the (erroneous) assumption that he was using homogenous, rather than heterogeneous, increments of labor (Sardoni 1994, 72–73).

34. This paragraph first appeared in the second edition. An abbreviated version replaced it in the fifth and subsequent editions (Marshall [1891] 1961, 1:332).

If Marshall engaged in some mythmaking here,[35] it should be remembered that he subsequently made clear that he had little faith that a supply and demand apparatus was of much help in a "temporary equilibrium" analysis. This was because the assumptions necessary to establish a unique equilibrium position were so restrictive that the analysis was of little practical use.[36] The use, in the passage above, of "equilibrium price" in quotation marks suggests that, even within that framework, commodities such as Old Masters posed particular problems when compared with, say, markets for financial instruments. Yet the reasons for this were not stated clearly. It does appear that Marshall now rejected the use of a market demand curve, based on marginal utility theory, due to the existence of heterogeneity, to which he referred as "grading." The references to utility suggest instead a restatement of Jevons's point that the purchase of such commodities should be couched in terms of total rather than marginal utility. Given the range of indeterminacy that followed, the unpredictable appearance of "rich" potential buyers on a particular day increased the variability of prices, although that would be tempered by the role of specialist "dealers." Marshall had replicated Ricardo's conclusion that no systematic explanation could be given for the prices of such irreproducible commodities and that they could be dismissed as of little "practical" significance. The difference between them was that Ricardo could argue their market prices could be discussed in terms of the "proportion" between supply and demand. For Jevons, Jenkin, and Marshall, there could be no determinate explanation for the prices of rare art, either in a market or in a long period. It was the reformulation of the laws of supply and demand in terms of functional behavior that produced that result.[37]

35. Apart from De Quincey, there seems little basis for Marshall's (and Walras's) claim that discussion of irreproducibles "has occupied a good deal of space in economic literature."

36. See Whitaker 1996, 2:391; also 1:275. For an attempt to identify more clearly the assumptions necessary in Marshall's argument in the *Principles*, see Kregel 1995.

37. Böhm-Bawerk's discussion of a horse market, albeit without Marshallian-type demand and supply fuctions, also discusses an "indeterminate" result. That analysis was referred to in the early literature on game theory in economics; see Endres 1996 and the references cited therein.

Conclusions

Echoes of the nineteenth-century problem of providing a systematic or determinate theoretical explanation for the prices of irreproducible commodities, such as rare art or books, can be found in more recent commentaries. Commenting on the peculiar prices posted in catalogs of rare economic books, for example, Arnold Heertje (1990, 100) referred to Ricardo's distinction between producible and irreproducible commodities, suggesting that "this important distinction has been neglected in orthodox economic theory, price theory being applied to both types of goods as if there is no difference at all." The peculiarity of such prices does not mean that no explanation can be given for them. Indeed, the factors Heertje identified as relevant in that regard were similar, though not identical, to those in Baumol's (1985, 1) analysis of "the market for the visual arts, particularly the works of noted creators who are no longer living." Using a time-series analysis, Baumol argued that the prices of such items were "inherently rudderless" or "unanchored" and that purchasing them for a financial return was akin to participating in a "floating crap game" (1, 2). The reasons for this were a zero elasticity of supply; the uniqueness of each item; the monopoly position of the supplier; imperfect information; the impossibility of detecting a "true" price as could be found on financial markets (if the strong form of efficient market theory prevailed); and, most importantly, "the fickleness of taste whose meanderings defy prediction" (8, 9, 17). Such prices were quite different from those for commodities such as steel bolts where there was a tendency toward a long-run position, given the mobility of capital and constant returns to scale. Casting the problem in that way, using a long-period method, produced a similar conclusion to that reached by the classical and early postclassical authors discussed in this article, although the theory reflects the postclassical theory of demand and supply. The reader, however, might gain the impression that the conclusion was a new one one as Baumol commented that, while "classical economics devoted considerable attention to the concept of natural [i.e., long-period] value . . . in the market for the visual arts . . . there exists no such equilibrium level, so that the prices of such art objects are strictly *un*natural in the classical sense. Their prices float more or less aimlessly and their unpredictable oscillations are apt to be exacerbated by the activities of those who treat such art objects as investments" (1). It does seem odd not to have mentioned here that the classical economists, such as Ricardo, were quite clear that a long-period analysis could not depict a "natural value" for such commodities and that a systematic or determinate theoretical explanation of market prices continued to be elusive.

References

Bailey, Samuel. [1825] 1967. *A Critical Dissertation on the Nature, Measure, and Causes of Value*. New York: Augustus M. Kelley.

Baumol, William J. 1985. *Unnatural Value: Or Art Investment as Floating Crap Game*. Research Report 85-25. New York: New York University, C.V. Starr Center for Applied Economics. Revised 1986. In *American Economic Review* 76.2:10–14.

Black, R. D. C. 1973–81. *The Papers and Correspondence of William Stanley Jevons*. Vols. 2–7. London: Macmillan.

Boyle, Robert. 1772. *The Works of the Honourable Robert Boyle*. Vol. 2. Edited by Thomas Birch, W. Johnston, et al. London.

Brown, Marilyn R. 1994. *Degas and the Business of Art: A Cotton Office in New Orleans*. University Park: Pennsylvania State University Press.

De Quincey, Thomas. 1897. *The Collected Works of Thomas De Quincey.* Vol. 9. Edited by David Masson. London: A & C Black.

Edgeworth, F. Y. 1881. *Mathematical Psychics: An Essay on the Application of Mathematics to the Moral Sciences*. London: Macmillan.

Endres, A. M. 1996. Some Microfoundations of Austrian Economics: Bohm-Bawerk's Version. *European Journal of the History of Economic Thought* 3.1:84–106.

Gordon, S. 1982. Why Did Marshall Transpose the Axes? *Eastern Economic Journal* 8.1:31–45.

Groenewegen, P. D. 1982. Thomas De Quincey: Faithful Disciple of Ricardo? *Contributions to Political Economy* 1:51–58.

Heertje, Arnold. 1990. Collecting Rare Economic Books. *Contributions to Political Economy* 9:99–105.

Heilbrun, James, and Charles M. Gray. 1993. *The Economics of Art and Culture*. Cambridge: Cambridge University Press.

Henderson, Willie. 1995. *Economics as Literature*. London: Routledge.

History of Economic Thought Newsletter. 1997. No. 59 (winter): 7.

Jenkin, H. C. Fleeming. 1868. Trade-Unions: How Far Legitimate? *North British Review* 48.95 (March): 1–62.

———. 1870. The Graphic Representation of the Laws of Supply and Demand, and Their Application to Labour. In *Recess Studies*, edited by Sir Alexander Grant. Edinburgh: Edmonston & Douglas.

———. 1871. On the Principles which Regulate the Incidence of Taxes. *Proceedings of the Royal Society of Edinburgh* (session 1871–72) 7.84:618–31.

Jevons, W. Stanley. [1862] 1866. Brief Account of a General Mathematical Theory of Political Economy. *Journal of the Statistical Society* 29 (June): 282–87.
———. [1871] 1970. *The Theory of Political Economy*. Edited by R. D. C. Black. Harmondsworth, England: Pelican.
———. 1873. Commercial Panics. *Pall Mall Gazette*, 17 March, 7.
———. 1878. *Political Economy*. London: Macmillan.
———. [1882] 1894. *The State in Relation to Labour*. 3d ed. Edited by Michael Cababe. London: Macmillan.
———. 1905. *The Principles of Economics*. Edited by Henry Higgs. London: Macmillan.
Kregel, J. A. 1995. Neoclassical Price Theory, Institutions, and the Evolution of the Security Market Organisation. *Economic Journal* 105.429:459–70.
Kurz, Heinz, and Neri Salvadori. 1995. *Theory of Production: A Long-Period Analysis*. Cambridge: Cambridge University Press.
Lindop, Grevel. 1995. English Reviewers and Scottish Professors. *Times Literary Supplement*, 29 December, 9–10.
Marshall, Alfred. [1891] 1961. *The Principles of Economics*, 9th variorum ed. 2 vols. Edited by C. W. Guillebaud. London: Macmillan.
Marshall, Alfred, and Mary Paley Marshall. 1879. *The Economics of Industry*. London: Macmillan.
Mill, John Stuart. 1909. *The Principles of Political Economy*. Edited by William Ashley. London: Longman Green.
Ricardo, David. [1819] 1951. *On the Principles of Political Economy and Taxation*. In vol. 1 of *The Works and Correspondence of David Ricardo*, edited by Piero Sraffa, with the collaboration of M. H. Dobb. Cambridge: Cambridge University Press.
Sardoni, Claudio. 1994. *The General Theory* and the Critique of Decreasing Returns. *Journal of the History of Economic Thought* 16.1:61–85.
Schaffer, Simon. 1989. The Nebular Hypothesis and the Science of Progress. In *History, Humanity, and Evolution*, edited by J. R. Moore. Cambridge: Cambridge University Press.
Scrope, G. Poulett. [1833] 1965. *Principles of Political Economy Deduced from the Natural Laws of Social Welfare and Applied to the Present State of Britain*. New York: Augustus M. Kelley.
Senior, Nassau W. [1836] 1951. *An Outline of the Science of Political Economy*. London: Allen & Unwin.
Smith, Adam. [1759] 1976. *The Theory of Moral Sentiments*. Edited by D. D. Raphael and A. L. Macfie. Oxford: Clarendon.
Streissler, Erich W. 1990. The Influence of German Economics on the Work of Menger and Marshall. In *Carl Menger and His Legacy in Economics*, edited by Bruce J. Caldwell. Durham, N.C.: Duke University Press.
Sylos Labini, Paolo. 1988. The Great Debates on the Laws of Returns and the Value of Capital: When Will Economists Finally Accept Their Own Logic?

Banca Nazionale del Lavoro Quarterly 106 (September): 263–91.

Thornton, William Thomas. 1869. *On Labour: Its Wrongful Claims and Rightful Dues: Its Present and Possible Future.* London: Macmillan.

Tooke, Thomas. [1826] 1996. *Considerations on the State of the Currency.* Edited by Matthew Smith. Reprints of Economics Classics, Series 2, No. 8. Sydney: University of Sydney.

Walras, Leon. [1874–77, 1926] 1954. *Elements of Pure Economics or the Theory of Social Wealth.* Translated by William Jaffe. London: Allen & Unwin.

Weintraub, E. Roy. 1974. *Conflict and Co-Operation in Economics.* London: Macmillan.

Whitaker, John K., ed. 1996. *The Correspondence of Alfred Marshall.* 3 vols. Cambridge: Cambridge University Press.

White, Michael V. 1987. Porter's "Hint"? A Note. *Australian Economic Papers* 26.49:328–31.

———. 1992. Diamonds Are Forever(?): Nassau Senior and Utility Theory. *Manchester School* 60.1:64–78.

———. 1994. "That God-Forgotten Thornton": Exorcising Higgling after *On Labour. HOPE* 26 (supplement): 149–83.

———. 1996a. Manufacturing the Smithian Paradox of Value. Unpublished manuscript.

———. 1996b. No Matter of Regret: The Cambridge Critique(s) of Jevons's Hedonics. In *Economics or Ethics?* edited by Peter Groenewegen. London: Routledge.

Wicksteed, Philip, H. 1934. *The Common Sense of Political Economy and Selected Papers and Reviews on Economic Theory.* Vol. 2. Edited by Lionel Robbins. London: Routledge.

Wilson, George. 1849. On the Early History of the Air-Pump in England. *Edinburgh New Philosophy Journal* 46:330–54.

Pacifying the Workman: Ruskin and Jevons on Labor and Popular Culture

Harro Maas

> On Monday we left Buxton for Manchester in a tremendous shower of rain. . . . Manchester is a most disagreeable town & we thought it the more so as we had hardly an hour of fair weather all the time we were there. . . . It is so full of manufactorys that you are enveloped in clouds of smoke & the place is so hot we could scarcely breath & we were very glad to breath the fresh air of the country again the next morning.
>
> —John Ruskin, *A Tour to the Lakes in Cumberland*

> How a painter would have enjoyed the sight which broke upon my waking eyes this morning! To my right is one of the tributaries to the Irwell, winding through the depths of a richly wooded and precipitous valley, or rather ravine. . . . Before me . . . is the Hall in the Wood, memorable for having been the residence of Crompton, the inventor of the spinning-jenny. . . . Beyond is the hill on which a great part of the busy town of Bolton is built. The intervening valley is studded with factories and bleach-works. Thank God, smoke is rising from the lofty chimneys of most of them! . . . it produces variations in the atmosphere which, to me at least, have a pleasing and picturesque effect.
>
> —William Cooke-Taylor, *Notes of a Tour in the Manufacturing Districts of Lancashire*

On the occasion of the opening of the academic year in 1865 at Queen's College, Liverpool, William Stanley Jevons was invited to deliver the

This paper greatly benefited from the help of Peter Nockles at the John Rylands University Library in Manchester, who kindly guided me through the Jevons archives. I would like to thank the John Rylands Library for their permission to quote from the archives. I would also like to thank Neil De Marchi, Mary Morgan, Marcia Pointon, Michael White, and an anonymous referee for their insightful and thorough comments on an earlier version.

opening address. Jevons started his address with a favorable reference to his attendance at a public lecture given one year earlier by John Ruskin at Rusholme Town Hall near Manchester, where Jevons at the time was affiliated as tutor at Owens College. Ruskin's lecture, which was to become "Of Kings' Treasuries" in his highest-selling book, *Sesame and Lilies*, so tells us Jevons, gave him the subject of his own lecture: "Reading and Study." Jevons clearly was impressed by Ruskin's abundant use of "imaginative names and figurative expressions," which were "either beautifully true, or suggestive of truth" (*LDP* 1865).[1] On a surface glance, we see many points of similarity between Jevons's and Ruskin's views of this subject: both are adverse to "cramming" students; students should be "active," "reflective," and not merely abandon their minds to be passively "dragged through a fixed course of instruction" (*LDP* 1865). Given Ruskin's examples of free libraries, well filled with valuable books, accessible art galleries, and so on, we can easily imagine that Ruskin's lecture resonated in Jevons's later essays on social reform. Indeed, the cultural and moral elevation of the working class was a subject that occupied Jevons's thoughts until the end of his life.

But the seeds of differences were already there. Jevons elaborates that "active use of the mind" means stimulation of the "process of judgement which the mind performs" using "mechanical devices" and says it is possible to get at conclusions "by the motion of wheels and levers, somewhat as Pascal worked an arithmetical question, or Mr. Babbage solves an equation, or calculates a page of logarithms by turning the handle of the calculating machine" (*LDP* 1865). But we look in vain in this inaugural address for a substantial explanation of what the "active, reflective" use of the mind might be.

De Marchi and Van Miegroet (this volume) show that ingenuity was important to the value of works of art in eighteenth-century Great Britain. Ingenuity, "the successful composing of apparently unconnected elements and notions into new products and systems of ideas" (379), directs the attention from a consideration of works of art as a product to the conditions of their production. My article follows this lead. It explores the considerations of one of the most famous English

1. This and subsequent citations of *LDP* 1865 refer to a supplement to the *Liverpool Daily Post* of 3 October 1865, in which Jevons's inaugural lecture was printed in full. I would like to thank Michael White for sending me a copy of it.

art critics ever, John Ruskin, of the conditions under which artistic production can flourish. These considerations brought him to a criticism of factory production in general and to a criticism of economists and their theories. In this criticism, Ruskin's conception of the "active part" of man—of inventiveness and the closely related concepts of imagination, genius, and ingenuity—plays a central role. Ruskin's criticism is contrasted with the viewpoints of William Stanley Jevons, the English founder of marginalist theory, on the "active, reflective" use of the mind. In particular, I will discuss the consequences of their respective analysis of the active use of the mind on their respective stances on labor and popular culture.

The structure of this article is as follows. After an exposition of Ruskin's views on invention, genius, and ingenuity, I will turn to his criticism of the factory system. William Cooke-Taylor's ([1841] 1969) apologetic description of the factory system serves, for reasons that will become clear, as a first step. Then, having expanded on Ruskin's art-driven criticism, we will be in a position to evaluate Jevons's picture of labor in *The Theory of Political Economy* ([1871] 1970) and his essays on social reform (reprinted in Jevons 1883) in the light of this criticism. As already indicated, Jevons's essays on popular culture will be emphasized.

Invention, Genius, and Ingenuity

Writing the chapter on Gothic architecture in his three-volume study *The Stones of Venice* (1851–53) made Ruskin aware of the conditions under which the production of art might flourish. For Ruskin the Gothic era represented an epoch in which the production of art was part of common life. At first Ruskin directed his attention only to the political economy of art in lectures he delivered in Manchester in 1857.[2] But he soon realized the broader implications of his thesis: from his construction of the Gothic past, Ruskin drew up a concept of craftsmanship, which he then used to criticize the conditions of production so rapidly spreading in nineteenth-century England under the factory system. It made him a critic not only of the factory system itself but also of those he blamed for its invention: the political economists, most notably John

2. These were printed as *The Political Economy of Art* and were later reprinted as *A Joy Forever (and Its Price in the Market)* ([1857] 1904).

Stuart Mill. In a letter of August 1862 to John Brown, he wrote, "The Science of Political Economy *is* a lie,—wholly and to the very root. . . . To this 'science,' and to this alone . . . is owing *All* the evil of the modern days. I say All" (Ruskin *Works*, 17:lxxxii).[3] Ruskin wrote this letter in response to the general public outrage that generated *Unto This Last* ([1862] 1985), the published book version of his essays on political economy.

Unto This Last went beyond the economics of art through art critics' eyes and might be better paraphrased as "political economy" through art critics' eyes. For Ruskin, the vocabulary of art furnished the clue to reveal the truths of political economy, which were hidden behind a veil of smoke. The aesthetic valuation of an object, the enjoyment of a commodity, be it a work of art or a "mere" consumer good—a distinction that Ruskin would have opposed—directed Ruskin's attention to the conditions under which it was produced. Ruskin emphatically argued that there was no enjoyment to be had from products made under modern factory conditions. According to Ruskin, the factory system obliterated the better part of the workman—his "thoughtful part," his genius. This, Ruskin argued, was just what was cherished in the much-despised Gothic era.[4] In Gothic man's genius, his imagination, his inventive or thoughtful part, embellished each and every product with uniqueness—with originality in design.[5] This was what could, and should, be enjoyed in any product. Of course, Ruskin did not believe everyone could be a William Turner, a James Watt, or an Isaac Newton, but everyone was able to use his imagination to create something new

3. Hereafter referred to as *Works*, followed by volume number.

4. The revival of the Gothic in Great Britain was influenced by Ruskin's work and was in no way unambiguously approved of by him.

5. Considering the relation of economists and art, one might be tempted to focus on real or assumed properties of works of art that differentiate them from other commodities. One such property is their uniqueness. We may question whether today uniqueness can still be seen as a distinguishing feature of art. Indeed, Walter Benjamin's famous and influential essay on the consequences of the modern technical reproducibility of a work of art departs from exactly the opposite thesis, as do most of the Marxist aesthetics (see, for example, Paetzold 1974). However, uniqueness was a feature of works of art, which, as Michael White shows in his contribution to this volume, definitely puzzled nineteenth-century economists. Being unique, a work of art resists one of the fundamental principles of the market: there is no quid pro quo for it, and consequently no market price can be determined. Not incidentally, many of those thinking about the value of art took and still have recourse to criteria outside the sphere of the market, like that of its contribution to the "national heritage," as in the case of Lionel Robbins (see Balisciano and Medema, this volume).

and unique, however limited in perfection. For Ruskin, genius was common to all men and was the *conditio sine qua non* to make life enjoyable. Modern conditions of work turned labor into a routine activity, alienating the workman from his "thoughtful part."

Ruskin, who by then was considered *the* outstanding art critic, had put his reputation in jeopardy. His work on political economy was referred to as "one of the most melancholy spectacles" of the year, and the *Saturday Review* wrote of "eruptions of windy hysterics," "absolute nonsense," "utter imbecility," and "intolerable twaddle" and characterized Ruskin himself as "a perfect paragon of blubbering." Indeed, the general opinion was that "it was no pleasure to see genius mistaking its power, and rendering itself ridiculous" (*Works*, 17:xxvii–xxviii). Ruskin directed his attention almost solely to Mill's reductionist image of man as only striving for the possession of wealth. Though our reception of *Unto This Last* may be different from those days, it is still generally acknowledged that there was an "extreme unfairness," to use Clive Wilmer's (introduction to Ruskin [1862] 1985, 26–27 and 27 n) words, in Ruskin's judgment of political economists. Reading his autobiography and his essays on Jeremy Bentham, for example, one is struck by Mill's struggles with Bentham's one-sided reduction of man to a "reasoning machine,"[6] a mechanically acting puppet.

At one point in his autobiography, Mill described this reduction to be a "perpetual worm at the root both of the passions and of the virtues" (*CW*, 1:143). The "excitement of beauty" occasioned by his reading of Wordsworth's poems, it is well known, made him argue that this half-picture of man should be complemented by the source of this excitement—the imagination: These poems "seemed to be the very culture of the feelings, which I was in quest of. In them I seemed to draw from a source of inward joy, of sympathetic and imaginative pleasure, which could be shared in by all human beings. . . . From them I seemed to learn what would be the perennial sources of happiness" (1:151). Elsewhere, Mill recognized that the power of the imagination, which he also termed the "daemon" that inspired poets and artists, "never was awakened" in Bentham (10:92). Indeed, he admitted that in utilitarianism this power of imagination "generally" was undervalued as a constituent of human nature (1:115).

6. See Mill, *Collected Works* 1:111, 10:112. Mill's *Collected Works* will hereafter be referred to as *CW*.

Mill's use of the Greek close relative of the Roman word *genius*—*daemon*—is informative. Daimonion, Socrates's famous inner voice, was a privileged source of godly truth and inspiration and had a highly irrational overtone. Mill's remark that Bentham gave a one-sided picture of man suggests that this daemon, the power of imagination, was a part of every man. In classical Rome, *genius* denoted man's soul or spirit and was connected to man's vital forces, as its root *gen* makes clear. Thus, without its irrational Greek overtones, genius was common to all men and functioned, in fact, as *principium individuationis*: one's genius determined one's uniqueness, one's character. In classical Rome, genius was not *ingenium*, or the extraordinary talent found in a limited number of people (and a closer relative of the Greek word *daimonion*). The history of the concept of genius is to a great extent determined by the way *genius* and *ingenium* became conflated, however. (See Zilsel 1926, 9–36 for a review of the history of the concept of genius.) The classical Roman flavor of genius was involved in Ruskin's use of the word. Ruskin feared that Mill's dissection of aesthetic and economic man transformed into a privilege for a selected number of people what according to him belonged to the life of all: the use of one's imagination. Indeed, Ruskin perceived the real source of distress in the industrializing towns to be the degradation of the workman.

There was some justness in Ruskin's fear of and anger toward the political economists, though Jevons would have provided a better target than Mill. My purpose is to show that in his writings on the common workman Jevons indeed squeezed out something like what Ruskin called the "thoughtful part" of man and what Jevons himself called the "active, reflective" use of the mind. In *The Theory of Political Economy* ([1871] 1970), Jevons narrowed the concept of economic man—which he presented as a universal and natural picture—to someone fitting the Victorian factory worker. For Jevons, genius did not consist in the use of the imagination at all but was a form of routine labor. This is a leading thread throughout Jevons's life and work, whether we look at his theory of labor, his essays on logic, or his essays on popular culture. In Jevons's (*Papers and Correspondence*, 1:58)[7] second entry into his diary, on 26 August 1852, we read:

7. Hereafter referred to as *PC*, followed by volume number.

> I have often thought much about what is called cleverness & genius. The oftener an action is repeated, the more easy is it to perform it again, & the more perfectly it will be performed. It is by long repetition that workmen or jugglers acquire such perfection, & the only credit given to them, is for their diligence. But I think it is exactly the same case with students, for if they have been accustomed for a long time to study diligently . . . they get *practised* or *clever* in acquiring knowledge.

Whereas Ruskin stressed "genius" as inherently linked to the imagination—that is, to human capacity for original design—for Jevons, the "thoughtful part" of man did not essentially differ from the routine activity of the workman.[8] In fact, much of his work on logic was driven by the idea that what in Ruskin's terms would have been called the "thoughtful part" of man could be as well mechanized as many other sorts of labor. His *Logical Abacus* made him comfortable with the idea that labor and human thinking followed mechanical rules (see Maas 1999). We can trace this routinized agent in Jevons's concept of the economic actor, living a dull and unenjoyable life. Although Jevons, we will see, implicitly acknowledged that English working conditions were to be blamed for the low culture of the working classes, his proposals for social reform, in fact, extended factory conditions to the leisure time spending of the workers. The use of the imagination—invention—came to be reserved for a separate class of men, whereas for Ruskin invention was very much the soul and spirit of every man.

For Ruskin the source of evil was the division of labor as practiced in the factories, these "Bastilles for Labour built by Capital" (quoted in Geddes 1884, 30), and successors of the "Houses of Terror," as they were named at the end of the eighteenth century (see Mumford 1946, 172–82; Ashworth 1998). It divided not labor, but the laborer, and turned the workman into a cripple. Many of the propagators of the factory system did not conceal this. Andrew Ure ([1835] 1967, 20), for example, stressed that the end goal of the factory system was "to substitute mechanical science for hand skill . . . on the automatic plan, skilled labour gets progressively superseded, and will, eventually, be

8. See also De Marchi and Van Miegroet, this volume, who show that practice was an important aspect to both Smith and Reynolds. But Smith, of course, never thought that a workman, who is capable of improving a part or an aspect of a given process, could conceive anew the whole principle behind his isolated activity.

replaced by mere overlookers of machines." And somewhat earlier Samuel Bentham, Jeremy's less-well-known brother, had stressed that skills and crafts of the workmen were a threat to the efficient working of the factory system. According to Samuel, these crafts and skills had to be broken down and made visible to be able to control the workmen (see Ashworth 1998).

One description of the factory system forcefully denied the degrading implications of the factory system on the workman's life, however. William Cooke-Taylor's *Notes of a Tour in the Manufacturing Districts of Lancashire* ([1841] 1969) was written only a couple of years before Engels's devastating description of life in Manchester. In its very rhetoric, Cooke-Taylor's book tried to conceal the effects of the factory system on the condition of the working class. The rhetoric is important, for not incidentally it had recourse to the language of art itself. Since this language was Ruskin's original biotope, we shall start with Cooke-Taylor's description of the factory system to begin to understand why Ruskin's concept of artistic production made him a critic of the factory system.

Lancashire Scenery: The Notion of the Picturesque

In May 1830 the Ruskins set off for a four-month tour to the Lakes of Cumberland. On their journey, they passed through Manchester, which made so uncomfortable an impression on the eleven-year-old John that he described it as a most "disagreeable town." They were far more pleased by the natural scenery of the lake district, and it would stimulate John Ruskin ([1830] 1990, 16) to find in the pleasure of landscape his "ruling passion."

Cooke-Taylor opened the second letter of his *Notes of a Tour in the Manufacturing Districts of Lancashire* by describing his early morning view with words referring to the arts: a "painter" would have "enjoyed" the Lancashire scenery, which produced a "pleasing" and "picturesque" effect. Although Cooke-Taylor was not the only one who wrote on the factory system, he was quite right when he noted that the factory system was so novel a creation that its importance and impact on society had only recently come to be estimated. And, "like most strangers," his first impressions were very "unfavourable." According to Cooke-Taylor ([1841] 1969, 3), the factory system affected life in England so deeply and permanently that one was better off to see it as an "established innovation" and to judge it on those terms. Cooke-Taylor's use of aesthetic vocabulary functioned to redress these first impressions and to reconcile all those who experienced the factory system as the source of ugliness, with the inevitable.

One aesthetic term suggested that there was no a priori distinction between a picture of a landscape and a picture of a smoking chimney: the picturesque. At the turn of the eighteenth century, the notion of the picturesque had become very popular. It gave travelers an aesthetically legitimized way of looking at scenery that, according to traditional classifications, could only be considered ugly. Ruins, litter, or disorderly lumps of stones, as in mountain scenery, became acceptable objects of admiration, if only they gave rise to morally elevated thoughts. One could admire Roman ruins, for example, because they stood for the Augustan age, the last "golden age" before the fifteenth century.[9] Originally, the picturesque denoted a class of objects that was outside the scope of the notion of the sublime, as developed, for example, by Burke and then by Kant to denote objects that filled the spectator with a sense of awe and terror, and so—paradoxically—strengthened man's superiority over nature. Picturesque objects simply were too small to convey this sense of horror. Contrary to the experience of the sublime, there was nothing threatening in the picturesque at all. In fact, the picturesque turned out to be a verbal chameleon that came to denote whatever was beautiful in a picture (Heffernan 1984, 4).

It was in the consoling terms of the picturesque, then, that Cooke-Taylor described his early morning view. There was something provocative in it, as there was in the whole book. It was quite generally thought at the time that the smoke of the chimneys in the Lancashire district gave towns like Manchester the appearance of a real inferno in which life was simply inconceivable. It was one of Cooke-Taylor's purposes to show that it was not the factory system as such that made life unbearable but a complex of accidental causes that laid a veil over the "moral worth and social importance" of this system. The direct political aim was to give support to the Anti-Corn Law League, which actually sponsored the publication of the book, a fact that was concealed from the public. If government politics on corn pricing were a hindrance to manufacturers, so ran the argument, they also blocked the

9. The example was suggested to me by Neil De Marchi.

spread of the factory system, which proved so beneficial to the social and moral conditions of the common workmen.

Cooke-Taylor did not underplay the enormous misery to be encountered in the city of Manchester. As a good rhetorician, he devoted his first letter to a description of this town. The message was obvious: If what was considered the most unhealthy place in England to live in was not, in fact, all that detrimental, how much better might life be then in all other manufacturing towns and villages? Of course, there could not be any misunderstanding that Manchester, the metropolis of the cotton industry, was not a place of pleasure, but related only to the business part of man. The crowd on the streets passed the visitor with "the look of thought and the step of haste." There were no amusements to be found. Like "insects," the inhabitants of Manchester had assumed the colors and character of the place; they were, however, not all living a shadowy life. At the Exchange of Manchester one was able to judge how the manufacturers were encouraged to use their intellect: "The genius of the place is talent and intelligence; genius and stupidity appear to be equally absent; but if the average of intellect be not very high, it is evident that not a particle of it remains unemployed" (Cooke-Taylor [1841] 1969, 11).

Although people lived in misery in Manchester, the causes for this were to be sought elsewhere. Factors like immigration into the city and the health state of the immigrants were judged to be more important than the factory system to the considerable amount of "distress." To be sure, considerable distress would occur wherever unskilled labor was used, but the mills needed predominantly skilled labor. And, admittedly, in Manchester, the chimneys were so close to one another that they produced a really filthy and unhealthy atmosphere. In fact, this was an important reason why the "rich" of Manchester knew so little about the living conditions of the poor, for they chose to live in the more lofty atmosphere outside of town.

To be able to judge the merits or demerits of the factory system, Cooke-Taylor thought it wise to study it at places where all these accidental factors were ruled out—for example, at the picturesque scenery he admired when visiting the Turton mill of Mr. Henry Ashworth. Of course, Cooke-Taylor used the painter's expression provokingly and deliberately. Generally, the smoking chimneys were not thought of as worth a painter's eye, but considering them to be picturesque made them, as with ruins, worth one's admiration. One could "admire" smokestacks because of their association with something else that was admirable: power, order, efficiency, and so on. Even the consoling effect was argued for: "Thank God, smoke was rising!" for otherwise the mills would have lain idle, providing no work, and consequently no income—no bread to the workmen. The interior of the mill itself was described as "lofty"—there was "so much space occupied by the machinery that crowding was physically impossible." Cooke-Taylor wrote he would have been "very well contented to have as large a portion of room and air in my own study as a cotton-spinner in any of the mills of Lancashire" (26).

The factory system proved to be a system of perfect order. The steam engine, the "common assistant and friend of all" and the "most impartial of arbitrators," apparently provided the sort of employment to the operators that "habits of order, cleanliness, and propriety" were impressed upon them. This made "the organization of the community complete, and the human agents work with all the exactness of machinery." The factory system was a complete novelty: "So strange a combination of perfect despotism with perfect freedom never before existed, and to have produced such a state is one of the noblest triumphs of morality and intelligence" (121–24). And though the human agent worked "with the exactness of machinery," this did not mean that the work itself was mechanical. In fact, the operator only surveyed the operations of the machinery, not interfering at all. And this, according to Cooke-Taylor, "gave frequent opportunities . . . for the exercise of skill, ingenuity, and contrivance" (115). The operator was able to sell these skills at a high price. In contrast, those branches of industry that were dependent on manual labor, and were not aided by machinery, turned man into a machine. In times of crisis in the economy, the workmen did not blame their employers for the reduction of the wages or the closing down of the mills but were well aware of the effect of government policy on trades and selling opportunities. For Cooke-Taylor this proved that a "vagrant cotton-spinner" possessed "[higher] attributes of genius" than were to be found at that time at English universities (28–29).

Ruskin's Criticism of the Factory System

Cooke-Taylor used the notion of the picturesque on another occasion, when he visited the Methodist chapel that was shown to him by the

Messrs. Whitehead. This visit amplified his wish to have the "pleasure . . . to repeat my visit to Rosendale and Hollymount":

> They took me to see the chapel which had been erected in Hollymount, a building of the Ionic order, and which to me, uninitiated in the rules of art, appears one of the prettiest specimens of the modern imitations of Grecian architecture I have ever seen. There is a defect in the position of the building: it is not easy to get a view of its full front, and the volutes of Ionic columns seen cornerwise invariably remind one of the rams' horns from which the first notion of these ornaments is said to have been derived. The interior of the chapel struck me as superior in arrangement and picturesque effect to any of the modern churches in the Grecian style I have yet seen. (65)

Cooke-Taylor's use of the word *picturesque* here reveals just those parameters of production under factory conditions that were so criticized by Ruskin. For Ruskin, who *was* initiated in the rules of art, the "defect" of the building would certainly not have been incidental; on the contrary, it revealed a structural defect of Grecian architecture. The criticism Ruskin most likely would have made of this building would have mirrored to a very high degree his criticism of the factory system. In fact, Ruskin's criticism of both the factory system and Grecian architecture stemmed from a common source: neither was a system of perfect order, as was suggested by the term "picturesque." It is widely held that the chapter "The Nature of Gothic" in *Stones of Venice* contains all those elements that transformed Ruskin from an art critic to a critic of society (Ruskin [1862] 1985, 17). Indeed, many of these elements are also in Cooke-Taylor's account: being an "imitation," not being able to get "a full view of the front," and the "invariableness" that the experience of the ornaments evoked.

Ruskin saw an obvious reason why spectators of modern (and classical) Grecian buildings would always find that they could not get a full view of Cooke-Taylor's picturesque chapel and would see the ornamentation as ill placed. Only the upper parts of Grecian buildings were ornamented, and almost always on such a small scale (given the distance) that it was impossible to discern what was depicted. Such ornamentation thus simply was useless. It conveyed no sensible message to an observer at all and consequently was only an expression of waste—a waste of the labor executed to produce it and a waste of money for paying the labor. Since only the upper part was ornamented, the rest of the building commonly was nothing more than "a wilderness of square-cut stone" (Ruskin 1854, 61). The only impression to be had from this wilderness was monotony.

This monotonous impression was deepened by the "invariableness" of the Ionic, Doric, and Corinthian columns. No enjoyment for the eye was to be had from monotony, but even worse, there was no enjoyment for the workman, either. The workman's labor invariably consisted in *imitating* the same ornamentation over and again, or executing no ornamentation at all. "Imitating" here means copying. Smith used imitating quite to the opposite, as not mere copying but as creating novelty (see De Marchi and Van Miegroet, this volume). In a lecture on architecture given in Edinburgh, Ruskin gave the example of sixty-six heads of lions, all "exactly the same," which he had seen on a recently constructed Grecian building, and he contrasted this with the way ornamentation was executed in Gothic buildings (figure 1). The west window of Dumblane Abbey in Edinburgh, for example, was ornamented with leaves. But no leaf was exactly the same as any other. All leaves reinforced the form of the window, which was itself a leaf (figure 2). This demanded what Ruskin called *invention*: Imagination, ingenuity, and judgment had to cooperate to produce this architectural arrangement. The workman had to *think* about the *design* of the window; he was not merely executing the thoughts and designs of others. There was no place for exact replication here. If you expect a workman to "think about what he is doing, and feel something about it," you cannot expect him to do the same thing twice. Since "men do not commonly think the same thought twice, . . . you are to expect another and a different thought of them, as soon as one thought has been well expressed" (105).

Consequently, invention fulfilled a double function, not only in the arts but in all production of goods. It gave these products something unique and distinctive: design.[10] If a workman was enabled to use his imagination and judgment, his "*thoughtful* part" (Ruskin [1862] 1985, 84), his work itself was raised beyond the level of simple manual labor, for which "brute animals would be preferable to man" (83). Thus, not only the *production* of goods would be an enjoyment to the worker but also the *con-*

10. As Marina Bianchi has pointed out to me, Ruskin, like many others, was in this influenced by William Hogarth's *Analysis of Beauty* ([1753] 1997).

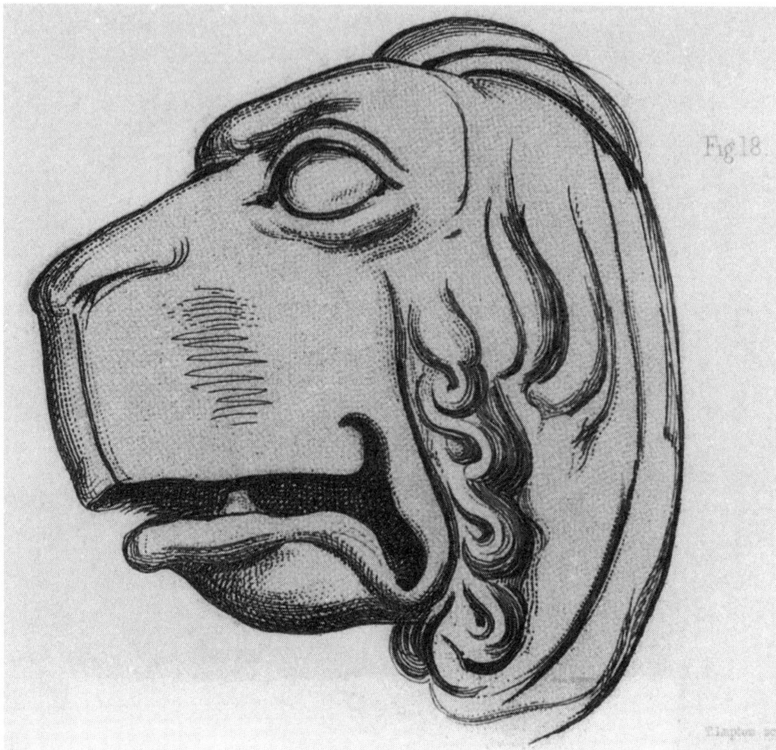

Figure 1

sumption of the product. As in the opposition of the leaf window and the uniform ill-placed ornament, Ruskin argued that there was no enjoyment to be found in sixty-six exactly similar lion heads, though there *was* enjoyment in a dozen or so not exactly similarly shaped leaves. Diversity, not monotony, provided nourishment for the eye.[11]

11. Steven Medema has suggested to me that Ruskin thus overlooked the fact that the emerging mass-consumption industry provided a different form of diversity—namely, an exploding variety of consumer goods. Ruskin argued, however, as in the case of the sixty-six identical heads of lions, that "exquisite invention," which was a marker of the use made of the imagination of the workman, could be found *within* a single good. Ruskin consequently did not limit his discussion of the lion heads to their all being equal but pointed out how a single exemplar might lack "exquisite invention." For Ruskin, the exploding diversity of consumer goods made possible by mass production was only an explosion of monotony.

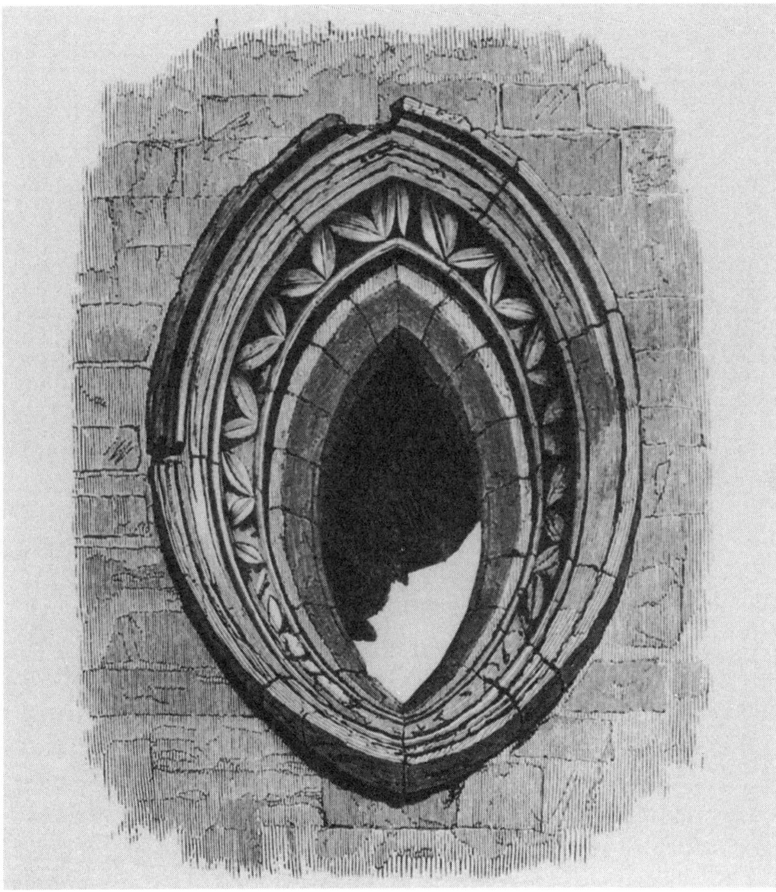

Figure 2

Ruskin consequently criticized the consumption of goods that did not embody some design, however imperfect, but only showed uniformity. The more expensive these uniform goods were, the more clear it was that they were only bought as a store of wealth, providing no enjoyment at all. And it was on this very point that he took offense at Mill's definition of economic man as "solely" striving for wealth, for this man was depriving both himself of the enjoyment of consumption and the workman of the enjoyment of production. The consumer could get his uniform goods cheap, but this cheapness also was a sign of their being "utterly unnecessary." When buying goods of "exquisite invention," one was paying also for the invention and not for mere finish or execution (88).[12]

In fact, someone buying goods without invention, according to Ruskin, was engaged "in the slave-trade" (88), for goods without design implied a degradation of the workman. His sometimes only "tardy imagination, torpid capacity of emotion, tottering steps of thought" (84) were taken from him, and nothing was left to him but simple, unenjoyable routine labor. Even if there was design in a product, this, under the modern conditions of production, mostly implied an enslavement of the workman. The evil here was the division of labor. Ruskin sensed a tendency to make from the inventive part of man a separate laborer, and thus to obtain the highest form of perfection from both the inventor and the manual worker (90). Even in Leonardo da Vinci, Ruskin noticed a peculiar paradox: This man, who according to Ruskin was always striving for perfection, in fact left all his works unfinished. His mind was always in advance of his powers of execution. Ruskin took this imperfection as a sign of life itself. For him it was a sign of a mortal body, of progress and change. An inventor, such as an architect, would be able to attain perfection in a building only by imposing *his* working conditions on the workmen and not leaving them any room to deliberate on their own.[13] Ruskin had a very simple index of the degree to which workmen were enslaved—namely, the extent to which the several parts of a building were or were not exactly similar. Specialization was a misunderstanding of what the conditions of production should be, and with respect to art, it was also a misunderstanding of the ends of art itself—its aim not being perfection, but original design.[14]

12. See Babbage [1835] 1963, 119: "The first object of every person who attempts to make any article of consumption, is, or ought to be, to produce it in a perfect form; but to secure to himself the greatest and most permanent profit, he must endeavour . . . to render the new luxury or want . . . cheap to those who consume it."

13. In this connection, Simon Schaffer (1994, §2, mn. 217) relates an interesting aspect of the struggle Charles Babbage had with the engineer Joseph Clement and Jarvis, Clement's draftsman, on the displacement of the engine project from Lambeth to wealthy Marylebone. Jarvis refused to work under the continual supervision of Babbage because, as Schaffer quotes, he would not become "party to my own degradation."

14. This does not mean that one should, or could, not demand the most of man's capacities. On the contrary, as a teacher of watercolor painting, Ruskin was known to be ill satisfied and to demand from every student the best he or she could give. This held equally for his drawing classes at Oxford and his lessons for the Working Men's College. (See for example Davies 1904 on Ruskin's years at the Working Men's College.)

Imperfection thus became a precondition for enjoyable work *and* for enjoyable consumption. It was a common feature of Ruskin's valuation of Gothic architecture as it was of Turner's landscapes. In fact, Ruskin argued, it was an essential element of our perception of nature itself. Ruskin considered a Gothic cathedral as one great sculpture, as one great work of art, which was so richly decorated that it was impossible to have full comprehension of it. Focusing on details, it was impossible to retain an image of the whole, and when taking a view of the whole, details became vague, though they still contributed to the whole image:

> Go to the top of Highgate Hill on a clear summer morning at five o'clock and look at Westminster Abbey. You will receive an impression of a building enriched with multitudinous vertical lines. Try to distinguish one of those lines all the way down from the one next to it: You cannot. Try to count them: You cannot. Try to make the beginning or end of any one of them: You cannot. Look at it generally, and it is all symmetry and arrangement. Look at it in its parts, and it is all inextricable confusion. Am I not, at this moment, describing a piece of Turner's drawing, with the same words by which I describe nature? (Ruskin 1995, 17–19)

In his analysis of Turner, Ruskin pointed out that the landscape's nourishment of the eye consisted in the perceptual bewilderment that took hold of a spectator. Not being able to grasp with the eye the details and variety of nature, an observer was forced to continually reexamine his visual impressions to form a coherent image. One of the things that fascinated Ruskin in Turner's landscape paintings was the optical complexity made explicit by suggesting details without wholly revealing them. Thus, one can see "the spots on the trout" as painted by Turner, without being able to "count" them (Smith 1995, 57). In this consisted Turner's inventive genius, according to Ruskin—not painting all details, but conveying the sense of bewilderment experienced by the observer: "Abundant beyond the power of the eye to embrace or follow, vast and various beyond the power of the mind to comprehend, there is yet not one atom in its whole extent and mass which does not suggest more than it represents" (Ruskin 1995, 15).

Ruskin criticized other landscapists, as well as Canaletto's paintings of Venice, because either they painted all aspects of nature fully detailed, but in a way the eye never could have grasped them in fact (in

Dutch landscapes), or they simply ignored nature's richness (in Poussin). The paradoxical effect of Turner's landscapes was that in their "truth to Nature" they conveyed the message of man's humility, of man's inadequacy to grasp the whole of nature. Ruskin's term for this effect was the *grotesque*, as distinguished from the sublime, the beautiful, and the picturesque. The grotesque was adversary to the subsuming and consequently violent attitude toward nature implied in these other terms. In reference to Turner's paintings, *grotesque* expressed the greatness and variety of nature, but it also showed the imperfections of man and the imperfection of the eye.

In Gothic architecture, the grotesque was also the expression of the liberty of the workman. Imperfection was not deliberately attained, but was an inevitable consequence of the appeal to the best in the workman, his thoughtful part. For Ruskin, we have seen, in Grecian architecture things were completely different. The ill-placed, useless, and uniform ornamentation and the undecorated lower parts turned these buildings into prisons, for the spectator as well as for the workman. In his lectures in Edinburgh, Ruskin (1854, 61–62) expressed himself as follows:

> Walk round your Edinburgh buildings, and look at the height of your eye, what will you get from them? Nothing but square-cut stone . . . so that your houses look like prisons, and truly are so. . . . These square stones are not prisons of the body, but graves of the soul; for the very men who could do sculpture . . . for you are here! still here, in your despised workmen: the race has not degenerated, it is you who have bound them down, and buried them beneath your Greek stones.

The "insects" Cooke-Taylor had encountered in Manchester were, for Ruskin, "despised workmen." According to Ruskin, the factory system forced men to produce "with the accuracy of tools, to be precise and perfect in all their actions," but this "verily" meant the "degradation of the operative into a machine" (84–86).

The Routinization of the Workman

There was an obvious incongruity in Ruskin's and Cooke-Taylor's descriptions of the effects of the factory system on working conditions. Whereas Ruskin claimed the factory system to be solely despotic,

Cooke-Taylor admitted a considerable and inherent degree of freedom for the workman, except when only manual labor was demanded. From the machine operators hardly any manual labor was demanded at all, but even then Cooke-Taylor ([1841] 1969, 110) observed that their work consisted mainly in controlling the working of the machine: "The operatives are rather tenders of machinery than actual labourers, and . . . the self-acting mule had greatly diminished the importance of the spinner." Cooke-Taylor did not conclude from this that the work of the operative became "purely mechanical"; on the contrary, there were "frequent opportunities in a mill for the exercise of skill, ingenuity, and contrivance" (115).

Obviously, there was a difference between the ingenuity Cooke-Taylor ascribed to the operative and the kind of inventiveness Ruskin argued for. If the "self-acting mule" got stuck, the operative had to have knowledge of the principles on which it operated to get it going. He had to be educated in them, and Cooke-Taylor observed an increasing demand for skilled labor in Lancashire. This sort of training is minutely examined in Veblen's *Theory of Business Enterprise* ([1904] 1975). The operative—at least to some extent—had to have knowledge of the principles underlying the working of the machine. This knowledge ran in quantitative terms, in terms of cause and effect. Veblen stressed that "other intelligence on the part of the workman is useless; or it is even worse than useless, for a habit of thinking in other than quantitative terms blurs the workman's quantitative apprehension of the facts with which he has to do." To be fitted for working at a machine, the "habits of life and thought of the workman" had to run along the lines of "regularity of sequence and mechanical precision." The effect was a "standardization of the workman's intellectual life in terms of mechanical process," and this not only accounted for his life at the factory but even standardized his tastes (308–9).[15] It was this standardization that Ruskin opposed, making life dull and monotonous and consequently depriving men of the enjoyment of their lives.

It is here, I think, that Ruskin's aesthetically driven analysis of labor helps clarify aspects of Jevons's analysis of labor in *The Theory of Polit-*

15. See Veblen [1904] 1975, 13: "Men are required to adapt their needs and their motions to the exigencies of the process whereby this civilized method of intercourse is carried into effect. The service is standardized, and therefore the use of it is standardized also." William Barber pointed out to me that Veblen's criticism of American university teaching runs along similar lines.

ical Economy ([1871] 1970). Foreshadowing Veblen's diagnosis of working conditions, Jevons combined Ruskin's evaluation of labor as a routine activity with Cooke-Taylor's contention that there was a high degree of ingenuity related to the workman's use of machinery. But in Jevons's work there is no trace of the same negative judgment of routine activities that one finds in Ruskin. That labor is painful is taken for granted. Jevons even compared man's thought processes to routine manual labor, thus effectively blocking what Ruskin viewed as the source of enjoyment of life. This becomes manifest, we shall see, in Jevons's essays on popular culture. Invention and the use of the imagination came to be reserved for a limited group of highly gifted individuals.

In *The Theory of Political Economy* ([1871] 1970, 188) Jevons conceived labor as a negative pleasure: a pain. It was a "painful exertion which we undergo to ward off pains of greater amount, or to procure pleasures which leave a balance in our favour." Measured along the dimensions of intensity and duration, a person can be laboring "*uniformly*" or can "exert more or less muscular and nervous effort" (190). Though Jevons admitted that "labour may be both agreeable . . . and conducive to future good," his two dimensions of labor should make it clear that labor, in fact, should be conceived of as a pain only (189–91). Jevons represented the disutility connected with labor in the diagram shown in figure 3.[16]

The curve *a–b–c–d* represents the disutility connected with the pain of the execution of labor. Positive utility is derived from the labor itself only in arc *b–c*. Though it is nowhere clearly expressed, we may think of this utility as the surplus of the enjoyment derived of the increasing dexterity of the workman over the pain of the execution of the work. Beyond point *c*, this balance turns to negative.

Balanced against the disutility of labor is the utility derived from the amount of produce *o–x*, representing the return on labor or his income. In the initial equilibrium the return on labour is *o–m*. Interestingly, Jevons added a discussion on the "general tendency" in Eng-

16. For a more extensive discussion of this diagram, see White 1994a, 434–37. It is interesting to notice that the shape of the labor curve closely resembles that of the Wundt curve discussed by De Marchi and Van Miegroet in this volume. But it is highly improbable that Jevons was influenced either by Fechner's psychophysics or by Wundt's work; psychophysics only became known in Britain with Sully's unsigned review article published in 1872 in the *Westminster Review*. Nicolas Chaigneau (1996a, 1996b, 1997) has shown convincingly that Edgeworth was influenced by reading both Fechner and Wundt.

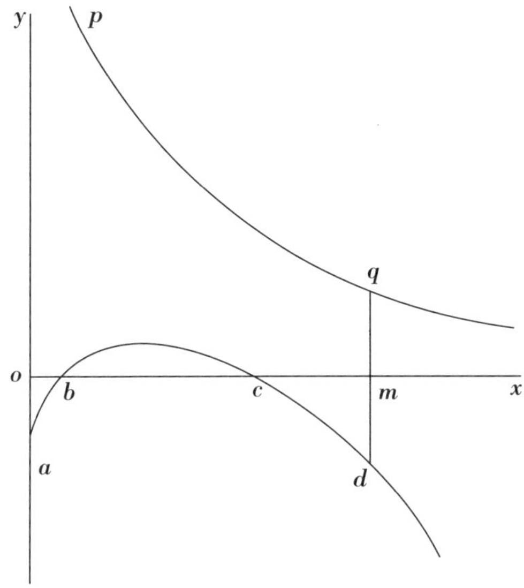

Figure 3

land to reduce working hours, "thus proving that the painfulness of labour varies so rapidly as easily to overbalance the gain in utility" (197). Apparently, for many occupations there was no intrinsic enjoyment to be derived from labor. The range of jobs Jevons mentioned—from artisans and millhands to the mercantile offices—covered all those that Cooke-Taylor ([1841] 1969, 115) had maintained "gave frequent opportunities . . . for the exercise of skill, ingenuity, and contrivance." The talent and intelligence demanded inspired workers only to save their own labor, just as Adam Smith's boy, Humphrey Potter, who preferred to play in the field with his friends, was induced to invent a device that would allow this. But Smith's ingenious young boy was, so Jevons assured us, an exception, for "all the greater inventions" were "the result of deliberate study" (197; see Smith [1776] 1976, 1:20).[17] Indeed, it was not always "possible to graduate work to the worker's liking" (Jevons [1871] 1970, 197).

17. Jevons expressed his skepticism of Smith's assurance that many inventions were made by the users of machinery in a side remark to Smith mentioning the boy and the boy's name. See JA6/6/7.

The only professions for which Jevons acknowledged that the work could be of "interesting and stimulating nature" were the inventive ones. Jevons listed "the philosopher, scientific discoverer, artist, etc." (197–98). I think it is not incidental that Jevons did not draw a graph of the utility of the labor for these professions. Imagine, for example, what should have been put on the *O–X* axis. One can imagine that the disutility of a farmer's labor increased when a greater amount of corn was harvested. But inventions of a scientific discoverer, or an artist, did not relate to a greater or lesser amount of produce. And even supposing a curve could be drawn, the picture would be completely out of balance, for the utility of the labor remained positive.[18]

Even these occupations, however, so Jevons ([1871] 1970, 198) assured the reader, in line with his early views on genius (see *PC*, 1:58), required "mental powers" that "must be kept in perfect training by constant exertion, just as a racehorse or an oarsman needs to be constantly exercised." And with regard to this "training," Jevons conceived mental powers to be as mechanical and routine as manual labor. In fact, he motivated the validity of his substitution principle in logic by drawing an explicit parallel between reasoning and routine activities:

> I need hardly point out that not only in our reasonings, but in our acts of common life, we observe the principle of similarity. Any new kind of action or work is performed with doubt or difficulty, because we have no knowledge derived from a similar case to guide us. But no sooner has the work been performed once or twice with success, than much of the difficulty vanishes, because we have acquired all the knowledge which will guide us in similar cases. . . . The whole practice of law in English courts, if not in all others, consists in deciding all new causes according to the rule established in the most nearly similar former causes, provided any can be found sufficiently similar. (Jevons [1890] 1971, 127)

What remained obscure in Jevons's views on the "laws of thought" was, as John Herschel pointed out in a letter to him, how "to decide what things *are* similar: so similar as to admit substitution for each other in the argument in hand; which is not a province of formal or Aristotelian logic, however largely supplemented by Dr Boole, Dr

18. On the importance of *increasing* marginal utility, see Bianchi 1998.

Thomson or yourself" (JA6/2/196).[19] Jevons had little to say to this. In his *Principles of Science*, invention became "the inexplicable action of a gifted mind" (Jevons [1874] 1958, 579). It had to do with the "rare genius" of Newton, Huygens, and Faraday (585). Jevons even went so far as to state that "the mind of a great discoverer must combine contradictory attributes" (592). The faculty of the imagination, which traditionally was involved in the explanation of invention, became fully irrationalized.[20]

Jevons thus made an inexplicable matter of natural gifts, or talents, what was for Ruskin to a greater or lesser degree common to all workmen: the power of invention.[21] In this respect, Ruskin had a more traditional inclination toward Adam Smith's contention that the division of labor was only to a very limited degree dependent on natural gifts and talents (see Smith [1776] 1976, 28). Ruskin believed there should be no division between manual and mental labor at all. In most professions, labor was a pain just because man's capability to use his mental powers, his imagination, was either severely restricted or not acknowledged. For Ruskin the curve *a–b–c–d* would have related only to circumstances of production in which the workman was forced to execute

19. In the handlist to the Jevons archives at the John Rylands University Library, Manchester (McNiven 1983), Herschel's letter to Jevons is wrongly dated 8 July 1863. The right year must be 1869, given that Jevons in his letter to Herschel 9 July 1869 (item no. 10327 of the Herschel-Jevons correspondence at the Royal Society) explicitly refers to Herschel's letter. I owe this information to Paul Byrne, researcher at the Royal Society's archives.

20. Till the end of the eighteenth century, the art of invention was considered closely related to the mind's faculty of imagination. A succinct example is given by Alexander Gerard's *Essay on Genius* of 1774: "*Imagination* . . . is the first author of all inventions. . . . It forms what we properly call genius in every art, and in every science. It is always necessary indeed, that *judgement* attend it in its operations, and assist it in discovering truth or beauty" (Mainusch 1969, 70, quoting Gerard). Under the general pressure of Bacon's *Novum Organon*, this conception of invention more and more gave way to a conception that identified invention with observation and recollection of data. Invention thus became identified with the problem of induction. In his *Principles of Science*, Jevons ([1874] 1958, 12) emphasized that "*induction is really the inverse process of deduction*," and in the second edition of *The Theory of Political Economy* in 1879, Jevons took this statement as his "principal objection" to Mill's theory of induction: "Possessing certain facts of observation, we frame a hypothesis as to the laws governing those facts; we reason from the hypothesis deductively to the results to be expected; and we then examine these results in connection with the facts in question" (19). This, of course, left the reader in the dark *how* a hypothesis was "framed." See also Eisler 1971, 544–73.

21. Michael White (1994a, 437) has shown how for Jevons talents and gifts were related to "character" or "race": One can hardly imagine a more irrational underpinning for the division between mental and manual labour (see also Jevons [1871] 1970, 198).

the *same sort* of labor time and again. And, we have seen, this was indeed the sort of labor Jevons's theory had as its object. For Ruskin, it was not so much labor per se that occasioned disutility, but the content of the work and the conditions under which the work was executed. If there was no originality to give to the product—that is, if man's inventive part was not involved in its production—labor would reduce to sheer monotony. In his arguments for labor being predominantly a disutility, Jevons separated the inventive part of man from his manual labor and relegated it to a specific gifted group of people. For the workmen, this was "to find their whole being sunk into an unrecognized abyss, to be counted off into a heap of mechanism numbered with its wheels, and weighed with its hammer strokes" (Ruskin [1862] 1985, 87).

Pacifying the Workman: The Regulation of Taste

We have seen how positively Cooke-Taylor evaluated the factory system and how much he stressed its beneficial working on the culture of the working class. Even though Cooke-Taylor had made some reservations with respect to social conditions in Manchester, his view on the workingman's life in Manchester tended to the positive compared with, for example, Engels's and Tocqueville's descriptions of Manchester life written around the same time. For Tocqueville, Manchester was a place "where civilized man is turned back almost into a savage" (quoted in Golby and Purdue 1984, 90).

However doubtful Cooke-Taylor's account may have been at the time he wrote his book, his positive evaluation of the culture of the working class was not shared by Jevons. Although we get a vivid impression of Jevons's enthusiasm for the manufacturing districts in London from his diary and his letters to his family—he even writes that he now definitely prefers to walk there instead of taking a tour in the countryside (*PC*, 1:90–91)—this enthusiasm did not entice him to the kind of propagandistic writing on the moral virtues of the factory system displayed by Cooke-Taylor. Though Jevons emphasized that not all manufacturing districts in London produced the same amount of "busy vice and crime" as, for example, "St Giles, Drury Lane, &c." (90), he, like many middle-class contemporaries, considered the violent and riotous ways that for the working class functioned as an outlet of their miserable lives to be a general evil that had to be combated.

This is the context in which we find his articles on social reform, such as the effects of women's labor, education, or popular culture. The more lengthy of them appeared mostly in the *Fortnightly Review* and were reprinted posthumously in *Methods of Social Reform* (1883). Of his articles on social reform, Jevons's essays and newspaper articles in the 1870s against women working in factories provoked the most controversy. One of those reacting was William Cooke-Taylor, who took offense at Jevons's suggestion that infant mortality rates in industrialized cities were higher than elsewhere. Even in the 1870s Cooke-Taylor was not prepared to admit the detrimental effects of factory work on worker's lives.[22]

How to redress the low culture of the working class would occupy Jevons's thoughts till the end of his life. But whereas Ruskin's solution to this problem pointed to the abolition of the factory system altogether, a solution for which he was ridiculed in the press, Jevons envisaged solutions that essentially *extended* the factory system outside the factory itself. As labor was conceived of as a routine activity to discipline the workman's life, so the amusements available to the people should regulate their leisure habits. Jevons's most relevant essay is "Amusement of the People," reissued in *Methods of Social Reform* (1883). In this essay, however, Jevons does not fully address by what mechanism popular entertainment regulates the workman's leisure habits. An incomplete and apparently unfinished manuscript on musical theory, cataloged in the John Rylands Library, University of Manchester, under the call mark JA6/47/1–17, gives more information on this. Since this manuscript is extensively discussed by Bert Mosselmans and Ernst Mathijs's contribution to this volume, I will focus on those elements that directly relate to my main argument. It will turn out that there is a parallel to be drawn between the routine labor in the factory, which Jevons addressed in *The Theory of Politi-*

22. Cooke-Taylor had a good point. Jevons's use of statistical material in this case was very hazy. In the end, Jevons was forced to admit that the "real proof" of his thesis was "not to be found in complicated statistical tables" (quoted in White 1994b, 64). For an excellent discussion see White 1994b.

cal Economy, and the appreciation of the arts as these, to a greater or lesser degree and most perfectly in musical entertainment, worked as a tranquilizer of the mind.[23]

In his essay on popular amusements, Jevons started with the observation that, due to "riotous and vicious assemblages" of people, most popular festivals had been suppressed by the authorities.[24] England, according to Jevons, had become a "dull England." In fact, the suppression of festivals left to the public nothing but the worst forms of leisure activity, such as drinking and violence: "The people seem actually to have forgotten how to amuse themselves, so that when they do escape . . . from their depressing alleys, there is no provision of music, no harmless games, nor other occupation for the vacant time." The effect of this was that the "English masses" only were able to amuse themselves in a "clumsy and vulgar way" (Jevons 1883, 4–5). On his journeys through Europe, it had struck Jevons as "extremely painful" that "the poor gentleman peasants of Scandinavia" were so much more well behaved than "the rich, rowdy, drunken artisans of England" (5). Shortening a workman's day or heightening salaries would only aggravate this, for Jevons feared most that workmen would spend more earnings on drink. The lower classes should be stimulated, he stated provokingly, in "aping [their] betters," thus in spending on culture instead of drink (7).[25] What was needed was an increase of cul-

23. Jevons's choice of music as a tranquilizer of the mind is remarkable. We only have to think of Schopenhauer's *Die Welt als Wille und als Vorstellung* and Nietszche's *Die Geburt der Tragödie aus dem Geiste der Musik* to realize that, at least on the European continent, music was not considered to function as a tranquilizer of the mind *at all*, but on the contrary poured into the very hidden and uncontrollable regions of our passions. One need not be a perfect Wagnerite to experience something of this when listening to the *Ring des Nibelungen*.

24. The authorities attempted to suppress these festivals partly as an offspin of the French Revolution. The violent and riotous turn these festivals often took was thought of as a hotbed for revolt against the social order. Support for suppression also came from manufacturers who by then needed a well-regulated workforce. For an extensive discussion, see Golby and Purdue 1984, chap. 4., esp. pp. 88–94. Golby and Purdue's discussion makes clear that in the light of recent research the then prevailing image of a decline in popular amusements is inaccurate.

25. Jevons used the expression "aping their betters" provocatively, foreshadowing Veblen's theory of emulation. The importance of emulation in Jevons's epoch is also emphasized by Golby and Purdue 1984. At the end of his essay, Jevons (1883, 24) attributes the "degradation of English amusements" to this tendency of living up to the Joneses. It is unclear, however, what other criterion than aping their betters the public has in judging culture since they lacked the mental capacity to decide for themselves on the worth of culture.

ture, and this could be attained by the provision of suitable entertainment.[26] For a reason already hinted at, Jevons considered music to be best fit to achieve this goal.

Interestingly, listening to music was described by Jevons as having the properties of both the absence of thought and of manual labor. It was "merely passive abandonment of the mind to the train of ideas and emotions suggested by the strains" (9). In this, there was no mental process involved—the appreciation of sounds, the building blocks of music, depended only "upon the nature of the *sense of hearing*" (JA6/47/4). There are then no thought processes involved separate from the involuntary working of that part of the brain that makes us recognize sounds. According to Jevons, we have to deal only with sensations "produced on the brain by minute mechanical impulses acting on the wonderful organism of the brain" (1). In listening to a great orchestra, "many hundreds . . . of waves and pulses of air" were continually reaching the ear, and it was by the "almost involuntary & instantaneous comparison of these waves" that the ear "received" the impression of a tone.

The function of music consists of "a general removal of the mind from its ordinary course of duties . . . causing it to forget ordinary affairs and thoughts." It causes a "feeling of Beauty or of Sublimity . . . often excited, more or less, by every pleasant country walk, by sightseeing, by beautiful and extensive views or grand and striking scenery on sea or land, by magnificent architectural . . . works or a fine piece of poetry" (8–9). This feeling, Jevons suggested, "belongs to the *perceptions*, not . . . reason and is far below the level of a somewhat analogous but feebler feeling produced by the contemplation of wonderful and beautiful facts of science or knowledge in general." In short, music belongs to what Jevons termed the class of "*perceptive pleasure* meaning any emotion . . . produced by subjects of nature or Art through the medium of the sense or mind but without the necessary exercise of the higher faculties of reason" (9). Thought being absent, happily there is also no labor spoiled. Of course, Jevons admitted, "there is some nervous waste even in the enjoyment of music, and it is greater as the attention is more

26. Jevons nowhere made the inference that the factory system was to be blamed for poor worker's habits, though it is striking that poor Scandinavian *peasants* behave better than the English working class. Apparently, these peasants did not need pacifying entertainment to behave properly.

excited," but music holds the mind "enchained just so long as there is energy of thought to spare; in the meantime the body remains in a perfect state of repose" (Jevons 1883, 10).[27]

The music that Jevons thought best fit to limit the "nervous waste" and so to be played in parks or music halls was highly conventional. It should consist of "the better class of dance music, old English melodies, popular classical songs." The public would not be suited for the "great musical structures" since they demanded "long musical training for their appreciation." Though it is nowhere said, it is not difficult to conceive that one of Jevons's reasons to exclude common man from the great musical compositions was that it would not lead the mind to a state of rest, but instead would excite the brain. Obviously, he considered the common man to be unfit for this sort of excitement and implicitly reserved the appreciation of complex music to those who were naturally gifted with imagination, in practice the higher classes. If, in other words, "small" art and not "great" art were provided to the public, the whole thing would be completely "harmless" and "devoid of coarseness or vulgarity" (16).

This negative description left obscure how listening to music could contribute in a genuinely positive way to the elevation of the cultural level of the lower classes. By suppressing the use of man's brain, the only enjoyment to be had, in fact, was simple relaxation. Popular entertainment thus served predominantly to pacify the workers. Indeed, the feeling of beauty or sublimity suggested to the listener a superiority over nature that could only be attained by "forgetting . . . the ordinary course of duties . . . [the] ordinary affairs and thoughts." This feeling consequently belied the listener over his true social position in which he was not in control, but the one controlled. In Jevons's conception of the effects of the arts, there was no positive evaluation at all of the "perceptual bewilderment" that, according to Ruskin, was the prime virtue of Gothic architecture and Turner's landscapes and which, far from putting the mind in a state of rest, stimulated man's imagination.

27. It is very hard at this point not to think of Ulysses and the Sirens. Enchained, Ulysses listened to the seductive hymns of the Sirens, while his deaf-made companions rowed past. In Ruskin's terms, this image might be taken as the ultimate and evil consequence of the division of labor, in which the manual workers are deprived of their senses and therewith of their power of imagination, the use of which comes to be reserved for the inventor. In Jevons's analysis, things are even worse, for there was no role to be played for the imagination at all, save for those rare geniuses which for Jevons were the real inventors. For an unsurpassed analysis of Ulysses, see Adorno and Horkheimer [1947] 1986, 50–87.

Ruskin's views on art contrasted strongly with those of Jevons, since art, for Ruskin ([1862] 1985, 99), "must confess that we have not reached the perfection we can imagine, and cannot rest in the condition we have attained." This "harmless" state of rest was exactly what Jevons had in mind.

Conclusion

At this point, let me return to where we started: the solemn inaugural ceremony at Queen's College, Liverpool. How sympathetic *was* Jevons to Ruskin's lecture? "Of Kings' Treasuries" not only dealt with the question of how to read (how to address) the great books of the past but also analyzed and commented on the adverse cultural climate toward reading. "We despised," Ruskin complained, all the great achievements of mankind: literature, science, the arts; worse, even, nature, "the deep and sacred sensations of scenery," and compassion were despised. In the course of his further lamentation Ruskin shifted from the use of "we" to "you": the audience as those despising. It is quite clear who this audience was: the middle and upper classes. They were not the workmen by "whose work, by whose strength, by whose life, by whose death, you live, and never thank them" ([1862] 1985, 281). These "common workmen" for Ruskin were the "body and nervous force" of the nation, but they were excluded from participation in the amusements of the better-off classes: "Our National religion is the performance of church ceremonies, and preaching of soporific truths (and untruths) to keep the mob quietly at work; and the necessity for this amusement is fastening on us, as a fevorous disease of parched throat and wandering eyes—senseless, dissolute, merciless" (281–82).

For Ruskin, the word "Dis-ease . . . literally" expressed the decline of morals and culture in England. It was a reflection of the conditions under which the majority of men was forced to work for a living with the awful consequence that "we pour our whole masculine energy into the false business of money-making" (282). Ruskin obviously played with the life-giving connotations of this "masculine energy" (and we may note again that the classical Roman translation for this masculine energy is genius). With an ironic allusion to the Corn Laws, Ruskin urged the establishment of "corn laws" of a better sort: for the old Arabian grain, sesame, "which opens doors—doors not of robbers', but of Kings' Treasuries": the great achievements of mankind in literature, art, and science (282).

Jevons's obvious admiration for Ruskin's many "imaginative names and figurative expressions" cannot conceal the differences between their stances, which in due time only became greater. When we read Jevons's original 1877 essay on "Cram" in *Mind* and compare this with Ruskin's scattered remarks on the same subject, the differences between their respective stances become manifest. By that time Jevons (1883, 90) had become of the opinion that a "well-ordered education is a severe system of well-sustained 'Cram' . . . the agony of the examination-room is an anticipation of the struggles of life. All life is a long series of competitive examinations." For Jevons, the "business" of the educator was to "impress indelibly upon the mind the useful knowledge which is to guide the pupil through life. This would be 'Cram' indeed" (99). Jevons's defense of "Cram" stemmed from the idea that it should be possible to control "the plastic fibres of the youthful brain" (88). Ruskin severely opposed "the school of Cram" in education exactly because he thought it deadened the inventive part of man, man's genius, and defended "the school of Culture" in its place. (See, for example, Geddes 1884, 40.) In *Fors Clavigera* he related the story of an art student who had "the finest powers of mechanical execution I have ever met with, but was quite incapable of invention, or strong intellectual effort of any kind" (*Works*, 25:150). Ruskin fully blamed the educational system for the "mischief done to the best faculties of the brain" whose sole interest it was "to keep order." According to Ruskin, the "best powers of the youth" could only be developed "without competition" (151–153).

Their diverging attitude toward "Cram" is paradigmatic for their different views on the mind's working, labor conditions, and the role of culture in society. We have seen that Ruskin's and Jevons's different conceptions of man's imaginative powers in the end were directed toward the distinction between "popular" and "high" culture. But there was a class distinction involved, also. The lower classes were preferably to be excluded from the appreciation of high culture, which was to be reserved for the higher classes. In fact, Ruskin's analysis of Gothic functioned to deny the relevance of both these distinctions, whereas Jevons intended to regulate the moral conduct of the workmen by the regulation of popular culture.[28] A

28. Mosselmans and Mathijs's (this volume) succinct reading of Jevons's manuscript confirms this point. According to them, the appreciation of popular culture served to both pacify *and* elevate the working classes. Though this indeed might be inferred from both the manuscript and Jevons's essays on social reform, it remains obscure what this elevation of the working classes consisted of other than their pacification.

remark in one of Ruskin's *Fors Clavigera*, his own letters in a bottle to the "Workmen and Labourers of Great Britain," confirms Ruskin's unwillingness to distinguish two levels of culture:

> A day seldom passes . . . without my receiving a remonstration on the absurdity of writing "so much above the level" of those whom I address. . . . I want to know why it is assumed so quietly that your brains must always be at a low level. Is it essential to the doing of the work by which England exists, that its workmen should not be able to understand scholar's English . . . , but only newspaper's English? . . . For my part, I cannot at all understand why well-educated people should still so habitually speak of you as beneath their level, and needing to be written down to, with condescending simplicity, as flat-foreheaded creatures of another race, unredeemable by any Darwinism. (*Works*, 27:181–82)

This criticism turned Ruskin from art critic into economist, as was most succinctly expressed by Patrick Geddes[29] in his short book *John Ruskin: Economist* (1884): "Criticism of the aesthetic consumption becomes the most needful of all conceivable contributions to production; and it is therefore for the economist to become an art-critic, or, failing him, the art-critic must supply his place and become an economist" (30). *If* man is in a position to use his imagination, he will be able to appreciate what others reserve for an elite group. Under modern conditions of production, however, man was not in such a position. There was a general agreement on the observation that the factory system, *as a whole*, forced the operative to work with the minuteness of a machine. Whereas this observation filled Ruskin with disgust, it was for Cooke-Taylor ([1841] 1969, 123) a source of "admiration": "The organisation of the community is complete, and the human agents work with all the exactness of machinery." For Ruskin ([1862] 1985, 84) it meant to "unhumanize" man: "Men were not intended to work with the accuracy of tools, to be precise and perfect in all their actions." Ruskin once gave an example that highlighted the difference between man working as an animated tool and as a thinking being:

29. Recently, there has been some increased interest in Geddes's work, which was a source of inspiration for Lewis Mumford. Geddes originally was a biologist who is best known for his work on the emergence of the metropole. In 1903 he helped establish the Sociological Society of London. See introduction in Novak 1995.

> You can teach a man to draw a straight line, and to cut one, . . . and to copy and carve any number of given lines or forms, with admirable speed and perfect precision. . . . but if you ask him to think about any of these forms, to consider if he cannot find any better in his own head, he stops; his execution becomes hesitating; he thinks, and ten to one he thinks wrong; ten to one he makes a mistake in the first touch he gives to the work as a thinking being. But you have made a man of him for all that. He was only a machine before, an animated tool. (84)

The thinking part of man, we have seen, was for Ruskin closely connected to the imagination. The type of ingenuity Cooke-Taylor referred to pointed in the wrong direction for Ruskin: it meant skill and dexterity and underplayed the role imagination had to play in daily life. But without imagination, Ruskin insisted, man's intellectual activities would reduce to routine operations. His labor would be only mechanical, and consumption would be without taste. The crucial point, for Ruskin in all instances, was that in no sphere of life should man *conform* to vested rules, but should himself deliberate and decide what path to follow.

In his criticism of modern working conditions, Ruskin retreated into the Gothic past to derive criteria for the enjoyment of life, which he saw rapidly declining around him. From the 1860s onward, his work turned on this, and it was widely thought to be completely quixotic. In a letter to Professor Norton, Sir John Simon wrote about Ruskin's "utterly spendthrift way in which (with imagination less and less controlled by judgment) he has for these last years been at work with a dozen different irons in the fire. . . . And his emotions all the while as hard worked as his intellect. . . . I wonder he has not broken down long ago" (*Works*, 27:xviii).

Jevons balanced "the pain of work" against the utility of the product or, as he equivalently said, the "desire of possession" ([1871] 1970, 192). One of Ruskin's main complaints was that Mill's economic man desired only possession, thus downplaying the importance of *enjoying* the wealth possessed. The enjoyment of goods evoked criteria Ruskin took from his analysis of art. They were inherently related to the nourishment of our imagination, and not only of the senses, as we have seen in Jevons's description of music. A product was enjoyable if it stimulated our imagination: "There is no want of genius among us, still less of industry . . . but there is a want among us, deep and wide, of discretion in directing toil, and of delight in being led by imagination" (Ruskin [1857] 1904, 227). This mirrored the working conditions under which a product was produced, however, and for Ruskin those conditions of the factory system should be completely reversed.

Such radical notions were completely alien to Jevons. His analysis of labor and popular culture mimicked the conditions of workmen in the factory system. This did not imply that Jevons simply took working conditions for granted, as he made clear, for example, in *The State in Relation to Labour* ([1882] 1968). What he did take for granted, however, was the monotony the factory system had imposed on the workman. His proposals for social reform coincided with this view in that reform should be directed to regulating more successfully the lives of the mass of the people. As he once stated: "As feelings [of pleasure and pain] are both the ends and instruments of the moralist and legislator, it especially behooves us to learn how to estimate these values aright" (Jevons [1890] 1971, 276). In his essays on popular culture Jevons's ultimate aim was to pacify the crowd.

Maybe the different analyses of Ruskin and Jevons in the end were motivated by the two different attitudes Cooke-Taylor discerned with respect to the factory system. Either one could judge the factory system "by an inapplicable standard" and retreat to "previous reading and experience"— as Ruskin did—or one could examine it as an "established innovation" (Cooke-Taylor [1841] 1969, 3), and this, of course, was what Jevons did. Clearly aware of the many vices and crimes associated with poor working and living conditions, Jevons nevertheless wrote in a diary entry at the end of February 1853: "I have been [on] one or two good walks lately, chiefly among the manufacturing parts. . . . I feel as if I could see nothing with so much pleasure now as a dirty pearl-ash manufactory or tar-distillery" (*PC*, 1:90–91). Ruskin's criticism of political economy clearly could not come to terms with a situation in which the factory system not only endured, but spread worldwide:[30]

30. Is it a coincidence that, when Ruskin retreated to the Lakes of Cumberland he had visited with so much delight in his early youth, William Pater and Oscar Wilde proclaimed the full independence of the arts of socioeconomic considerations? Where this essay has argued that Ruskin opposed the factory system and the consumer culture that emerged from it, Regenia Gagnier (1993, 126) convincingly argues that Pater's and Wilde's aesthetics accommodated the newly developing consumer culture: "Indeed, Wilde captured the essence of modern economic man when he named the cigarette the perfect type of pleasure because it left one unsatisfied. For this reason, of course, the cigarette is the perfect commodity."

> All England may, if it so chooses, become one manufacturing town; and Englishmen, sacrificing themselves to the good of general humanity, may live diminished lives in the midst of noise, of darkness, and of deadly exhalation. But the world cannot become a factory nor a mine. No amount of ingenuity will ever make iron digestible by the million, nor substitute hydrogen for wine. ([1862] 1985, 225)

References

Adorno, Theodor W., and Max Horkheimer. [1947] 1986. *Dialektik der Aufklärung*. Frankfurt am Main: S. Fischer Verlag.

Ashworth, William J. 1998. "System of Terror": Samuel Bentham, Accountability, and Dockyard Reform during the Napoleonic Wars. *Social History* 23.1:63–79.

Babbage, Charles. [1835] 1963. *On the Economy of Machinery and Manufactures*. Reprints of Economic Classics. New York: Augustus M. Kelley.

Bianchi, Marina. 1998. *The Active Consumer: Novelty and Surprise in Consumer Choice*. London: Routledge.

Chaigneau, Nicolas. 1996a. A Case of Swinging Boundary: Edgeworth versus Fisher on Utility Measurement. Presented at the BSHS/AHSC Conference, 23–26 July, Edinburgh.

———. 1996b. Utilitarisme et psychophysique dans les *New and Old Methods of Ethics* d'Edgeworth. Paper presented at the Colloque de l'Utilitarisme: Analyse et Histoire, 25–26 January, Lille, France.

———. 1997. Contrat et utilité: Origines et fondements de la théorie de l'échange de Francis Ysidro Edgeworth. Ph.D. diss., Université de Paris I Panthéon-Sorbonne.

Cooke-Taylor, William. [1841] 1969. *Notes of a Tour in the Manufacturing Districts of Lancashire*. Reprints of Economic Classics. New York: Augustus M. Kelley.

Davies, J. Llewelyn. 1904. *The Working Men's College 1854–1904*. London: Macmillan.

Eisler, Rudolf. 1971. Lemma on Invention. In *Historisches Wörterbuch der Philosophie*. Basel/Stuttgart: Schwabe & Co. Verlag.

Emerson, Sheila. 1993. *Ruskin: The Genesis of Invention*. Cambridge: Cambridge University Press.

Gagnier, Regenia. 1993. On the Insatiability of Human Wants: Economic and Aesthetic Man. *Victorian Studies* 36.2:125–53.

Geddes, Patrick. 1884. *John Ruskin: Economist*. Edinburgh: William Brown.

Golby, J. M., and A. W. Purdue. 1984. *The Civilisation of the Crowd: Popular Culture in England 1750–1900*. London: Batsford Academic and Educational.

Heffernan, James A. W. 1984. *The Re-Creation of Landscape: A Study of Wordsworth, Coleridge, Constable, and Turner*. Hanover, N.H.: University Press of New England.

Hogarth, William. [1753] 1997. *The Analysis of Beauty*. New Haven, Conn.: Yale University Press.

Jevons, William Stanley. Jevons archives. John Rylands University Library, University of Manchester. [JA]

———. [1871] 1970. *The Theory of Political Economy*. Edited and introduced by R. D. Collison Black. Harmondsworth, England: Penguin.

———. [1874] 1958. *The Principles of Science: A Treatise on Logic and Scientific Method*. New York: Dover.

———. 1879. *The Theory of Political Economy*. 2d ed. London: Macmillan.

———. [1882] 1968. *The State in Relation to Labor.* Edited by Francis W. Hirst. New York: Augustus M. Kelley.

———. 1883. *Methods of Social Reform*. London: Macmillan.

———. [1890] 1971. *Pure Logic and Other Minor Works*. Edited by Robert Adamson and Harriet A. Jevons. New York: Bert Franklin.

———. 1972. *Papers and Correspondence of William Stanley Jevons*. Vol. 1. Edited by R. D. Collison Black and Rosamond Könekamp. London: Macmillan.

Liverpool Daily Post, 1865. Supplement, 3 October, 7.

Maas, Harro. 1999. Babbage, Jevons, and the Machinery of the Mind. Working Paper on Measurement in Physics and Economics. London School of Economics.

Mainusch, Herbert. 1969. *Romantische Ästhetik: Untersuchungen zur englischen Kunstlehre des späten 18. und frühen 19. Jahrhunderts*. Bad Homburg v.d.H.: Gehlen Verlag.

McNiven, Peter. 1983. Hand-list of the Jevons Archives in the John Rylands University Library. *Bulletin of the John Rylands University Library* 66:213–55.

Mill, John Stuart. 1981; 1969. *Collected Works*. Vols. 1 and 10. Edited by J. M. Robson. Toronto: University of Toronto Press.

Mumford, Lewis. 1946. *Technics and Civilization*. London: Routledge.

Novak, Frank G. 1995. *Lewis Mumford and Patrick Geddes*. London: Routledge.

Paetzold, Heinz. 1974. *Neomarxistische Aesthetik*. 2 vols. Düsseldorf: Schwann Verlag.

Ruskin, John. [1830] 1990. *A Tour to the Lakes in Cumberland: John Ruskin's Diary for 1830*. Edited by James S. Dearden and introduced by Van Akin Burd. Aldershot, England: Scholar Press.

———. 1854. *Lectures on Architecture and Painting*. London: Routledge.

———. [1857] 1904. *A Joy Forever (and Its Price in the Market)*. London: George Allen.

———. [1862] 1985. *Unto This Last and Other Writings*. Edited and introduced by Clive Wilmer. Harmondsworth, England: Penguin.

———. 1903–12. *The Works of John Ruskin*. 39 vols. Edited by E. T. Cook and Alexander Wedderburn. London: Allen.

———. 1995. *Selected Writings*. Edited by Philip David. London: Everyman.

Schaffer, Simon. 1994. Babbage's Intelligence: Calculating Engines and the Factory System. *Critical Inquiry* 21.3:203–27.

Smith, Adam. [1776] 1976. *An Inquiry into the Nature and Causes of the Wealth of*

Nations. Edited by R. H. Campbell and A. S. Skinner. Oxford: Clarendon Press.

Smith, Lindsay. 1995. *Victorian Photography, Painting, and Poetry: The Enigma of Visibility in Ruskin, Morris, and the Pre-Raphaelites*. Cambridge: Cambridge University Press.

Ure, Andrew. [1835] 1967. *The Philosophy of Manufacturers; or, An Exposition of the Scientific, Moral, and Commercial Economy of the Factory System of Great Britain*. London: Frank Cass.

Veblen, Thorstein B. [1904] 1975. *The Theory of Business Enterprise*. Reprints of Economic Classics. Clifton, N.J.: Augustus M. Kelley.

White, Michael V. 1994a. Bridging the Natural and the Social: Science and Character in Jevons's Political Economy. *Economic Inquiry* 32.2:429–44.

———. 1994b. Following Strange Gods: Women in Jevons's Political Economy. In *Feminism and Political Economy in Victorian England*, edited by Peter Groenewegen. London: Edward Elgar.

Zilsel, Edgar. 1926. *Die Entstehung des Geniebegriffs: Ein Beitrag zur Ideengeschichte der Antike und des Frühkapitalismus*. Tübingen: J. C. B. Mohr Verlag.

Jevons's Music Manuscript and the Political Economy of Music

Bert Mosselmans and Ernest Mathijs

Here we investigate an unpublished manuscript on music by William Stanley Jevons. First, we analyze the origin of the manuscript and show that it should be seen as a part of Jevons's utilitarian "science of man" project. The manuscript also serves as a justification for the time Jevons devotes to playing music, and it was meant as an improvement of already existing literature on the subject. Second, we summarize the chapter "On the Functions of Music" and highlight several aspects. Music is partly an object of enjoyment, but it fulfills educational and moralizing purposes as well. An "intellectual cleavage" in Jevons's ideas on music appears when he argues that everyone may enjoy lower forms of music, but that higher forms require education and training. His diagrams on the classification of the arts reflect this cleavage. Third, we investigate the aesthetic context of Jevons's manuscript, and we argue that it belongs to the Anglo-Saxon aesthetic tradition of Shaftesbury. Although Jevons remains

This essay contains hitherto unpublished material by Jevons (see appendix), which was found in the Jevons archives at the John Rylands University Library of Manchester University. For a complete list, see McNiven 1983. Parts of the archives ("On the Functions of Music," JA6/47/8, and a diagram, JA6/45/4) are reproduced by courtesy of the Director and University Librarian, the John Rylands University Library of Manchester. We would like to thank Peter Nockles for his kind help with the archives and John Vint and the Manchester Metropolitan University for their support during the stay in Manchester. This essay is part of the OZR-project no. 1971131490 financed by the Research Council of the Free University of Brussels. We received many interesting comments at and after the 1998 *HOPE* conference, and we would like to thank Neil De Marchi, Craufurd Goodwin, Judy Klein, Harro Maas, and Michael V. White for their specific remarks. Michael White's comments were especially useful, as he directed our attention to several aspects of Jevons's context and to some additional archival material.

within this tradition, his general disinterest in aesthetic categories (the beautiful and the sublime) is explained by his utilitarian approach. Art in a utilitarian sense—its usefulness—is Jevons's concern, and not the metaphysics of the beautiful. This becomes clear in the last section, in which we investigate Jevons's policy prescriptions regarding public performances of music. These cheap and easily accessible means of spreading culture may operate as tools to elevate moral consciousness among the people. We argue that Jevons's solitary and intellectual conception of music may be ill suited for this purpose.

The manuscript "On the Science and Art of Music" is located at the John Rylands University Library with reference JA6/47/1–17,[1] and it consists of fifty pages. Most of the chapters deal with physical and technical aspects of music: The Nature of Sound and the Undulatory Theory (chap. 1); On the Harmony of Sounds (chap. 2); On the Complete or Chromatic Scale and the Adjustment of Notes or Temperament (chap. 3); On Melody (chap. 4); On the Functions of Music (unnumbered chap.); On Musical Rhythm and Time (unnumbered chapter); and some preparatory writings.[2]

We focus here on the chapter "On the Functions of Music" as it contains Jevons's most explicit aesthetic ideas. We provide a general overview of the content of this chapter, and then we examine several aspects in detail: the essential character of music, its intellectual aspects, and Jevons's concept of "perceptive pleasure." We then examine and compare three different illustrations to be found at different places in the archive (JA6/45/4, JA6/45/5, and JA10/1/32b). To clarify our arguments, we add material from the correspondence between Jevons and his sister Henrietta (JA10; Black 1973). Appendix 1 to this essay contains a complete transcription of the "Functions" chapter (JA6/47/8), and appendix 2 provides the most elaborate diagram, JA6/45/4.

The Origin of Jevons's Music Manuscript

The music manuscript is one of the numerous products of Jevons's lonely hours in Australia. In October 1854, Jevons arrives in Sydney,

1. This and all subsequent citations beginning "JA" refer to items in the Jevons archives.

2. White notes that the chapter "On the Functions of Music" was to follow the chapter "On Musical Rhythm and Time" and that Jevons intended to add at least one chapter to appear between these two chapters. As there is no trace of this chapter, it may be possible that it has never been written. See White 1996, 2.

where he starts his position as an assayer at the Australian Mint. His acceptance of this position was partly motivated by the narrow financial situation at home, after the bankruptcy of his father following the railway boom crisis of 1847–48. On 5 January 1855, Jevons writes in his journal that he does not intend to stay in Australia and remain an assayer for the rest of his life; on the contrary, he looks forward to returning to England after having collected a small sum of money. He would like to start over again at home, but with some capital and with several years of colonial experience (Black and Könekamp 1972, 110). Jevons fills up his spare time with various scientific investigations (meteorology, botanics, and geology), excursions, and music.

In February 1856, Jevons receives the news of the sudden death of his father, Thomas Jevons. Elsewhere we argue that this sad news enters Jevons's reflections on subjects regarding selfishness (Mosselmans in press). He has always been somewhat preoccupied with this subject, but the death of his father brings in a stronger personal dimension.[3] Jevons would be pleased if he knew that he had pleased his father, and he wonders whether this reasoning is induced by feelings of love toward his father or simply by selfishness. He concludes that "all our thoughts and motives . . . never seem to spring from a perfectly pure source" (Black 1973, 212). Moreover, his father's death leads Jevons to a general questioning of what ought to be achieved in life. The outcome of his reflection is a utilitarian framework in which a "science of man" emerges; we argue here that the music manuscript is part of this science. Jevons's personal worries are mixed up with his scientific investigations, and he seems to derive the basic principles of this framework from what he had

3. Michael White urged us not to neglect other important contextual aspects. Indeed, Jevons did not start his reflections on selfishness after the death of his father, as earlier remarks in his journal indicate (White 1989, 624; Black and Könekamp 1972, 112). Woolley's lecture "The Selfish Theory of Morals" should be seen as a major influence, as it enabled Jevons to couch his analysis of selfishness in terms of pleasures and pains (White [1982] 1988, 337–38; White 1989, 625; Black and Könekamp 1972, 132–34). This lecture therefore crystallized Jevons's thoughts on this subject. However, whereas Jevons visited the lecture in September 1856, he had received the news of his father's death in February of the same year. We agree with White that the lecture provided Jevons with more analytical rigor, but the death of his father gave his reflections a more personal and existential dimension. This becomes clear from a review of Jevons's letters to his sister Henrietta, which are filled with matters of a more intimate nature.

learned from his father.[4] Thomas Jevons had always defended the idea that a person should "be *good* and *honourable*" and should "strive to make himself of *use & value* in the world" (214). Jevons's reflections on selfishness and usefulness are expressed in a letter to his sister Henrietta:

> I have enough ado indeed to find out what I am myself exactly and to persuade myself that it is what is right, and to this end I have often entered into sorts of long mental discussions as to what the word (of all the most disagreeable) "*selfish*" really means. Generally, however, they terminate much about where they began, and I have lately begun to accept the wish to be *unselfish* as tantamount to the fact. (240–41)

Jevons states that human behavior should be judged by an investigation of motives, and these motives should be guided by principles of truthfulness and honesty of purpose, with a real regard for the sake of others and for oneself. This procedure may be too indefinite and uninviting for most minds, but Jevons does not see other options. He would like to be as unselfish as possible, but he is not at all convinced that similar processes of mind go on in other persons. Since words are insufficient to prove the purity of purposes, acts may be the only way to show one's honesty (241–42).[5] Jevons uses this utilitarian framework to judge his own daily activities, and here he arrives at some trouble. He is always occupied with intellectual activities, and he even complains that he does not have enough time to undertake everything he would like to (225). He is very worried about how to allocate his scarce time to his various occupations because he would like to maximize his use and value for the world. Nevertheless, Jevons does not give the impression of being concerned with others. He reports to Henrietta that he had visitors, but he could not spend more than twenty minutes with them because he was buried in a particular subject. He wonders whether

4. This is, once again, not to neglect other influences. See the previous note for the argument that Woolley's lecture supplied Jevons's reflections with more analytical rigor. For the discussion of Jevons's early influences, see the successive articles La Nauze [1941] 1988, White [1982] 1988, Hutchison 1982, White 1984, Hutchison 1984, Bostaph and Shieh 1986, Bostaph 1989, and White 1989.

5. This is in accordance with White's (1994a, 431) description of Jevons's "naturalistic theory of ethics": "What was good or ethical could be characterized in terms of 'sensible' properties of the world and hence could be discussed and identified in empirically meaningful terms."

his sisters will tolerate his "abstract attitude" once he returns to England (JA10/1/37a). He writes to Henrietta:

> Sometimes I begin to feel more like a misanthropist than is comfortable although in theory I profess the very opposite. I am not very amiable or well fitted to please small tea parties; it may be very well to amuse and please people in general but it scarcely seems my vocation. Cannot a division of labour be allowed so that those who are amiable may exercise their talents in small talk and good humour, while I betake myself to dreary work and thought? This is all that I ask and surely I offer people in general a very favourable bargain. It is a pity that they cannot see it as I see it. (JA10/1/40a)

Elsewhere Jevons writes that it would be "bad economy" to drop his current activities and to work solely for others, although it would certainly be an action induced by good motives. It may be more profitable in the long term to devote much time to reading and scientific study, although it may appear to be selfish at first sight (Black 1973, 276–77). Jevons would like to be "powerfully good," not to just one or several persons, but toward a nation or even the world. He would therefore like to use the powers of his mind to maximize his usefulness for the world. He thinks that the most powerful ability of his mind lies in a strong disposition to classify things. He is not so good when it comes to forming new thoughts and opinions, but his strength consists in developing already existing ideas "into something symmetrical" (308). Although Jevons would like to be a practical man who sees the effects following the cause, he is more suited to become a student of remote and abstract causes, and in this sense he could be a "great good to all succeeding generations" (335). Jevons illustrates the difference between a practical and a theoretical life by a reference to "performance and preparation," or even "labour and capital." It may be "good economy" to delay hammering and to spend some time in acquiring strength and skill to use the hammer with more power in the future. Jevons's justification of his own "dreary work and thought" is an important road to his 1871 *Theory of Political Economy*: "We enter here into one of those deeply laid and simple propositions of Economy which I hope some day to work out into a symmetrical and extensive manner hitherto unattempted even by Mill or Adam Smith" (Black 1973, 359–60). Jevons's collection of the "fragments of a scattered science" is therefore an outcome of the utilitarian framework he constructed in Australia. It is also quite reasonable to suppose that Jevons's ideas regarding "preparation and performance" at least partly operate as justifications for his wish to return to England and to continue his education.

The same utilitarian framework enables Jevons to justify his scientific investigations and his aversion toward small talk and tea parties. But he remains unsatisfied with other people considering him "strangely unsociable and uncompromising" (Black 1973, 302). Jevons complains about not having a "mind" to talk to: it would be absurd to express serious thoughts to persons who cannot respond to them or think them absurd (311). He prefers solitude, as this is a requisite in order to form "earnest thoughts"; almost nothing can be learned from experiences with ordinary people (337). Although Jevons may exaggerate his solitude,[6] it is clear that he prefers solitary scientific investigations to social gatherings. He does not sleep much, and he spends a lot of his spare time on the science of man, a collection of scientific studies based on Jevons's utilitarian framework. Jevons describes his project of the science of man in a letter to Henrietta:

> Within the last hundred years, sciences almost innumerable have sprung up, but mostly devoted to physical Nature. Comparatively few have perceived that Human Nature may also be the subject of a science. It is indeed a many-sided subject. Religion, metaphysics, ethics, jurisprudence, political economy, politics, and even medicine, art, poetry and many other studies all have man for the subject. (336)

Just as in physics, the science of man is directed to the discovery of general principles and laws. The science rests on the suppositions that man is "a phenomenon in which *effect* is always connected with *cause*" and that there have to be "causes to make people good and bad, happy and miserable, rich and poor, as well as strong and feeble." The science of man should take numerous data into account, because each human being possesses animal powers, a logical mind, and a series of emotions and is placed in circumstances that are continuously changing (Black 1973, 361–62). Jevons's project is therefore a heterogeneous collection of different disciplines, and he devotes much time to different surveys.

6. According to White, Jevons made some misleading statements regarding his solitude, and he tended to exaggerate his intellectual isolation. See, for example, Jevons's activities as a photographer (Burke [1955] 1988). His numerous articles for newspapers (Inoue and White 1993) indicate that Jevons did not live in intellectual isolation. We argue here, however, that Jevons's solitude remains important for his ideas on music (and religion).

One part of this large project concerns "towns and cities" and is directed to the discovery of the "nature" of particular cities. It would consist in analyzing the constitution and causes of cities, the relative character of their parts, and the relative character of particular cities (327).[7] Another part is economics, "a sort of vague mathematics which calculates the causes and effects of man's industry, and shows how it may best be applied" (321). Jevons's music manuscript is another part of this science of man. The chapter "Functions" opens with the observation that music is an "integral part of man" (JA6/47/8). Moreover, Jevons's comparison of different art forms is couched in utilitarian terms (see below). A first motivation for Jevons to prepare the manuscript is therefore that it is a part of the science of man project. We elaborate on this subject in the next section.

We already stated here that Jevons's project is mixed up with personal worries. A second motivation for the manuscript is as an attempt to justify his love for music and the time he devotes to playing his harmonium. Jevons buys the harmonium in 1855 and considers it a "first rate thing" to have an instrument in the "Australian wilds" (Black 1973, 162). He purchases several pieces of music and practices a lot. He reports about his progress and his judgment of the pieces to his sister Henrietta, who is very fond of music as well. She is, in fact, the only person Jevons communicates with on musical topics. Jevons states that he does not play to please other people, but he would like to understand the music in his own way. He compares this with reading a book, which is also an activity never to be performed to please others (225).

Although Jevons's solitude may be exaggerated when it comes to his scientific work, it may be a proper characterization of his attitude toward music. We argue later that Jevons's solitary conception of music has severe consequences for his policy recommendations. Jevons spends a lot of time playing the harmonium. On 25 November 1856 he writes that "music proceeds well and I shall know half the music in the world in a few years if I play as much as I do now" (JA10/1/27). Music is very important for Jevons:

7. In an article for the *Sydney Morning Herald*, published on 7 October 1858, Jevons makes clear that the character of a city is connected with the character of its inhabitants. Jevons describes the "Rocks" as a dirty and unhealthy part of Sydney, inhabited by immoral and drunken people. Here, the complete absence of sanitation should be condemned. A proper sanitation may be a step in the direction of the elevation of the morality of the masses (Jevons 1858). For the role of music in the process of civilization, see our section "The Political Economy of Music."

> Music is always to me the same, a condition of my existence, a part of me. I believe I could live a *life of Music*. If our physical nature did not interfere, I can almost conceive it possible that a man might play music *ad infinitum* and still never tire. . . . Now I think that nothing less than a life time would quite satisfy my musical thirst while I find with concern that a single hour per day out of the 24, considerably interferes with other affairs equally or more important. Music thus ought to be a rare but still a legitimate and occasional delight. (Black 1973, 319–20)

This quotation suggests that the music manuscript should also be seen as an attempt to justify the time Jevons devotes to playing music, as it interferes with other activities.

A third motivation to write the manuscript is Jevons's general dissatisfaction with the already existing literature on the subject. On 3 May 1856 he reports reading Spencer's *Rudimentary and Practical Treatise on Music* (1850), which he considers "*excessively dull* as well as rather difficult" (Black 1973, 227). On 3 July 1856 he writes to Henrietta:

> I enclose you a long affair which I have been writing lately. Wishing to read and understand a little of the principles of music, and being rather disgusted with the superficial uninteresting sort of books I can find on it, I thought I would write a book of my own which however imperfect would indeed teach me more than any body else's. . . . Voici Chapters 1 and 2. As it must be so very short, I do not know whether I make it very plain, if not get other books to help you out, for instance Spencer's *Rudimentary Treatise on Music*. (JA10/1/25)

Black and Könekamp (1972, 32; see also Black 1973, 243) argued that Jevons's music manuscript contained a new system of notation and that it has not survived. There is no evidence, however, that the book was on notation of music. Jevons indeed writes in a letter that the current system of notation is "stupidly contrived," but he adds that "I should improve it if I think I had much to do with it" (Black 1973, 227).

It seems clear that the manuscript contains a general survey of music theory instead, as it was intended as an improvement of already existing literature on the subject. Moreover, the Henrietta section of the John Rylands University Library in Manchester contains a document (JA10/1/32b) that is certainly a part of the larger manuscript to be found in the same archive (JA6/47/1–17). Since Jevons sent the manuscript to Henrietta, this is good evidence that the manuscript under consideration is the one mentioned in Jevons's letters.[8] Jevons reports sending a new chapter of the book on 1 October 1856 (Black 1973, 243) and another chapter ("a longer one than ever") on 25 November 1856 (JA10/1/27). On 4 April 1857 Jevons states that he does not have time to continue the book, nor does he have something in his head to write about.

We therefore conclude that the "missing manuscript" is archived at the John Rylands University Library and that it was written in the last quarter of 1856 and the first quarter of 1857. It should be seen as a part of the larger "science of man" project, as a justification of Jevons's love for music, and as his attempt to improve the already existing literature on the subject. In the next section we investigate this manuscript in detail.

Analysis of the Chapter "On the Functions of Music"

In the first paragraph of the "Functions" chapter, Jevons states that the function of music should not be reduced to its use, as music is more than a simple instrument of pleasure. It is an integral part of every individual, although the importance attached to music is not equal for every person. When the sense for music is once developed, it becomes an indissoluble part of the person (like the other senses). Jevons would like to investigate the precise place music occupies "among the occupations and capacities of men." Music is essential because its experience gives rise to essential feelings. Everybody knows these feelings "to a greater or less degree": They result from the contemplation of "subjects of interest, beauty, or sublimity." These feelings remove the mind from its ordinary affairs and thoughts, but do not lead to conclusions or future purposes. The hearer receives "a sort of confident moral strength" which is not lasting, as it disappears as soon as the music is over and the daily duties and sorrows appear again (JA6/47/8).

Jevons lists other means of achieving these feelings: a walk in the countryside, sightseeing, observation of architectural or engineering

8. We would like to thank Michael V. White for drawing our attention to the music material in the Henrietta section. We analyze it at the end of the next section.

works, or listening to poetry. The feelings arise from the contemplation of anything that possesses "a degree of fresh interest, beauty, or grandeur." Jevons is unable to investigate the cause of these feelings, but it is clear that they do not depend on knowledge. No scientific knowledge of the subjects of "interest, beauty, or grandeur" is required: the beauty of a forest does not increase if the perceiver gains botanical acquaintance, and the enjoyment of music does not presuppose knowledge of harmonical composition. These feelings belong to the perception and not to the reason, and they are inexplicable. These feelings are similar to the feebler feelings that are produced by the contemplation of "beautiful" scientific facts or knowledge, or of "fixed principles and enduring convictions and emotions which form religion and all our sense of love and duty." This fact notwithstanding, Jevons considers the former feelings to be "far below the level" of the latter feelings.

He then defines the concept of "perceptive pleasure" as the emotions "produced by subjects of nature or art, through the medium of the senses or mind, but without the necessary exercise of the higher faculties of reason." These emotions can arise from different sources, and Jevons classifies them by the "sense or means through which they act on the mind": the sense of hearing, the sense of sight, and "poetical ideas or mental pictures of beauty" that arise through the medium of the mind itself (JA/47/8). Only a small part of emotions does not fit into this framework, but even these emotions are closely dependent on the three categories mentioned. Finally, Jevons introduces a table (which we investigate later in this section).

The first part of the chapter makes clear that the manuscript belongs to Jevons's larger project of the "science of man." Music is not merely an instrument of pleasure, it is an essential part of every human being. The aim of the "Functions" chapter is to identify the precise place music occupies among the activities of a person. Everyone should experience the feelings that originate from listening to a piece of music from time to time, because these feelings let us forget the daily sorrows. Moreover, they lead to the experience of a certain "moral strength" that enables us to survive in the context of the difficulties of our lives. All this may suggest that music should merely be seen as a "tranquilizer" of the mind, an interpretation to be found elsewhere.[9] Although this

9. See Harro Maas's contribution, "Pacifying the Workman: Ruskin and Jevons on Labor and Popular Culture," this volume.

aspect is certainly present, a prime nuance of this statement should be that it is an *essential* tranquilizer—necessary for every person. More important, music is not a simple instrument of pleasure, because the feeling associated with the music has a certain intellectual dimension.

This becomes clear in the text under consideration when Jevons states that music is not equally important for everyone, and when he argues that everyone already experienced the feelings associated with music to a greater or less degree. Although Jevons maintains that these feelings have nothing at all to do with reason or knowledge, there has to be something "intellectual," which implies that some people enjoy music more than other people do and that it is more important in some people's lives than in others'. We can clarify this point by taking other sources into account. Jevons states that it is possible to understand and appreciate music without being able to play it brilliantly. This indicates that this ability does not stem from some manual or technical ability. Jevons compares playing music with reading poetry (Black 1973, 257). He even writes: "I regard a fine piece of music like a fine poem, or essay or philosophical work, that is as a thing to be studied, understood and remembered. In this point of view playing music though it may *bore* others is still as good an employment of time *to a certain extent* as reading" (225).

This quotation clarifies Jevons's statement in the manuscript that although the feelings associated with the contemplation of scientific, ethical, or religious subjects are somewhat feebler than the feelings associated with music, they still have intellectual superiority. The study of art forms is similar to scientific study, but emotionally stronger and intellectually lower. Moreover, we show in the following section that art forms concerned with subjects that may also become topics of scientific investigation are valued higher in Jevons's utilitarian framework. All this implies that Jevons attributes to art and music an important intellectual dimension. A closer reading of other letters indicates that there are really different kinds of music, which are associated with different kinds of persons. Jevons writes about Handel's *Israel in Egypt*:

> As you are aware it consists of little except grand heavy choruses describing the plagues of Egypt and the Exodus of the Israelites. The subject is one perhaps which no writer but Handel dared to attempt; ordinary music and ordinary art usually appeal to the more common and immediate feelings of the heart, which every one comprehends

> more or less. To paint such feelings or describe them in poetry is no very difficult thing, but as it is only the very greatest artists that can reproduce historical scenes, or embody things with which the mind always associates vague ideas of extreme grandeur, so it is only the highest master-hand that could take music from its ordinary sphere, and make it describe events of strange and miraculous nature as those which are the subject of Israel. (JA10/1/40a)

This quotation indicates that Jevons regards this "descriptive music," which reproduces historical scenes with "extreme grandeur," as a high form of music. Jevons's letters to Henrietta are filled with descriptions of parts of musical pieces that express, for instance, the movement of frogs and the falling of hail (JA10/1/40a), and elsewhere Jevons describes a passage that "reaches the ultimatum of expression, the difference of Heaven and Hell. It is the highest effect of art" (JA10/1/37c).[10] This indicates that a real masterpiece deals with historical or religious subjects, which are reproduced emotionally in the inner eye (or ear) of the reader. This explains the lower status of music in comparison with science and religion: Although they deal with similar subjects, science and religion are concerned with the contemplation of these subjects themselves, whereas music merely reproduces the feelings of grandeur associated with these subjects. Although the latter feelings are more forceful than those produced by scientific or religious contemplation, they still remain intellectually at a lower level. Jevons's emphasis on the intellectual content of music also implies that, although (strictly speaking) no knowledge is required to appreciate a masterpiece, some knowledge may help. A person completely unfamiliar with the biblical or historical scenes reproduced in the piece will not

10. This observation gives a new dimension to Klein's (1995, 136) remark that Jevons had low qualities of visualization. He responded to a query by Francis Galton that he had severe difficulties in forming geometric conceptions in his mind. This low visualization capability may partly explain why Jevons seems not to be at all interested in art forms other than music. His detailed descriptions of musical pieces contrast heavily with other very superficial descriptions of art, like his visit to the Louvre: "It is a magnificent palace filled with all sorts of collections of pictures, sculpture antiquities, etc., etc., but the most celebrated I believe are the pictures by the old painters" (Black 1973, 58). He writes about an exhibition of paintings in London that "there were of course a great many fine paintings, but also a great many foolish and absurd ones, and a very large number of portraits which are very dull" (76). As the contrast with his descriptions of music is indeed very striking, we may conclude that although Jevons had a low capability of visualization when it came to graphics, he had a very high capability of visualization for music. And this may (at least partly) explain his interest in music and his disinterest in other forms of art.

be able to perceive the intellectual significance of the music. He might be able to discover the beauty of the piece as such, but he could not relate it to the occurrences Jevons describes in his letters. This point is reinforced in a manuscript to be found in the Henrietta section at the John Rylands University Library (JA10/1/32b), which appears to be an earlier draft of a part of the "Functions" chapter that is not in the archives.[11] Jevons writes: "Music, on the other hand, never attains its highest pitch of beauty and interest unless accompanied by words which giving a *poetical* meaning to its otherwise inanimate expression, intensify as well as define its influence on the mind. All the greatest musical compositions are, I believe, *vocal*" (JA10/1/32b). All this implies that Jevons considers music to be more than simply a "tranquilizer" for the mind. It has an intellectual and religious dimension. But there exist different kinds of "higher and lower" forms of music, and not every person is in a similar need for music of high quality.

We already stated that Jevons does not consider himself a scientific genius who creates scientific inventions, but that he thinks his ability consists of developing already existing ideas into something symmetrical. Ordinary people, on the contrary, may not at all be suited for intellectual work and should therefore confine themselves to routine labor. A similar picture emerges in Jevons's view on music. A musical genius creates high forms of music, as we saw earlier. Jevons does not consider himself a musical genius, but he is able to play and appreciate the higher forms of music in his way. Ordinary people, by contrast, may only be able to enjoy the lowest and simplest forms of music that are immediately clear to anybody (due to a natural propensity of every human being). We return to this issue when we discuss Jevons's critique of Archibald Alison (who neglects the difference between higher and lower forms of music) and when we discuss Jevons's policy prescriptions regarding public performances of music.

At any rate, Jevons does not distinguish clearly the intellectual from the nonintellectual aspects of music. The feelings associated with music

11. Jevons refers in this manuscript to a chapter on musical harmony, which indicates that it is in fact a part of the project on the science and art of music. Moreover, the reference is to an unnumbered chapter, whereas the chapter on harmony in the science and art manuscript is marked as chapter 2. This suggests that the writings found in the Henrietta section are from an earlier date, since otherwise Jevons probably would have referred to chapter 2. This manuscript elaborates on the division of the arts (where the chapter reproduced in the appendix stops) and on Jevons's criticism on Alison's *Essays on Taste*. We return to both issues later in this essay.

belong to perception, not to reason, and this may explain why they are in fact inexplicable. Although the emotions do not depend on knowledge, there certainly is a connection between the two, but this connection is not stated clearly. Instead, the concept of "perceptive pleasure" serves to cover this tension in Jevons's music theory. In the first place, it seems strange that Jevons includes in his definition of perceptive pleasure emotions that arise through the medium of the mind. He does not recognize explicitly that when the "mind" is at stake, intellectual aspects will certainly interfere. In the second place, he writes that there is no "necessary exercise of the higher faculties of reason," but he does not exclude the possibility that reason may interfere. And, finally, the feelings that arise from the contemplation of religious and scientific subjects are somewhat similar but feebler. The concept of "perceptive pleasure" covers this tension, which is also present in Jevons's diagrams depicting his classification of the arts.

The Jevons archives contain three separate illustrations: JA6/45/4, JA6/45/5, and JA10/1/32b. JA6/45/5 and JA10/1/32b are simple tables; the elaborate diagram JA6/45/4 is reproduced in appendix 2. They are classified in different sections of the archives, but it is highly probable that Jevons does not refer to any of these illustrations in his chapter on the functions of music, but to a similar (missing) table instead. Jevons writes that a diagram is represented on the following page, but this page is missing. However, no doubt remains that these illustrations express the classification Jevons refers to in his description.

Jevons sums up the classes of art he differentiates with regard to the senses on which they operate. He establishes a natural distinction between the sense of hearing, the sense of seeing, and a so-far-unnamed sense, a "third and highest division," in which he places poetical ideas and mental pictures of beauty. For each of these senses, Jevons intends to sum up the several subclasses of subjects and objects. The three illustrations represent three different versions of the same classification. All three figures contain sight and hearing as main classes; the name of the third class varies. JA6/45/5 mentions "memory and understanding"; JA10/1/32b mentions "mind and feeling"; and JA6/45/4 mentions "feelings." All three illustrations mention a small fourth class of motion (marching, dancing), which we reconsider later in this essay.

In the "Functions" chapter Jevons seems to refer to one of the two tables, because he writes that "poetical ideas" form the central and main division, but due to their close connection with "natural objects" this last column is placed alongside in a column under the heading of "sight." On either side are placed the artificial representations of these objects and ideas, by both sight and hearing. This is precisely the structure of the two tables, JA6/45/5 and JA10/1/32b: in both cases, the columns are named (1) "sight art," (2) "sight nature," (3) "memory and understanding" or "mind and feeling," (4) "hearing," and (5) "motion." Jevons stresses that the tables provide insights into the close connection between the different forms of perceptive pleasures. For example, "landscape and painting in general," "natural scenery," "descriptive poetry," and "descriptive music" are placed at the same height in both tables. We show later that the additional material (JA10/1/32b) elaborates on the similarities between the different art forms, but it is highly improbable that Jevons refers to one of the tables in the manuscript (JA6/47/8). In the "Functions" chapter, Jevons refers to a column of "Poetical Ideas," and not to "memory and understanding" or to "mind and feeling." All this suggests that he refers to a table with a layout similar to that in both tables from the archives (JA6/45/5 and JA10/1/32b), but not to either one of these specific tables.

The different layout of the diagram, JA6/45/4, suggests a different approach to the classification. Many other differences substantiate this claim. Under the heading of sight, the tables mention a division between art and nature, whereas the diagram has no such division. In the diagram, the "exterior of nature and art" is mentioned as one of several subclasses. In the category of sight, the diagram makes mention of a division between "beauty" and "symmetry," whereas the two tables do not. A section on "Harmony of colours" does not appear in the diagram, nor do "ballads." "Oratories and opera" are classified under the class of feelings in the diagram JA6/45/4, instead of under hearing. This diagram also contains a division between "harmony" and "melody" under the section of hearing, whereas the two tables have no such division.

Although there cannot be any certainty on this issue, it seems reasonable to suppose that the more elaborate diagram, JA6/45/4, should be seen as the latest and most definitive version, and we therefore decided to reproduce it here. We take special interest in two aspects of the classification: the structure of the diagrams and the way of presenting concrete art forms and objects. We take JA6/45/4 as the main focus of attention and refer to differences or similarities with the two tables when required. We argue that all three illustrations contain a hierarchy of "levels of abstractness," but only the diagram, JA6/45/4, contains an elaborate second hierarchy that expresses the intellectual significance of the different forms of art. Rather, the tables are intended to represent similarities, as argued earlier in this essay.

The general structure of Jevons's tables and diagram seems very clear. He presents a classification of art forms on the basis of abstract categories of perception. By inferring such abstract characteristics of perception from concrete art forms, Jevons is able to construct a hierarchical view of the perception of art. At the center of the diagram (or at the top of both tables), we find the most general divisions. These are also the most abstract instances of perception of art. The more we approach the outer end of the circle, the more concrete the perceptions become: Poems, paintings, and choruses are more sensible than beauty, melody, and harmony. Jevons uses the biological origin of perception as the criterion to classify different kinds of perceptive pleasures: hearing is not seeing because we don't see with our ears. In between, however, Jevons looks for a denominator as general as possible. He comes up with the concepts of "symmetry" and "beauty" under the general heading "artistical" for sight, and the concepts of "harmony" and "melody" under the general heading "musical" for hearing. He does not succeed in mentioning a similar term for the category of feeling, although "poetical" is placed under this heading. Further off the center of the circle we find more sensible examples of the arts: Under the heading of "beauty," Jevons recognizes, among others, "sculpture" and "painting"; under "symmetry," he places, for instance, "grand scenery" and "architecture." The "exterior of nature and art" separates beauty from symmetry, which apparently indicates that it possesses characteristics of both categories. Under "melody" Jevons places, among others, "vocal music," and under "harmony" he places, for instance, "military music." Under the category "poetical" Jevons places "poetry," "rhythm," and "opera" as the most sensible examples of the class of poetical ideas. The furthest from the center of the diagram is the category of "regularity of motion," including "dancing," "military marching," and "military display." These very sensible art forms, on the overlap between sight and hearing, produce as much emotion as any other, but cannot be represented directly by one of the three main classes.

At first sight, Jevons seems to classify art forms through their levels of abstractness. The individual is at the center of the diagram, surrounded by different kinds of senses and the perceptive pleasures with which they are associated; and the events capable of producing these pleasures are listed at the outer end of the circle.

There is also another hierarchical structure in Jevons's classification, however: from top to bottom. It visualizes a classification on the basis of Jevons's most problematic conception—namely, the intellectual characteristics of art. We already argued here that although Jevons states that music may be a tranquilizer of the mind, he clearly maintains some intellectual aspects. Jevons remains vague in his conceptualization of this intellectual function, but a close examination of the diagrams reveals that they refer to it. The intellectual hierarchy may even be said to govern the structure of the diagram, JA6/45/4. The top of the circle diagram presents the art forms that, in Jevons's opinion, require the most intellectual perception. The more we approach the bottom, the more the art forms become less intellectually stimulating. Following this classification, a hierarchy from poetry through visual arts and music to motional art forms becomes visible. The best example may be the higher rank of "melody" over "harmony," which indicates the intellectual superiority of "melody." Jevons writes in chapter 4 of the music manuscript, "On Melody": "Harmony, indeed in some inscrutable manner *pleases* the *ear*; melody appeals to the *mind*, and it is merely by a succession of sounds, rising or falling, or varied in an infinite number of ways, that the musical composer has to express his thought and feelings and give that *meaning* or *soul* to his sounds which constitutes their intrinsic value" (JA6/47/7).

This is perhaps the most explicit statement on the intellectual cleavage in Jevons's thought on music. A melody is a meaningful collection of words, like a book is a meaningful collection of sentences. Melody appeals to the mind and expresses thoughts, but the feelings associated with it nevertheless fall under the class of perceptive pleasures. Although Jevons does not explicitly recognize these intellectual aspects, he ranks intellectually higher art forms above intellectually lower forms. Other examples from the class of music provide the same insights. Jevons places vocal music (opera, songs, oratories) on a higher level than instrumental music. We already saw that Jevons prefers vocal music, as it depicts descriptive scenes (of historical significance) that require a more intellectual attitude and perception. The only exception in the distinction between vocal and instrumental music, the choruses, reinforces this argument. Jevons considers choral music outside the opera of less intellectual importance since it operates mainly within the context of less cerebral manifestations and grand performances. The same intellectual cleavage explains why "historical painting" is ranked above "painting in general" and "landscape" and why "pyrotechny" receives a low hierarchical status. Similarly, the low position of the motional class outside the diagram, on the overlap between symmetry and harmony, gives utterance to its insignificance not only on a perceptive level of abstraction but also on that of intellectual perception.

This second classification reinforces our point that the diagram—reproduced here in appendix 2—contains the most definitive and structural view on Jevons's classification. The two tables contain the (first) abstraction hierarchy, but they do not visualize thoroughly the intellectual degree (the second hierarchy). The tables do express some hierarchies of this kind, like the superiority of "descriptive music" over "vocal music and melody and general," but they do not express more general hierarchies (e.g., the poetical, artistical, and musical are placed alongside in the tables). Moreover, the fact that the two tables mention "memory and understanding" and "mind and feelings," respectively, suggests that in the tables Jevons was not fully aware of the intellectual cleavage in his classification. The final diagram mentions only "feelings," which may indicate that Jevons tried to demarcate perceptive pleasures more clearly from intellectual activities. Of course, he could not annihilate this tension by simply changing a concept, but the more detailed visualization of the second hierarchy brings more clarity in the classification. Whereas the tables emphasize the similarities between the different forms of perceptive pleasures, the diagram puts a stronger emphasis on the intellectual hierarchy of different feelings.

The additional music material to be found in the Henrietta section at the John Rylands University Library (JA10/1/32b, see above) complements Jevons's classification of the arts and plays down the strictness of his divisions. In this manuscript Jevons elaborates on the hierarchy of the arts:

> Music is the pleasurable exercise of one of our senses and in this view stands in the same rank as the other two divisions of perceptive pleasures. It must be allowed however that if we consider the comparative values of the three kinds of perceptive pleasures that the balance is somewhat against our Musical Art, as being more abstract and of less general meaning and appliance than the visual and poet-

> ical dimensions of Art. It is not like these latter occupied with subjects for instance nature or man the contemplations of which in a scientific, metaphysical or other point of view are of much superior importance and interest. Hence Art and Poetry must be allowed to take precedence, not that they are in themselves better or more easy sources of *perceptive* enjoyment but because they are likely to lead the mind to higher pursuits and more valuable acquirements. (JA10/1/32b)

This quotation indicates once again that music, and art in general, have an intellectual dimension that is somewhat covered in the concept of "perceptive pleasure." Whereas "descriptive music" is more important to Jevons because it reproduces historical and religious scenes of "beauty and grandeur," art and poetry should take precedence over music because their subjects may be investigated scientifically as well. In this sense, art may become the first step for the mind to become interested in scientific investigations. However, Jevons continues by arguing that "more fairness" should be brought in this comparison. If the money that was spent on erecting a building of "architectural beautification" would instead have been invested in the maintenance of a small staff of musicians who would perform publicly and gratuitously, the town might be more pleasant and beautiful than in the first case (JA10/1/32b).

The argument that the public performance of music is rather inexpensive is an important one; it returns in Jevons's writings on the policy of public performances (see later in this discussion). Moreover, these writings once more confirm that the music manuscript is a part of the larger science of man project. In a typically utilitarian fashion Jevons balances costs and benefits of several forms of perceptive pleasures against each other. Moreover, Jevons underlines the importance of artistic expressions for the science of man: Although the production of objects with an agreeable and beautiful shape "is entirely useless in an utilitarian point of view, still in all ages much attention has been given to it, and more and more value depended upon it as he [man] became more and more refined" (JA10/1/32b). The performance of art in a culture therefore expresses its level of civilization.

The additional material also contains some arguments regarding the incompleteness of Jevons's divisions. A "new but insignificant class of motional perceptive pleasures" is formed by joining the idea of rhythm in music with regularity of motion, as in marching and dancing (JA10/1/32b). We already stated that this small class is depicted in Jevons's diagram: It is not included in one of the three main divisions, and the fact that it appears at the bottom of the diagram illustrates its low status in Jevons's classification. Indeed, elsewhere (in 1878) Jevons reports that he always considered dancing to be something vulgar, until he learned from his visits to Denmark that this was a prejudice against this art form:

> But we are so accustomed to see ballet girls in evanescent skirts, in ambiguous attitudes, or dressed up as wasps or cupids, or something extravagant and low in taste, that we have established an inseparable association of ideas between dancing and immorality. I retain a grateful recollection of the Froeken Carey, who opened my eyes more than anything else to the degradation of public taste in England. I afterwards learned that Copenhagen is considered a great school of graceful and chaste dancing. (Jevons [1883] 1965, 22)

Besides the introduction of this "new and insignificant class," Jevons plays down the strictness of his classification by arguing that several classes may be joined to form sensations that may not belong entirely to one of the three main divisions. Poetry is usually rhythmical and may be joined with the sounds of a melody; and opera should be seen as a combination of poetry, music, and artistical representation (JA10/1/32b). The three main divisions can even be defined by reference to each other: "Poetry is the Artistical or Melodious Arrangement of Ideas. Art is the Poetical Arrangement of Natural Objects. Music is the Poetical or Artistical Arrangement of Sounds" (JA10/1/32b).

Jevons's divisions should therefore not be taken too strictly. There is also no strict hierarchy among these divisions: Music is more abstract and therefore less likely to lead the mind to subjects of scientific interest; nevertheless, music is not expensive, is more universal, and is better suited for many different occasions—and it does not require much concentration and reflection (JA10/1/32b). Similar arguments can be found in Jevons's utilitarian judgment of public performances of music (see later in this discussion).

Still, there is an intellectual cleavage in Jevons's music theory, when he argues that the lower forms of music are easily accessible to everyone, whereas the possibility to appreciate higher forms depends on the formation of the ear. This cleavage appears in Jevons's discussion of

Alison's *Essays on Taste*, which is to be found at the end of the additional material JA10/1/32b. A review of Jevons's remarks on Alison is also a good starting point for an investigation of the relation between Jevons's music manuscript and other writings on music, art, and aesthetics in his time.

Jevons's Remarks on Alison's Aesthetics

We already mentioned that the intellectual cleavage in Jevons's writings on music is especially visible in his arguments on the intellectual superiority of melody over harmony. Precisely this argument forms the core of Jevons's criticism of Archibald Alison's ([1790] 1968) *Essays on the Nature and Principles of Taste*. Although Alison distinguishes between different kinds of sounds, he does not establish a hierarchy in Jevons's sense, nor does he emphasize the necessity of musical training and education for an adequate perception of higher forms of music. According to Alison, all sounds may be sublime, though not to the same extent. The level of sublimity of each sound or series of sounds depends on the precise nature of the sound (e.g., thunder, tempest, or cascade), but also on the association the perceiver makes. Alison ([1790] 1968, 153) acknowledges that every perceiver does not have the same ability to form such associations and is not equally sensible to the sublimity of sounds. He attributes these differences to several reasons, as, for instance, the temper of the perceiver or the regularity of occurrence. A musical composition affects the emotions of sublimity or beauty as a result of either (1) the nature of the single sounds, (2) the nature of the whole composition, or (3) the associations the listener connects with it. According to Alison the ability to create associations is the key in the perception of music (194–95).

Jevons criticizes Alison for not establishing a firm hierarchy of different kinds of music: whereas everyone may experience rhythm and harmony, the proper appreciation of melody requires a genuine formation of the ear. He writes:

> He [Alison] has not sufficiently entered on the Theory of Music, to see the complete distinctions of melody, rhythm and harmony, which all contribute to the pleasures of music, but independently of each other. . . . Still if anything more were required to prove the independence of associated feelings, we may be convinced by the fact

> that rhythm and harmony are naturally discriminated and enjoyed by all persons and at all ages, while the enjoyment of a melody depends absolutely on the character and education of the hearer. (JA10/1/32b)

Whereas Jevons relates the sense for higher art forms to training and education, Alison refers to the aesthetic categories of the beautiful and the sublime. Jevons refers to these concepts as well, but does not put much emphasis on them because of his utilitarian orientation. According to Alison, the perception of art is attended with a specific pleasurable emotion, incomparable to other emotions. This particular emotion is then called "taste." But, unlike other emotions, taste has a particular interaction with the mind: "Taste is that Faculty of the human Mind, by which we perceive and enjoy, whatever is BEAUTIFUL or SUBLIME in the works of Nature or Art" (Alison [1790] 1968, vii).

Although Alison tries to connect taste with the human mind, he does not elaborate on the function of the mind in the act of perception. Alison tries to isolate what he calls the most important elements of the pleasurable perception: the aesthetic concepts of the sublime and the beautiful. When the artist tries to strive for truly great art, which is permanent and genial, he has to employ the concepts of the sublime and the beautiful. Throughout his essays, however, Alison hardly succeeds in isolating the pleasures associated with beauty or sublimity from other pleasures. On the whole, he seems unable to connect the emotion of pleasure with the effect that it has on the human mind. Rather, his use of the sublime and the beautiful as acknowledged intellectual concepts keeps him from bridging the gap between emotion and intellect.

Alison's vocabulary of beauty and the sublime belongs to a specific Anglo-Saxon aesthetic tradition that considers the sublime to be the ultimate goal and structure that governs the arts. That goal is the attempt to find a natural foundation of the perception of the arts, and of taste. One of the most prominent pioneers of this tradition is the third Earl of Shaftesbury. His contribution deals with the specific characteristics of sublimity, especially in its connection with the religiosity of art, but also, and perhaps more importantly, it attempts to find a natural and anthropological foundation of the sublime. A pupil of John Locke, Shaftesbury tried to incorporate his empiricism into aesthetic inquiries. As such, he is one of the first who tried to establish an empiricist foundation of sublimity. His view of mankind as harmonious and virtuous was, in the early eighteenth century, particularly reflected in classical architecture and music (especially in the proportionality of the sonata). In short, Shaftesbury argued that mankind is good by nature and therefore able to recognize other good aspects in the world (like the works of nature and true art). Shaftesbury's empiricism implies that this recognition is based on the senses. Although his influence remains implicit and vague, his views on the subject of the foundation of aesthetics have been of great importance for the further development of thought on art and music (Shaftesbury 1790).[12] Alison tried to complete Shaftesbury's empiricist foundation by combining it with his emphasis on the intellectual aspects of the perception of art. He enlarged Shaftesbury's concept by adding, apart from the sensorial recognition, the appeal to the mind as well (Kallich 1948, 324). We already argued here that Alison introduces the categories of the sublime and the beautiful for this purpose, but he does not succeed in bridging the gap between emotion and intellect.

Alison's conceptualization brings Jevons's to mind. Both use the same vocabulary and adhere to the same established tradition of aesthetics. Like Alison, Jevons recognizes the importance of the concepts of sublimity and beauty, especially when he refers to the difference between the intellectual and nonintellectual characteristics of aesthetical perception: "[A certain feeling] is excited by the contemplation of subjects of *Interest Beauty* or *Sublimity*. . . . It arises in short from the *contemplation* of anything possessing a degree of fresh *interest beauty or grandeur*" (JA6/47/8).

Precisely in this section, in which Jevons tries to define or describe the feeling he perceives when confronted with great objects of art, he resorts to the terms connected with the Anglo-Saxon tradition. But while Alison clearly places himself within this tradition and tries to continue it, Jevons does not consider aesthetical concepts as essential for an investigation of its effects on the mind and emotions. This may be explained by Jevons's utilitarian approach to the subject. Whereas Alison would like to enlarge Shaftesbury's empiricist foundation of aesthetics by taking intellectual aspects into account, Jevons would like to examine the "use" of music in the context of the "science of man." Jevons wants to know the precise place of music among human occu-

12. For a concise treatment of Shaftesbury's connection with Locke, see Marsh 1961.

pations, and he would like to develop utilitarian guidelines for using music. Many of the writings on art from the middle of the nineteenth century onward treat art in a utilitarian way.[13] Resulting from a desire to preserve art (or deal with it) in a more industrialized society, the main argument is that, if nothing else, art serves as an educator of man, to make him perceptive to nature and the beauty in it. Evidently, this argument is connected strongly with a moralist view on the matter. Jevons is therefore not so much interested in the nature of the sublime as such, but rather in the capability of art to raise the level of morality. This is especially visible in Jevons's writings on what we might call the "political economy of music." In the next section we show that these writings are compatible with our examination of the music manuscript. Although written more than twenty years after the manuscript, it may be seen as a policy outcome of Jevons's ideas on aesthetics.

Political Economy of Music

We showed earlier that Jevons uses utilitarian notions in his comparison of different art forms. Several of Jevons's arguments return in his article "Amusements of the People," which appeared originally in the *Contemporary Review* of 1878 and was reprinted in *Methods of Social Reform* (1883). In this essay Jevons complains about the attitudes of lower-class people in England. He argues that the behavior of drunken English "blackguards" differs fundamentally from the behavior of Continental or American lower-class people, who are, "comparatively speaking," ladies and gentlemen of refinement. Jevons states that it is difficult to change these bad habits, especially because they have been confirmed by centuries of ignorance and mistaken legislation. Lower-class people in England do not have access to good moral public amusements, and therefore their only option is to get drunk in their spare time and to cause trouble. In Continental Europe these morally elevating amusements exist, and this explains why the lower-class people in these countries have a much more refined behavior. In England, on the contrary, the aristocracy suppressed the existing amusements but did

13. Jevons's utilitarian treatment of art is similar to Bentham's fragmentary remarks on the subject. Bentham ([1825] 1998) states that art is a source of pleasure and should be used for a moral elevation of the masses; he even argues that art may be a good substitute for drunkenness. These ideas appear in Jevons's policy prescriptions as well (see the next section in this essay).

not offer alternatives. The earlier amusements had to be suppressed, as they were only covers for crime and immorality, but the people are in need of amusements. Lower-class people are mostly excluded from natural enjoyments because they do not have any property, and the existing public amusements are usually too expensive. The aristocracy lives a life of amusements, and the hardworking laborers should get a harmless and healthy counterpart. This should give rise to moral improvement of the lower classes, through a change of habits and attitudes (Jevons [1883] 1965, 2–7).

Jevons has two purposes in mind: entertainment and civilization of the people. Both purposes are interconnected, because the necessary entertainment of the people should lead their habits in a more civilized direction. Especially music seems to be the best means of popular recreation, as it fulfills all the requirements. Jevons lists three arguments similar to his earlier remarks on the utility of music in relation to other forms of art. First, listening to music involves no bodily fatigue; no efforts are required, only a "passive abandonment of the mind to the train of ideas and emotions suggested by the strains" (9). Other possibilities, like visiting galleries or museums, involve rather tiring body movements and are therefore less suited for the purposes of entertainment and civilization. Second, music costs little. The cost of a theater is necessarily higher than the cost of a music performance, because theater is drama plus the music. Institutions designed for higher-class people generally cost more, which necessitates a higher entrance fee. Third, music is more pure and removed from concrete life than a drama. This is important because the public performance should distract the laborers from their daily work and sorrows. Jevons recognizes that there exist "lascivious" songs, but the impurity lies in the words, not in the music (8–11). This clarifies Jevons's statement in the music manuscript about the attainment of "a sort of confident moral strength": the music serves as a "tranquilizer" of the mind (entertainment), but the songs have to be pure and morally elevating (civilization). All this is also compatible with the importance Jevons attaches to music that reproduces scenes of historical and religious grandeur, and it illustrates the importance Jevons attaches to vocal music. While music serves as a "tranquilizer" to a certain extent, it should contain an intellectual and moral component in order to elevate the moral attitude of the listener. This would also annihilate the unhealthy habits of lower-class people: "What some seek at the cost of health, and life, and reputation, from alcohol, and from opium, that they might obtain innocuously from music, if they could cultivate true musical taste" (10).

The cultivation of musical taste is therefore a prerequisite for the moral elevation of the people. Jevons argues that the low quality of musical education among the masses explains their "helpless state" when seeking recreation. Their musical education should somehow be "triggered" by the organization of free public musical performances. As this would not cost too much, there are no real financial burdens. Middle- and upper-class people are afraid, however, that these performances will attract "a horrid crowd of roughs and pickpockets." But as soon as "the novelty of the thing had worn off" and the roughs and the pickpockets would stay away because of the presence of the police, middle-class people would no longer be reluctant to go to these performances and bring their families with them (12). Moreover, higher- and upper-class people might be willing to pay for reserved chairs or by a subscription list, and this would possibly cover the expenses. Local movements should organize the performances. Jevons claims that especially religious and sacred music is important, and people from all ranks may attain it. The elevation of the tastes of the poorer classes should be achieved by a mixture of different kinds of music—the better class of dance music, old English songs, and popular classical songs—but a careful intermixture is certainly appropriate. Jevons seems to suggest that people would be attracted by the more popular and easier parts of the performance, and that the careful injection of some "higher" musical pieces would gradually raise the musical tastes. Jevons's own observation is that every person is able to appreciate a really beautiful melody; only musical symphonies require a long training (11–16). This is in accordance with Jevons's earlier views, as in his criticism of Alison as already discussed.

The government cannot interfere directly in the private organization of already existing music halls; the audience has to demand better entertainment. By contrast, the already existing public places of recreation (the Crystal and Alexandra Palaces and the Westminster Aquarium) should maintain a high tone in order to avoid degradation to a vulgar level, but meanwhile they have to "make a point of mingling all classes together" (17–18). This argument resembles Jevons's discussion of trade unions in *The State in Relation to Labour*, where he raises hands for heterogeneous cooperation. A partnership binding together the interests of employer and worker should be the solution for the labor problem. Industrial divisions should be perpendicular, not horizontal: the worker's interests should be bound up with those of his or her employer. The worker will then become a shareholder of the firm (Jevons [1882, 1910] 1968, 143–49). A careful intermixture of higher- and lower-class people would give rise to moral improvement, on the work floor as well as at public performances. In this sense, Jevons ([1883] 1965, 18) remarks that those who would like to elevate the tastes of the masses place the means to achieve this goal as far away as possible from these masses. On the contrary, a proper method to improve habits and morality should be that higher-class people visit popular performances in order to give a good example that may be imitated by lower-class people (24). Middle-class people love to imitate their betters, but they should also be willing to visit "lower" performances. The careful intermixture of classes would give rise to social improvement through "aping the upper class." Jevons writes at the end of his essay:

> There are none so blind as they who will not see, and this is the kind of blindness which prevents us from seeing that the vulgarity of the cheap trip, the inanity of the music-hall, and the general low tone of popular manners, are no necessary characteristics of hard hands and short purses, but are due to the way in which for so long a time popular education and popular recreation have been discountenanced. Of course the question of recreation is subordinate to that of education. (26)

The last sentence once more shows that the intellectual and moral aspects of music are more important than its recreative function. Jevons's policy prescriptions are not limited to the case of music; several other policies with an even greater emphasis on intellectual aspects are present in *Methods of Social Reform*. Public libraries should receive sufficient funding, as this would give rise to a reduction of poor rates and less expenditure on crime. Jevons does not condemn reading literature as a distraction from practical subjects, because the alternative would be even worse: reading of vulgar works or no reading at all. Public libraries should therefore be seen as progressive institutions: they increase education and general intelligence (32–48). The same may be said about museums, at least if there is no accidental ordering of subjects and no political influence (58–73). Jevons's educational project struggles with some difficulties, however, as the *Spectator* remarks in

October 1878:[14] "Mr. Jevons's advice to give the people music may be sound, but where is the evidence that the people wish for it, in place of more objectionable entertainment? Why, in fact, does not the people, if it would like music, subscribe its twopences, and have music?" (Black 1977, 291).

This criticism points to a vicious circle in Jevons's policy prescriptions: He would like to alter the musical taste of the masses through public performances of music, but in order to be able to appreciate refined forms of music, a certain musical taste already has to be present. People might be more attracted to lower and possibly more "vulgar" forms of music because of their bad tastes, whereas precisely "higher" forms of music would be required to improve morality. Here we encounter the "cleavage" in Jevons's music theory already identified; the music manuscript refines this observation.

It is clear that Jevons has a somewhat solitary, intellectual, and high-class conception of music. He prefers descriptive music that recreates biblical and historical scenes of beauty and grandeur for the listener. A piece of music should be studied like a book; it should be understood and remembered. This conception of music (or art in general) indeed allows moral elevation—along with intellectual elevation if the theme of the artwork may become a subject of scientific investigation. The concept of "perceptive pleasure" covers the tension between the intellectual and emotional aspects of music, and it is not a valid analytical concept to differentiate "higher" from "lower" forms of music. It is unclear whether a "careful intermixture" of different kinds of music (and classes) is possible.

Here we encounter a general problem in Jevons's thought. White (1994a) elaborates on a general cleavage in Jevons's political economy between the individual of the theory and the character of a concrete person. This is especially visible in Jevons's discussion of the reduction of working hours, which he opposed. A reduction of working hours would only give rise to a greater drunkenness. Moreover, the majority of the population (laborers, artisans, white-collar workers) would prefer "greater ease" in case of rising wages, whereas a small exceptional

14. Another criticism was raised by Charles Corkran, a Unitarian minister, who remarked in a letter to Jevons that he agrees with Jevons's suggestions, but he states that concerts in London are difficult because of reasons of climate and distance. He already proposed a similar policy to "a very active Broad Church vicar," but the proposal fell through (Black 1977, 292).

class of "learned professionals" would work more severely in case of increasing incomes. Jevons's economic theory is constructed around the notion of a "representative individual," but in his practical surveys, terms of class and character should bridge the gap between theoretical agent and concrete individuals. The representative individual is based on Jevons's image of the Victorian middle class: the laborer in Jevons's theory would, in the absence of other motives, devote all energy to the accumulation of wealth. Since this definition does not fit in the case of lower-class people, Jevons's description of character and class behavior relaxes his ceteris paribus definition of the laborer. Different solutions for economic problems emerge when different categories are involved.[15] In this case, Jevons's intellectual, solitary, and upper-class conception of music may be ill suited to the problem of the elevation of the taste of the aggregate of low-class people.[16]

Conclusion

Our reading of Jevons's music manuscript confirms once more that his large oeuvre should be considered a unified whole.[17] Jevons's utilitarian project of the science of man consists of many surveys from several disciplines, including the science and art of music. His general methodology entails the construction of a (representative or average) individual and the application of this notion to a concrete case by taking elements of character into account. In the case of music, the manuscript may be seen as the toolbox in which the individual perceiver is created. This individual is then used in Jevons's "Amusements of the People." Unfortunately, Jevons's solitary and intellectual conception of music is unsuitable for an elevation of the morality of the masses. It is therefore doubtful whether his program of moral elevation can be brought into practice. We showed that the *Spectator*, in 1878, questioned whether the masses ask for morally elevating art. This argument can be put otherwise: Jevons does not take the role of demand for art into account. This is an important problem, as the role of art

15. See White 1993 and 1994b for Jevons's use of the category *race*, and see White 1994c for Jevons's use of the category *gender*.

16. Elsewhere (Mosselmans 1998) we elaborate on the general problem in Jevons's thought that he is unable to link conceptions of individuals with conceptions of aggregates of individuals.

17. See Mosselmans 1998 for similarities between Jevons's logic and economics.

changes in the nineteenth century, and the importance of demand increases heavily.

The second half of the nineteenth century saw the emergence of a new function of the artist, depending increasingly on markets and sales instead of traditional patronage. Pierre Bourdieu ([1979] 1984, 1994) refers to this change as the battle of artistic legitimacy. One of the main effects of this change was that artworks no longer resulted from a reflection on the world, but rather became anticipations of public demand. Attention was diverted from large, officially sponsored historical pieces in favor of more portable forms, such as picturesque landscapes and portraits. Alexis de Tocqueville ([1845, 1850] 1966) made similar remarks in his *Democracy in America*. He argued that the role of art in a democracy differs fundamentally from its position in an aristocratic society. In an aristocracy all art is consumed by a small group of privileged people who are difficult to please, and therefore art is created by craftsmen who strive for perfect workmanship in order to maximize profits. When the privileges have been abolished, this situation changes dramatically. As soon as the standards of wealth are generally moderate (without, however, introducing superfluity), the universal desire for comfort among the people encourages the taste for the useful, rather than the love of beauty. This explains, according to Tocqueville, that the painters in his days tried to copy nature as exactly as possible, whereas earlier artists tried to do better by adding beauty to beauty and by showing glimpses of divinity. The modern craftsperson maximizes his or her profit by selling products of average or inferior quality to as many people as possible. Tocqueville ([1845, 1850] 1966, 434) writes: "To arrive in a country and find some things admirably made tells one nothing about the social conditions or political institutions of that country. But if one finds quantities of things generally shoddy and very cheap, one can be sure that in that country privilege is on the wane and classes are beginning to mix and will soon lose their identity."

This is precisely the goal of Jevons's music policy: to establish an intermixture of classes that would raise the morality of the lower classes ("aping the upper class"). But Tocqueville's analysis of the role of art in democracy and aristocracy shows that Jevons maintains an inadequate view on the content of artworks. His higher forms of music should be seen as examples of Tocqueville's aristocratic art forms, which are therefore inadequate in a democratic society. Unlike Tocqueville, Jevons did not perceive the changing role of art in his days, which led to a greater emphasis on demand in the art market. The popularization of culture, which started in the early nineteenth century, has been a slow process. It required mass media interest and a receptive middle class, elements that Jevons ignored in his analysis.[18]

Appendix 1: JA6/47/8
On the Functions of Music

By functions of music is partly meant what one should call the *use* of music, but not exactly so. If we were to speak of *using* music, we should imply that it was a sort of instrument, one of pleasure no doubt, which we could employ or may avoid at will.

But music is more than this; it is an integral part of a man, of the musician of course more especially, but of all men more or less; they could not lay it aside any more than they could one of the perceptions or faculties of their minds when once developed; and they use it by nature as they use any of their senses, rather than as an instrument supplied by art. By "functions" of music then is meant more exactly the part or position occupied by it among the occupations & capacities of men.

Before attempting to explain what I believe the part of music really to be, I must call upon the reader to bring before his mind as distinctly as possible a certain feeling that all have no doubt been conscious of, to a greater or less degree, on innumerable occasions. It is excited by the contemplation of subjects of *Interest Beauty* or *Sublimity*, and consists of a gentle excitement, an engrossment of the thoughts by agreeable subjects and a general removal of the mind from its ordinary course of duties & frailties, and its continual mixture of slight pleasures and pains.

When rising to an unusual pitch, the feeling of which I speak becomes an intense delight; it absorbs the attention completely, and causing it to forget ordinary affairs and thoughts, elevates it to a region of pleasurable sensations nowhere else discovered. It is indefinite however, leads to no conclusion, suggests it may almost be said no leading or strong thought or purpose and even of one's future path in life, or unavoidable duties happen to occur to the mind in the midst of this sort of intoxi-

18. See Grindhammer 1975 for a description of this process in America.

cation, they appear smoother than ever before, the difficulties have entirely vanished and *oneself* feels such a sort of confident moral strength, as will only too soon be found to disappear when this state of feeling has ended and the petty or great difficulties of life are once again visible in all their reality. Who that has attended a concert, play or other public performance, has not experienced this sudden and almost disgusting *revulsion* of feelings at its termination when the music has finally ceased & no longer rivets the attention, and a dreamy progress home, and a renewed circle of duties and the sorrow are all that seem to await one.

This feeling, too, is often excited more or less, by every pleasant country walk, by sight-seeing by beautiful and extensive views or grand and striking scenery on sea or land, by magnificent architectural or engineering works or a fine piece of poetry, or lastly by *music* whether in the wonderfully grand and sublime Oratories or the sweet and exciting Song. It arises in short from the *contemplation* of anything possessing a degree of fresh *interest beauty or grandeur* and is accompanied by cheerfulness or good humour, often rising to excitement or a sense of impressiveness. Let the reader bring to his recollection as many occasions as possible when this has been felt and by a short reflection try to obtain as clear and definite an idea of its nature as he possibly can.

To investigate its cause would be to enter one of the most difficult and least certain of metaphysical subjects and be quite beyond our purposes. It will suffice to say that it does not depend in any particular degree on knowledge. A pile of rocks is no grander in this point of view after their geology has been examined, the beauty of a forest scene is not increased by a botanical acquaintance with the trees and plants composing it, nor is a knowledge of *colouring* or *harmonical composition necessary* for the enjoyment of excellent painting or music, though no doubt all knowledge & such acquirements refine the mind and tend to make it more susceptible of such impressions. A large & well-designed piece of architecture is pleasing and distinguishable from less masterly works in a manner that it is hard to understand; the essential nature of Poetry it is universally acknowledged to be almost impossible to define, and lastly the sense of *beauty* or of melancholy arising from a simple succession of sounds, that is to say an air or melody, is equally inexplicable.

But this feeling belongs to the *perception*, not the *reason* and is far below the level of a somewhat analogous but feebler feeling produced by the contemplation of wonderful and beautiful facts of science or knowledge in general, or those fixed principles and enduring convictions & emotions which form religion and all our sense of love and duty.

I have occupied so much space in considering this abstract subject, because this feeling it is, which proves the high position really held by music and which naturally suggests itself as a means of classification that is to say as the characteristic of the class in which music falls. We may define it conveniently by the somewhat comprehensive term of *Perceptive Pleasure* meaning any emotion, usually an agreeable one, produced by subjects of nature or art through the medium of the senses or mind but without the necessary exercise of the higher faculties of reason. Now it will be remembered that I have spoken and I believe with truth, of a large number & variety of objects or circumstances capable of producing perceptive pleasures. I enumerate them all and place them in one grand class, because the relation of each to the mind and its faculties are throughout of much the same nature or *order*, but they naturally fall into subclasses according to the *sense* or means through which they act on the mind. Music evidently belongs exclusively to the sense of hearing. The Exterior of nature and artificial works of beauty and grandeur, as well as their artificial representations by pictures, sculpture etc., act principally on the *eye* in the sense of *sight*, but these as well as music it must certainly be allowed, are more or less connected with the third and highest division of *perceptive objects*, viz. *poetical ideas* or mental pictures of beauty, and though even these may not quite comprise the origin of every form of what I have called perceptive enjoyment, the remainder are but insignificant in proportion & closely dependent on these.

All these objects and subjects which occur to me are fully represented in the diagram on the following page, under their respective subclasses.

The central & main division is that of Poetical Ideas which are however so closely connected with & derived from Natural Objects that the latter are placed along side in corresponding order in a column of their own but under the heading of *Sight*. In parallel order likewise on either side are the artificial representations of these ideas and objects by both sight & hearing, in the columns respectively of Art & Music and we have thus exhibited to us both the close connection yet evident distinction of all these sources of perceptive pleasure.

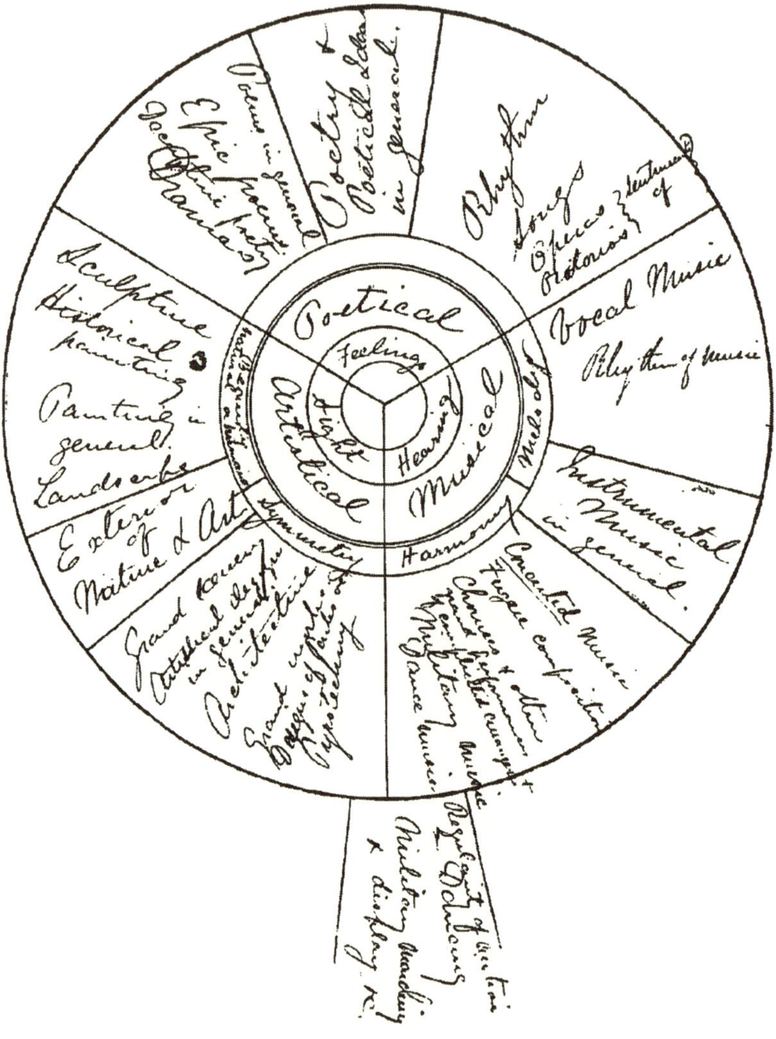

Appendix 2 : JA6/45/4

Diagram depicting the classification of the arts.

References

Alison, A. [1790] 1968. *Essays on the Nature and Principles of Taste*. Hildesheim: Olms.

Bentham, J. [1825] 1998. Reward Applied to Art and Science. In *Art in Theory (1815–1900)*, edited by P. Harrison, C. Wood, and J. Gaiger. Oxford: Blackwell.

Black, R. D. C., ed. 1973. *Correspondence 1850–1862*. Vol. 2 of *Papers and Correspondence of William Stanley Jevons*. London: Macmillan.

———.1977. *Correspondence 1873–1878*. Vol. 4 of *Papers and Correspondence of William Stanley Jevons*. London: Macmillan.

Black, R. D. C., and R. Könekamp, eds. 1972. *Biography and Personal Journal*. Vol. 1 of *Papers and Correspondence of William Stanley Jevons*. London: Macmillan.

Bostaph, S. 1989. Jevons's "Antipodean Influence": The Question of Early Influences. *HOPE* 21.4:601–23.

Bostaph, S., and Y.-N. Shieh. 1986. W. S. Jevons and Lardner's "Railway Economy." *HOPE* 18.1:49–64.

Bourdieu, P. [1979] 1984. *Distinction*. London: Routledge.

———. 1994. The Link between Artistic and Literary Struggles. In *Artistic Relations*, edited by P. Colhier and R. Lethbridge. New Haven, Conn.: Yale University Press.

Burke, I. [1955] 1988. Australia's First Pictorialist. *Australian Photo Review* 62:6–22. Reprinted in *William Stanley Jevons: Critical Assessments*, vol. 1, edited by J. C. Wood. London: Routledge.

Grindhammer, L. W. 1975. *Art and the Public: The Democratization of the Fine Arts in the United States, 1830–1860*. Tübingen: Metzler.

Hutchison, T. W. 1982. The Politics and Philosophy in Jevons's Political Economy. *Manchester School* 50.4:366–78.

———. 1984. Mr. White on Jevons: A Rejoinder. *Manchester School* 52.1:73–74.

Inoue, T., and M. V. White. 1993. Bibliography of Published Works by W. S. Jevons. *Journal of the History of Economic Thought* 15:122–47.

Jevons, W. S. Jevons archives. John Rylands University Library, University of Manchester.

———. 1858. The Social Cesspools of Sydney No. 1.—The Rocks. *Sydney Morning Herald*, 7 October. Typescript provided by Michael V. White.

———. 1871. *The Theory of Political Economy*. London: Macmillan.

———. 1878. Amusements of the People. *Contemporary Review* 33 (October): 498–513. Reprinted in Jevons [1883] 1965.

———. [1882, 1910] 1968. *The State in Relation to Labour*. London: Macmillan.

———. [1883] 1965. *Methods of Social Reform*. New York: Augustus M. Kelly.

Kallich, M. 1948. The Meaning of Archibald Alison's *Essays on Taste*. *Philological Quarterly* 27:314–24.

Klein, J. 1995. The Method of Diagrams and the Black Arts of Inductive Economics. In *Measurement, Quantification, and Economic Analysis*, edited by I. H. Rima. London: Routledge.

La Nauze, J. A. [1941] 1988. Jevons in Sydney. *Economic Record* 17:31–45. Reprinted in *William Stanley Jevons: Critical Assessments,* vol. 1, edited by J. C. Wood. London: Routledge.

Marsh, R. 1961. Shaftesbury's Theory of Poetry: The Importance of "Inward Colloquy." *English Literary History* 28:54–69.

McNiven, P. 1983. Hand-List of the Jevons Archive in the John Rylands University Library. Bulletin of the John Rylands University Library 66:213–55.

Mosselmans, B. 1998. William Stanley Jevons and the Extent of Meaning in Logic and Economics. *History and Philosophy of Logic* 19:83–99.

———. In press. Cracking the Canon: William Stanley Jevons and the Deconstruction of "Ricardo." In *The Canon in the History of Economics: Critical Essays,* edited by M. Psalidopoulos. London: Routledge.

Shaftesbury, A. 1790. *Characteristics of Men, Manners, Opinions, Times with a Collection of Letters.* Basil: Tourneisen & Legrand.

Tocqueville, Alexis de. [1845, 1850] 1966. *Democracy in America.* New York: Harper & Row.

White, M. V. [1982] 1988. Jevons in Australia: A Reassessment. *Economic Record* 58.160:32–45. Reprinted in *William Stanley Jevons: Critical Assessments,* vol. 1, edited by J. C. Wood. London: Routledge.

———. 1984. Jevons in Australia: Response to Professor Hutchison. *Manchester School* 52.1:70–72.

———. 1989. Jevons's Antipodean Interlude: Rejoinder. *HOPE* 21.4:623–31.

———. 1993. The "Irish Factor" in Jevons's Statistics: A Note. *History of Economics Review* 19:79–85.

———. 1994a. Bridging the Natural and the Social: Science and Character in Jevons's Political Economy. *Economic Inquiry* 32:429–44.

———. 1994b. A Five Per Cent Racist? Rejoinder to Professor Hutchison. *History of Economics Review* 21:71–86.

———. 1994c. Following Strange Gods: Women in Jevons's Political Economy. In *Feminism and Political Economy in Victorian England*, edited by P. Groenewegen. Aldershot, England: Edward Elgar.

———. 1996. Notes on Jevons's "On the Science of Art and Music." Unpublished manuscript.

The Economics of Art through Art Critics' Eyes

Craufurd D. W. Goodwin

During the first three quarters of the twentieth century, a number of art critics—or what we might call today "public intellectuals"—set out to explain the circumstances that surround the production and consumption of art. Although they had little formal acquaintance with economics, in their backgrounds and intent these writers were quite similar to the economists who initiated the marginal utility revolution during the second half of the nineteenth century; indeed, the art critics attempted to answer questions very similar to those that had captivated the marginalist economists. This chapter examines how these noneconomists engaged these economic questions and how well they succeeded with their explanations.

The art critics came from the same comfortable upper-middle-class backgrounds as the marginal revolutionaries, and they were educated in the same prominent universities where they developed a passion to explain the world around them. But there were important differences in their careers. The critics were not scholars in the traditional sense. They did not hold conventional university posts, did not adhere to professional rules of conduct, and did not address any single disciplinary audience. They wrote for a broad-based elite throughout civil society, where, indeed, they made their living. Moreover, unlike the scholars in economics, they had highly varied careers as journalists, museum directors, and entrepreneurs. They supported themselves in part as independent contractors and in part with private wealth. They wrote close to and against a backdrop of international affairs that included two world wars and a major depression. And, because they wrote several decades later than the pioneer marginalist economists, they had a clear consciousness of a revolution in biological science in progress, rooted in both the evolutionary theory of Charles Darwin and the behavioral theory of Sigmund Freud.

The art critics examined here are the British writers Roger Fry, Clive Bell, and Kenneth Clark. I am concerned with how these three explored and came to understand developments in that segment of the economy that economists call the market for art; where their ideas came from; and what they did with their ideas. The most striking conclusion here is that these critics behaved and approached their subject in some ways remarkably like the economists, although they ended up with very different results.

Fry, Bell, and Clark were all prominent public figures in the art world and beyond. Roger Fry was one of the founders of the *Burlington Magazine*, a curator at the Metropolitan Museum of Art in New York, an organizer of the two revolutionary Postimpressionist exhibitions in London (in 1910 and 1912), and a proprietor of the Omega Workshops (1913–19). Clive Bell, like Fry a member of the Bloomsbury Group, gained fame as a crusading pacifist in World War I and went on to become a prolific essayist and an interpreter of modern art in Great Britain. Kenneth Clark, later Lord Clark, was heir to a substantial fortune and held several of the most powerful positions in the British art world. He was Keeper of Fine Arts at the Ashmolean Library in Oxford, and at age thirty he was appointed director of the National Gallery in London. He also served as Surveyor of the King's Pictures, as chairman of both the Arts Council and the Independent Television Authority, and as a member of the boards of numerous other institutions.

There are many differences among these three critics that cannot be explored here. The focus will be instead on things they held in common, in particular a model of how art is produced and consumed that was worked out in detail by Fry and was accepted substantially by the other two. The model was applied to large issues of public policy by Bell and to the history of art by Clark.

Wiping the Slate Clean: Tolstoy's *What Is Art?*

Leo Tolstoy's long essay *What Is Art?,* published in English in 1898, was a foundational work for these critics. On the question of what determines beauty, or value, in art, Tolstoy rejected most of what had gone before, and he offered suggestions for a new direction ahead. In particular, Tolstoy turned away from the two determinants of value proposed by aestheticians thus far, and that would have been understood by an economist: the circumstances of production on the one hand and the desires of demanders on the other. Fry explained the impact of Tolstoy in his own case:

> In my youth all speculations on aesthetic had revolved with wearisome persistence around the question of the nature of beauty. Like our predecessors we sought for the criteria of the beautiful, whether in art or nature. And always this search led to a tangle of contradictions or else to metaphysical ideas so vague as to be inapplicable to concrete cases. It was Tolstoy's genius that delivered us from this *impasse,* and I think that one may date from the appearance of *What Is Art?,* the beginning of fruitful speculation in asthetic." (Fry [1920] 1956, 192)

Tolstoy began his essay with a short history of aesthetics, which he claimed appeared as a separate subject of inquiry only in the mid-eighteenth century. Aesthetics, he said, had been characterized by two kinds of theorist. One found value to be inherent in a work of art and believed that "beauty is something having an independent existence (existing in itself), and that it is one of the manifestations of the absolutely Perfect, of the Idea, of the Spirit, of the Will, or of God" (Tolstoy [1898] 1960, 41). This approach bears some resemblance to a supply-side theory of value in economics in that value is seen as determined by actions of the artist-suppliers. The other found value on the demand side in the reaction of audiences: "Beauty is a kind of pleasure we receive which does not have personal advantage for its object" (41). Tolstoy found the roots of this utilitarian explanation of the value of art in the writings of Adam Smith's patron Lord Kames (1696–1782), who had argued that "beauty is defined by taste alone. The standard of true taste is that the maximum of richness, fullness, strength, and variety of impressions should be contained in the narrowest limits" (27).

Tolstoy observed that the supply-side "objective-mystical definition of beauty is held by a majority of the educated people of our day" (41) while the "very simple and intelligible subjective [demand-side] one, which considers beauty to be that which pleases . . . finds favor chiefly among the English aesthetic writers and is shared by the other part of our society, principally by the younger generation" (42). Tolstoy concluded that neither the objective supply-side nor subjective demand-side approaches yielded "laws" that could give predictions about the value of art. Some new approach was needed.

The new approach he suggested was to think of art not as a collection of goods that embodied certain peculiar qualities, or that gave pleasure in a utilitarian sense, but as a mechanism for human communication:

> In order correctly to define art, it is necessary . . . to consider it as one of the conditions of human life. Viewing it in this way we cannot fail to observe that art is one of the means of intercourse between man and man. . . . Art is not, as the metaphysicians say, the manifestation of some mysterious Idea of beauty or God; it is not, as the aesthetical physiologists say, a game in which man lets off his excess of stored-up energy; it is not the expression of man's emotions by external signs, it is not the production of pleasing objects, and, above all, it is not pleasure; but it is a means of union among men, joining them together in the same feelings, and indispensable for the life and progress toward well-being of individuals and of humanity. (49, 51–52)

Art by this conception—a means of communication rather than a consumption good—was not simply welfare-enhancing; it was central to the successful operation of a civilized society: "Art is a human activity having for its purpose the transmission to others of the highest and best feelings to which men have risen" (66). Tolstoy was hard-pressed to come up with a metaphor to explain how communication through art in fact took place, and he speculated about the similarity to the spread of infectious disease: "If men lacked . . . this capacity of being infected by art, people might be almost more savage still, and, above all, more separated from, and more hostile to, one another" (52).

Religious ideas, Tolstoy thought, were the earliest messages communicated through works of art. However, loss of faith during the Reformation robbed Christian art of its message, and "counterfeit" art began to be produced by religious artists, who "could have no standard wherewith to estimate what was good and what was bad art but that of personal enjoyment" (60). When the true function of art as communication was lost, what was left was a collection of consumption goods masquerading as art. One "consequence of this absence of true art showed itself, inevitably, in the corruption of that class which nourished itself on the false art" (66). Another consequence was that potential artists, having nothing to communicate, found commercial success through "obscurity elevated into a dogma" (79). Tolstoy estimated that of all the supposed works of art and literature produced in his own time only a minute fraction were the real thing: "Scarcely one in a hundred thousand proceeds from an emotion felt by its author, all the rest being but manufactured counterfeits of art in which borrowing, imitation, effects, and interestingness replace the contagion of feeling" (131).

Tolstoy pictured the art market as the mechanism through which artistic communication should occur. But the art market was also where the corruption of art could be most readily recognized. He looked to the time when the production of art would be done by those who felt "impelled to do so by an irresistible inner impulse" (179). Effective communication should be the only criterion of success among artists. He mistrusted guilds and other monopolistic devices by which artists attended only to their own comfort and set themselves apart from competition:

> And sound feeling can only be engendered in a man when he is living on all its sides the life natural and proper to mankind. And therefore security of maintenance is a condition most harmful to an artist's true productiveness since it removes him from the condition natural to all men—that of struggle with nature for the maintenance of both his own life and that of others—and thus deprives him of opportunity and possibility to experience the most important and natural feelings of man. There is no position more injurious to an artist's productiveness than that position of complete security and luxury in which artists usually live in our society. (176)

Part of the reason for the characteristic monopoly to be found in an art market was the network of dealers: "Until the dealers are driven out, the temple of art will not be a temple" (177). Tolstoy appreciated that he might have looked for reform of the art market and defense of competition to the science of political economy, but he found that this subject, like contemporary theology, philosophy, and history, was "chiefly occupied in proving that the existing order is the very one which ought to exist, that it has come into existence and continues to exist by the operation of immutable laws not amenable to human will, and that all efforts to change it are therefore harmful and wrong" (182). Tolstoy speculated that the time might be close when the parallels would be appreciated between the need for pure science ("science for science's sake") and pure art ("art for art's sake"). Science and art were activities that had, at least in the short run, "no direct relation to human life" (182). But because they were also the two ultimate sources of human advance, they should receive the most serious attention from society's leaders. "Art," he wrote, "is one of the two organs of human progress. By words man interchanges thoughts, by the forms of art he interchanges feelings, and this with all men, not only of the present time but also of the past and the future" (159).

All three writers examined in this essay pay their respects from time to time to Tolstoy. But it is especially interesting that Clark ends his celebrated book and television series *Civilisation,* the last work to be examined here, with a meditation on Tolstoy's death in 1910. Clark (1969, 344) saw the departure from the scene of Tolstoy—"the hero of almost all generous-minded men in the late nineteenth century"—as ushering in a "new era" in which we are still living that was dominated not by religion or the humanities but by the physical science of Rutherford, Einstein, and Bohr. It is significant, then, that we now turn to an art critic trained in the scientific method, who attempted to construct an explanation of the art market using the new social and behavioral sciences.

Constructing a Model of the Art Market: Roger Fry

The young art critic and budding aesthetician Roger Fry read Tolstoy's essay early in the century and was much affected by it. He did not accept Tolstoy's ideas unconditionally; in particular, he did not agree with Tolstoy's heavy moralizing about the necessity that true art must have positive social significance, just as he did not accept similar ideas coming from John Ruskin and William Morris. But Fry found Tolstoy liberating and highly stimulating. Above all, the tentative portrayal of art as a process of communication through the emotions rang true at a time when the discipline of psychology was just beginning to attract widespread attention. Other writers, whom Fry much admired, made suggestions at the time that seemed consistent with this interpretation—in particular, these were the Cambridge philosopher G. E. Moore with his discussions of "states of mind" and his fellow critic Bernard Berenson with his conception of "ideated sensations."

When Fry began to think and write provocatively about aesthetics in the first decade of the twentieth century, most notably in an article entitled "An Essay in Esthetics"(1909; republished in the first collection of his essays, *Vision and Design,* 1920, reprinted 1956), he was just completing a crash course of practical exposure to the art market. He had been buyer for the Metropolitan Museum, several American collectors, and himself as a minor speculator. He had also been seller as a professional painter, gallery operator, and exhibition entrepreneur. And so it is not surprising that, unlike Tolstoy, who saw the art market from afar, he approached the market with a peculiar intimacy and explored the process of art creation in a market context. The suggestion made by Tolstoy that the true artist was engaged in communicating an emotion rather than in producing a good simplified Fry's analytical task on the supply side. He took from this the conclusion that some sort of psychological explanation, yet to be provided, was needed for the moment of vision and the process of transformation of an artist's vision into a piece of artwork. To understand the aesthetic emotion that accompanied the vision and stimulated the process, the conventional market variables of output price and input cost seemed largely irrelevant. The creation of most great art involved the artist working alone, away from the market, with pencil or brush. The real artist danced to an internal drummer of some kind rather than to external market signals.

However, Fry observed that market characteristics were still important determinants of the performance of artists. First, artists needed enough income from the sale of their products at least to survive and remain artists. Second, like other humans they could be corrupted by too much market success, and if too generously rewarded they could be persuaded to abandon the communication of emotion in favor of some more prosaic task. So even when rewarding the artist abundantly, the market could be a danger to art. Finally, as Tolstoy had hinted, certain market conditions seemed to provide a more agreeable environment for true artistic creation than others. Fry came to agree with Tolstoy that moderate market competition seemed a more salutary condition for most artists than either monopoly or government patronage.

The limited number of answers that could be given to questions about the production of art on the supply side before there had been some breakthrough in the new science of psychology led Fry to move to the demand side of the market. In a small pamphlet entitled *Art and Commerce* (1926), published by Leonard and Virginia Woolf's Hogarth

Press, he focused on the nature of the demand for art, and, using large categories, he speculated about who the demanders of art really are. Here his training in biological taxonomy, gained from a first-class degree in natural science at Cambridge University, shone through.

Fry suggested that human consumption activities fall into three categories. The first category included consumer demand in areas that are biological in origin, reflecting the need for food, shelter, defense against aggressive neighbors, and so on. These, he implied, could be explained adequately by economists through market analysis of price responses on the demand and supply sides. This was the part of human life that Fry believed could be illuminated well through the lens of Darwinian evolutionary biology. Consumers who were driven by biological urges made selections among those goods that were provided by farmers, manufacturers, and service workers according to familiar utilitarian criteria. So far, so good! Fry recognized in a general sense that in the biological arena, consumers optimized their utility functions subject to budget constraints.

The second category presented more complexity. Here consumers responded to the universal human need for repute, prestige, and display—the desire to appear superior to one's fellows. For an explanation of these activities, Fry and the other critics recognized inadequacies in conventional market analysis, and they made use of the writings of Thorstein Veblen and various anthropologists who observed emulative traits in both primitive peoples and modern man. Tolstoy had referred to those goods destined only for display as "counterfeit art." Fry puzzled over a new, less pejorative vocabulary.

In the third category, the use of goods to sustain the imaginative life of mankind, Fry placed the practice of true art, true science (science for its own sake, rather than applied science), and religion. In all three of these activities humans experienced an emotional reward rather than the satisfaction of a biological need or an increase in their prestige.

A complication Fry discovered in distinguishing among these three categories of demand for consumption goods is that suppliers of these goods are sometimes required to respond to more than one kind of demand, and occasionally all three, at the same time. For example, a structure might answer the biological need for shelter, the desire of the owner for prestige in the community, and the need of the architect to convey aesthetic emotion through a genuine work of art. For another example, the scientific community, through its applied scientists, responded to biological needs by improving the quality of goods and the processes that produced them. But, while so doing, pure scientists also achieved improvements in human understanding that, in the short run at least, brought nothing more than emotional satisfaction to other scientists in their imaginative life. In the case of art, the circumstances were usually complex because suppliers were almost always required to respond at the same time to those who sought only prestige and those who responded to genuine aesthetic emotion. To remove this confusion, Fry called all those goods popularly called art and destined for the second and third categories of consumption *opifacts* and their producers *opificers*. In all societies, a portion only—and in most societies, a small portion—of opifacts were genuine works of art that conveyed aesthetic emotion to viewers in their imaginative life. The rest were merely opifacts that conferred status, the equivalent of Tolstoy's "counterfeit art."

Undoubtedly influenced very much by his own recent adventures in the art market, Fry produced another taxonomy of seven kinds of purchasers of opifacts, including opifacts that are works of art and those that are not. He found this taxonomy to be of both historical and contemporary relevance. First among the purchasers historically, he suggested, was organized religion and, in the case of Western Europe, the Roman Catholic *Church*, which in its early history, at least through the Middle Ages, had been the most important consumer of both works of art and other opifacts; some church leaders experienced aesthetic emotion from their purchases, while others merely sought prestige. Second, *the monarchy and the aristocracy* became major purchasers of opifacts, leaving in older countries large collections of their trophies for someone else to maintain. Third, beginning in the nineteenth century at least, *the modern state* had taken on an important new role as preserver of opifacts in public museums, as purchaser of some works by individual artists (especially monuments and public buildings), as provider of sinecures to favored opificers, and as mobilizers of public art projects. Unfortunately, Fry found, the proportion of true art in the opifactual purchases of the state was usually quite low.

In the modern industrial economy that had appeared in the nineteenth century, there were four additional groups of purchasers of opifacts. The first category, the mass of the people—or *the herd*, as Fry liked to call them, using a popular term from the psychological literature of the time—were inclined to purchase opifacts when persuaded to do so by some leader who caught their ear (like the Prince Consort or William Morris). But since there were so many members of the herd, each one could not reasonably think of these opifacts as giving them, individually, prestige among their neighbors. In particular, mass-produced opifacts could hardly be expected ever to satisfy the desire for display. Moreover, since the herd had Philistine tastes (a term taken from Matthew Arnold), it was highly unlikely that their opifacts would include works of art.

The second category was *the plutocrats*, the leaders of commerce and industry, who engaged in collecting on a grand scale. Fry called these purchasers "classicists" because they were exceptionally cautious and purchased only the works of dead artists whose art had been certified as of high quality by reputable experts. The classicists performed a useful function in gathering together and caring for the past achievements of the imaginative life, but they did little to encourage or sustain living artists. During the years in which Fry was writing about the art market, the plutocrats were busily arranging for the transfer of much classic art from the collections of the declining aristocracy to their own, a process in which Fry was involved as adviser and agent. The problem that was presented when the plutocrats were in one country and the aristocrats in another, discussed by Helen Rees (this volume), attracted Fry's attention.

The third category contained what Fry called *snobbists* (a term taken from William Makepeace Thackeray), who purchased opifacts they perceived to be in style, or better yet just coming into style. The snobbists attended little to the artistic quality of the opifact but worried about the impression their purchases were making on persons whose opinions they valued. Snobbists were speculators attempting to judge where the market will jump, but they were unlike conventional speculators in that the returns they sought were increases in their own repute rather than profits. The snobbists, unlike the herd and the classicists, were able inadvertently to assist in the creation of new art when they identified a true artist as likely soon to come into fashion.

The fourth category was *the true middle-class aesthete* who purchased a work of art because of the aesthetic emotion received and not because of any herd instinct, collecting mania, or pursuit of fashion. These were the purchasers that Fry thought had nurtured the French Impressionists and Postimpressionists. Sometimes these aesthetes were quite sophisticated and educated about the arts they patronized, but often they were simple people who merely rejoiced in their personal aesthetic experience. Fry did not pretend to understand everything that transpired in the minds of the true aesthete, but he concluded confidently that upon their existence, as much as upon the presence of creative artists, depended the vigor and richness of the imaginative life of humankind.

Over the course of his career, Fry worked out and defended many of the policy implications of his model of the art market (Goodwin 1998). In addition, however, his ideas lived on in the works of various close friends and admirers. We turn now to writers who make use of the Fry model, Clive Bell and Kenneth Clark, who wrote two popular and highly controversial books with the same title, *Civilization*, but separated in time by forty-one years.

The *Civilization* of Clive Bell

Clive Bell graduated from Cambridge a generation after Roger Fry with thoughts of becoming a historian or lawyer. Happily, he was independently wealthy and could enjoy life instead as occasional journalist, critic, and bon vivant. He spent much time in Paris and was one of the first British commentators to write enthusiastically about the Postimpressionists. After he met Fry in 1910, they remained close friends. Bell gained a reputation in the art world for a book entitled *Art* ([1913] 1958) and for a collection of his essays, *Potboilers* (Bell 1918; Bywater 1975). In *Art*, Bell acknowledged a debt to Fry "that defies exact computation," and he called Fry's "Essay in Aesthetics" "the most happy contribution to the science that had been made since the days of Kant" (Bell [1913] 1958, 7, 8). Bell reported that "for some years Mr. Fry and I have been arguing, more or less amicably, about the principles of aesthetics" (8). It appears to the later observer that Bell's main contributions to the argument were his intimate knowledge of modern Continental painting and the idea for a shorthand term, *significant form*, to denote the capacity of an artwork to convey aesthetic emotion, a term with which Fry was never comfortable. Bell's *Art* may be seen, in fact, as mainly an elaboration to book length of the ideas contained in Fry's "Essay in Aesthetics" (reprinted in Fry [1920] 1956).

In *Civilization* ([1928] 1973), Bell went beyond the discussion of art to address the question of what constituted improvement in human life and what signified an advance in civilization. On this occasion he extended rather than simply restated Fry's ideas. In using the term *civilization* he was still smarting from the suggestion made by critics of his pacifist position a decade earlier that World War I was fought to preserve civilization. He thought the opposite was true: war had threatened civilization. To make his case, he gave a long list of conditions that did not, as some claimed, characterize civilization; these included respect for property, patriotism, "submission to nature's law" of survival of the fittest, technical virtuosity, and creature comfort. (If writing thirty years later, he might have added rising Gross Domestic Product per capita.) Fry would have said that all of these things that civilization was *not* were features of the biological life of humans. Instead, civilization lay with the higher imaginative life. Thus Bell entered the debate that would continue in macroeconomics until now about how to measure the performance of a society and the true state of human welfare.

Bell concluded that even if we have difficulty defining civilization, or specifying genuine human well-being, we know it when we see it. The main characteristics, he said, are "a sense of values and reason enthroned" (50). By "sense of values," Bell meant the presence among the citizenry of the capability "of sacrificing obvious and immediate goods to the more subtle and remote. People who deliberately sacrificed comfort to beauty—with no practical or superstitious end in view—would appear to me to possess a sense of values" (51). By "reason enthroned," Bell meant an overwhelming urge to explain and to understand and to take inquiry wherever it might lead, regardless of the apparent immediate utility. A willingness to emphasize the imaginative life over biological needs could be seen in many aspects of a civilized society, for example in the system of education: "To prefer a liberal to a technical education, an education that teaches how to live rather than one that teaches how to gain, is another manifestation of this highly civilized sense" (51). In terms of Fry's model, Bell argued that an advancing civilization exhibited consumption patterns in which the citizens consciously responded to the imagination at the expense of instinctive biological needs and the desire for prestige: "So long as man remains natural and follows instinct he will not go far towards civilization. Civilization comes from reflection and education. Civilization is artificial" (53).

A civilized society, Bell insisted, honored poets and painters above trade, politics, and war: "The essential characteristic of a highly civilized society is not that it is creative but that it is appreciative" (57–59). Where appreciation is well-developed, creativity tends to follow automatically. Civilization is concerned with quality not quantity, and with "standards"—even in cooking and manners. A civilized society made hard choices that juxtaposed the imaginative life squarely against the biological life, pure art against applied (useful) art, pure speculative science against applied (useful) science. One of the glories of the Renaissance, Bell wrote, was that it "devoted itself to such purely speculative sciences as mathematics and geometry, rather than to the more useful Biology and Chemistry" (76). A truly civilized society recognized that those people who really made a difference were involved with the imaginative life, not with the biological side of man: "It is amongst artists, philosophers, and mystics, with their intense and interminable ecstasies of contemplation and creation, that we must turn for our saints" (123). Progress in civilization implies change, and genuine change comes only from the bubbling yeast of the imagination.

Bell seemed to anticipate conflict with the discipline of economics over the importance he attached to the imaginative life ahead of the biological life and the need to educate humans to enjoy the arts. Economics, he found, was one of those disciplines "useful" mainly in the relatively static biological life of man. It had little to say about the complex dynamic imaginative life. The only direct confrontation of Bell's view with economics on that point is a reference by A. C. Pigou in *The Economics of Welfare* (1924) to a book by Fry's and Bell's close friend and kindred spirit, Goldsworthy Lowes Dickinson (1901), who had made the point that human welfare might be increased as much by improving the capacity of humans to enjoy goods as by providing them with more goods. Education for production might be less cost effective than education for consumption. Pigou (1924, 14) acknowledged that "at all events it brings out vividly the point which is here at issue; that efforts devoted to the production of people who are good instruments may involve a failure to produce people who are good men." But Pigou did not pursue the matter further.

When Bell spoke of civilization, it is clear that he was talking of a society that placed a premium on innovation throughout the arts and sciences and that was prepared to sustain creativity against the strong competing demands for conventionality backed by biological instinct and the desire for emulation. The truth was, he said, that the biological life simply could not sustain change of a fundamental kind, and a society that devoted all of its resources to filling biological needs would ultimately be consigned to stagnation, both in the production of goods and services and in the appreciation of works of art. A society that desired civilization and human progress must nurture a citizenry that appreciated the necessity of a rich imaginative life and was willing to devote its time and treasure to the cause: "The thoroughly civilized person will be willing at any moment to follow intellect into the oddest holes and corners, while his instinctive reaction to life will be ever conditioned by taste" (Bell [1928] 1973, 122).

It was his discussion of how actually to advance civilization, as much as how to describe its growth, that brought a storm of criticism down on Bell's head. He argued that a lively imaginative life—the source of progress in society—absolutely required the existence of a vigorous elite on the demand side of the market for the arts and sciences. This elite must contain individuals with the taste and the means to choose wisely and sustain the artists and scientists, either through their private actions or through support for appropriate public policies (130). The demand for the products of the imaginative life, rather than their supply, was most crucial to the dynamism of a society—and was also most fragile. Like the citizens of Athens, this elite should "live richly rather than . . . be rich." They should have "a tendency towards cosmopolitanism, based on individualism, a movement of liberation from the herd instinct" (81). They should have a "taste for truth, beauty, tolerance, intellectual honesty, fastidiousness, a sense of humour, good manners, curiosity, a dislike of vulgarity, brutality, and overemphasis, freedom from superstition, prudery—a fearless acceptance of the good things of life, a desire for complete self-expression and for a liberal education—a contempt for utilitarianism and Philistinism—in two words sweetness and light" (120). It was essential to maintain the elite at a sufficient size to resist the forces pressing for stagnation: "A civilized nucleus becomes civilizing when it is sufficiently numerous and powerful to colour the mass" (122). Moreover, a civilized society had always to nurture this nucleus: "The civilized man is made not born; he is artificial; he is unnatural" (134). Dynamism is the essence of the nucleus: "For ever challenging accepted beliefs and instinctive reactions, reason alone keeps personality clear of fixed ideas and foregone responses" (135). Some member of the nucleus "will be trying always to improve on nature, and probably he will succeed" (136).

Bell's most controversial observation about the public policy implications of the Fry model was that the maintenance of a civilizing nucleus able to sustain the imaginative life of a society required acceptance of some inequality of income and wealth in the society. He insisted that it took funds and leisure among a substantial part of society to develop the taste and sophistication necessary to appreciate and sponsor a vigorous imaginative life. Incautiously, in the offhand style of the Bloomsbury Group, he remarked that the Athenian citizens had slaves to lighten their burdens and accomplish this end. Bell's position was interpreted by his critics as being nothing more than a smug, callous, self-serving defense of the privileged lives and ways of the Bloomsburys who wished to remain independent and unaccountable aesthetes while dining at the public trough.

A more sympathetic and plausible interpretation of Bell's observation, and one consistent with Bloomsbury social philosophy overall, is that it expressed the belief that true dynamism lies only in certain parts of the private sector of a free society, and the challenge is to devise structures that will nurture and sustain these essential roots of creativity. In Fry's terms, the case was being made that only an aesthetically sensitive middle class, and a few snobbists, were able to discern, and willing to support, this creativity. They were the friends and admirers essential to the strength of the arts and sciences. Therefore, any social and economic policies that weakened these groups had to be weighed against the stagnation that could result. In terms of the political landscape of Great Britain at the time, this was an appeal to Liberal Party values, over and against the Labour Party emphasis on the welfare of "the herd" and the Conservative Party defense of the aristocracy and plutocracy. The sorts of institutions and practices that, it can be inferred, Bell would have supported (and Americans would understand well still today) include liberal arts colleges sustained by private endowments, tax deductions for private contributions to "education and culture," and such public funding agencies as the National Science Foundation and the National Endowments for the Arts and the Humanities that channel funds to the arts and sciences with minimal intrusion from the heavy hand of the state.

The *Civilisation* of Kenneth Clark

In his autobiography, Kenneth Clark testified to the influence upon him of Bell and Fry, but mainly of Fry. It began when he was a student:

> I had admired Roger Fry's writings since the publication of *Vision and Design* in 1920, but when I heard him lecture in Oxford on Poussin and Cézanne my admiration turned to idolatry. The wit, the grave, resonant voice and the air of perfect reason with which he would propound incredible theories made him the most bewitching lecturer I have ever heard, and these magical powers were united to a gift of pictorial analysis which, when they were applied to Poussin or Cézanne, was a revelation. (Clark 1974, 109)

Like most students of art in the early years of the century, Clark was raised on the "turgid and over-insistent" prose style of John Ruskin. Thus "it was a relief to turn to the clear contemporary language of Roger Fry, whose skill in analysing the components of a design, be it a drawing by Daumier, a painting by Poussin, or a Ch'ang bronze, was the finest education in art-criticism I ever received" (75–76). Clark went on to a long and highly successful career as writer and lecturer in the arts, administrator, and intimate of prominent figures in the cultural and political life of Britain. He was involved with most significant institutions in the arts during his lifetime, including, with John Maynard Keynes, another friend of Fry's, the Arts Council, an organization that was fully consistent with Fry's insistence on an arm's-length role for the state in supporting the arts. Late in life, Clark was persuaded to serve as narrator in a highly ambitious British Broadcasting Corporation television series on which ultimately more funds were lavished than on any similar endeavor to date. A handsome volume that was essentially the script emerged from the series.

In contrast to Bell's *Civilization,* which was a polemic for support of the arts and sciences by attending to the demand side of the markets for their products, Clark's *Civilisation* (1969) was a broad-brush meditation on the history of Western art and science, aimed at a very large television and reading audience and presented substantially through the filter of the Fry model. Even though, perhaps symbolically, an African mask from Fry's collection is pictured at the start of the series, the influence of Fry is not acknowledged directly and must be inferred from the approach taken.

Clark understood the advance of civilization very much as did Fry and Bell—"in terms of creative power and the enlargement of human faculties" (Clark 1969, 323). Although he did not employ quite the same terms as Fry, Clark used for his story line rewards for those who sustained the imaginative life juxtaposed through history against the pressures for attention from the biological life and the instinct of emulation. In his account, as in the works of the other two critics, painting, architecture, and sculpture are linked with music, dance, literature, pure science, and other mystical elements in a society. These all tend to rise and fall together as part of what Fry called the imaginative life of humans. Clark developed this notion at the start of his first chapter:

> At certain epochs man has felt conscious of something about himself—body and spirit—which was outside the day-to-day struggle for existence and the night-to-night struggle with fear; and he has felt the need to develop these qualities of thought and feeling so that they might approach as nearly as possible to an ideal of perfection—reason, justice, physical beauty, all of them in equilibrium. He has managed to satisfy this need in various ways—through myths, through dance and song, through systems of philosophy and through the order that he has imposed on the visible world. The children of his imagination are also the expressions of an ideal. (3)

Clark associated progress of civilization with the accumulation of works of art, a process analogous to improvements in the stock of certain kinds of social capital, and he recognized that special conditions were required for the accumulation of this type of capital as for any other kind. In particular, he found that fear and insecurity were the enemies of the augmentation of the artistic capital that enriched the imaginative life. The fear took many forms: "Fear of war, fear of invasion, fear of plague and famine, that make it simply not worthwhile constructing things, or planting trees or even planning next year's crops. And fear of the supernatural, which means that you daren't question anything or change anything" (3–4). Confidence, the obverse of fear, was necessary for civilization to move forward—"confidence in the society in which one lives, belief in its philosophy, belief in its laws, and confidence in one's own mental powers" (4). In addition, civilization required "a vigorous belief in law and discipline." It also took hard work: "Vigour, energy, vitality, all the great civilizations—or civilizing epochs—have had a weight of energy behind them" (4). The particular capital accumulation required for civilization required also "a sense of permanence. The wanderers and the invaders were in a continual state of flux. They didn't feel the need to look forward beyond the next March or the next voyage or the next battle. And for that reason it didn't occur to them to build stone houses, or to write books" (14).

When a society lost its energy, then its civilization—its imaginative life—simply crumbled from inattention. The barbarians destroyed the buildings of Rome mainly through lack of preventive maintenance: "The idea of keeping them up never entered their heads. They preferred to live in pre-fabs and let the old places fall down" (4). Clark found that one way in which works of art had survived hard times was through masquerading as what Fry had called opifacts for emulation: "It is arguable that western civilization was saved by its craftsmen. The wanderers could take their craftsmen with them. Since the smiths made princely weapons as well as ornaments, they were as necessary to a chieftain's status as were the bards whose calypsos celebrated his courage" (9).

Clark traced the origins of civilization in Europe to around 1100 A.D. when there came to be enough "wealth, stability, technical skill and, above all, the confidence necessary to push through a long-term project" (34). The Roman Catholic Church was the initiator of civilizing projects, taking advantage of economies of scale and social mobility: "The church was powerful for all kinds of negative reasons; she didn't suffer many of the inconveniences of feudalism; there was no question of divided inheritances. For these reasons she could conserve and expand her properties. And she was powerful for positive reasons. Men of intelligence naturally and normally took holy orders, and could rise from obscurity to positions of immense influence" (35). From the start, the Church, like later patrons of the arts, had mixed motives for supporting the imaginative life of their flock and for producing the stuff of civilization. Churchmen, like other men, had both a Veblenian instinct of emulation and a belief in God. Civilization fared best when they responded to both.

The Abbot of the Royal Abbey of St. Denis in France was a case in point. He was a classicist and collector on the scale of the great American plutocrats of the twentieth century. He had "the love of brightness and splendour and antiquity—and a love of acquisition" (49). But he also was a mystic:

> [What he] did was genuinely done to the glory of God. And he was not merely a collector—he was creator. His work had a philosophic basis that is very important to western civilization. . . . He argued

> that we could only come to understand absolute beauty, which is God, through the effect of precious and beautiful things on our senses. He said: "The dull mind rises to truth through that which is material." This was really a revolutionary concept in the Middle Ages. It was the intellectual background of all the sublime works of art of the next century and in fact has remained the basis of our belief in the value of art until today. (50)

The aristocracy and the monarchy complemented the Church in supporting the imaginative life of the Middle Ages. But they were a less-predictable and dependable source, dependent on the individual characters of the rulers and involving a smaller part of the population than the Church: "Even in republican Florence, the Renaissance touched relatively few people, and in places like Urbino and Mantua it was practically confined to the court" (112). The Renaissance demonstrated how necessary it was for the elite who enjoyed the imaginative life to become large enough to be self-sustaining: "The few had gone too far away from the many, not only in knowledge and intelligence—this they always do—but in basic assumptions. When the first two generations of humanists were dead their movement had no real weight behind it, and there was a reaction away from the human scale of values" (116).

Like Bell's *Civilization,* Clark's is concerned continuously with the need for adequate patronage of the arts. Theirs is substantially a demand-side perspective. By the end of the fifteenth century the Church as patron of the imaginative life was in trouble: "The great civiliser of Europe was aground, stranded on forms and vested interests" (143). With the Reformation, Martin Luther gave the Church self-confidence once again, but he also "released . . . latent violence and hysteria. And beyond this was another northern characteristic that was fundamentally opposed to civilization: an earthy, animal hostility to reason and decorum that Nordic man seems to have retained from his days in the primeval forest" (158). Indeed, during the Reformation, civilization took some backward steps: "Whatever the long-term effects of Protestantism, the immediate results were very bad: not only bad for art, but bad for life. The North was full of bully boys who rampaged about the country and took any excuse to beat people up" (160–61).

Baroque art of the sixteenth and seventeenth centuries, rooted in a Catholic revival, was the first popular art on a grand scale that reached for support across a wide spectrum of social classes: "The art of the Renaissance had appealed through intellectual means—geometry, perspective, knowledge of antiquity—to a small group of humanists. The Baroque appealed through the emotions to the widest possible audience. The subjects were often obscure, thought out by some theologian: but the means of communication were popular, and even remind one of the films" (182). The downfall of the Baroque came because the instinct of emulation was as alive and well within the church as without and more and more of the patronage went not for genuine art but for display: "The colossal palaces of the Papal families were simply expressions of private greed and vanity" (192).

The most serious challenge to the strength of the imaginative life in Europe came with the evolution of the modern market economy. The question was posed, Could the arts and sciences thrive in "the world of trade and of banking, of cities full of hard-headed men whose aim in life was to grow rich without ceasing to appear respectable" (79)? The Italian merchants of the fourteenth century began the shift in patronage of the imaginative life away from the church and the aristocracy with results that were clearly reflected in the works of art that emerged: "The painting they commissioned had a kind of solid reality that was to be the dominant aim of western art up to the time of Cézanne" (80).

It was left to the mercantile community of the Netherlands to demonstrate that civilization could be compatible with a vibrant market economy. Both the means and the will were there for patronage of the arts on a grand scale: "At a certain stage in social development fluid capital is one of the chief causes of civilisation because it ensures three essential ingredients: leisure, movement and independence. It also allows that slight superfluity of wealth that can be spent on nobler proportions, a better door-frame or even a rarer and more extraordinary tulip" (197). But among the merchants, just as earlier among the churchmen and aristocrats, the corrupting influence of the instinct of emulation soon raised its ugly head. Funding that could have gone to support the arts was spent instead on mere magnificence:

> This kind of visual self-indulgence very soon leads to ostentation and this, in bourgeois democracy, means vulgarity. One can see this happening in Holland in the work of a single painter, Pieter de Hooch. In 1660 he was painting pictures of clean, simple interiors, their ordered space full of light. Ten years later his interiors were very

elaborate, and instead of light whitewashed walls there was gold Spanish leather. The people are richer: and the pictures are much less beautiful. Bourgeois capitalism led to a defensive smugness and sentimentality: no wonder that earlier Victorian painters imitated the genre pictures of Metsu and Terborch. (197–99)

A redeeming feature of the imaginative life of the Dutch commercial economy, Clark conceded, was that while it corrupted some great artists like de Hooch and turned out a great deal of "vulgar trivial art," it also sustained genius: "Well—they also got Rembrandt" (201).

A most important development in the seventeenth century in Clark's view was that science replaced religion as a "dominating factor" in the imaginative life of humankind: "Mathematics became, in fact, the religion of the finest minds of the time—the means of expressing a belief that experience could be united with reason" (208). One consequence was that subjects of attention emerged in common between the arts and sciences—for example, light, proportion, vision, and astronomy. Science affected all the arts and the great artists, including Wren in architecture, Purcell in music, and Vaughn in poetry.

The eighteenth and nineteenth centuries presented sharp contrasts for Clark in the economy and the arts. The eighteenth century was a great age of amateurism, of enlightenment, of salons, of good conversation, of Voltaire, and of "douceur de vivre" as Tallyrand put it. For the most part, the players in the arts were no longer priests, aristocrats, or wealthy merchants but instead upper-middle-class intellectuals and aesthetes with property enough to pursue their interests into any direction that had appeal. Although Clark took pains to distance himself from Bell's extreme position on the importance of leisure and privilege, Clark's vision of the eighteenth century does look very much like Bell's picture of civilization.

The eighteenth century was the first period in modern times, Clark concluded, when it could be demonstrated convincingly that the pattern of income distribution in society affected creativity. He observed that "a margin of wealth is helpful to civilisation, but for some mysterious reason great wealth is destructive. I suppose that, in the end, splendour is dehumanising, and a certain sense of limitation seems to be a condition of what we call good taste" (253). But, he asked, was civilization in the eighteenth century therefore achieved through "injustice" to those who received less than an equal share of national output? Was the imaginative life of society based on exploitation? Clark thought not. He said "our whole society is based on" what some might consider to be "different sorts of exploitation" (256). In reality, though, the support of creativity and the progress of civilization simply required inequality. If these ends were admirable, as he thought they were, the means could not be considered exploitation.

Clark believed that far more ominous for the future of the arts than their dependence on private property and inequality of income distribution were economic "progress" and the new behaviors that were emerging from the modern industrial economy of the nineteenth century. He noted that "every civilization seems to have its nemesis," and for the past century and a half this had become the Malthusian specter of "growth of population" accompanied by rapid industrial development. The consequence of these changes for the arts was that middle-class aesthetes were becoming an endangered species, displaced by insensitive plutocrats and the Philistine herd, neither of which could be expected to make available the resources to sustain a vigorous imaginative life, nor even to construct such great works of art as those by, say, Christopher Wren: "The greedy became greedier, the ignorant lost touch with traditional skills, and the light of experience narrowed its beam so that a grand design like Greenwich [The Royal Hospital, Greenwich, by Wren] would now be thought of as a waste of money that no accountant could condone" (220).

With respect to the arts, Clark saw the twentieth century as just a projection of the nineteenth. Although resources had become much more abundant, they were not directed generously toward the arts. Great monuments had been constructed aplenty, but they were simply for display or for the worship of a new deity—mammon. "New York was built to the glory of mammon—money, gain, the new god of the nineteenth century. So many of the same human ingredients have gone into its construction that at a distance it does look rather like a celestial city. At a distance. Come closer and it's not so good. Lots of squalor, and, in the luxury, something parasitical" (321). While industrialization had made few additions to the store of beauty, it had made numerous subtractions. In the case of Great Britain, "by failing to control her industrial development she had suffered a defeat, in terms of human life, far more costly than any military disaster" (324). One of the culprits leading Great Britain to ignore the decline of its imaginative life was a classical political economy that counseled only laissez-faire: "When I call them sacred books I am not joking. Malthus and Ricardo were taken as gospels by the most serious and even pious men, who used them to justify actions they would never have thought of defending on human grounds" (327). Clark was saying, of course, what Fry and Bell had said before him—that economics was a science designed for the biological life of humans, and as a guide to the rest it was seriously flawed.

Clark concluded his history of civilization on a querulous note. He was very doubtful that substantial resources could ever flow to the imaginative life of humans as long as their biological life was in disarray. At the end of the 1960s, it seemed utopian to anticipate the strengthening of a middle-class elite able to press successfully for support of the arts from either public or private sources. The prospect for civilization was dim. Clark even found fault with the other major participant in the imaginative life—science—because of its contemporary impact on the arts. With the decline of religion, pure science was now the principal compatriot of the arts in the imagination. But this compatriot was leading the arts astray: "Artists who have been very little influenced by social systems, have always responded instinctively to latent assumptions about the shape of the universe. The incomprehensibility of our new cosmos seems to me, ultimately, to be the reason for the chaos of modern art" (345).

Civilisation made Kenneth Clark the best-known commentator on the arts of his age. Praise flowed in from all sides (Secrest 1986, 230), but the praise was not unalloyed. Some of the most intense criticism was, perhaps, rooted in jealousy because the project was so successful (more than a million copies of the book sold in America alone) and because the work was seen as a political and ideological statement. John Bussy in the *New Statesman and Nation* (3 April 1970) saw it as "an essay in contemporary polemic" masquerading as history. The television series aired in the late 1960s when much of European and American society was consumed with issues of race, class, and postcolonial warfare, and Clark's emphasis in his historical narrative on the need in civilized society for self-confidence, security, the rule of law, discipline, and a sense of permanence was perceived by many of his listeners as a commentary on the current turmoil—as to some degree it was. In any case, he was hailed by some, as Clive Bell had been before, as spokesman for conservatism and reaction, careless of the interests of the common man. Howard Clurman wrote in *Harpers Magazine* (13 September 1970):

> Brave words! They satisfy something in us which is oppressed by our presentday burdens. Embedded in Sir Kenneth's anathema of contemporary blights lurks a troublesome question he avoids except in passing reference. He is so enraptured by the bloom of beauty that he does not seem to examine the soil from which it rises: the immense number of simple toilers at the bottom of civilization's splendors. What is their relation to the arts whose wonders he records for our delight? (101)

Coded messages could be found by critics throughout Clark's interpretation of history. For example, his commentary on Baroque art—that much of it appealed only to a narrow intellectual elite and therefore failed—could be seen as an attack on abstract modern art. His suggestion that science was gaining a new and baleful influence over art was distasteful to many in the art world who, at this time, were anxiously proclaiming their separate and distinct identity and therefore a need for such institutions as the National Endowment for the Arts. Clark's enthusiasm for the cultured middle class as it emerged in the eighteenth century, even though not accompanied by such inflammatory terms as those used by Bell and Fry (herd, plutocrats, snobbists, etc.), was nevertheless "politically incorrect" for the 1960s.

Clark was far from thrilled by the polarized political image created for him by *Civilisation.* At a ceremony in the National Gallery of Art in Washington, where he was faced with hundreds of adoring fans and presented a medal, he burst into tears (Clark 1977, 225).

Conclusion

What can we take away from this account of how three prominent twentieth-century art critics set out to explain various aspects of the production and consumption of art? For a start, it is striking that, very much like the economists of the time, they operated to some extent as a community and within the confines of an agreed model that helped them organize and understand their material. Any stereotype of the humanists of this period operating independently of their fellows, without theory and through simple narrative, is belied by this case. Like the models of the economists, the model of these art critics was used not only in theoretical speculation but also in policy debate and the telling of history. The critics' model was considerably more complex than that of the economists, who, a half century earlier, had settled on a Benthamite calculus of pleasure and pain to explain human behavior in markets. The critics conceded that the economists' model might be satisfactory to explain what they called the "biological life" of man, but for them that was not the whole story—or even the most important part of the story. For an understanding of why humans demanded goods for display, the critics turned to a heretical part of economics—to the American Institutionalist Thorstein Veblen and his discoveries from anthropology of an instinct in humans of emulation and a yearning for display. Whereas the economics discipline at the time tended to see the neoclassical and Institutionalist explanations of behavior as alternatives and in conflict with each other, these art critics saw them as complementary and explaining different realms of human behavior.

But it was in the third part of human activity, what Fry called the imaginative life, that the critics were most interested. This was where pure science was practiced, the arts were performed, and various mystical experiences took place. To understand the imaginative life, the critics turned away from the economist's metaphors and what they took to be an essentially Darwinian process, and they looked for enlightenment to psychology and the study of communication. The imaginative life they found was not about the production and consumption of goods and services in any conventional sense; it was about emotion, and novelty, and the transmission of ideas and feelings. It was about fundamental and thus far unpredictable, dynamic change.

Since neither the critics themselves nor anyone else to date had successfully predicted or explained the process of creation that was central to the imaginative life, the critics settled for making a study of conditions in which creativity seemed to be at its greatest. For this they stayed with market metaphors and were led naturally to the demand side of the market and a concern for the strength of those in society who could sustain this creativity. Economists who have engaged in comparable explorations have been few, and not always well appreciated. In the mid-nineteenth century, John Rae (1834) tried to explain the process of capital accumulation and technological innovation, and at about the same time as these critics were writing, Joseph Schumpeter ([1912] 1934) examined the conditions favorable to entrepreneurship. It is interesting that both Rae and Schumpeter were accused by economists of being closet sociologists, a charge that might have been leveled at the art critics as well.

This chapter gives an account of art critics operating far apart from economists on topics that were, in fact, quite close and where both groups might well have benefited from interaction. "What if" history should not be pushed very far. Nevertheless, four questions may be suggested on which, under the right circumstances, economists and art critics might have had a lively conversation.

1. What is the best way to improve human welfare (as the economists called it) and to advance civilization (as the art critics understood the matter)? Was it simply by the efficient production and just distribution of more goods and services in what the critics called "the biological life," or was it more complex? Was excellence in the imaginative life, perhaps, an alternative to be considered? That Pigou, at least, recognized the question is reason to believe that a more extensive exchange might have been fruitful. The intellectual struggles that William Stanley Jevons underwent after discovering the special qualities of the consumption of music, described by Bert Mosselmans and Ernest Mathijs in this volume, suggest that this one marginalist pioneer at least was ready for new ideas. Trapped as he was in a utilitarian straitjacket of his own making, Jevons went to great lengths to find justifications for more public attention to music than would occur naturally from the spontaneous demands expressed in the market. But, like John Ruskin and William Morris at about the same time, Jevons could not get beyond a primitive notion of positive externalities. At a minimum, Jevons's successors might have profited from a vigorous exchange with the art critics who dismissed utility as an explanation of behavior in the imaginative life and called instead for study of the arts as a process of communication.
2. What stimulates human creativity? Genuine art, as Fry distinguished it from mere opifactual production, is all about novelty and change, about invention and innovation. What, the economists asked, made the inventor discover new ways to transform materials? What, the art critics asked, made the artist experience a creative vision and then transform it into a work of art? In essence, these are the same question, and the questioners were led naturally to similar subquestions: What are the effects of price, income, and wealth on the innovative process? How can government or private initiative stimulate the process? Neither

economist nor art critic has worked out satisfactory answers to these questions, even unto this day, and it is reasonable to speculate therefore that they might have come closer if they had worked together.

3. What understanding is to be gained by economists from an intimate familiarity with the art market? Perhaps the only economist who benefited directly from this intimacy was John Maynard Keynes, who knew all three critics discussed here but was closest to Fry. Keynes's representation of the stock market as a beauty contest, where the speculation of participants about the perceptions of other participants is more determinative than market fundamentals, is highly reminiscent of Fry's portrayal of the art market dominated by snobbists who respond to fashion much more than to anything approaching objective beauty (Goodwin 1998, 53–54). Keynes, of course, was immersed with Fry and Bell in the Bloomsbury Group—that quintessential multidisciplinary community in which prejudices against unfamiliar disciplines, paradigms, and points of view were simply not tolerated. The Fry-Keynes connection may, indeed, be seen as a test case of what might emerge from more art and economics interaction.
4. Might the very different intellectal styles of the economists and art critics perhaps have promoted a useful exchange about method? The former were engaged in a process of enclosure and academicization just at a time when the critics were reaching out to a much wider lay elite, not simply through the conventional written word but, in the case of Clark, through the new medium of television as well. It is not obvious that either group would have persuaded the other to change its path by exposure to an alternative, but the experience would have provided food for thought.

References

Bell, Clive. [1913] 1958. *Art*. New York: Capricorn.

———. 1918. *Potboilers*. London: Chatto and Windus.

———. [1928] 1973. *Civilization*. Chicago: University of Chicago Press.

Bussy, John. 1970. Review of *Civilisation* by Kenneth Clark. *New Statesman and Nation* (3 April): 480.

Bywater, William G., Jr. 1975. *Clive Bell's Eye*. Detroit: Wayne State University Press.

Clark, Kenneth. 1969. *Civilisation*. New York: Harper & Row.

———. 1974. *Another Part of the Wood*. New York: Harper & Row.

———. 1977. *The Other Half*. London: John Murray.

Clurman, Howard. 1970. Review of *Civilisation* by Kenneth Clark. *Harpers Magazine* (13 September): 100–102.

Dickinson, Goldsworthy Lowes. 1901. *Letters from John Chinaman*. London: R. Brimley Johnson.

Fry, Roger. [1920] 1956. *Vision and Design*. New York: Meridian.

———. 1926. *Art and Commerce*. London: Hogarth Press.

Goodwin, Craufurd. 1998. *Art and the Market: Roger Fry on Commerce in Art*. Ann Arbor: University of Michigan Press.

Pigou, A. C. 1924. *The Economics of Welfare*. 2d ed. New York: Macmillan.

Rae, John. 1834. *Statement of Some New Principles of Political Economy*. Boston: Hilliard, Gray.

Schumpeter, Joseph A. [1912] 1934. *The Theory of Economic Development*. Cambridge: Harvard University Press.

Secrest, Meryle. 1986. *Kenneth Clark: A Biography*. New York: Fromm International.

Tolstoy, Leo N. [1898] 1960. *What Is Art?* New York: Macmillan.

Part 2

Art and Economic Policy

Art Exports and the Construction of National Heritage in Late-Victorian and Edwardian Great Britain

Helen Rees

The "Old Masters Question"

In November 1911, the Board of the National Gallery, London, appointed a sub-committee of trustees to conduct an "Enquiry into the Retention of Important Pictures in This Country."[1] The focus of the trustees' concern was what had become known as the "Old Masters question"—that is, the apparently incompatible ambitions of vendors, the British state, and the National Gallery in the face of an increasingly competitive market in Old Masters paintings. New and wealthy collectors—primarily, but not exclusively, from the United States of America—were creating an escalating demand for such pictures, and the art collections of the British peerage provided a ready supply. The result was a discernible and, to the British art establishment, alarming increase in the pace of art exports (Witt 1911).

In an attempt to quantify the problem, the National Gallery committee compiled a list of five hundred "Important Pictures Sold out of the United Kingdom in Recent Years" (National Gallery 1915, 52–60). The list maps a process of dispersal that had begun in the 1880s and had

Special thanks to the National Gallery Archive, London, and National Art-Collections Fund Archive, London, for access to their resources.

1. The full title of the report of the committee was *Enquiry into the Retention of Important Pictures in This Country and Other Matters Connected with the National Collections*. The report of the committee is dated 13 December 1913, but it was not finally approved by the full board for publication until 16 March 1915. It was eventually published by His Majesty's Stationery Office, London, in 1915, as Cmmd Paper 7878. The *Minutes of Evidence* were published simultaneously as Cmmd Paper 7879.

continued for over twenty-five years. It is dominated by sales of European paintings from the fifteenth to the eighteenth centuries, and of British portraits from the eighteenth and early nineteenth centuries, primarily from aristocratic collections.[2] Of course, Great Britain was not the only source of Old Masters paintings at this time. Obviously, Italy was incomparably richer in indigenous works of art which, despite the official prohibition on the export of national treasures, were frequently removed from the country, albeit illegally (Baldwin Brown 1905). Equally, not all art exports from Great Britain were destined for the United States of America: for example, all four works by Albrecht Dürer included in the National Gallery list were bought by the Kaiser Friedrich Museum, Berlin.

However, it was the increasing competition from New World collectors that excited the greatest apprehension, envy, and, occasionally, approval among commentators in Great Britain. Responses to the crisis were certainly not uniform, let alone predictable. Roger Fry (1911b, 66) commented that "the American side of this vexed question is by far the brightest. . . . It is excusable for Englishmen to resent the acquisitiveness of these magnates, but no one in his senses can deny that by the employment of their vast powers they are doing national service to their own country." Others were less even-handed: D. S. MacColl (1912, 25) believed that "fortunes there [i.e., America] have reached a wicked scale that throws into the shade the old-fashioned fortunes of our treasures." For Henry James (quoted in Edel and Powers 1987, 126) 1895 was "the age of Mrs Jack," his friend Isabella Stewart Gardner, whom he described as "the American, the nightmare" and whom he compared with the barbarian at the gates of Rome.

Fourteen years later, in 1909, James wrote a comic play entitled *The Outcry* (reprinted in Edel 1949, 761–807), in which he satirized the attitudes toward the ownership of works of art. The central, contrasting

2. Thus, for example, Isabella Stewart Gardner of Boston had acquired nineteen paintings from Great Britain between 1885 and 1910, including *The Rape of Europa* by Titian (from the earl of Darnley), *The Death of Lucrezia* by Botticelli (from Lord Ashburnham), Rubens's *Portrait of the Earl of Arundel* (from the earl of Warwick), and *The Presentation in the Temple* by Giotto (from the Willett collection). Meanwhile, Henry Clay Frick had bought thirty-two paintings from Great Britain during the same period, including a portrait of Sir Thomas More by Holbein the Younger (from the Huth collection), a portrait of Frans Snyders by Van Dyke (from the earl of Carlisle) and its pendant of Margareta Snyders (from the earl of Warwick), and two portraits by Reynolds of Lady Skipwith and Lady Elizabeth Taylor (both from the earl of Egremont).

characters are a proud and unworldly English aristocrat, the earl of Theign, and an acquisitive American tycoon, Mr. Beckenridge Bender. Much of the humor of the piece derives from the apparently paradoxical behavior of the protagonists: Theign appears to be willing to contemplate a sale, at the same time as he recoils from market forces; and Bender undoubtedly wants to buy, but only for a very high price. Lord John, who is a friend of both men, suggests to Theign that a degree of compromise is required of each:

> LORD JOHN: Would you mind an agreement on such a basis as this? that you shall resign yourself to the biggest equivalent you'll squeamishly agree to take, if it's at the same time the smallest he'll squeamishly consent to offer? (Edel 1949, 800)

The Outcry is generally regarded by Jamesian scholars as of marginal interest (Hopkins Winner 1970, 146). Inevitably, as a three-act comedy it lacks the metaphorical range and subtlety with which James interrogates the moral implications of art appreciation and possession in, say, *The Golden Bowl* or even *The Spoils of Poynton*. Due to the circumstances of James's ill health and the death of Edward VII in May 1910, the play was never produced in the author's lifetime, and so we cannot access an immediate critical response to the drama. Nonetheless, James clearly believed that a contemporary audience would not only recognize but also relish the comic potential of his mise en scène. Certainly, the subsequent success of a novella based on the play, which ran to three editions when it was published in 1911, suggests that moral and economic implications of the transatlantic trade in art had entered the currency of contemporary popular culture.

The purpose of this article is to map the historical events that inspired James's play and thus to investigate how the associative discourses of art and nationhood were activated by the export of paintings in the years before World War I. I shall also describe how a succession of Jamesian "outcries" shaped the formation of British public policy through the appointment of the 1911 National Gallery committee. My focus is on the linked dramas of two transactions that acquired immediate notoriety on both sides of the Atlantic: namely, the sale of Holbein's portrait *Christina of Denmark* to the National Gallery in 1909, and the export of Rembrandt's landscape *The Mill* to Peter Arrell Brown Widener of Philadelphia in 1911. The sales of these two paintings—one "saved" and the other "lost"—were the most fiercely contested in the decade before 1914. In the process, each acquired an emblematic status in the discourse of threatened patrimony that exceeded its singular history as a privately owned painting, depicting a non-English subject, and created by a foreign artist.

Sale of the Norfolk Holbein, 1909

At the time James was writing *The Outcry*, some of his English friends, including Edmund Gosse and Sidney Colvin,[3] were actively campaigning to prevent the sale of the duke of Norfolk's portrait by Holbein, *Christina of Denmark, Duchess of Milan* (probably 1538) (Tintner 1981). The prospective purchaser was the American millionaire industrialist, Henry Clay Frick. On this occasion, the American collector was thwarted and, as a result of a dramatic public appeal, the painting was bought for the National Gallery, London.

Whether or not James intended to draw a direct parallel between the protagonists involved in the sale of the Holbein and the characters in *The Outcry* is moot. However, in both the historical and fictive dramas, the actions of aristocratic vendors aroused as much controversy as did the ambitions of American collectors. For the outrage provoked by such sales was directed not only at overseas predators but also, to quote James, at "the fortunate owners of precious . . . works of art [who] hold them in trust, as it were, for the nation and may themselves, as lax guardians, be held to account for public opinion" (Edel 1949, 763). Not surprisingly, many vendors were unwilling to subject their actions to public scrutiny and preferred to deal discreetly, thus begging the question asked by Beckenridge Bender: "If they don't sell their Ancestors, where in the world are all the Ancestors bought?" (Edel 1949, 775). The force of Bender's irony would not have been lost on James's contemporaries: in 1909, the scandal surrounding the sale by the Norfolk Holbein was certainly exacerbated by the duke's insistence that his plans for a sale be kept secret, until it was almost too late to mount a public appeal for its purchase for the national collection. As a result, the duke was regarded by many as a "lax guardian" of his

3. Edmund Gosse (1849–1928) was a poet and critic. In 1909 Gosse was librarian to the House of Lords and also a member of the council of the National Art-Collections Fund. Sidney Colvin (1845–1927) was a literary and art critic. In 1909 Colvin was keeper of prints and drawings at the British Museum and a member of the executive committee of the National Art-Collections Fund (*Concise Dictionary of National Biography* 1992).

property, who had failed to acknowledge the national interest in his dynastic inheritance.

The portrait of sixteen-year-old Christina had been painted for Henry VIII, king of England, in 1538 to assist his search for a fourth bride among the royal families of Europe. Although the picture was delivered to the king,[4] negotiations for the marriage foundered, and Christina herself never came to England. By the middle of the seventeenth century, the painting had been acquired by Thomas Howard, second earl of Arundel,[5] and thereafter was transferred by descent through the line of the dukes of Norfolk, until it was inherited in 1860 by the fifteenth duke—its eventual vendor. In 1880, the fifteenth duke lent the picture to the National Gallery, where it remained until 1909; during those twenty-nine years, the boundary between private ownership and public trusteeship was effectively erased, and the national interest in the painting was implicitly asserted by virtue of its apparent assimilation into the national collection (Holmes 1909, 135). Consequently, the duke's decision to sell the work was perceived as an unpatriotic reversion to aristocratic privilege.[6]

The erasure of the distinction between the family and the nation substantiated the claim that *Christina of Denmark* was part of the British patrimony, despite the fact that the painting still belonged to a private individual. This contention was reinforced by a further rhetorical elision, whereby Princess Christina herself was revivified and invoked as symbol of English womanhood and, by extension, of the nation. Thus, Christina, the daughter of a Danish father and an Austrian mother, was repeatedly described as an ideal English type and the embodiment of a "charm [that] we Northerners understand. Her delicate complexion and slightly rounded contours speak to us of a beauty specially belonging to *our* womenfolk" (National Art-Collections Fund 1910, 20; emphasis added). The portrait of Christina was no longer secure within the sanctuary of the English National Gallery; and the nation itself was violated by the attempt to remove it. The

4. It is listed in an inventory of 1542 (Baker and Henry 1995).

5. Bätschmann and Griener (1997, 202) comment that "not only aesthetic, but historical values were at stake: a strong sense of nostalgia for the Tudor period drove a collector like Thomas Howard, 2nd Earl of Arundel, to purchase Holbeins at almost any cost."

6. Evidence of widespread recognition of the National Gallery's claim on the picture comes from the fact that both the Kaiser Friedrich Museum, Berlin, and the Metropolitan Museum, New York, declined to make an offer for it (Holmes 1909).

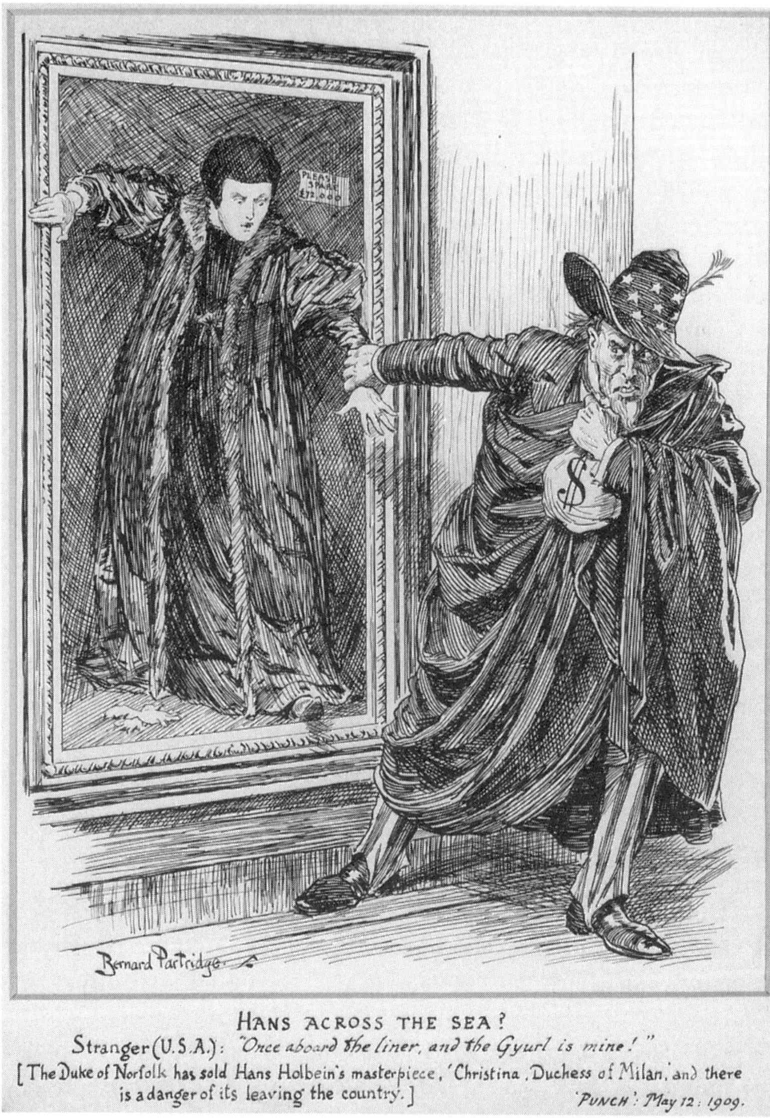

Figure 1 Bernard Partridge, *Hans across the Sea*. Reproduced in *Punch*, 1909.

drama was caricatured in a famous cartoon by Bernard Partridge, published in *Punch* magazine (see figure 1): Uncle Sam, in the guise of a robber baron, clutches a sack of dollars in one hand and pulls Christina out of her frame with the other. In the caricature, the greedy millionaire stands for America, and *Christina*/Christina is England personified—and despoiled.

Yet the concept of nationhood that *Christina* emblematized was fractured and contested, both in 1538 when the painting was made and in 1909 when it was sold for the first and only time. The historical Christina's relationship with the Tudor court was limited to just one sitting for Holbein;[7] her proposed marriage to the king of England never took place, and thus for Henry, and for England, her portrait represents absence and desire. It was therefore ironic that the 1909 campaign to "save the precious Duchess from exile" sought to retain the painting of a woman who never came to England and whose failure to become Henry's consort was regarded as something of a lucky escape (National Art-Collections Fund 1910, 16). Moreover, as an iconic image of Henry's search for a Protestant bride, Holbein's *Christina* represents the patronage of the Reformation court; yet for 250 years, the portrait had belonged to the Howard family, one of the leading Catholic dynasties in England. Henry Fitzalan-Howard, the fifteenth duke of Norfolk, was not only the premier duke but also the leading Catholic layman in the country. In 1902, as earl marshal of England, he had organized the coronation of Edward VII according to the rites of the Protestant succession; in 1909, he cited the proposed government reform of Catholic education as the reason for his decision to sell *Christina*. His avowed desire to raise funds for Catholic schools—and the means by which he chose to do so—revealed the alienation of Catholics, however high their rank, within the British state.

Having announced his decision to sell, the duke was widely criticized for giving the National Gallery just ten days to raise the purchase price of £61,000.[8] As a result, the deadline for the sale had already passed before the next scheduled meeting of the trustees took place, by which time the painting had been bought by the dealers, P & D Col-

7. 12 March 1538 (Baker and Henry 1995).

8. Letter from the duke of Norfolk to the director of the National Gallery, dated 22 April 1909 (National Gallery Archive, London). At the time, £1 sterling was worth approximately $5 US.

naghi. They, in turn, offered it to the gallery for the increased sum of £72,000.[9] However, when the possibility of a sale had been raised the previous year, the duke had explicitly objected to the suggestion that a public appeal be launched to raise funds for the purchase.[10] Now that he had already sold the painting, no such constraint applied, and a fundraising appeal was organized on behalf of the gallery by the voluntary society, the National Art-Collections Fund.[11] The government gave £10,000 toward the purchase. Of the remaining target of £62,000, less than £12,000 was raised by some six hundred donations of £1,000 or less. The bulk of the money was made up from three large, anonymous contributions, including one of £40,000 pledged just the day before the deadline for the purchase was due to expire.[12] Despite the outcry surrounding the sale, the campaign revealed that far fewer than a thousand individuals were willing to subscribe to the purchase. The desirability of retaining the portrait in England was not contested, but the price of doing so was. In particular, the trustees of the National Gallery were criticized for having acceded to the duke's wish that they should not organize a preemptive public appeal, with the result that the cost of the painting was greatly increased (Holmes 1909, 135).

The episode revealed the existence of American collectors who combined both the means and the desire to pay high prices for famous paintings—although some commentators continued to doubt the reality of "that mysterious anonymous . . . millionaire" whose supposed interest in a picture was vaunted by the dealers whenever a celebrated masterpiece came onto the market (*New York Times* 1909a). The *New York Times* (1909b, 6) was dismissive of "stories of enormous prices paid by American art lovers," which, it believed, were being "coddled in London for the sake of boosting the value" of such pictures; in its view, American buyers were more cautious and thrifty than was gen-

9. In 1909, the annual grant to the National Gallery for acquisitions was £5,000. In addition, the government could, with the consent of Parliament, make individual special grants for the purchase of singular masterpieces. The *New York Times* of 1909 calculated the sum of £72,000 as the equivalent of $330,000.

10. "A premier Duke of England does not show to advantage when he is the subject of a public appeal. That the condition [imposed by the duke] was also vain and foolish events have proved too clearly" (Holmes 1909, 136).

11. The National Art-Collections Fund (NA-CF) was a voluntary society, funded by subscriptions, founded in 1903 under the slogan "Save Art for the Nation."

12. The bulk of the private money was raised thus: Anonymous, £40,000; Anonymous, £5,000; Anonymous, £3,050; and Messrs P & D Colnaghi, £2,000 (National Art-Collections Fund 1910, 66).

erally supposed in Europe. In many cases this was true, but it was the occasional, highly conspicuous purchase that belied the norm and reinforced the stereotype of the collector whose acquisitiveness was excited, rather than deterred, by record prices. In *The Outcry*, Beckenridge Bender is just such a millionaire whose desire is "to be cited and celebrated as the biggest buyer that ever lived" (Edel 1949, 799).

In 1909, American speculation about the identity of the putative purchaser of *Christina* was entwined with the continuing debate at home about the desirability of amending the U.S. import tariff on works of art (Barber "International Commerce," this volume).[13] As far as *Christina* was concerned, the arithmetic was simple: "Under the existing tariff an American purchaser would have to pay 20 per cent of the value of the picture, i.e. $70,000. . . . Under the amended tariff there would be no duty upon its entry into America" (*New York Times* 1909b, 2). It therefore seemed reasonable to suppose that the revelation of the prospective purchaser's identity "will probably depend on the tariff legislation in Washington" (2). Although we now know that it was Henry Clay Frick who had offered to buy the picture from the Colnaghis, contemporary commentators thought it more likely to have been J. Pierpont Morgan. For, unlike Frick who did not have property in Europe, Morgan kept that part of his collection that he had bought outside America in his London house, 13 Princes Gate—and so avoided paying duty on its import into the United States (Chernow 1990; Saarinen 1959). Morgan thus combined the means both to buy *Christina* and to evade the tariff. However, in 1909, the *New York Times* was unaware that the year before *Christina* was sold, Morgan had promised the director of the National Gallery that not only would he not compete for the picture but also he would contribute to its purchase for the nation (National Gallery 1908). This was not the first time that Morgan had supported the acquisition of an Old Masters painting for the British national collection: in 1904, he had given £5,000 toward the purchase of Lord Darnley's *Titian, Portrait of Man*. Morgan's name is not listed among the individual contributors to the appeal for Christina organized by the National Art-Collections Fund, but it is unlikely that he broke his promise, and he may well have been the source of £5,000 given by an "Anonymous" donor.[14]

13. Barber has shown the increase in imports into the United States of foreign works of art over twenty years old in the immediate aftermath of tariff reform enacted in August 1909.

14. Morgan gave a further £5,000 toward the purchase in 1911 from the Dowager Countess Carlisle of *The Adoration of the Kings* by Jan Gossaert.

Meanwhile, Charles Holmes (1909, 69), writing in the *Burlington Magazine*, voiced the anxiety aroused in Great Britain by the prospect of tariff reform: "The removal of the import duty inevitably accelerates this process of spoliation. . . . it will give a further impetus to the forces making for the dispersal of the comparatively few important works of art which still remain in private possession here."

Certainly the prospect of further sales from English country seats troubled Holmes, but, in addition, he was worried that removal of the tariff would prompt American collectors to remove the works of art they had hitherto lent to museums and kept in their private houses in Britain (Holmes 1909, 69). This concern was a thinly disguised reference to Morgan, who was both a benefactor of the *Burlington Magazine* and a persuasive advocate of tariff reform. As predicted by Holmes, Morgan began the vast process of shipping his collection from London to New York in 1912, including not only the contents of Princes Gate but also the celebrated "Colonna Altarpiece" by Raphael, which had been on loan to the National Gallery since 1901.[15] As David Alan Brown (1983, 69) has commented: "From the walls of the National Gallery in London, the Colonna altarpiece went on exhibition at the Metropolitan Museum in New York in 1913."

Sale of the Lansdowne Rembrandt, 1911

Work had not yet begun on the removal of the Morgan collection when, two years later, the National Gallery faced an even greater acquisitions crisis than that provoked by the Norfolk Holbein. In 1911, Henry Petty-Fitzmaurice, the fifth marquis of Lansdowne, announced that he had accepted an offer of £100,000 for his Rembrandt, *The Mill* (ca. 1643–45). The gallery had just over a month to match the offer, to which Lansdowne said he would contribute £5,000. (At this point, the name of the prospective purchaser—in fact, Peter Arrell Brown Widener—was not disclosed.)[16] The gallery had just £2,283 to spend on the purchase. Once again, the government offered a maximum of £10,000 toward any deficit arising from a public appeal.[17]

15. Brown (1983, 69) estimates the duty payable on the "Colonna Altarpiece" prior to the 1909 tariff reform at $100,000.

16. The London art dealer Arthur Sulley was acting on behalf of the unknown buyer.

17. By now, the formula was familiar to those concerned. Later that year, Robert Witt (1911, 22) published a polemical little book entitled *The Nation and Its Art Treasures* in which he observed that "the public not unnaturally looks for a lead to the Government. The Government with equal astuteness looks to the public."

However, the difficulties faced by the National Gallery trustees were even more intractable on this occasion than they had been in the case of *Christina*. Lord Lansdowne himself had been a member of the National Gallery board since 1894, and the trustees could hardly mount a public appeal that would have the effect of directly enriching one of their own number. The crux of the matter was the perception that not only had Lansdowne failed to recognize his public obligations as a trustee but also the entire system of appointing trustees was thereby discredited (Fry 1911b; MacColl 1912). The sale of *The Mill* stimulated demands for both a diminution of aristocratic control over the national collection and an increased acknowledgment of the public interest in patrician property—demands which, in turn, echoed the call for a reduction of patrician privilege in Parliament. As leader of the Unionist peers in the House of Lords, Lansdowne was also at the center of the constitutional debate that dominated British parliamentary politics during the years 1909–11, and which reached its climax with the passing of the Parliament bill to restrict the power of the lords in the summer of 1911.[18] Lansdowne's actions as a trustee of the National Gallery and as an heir to a famous art collection both intersected with and instantiated the parliamentary battle over the privileges and responsibilities of the peerage.

The Mill was put on show in the National Gallery from 6 to 31 March, during which time it was seen by an estimated 11,000 people.[19] As an attempt to attract support for its purchase—although there was no direct appeal for funds—the display was a failure.[20] The loan of *The Mill* created a spectacle of a work of art whose fame now depended as much on its price as on its aesthetic quality or significance in art history. In effect, the trustees had invited the market into the museum, with no apparent purpose other than to publicize a work of art which was now so expensive that its retention in Britain appeared highly

18. The Parliament Act of 1911 limited the power of the House of Lords to only a temporary veto on bills passed by the House of Commons.

19. It was insured for £100,000 by London art dealer Thomas Agnew & Sons. This information and other practical arrangements concerning the loan are given in a letter from Lockett Agnew to Sir Charles Holroyd, dated 6 March 1911 (National Gallery Archive, London).

20. The London correspondent of the *Nation* satirized the gallery's attempt to convince the public of "the urgent need of raising one hundred thousand pounds . . . , and so save it for the nation before it has fallen into the rapacious grasp of the inconsiderate American who has offered to buy it at the price" (*Nation* 1911b, 352).

unlikely.[21] At the end of the month, the trustees' option on the painting expired, and the painting was sold to Mr. Widener.

Why was *Christina of Denmark* "saved" in 1909 and *The Mill* "lost" in 1911? Was the national claim on *Christina* somehow more plausible than the assertion of the British interest in *The Mill*? In 1911 there were already eighteen works attributed to Rembrandt in the National Gallery, London (but no landscape painting on the scale of *The Mill*), compared with just two Holbeins.[22] Meanwhile, eleven portraits by Holbein were exported from British collections between (roughly) 1885 and 1910, compared with over fifty paintings by Rembrandt (National Gallery 1915). The prevalence of paintings by Rembrandt in both private collections and in the National Gallery attests to the enduring taste for seventeenth-century Dutch paintings among British collectors, as well as to a ready supply on the art market.

The Mill had been brought to Great Britain in 1793, as part of the first wave of pictures from the celebrated collection of Philippe-Egalité, Duc d'Orléans.[23] As such, it was already inscribed in a narrative of dispersal and recovery, for the Orléans sales signaled the fragmentation of one of the greatest collections of paintings ever formed, at the same time as they reinvigorated the collections of the British aristocracy and gentry.[24] And as part of the "Orléans Gallery," *The Mill* achieved immediate fame. The painting was bought at the Orléans sale for £500 by William Smith, a Norwich politician and a friend of J. M. W. Turner. Smith subsequently sold it to the third marquis of Lansdowne some time before 1824. The reputation of the painting was further reinforced

21. Henceforth the trustees were more cautious about displaying works of art that were for sale in the public rooms of the gallery. Later that year, the campaign to raise funds to purchase *The Adoration of the Kings* by Jan Gossaert was organized very differently: the trustees asked the National Art-Collections Fund "to collect donations" by private appeal only, and access to view the painting in a private room of the gallery was restricted "to any person bearing the card of a member of the Fund Committee."

22. *The Ambassadors* (1533) by Holbein was bought from the fifth earl of Radnor in 1890. Contemporary critics compared it unfavorably with *Christina of Denmark* (National Art-Collections Fund 1910, 34).

23. In 1792, the picture dealer and agent Thomas Moore Slade had bought the German, Dutch, and Flemish pictures in the Orléans collection for 350,000 livres. The following year, they were exhibited for sale at 125 Pall Mall, the former home of the Royal Academy, which was immediately dubbed "the Orléans Gallery."

24. The Orléans dispersal was typically described in Great Britain as the single greatest opportunity since the Restoration to recover works of art sold from and since the dispersal of the collection of Charles I (Buchanan 1824; Waagen 1838).

by its exhibition at the British Institution in 1806[25] and again in 1815. Later in the nineteenth century, *The Mill* was shown in the Royal Academy Winter Exhibitions of Old Masters in 1878 and 1888. Meanwhile, the painting had become further embedded in the national artistic consciousness that exceeded the walls of the National Gallery, through the copies that were made from it, paintings that related to it or were inspired by it, and its publication as a print (Schneider 1990). Therefore, it was not just the apparent fame of *The Mill* throughout the nineteenth century that was effectively and plausibly invoked by those who deplored its export in 1911: through its profound impact on both Constable and Turner, it had, in effect, been assimilated into an English landscape tradition (Leslie 1845; Burnet 1852).

My contention is that the "loss" of *The Mill* was no more explicable in terms of its inherent qualities or its significance in art history, than was the "saving" of *Christina of Denmark*. In both cases, although the arguments for retention were—ostensibly—aesthetic and cultural, the outcome was determined by financial and political factors. In 1909, it was an unexpected donation of £40,000 that secured the purchase of *Christina of Denmark*, but in 1911, it was politically impossible even to organize an appeal for *The Mill*, let alone to raise the money required. Both episodes had exposed the unwillingness of aristocratic vendors to resist the temptations of the transatlantic art market, along with the impotence of the National Gallery trustees as guardians of the national patrimony.

The National Gallery and Its Critics

In the British press, criticism of the National Gallery resonated beyond the circumstances of the sale of *The Mill*. The episode invoked complaints about the trustees that echoed the broader demand in the country and in Parliament that the ownership of land should no longer confer political privilege without constraint. Indeed, the events of 1911 staged the climax of a rhetorical attack on the gallery that had been gathering force throughout the 1900s. The assault was led by a loose coalition of journalists and critics, including Claude Phillips in the *Daily Telegraph*, Roger Fry in the *Athenaeum* and later the *Burlington*

25. In 1806, it was also selected as one of the loan paintings from which the artists could make copies.

Magazine, D. S. MacColl in the *Saturday Review*, and Charles Holmes in the *Burlington Magazine*, all of whom had been involved (to some degree) in the founding of the National Art-Collections Fund (NA-CF) in 1903. Two years later, in 1905, D. S. MacColl had argued that three of his colleagues on the founding executive committee of the NA-CF—Sidney Colvin, Claude Phillips, and Roger Fry—were among the best qualified candidates for the directorship of the National Gallery, which had become vacant the previous year. It was a direct assertion of the superior expertise and authority of the voluntary NA-CF, in contrast to the collective timidity and ineptitude evinced by the official guardians of the national collection by, for example, their (mal)administration of the Chantrey Bequest, the acquisition of the Northampton "Dürer" in 1904, and the trustees' failure to appoint a director from 1904 to 1906. Holmes (1906, 226) thus expressed the anxiety of his friends and colleagues in the NA-CF and the *Burlington Magazine* when he wrote, "The Trustees represent what may be termed hereditary patronage. They have political and social influence; they represent great private accumulations of art treasures; and they directly control the National Gallery." The attack was later renewed by MacColl (1912, 27), who described the board of trustees as being "of the old-fashioned type, consisting of territorial magnates and men of wealth of leading position in public affairs, all of them in some degree interested in art, and possessed of art collections, inherited or acquired."

Such criticisms were an attack on the hegemony of the trustees, rather than on the institution itself. By attacking the management of the National Gallery, Holmes and MacColl were seeking to shift what Gordon Fyfe (1996, 218) calls the "balance of power within the cultural state"—that is, they employed the rhetoric of disapproval to press their influence on the management of the gallery, which they regarded as incompetent and misguided. The result was what Fyfe describes as "an aesthetic partnership between the state, the professional class and a declining aristocracy."

Of all the trustees' critics, none was more outspoken or occupied a more ambivalent position as scholar, critic, and occasional dealer than Roger Fry. In 1905, Fry's candidacy for the directorship of the National Gallery in London had failed as a result of the vacillation of the trustees; by the time he was eventually offered the position, he had already accepted the post of curator of paintings at the Metropolitan Museum, New York, where J. Pierpont Morgan was president of the board. Now, in 1911, having returned from New York the previous year, Fry had taken over as editor of the *Burlington Magazine*, while continuing to advise and act as agent for American collectors such as Morgan, Frick, and John Graver Johnson. Commenting on the passing of Rembrandt's *Mill*, Fry (1911b) applauded the acquisitive ambitions of American collectors, "who were prepared to devote a considerable portion of [their] wealth to the acquisition of certain objects of historical and artistic interest which the country itself cannot produce or acquire in any other way." Yet in his private letters, Fry described his continuing freelance activities on behalf of American collectors as "rather tiresome and hateful work" (Sutton 1972, 330). Fry himself had been criticized by friends and colleagues when he first went to work in New York (Woolf 1940, 106). Now he was once again exasperated by the collective timidity of the trustees of the National Gallery: "The time has come when it is no longer possible to conceal the deep indignation of those who have the interests of our National Collections at heart. . . . it is now our duty to state plainly that the Trustees of the National Gallery have, as a body, conspicuously failed in the trust which has been placed upon them" (Fry 1911a, 3).

Fry was similarly critical of Lord Lansdowne himself: "No doubt it may be urged that *The Mill* belongs to Lord Lansdowne and he has a perfect right to dispose of it as seems good to himself, but in point of fact the great consideration and esteem, the actual predominance in social and political life that is accorded to men in Lord Lansdowne's position is based on a traditional understanding that they recognize a corresponding obligation to the public" (3). Fry's point was that the nation had a legitimate interest in the disposition of privately owned works of art and that private owners had public responsibilities, as well as legal rights—whether or not they were trustees of the National Gallery. Certainly, Lansdowne's singular position as a trustee heightened the uproar provoked by the sale of *The Mill*, but it was not the cause of it. For, as the American weekly magazine the *Nation* (1911a) commented, with some skepticism: "Legally the noble lord's property, the threatened Rembrandt is characterized as being a national treasure of which its owner ought to regard himself as merely the steward."

However incredible it appeared to the American mind, it was precisely this requirement for self-restraint over the disposition of inherited property that had underpinned the English estates system for the past two hundred years and was now straining under the pressures of changing economic and social circumstances of landowning families. One response to those pressures—in particular, the effects of the chronic agricultural depression that had already lasted for over ten years, and which threatened the viability of many estates as a result of the concomitant fall in the value of rents—was the Settled Land Act of 1882. The act was an acknowledgment that the old, inflexible system of property could no longer serve the interests of landowners—or, by implication, the nation. It was an enabling measure: Henceforth a tenant for life could apply to the Court of Chancery for consent to sell land and chattels, provided the proceeds remained under settled property.[26] The Settled Land Act of 1882 provided the means to an end; it did not, in itself, cause the disposal of land or heirloom property. However, the new freedom that it offered to owners signaled a decline in both the usefulness and the authority of land and, by implication, in the aristocratic virtues of stability and disinterestedness that had been manifest in the retention of property.

What did this mean with respect to works of art? How many paintings, sculptures, and other objects were counted as heirlooms as opposed to unfettered chattels and thus were rendered alienable for the first time under the act? It is impossible to quantify just how many collections were subject to restrictions prior to 1882, and, in any case, quantification would obscure the complex and dynamic relationship between the framework of law and the interests of families. Evidence of prevailing attitudes to property derives from the restrictions that families imposed on themselves, as well as the extent to which they took recourse to legal sanctions. Thus, the doctrine of estates that subjected an heir to the control of trustees with regard to the disposition of "his" property also demanded adherence to the practice of economic primogeniture—for without the dynastic discipline of primogeniture, the individual could not be locked into a system of planned and predictable settlement.

26. Section 37 of the act states: "(1) Where personal chattels are settled on trust so as to devolve with land until a tenant in tail by purchase is born or attains the age of twenty one years, or so as otherwise to vest in some person becoming entitled to an estate of freehold of inheritance in the land, a tenant for life of the land may sell the chattels or any of them. (2) The money arising by the sale shall be capital money arising under this Act, and shall be paid, invested or applied, and otherwise dealt with in like manner in all respects as by this Act directed with respect to other capital money arising under this Act, or may be invested in the purchase of other chattels of the same or any other nature, which, when purchased, shall be settled and held on the same trusts, and shall devolve in the same manner as the chattels sold. (3) A sale or purchase under this section shall not be made without an order of the Court."

If the Settled Land Act of 1882 can be read as an assault on the ideology of the English estates system, then the Finance Act of 1894 was widely regarded at the time as a fiscal offensive against the landed interest. In short, the Finance Act aimed at wholesale reform of the complicated system of inheritance tax that had grown up over the previous one hundred years, and it introduced the first graduated taxation on death: a new estate duty was introduced on all property—real and personal, settled and unsettled—starting at 1 percent on an estate valued at £100, and rising to 8 percent on an estate worth more than £1 million. The quantifiable effects of the 1894 budget are still debated among economists: although the incidence of taxation inevitably varied greatly, the 1894 budget provided the landed interest with a pretext for citing fiscal pressure to justify the disposal of property that had been facilitated by the Settled Land Act of 1882.

Curzon Committee: A Response to the Crisis

It was against this backdrop of social, legal, and fiscal change—as well as in response to the trauma of the sale of *The Mill*—that the National Gallery trustees at last took action to address the art export crisis. In the English tradition, they appointed a Committee of Enquiry (to which I referred at the beginning of this essay), chaired by Lord Curzon,[27] to investigate and recommend a solution to the Old Masters problem.

Curzon's appointment to the National Gallery board had been approved by the Treasury in April 1911; by December, he established the "Curzon Committee" of inquiry "Into the Retention of Important Pictures in This Country and Other Matters Connected with the National Collections."[28] The formation of the committee was a demonstration of the active formation of Fyfe's aesthetic partnership between the gallery trustees and their erstwhile critics: Robert Witt, the founding secretary of the National Art-Collections Fund, was appointed honorary secre-

27. George Nathaniel Curzon (1859–1925) was viceroy of India from 1898 to 1905. On his return from India he was created earl Curzon of Kedleston (and marquess of Curzon in 1921) and was appointed chancellor of Oxford University. He served in successive Conservative administrations and was appointed foreign secretary in 1919.

28. Members of the committee were the earl Curzon of Kedleston (chairman), Sir Edgar Vincent and Mr. R. H. Benson (trustees), and Sir Charles Holroyd (director of the National Gallery). Robert C. Witt, founding secretary of the National Art-Collections Fund, acted as honorary secretary.

tary, and for six days in December 1911, the committee heard evidence from witnesses, including Fry, MacColl, and Holmes.

Curzon's achievement was to construct a debate in terms that coalesced the interests of owners, dealers, and the national collection. The keystone of consensus was a robust defense of private property, in return for which owners would be expected to acknowledge a legitimate public interest in the disposal of their possessions. The report objected strongly to any interference with, or modification to, the rights of property and recommended that the cooperation of owners be encouraged, rather than enforced: "To place upon owners the burden of very heavy taxation and then to deprive them of what are in many cases the sole means of meeting it would be almost a refinement of cruelty . . . at the very moment when [the government] ought to conciliate the sympathy and to secure the co-operation of the class to whom these masterpieces belong" (National Gallery 1915, 37). The practical and administrative difficulties encountered by the Italian authorities in their efforts to enforce proscription (under the Pacca Edict of 1820) were cited as evidence to support the principle of a voluntary system in Great Britain. Any attempt at proscription in Great Britain would be counterproductive because it would "arouse a widespread antagonism and defeat the object in view" (19).

The committee assumed that the property rights of the individual were best served by the preservation of free and unfettered trade and that any constraint on the London art market would be objectionable in principle, as well as damaging to the economy. Curzon also recognized that "if the ancestors of a nobleman in England purchased his masterpiece abroad two centuries or less ago, it is difficult to contend that the picture has now become so English that the law can be legitimately invoked to prevent it from ever going abroad again" (11). It was a view echoed elsewhere by Witt (1911, 13): "We are but being treated as we treated the Continent during the seventeenth, eighteenth and early nineteenth centuries. Any feeling of resentment is wholly out of place."

Curzon diagnosed the primary cause of the Old Masters problem as financial: if only sufficient funds were made available by government, then important works of art could and would be saved. The report argued that if it is unacceptable and impractical to prevent export by force of law, then the government must "provide the means—the existing resources having been shown to be inadequate for the purpose" (National Gallery 1915, 10). The Curzon report recommended that the annual grant to the National Gallery be increased from £5,000 to £25,000 "and that the Trustees be not required to return any unspent balance at the end of the year" (37). In addition, the custom of voting individual special grants for the purchase of singular masterpieces should be continued. The question then arose: What should be the means of raising the necessary additional revenue?

An export duty on the sale of works of art was rejected on the grounds that it would be very difficult to determine what was—and what was not—a work of art. Administrative problems were also envisaged when the committee considered an ad valorem stamp duty on sales of works of art: it would be impracticable to apply such a tax to private sales which, by their nature, were not publicly recorded, but it could be applied to public auctions. Another proposal was that the death duties payable on works of art should be earmarked for acquisitions. Curzon believed that the idea would be acceptable in principle, but that, in practice, it could be difficult to separate the value of works of art from the rest of an estate. However, the committee argued that such a division should not prove impossible, or else some formula for the calculation of the value of art could be agreed. Curzon thus recommended a combination of two new hypothecated taxes: a tax on the sale of works of art at public auction, and the allocation of death duties on works of art to the purchase of pictures for the national collection. Curzon also advocated a proactive and systematic acquisitions policy whereby the gallery would draw up a list of desiderata and then approach owners privately with a request of first refusal should they decide to sell a particular work. In case patriotism alone did not provide an adequate incentive, the committee suggested that the government should offer certain privileges or concessions in return—for example, the proceeds of such a sale should be exempt from the calculation of estate duties on the death of the vendor.

A succession of delays, followed by the outbreak of war, prevented the publication of the Curzon report until 1915. By then, the attention of the gallery and the nation had turned elsewhere. The effect of the Curzon report was thus slow-burning; however, a system of tax concessions on private treaty sales of works of art to national institutions was introduced in the 1921 Finance Act, and the following year the government agreed to support the purchase of works of art on a list of desiderata submitted by the National Gallery, known as the Paramount List of 1922. Both of these measures proved problematic in practice, and Great Britain remained a valuable source of supply of Old Masters in the interwar years. The lasting legacy of the Curzon committee was philosophical and rhetorical; its immediate political impact was negligible, but it remains the locus classicus of the British position on export controls (and was a defining influence on the Waverley Report of 1952, which, eventually, formulated a regulatory system). Prompted by the crisis of *The Mill*, the report was above all an exercise in reconciliation: between the rights of private owners with the interests of the national collections, between the reality of government and the ambitions of the National Gallery, between the existing trustees of the gallery and those who sought reform, and between an eighteenth-century ideology of property and the demands for reform and enfranchisement on the eve of the First World War.

Epilogue

What, finally, have been the respective histories of *Christina of Denmark* and *The Mill* since their dramatic sales some ninety years ago? *Christina* has been joined by a third Holbein in the National Gallery, London: *A Lady with a Squirrel and a Starling* (ca. 1526–28), acquired from the collection of the marquis of Cholmondeley in 1993. The circumstances of this acquisition—in particular, the decision of the marquis to consign the painting to auction without giving the gallery prior notice and the price of £10 million—aroused an outcry that would have been familiar to Henry James and was entirely reminiscent of the events of 1909. Notwithstanding the panoply of measures designed to protect the national patrimony that are now in place in Great Britain, the narrative of heritage is still continuously and necessarily reinvigorated through crises of dispersal and acquisition.

Meanwhile, after 1911, for some thirty years *The Mill* was the central focus of the picture gallery at Lynnewood Hall, a Philadelphia estate built by Peter Widener. In 1942 it entered the National Gallery of Art, Washington, D.C., as part of the Widener collection given by his son, Joseph, in accordance with his father's wishes.[29] Today the catalog of

29. The canvas has been cleaned and conserved twice since 1911: first in Berlin, immediately after its sale and prior to being transported to the United States of America, and then in Washington between 1977 and 1979. Both occasions provoked controversy regarding the issue of its attribution, and each time, the majority of scholars reaffirmed its status as autograph Rembrandt (Wheelock 1995).

the National Gallery of Art (1998) describes *The Mill* as "one of those few paintings that are significant not only because they are beautiful but because they have profoundly influenced the history of taste." The history of *The Mill* as part of "important eighteenth- and nineteenth-century collections" is explicitly invoked in order to assert its status within the national collection of the United States of America, just as it was once employed in the argument for its retention in England.[30] The outcry over its sale in 1911 is now an episode in a history of ownership that reinforces its value within the triumphant discourse of the American museum.

References

Baker, Christopher, and Tom Henry. 1995. *National Gallery Complete Illustrated Catalogue*. London: National Gallery Publications.

Baldwin Brown, G. 1905. *The Care of Ancient Monuments*. Cambridge: Cambridge University Press.

Bätschmann, Oskar, and Peter Griener. 1997. *Hans Holbein*. London: Reaktion Books.

Brown, David Alan. 1983. *Raphael and America*. Washington, D.C.: National Gallery of Art.

Buchanan, William. 1824. *Memoirs of Painting*. 2 vols. London.

Burnet, John. 1852. *Turner and His Works*. London: Bogue.

Chernow, Ron. 1990. *The House of Morgan: An American Banking Dynasty and the Rise of Modern Finance*. New York: Simon & Schuster.

Concise Dictionary of National Biography. 1992. Oxford: Oxford University Press.

Duncan, Carol, and Alan Wallach. 1980. The Universal Survey Museum. *Art History* (December) 3:447–69.

Edel, Leon. 1949. *The Complete Plays of Henry James*. London: Rupert-Hart Davis.

Edel, Leon, and Lyall H. Powers. 1987. *The Complete Notebooks of Henry James*. New York: Oxford University Press.

Fry, Roger. 1911a. Rembrandt's Mill. *Burlington Magazine* 19.97:3–4.

———. 1911b. The Passing of Rembrandt's Mill. *Burlington Magazine* 19.98:66.

Fyfe, Gordon. 1996. A Trojan Horse at the Tate. In *Theorizing Museums,* edited by Susan MacDonald and Gordon Fyfe. Oxford: Blackwell.

Holmes, Charles. 1906. The Lesson of the Rokeby Velasquez. *Burlington Magazine* 8.34:225–28.

———. 1909. Unanswered Questions about the Norfolk Holbein. *Burlington Mag-*

30. The assimilation of *The Mill* into the Washington collection is thus a reminder that the National Gallery, London, and the National Gallery of Art, Washington, are more accurately understood as "universal survey museums," reflecting the desire of the nation-states of Great Britain and the United States to demonstrate their allegiance to the highest, internationally recognized, cultural values (Duncan and Wallach 1980).

azine 15.75:135–37.

Hopkins Winner, Viola. 1970. *Henry James and the Visual Arts*. Charlottesville: University Press of Virginia.

Leslie, Charles Robert. 1845. *Memoirs of the Life of John Constable, Esq.RA: Composed Chiefly of His Letters*. 2d ed. London: Longman, Brown, Green, and Longmans.

MacColl, D. S. 1912. The National Gallery—Its Problems, Resources, Administration. *Nineteenth Century and After* (January): 24–39.

Nation. 1911a. Untitled. 92.2385:257.

———. 1911b. At the National Gallery, London March 25. 92.2388:351–52.

National Art-Collections Fund. 1910. *Sixth Annual Report, 1909*. London: National Art-Collections Fund.

National Gallery. 1908. *Minutes of Meeting of the National Gallery Board, 10 March*. Vol. 7. London: National Gallery Archive.

———. 1915. *Report of an Enquiry into the Retention of Important Pictures in This Country and Other Matters Connected with the National Collections*. Cmmd Paper 7878. London: His Majesty's Stationery Office.

National Gallery of Art. 1998. Washington, D.C. Website: http://www.nga.gov/home/htm

New York Times. 1909a. Call Holbein Option Trick. 9 May, 4.

———. 1909b. England Not Likely to Save the Holbein. 16 May, pt. 3, 2–6.

Saarinen, Aline B. 1959. *The Proud Possessors*. London: Wiedenfeld & Nicolson.

Schneider, Cynthia P. 1990. *Rembrandt's Landscapes*. New Haven, Conn.: Yale University Press.

Sutton, Denys. 1972. *Letters of Roger Fry*. London: Chatto & Windus.

Tintner, Adeline. 1981. Henry James's *The Outcry* and the Art Drain of 1908–09. *Apollo* 93.228:110–12.

Waagen, Gustav. 1838. *Works of Art and Artists in England*. London: J. Murray.

Wheelock, Arthur, Jr. 1995. *Dutch Paintings of the Seventeenth Century*. Washington, D. C.: National Gallery of Art.

Witt, Robert. 1911. *The Nation and Its Art Treasures*. London: William Heinemann.

Woolf, Virginia. 1940. *Roger Fry: A Biography*. Oxford: Blackwell.

International Commerce in the Fine Arts and American Political Economy, 1789–1913

William J. Barber

For roughly 80 percent of the first century and a quarter of the nation's existence, the American federal government imposed tariff duties on imported works of art. Among economists, this phenomenon has passed largely unremarked. The careful reader of such standard works as F. W. Taussig's *Tariff History of the United States* (1914) and Edward Stanwood's *American Tariff Controversies in the Nineteenth Century* (1903) might well be excused for being unaware of it: neither of these studies contains a single index reference to the tariff on art.[1]

It is small wonder that this topic should have been treated so dismissively by economic historians. By comparison, say, with iron and steel producers or with the manufacturers of woolen goods, those interested in art markets—whether as buyers or sellers—had little political leverage and were remote from the main action. In addition, the dollars Americans spent on artworks from abroad were trivial in the nation's aggregate import bill, and even when art duties were stiff their contribution to total customs revenues was slight.

There was an asymmetry here. The treatment of imported art may have counted for little in the larger story of tariff-making in the United

1. Taussig, it should be noted, was well acquainted with the pertinent facts. In his appearance before the Ways and Means Committee of the House of Representatives in 1908, the following exchange was recorded:

Mr. Longworth: You favor the abolishing of the duties on objects of art?

Mr. Taussig: Yes; I do.

Mr. Longworth: Would you suggest a definition of art which would enable us to accomplish that purpose?

Mr. Taussig: I am sorry to say I can not; no. I wish I could. (Taussig 1908, 7731)

States. Within the arts community, however, this topic took on high significance; indeed, it came to be regarded as a litmus test of the government's posture toward the nation's cultural life. To critics of the tariff on art, the central issues could be starkly posed: Would policy be controlled by Philistines who regarded art as a luxury enjoyed by the rich—and thus compellingly attractive for taxation? Or would policy be guided by the enlightened who were convinced that any impediment to the free importation of art compromised the national culture? The United States was not the only country to tax artworks created beyond its borders. From 1660 until well into the eighteenth century, England did this (see Ormrod 1998, 167–86). By the nineteenth century, the United States stood alone among Western countries in its systematic indulgence in a practice deemed by many to be "uncivilized."

Arguments before the Tariff Commission of 1882

Controversy over the art duties had a bite to it in the 1880s. But the dutiability of art did not begin then: it had, in fact, dated from the founding of the republic. In antebellum America, few saw anything improper about taxing imported art objects. The federal government's ability to pay its bills was overwhelmingly dependent on tariff receipts, and there appeared to be no persuasive reason why any category of imports for private use should be accorded tax immunity altogether. Even so, imported art enjoyed a number of special privileges at the customhouse. The ad valorem rate of duty on works of art was consistently below that charged on dutiable imports overall. It was striking as well that the art duties were waived completely in seasons when the Treasury's accounts were in surplus. (Thus, the duty was zero from 1832 to 1841 and from 1846 to 1861.) In addition, beginning in 1816, the imports by "any society incorporated for philosophical or literary purposes and for the encouragement of the fine arts" were placed on the free list. This exemption for "nonprofit" institutions was to become a permanent feature of the tariff codes, even though it was to be a long time before its impact on the volume of imports would become quantitatively significant. A further exemption was added in the Tariff Act of 1842: the "productions of American artists residing abroad" were accorded free entry. This feature of tariff legislation was also to continue. (See table 1.)

Table 1 Highlights of Official Treatments of Imported Paintings and Sculpture, 1789–1865

Year	Duty on Paintings and Statuary (ad valorem) (%)	Approximate Average Rate on Dutiable Imports (ad valorem) (%)	Exemptions in Art Duties	Context of Change
1789	5			
1790	10			A general increase in duties was prompted by revenue requirements.
1800	12.5			Upward revisions were made to "defray expenses in relation to the Barbary States."
1804	15			
1812	30			Duties were doubled to finance the war with Britain.
1816	15	20	Imports of "any society incorporated for philosophical or literary purposes or for the encouragement of the fine arts" were placed on the free list.	General postwar reductions in rates were made.
1824	15	38.5		Protectionist pressures generated advances in duties, overall, but duties on imported art were not changed.
1828	15	41.2		
1832	0	29.8	All paintings and sculpture were placed on the free list.	Though the Tariff Act of 1832 remained protectionist in spirit, the imposition of low duties (or none at all) on goods not produced in the U.S. (such as tea and coffee) reduced the overall average rate.

Table 1 (continued)

Year	Duty on Paintings and Statuary (ad valorem) (%)	Approximate Average Rate on Dutiable Imports (ad valorem) (%)	Exemptions in Art Duties	Context of Change
1841–42	20	36.6	Though art duties were reimposed, the "productions of American artists residing abroad" were added to the free list, along with imports of nonprofit cultural institutions. Indecent and obscene paintings and prints were prohibited.	The overall increase in rates was driven by the needs of an empty Treasury.
1846	0	25.5	All paintings and statuary entered free when imported as an object of taste and not of merchandise.	Protectionism was moderated with a general reduction in duties.
1857	0	20.3	Status quo was maintained.	A general reduction in duties was justified by redundant revenues.
1861	10	19.1	The usual exemptions were continued.	The requirements of the Civil War finance elevated overall rates.
1862–63	10	42.8		

Source: Data on duties are drawn from DeForest 1908, 7213, 7215.

The economic environment generated by the Civil War radically altered the character of discourse on tariff policy in general and on the art duties in particular. As a matter of fiscal necessity, wartime tariff rates had risen to record-setting heights. Meanwhile, a fair number of domestic producers of goods subject to high duties learned agreeably how the protective effects of this policy augmented their profits. In their view, this experience seemed to validate the arguments for a protective system advanced by Henry C. Carey (1793–1879) in the 1840s, which for the rest of his life he had promoted vigorously as the model for an "American system." It was now apparent that the war had produced a well-heeled interest group that understood its stake in a regime of high tariffs and was willing to flex political muscle to preserve it.[2] The income redistribution produced by wartime policies had a further implication: it fed buying by the nouveaux-riches that markedly expanded the importation of dutiable art. (See table 2.)

Discussion of tariff-making—both in principle and in practice—entered a new phase in 1882 with the appointment of a Tariff Commission of seven so-called civilian experts who were charged to review tariff policies and to recommend appropriate changes. President Chester A. Arthur had created this body, hoping that the commission's report would frame the agenda for future legislation and constrain the congressional logrolling that typically accompanied tariff-making. The commission could not be faulted for lack of thoroughness in the way it went about its business. Over a span of five months, it heard testimony in various parts of the country, and its proceedings (Tariff Commissioners 1882), published in two volumes, came to more than 2,600 pages. Though the commissioners were thought to be protectionist in their sympathies, they provided a platform from which a diverse range of views was articulated.

With respect to the overall strategy that should inform tariff policy, the commission heard spokesmen for positions that were polar opposites. William Graham Sumner (1882), the social Darwinist from Yale,

2. Though wartime economic policies won important converts to Careyite doctrine within the business community, there was also an important defection. David A. Wells had originally been a Carey disciple, but after service as Commissioner for the Revenue from 1866 to 1868, he reversed direction. His experience in that post convinced him that protection produced unseemly and unwarranted profits and that its continuation would lock in inefficiencies in American industry and invite corruption in the political process. Thereafter, Wells was a militant crusader for free trade.

Table 2 Imports of Artworks (Fiscal Years Ending 30 June), 1872–83

Year	Total ($000)	Free List ($000)	Dutiable ($000)	Dutiable (% of Total)	Rate of Duty (%)
1872	1,209	261	948	78	
1873	1,589	237	1,352	85	
1874	1,437	267	1,170	81	
1875	1,448	295	1,153	80	
1876	1,944	308	1,636	84	
1877	1,227	228	999	81	10
1878	968	174	794	82	
1879	1,269	194	1,075	85	
1880	2,320	215	2,105	91	
1881	2,547	325	2,222	87	
1882	3,038	237	2,801	92	
1883[a]	3,404	275	3,129	92	

[a]The Tariff Act of 1883, which raised the tariff on dutiable art to 30 percent, became law on 3 March 1883.
Source: *Statistical Abstracts of the United States,* 1872–83.

made a forceful statement in support of free trade—or, more strictly speaking, the case for a revenue tariff only, from which all protectionist elements would be purged. Sumner presented himself as "a professional student of political economy" who felt under obligation to expose the fallacy in doctrines that had been placed before the commission. In particular, he denounced the protectionist position as based on "superstition . . . more wild than feti[s]hism or astrology." He characterized the protected industries as "parasites on the naturally strong industries." The essence of the matter, as he saw it, was that protective tariffs "interfere[d], on behalf of certain persons, with the conditions of production and the relations of competition." Sumner received a respectful, if skeptical, reception. As one of the commissioners remarked, "You have announced yourself as a political economist, as a theorist," whereas members of the commission were "practical men with a practical object in view" (Sumner 1882, 2314, 2315, 2319, 2327).[3]

3. A future president of the United States, Woodrow Wilson (then a struggling attorney in Atlanta), also endorsed the elimination of protective duties. The bankruptcy of that policy, he maintained, was apparent because "infant industries were at first protected by very small duties, but, instead of growing into manhood and strength, they have gone into weaker decrepitude. . . . I maintain that manufacturers are made into better manufacturers whenever they are thrown upon their own resources and left to the natural competition of trade" (Wilson 1882, 1296).

Sumner's position was brought under direct attack in testimony presented by Cyrus Elder, a Pennsylvania attorney and sometime secretary of the Industrial League. Sumner's views, Elder (1882, 2355) observed,

> seem to have attracted some consideration, or claim to consideration, from the fact that they are supposed to be delivered by a man of science, who is thoroughly familiar with the science known as "political economy," as taught in our schools and colleges. He has given you what is now known and recognized as English political economy. He has stated certain abstract propositions in logical form, but they are not based on facts; they are the results of the deductive method of investigation.

In Elder's view, it was unfortunate in the extreme that these "unsound and un-American theories" dominated teaching in most of the nation's colleges. Students should instead be educated in American political economy, as proclaimed in the writings of Henry C. Carey. Elder was unstinting in his admiration for Carey, arguing that

> before his time, outside of his writings, this so-called science was in chaotic condition. The principal maxims of the political economist, upon which the so-called science rests, apart from free trade, are the doctrines of the theory of population and the doctrine of rent. These doctrines assume that the world is out of tune and out of harmony. . . . These two doctrines have been conclusively and absolutely refuted; and Mr. Carey has done great service to humanity by his efforts in this direction. . . . It gave a Christian basis to the great system of American political economy. (2356)

When the commission shifted its focus from grand designs for tariff policy to the particulars of specific markets, the arts had low priority. But the matter of imported works of art was far from being overlooked. The president of the American-Belgian Chamber of Commerce—an organization that had recently sponsored an exhibition of Belgian works of art in Philadelphia (a project that had not lived up to expectations)—submitted a statement appealing for elimination of art duties and deploring that the American people were "certainly the poorest in the world as far as artistic wealth is concerned." The customhouse, he maintained, bore a heavy responsibility for that state of affairs:

> Not only do the duties increase the cost of paintings and statues, but their shipping is thereby surrounded by difficulties; they encourage fraud and plagiarism; they disgust and discourage the dealers, who would often furnish the public and the American artists opportunities to admire the masterpieces of the different schools, if they did not fear the whims of the custom-house officer, his ignorance, his often irreparable carelessness in opening boxes. (Sève 1882, 2239)

Other grievances were aired. A spokesman for the Brooklyn Revenue Reform Club argued that "duties might justifiably be remitted from all works of art, on account of their beneficial influence upon taste and manners." But it was especially important that they be removed from "the cheaper class of productions" on grounds that these were the only works of art that the poor could afford. He complained as well about the "unjust discrimination" involved in taxing copies of statuary at rates substantially higher than those levied on originals. This arrangement favored the rich, "for it is only the very wealthy who can afford to buy original works of art, while persons in very moderate circumstances can buy copies, if not burdened with excessive duties" (Shearman 1882, 1542). An importer of statuary also registered a protest about the differential treatment of originals and copies; both, he insisted, were genuine works of art (Viti 1882, 336). And an appraiser at the New York Custom House also championed reform in the law governing statuary, arguing as follows: "Each copy of the hard-metal statue, even when reproduced twenty to fifty times, would be exactly like the first one, and yet we are compelled to pass on the first one as being the original. . . . No expert can tell the difference between the first, second, third or twentieth copy" (Stevens 1882, 527).

The commission was also treated to a vigorous defense of the art duties—including a recommendation that the tariff be raised from the 10 percent rate then prevailing to at least 40 percent. This proposition was advanced by one Thomas Donaldson (1882, 2461), a Philadelphian, who described himself as a picture buyer. Congress, he insisted, had an obligation to "place a duty on foreign art productions that will enable our men and women art-workers to live while they produce true American art and rival or excel the famous workers of the Old World." Given the proper policies, he saw no reason why an indigenous art should not flourish, "for we have as fine skies here and as beautiful women for models as in any country of the world" (2461). This would bring social as well as cultural advantages because "the practice of art has opened new fields of labor for women and for persons physically incapacitated from manual labor" (2464). He diagnosed the core problem as follows: "American art finds its worst enemy in a portion of its own people—people, usually, who are educated to believe that the art productions of their own country are crude and new. It is to be regretted that this class do not die more rapidly than they do" (2464). In light of the prevalence of such attitudes, dealers preferred to import cheap works from Europe, while shunning the creations of local artists. But a major hike in the tariff would turn things around: it would "especially benefit our younger artists, men and women, who cannot now sell their pictures to dealers at any price," and "it would result in putting better foreign pictures on our market, and stop the bringing in of the trash that now comes from Europe and is sold here and placed on our walls" (2461). A tariff of at least 40 percent, Donaldson further maintained, would have no impact on the importation of "high-priced" and "high-class" pictures: "Men who can afford these luxuries are willing to pay for them" (2463).

One group of artists—Americans residing abroad—engaged in a bit of special pleading. Although they were already the beneficiaries of tariff immunity when shipping their works to the United States, they were not satisfied. Existing law required American artists overseas to execute a certificate before an American consul to validate that the work in question was their own. There was a fee for this service—$2.50 for the certificate and a further $2.50 was required for an invoice. The petitioners (who did not identify themselves) held these charges to be "excessive and exorbitant" and urged that they be removed. In addition, they noted that "under present law an artist is obliged to pay a duty of 35 percent on the value of his frame, which effectively prevents him from sending his picture to America framed. This we consider not only detrimental to his artistic interests, but injurious to the cause of art" (Petition of American Artists 1882).

The Report of 1882 and Its Reception

On 4 December 1882, the Tariff Commissioners submitted their report. "It [was] their desire," this document noted, "that their recommendations shall serve no particular party, class, section, or school of political economy" (Tariff Commissioners 1882, 4). While the commissioners were opposed to radical departures from the status quo, they nonetheless were "convinced that a substantial reduction of tariff duties is demanded, not by a mere indiscriminate popular clamor, but by the best conservative opinion of the country, including that which has in former times been most strenuous for the preservation of our national industrial defenses" (5). Accordingly, they recommended reductions in existing rates which, on average, would be "not less than 20 percent" (6). They made clear that this reform should not be a straight across-the-board cut. On this point, the commissioners wrote that they "ha[d] not hesitated to withhold the application of the general rule of reduction in many cases, and in some, though comparatively few, cases to recommend an increase of duties where such increase seemed to be required to preserve the 'scale of justice'" (7). They further noted that they had sought "to make the reduction apply to commodities of necessary general consumption, and to diminish or withhold reduction upon commodities of high cost, requiring more labor, and which being consumed principally by the more wealthy classes could bear higher duties" (7). And they drew attention to two instances in which their recommendations were made quite independently from revenue considerations, but were intended for other purposes. Thus, duties on books should be reduced "in the interests of the diffusion of knowledge" (7). But duties on works of art should be advanced "for the encouragement of original American art" (7). Though his name was not mentioned in this connection, it would appear that the commission had found the argument of Philadelphian Thomas Donaldson to be persuasive.

If President Chester A. Arthur anticipated that the work of a body of "experts" could provide useful discipline to the congressional agenda, he was quickly disabused of that notion. Both houses of Congress approved legislation calling for duties higher than those proposed by the Tariff Commission. Moreover, the report of the joint Conference Committee—which formed the basis for the Tariff Act of 1883—produced a schedule of duties even higher than the ones initially approved separately by the Senate and the House of Representatives. As of 3 March 1883, the new law of the land imposed ad valorem duties of 30 percent on imported works of art. Imports by nonprofit institutions and the works of American artists residing abroad, however, remained on the free list.

The hike in the art duties in the Tariff Act of 1883, combined with the continued provisions for the free entry of works produced by Americans overseas, sparked a firestorm. (For a discussion of this episode, see Boime 1989.) The Italian government registered a protest, drawing particular attention to the differential treatment of artworks created by Italians and by Americans resident in Italy. This feature of American law, it maintained, ran counter to the commercial treaty that the two countries had negotiated in 1871. The French, Belgian, and Austro-Hungarian governments were shortly to follow suit. At home, the *Nation* magazine ("Italy and the Art Tariff" 1883) expressed editorial outrage in 1883, warning that the French might well retaliate "for what they regard as a prohibition in our tariff upon works of art, by excluding Americans from the gratuitous advantages of their Government schools of art, and their works from the awards of the Salon." The Italians could also be expected to take exception to "our national theory that all nations may help our boys, teach them and reward them, but purely gratis—no favors allowed in return." The *Nation* further understood that the Italian government was considering the imposition of a stiff export tax on the works of American artists in Italy.

By March 1884, there were signs that the representations of foreign governments on these matters had stimulated stirrings in Washington. The House of Representatives (1884) then passed a resolution requesting the Arthur administration to release relevant correspondence—which it duly did. Shortly thereafter, the Ways and Means Committee revisited the issue and produced a report, dated 21 April 1884, recommending elimination of discrimination between imported works by Americans and foreigners (*Congressional Record, House* 1884, 4294–95). Its proposed amendment to the 1883 act called for a reduction in the tariff rate from 30 percent to 10 percent, which would be applied uniformly to all imported art: that is, the productions of Americans abroad—as well as imports by schools, universities, and museums—would now be dutiable.

The floor debate in the House of Representatives on the motion introduced by the Ways and Means Committee throws arresting light on the polarization of American opinion with regard to the federal government's relationship to the arts. As one of the chief sponsors of the proposed tariff amendments, Congressman Frank H. Hurd (Democrat of Ohio) spoke eloquently in support of the bill, even though he regarded its provisions as less than ideal. He would much have preferred to have the art duties waived altogether: "It is humiliating that our tariff laws should place restrictions upon foreign art. Art is an educator. It refines, elevates, civilizes. It develops and perfects the tastes of a people. It is at once the evidence and the cause of culture. . . . How short-sighted this policy of art exclusion! It is a blow at beauty" (*Congressional Record, House* 1884, 4296).

Hurd regretted that he had not succeeded in persuading a majority in the Ways and Means Committee to follow his preferred course. But the bill he introduced, though decidedly suboptimal, was still "urgent." It was essential to eliminate the distinction at the customhouse between works by Americans and those by foreigners. As he saw matters:

> American artists abroad, for whose benefit the discrimination was made, are nearly unanimous in their request for its removal. Its continuance is a confession by their Government of their inferiority. It places them in embarrassing relations to foreign artists and governments. . . . It savors of ingratitude for our people to enjoy foreign courtesies, and then thus to effront those from whom they receive them. (4296)

Hurd also drew attention to the Italian government's charge that the discriminatory duties violated the commercial treaty between the two countries. He noted as well that the French government—which had banned imports of American pork since 1881, alleging that they posed health hazards—regarded the art duties as an obstacle to a "satisfactory adjustment of commercial relations." Thus, American farmers were "made seriously to suffer" for their government's handling of French art (4296).

To the most vocal opponents of the proposed bill, neither its implications for protection nor those for revenue particularly mattered. The crucial point for them turned on its impact on income redistribution. As Congressman Poindexter Dunn (Democrat of Arkansas) put it:

> This reduction in taxation is on the luxuries and fine ornaments of the very rich. Not only can the poor not afford those things, but people of average and good fortunes can not. The burdens, galling as they are, that rest upon the great masses of the people are to remain. . . . Tax the salt of the humblest laborers of the land and take off the tax from the one-hundred-thousand-dollar painting and other works of art of the millionaire! Is that justice? Tax the wool hat or the blanket of the toiling millions and take it off the luxuries of the rich? (4296)

Congressman Roger Q. Mills (Democrat of Texas) echoed this theme:

> The necessaries of life in the shape of clothing and food come in under a rate of duty of 100 percent, and you refused to reduce it to 50

> or 60 percent. And at the same time you propose to bring it down on the magnificent paintings which are imported to adorn the parlors of a Gould or a Vanderbilt to 10 percent. . . . What a record we are making to go before the country upon! (4296)

Other members of the House objected because the bill would impose a 10 percent duty on works produced by Americans overseas and on imports destined for nonprofit institutions. In the end, the bill was resoundingly defeated by a vote of 179 to 52.

The issue of tariff discrimination that favored American artists came back on the public agenda in late 1885. In his first State of the Union message, President Grover Cleveland ([1885] 1967) characterized this policy as "odious" and strongly recommended that it be scrapped. Meanwhile, Congressman Perry Belmont (Democrat of New York), who had spoken in favor of the bill that failed in the House in 1884, signaled his willingness to sponsor legislation for this purpose.[4] The *Critic,* a weekly magazine of opinion, took note of these events. The nation was being held hostage, it editorialized, "by the kind of protection to industries which it is the special mission of the state of Pennsylvania to champion" (Editorial 1885, 289). In the case of the arts, tariffs worked perversely and were better calculated to destroy than to protect. "The sapient legislator," it observed, "has aimed, under pretense of doing good to native art, a deadly blow against every American artist" (289). The attempt to protect American artists amounted to a "stigma" and a "blight" because world opinion held that "if . . . they were equal or superior to foreign works, no protective tariff would be necessary." At home, "the wealthy buyer has turned all the more to the costly foreign canvas because of this placard setting forth inferiority in the native product" (289). The editorial closed on the following note:

> Is Philadelphia to be permitted to dictate the ruin of American art under the guise of protection? Philistia is in Boston and New York; Philistia is in Chicago and New Orleans; but its complete paradise is in the Quaker City, where, so far as can be learned, the remarkable clause which raised the tariff on works of art from ten to thirty percent was concocted. (289–90)

4. Belmont represented Staten Island and most of Long Island. In his memoirs, he observed that his interest in putting works of art on the free list during his congressional service had brought him "into close relations with the painters, sculptors, and architects of New York" (Belmont 1940, 608).

As part of its campaign against the art duties, the *Critic* solicited and published letters in support of its position from the presidents of the National Academy of Design, the Society of American Artists, and the Art Students' League. In addition, a number of prominent artists wrote individually in favor of reform: among them were Frederick Church, John S. Sargent (writing from Broadway, Worcestershire), J. Alden Weir, Augustus St. Gaudens, and Kenyon Cox (290–94). Despite this testimony, the lobby for change in the art duties went nowhere in Congress. A further appeal from President Cleveland was also ignored.[5]

In the later 1880s, contemporary commentators continued to remark on an anomaly inherent in this situation: members of the American art "industry" were the only domestic producers to object to being "protected" and yet their protests seemingly went unheard in Washington. But, as the *Nation* (Editorial 1889, 24–25) noted, two categories of persons benefited from the art duties: (1) "the forger of imitation foreign pictures" and (2) certain dealers who traded in imported art. The latter stood to gain because "the ordinary picture-buyer knows little of the artistic merit of a painting, and the dealer can always point to the fact that he has found it worth his while to pay a 30 percent duty upon it as proof positive of the superiority of the foreign work over domestic production." The member of the U.S. commission assigned to report on the fine arts at the Universal Exposition of 1889 in Paris expressed himself bluntly on a related matter. In his judgment, statutory restrictions on imported works of art had "raised up a class of dishonest tradesmen who, presuming upon the credulity born of ignorance, produce rubbish which is passed off upon those unable to discriminate" (Hawkins 1891, 3). In addition, it had "encouraged the production of bogus pictures" and had "assisted a newly fostered set of knaves to cheat the ignorant" (8). The "vanity" of Americans who had suddenly acquired wealth made them easy prey for the unscrupulous. Moreover, the power of the wealthy in American society had become a "national misfortune" and the "conceit" that went with it "constitute[d] a sort of intangible Chinese wall, which stands as a barrier against general improvement in matters of taste and artistic accomplishment" (9).

5. In his Second Annual Message to Congress ([1886] 1967), Cleveland wrote as follows: "Representations continue to be made to me of the injurious effect upon American artists studying abroad and having free access to the art collections of foreign countries of maintaining a discriminatory duty against the introduction of the works of their brother artists of other countries, and I am induced to repeat my recommendation for the abolition of that tax" (1563).

Art and Tariff Legislation, 1890–1909

During the decade of the 1890s, three major tariff revisions were enacted. The champions of "free art" could find something to cheer about in the first two. But the third was a serious setback.

The Tariff Act of 1890 was designed as a high protectionist statement in which rates on most dutiable imports were advanced. The treatment of imported works of art was an arresting exception: rates were cut in half—to 15 percent ad valorem from 30 percent. The discrimination between the productions of Americans abroad and those of their non-American counterparts remained in place, despite President Benjamin Harrison's appeal for its elimination. A thoroughgoing breakthrough seemingly was accomplished in the tariff legislation of 1894. Duties on works of art were then waived altogether. (See table 3.) Two features of the political environment had contributed to this result. In the first instance, the second administration of President Grover Cleveland had been returned to office with a commitment to tariff reductions. Even though the usual congressional horse trading meant that the final bill failed to reduce duties to Cleveland's liking, there was still more official receptivity to freer trade doctrines than had been in evidence for some time. Another consideration probably had more impact on the outcome as it affected the art market: the Tariff Act of 1894 contained a proviso creating a federal income tax. Even though the Supreme Court soon thereafter declared this version of an income tax to be unconstitutional, its inclusion in tariff legislation at the time must have made duty-free art much more acceptable than would otherwise have been the case. The argument that steep tariffs on imported art were necessary because they were the major tax bite on the wealthy thus lost much of its force. When the art duties fell to zero as of 27 August 1894, the import traffic increased markedly. (See table 4.)

This triumph for "free art" was to be short lived. Republican victories in the elections of 1896—which brought William McKinley to the White House—populated both the executive and legislative branches with aggressive protectionists.[6] Official Washington was then also concerned about sizable federal deficits. Since 1893, the economy had been in depression: curtailment of demand for imports, combined with the 1894 reduction in tariff rates, had thus led to revenue shortfalls. The

6. The adjective *aggressive* is borrowed from Taussig's account of the legislative history of the Tariff Act of 1897. See Taussig 1914, esp. chap. 7.

Table 3 Imports of Artworks (Fiscal Years Ending 30 June), 1884–90

Year	Total ($000)	Free List ($000)	Dutiable ($000)	Dutiable (% of Total)	Rate of Duty (%)
1884	1,192	361	831	70	
1885	1,756	372	1,384	79	
1886	1,343	396	947	71	30
1887	2,806	474	2,332	83	
1888	2,211	531	1,680	76	
1889	1,647	338	1,309	79	
1890[a]	2,196	400	1,796	82	

[a]The Tariff Act of 1890, which lowered the art duties to 15 percent, became law on 1 October 1890.
Source: *Statistical Abstracts of the United States,* 1884–90.

Table 4 Imports of Artworks (Fiscal Years Ending 30 June), 1891–97

Year	Total ($000)	Free List ($000)	Dutiable ($000)	Dutiable (% of Total)	Rate of Duty (%)
1891	2,411	396	2,015	86	
1892	2,337	306	2,031	87	15
1893	2,796	429	2,367	85	
1894[a]	1,725	241	1,484	86	
1895	3,843	3,656	187		
1896	4,820	4,820	—		Free
1897[b]	4,799	4,424	375		

[a]The Tariff Act of 1894, which became law on 27 August 1894, removed duties on imported art.
[b]The Tariff Act of 1897, which raised the duty on nonexempt art to 20 percent, became law on 24 July 1897.
Source: *Statistical Abstracts of the United States,* 1891–97.

Tariff Act of 1897 was structured to undo the work of 1894, and it did so with a vengeance. Duties were raised overall, and the tariff on imported art moved from zero to 20 percent, with exemptions for works by Americans abroad and for the acquisitions of nonprofit cultural organizations. In the absence of a federal income tax, the "soak the rich" argument again had political resonance.

It was some time before the "free art" lobby could effectively regroup. A renewed campaign was launched in 1902 with an open letter signed and circulated by a number of the nation's most prominent painters, sculptors, and architects.[7] This document reiterated a number of arguments that were by now familiar—for example, that the art duties were a "tax on civilization"; that it was a national embarrassment that the American government, "alone among those of civilized peoples, [should] treat art as a luxury, the indulgence in which must be penalized" (Cox 1902, 371). But the presentation of the case also took some novel turns. This was an opportune moment to call for abolition, it was argued, for a number of reasons. In the first instance, public interest in the matter had been "roused" because "several Americans of great wealth and liberality" had recently purchased some of the world's great masterpieces (371). Owing to impediments imposed by American tariff policy, it was noted, "many great works actually owned by American citizens are retained abroad." The country should instead welcome these treasures and encourage their importation. As the richest country in the world, the United States now had an opportunity to use its wealth to enrich its culture. "Financial embarrassment in many countries of the Old World," the document observed, meant that treasures were now being placed on the market which formerly "could not have been purchased at any price" (371). Though the petitioners urged the repeal of all art duties, they recommended—as a first step—that all works more than fifty years old should be placed on the free list. (For the text of the open letter, see Cox 1902.)

A number of the more prestigious periodicals with a national readership threw their weight behind fundamental reform in the treatment of imported art. In 1903, for example, *Harper's Weekly* (10 January 1908, 60) described the tariff on art as "monstrous" and asserted that "there is hardly any law in the statute-book so inherently vulgar and so inspired by the evil spirit of sordidness as that which imposes a tariff tax on art." It challenged the "reasoning of the political mind" that concluded that "if art was to become a paying trade in the United States, the practice of buying foreign works should be discouraged by a tariff tax. . . . Art is not confined by national boundaries, and those who endeavor to breed it in narrow confines bring forth at the best, an abor-

7. The following were signators: J. Carroll Beckwith, Kenyon Cox, William M. Chase, Edwin H. Blashfield, F. P. Vinton, William A. Coffin, Frederick Dielman, J. G. Brown, John LaFarge, J. Alden Weir, Thomas Eakins, Frederick W. Kost, C. E. Cookman, Childe Hassam, John W. Alexander, Edwin A. Abbey, H. Siddoms Mowbray, Augustus St. Gaudens, R. W. Gibson, Abbott H. Thayer, George de F. Brush, and Charles F. McKim.

tion." The *Outlook* (20 January 1906, 98) sought to instruct those members of the public—and, at one remove, members of the political establishment—who believed, wrongly, that a tax on art was a tax on the rich. As its editorialist argued:

> Works of art are not altogether the possession of their owners; the canvas or the marble may be the property of the rich, but the art, which gives value to the canvas or the marble, belongs to any one who can enjoy it. Thus persons of moderate means and even of downright poverty may share with the wealthy every benefit that a work of art bestows. . . . Many paintings and sculptures find their way from private collections and into public museums; but even those which remain private property are to a great degree made accessible by loan exhibits.

Later, the *Nation* (18 October 1906) drew attention to an inconsistency in national policy:

> It may occur to certain visitors to the Columbia University Library, where splendid illuminated manuscripts belonging to J. Pierpont Morgan are temporarily exhibited, to inquire: Why are these treasures of art in America, whereas Mr. Morgan's paintings, bronzes, enamels, tapestries, etc., remain in Europe? The answer is simple: the manuscripts are not in the eye of the law works of art, and come in free of duty, whereas the rest are included under the category of paintings and statuary and must pay 20 percent *ad valorem*.

It was to be 1908 before the duty on art again received systematic legislative attention. By that time, the "free art" lobby had reenergized its core constituencies. In hearings before the House Ways and Means Committee, Robert W. DeForest, president of the Municipal Art Commission and chairman of the executive committee of the Free Art League of New York City, appeared as the lead witness, recommending that the law be amended to add works produced before 1850 to the free list. He allowed (1908, 7207) that it had been important for the government of a "new nation" to encourage industries, but now—when they were firmly in place—it was time to "provide for the encouragement of the fine arts." He emphasized that the strategy best calculated to bring American art to its "highest development" should provide for "the fullest knowledge of the art of the past and the unhampered flow of ideas from other countries. Having no art traditions of its own, the young nation should have the benefit of all that the art treasures of the Old World can teach or suggest, without hindrance from tariff barriers" (7208). DeForest reminded his listeners of the extraordinary expansion of museums in the recent past and of their rising popularity. This fortunate development deserved to be accelerated and spread throughout the country, and that objective would be best served if individuals were permitted to bring art freely into the country. This was crucial to the welfare of the public museums because they depended "upon the gifts, bequests, and loans of individuals . . . not only for their growth, but for their very existence" (7211). He further noted that four-fifths of the foreign works displayed at the Metropolitan Museum in New York had been so acquired. In his concluding remarks, DeForest informed the committee that the American Free Art League for which he spoke represented the views of some two hundred presidents of colleges and some two hundred artists, as well as the positions of directors of the nation's major museums (7216).

As the hearings before the House Ways and Means Committee proceeded, DeForest's position was seconded in the testimonials of leading figures in the arts community. Their statements were not all carbon copies of one another. Leslie W. Miller (secretary of the Fairmount Park Association, principal of the Pennsylvania Museum and School of Industrial Arts, and vice-president of the Art Club of Philadelphia), for example, struck a note that was distinctive: "I want it distinctly understood," he emphasized, "that . . . the organizations I represent stand for free art, not from any want of loyalty to the idea of protection, but because we believe that art is very strictly and truly a thing apart from anything in connection with commercial considerations under which all of our protective policy has been shaped. . . . I wish it distinctly kept from considerations of any commercial character whatever" (Miller 1908, 7220–21). Miller apparently felt a need to stay in tune with his Philadelphia political base when distancing himself from the views of Philadelphian Thomas Donaldson, vintage 1882.

The recommendations of the American Free Art League did not go unchallenged. The case for protection—in a mutated form—was presented most forcefully by James B. Townsend, editor of the *American Art News*, a weekly journal, who claimed to represent some sixty-two American artists.[8] Townsend (1908, 7235–38) advanced two proposi-

8. It would be fair to say that none of the sixty-two allied with Townsend would be candidates for an artists' "Hall of Fame" in the judgment of latter-day art historians.

tions: (1) that duties should be waived on a work of art more than one hundred years old and (2) that a specific duty of $100 be levied on imported works that were less than one hundred years old, including those created by Americans abroad. Part of the rationale offered for the latter proposal had the ring of the old-fashioned "pauper labor" argument for protection. Townsend maintained that "there must be some limitation . . . upon the importation of the cheap art of Europe from the fact that its artisans and artists can live much more cheaply there than we do here; and that they have a natural faculty for the production of art, particularly in the south of Europe" (7235). The case for the $100 specific duty on art less than a century old also rested on another premise—namely, that the American public was deficient in art knowledge and taste. The $100 duty was necessary to keep the country from being flooded with cheap "trash" and forgeries, "with resultant demoralization of public taste" (7235). The American artist, Townsend and his co-petitioners insisted, "asks for no protection from the old masters or even their later followers up to a century ago" (7237). Those works should come in duty-free:

> He does ask, however, that the product of his brain and hand should have some protection when it goes before persons not having art knowledge and taste as against the trash of modern Europe. Why should an American figure painter, for example, who produces good genius and whose living costs him far more than his fellows in Europe, be obliged to meet the prices which . . . can be taken for inferior European works? (7237)[9]

When the Tariff Act of 1909 emerged from the congressional pipeline, it contained two striking departures: first, the standard rate of duty on nonexempt works of art fell from 20 percent ad valorem to 15 percent; second, and more important, all works of art more than twenty years old were added to the free list. The new legislation became the law of the land on 6 August 1909. Immediately thereafter, imports of art mushroomed in value. (See tables 5 and 6.)

9. Townsend and his fellow petitioners were quite direct about urging Congress to ignore entreaties from American artists abroad: "Those American artists who choose to expatriate themselves and live abroad and complain that the feeling in Europe against an art duty is embarrassing to them, should, we feel, not be quoted so freely in favor of free art. They do not live here and vote here" (Townsend 1908, 7236).

Table 5 Imports of Artworks (Fiscal Years Ending 30 June), 1898–1909

Year	Aggregate of Indicated Categories ($000)	Works of American Artists Residing Abroad ($000)	Dutiable ($000)	Dutiable (% of Aggregate)	Rate of Duty (%)
1898	2,263	701	1,562	69	
1899	2,459	419	2,040	83	
1900	2,609	345	2,264	87	
1901	3,304	481	2,823	85	
1902	3,517	337	3,180	90	20
1903	4,311	297	4,014	93	
1904	3,286	604	2,682	82	
1905	4,381	385	3,996	91	
1906	4,909	767	4,142	84	
1907	5,867	707	5,161	88	
1908	4,311	400	3,911	91	
1909[a]	3,797	558	3,239	85	

[a]The Tariff Act of 1909, which became law on 5 August 1909, added all artworks over twenty years old to the free list.
Source: *Statistical Abstracts of the United States,* 1898–1909.

Table 6 Imports of Artworks (Fiscal Years Ending 30 June), 1910–13

Year	Aggregate of Indicated Categories ($000)	Works of American Artists Residing Abroad ($000)	Works of Foreigners Free of Duty (i.e., More than 20 Years Old) ($000)	Dutiable Works of Foreigners (i.e., Less than 20 Years Old) (No.)	Rate of Duty on Nonexempt Artworks (%)
1910	21,089	753	18,634	1,701	
1911	22,496	641	20,264	1,591	15
1912	36,093	801	34,250	1,043	
1913[a]	52,876	640	50,749	1,487	

[a]The Tariff Act of 1913, which became law on 4 October 1913, exempted all original works of art, without regard to age or nationality of the producer.
Source: *Statistical Abstracts of the United States,* 1910–13.

Victory for Free Art in 1913

Members of the American Free Art League got more than they had originally asked for in the tariff amendments of 1909. Whereas they had proposed that works more than fifty years old should enter duty free, Congress was willing to exempt all works more than twenty years old. This meant that import impediments applied only to contemporary art. To one American collector in particular—John Quinn (1870–1924)—this provision stuck in the craw.

Quinn was a lawyer who had built a very successful practice on Wall Street. He had also developed a taste for modern art, particularly for contemporary French works. This enthusiasm led him into becoming one of the prime movers behind the Armory Show. In mid-1912, it was he who drafted the articles of incorporation for an Association of American Painters and Sculptors (which became the parent body for that project). By the standards of the time, the Armory Show of February–March 1913 was a blockbuster. For most Americans, this was their first exposure to the French avant-garde. Not so for Quinn: he lent seventy-seven items from his own collection for display there (see Reid 1968, 142–45).

When it came to negotiating with official Washington, Quinn had talents that few other advocates of free art could match. He had long been active in Democratic Party politics: In 1908 and 1912, he was a New York delegate to the Democratic convention. On the latter occasion, he was a well-identified supporter of the unsuccessful candidacy of Oscar W. Underwood for the presidential nomination. This did his cause no harm when Underwood served as chairman of the Ways and Means Committee of the House of Representatives in 1913. In addition, Quinn commanded impressive skills in legal draftsmanship.

Quinn brought the case for eliminating the penalty on imported modern art to the halls of Congress in January 1913. Testifying before the House Ways and Means Committee, he presented himself as representing the Association of American Painters and Sculptors, though he was really speaking for himself. Art, he maintained, should be regarded as a necessity, not a luxury, and one from which an economic payoff might be expected. He cited the example of France, where millions of dollars worth of goods were sold to the rest of the world as by-products of the artistic sense cultivated among its people. Sophisticated art was not something to be observed only in museums and galleries but in "everything where form, design, color, molding, modeling, or decoration may possibly enter." Making America more competitive in these matters should begin by encouraging the "practice, study, and knowledge of contemporary art" that would come from unobstructed exposure to what was going on in the rest of the world (Quinn 1913, 5694–95).

Scrapping the duties on contemporary art, Quinn further argued, would improve distributional fairness. Taking the tariff off old art—as had happened in 1909—was a benefit to the rich, for only they could afford to be purchasers. Quinn entered the following plea:

> The committee should bring within the means and within the power of the man of moderate means—yes, even before the poor man—to acquire works of contemporary art before they become 20 years of age and appreciate in value and then fall into the hands of dealers and then become merely the hobby or exclusive possession of the rich. . . . I do not belong to the class of rich men who can indulge in Rembrandts, or Velasquezs, or Frans Hals, and other old masters, some of them good and some of them bad, and perhaps many of them forged. I want to buy the art of my own time. (5696)

In addition, Quinn provided the Ways and Means Committee with legislative language cut to specifications of his choice. There was an artfulness in his approach. He did not propose that the standard ad valorem rate on dutiable art—set at 15 percent in 1909—be changed; to have done so would no doubt have invited some nasty political contention. He proposed, instead, to widen space for the nondutiable by exempting all "original works" without regard to age. As Quinn explained this "new feature" to the Ways and Means Committee:

> The addition of the word "original" would, it is confidently believed, go a long way to check the importation of mere copies and forgeries of old masters now imported and sold as original works of art. Besides the law in its application would thus secure a record of works of art that would be in the custody of the examiners, appraisers, and other official bodies, and the danger of multiplying forgeries and copies of works already imported would be greatly lessened. (5706)

The beauty of this formulation was that it did not disturb the standard rate on what was dutiable. But the dutiable category was now reduced to copies and fakes. Tariff policy implemented in this vein amounted to a form of quality control.

Quinn's version of reform cleared the House of Representatives, but it ran into heavy weather in the Senate. In fact, the Senate Finance Committee was disposed to move two steps backward by raising the dutiable rate to 25 percent and by widening the age range of art subject to the tariff from twenty years to fifty years (see Zilczer 1978). Despite vigorous lobbying by Quinn and others, the outcome was touch-and-go in the midsummer of 1913.[10] The bill that became law on 14 October 1913 incorporated Quinn's language and scrubbed duties from "original" art. Underwood's clout on the six-member Conference Committee—and Quinn's connection with Underwood—had a lot to do with that outcome.

For all practical purposes, Quinn's interventions had opened the American market to international art. His complaints about governmental treatment of art, however, did not end there. He opposed the federal sales tax on works of art, which had been enacted in 1918 as a fiscal measure during World War I, and he spoke out forcefully for its repeal in 1921. He again felt obliged to lead the "recurrent fight against Philistinism, against Puritanism, and against false commercialism that would tax art."[11]

A Closing Word

Within the American polity, there were struggles aplenty over the posture the federal government should adopt toward the fine arts. The fact that most European governments were active sponsors of the arts—through state support for art schools, museums, and (in some instances) direct subsidies to individual artists—was well known and frequently remarked on. But the issue of whether the United States should imitate those models was never seriously debated. It seemed to be taken for granted that they were ill suited to American conditions. Controversy over government policy toward the arts was thus framed by the terms on which Americans could participate in the world's art markets.

But there was an arresting irony here. Both the advocates of "free art" and the champions of restrictions proceeded from a shared presupposition—namely, that America suffered from cultural inferiority. Much of the case for free art was built around the notion that there was little hope

10. An informal lobbyist was the president's wife, herself an amateur painter. Reacting to reports of the Senate Finance Committee's position, she wrote to Wilson: "Can't something be done about it? It is actually worse than the one it replaces, for that admitted pictures free if they were 20 years old and this requires that they be 50 years old. It is well known that the persons back of this change in the bill since it went to the Senate are certain rich art dealers in N.Y. who do thriving trade in 'antiques' largely faked. Really, dear, it is the sort of job that ought to be looked into. You know the regular House bill admitted all art free" (Wilson [1913] 1978, 120).

11. Quinn's enthusiasm for modernism, it should be noted, was not limited to contemporary art. He also gave strong support to James Joyce, Ezra Pound, and T. S. Eliot.

that the American artistic community could be elevated to world-class standards without uninhibited exposure to the best work produced elsewhere. Certainly John Quinn—who made no secret that he regarded most American art (apart from landscapes) as bad—believed that his countrymen were sorely in need of such stimulus. But those who urged some form of protection as national policy also invoked a cultural inferiority argument as at least a partial justification for their position. Unsophisticated and undiscriminating public tastes, it was argued, put American artists at a disadvantage, even when—on the merits—they might be able to hold their own in an openly competitive international art market.

References

Beauties of the Art Tariff. 1906. *Nation,* 18 October.

Belmont, Perry. 1940. *An American Democrat: The Recollections of Perry Belmont.* New York: Columbia University Press.

Boime, Albert. 1989. The Chocolate Venus, "Tainted" Pork, the Wine Blight, and the Tariff: Franco-American Stew at the Fair. In *Paris 1889: American Artists at the Universal Exposition*, edited by Annette Blaugrund. Philadelphia: Pennsylvania Academy of the Fine Arts.

Cleveland, Grover, President. [1885] 1967. First Annual Message to Congress, 8 December. In vol. 2 of *The State of the Union Messages of Presidents.* New York: Chelsea House.

———. [1886] 1967. Second Annual Message to Congress, 6 December. In vol. 2 of *The State of the Union Messages of Presidents.* New York: Chelsea House.

Congressional Record, House. 1884. 19 May. Vol. 15, 48.1. Citing Frank H. Hurd, Poindexter Dunn, and Roger Q. Mills.

Cox, Kenyon. 1902. The Tariff on Works of Art. *Brush and Pencil* 10:371–72.

DeForest, Robert W. 1908. Statement before the Committee on Ways and Means, House of Representatives, 28 November. 60.2:7206–18.

Donaldson, Thomas. 1882. Testimony in Philadelphia, 16 October. *Tariff Commission Report.* House Misc. Doc. 6. Washington, D.C.: Government Printing Office. 2:2461-64.H

Editorial. 1885. *Critic,* 17.102 (19 December): 289–94.

Editorial. 1889. *Nation,* 11 July, 24–25.

Elder, Cyrus. 1882. Testimony in Philadelphia, 14 October. Tariff Commission Report. House Misc. Doc. 6. Washington, D.C.: Government Printing Office. 2:2355–57.

Hawkins, Rush C. 1891. Report on the Fine Arts. In *Reports of the United States Commissioners to the Universal Exposition of 1889 at Paris*, vol. 2. Washington, D.C.: Government Printing Office.

Italy and the Art Tariff. 1883. *Nation,* 24 May, 440–41.

Miller, Leslie W. 1908. Statement before the Committee on Ways and Means,

House of Representatives, 28 November. 60.2:7220–21.

Ormrod, David. 1998. Origins of the London Art Market, 1660–1730. In *Art Markets in Europe*, edited by Michael North and David Ormrod. Aldershot, England: Ashgate.

Petition of American Artists. 1882. 5 October. *Tariff Commission Report*. House Misc. Doc. 6. Washington, D.C.: Government Printing Office. 2:1598.

Quinn, John. 1913. Testimony. Hearings before the Committee on Ways and Means, House of Representatives, 30 January. 62.3:5692–5708.

———. 1921. Testimony. Hearings before the Committee on Finance, U.S. Senate, 26 May. 67.1:675.

Reid, B. L. 1968. *The Man from New York: John Quinn and His Friends*. New York: Oxford University Press.

Sève, Hon. Edward. 1882. Statement in Philadelphia, 13 October. *Tariff Commission Report*. House Misc. Doc. 6. Washington, D.C.: Government Printing Office. 2:2238–40.

Shearman, Thomas G. 1882. Testimony on behalf of the Brooklyn Revenue Reform Club, New York, 5 October. *Tariff Commission Report*. House Misc. Doc. 6. Washington, D.C.: Government Printing Office. 2:1539–52.

Stanwood, Edward. 1903. *American Tariff Controversies in the Nineteenth Century*. 2 vols. Boston: Houghton, Mifflin.

Stevens, Cyrus A. 1882. Testimony of Assistant Appraiser, New York Custom House, at Long Branch, New Jersey, 18 August. *Tariff Commission Report*. House Misc. Doc. 6. Washington, D.C.: Government Printing Office. 1:527.

Sumner, W. G. 1882. Testimony in Philadelphia, 14 October. *Tariff Commission Report*. House Misc. Doc. 6. Washington, D.C.: Government Printing Office. 2:2313–33.

Tariff Commissioners. 1882. *Tariff Commission Report*. 2 vols. House Misc. Doc. 6. Washington, D.C.: Government Printing Office. 47:2.

Taussig, F. W. 1908. Statement of Professor at Harvard College, Relative to Tariff Systems, 15 December. Hearings before the Committee on Ways and Means, House of Representatives. 60.2:7731.

———. 1914. *Tariff History of the United States*. 6th ed. New York: Putnam.

Townsend, James B. 1908. Statement before the Committee on Ways and Means, House of Representatives, 28 November. 60.2:7229–31, 7235–38.

Viti, Alonzo M. 1882. Testimony in Long Branch, New Jersey, 3 October. *Tariff Commission Report*. House Misc. Doc. 6. Washington, D.C.: Government Printing Office. 1:335–37.

Wilson, Ellen Axson. [1913] 1978. Letter to Woodrow Wilson, 5 August. *Papers of Woodrow Wilson*. Vol. 28. Princeton, N.J.: Princeton University Press.

Wilson, Woodrow. 1882. Testimony. *Tariff Commission Report*. House Misc. Doc. 6. Washington, D.C.: Government Printing Office. 2:1294–97.

Zilczer, Judith. 1978. *"The Noble Buyer": John Quinn, Patron of the Avant-Garde*. Washington, D.C.: Smithsonian Institution Press for the Hirschhorn Museum and Sculpture Garden.

"Sweet Are the Uses of Adversity": Federal Patronage of the Arts in the Great Depression

William J. Barber

> Sweet are the uses of adversity,
> Which, like the toad, ugly and venomous,
> Wears yet a precious jewel in his head.
> —Shakespeare, *As You Like It*

The Great Depression of the 1930s stands unrivaled as the greatest tragedy in American economic history. Whether one takes the measure of this episode through the number of bankruptcies, bank failures, and foreclosures; through the length of the breadlines; or through the official statistics on the shrinkage of national income and employment, the conclusion is always the same: this period in the nation's history was an economic disaster.

Such conditions, one might reasonably suppose, would be highly unpromising for substantial public support for the arts; nevertheless, American painters and sculptors enjoyed a higher visibility then ever before. Indeed, when measured as a share of Gross National Product, public monies committed to the arts were higher in the 1930s than at any earlier or subsequent moments in our national experience. This stands out as all the more remarkable when juxtaposed against the climate toward arts funding in the late 1990s: today, at a time when the country is enjoying unparalleled prosperity, the National Endowment for the Arts—the financial support for which has never been overly generous—is struggling to survive at all.

The Conception and the Mexican Connection

Much of the explanation for federal patronage of the arts during the Great Depression can be traced to the convergence of a number of strong personalities, with uncanny abilities to make acceptable what would otherwise have been unacceptable. Not the least among them was the president himself. During the electoral campaign of 1932, Franklin Delano Roosevelt had signaled clearly that he was ready to experiment and that he would not be bound by conventional taboos about limits on what was proper in the behavior of the federal government. More particularly, he affirmed his willingness to commit resources to assist society's most distressed. When he took office on 4 March 1933, there was no lack of worthy candidates for such relief—and artists were among them. Not that many artists are in the upper end of the income distribution in the best of times. In the worst of times, their ranks were dominated by people in real need, and with the collapse in the stock market, private patrons were in shorter supply than ever.[1]

In the administration's first hundred days, Roosevelt's White House was a busy place. Emergency measures intended to salvage the banking system and to strengthen the economy's farming and manufacturing sectors commanded a self-evident priority. Even so, the president made time to attend to a memorandum prepared by George Biddle, a prominent artist whom he had come to know in student days at Groton and Harvard. On 9 May 1933, Biddle reported that artists in Mexico had "produced the greatest national school of mural painting since the Italian Renaissance" and, though working at "plumber's wages," they had "express[ed] on the walls of the government buildings the social ideals of the Mexican revolution." Biddle (1939, 268) advanced a programmatic suggestion:

> The younger artists of America are conscious as they have never been of the social revolution that our country and civilization are going through; and they would be eager to express these ideals in a permanent art form if they were given the government's cooperation. They would be contributing to and expressing in living monuments the social ideals that you are struggling to achieve. And I am con-

1. It should be noted that the big-money American buyers of art had typically given scant support to the output of living American artists. Up through the 1920s, acquisitions of European works accounted for the overwhelming bulk of their purchases.

> vinced that our mural art with a little impetus can soon result, for the first time in our history, in a vital national expression.[2]

Roosevelt responded on 19 May 1933, suggesting that Biddle take up the matter with Assistant Secretary of the Treasury L. W. Robert Jr., who had jurisdiction over the decoration of public buildings (a function handled through the department's Procurement Division).

Armed with this encouragement, Biddle drafted a document entitled "A Revival of Mural Painting" and proceeded to circulate it among various New Deal "insiders," including Harold Ickes (Secretary of the Interior), Frances Perkins (Secretary of Labor), Rexford Guy Tugwell (Assistant Secretary of Agriculture and charter member of Roosevelt's "Brains Trust"), and Eleanor Roosevelt. In addition to elaborating on the timeliness of governmental support for a "national school of mural painting," Biddle described what he thought this required:

> Three things are needed to give the necessary impetus to such a movement:
>
> 1. A few social-minded, creative artists of the first rank, representing the modern movement, and experienced in mural painting.
>
> 2. The assignment to them by the government of public wall space on which to express the social ideals of the government and people.
>
> 3. The understanding that in the personal expression and technical execution, the artist be given as complete freedom as possible. Interference would only tend to emasculate his work.

Biddle pointed out as well that a number of leading artists had "expressed their enthusiasm"—among them, Thomas Hart Benton, Edward Laning, Reginald Marsh, Henry Varnum Poor, Boardman Robinson, and Maurice Sterne. Once a commitment of federal support had been obtained, he recommended that a major publicity effort be mounted, involving "the press, liberal magazines and other agencies to strengthen the movement in other cities."[3]

This project came close to being stillborn—and would have been if the president had chosen to accept the advice of the body he was obliged to consult on federal art and architecture. The Fine Arts Commission,

2. Biddle came from a socially and politically prominent Philadelphia family. His brother, Nicholas, was later to serve in Roosevelt's cabinet as Attorney General.

3. Biddle's "Revival of Mural Painting" was attached to a letter from Biddle to Eleanor Roosevelt, 28 June 1933, Franklin D. Roosevelt Presidential Library (hereafter FDRPL).

created during the administration of President Theodore Roosevelt, was charged to rule on the artistic merit of proposed government projects. The commissioners—who regarded themselves as the custodians of the "classical" harmonies of L'Enfant's Washington—had no use for the "modernism" of the Biddle group or for its social message. In their judgment, the mural program should be rejected as "ephemeral" and "unsound." Roosevelt relayed the opinion rendered by the Fine Arts Commission to Biddle, observing that "it does not sound very encouraging for the mural paintings" (quoted in Biddle 1939, 273; see also McKinzie 1973, 6–7).

Biddle was undeterred by this obstructionism—it was "not unexpected," he told the president (Biddle to Roosevelt, 10 August 1933, FDRPL). Instead, he intensified his lobbying. He correctly sensed that the crisis atmosphere of the First New Deal created unusual opportunities to move outside the standard bureaucratic channels. Congress, after all, had broken with precedent by voting a record peacetime appropriation to address the "emergency." But it was not just the size of the lump sum that mattered. No less important was the scope for presidential discretion that went with it. Those campaigning for government dollars for their pet schemes were relieved from petitioning Congress for a specific appropriation—at least for a season. The champions of causes could instead direct their attention to lobbying for an allocation from the "emergency" funding that Congress had provided. The president had already appointed Harold Ickes (Secretary of the Interior and also Public Works Administrator) to be his delegate in the allocation of a large chunk of that money. By mid-November 1933, Biddle and his allies had persuaded Ickes to sanction the release of just over $1 million from funds he had earmarked earlier for an employment relief program administered by Harry Hopkins. These monies were transferred to the Procurement Division of the Treasury for its use in the ornamentation of federal buildings and as a relief program for artists. Even though the sums involved were trifling when compared with the $400 million Hopkins had at his disposal for the fiscal year ending 30 June 1934, they promised to have significant impact on the well-being of artists.

Launching the Treasury's Public Works of Art Project

The man chosen to administer the Public Works of Art Project (PWAP) funded through this maneuvering had an unusual background. Edward Bruce (1879–1943) was an artist in his own right, so when he spoke on aesthetic matters, his views commanded respect. One could hardly describe his career path as a linear progression, however. He was trained as a lawyer and had practiced in New York City and in Manila before pursuing business interests in the Far East. In 1923 he turned his back on all that and moved to Italy to take up painting, an activity that occupied him for the next six years. Upon his return to the United States, he settled in California, but soon moved to Washington as a Pacific Coast lobbyist on Far East interests: his experience with Asian silver markets was thought to be a qualification for that assignment. Thus his expertise on silver—not on art—had brought him to the Treasury's staff, and he was wearing that hat when he attended the ill-fated World Economic Conference in London in June–July 1933 as a member of the U.S. delegation.

Bruce shared Biddle's enthusiasms for promoting art with a distinctive American identity. There were fundamental differences in their approaches, however. Bruce was not attracted to the idea that public wall space should become a vehicle for social commentary. He preferred to see the national experience celebrated in ways that braced the country's badly bruised morale. If things worked out as he wished, government-sponsored art would educate and elevate popular tastes, thereby stimulating an increase in private demand for the artist's product. This was important because he did not believe that painters and sculptors could expect government to be their principal patron over the longer term. And he drew attention to yet another constructive attribute of the system he administered:

> It brought to the artist for the first time in America the realization that he was not a solitary worker. . . . It gave a sense of powerful encouragement, which inspired in him both a broader and more realistic conception. . . . No longer was he limited in his appeal to a group of fellow artists or to pleasing a small minority of specialists. Symbolically he had become the spokesman of his community. (Bruce and Watson 1936, xi)

From his "real world" experience, Bruce was sensitive to vulnerabilities inherent in this novel venture. It was bound to attract critics who would challenge the legitimacy of subsidies for what they would claim to be unnecessary frills that had no redeeming social utility. It was thus imperative to build a broad base of support. He quickly reached toward the "grass roots" by creating sixteen regional committees with authority to hire and supervise local artists. Instructions sent out from PWAP headquarters in Washington called on selection committees to be guided by two considerations: (1) they should encourage works that interpreted the "American scene," and (2) they should be mindful that PWAP was an employment program, not a relief program. The latter was intended as a reminder that commissions should go to the competent, not just to the needy.

The program got off to a fast start. The first artist joined the payroll on 9 December 1933 (the second day of PWAP's existence). Within two months, PWAP had an operational presence in every state in the union. By the time funding expired with the end of fiscal year 1934, more than 3,700 artists had participated, and they had produced nearly 16,000 items of art or craft (McKinzie 1973, 27).[4]

Hoping that this artistic production would help him win friends in high places, Bruce mounted an exhibition of the best works from around the country at Washington's Corcoran Gallery in April–May 1934 to which prominent figures in the political establishment were invited.[5] There was no lack of ballyhoo in its promotion. Forbes Watson, a well-known art critic whom Bruce had brought to Washington as PWAP's technical director, predicted that this would be the "greatest art event in the country since the Armory Show" of 1913 in New York and would demonstrate that American artists had "cut themselves loose from foreign influence" (quoted in McKinzie 1973, 29). But part of the publicity was not welcome. There was an outcry over the withdrawal from the show of a painting by Paul Cadmus—entitled *The Fleet's In*—which depicted a number of inebriated sailors cavorting

4. Some 400 murals were completed, along with 3,821 oils, 2,938 watercolors, and 1,518 prints. Quite a range of items—for example, Indian blankets, Pueblo pottery, batiks, and decorative maps—were represented in PWAP's inventory.

5. This strategy for mobilizing supporters was sometimes counterproductive. Public Works Administrator Ickes (1954, 162), for example, reported in his diary entry for 23 April 1934 that President and Mrs. Roosevelt had asked him to visit the Corcoran show. He then remarked: "I will say that most of these paintings were terrible from my point of view and I left wondering why men who turned out that kind of stuff should be supported as artists."

with several women of questionable repute. The Navy had objected (McKinzie 1973, 29–30). McKinzie has summarized the general reaction to the Corcoran exhibition as follows: "Critics noted the absence of nudes, night club subjects, pretty women, aristocratic-looking men, and genteel houses. They noted a predominance of machinery, locomotives, steamships, workers, and common subjects of village and farm life" (30). Bruce also saw another use to which PWAP works of art could be put. They were, after all, federal property. He felt free to present them to the White House, to various cabinet departments, and to the House of Representatives office building.

Sustaining the PWAP

The Public Works of Art Project ended when its parent agency went out of business on 30 June 1934. But Bruce's career as an entrepreneur for government-sponsored art was just beginning. He was shortly to be named to head the Section of Painting and Sculpture (subsequently restyled as the Section of Fine Arts) in the Treasury's Procurement Division. From this post, he had jurisdiction over placement of all works of art in federal buildings. Arrangements had already been made to ensure at least minimal funding for his operations: a provision in the legislation authorizing appropriations for new federal buildings stipulated that 1 percent of construction costs should normally be set aside for their decoration. Depression conditions had swollen outlays for the construction of post offices and courthouses. This meant that Bruce had an opportunity to leave a mark in virtually every congressional district.

As Bruce saw matters, the new public art with the highest visibility would be that displayed in the buildings erected for the Department of Justice and the Post Office Department in Washington's Federal Triangle. What he wanted there—in all likelihood—would clash with the orthodoxies of the Fine Arts Commission. To negotiate passage around that obstacle, he created an advisory committee with political clout. Though the chairman of the Fine Arts Commission was a member, he was surrounded by two members of the president's cabinet, the chairman of the National Planning Board (who was also the president's uncle), and an Associate Justice of the Supreme Court. As well, the committee included the architects of the buildings in question, directors of the nation's leading museums, and several highly regarded painters and sculptors. Discussions within the advisory committee led to the recommendation that the "best possible contemporary art" should be commissioned for the Federal Triangle. In the end, the Fine Arts Commission, though sullen, was not mutinous.[6]

Bruce insisted that this undertaking should be executed by the nation's best talents. What counted was quality in production, not an artist's financial circumstances. Committee members were asked to identify those painters and sculptors best qualified for the work. The results of their balloting (in alphabetical order) were as follows:

> *Painters*: Thomas Hart Benton, George Biddle, John Steuart Curry, Rockwell Kent, Leon Kroll, Reginald Marsh, Henry Varnum Poor, Boardman Robinson, Eugene Savage, Maurice Sterne, and Grant Wood
> *Sculptors*: Paul Manship and William Zorach (Press Release, Treasury Department [Procurement Division], 24 March 1935, FDRPL)

All of those so identified were invited to compete for commissions, though some elected not to rise to that challenge. Grant Wood chose not to participate out of concern that the patron might attempt to control his work. Benton had a brief flirtation with the project but soon took flight.[7] Among the participants, a number of them chafed over what they took to be bureaucratic regimentation. Biddle, for instance, was incensed by the hostile reaction of the Fine Arts Commission to his plans for murals in the Department of Justice, even though Treasury's Procurement Division ultimately told him to ignore it and proceed.[8] The fate of

6. Bruce did his best to discredit the Commission of Fine Arts in the eyes of his superiors. A memorandum to Secretary of the Treasury Henry C. Morgenthau Jr., for example, argued that the commission "did not give serious thought or consideration to new work" when commenting on designs submitted in the competitions for the jobs at the Departments of Justice and the Post Office. And the contrast between the styles of the commission and Treasury's Section of Painting and Sculpture was sharply drawn: "The Commission of Fine Arts was organized as a protective, rather than a productive, commission. Its purpose has been to prevent structures out of harmony with the general plan of the city of Washington from being erected. The Section of Painting and Sculpture, on the other hand, is a productive organization. Its purpose is to encourage the production of American Art, and to install the various works produced in fitting places" (Memorandum to the Secretary of the Treasury from the Section of Painting and Sculpture, 19 December 1935, Morgenthau Papers, FDRPL).

7. In his autobiography, Benton (1969, 71) wrote that he had worked on plans "for a Treasury Department mural in the new post office in Washington, D.C., [but had] difficulties accommodating [himself] to the views of Treasury's supervisory committee, the aesthetic temper of which was less than sympathetic to [his] way of doing things."

8. Biddle characterized the commission's attitude as a form of "censorship" through its "rigid insistence on a particular style, the deadliest of the world we live in: a weak, thin-blooded, sugar-coated imitation of the French Beaux Arts–Prix de Rome, which in itself is the last vulgar, middle-class death agony of the pseudoclassicism of David, which even in 1800

Kent's mural for the cycle on the "History of Communications" in the Post Office Department headquarters was especially notorious. To depict the geographical sweep of the postal service, Kent traced the delivery of a letter sent to Puerto Rico by Alaskan Eskimos. Its message—when translated from the Eskimo dialect—turned out to be a statement supporting Puerto Rican independence. This was deleted on orders from above (McKinzie 1973, 63–65).

Artwork in the Federal Triangle grabbed headlines, far more than did section-funded projects elsewhere in the country. Even so, the scope of activities outside the District of Columbia was impressive. Altogether, more than 1,100 buildings were decorated in 1,083 cities. Post office murals accounted for more than half of the total (66). Bruce drew great satisfaction when forwarding letters he had received from postmasters to his superiors: the messages he relayed typically applauded the government's initiative in making original art available to many who had not before been exposed to it. He regularly kept Roosevelt apprised of what was going on. In January 1939, for example, he urged the president to visit the offices of the Section of Fine Arts to inspect designs submitted in the competition to decorate the post office in Wausau, Wisconsin (Bruce to Roosevelt, 12 January 1939, FDRPL).[9] Roosevelt declined this invitation but suggested that Bruce "arrange to have some of the exhibition set up in the Cabinet room for next Friday's meeting and come and tell us about them" (Roosevelt memo, 14 January 1939, FDRPL).

Bruce made the most of this opportunity to articulate his core convictions. This moment in the White House, he remarked, was probably the "first time in history that the head of a great state has asked his advisers to consider the work of a group of unknown but very talented artists." He considered this "an accomplishment of democracy." Formerly, he observed, political favoritism had been decisive when commissions to decorate public buildings had been awarded. As head of the Section of Fine Arts, he took great pride in changing all that. Its com-

---

was a dry, papier-mâché, schoolboy conglomeration of bad Poussin and seventeenth-century Italian decadence; of helmets and urns and fasces and white triumphal bulls and chariot wheels and little cuty girls with budding breasts and French empire dresses" (Biddle 1939, 290).

9. Bruce remarked that "it would really refresh your soul to see the designs" because "the work expresses the amazing vitality of this country and carries with it the promises of things hoped for" (Bruce to Roosevelt, 12 January 1939, FDRPL).

petitions were open to all, and awards were made on the merits based on the recommendations of impartial juries who judged proposed designs without knowing the identity of the artists submitting them. With respect to the mural designs entered in the competition for the Wisconsin post office, Bruce observed:

> These pictures are typical of the thousands of pictures that have been sent in to our office under competitions. There has been no sign of defeat or social unrest among any of them. They have spread out before us a panorama of America, triumphant, clear-eyed, and unafraid and I like to think that as time goes on we will continue to develop through our Post Offices little cultural centers where we are raising the taste of our country and helping to develop our native art.

Bruce even suggested that this program was highly cost-effective. He noted that the average cost per square foot of the pictures that Andrew Mellon had presented to the National Gallery in "his magnificent gift" came to $31,622. By contrast, the average cost of all the mural work sponsored by the Section of Fine Arts was $14 per square foot. "I do not say that our pictures are now worth Mr. Mellon's prices," he added, "but I do say, with absolute belief, that in the due process of time, the Government will find that it has made a very good bargain and that these pictures will be valued at 100 fold the prices which the Government has paid for them" (Bruce, Transcript of Remarks to President Roosevelt and His Cabinet, January 1939, FDRPL).

Bruce could also point to some other victories during his career as a bureaucratic entrepreneur. He had been a prime mover, for example, in generating work for artists as stamp designers (e.g., the presidential stamp series) and coins (e.g., the Jefferson nickel). But there had been defeats as well. He was bitterly disappointed that his battle for a gallery for modern art on the mall in Washington—which he hoped would serve as a counterpoise to the National Gallery, which he regarded as a monument to dead European art—was not successful. (The National Air and Space Museum later came to occupy the site he had in mind.) Another proposal laid before Secretary of the Treasury Morgenthau in November 1937, when planning for the Jefferson Memorial was under way, was also derailed. Bruce suggested that the secretary release "enough of the Treasury's silver to cast a silver statue" of the nation's third president. Apart from its contribution to beautification in the national capital, this action had a further point in its favor: "The fact that a part of the Treasury's silver was dedicated to the statue would relieve the Senate block from the fear that surplus stocks of silver might be dumped on the market so as to interfere with the beneficent service silver does in stabilizing world prices" (Bruce to Secretary of the Treasury Morgenthau, 30 November 1937, Morgenthau Papers, FDRPL).

The Section of Fine Arts closed shop in July 1943. During the nine years of its existence, more than 1,200 artists had placed work in federal buildings. The government's outlays aggregated just over $2 million: approximately three-quarters of this expenditure was for murals; the remainder went to sculpture (Dows 1972, 20).

Support for Artists from the Works Progress Administration

The federal arts program that swamped all others—both in the magnitude of its financial support and in the numbers of participating artists—began in mid-1935 under the sponsorship of a newly created agency, the Works Progress Administration (WPA). Harry Hopkins, a long-standing Roosevelt aide, was selected to head this organization. From his experience directing a program of direct relief in the first year of the New Deal, Hopkins had developed hatred for the dole. Handouts for which nothing was expected in return, he insisted, were an offense to human dignity and destructive to the recipient's self-respect. A system of "work relief" would be far superior, even if there was something a bit contrived about the jobs that could be put on offer. "Work relief" for artists became a reality in October 1935 when Roosevelt allocated nearly $3 million for the Federal Arts Project component of WPA to cover the next six months. In its first year, some 5,300 joined the payroll (1,000 of whom had participated in the Public Works of Art Project of December 1933 through 1934) (McKinzie 1973, 82).

Hopkins turned to an extraordinarily colorful figure, Holger Cahill (1887–1960), to run WPA's Federal Art Project (FAP). In the 1920s, Cahill had built up the collections of contemporary American art at the Newark Museum (which was one of the pioneering exhibit spaces for American works). Subsequently, he joined the staff of the Museum of Modern Art. By this time, he had acquired a reputation as an expert on American folk art. Cahill had also flirted with the notion of founding a new theory of aesthetics—called "Inje-Inje"—premised on the proposition that there was "something outrageous, something violent, something vulgar, something in bad taste in American life." Art should reflect these phenomena but should aim to transcend the vulgar "into the beautiful" (Cahill, quoted in McKinzie 1973, 79). In addition, Cahill had been exposed to the thinking of the iconoclastic economist, Thorstein Veblen, with whom he studied at the New School for Social Research.[10] There was more than a touch of Veblenianism in the diagnoses of the plight of American art that he advanced in 1936. Cahill (1936, 11) then wrote:

> After the Civil War . . . the rapid expansion of industrialism made for the dominance of social groups which had no tradition of art patronage and little interest in art except as it might serve as a badge of newly-acquired social distinction or as object of conspicuous display. . . . the new generation of art patrons demanded the grandiose, the vulgar, the spectacular, the over-embellished, and the over-genteel. . . . Archaeology and astute dealers supplied them with art objects which had somehow been associated with grandeur in the past and were still associated with the taste of the socially powerful in Europe.

In consequence, few American artists could flourish in their native land. The moral of this tale was that a "rediscovery of the American scene" was imperative. He applauded the artists who had made a "clear return to the interest of the average man" and who had "brought the gusty vitality of city streets into the staid salons of the genteel tradition" (14–15).[11]

Dedicated though he was to nurturing indigenous art, Cahill was still conscious that FAP/WPA was likely to confront a skeptical—if not hostile—public. It thus behooved him to present the program as something that went beyond work relief, as ordinarily understood. Cahill maintained that an invaluable piece of the nation's cultural heritage was in jeopardy. Without federal assistance to maintain their skills, the country's craftsmen were likely to suffer the fate of the traditional craftsmen in India and China. When the market for their works dried up, those skills died with them. Hopkins invoked this feature of the pro-

10. By Cahill's own account, he was one of Veblen's favorite students. See Cahill 1957, 115.

11. Cahill (1936, 15) cited John Sloan, George Luks, and George Bellows in this connection, adding that it was "an indication of the insecurity of American taste and of the influence of the genteel tradition upon American criticism that when these men appeared before the public . . . they were hailed as the 'ash can school.'"

gram's rationale in public statements—using lines fed to him by Cahill—and pledged that what had happened in Asia would not be repeated in the United States. It was altogether in keeping with this purpose that slightly more than half of those on the project's payrolls were "craftsmen, workers in commercial and applied art," while slightly less than half were "working in the fine arts" (17).

There was an element of tactical calculation as well in the decision to embrace craft workers: this step promised to enhance the program's political acceptability. Cahill, after all, was the director of a *national* program. But a question remained about just how "national" its operations could be. It was well known that the fine arts community was heavily concentrated in an area of fewer than fifty square miles: in the mid-1930s, about 45 percent of the country's practicing artists lived in New York City. Bringing the crafts under FAP/WPA's umbrella made obvious sense to those sensitive to the importance of extending the program's geographical scope. This consideration set the context for the allocation of FAP/WPA monies to support the preparation of the Index of American Design (see Rothschild 1972). Applied artists and craftsmen throughout the land could thereby be engaged to compile a comprehensive record of American tastes in day-to-day living. In the end, some 23,000 index plates were prepared, and they became part of the permanent collection of the Smithsonian Institution.[12] Even though work on the index provided useful base-broadening, some sixteen states were still not involved in the enterprise. Later some of them were brought into contact with FAP/WPA through its creation of community centers for art instruction.

By contrast with the policies of the Treasury's Section of Fine Arts—which mandated that artistic quality counted, but that an artist's needs did not—eligibility for FAP/WPA was to depend on whether the applicant satisfied the need criterion for relief.[13] This meant that some of the country's strongest talents did not participate.[14] It was perhaps

12. Categories into which the index was subdivided included carving, ceramics, costume, furniture, glassware, metalwork, and textiles (including floor coverings) (Rothschild 1972, 194–95).

13. With funding transferred to it from WPA, the Treasury agreed to hire some relief artists—but no more than 25 percent of the total—to ornament old buildings. The Section of Fine Arts was confined to new ones. The Treasury Relief Art Program (TRAP) was modest in scale and did not flourish.

14. Thomas Hart Benton (1969, 69), for example, regarded himself as "ineligible for participation in one of the most interesting occurrences of our national life—the entrance of the

not surprising that the placement of an arts program within the administrative structure of a relief bureaucracy bred a myriad of problems; some were petty, and all of them were irritating. Artists and sculptors, for example, were suspected of boondoggling because their work habits did not lend themselves to punching a time clock that could be observed by a supervisor. Misunderstandings arose as well from the obligation of FAP administrators to implement policies sent down by their superiors in WPA headquarters. When WPA ruled from Washington in March 1936 that relief employment should be frozen, a number of artists in New York who qualified (according to the "means test" standard) were excluded. This sparked some ugly sit-in strikes in FAP offices in New York City. Such activity left some scar tissue, but did not bend WPA's policy (McKinzie 1973, 96).

With the passage of time, it became more and more evident that the mind-sets of artists, on the one hand, and of bureaucrats and politicians, on the other, were fundamentally different. A crisis of sorts developed in 1937 as a by-product of Roosevelt's instructions for the fiscal year beginning on 1 July 1937. His administration to that point had run precedent-shattering peacetime deficits, and he had always found them to be politically embarrassing. Roosevelt was determined that the story would be different in his second term (which began in January 1937). After all, 1936 had been a good year for the economy—much the best since the collapse of 1929—and momentum for recovery appeared to be firmly established. It thus seemed to be timely to curtail "emergency" spending and to aim for a balanced budget in fiscal year 1938. WPA was a ripe target for retrenchment. As far as its arts program was concerned, the president indicated his desire to effect a further change: he no longer wished to approve "blanket projects on a nationwide or statewide basis" but preferred to scrutinize "an application for each type of work in each community only where such projects are justified by existing unemployment conditions" (Roosevelt to Hopkins, 9 July 1937, quoted in McDonald 1969, 223–24). Hopkins entered a vigorous protest, arguing that centralized control was essential to the quality of

---

Federal government into the support of art through the Works Progress Administration of the Roosevelt regime." He already had all the work he could handle and was not in need. He attributed his agreeable market position to "an immense regrowth of interest in American history and social behavior, which the depression had accelerated, and this established an intellectual background for the Americanism of my painting."

the arts program: state or local programs would inevitably be "less professional." "Within the past year and a half," he wrote, "we have received ample evidence of the creation and steady growth of new audiences which offer the only basis for the future livelihood of these workers, whether in private employment or in a national cultural program." Only work of the highest standards would defend this achievement (Hopkins to Roosevelt, quoted in McDonald 1969, 225). Hopkins's views on this point prevailed in this round, but he paid a price. William F. McDonald (1969, 227) has cogently identified the problem:

> National standards, as Hopkins insisted, could not be maintained unless the Washington office controlled authorization of funds to the states, and could increase, decrease, or withhold funds in accordance with the degree of competence that the arts projects in the several states manifested. In short, the criterion of professional standards . . . encouraged the flow of funds to metropolitan centers, where they were least needed, and discouraged their flow to less urban areas, where they were most needed. As a result, [the program] largely lost, if it ever possessed, rural support not only in Congress but also in the country, and that loss spelled its doom.

With the exception of a brief period in 1938—when work relief activities were reenergized to respond to the impact of the sharp recession of 1937–38—FAP/WPA was generally under pressure to shrink its operations. Formal termination of this enterprise did not occur until 1943, however, and there was an impressive volume of production to show for the eight years of this experiment. FAP/WPA's output included:

- More than 2,250 murals (including frescos, mosaics, and photo murals) that were placed in tax-supported public buildings: e.g., courthouses, hospitals, schools, the New York Public Library, the reception halls at Ellis Island
- More than 13,000 pieces of sculpture that were positioned in such places as parks, housing projects, and historic battlefields
- More than 100,000 paintings, the overwhelming bulk of which were placed in public institutions on permanent loan
- Nearly 240,000 prints from more than 12,500 original designs (Dows 1972, 43)

For an outlay of roughly $35 million, the federal government was responsible for the creation of all this. That funding also covered the work on the Index of American Design and the organization of some 103 community arts centers (most of them located in the South and West).

Lobbying for a Bureau of Fine Arts

By 1936, the federal government had become the largest employer of American artists. In consequence, artists acquired a group identity that they had not formerly possessed. Such conditions were favorable to organizational activities which, in turn, were to have a bearing on the terms under which future federal patronage would be dispensed.

Two bodies that claimed to speak for artists emerged in this period. The American Artists' Union—with a membership of about 5,000—focused primarily on "pork chop" issues (such as work rules and pay schedules). The American Artists' Congress—with roughly eight hundred members—addressed a more sweeping set of concerns. The "call" issued for the congress's first meeting, in February 1936, indicated that the following items would appear on the agenda:

> Fascism and War; Racial Discrimination; Preservation of Civil Liberties; Imprisonment of Revolutionary Artists and Writers; Federal, State, and Municipal Art Projects; Municipal Art Gallery and Center; Federal Art Bill; Rental of Pictures; the Art Schools during the Crisis; Museum Policy in the Depression; Subject Matter in Art; Aesthetic Directions; Relations of Media and Material to Art Content; Art Criticism. (Quoted in Rothschild 1972, 208)[15]

In the conditions of the Great Depression, it was readily understandable why members of the American Artists' Congress would throw all the weight they could muster behind measures to enhance their economic security. Self-evidently, programs such as FAP/WPA lacked certainty. In early 1938, the Artists' Congress joined the lobby behind a bill sponsored by Senator Claude D. Pepper (Democrat of Florida) and Congressman John M. Coffee (Democrat of Washington) that called for the creation of a permanent Bureau of Fine Arts. The bill also stipulated that "all persons presently employed upon Federal art projects of the W.P.A. and artists on other projects under W.P.A. who are competent to carry out the objectives of this Act, shall continue in

15. The following served as officers of the congress: Max Weber, chairman; George Biddle, Rockwell Kent, Paul Manship, Arnold Blanch, and Joe Jones, vice-chairmen; Stuart Davis, executive secretary.

such employment without interruption of time or salary under the jurisdiction of the Bureau of Fine Arts" (quoted in Taylor 1938, 157). Stuart Davis, now the national chairman of the American Artists' Congress, testified to his organization's strong support for this legislation, noting that artists on WPA projects "had been hampered in their work by the knowledge that their employment was precarious and subject to discontinuation at almost any time." A vital artistic culture deserved to be backed by government through mechanisms that were permanent and stable. For a number of reasons, private patronage could never provide a reliable substitute. In Davis's judgment, "private patronage has not in the past and does not today accept any social responsibility to the artist. . . . Private patronage has no conception of the meaning of democracy in culture which includes a broad participation by the masses of the people both in the production and enjoyment of art. Private patronage considers art as a private affair, reserved exclusively for an aristocracy of cultivated tastes and wealth." Government instead should promote a "democracy in culture," which Davis (1938, 16–19) insisted was "an essential part of political democracy."

Reactions to the Coffee–Pepper bill brought into sharp relief the wide divergence in contemporary perspectives on the role government ought properly to play over the longer term. Bruce and Watson of the Treasury's Section of Fine Arts called for the bill's defeat, arguing that its enactment would compromise artistic quality. Cahill took no public position on the bill but let it be known privately that he regarded the proceedings as "most foolish and annoying" (McKinzie 1973, 152).[16]

The Coffee–Pepper bill went nowhere. Neither did a proposal prompted by a similar motivation—sponsored by Congressman William I. Sirovich (Democrat of New York)—make much headway. (Sirovich's plan called for the creation of a Bureau of Fine Arts, to be housed in the Department of the Interior, that would support painting, sculpture, music, theater, and literature.) The debate in the House of Representatives, though brief, exposed the political fragility of propositions such as this. A number of speakers chose to drown it in sarcasm (U.S. House of Representatives 1938). Congressman Dewey J. Short (Republican of Missouri) spoke to the issue as follows: "All we need to do, with 12,000,000 people out of employment and with many more mil-

16. Illness prevented Cahill from testifying before Senator Pepper's subcommittee. An assistant director of FAP/WPA, Thomas C. Parker, did appear, but he confined himself to describing the agency's work and took no position on the merits of the legislation.

lions upon the Government pay roll and upon the dole and on relief, is to enact this legislation, in order that we may teach toe dancing so we can restore prosperity to the poor American farmer or the wage earner that is out of work" (9497). Two of his colleagues found the bill deficient because it made no provision for acrobats, an omission characterized as "an unjust discrimination against a great artistic profession" (9496). Another pointed out that the bill "seems to lack the one face-saving provision of providing for beauticians" (9497). The motion to table was approved by a vote of 195 to 35.

The debates in Washington in 1938 had negative consequences for WPA-sponsored arts programs. Since their inception in mid-1935, WPA monies had been channeled not just to painters and sculptors but to musicians, actors, playwrights, and creative writers. While WPA funding was a lifeline for each of these respective constituencies, the aggregate outlays for these purposes were still trifling as a percentage of WPA's total budget for work relief. For a time, these programs thus enjoyed an immunity that goes with being inconspicuous. That changed when the proposals for a Bureau of Fine Arts were opened up for public debate. It was natural that those drafting legislation toward that end should design a bureau that would maintain continuity with WPA's practices—that is, one that embraced all its components (the art, music, theater, and writers' programs). The congressional scrutiny that followed revealed what had actually been going on in WPA's cultural activities. This helped torpedo a Bureau of Fine Arts, and it also wounded the WPA arts programs that were already in place.

In the first instance, congressional displeasure was focused on the theater project because some of its productions had offended congressional sensibilities. Dissatisfaction was subsequently fueled by suspicions of Communist influences that were fanned in the notorious hearings before the House Un-American Activities Committee, chaired by Congressman Martin Dies (Democrat of Texas). Congress terminated WPA's theater program altogether in 1939. The art program managed to survive, though on a reduced scale and in a radically altered form. Congress then mandated that the art program should be administered through the WPA apparatus at the state level and that projects should be funded only when 25 percent of their cost would be met locally. Cahill lamented this change, which, he feared, spelled deterioration in quality. New York City was particularly hard hit: the WPA administrator on the spot was a lieutenant colonel in the Army who had no sympathy for the art program and who was skeptical about the political orientation of some of his clients; on his insistence, some mural work was destroyed (McKinzie 1973, 155–56).

FAP/WPA had never been in the front seat of national priorities, and as war clouds gathered in Europe, it moved even further back. Some of its alumni later found work designing posters to mobilize public support for the national defense effort. Cahill wrapped up his duties as director with a search for homes for the project's creations. In that connection, he wrote Harry Hopkins (then a special assistant to the president in the White House), to whom he had already shown some samples: "I'm glad you like the pictures. They are as fine, it seems to me, as anything produced by young American artists in our time. Any of these paintings or prints which you cannot use either at the White House or at the President's Library would be gratefully received by the museums around New York, the Metropolitan, Brooklyn, Modern, or Newark" (Cahill to Hopkins, 30 June 1943, Hopkins Papers, FDRPL).

Reflections on a Remarkable Period

In the adversity of the Great Depression, American governmental benefits to artists—when adjusted to the scale of the economy—were larger than at any moment before or since. The fact that special programs were mounted for this purpose was itself precedent-shattering. Could such arrangements have survived in times of prosperity? Probably not. Roosevelt never thought of the Federal Arts Project as a continuing governmental responsibility. Like other kinds of work relief, it was a stopgap in times of economic emergency and one that should be phased out as the economy recovered. In the environment of the 1930s, this program had something remarkable going for it: this was a moment when American artists were experiencing an identity crisis and when the populace at large was suffering a crisis of confidence. Artists and the public managed to connect: both producers and consumers appreciated art expressed in an identifiable American idiom. But such aesthetic nationalism would not be for all seasons.[17] Before the decade of the 1930s was out, some of the artists on the federal payroll were ready to bolt; to their taste, American provincialism had begun to lose its

17. The term *aesthetic nationalism* is borrowed from Mathews 1975.

charms. Abstract expressionism—its foreign roots notwithstanding—promised to be more satisfying.

It is remotely conceivable—but only remotely—that a foundation for a longer standing governmental commitment to the arts could have been laid if the implications of a revolutionary economic model had been embellished. This happened in Great Britain. John Maynard Keynes offered a blueprint for economic recovery, calling for increases in aggregate demand. Within this analytic framework, it made sense to encourage private consumption and to discourage saving. That objective could be served by aiming at reducing inequalities in the income distribution—by combining steeply progressive taxation of incomes of the wealthy with redistributive transfer payments to society's less fortunate. Keynes realized that private patronage of the arts would suffer from such policies. Nonetheless, he insisted, social stability required conditions of full employment, even when its price was "euthanasia of the rentier." The patronage function that the wealthy might otherwise have performed should thus be absorbed by the state. With this rationale, Keynes became an enthusiastic supporter of the Arts Council. In Roosevelt's Washington, a breed of Americanized Keynesians had risen to the top of the policy-making ladder by the late 1930s. They understood the policy lessons for the pursuit of full employment, but they did not take the further step of asking what those lessons might imply for patronage of the arts.

The experience of federal patronage of the arts in the Great Depression left no lasting mark on American institutions, but at least one aspect of its legacy is memorable. Thanks to governmental support, a number of major contributors to the American art scene kept going through some dark days; among them were Jackson Pollock, Ben Shahn, Willem de Kooning, Mark Rothko, Philip Gustan, and Arshile Gorky.

References

Benton, Thomas Hart. 1969. *An American in Art.* Lawrence: University Press of Kansas.

Biddle, George. 1939. *An American Artist's Story.* Boston: Little, Brown.

Bruce, Edward, and Forbes Watson. 1936. *Art in Federal Buildings.* Vol 1, *Mural Designs, 1934–1936.* Baltimore: John D. Lucas.

Cahill, Holger. 1936. *New Horizons in American Art.* New York: Museum of Modern Art.

———. 1957. *Reminiscences of Holger Cahill.* New York: Columbia University Oral History Research Office.

Davis, Stuart. 1938. Testimony before the Subcommittee of the Committee on Education and Labor, U.S. Senate, 75.3 (28 February):16–19.

Dows, Olin. 1972. The New Deal's Treasury Art Program. In *New Deal Art Projects: An Anthology of Memoirs,* edited by Francis V. O'Connor. Washington, D.C.: Smithsonian Institution.

FDRPL. Franklin D. Roosevelt Presidential Library. Various archives. Hyde Park, N.Y.

Ickes, Harold L. 1954. *The Secret Diary of Harold L. Ickes: The First Thousand Days, 1933–1936.* New York: Simon & Schuster.

Mathews, Jane DeHart. 1975. Arts and the People: The New Deal Quest for Cultural Democracy. *Journal of American History* 42.2:316–39.

McDonald, William F. 1969. *Federal Relief Administration and the Arts.* Columbus: Ohio State University Press.

McKinzie, Richard D. 1973. *The New Deal for Artists.* Princeton, N.J.: Princeton University Press.

Rothschild, Lincoln. 1972. The Index of American Design of the WPA Federal Art Project. In *The New Deal Art Projects: An Anthology of Memoirs*, edited by Francis V. O'Connor. Washington, D.C.: Smithsonian Institute Press.

Taylor, Francis Henry. 1938. Pork Barrel Renaissance. *Magazine of Art* 31.3:157, 186–87.

U.S. House of Representatives. 1938. *Congressional Record.* Washington, D.C.: Government Printing Office. 73.3 (15 June): 9490–99.

Positive Science, Normative Man: Lionel Robbins and the Political Economy of Art

Márcia L. Balisciano and Steven G. Medema

When scholars look at the world around them, they do so through lenses colored by the disciplines in which their lives are immersed. An economist is apt to see the world as a symphony of benefits and costs, melded together to create pictures of efficiency and inefficiency. An artist is apt to see the world rather differently, as one of aesthetics and marked by perceptions of beauty, emotion, and other sensitivities. Perhaps it is not surprising, then, that there is no long and deep history of the intermingling of economics and the arts. Although the last twenty-five years have witnessed an increasing interest in the economics of the arts, this relatively thin history makes all the more interesting the cases of interaction between these two important components of Western thought and culture.

Perhaps no economist was more heavily involved in the culture of the art world than John Maynard Keynes, who, through his association with the Bloomsbury Group, had his thought processes shaped—at least to some extent—by the art culture (see, e.g., Moggridge 1992, 216–22, and Skidelsky 1986, 244–51). Lionel Robbins was also extensively involved in the arts, especially in the realm of arts administration, an area where his involvement was no doubt deeper than that of any other economist. Because his involvement with arts administration began after his economic views were already solidly in place, Robbins

We would like to thank Christopher Johnson, Sir Claus Moser, and Richard Robbins for their willingness to provide their insights into Robbins's work in the arts, and two anonymous referees for their useful comments on a previous draft.

is an excellent case study in the movement of an economist within the art world.

Introduced to the world of art as a young boy, Robbins made regular visits to the National Gallery in the company of his parents and extended family. But these visits hardly served to stimulate the interest in art that was so large a factor in Robbins's later life; he described them as leaving him feeling only a strained neck and the resulting "overwhelming desire that the excursion should soon be over" (Robbins 1971, 242). It was through his friendship with his brother-in-law, Clive Gardiner, whom Robbins met in the winter of 1916–17, that his interest in art began to flower, as Gardiner educated him in the nuances of art appreciation in galleries at home and abroad.[1] Then, rather than a source of physical discomfort, for Robbins, "the galleries of London became what the conventicles had been for my ancestors—continual sources of spiritual refreshment and contemplation" (244).

Robbins's work in art administration began in the interwar period, when he was appointed to the Committee of Management of the Courtauld Institute. In 1953, Robbins was appointed to be a trustee of the National Gallery, a position that he held until 1974, including twice holding the chair and serving as the National Gallery's representative to the Tate Gallery (1953–59, 1962–67). About this association with the National Gallery, Robbins wrote that "of all the good things that have happened to me in public life, I count this connection with the Gallery to have been outstandingly the most gratifying. To share responsibility for the care of these marvellous treasures, to participate in discussions regarding presentation and acquisition, to have the companionship of the scholars and experts intimately concerned with their records and preservation, what greater pleasure—or honour—could come to any lover of the arts?" (250). Robbins's expertise in the arts and in economics led to his service, in the 1950s, on two governmental commissions whose scope of operations included issues pertaining to the political economy of the arts: the Committee on the Export of Works of Art, Etc. (the Waverly Committee) and the Committee to Consider a New Queen's Hall. His work on these committees afforded Robbins the opportunity to bring the insights of economics into arts policy, along with the challenge of balancing his emotional attitude toward the arts

1. For a discussion of his relationship with Clive Gardiner, see Robbins 1971, 44–45, 241–44.

with the colder realities of economics.[2]

Apart from work in arts administration, Robbins also wrote on the political economy of art, attempting to bring economic analysis to bear on questions of policy pertaining to works of art. As such, Robbins presents an interesting case study of the interaction between economics and art in two senses: first, in providing some insight into how the lessons of economic analysis can potentially be applied to art-related questions and, second, in showing how an economist's approach to arts administration is similar to or different from that of noneconomists.

Economics, Political Economy, and the Arts

Robbins is perhaps most well known for giving to economics its modern choice-theoretic definition. Arguing against the extant definition of economics as "the study of the causes of material welfare" ([1935] 1946, 4), Robbins contended that an examination of the work of economists reveals that economics is "the science which studies human behavior as a relationship between ends and scarce means which have alternative uses" (16). As such, economics focuses not on "the wealth of nations" but on behavior undertaken under the influence of scarcity.

The implications of this for the present subject are quite forceful. Under the material welfare—wealth-based—definition, economics has little, if anything, to say regarding the arts (or the aesthetic generally), and attempts to make "economic" pronouncements in this arena are liable to lead to almost embarrassing overreaching.[3] Robbins nicely illustrated this by referring to Sir Josiah Stamp's (1929) essay "Æsthetics as an Economic Factor," where, in attempting to make an *economic* case for things aesthetically pleasing, Stamp is forced to argue that "indifference to the æsthetic will in the long run lessen the economic product [whereas] attention to the æsthetic will increase economic welfare" (quoted in Robbins [1935] 1946, 29). Robbins was quick to point out the dubious nature of this claim that society's pursuit of the aes-

2. In addition to this work in administering the visual arts, Robbins was also involved with, and had a great love for, the performing arts; he served on the board of Covent Garden from 1955 to 1981. As this volume deals with the visual arts, we have largely ignored Robbins's work on the performing arts.

3. It is interesting to speculate whether Robbins's love for the arts played a role in his rejection of the wealth-based definition of economics. Given his extensive exposure to the arts prior to the formulation of his methodological views, this may indeed be the case.

thetic will lead to increased material wealth,[4] and, further, to point to the true nature of the relationship here—one revealed by the conception of economics as the science of choice: that there are cases (perhaps many or most) in which we are faced with a *choice* between material welfare on the one hand and aesthetic interests on the other (29–30). But while it is wrongheaded to make the case for art on the grounds of its positive effects on national wealth, it is equally wrongheaded to consider art outside the bounds of economic science. Robbins argued that "in so far as [an] activity involves the relinquishment of other desired alternatives, it has an economic aspect" (17).[5] Thus, since "both the services of cooks and the services of opera dancers [and, one might add, painters, sculptors, and curators] are limited in relation to demand and can be put to alternative uses" (16), the arts do indeed have an economic aspect.

One of the most important implications of the choice-theoretic definition of economics given by Robbins is that it takes ends as given and rules the choice among competing ends outside of the scope of economics (24–45).[6] Economic science cannot say whether a particular class of activities is good or bad, desirable or undesirable, relative to others. Rather, "it takes the ends as given in scales of relative valuation, and enquires what consequences follow in regard to certain aspects of behavior" (30). As such, economics cannot tell us whether we ought to have art, or in what form or amount, whether the arts ought to be subsidized, public museums built, and so on. Robbins (1976b, 175–76) recognized as much in his discussion of the question of whether taxpayer money should be provided for the support of the arts, pointing out that "clearly this is not a question which can be answered by reference to scientific economics. It is a question of ultimate values, a question of what you think to be the purpose and function of the state as the authoritarian element in society, a question of political philosophy." "Economics," he said, "comes in only when you want to know the impli-

4. "It may be perfectly true . . . that the wide interests fostered by the study of ancient monuments and the contemplation of beautiful objects are both stimulating to the intelligence and restful to the nervous system, and that, to that extent, a community which offers opportunities for such interests may gain in other, 'more material' ways. But it is surely an optimism, unjustified either by experience or by *a priori* probability, to assume that this *necessarily* follows" (Robbins [1935] 1946, 29).

5. Robbins ([1935] 1946, 17) goes on to say that "there are no limitations on the subject-matter of Economic Science save this."

6. "Economics is entirely neutral between ends" (Robbins [1935] 1946, 24).

cations of your decisions in this respect, implications as regards proportions, incentives and machinery" (176).

All of this appears to relegate the economist to the position of little more than a sideline observer, content to sit by and toss out information regarding the potential consequences as the policy game is being played. But Robbins was clearly of the mind that economists have much more than this to offer to debates over governmental policy. Doing so, however, involves pulling off the cloak of economic science and putting on that of political economy. Political economy, said Robbins (1976a, 2–3),

> is not scientific economics, a collection of value-free generalisations about the way in which economic systems work. It is a discussion of the principles of public policy in the economic field: and while it makes appeal to the findings of economic science, it also involves assumptions which, in the nature of things, lie outside positive science and which are essentially normative in character. It consists of prescription rather than description; although, since it is concerned with practice, its recommendations make use of what aspires to be a scientific examination of the results of action rather than wishful thinking regardless of consequences.

Since, for Robbins, "Political Economy thus conceived is essentially a search for solutions to problems of policy" (3), and as government policies toward the arts have important economic components, it should come as no surprise that Robbins, with his devotion to the arts, jumped into the arts policy debates of his day as activist political economist rather than as disinterested economic scientist.

Art Meets Political Economy

Robbins's strong classical liberal leanings and his championing of free markets are well known within the economics community, and his stance against trade barriers, regulation of markets, and state (or state-sponsored) monopolies are evident throughout his writings. Whether this pro-market stance is strong in absolute terms or simply stands out in contrast to the more interventionist tendencies of the Cambridge crowd is not for us to examine here. However, Robbins's discussion of the relationship between the state and the arts is instructive, as to either the pragmatic nature of his views or the selectivity with which he evaluates the efficacy of government interventions in the marketplace.

Art and the Liberal State

Robbins's two major academic pieces on art are concerned with government action in the sphere of the arts. "Art and the State" (1963, 53)[7] begins with Robbins posing two questions (which for him are really one): "Is the encouragement of the arts a proper function for political bodies? Is such encouragement compatible with liberal notions of the duties of the state?" Robbins's answers to these questions were strongly affirmative on both counts, and to make his case he found it necessary to deflect the negative responses coming from camps on both the right and the left.

From the right came the standard argument regarding the paternalistic nature of government involvement with the arts: that the use of taxpayer money in this way constitutes an illegitimate attempt by the state to influence (or set) cultural standards, and as such conflicts with democratic principles and free markets (57). "Why," it was asked, "should the taxpayer provide money for the arts? Why should not the whole business be left to consumer demand? If people want art they will buy it: if not, why should it be produced?" (Robbins 1976b, 175).[8] The objection from the left, stated by, for example, Clive Bell and Roger Fry (from whose books Robbins received a great deal of his education in the arts), was that artists would be better off if the government were to simply leave them alone—both in terms of the provision of financial resources and in terms of the cultivation of particular forms of art (Robbins 1963, 53–54; see also Bell 1928, 252; Fry 1921, 36–51). So there you have it: one group arguing that support for the producers of art is inimical to the interests of consumers, and the producers themselves arguing that this support is inimical to the interests of producers and, presumably, to the overall quality of the art produced!

While this would seem like an obvious instance in which a champion of free markets would assail government intervention, Robbins does just the opposite. He is in full agreement with the Bloomsbury Group's negative attitude toward the official art of their era—Robbins (1963,

7. This is the published version of an address by the same title delivered to the annual meeting of the Friends of the Birmingham Art Gallery on 19 March 1958. The published version is expanded in certain respects from the original address.

8. Interestingly, another major figure within the LSE tradition, Ronald Coase, has made exactly this argument regarding government support for public television in the United States. American public-television programming is primarily educational and cultural, and Coase (1968) argues that it ought not to be provided if the audience is not willing to pay for it.

54) called it "an all-time low in the history of visual art in this country" up to that time—but he rejected Bell's and Fry's general impression of a negative relationship between the state and the arts. Against such a view and along rather Smithian lines, Robbins constructed a set of arguments for the appropriateness of government support for the arts and its consistency with the principles of the liberal state. Robbins noted elsewhere that Adam Smith's ([1776] 1937, 651) third duty of the state—"the duty of erecting and maintaining certain public works and certain public institutions, which it can never be for the interest of any individual, or small number of individuals, to erect and maintain; because the profit could never repay the expence to any individual or small number of individuals, though it may frequently do much more than repay it to a great society"—is an important component of the activities of the liberal state. The question, of course, is how the boundaries of this duty are to be set. Robbins (1981, 9) believed that political economy can help society elucidate the appropriate boundaries, and for him, at least, its insights clearly revealed that government support for the arts falls within these boundaries.

Both Robbins and Smith regarded the education function as an important piece of the role of the state.[9] Within this, Robbins (1976b, 176) saw cultivation of the arts—"the provision of examples of the highest standards of cultural achievement in the visual arts, [etc.]"—standing alongside the encouragement of higher learning generally as an "obligation" of the state. In making his case, Robbins (1963, 56–57) linked "encouragement of high excellence in culture" with "the maintenance of sources of excellence in high learning and pure science, Archaeology, Pure Mathematics, [and] Astronomy, for instance—subjects with no special relevance to practical affairs as such, but which impart quality and meaning to life on this planet by reason of their mere existence." And, because it would be very difficult for arts and learning to flourish in a market environment without a substantial dose of support from the state, such support is necessary if the arts are to

9. Robbins did not go all the way with Smith on this score, however. For instance, Smith appears to advocate only minimal government financing for higher education, suggesting that professors would be more diligent if they were forced to rely for their incomes on fees paid by their pupils. Perhaps not surprisingly, Robbins took a rather dim view of this proposal. See Robbins 1998, 155–60.

bring to society the kinds and level of benefits of which they are capable (58–59).[10]

One particularly important manifestation of this, for Robbins, is the erection and maintenance of galleries and museums—"the public collection, accessible to all and specifically designed to preserve the manifestations of past culture" (59). Robbins contended that the whole of these collections is far greater than the sum of the individual parts, but yet it was not in the private interest to provide them. However, the benefits to society—through the educational function—are so substantial as to make state provision worthwhile.

By placing art within the general education or knowledge promotion function of the state, Robbins was able to offer a rebuttal to those who claimed that the use of tax dollars to support the arts is undemocratic. Robbins was clearly of the mind that the educational functions of the state, including support for the arts, provide benefits that are diffused through the population and cut across *all* classes of society—"that the positive effects of fostering art and learning and the preservation of culture are not restricted to those immediately prepared to pay cash but diffuse themselves to the benefit of much wider sections of the community in much the same way as the benefits of the apparatus of public hygiene or of a well-planned urban landscape" (58).[11] He rejected the argument (made by Bentham, among many others) that such collections are of interest only to the rich and thus the assertion that their provision involves catering to the minds of the rich using the money of the middle and lower classes. If one looks at the crowds in the galleries and museums, said Robbins, one sees the whole spectrum

10. While Robbins used the constant marginal productivity argument (à la Baumol) to justify subsidies for the performing arts, he does not appear to have used this argument in the visual arts context. It is also not clear that the constant marginal productivity argument is accurate with reference to the performing arts since, with positive income elasticity, marginal revenue product is increasing.

11. In his classic piece on the economics of government support for the arts, Alan Peacock (1976, 77) imputes an externality motive to Robbins's discussion here and criticizes him on that score, questioning how the average individual receives positive spillovers, particularly from the performing arts. Peacock's criticism is a bit wide of the mark, and for two reasons. First, the externality argument has merit to the extent that cultural excellence is part of a national identity to which the average citizen holds dear. Second, Robbins was speaking to the visual arts in this statement, and it is not at all clear that he was referring to spillover benefits. As individuals could then view the national collections free of charge, the benefits could be experiential, just as with the well-planned urban landscape to which he refers in this passage.

of social classes, with little discernable difference in "interest and enjoyment" across the classes (60). He also made the case that the galleries and museums serve an important educational function within the arts community—that the ability to observe the works of the past provides an important stimulus to excellence in contemporary art: "The greatest creative minds," he said, "are not bound by the past, but they are aware of it and derive strength and understanding from the contact; and for the visual arts that contact is perhaps best provided by the museums" (61).[12]

Robbins (1976b, 176) also considered "the provision of an accompaniment of enjoyment and amenity" to be "part of the legitimate and psychologically desirable manifestations of state activity." Such was the underlying rationale for state provision of parks and open spaces, for example, and Robbins saw galleries and museums serving (in part) a similar purpose. Complementary to this, for Robbins, was the issue of the aesthetics of state buildings. Since the state requires buildings to house its assemblies and offices, and although utilitarian functionality is the central aspect here, Robbins (1963, 56) saw no reason to be self-denying as to the aesthetics of these, arguing that, in tandem with functionality, the state should "aim at the highest excellence in the design and decoration of our public buildings." Beyond this, welfare-state-induced redistributions of wealth had seemingly everywhere reduced "private demands for works of art on the grand scale" (56). The failure to make public buildings a block for the sculptor and a canvas for the painter would serve to restrict "all painting and sculpture [to] the dimensions appropriate to the walls and mantelpieces of flats and suburban villas" of the rich—implying, of course, that such would be a great loss for society (56).

Robbins (1963, 57–58; 1976b, 176–77) was careful to distinguish between state *support* for and *encouragement* of the arts and a state *monopoly* in this area. In his view, the latter is unduly paternalistic and injurious to the notion of liberal democracy—not to mention injurious to the arts, as exemplified by the ill effects of the "artistic dictator[ship]" that existed during the Stalin regime. But state support for the arts in a context in which all members of society are also free to lend their sup-

12. This same logic led Robbins (1966, 112), in his work on the reform of university education, to advocate art history as an essential component of arts education, in that it has "all the characteristics required of liberal education."

port to the arts in accordance with their particular tastes, he said, "is completely harmonious with the principles of a free society" (1963, 57).[13] To prevent government from exercising too much control over the form and direction of art, he advocated the use of so-called buffer committees, such as the Arts Council, which, along with the boards of trustees of national museums and galleries, serve as a conduit for state assistance "without stultifying controls" (Hansard 1963–64, 1268).[14] This naturally leads to the question of how much state support is good or necessary—a question to which Robbins (1976b, 177) provided no specific answers, noting only that the amount should be that "necessary for the adequate maintenance of a sufficient volume of the various activities involved" and that "no sensible person will deny that this is a matter for argument and will vary from time to time and place to place."

This much having been said, Robbins's arguments here are by no means immune from criticism. First, some might question whether Robbins's use of the public good argument is legitimate in this case. If one thinks of a public good in terms of a well-defined commitment to provide a particular good or service—a road or a bridge, for example—then something like art, which is more open-ended (both definitionally and in terms of the expenditure commitment) may not qualify. The same could be said of national defense, however. If one adopts the Samuelsonian definition of a public good—a good exhibiting (substantial elements of) nonrivalry and nonexcludability in consumption—then art appears to fit the bill, in this case more along the lines of impure public goods such as roads and bridges than pure public goods such as national defense. In the end, Robbins's public good argument really comes down to desirable public amenities that the market cannot provide in sufficient amounts—a criterion whose practical implementation, we would argue, ultimately involves the evaluation of competing visions of what is in society's best interest. Robbins's position on this score is quite obvious. Second, it also seems clear that Robbins very much believed that the benefits from the provision of galleries, museums, and public displays flowed throughout socioeconomic classes. Yet it is not obvious that the facts regarding the distribution of

13. Robbins (1963, 57–58) finds a parallel in British broadcasting, seeing a government—through the BBC—monopoly as unduly authoritarian, but finding it perfectly acceptable for the government to be *a* player in the provision of broadcasting services.

14. Robbins applied this same "buffer committee" notion to his recommendations regarding the reform of university education, and for the same reasons.

benefits would sustain Robbins's casual empiricism. It would be difficult to refute the proposition that the middle and upper classes benefit disproportionately from government support for art—albeit probably to a lesser extent than in the performing arts, where admission fees tend to be more prohibitive. Third, Robbins's optimism concerning the wide diffusion of benefits seems to be matched by that of his views on the benign nature of government support that overtly avoids monopoly. In particular, state support runs the risk of creating a culture of dependency within the art community that could lead over time in a monopoly direction. The state, in choosing to whom it allocates funds, may substantially influence the direction of artistic creation and stifle certain forms of innovation, although the same charge can be leveled against strong power bases within private philanthropy (Baumol and Bowen 1966, 375–76).

Defending National Culture

A particularly pressing problem in British arts policy was the substantial outflow of significant works of art from England. Robbins (1963, 64) viewed these exports with great alarm, noting that "a stock of treasures which was once the envy and admiration of the entire world" had been substantially diminished and was in danger of disappearing altogether. The need to devise a means to stem the tide of art exports is a theme that recurs in his speeches and writings from the 1950s through the early 1970s. The high prices being paid on world art markets had combined with progressive taxation and high death duties to provide a substantial incentive for private collectors to dispose of their works of art.

Robbins traced the dramatic increase in art prices to four sources. First, the proportion of art remaining in private hands was diminishing and, as this was the source of supply for the world art market, this meant rising prices even in the face of constant demand (66). Second, "with the spread of education and the increase of population, interest in the arts is more widespread and intense in many parts of the world." This, coupled with rising global real incomes and favorable tax treatment for art donated to public institutions in the United States, he said, means strong, and relatively permanent, increased demand and thus higher prices (67). Other influences, perhaps more temporary, were the depreciation of the pound sterling and, working in tandem with this, the fact that "well-chosen works of art" are excellent hedges against inflation in times of monetary instability, giving rise to additional, speculative demand (67–68). But as Robbins had little confidence in the political will of governments to keep inflation low, he saw this, too, as a relatively long-term force in the market.

Given that the market itself gave no cause for optimism regarding the outflow of significant works of art, state action was, for Robbins, the only available remedy. Although he was a staunch proponent of free trade, Robbins (1931, 45) noted already in the 1930s that nations might wish to make the choice to forgo some of the efficiency advantages of free trade "in the interests of aesthetic valuations not formulated in consumers' price bids." While Robbins was thinking here along the lines of, for example, preserving some countryside by protecting certain farming interests, it seems fairly clear that he subsequently applied this same notion to art export policy. He was clearly of the mind that the export of significant works of art had to be stopped, and he saw government-imposed restrictions as the only means available.

Robbins (1963, 63) recognized the potential inconsistency of an Englishman arguing against art exports, given that England had originally acquired most of its significant works via export from their lands of origin:

> Now there can be no objection in principle to the movement of works of art across frontiers. Art, thank heaven, is not specifically national; and it would ill become us in this country, who gained so much from import of this kind in earlier centuries, to argue that import by the citizens and galleries of other countries is an international outrage. I confess to a feeling of acute pain when I think of some of the migrations—the great *Feast of the Gods* by Bellini and Titian, for instance. But I do not doubt that the general culture of the West has benefited by some at least of the diffusion which has taken place.

Nevertheless, he argued, these works had become a part of Britain's national heritage, and their continued departure served to rob the country of both an important piece of its heritage and a prime component of its national culture. Moreover, as other countries had acted to prohibit exports of art except with explicit government permission, Robbins (1963, 63; 1976b, 180) maintained that England would not be remiss if it did likewise.

While Robbins (1976b, 180–81) saw no problem with a flat export prohibition as it affected churches and charities, which already enjoyed special tax treatment from the state, he was concerned that such a policy, applied to individual or corporate owners, effectively involved "nationalisation without compensation" and offended one's sense of equity, particularly because those who owned less significant works of art would still be free to sell. Robbins thus recommended that the government have the right of first refusal to purchase significant works before they were sold abroad. A policy along these lines was exactly what the Waverley Committee, of which Robbins was a member, had recommended (see later in this essay), and it was in certain respects implemented. The problem is that the government had not allocated sufficient funds to fully accomplish its end of the bargain—that is, to put up the purchase prices necessary to prevent export.

The process of deterring art exports illustrated, for Robbins, the important role played by the public collections, which he saw as the appropriate agents for state art purchases. While these purchases could be funded through special grants provided by the state as needs arose, Robbins argued for the establishment of a special fund that the institutions could have at their disposal, noting that maneuvering through the political process would be "cumbersome *vis-à-vis* the surprises of the market." Moreover, as many sellers are willing to deal "on generous terms with national institutions," the ready availability of funds would allow the museums and galleries to act quickly to secure these works, avoiding the risk and expense that can result from having to bid against others on the world market (181–84).

Funding the Preservation

All of this, according to Robbins, implied the need for an enormous infusion of cash into the museums and galleries to finance art purchases. "It is no exaggeration," he wrote, "to describe their present position in this respect as pitiful and a disgrace to civilized standards" (1963, 68)—the amount then available to the National Gallery for such purposes being barely sufficient to allow for the purchase of a single major Impressionist work every five years or so. Robbins laid the responsibility for this state of affairs not at the feet of the civil servants, members of Parliament, or the general public but with the government ministers, "who have abdicated their responsibility in pushing through legislation providing such funding" (70).[15]

Robbins was quick to acknowledge that economic conditions and the state of the government's budget situation at the times of his writings pointed to the need for some governmental belt tightening. Indeed, he was himself a staunch proponent of, and active campaigner for, reductions in aggregate government expenditures during this era. Yet, he said, this "does not, in my judgment, imply that we should spend less on culture and learning, in relation to which, on any comparative standard, our spending is so much in arrears. *The necessity to curb spending in general does not in the least imply a necessity to apply the curb equally in all directions.* . . . it only means that there have to be further balancing cuts elsewhere" (71). Indeed, just "because one has wasted one's substance on wine and women does not mean that it is wise to economise the proper care of one's eyes and teeth" (1976b, 187). The arts, he argued, have been "starved," while at the same time government expenditures in other areas have grown "disproportionate[ly]"—indeed, have grown to such an extent that a small reduction in the enormous subsidies provided to agriculture (£2 million out of the £300 million), or a "tiny fraction" of the amount spent on the Concorde, would provide plenty of funds to allow the museums and galleries to make important purchases and adequately maintain their operations, as well as rescuing the national opera and ballet, the Arts Council, and the British Academy from their precarious financial situations. The end result, he maintained, would make "the difference between the memorable and the mediocre in the spiritual life of the community" (187).[16]

Beyond recommending increased funding for art purchases, Robbins also recommended that the death duties be revised to reduce the incentives for sale abroad. Although not opposed to death duties in principle, Robbins (1955, 13–15) was against what he considered the excessive leveling of wealth under the duties then in place, and he was especially critical of their stimulation of art exports. Robbins (1963, 64) went so far as to argue that this consequence of death duties was not the will of

15. In an earlier speech, Robbins had placed most of the blame on the members of Parliament. However, he subsequently changed his mind on this score (1963, 70 n. 1).

16. Robbins restated these very same sentiments in a speech in the House of Lords on 19 April 1967. See Hansard 1966–67, 265–66.

the people and that "if they knew that this was the by-product of the present tax system, they would be very willing indeed to take measures which, consistent with common justice to the owners, would prevent it," particularly as these owners frequently make their works available for public viewing in the nation's museums and galleries. While the death duties were subsequently modified to more favorably treat important works of art,[17] ever-increasing prices on world art markets still left many favorably disposed to going to auction with their works, suggesting that additional incentives were needed.

Toward this end, Robbins suggested that preservation become a partnership between the state and the citizens by encouraging citizens to make financial gifts in support of the arts. While bequests of art to national institutions avoided estate duties, financial bequests to these institutions were generally subject to duties and thus both provided no incentives to leave cash to the arts as opposed to other potential recipients and, because of the high duty rate, greatly diminished the net proceeds from the bequest ending up in the hands of the museums and galleries. Robbins (1976b, 185) saw absolutely no justification for this distinction between cash and in-kind bequests to the arts, opining that "if a cretinous village imbecile had set himself to do something perverse he could not have done better." Yet, in spite of the government's awareness of this inconsistency, no steps had been taken to remedy the problem.

Added to this, said Robbins, was the absence of favorable tax treatment of gifts made out of income to support of the arts—a situation quite different from that in the United States, for example. Such tax deductions, he believed, would not only serve as a source of funds for the arts but also allow for greater decentralization of decision making as to what forms and institutions of art receive more or less encouragement—a sentiment consistent with his views of the liberal state and against a high degree of state monopoly power. Robbins contended that the argument continually leveled against such tax inducements—that the donors would thereby avoid paying their fair share of taxes—was incredibly "myopic and second-rate stuff" in that these incentives would serve as a useful form of indirect taxation and are consistent with the empirical fact that different patterns of expenditure across

17. If works are not sold at the time of the passage of the estate, there is no death duty imposed, and a financial incentive is provided if one sells to a national institution rather than to a private individual or foreign institution.

individuals generally subject people to varying degrees of tax liability in any event (185–86). And, he said, one needs only to examine the American system and the magnitude of the tax-incentive-induced contributions to galleries, museums, institutions of higher learning, and so on to see the enormous benefits of such a policy.

While Robbins was very much in favor of government provision of inducements for private individuals to make contributions to the arts, he was steadfastly against the notion—"a somewhat half-baked doctrine," as he called it—that charges should be instituted for admission to state-subsidized galleries and museums (179). While most opponents of the institution of admission fees claimed that they would cause a dramatic fall-off in visitors or impose an inordinate hardship on the lower classes (or both), Robbins believed that the minimal nature of the fees could have no such tragic impacts. Nonetheless, he maintained that there were good reasons to maintain the free-entry policy.

The basic thrust of the argument for admission fees was their utility as a source of funds, and the justification was that charges were levied for admission to state-subsidized opera and theater, so why not also for, say, the National Gallery and the British Museum? Robbins was able to easily counter this argument with a bit of elementary economic theory. The issue, he pointed out, is that of capacity versus demand. In the case of the theater and opera, there would be enormous excess demand at a zero price, and it seemed reasonable to him to ration by price rather than by queuing—and, in fact, he recommended that theater and opera ticket prices be set at a level approximately sufficient to clear the market, rather than to maximize profits. The museums and galleries present a very different situation, he argued, because they are not in the same capacity-constrained situation: Except in situations when special temporary exhibitions take place, the demand at zero price is not generally such as to create any difficulties. Moreover, entrance fees are (correctly, in Robbins's view) instituted for the special temporary collections when capacity would be a problem (both absolutely and in the sense that individual visitors' enjoyment would be diminished by crowding) at zero price. The proper analogy, he suggested, is not to the opera and theater, but to parks and libraries—which, like museums and galleries have not entirely insignificant operating costs, but for the entrance to which no one was advocating the institution of charges (178).

We have already noted the links between Robbins's and Smith's views on the role of government, but Robbins would appear to part company with Smith on the fees issue. Smith ([1776] 1937, 681–766) was an ardent proponent of user fees to finance and maintain public works and activities—including education—and he made his case on both equity and efficiency grounds. One might be tempted to argue that Robbins's position on user fees is somewhat inconsistent, given that he goes on at such length about the dreadful state of funding for the arts. In particular, to insist that a market-clearing rather than a profit-maximizing price be established for the opera and theater, and that admission to museums and galleries be free, serves to rob the arts of a nonnegligible source of revenues—revenues that, by his own admission, would not impose a tremendous burden on the citizenry. And as he advocated a public-private partnership to help justify his position in favor of tax-deductible contributions to the arts, it seems that entrance fees would be consistent with such a partnership. Furthermore, even though basic price-theoretic principles demonstrate the basic optimality of differential, congestion-based pricing, a zero price for consuming the services of museums and galleries does not necessarily follow. It would appear that equity is the driving force behind Robbins's (1976b, 179) position here:

> Once it has been decided in the interests of amenity or culture to provide a park or gallery—admittedly a non-commercial enterprise—there seems no very convincing argument against making the amenities available to a larger rather than a smaller number of people, until the point at which increased use becomes gravely inimical to individual enjoyment. To impose a charge is likely to keep away just those members of the public in whom—in the interests of the educational and amenity function—it would be most desirable to kindle interest.

Yet one could make the same argument for equity in regard to access to the opera and theater—that is, that the congestion argument is not a valid ground for pricing people out of cultural activities and education. Robbins refused to go all the way with either efficiency or with equity, and his position here is emblematic of the types of potential inconsistencies and selectivity that are inevitably present in political economy.

While Robbins doubtless had in him a good deal of the classical liberal, one would do him an injustice to claim that he was simply an opponent of big government who was nonetheless advocating large doses of government expenditure on his pet projects. Writing on the subject of public finance in the mid-1950s, Robbins (1955, 3) allowed that "many of the extensions of the functions of the State which we have witnessed in our time seem to me to be necessary and desirable, in particular all those which serve positively to create greater equality of opportunity." That much having been said, while Robbins saw the necessity for government to use its coercive powers and play the role of savior in sustaining the arts, he seemed at the same time to share the classical liberal's pessimism about the ability of government to discharge its functions in the best interests of society. He noted, for example, that "Chancellors of the Exchequer are sensitive creatures, apt to be deflected from action which may well be in the long-run interests of everybody, by transitory and irrelevant circumstances which make it seem unsuitable at the moment to give extra money for a particular purchase" (1976b, 182). And in defending his support for tax deductibility of gifts to the arts, he offered that individuals are likely to give more contemplation to the use of their monies than would the members of political assemblies.

The Political Economist Meets Art

Robbins's analysis of the interplay between art and economics was undoubtedly fueled by his work in art administration. Indeed, the love of the arts he discovered in his youth—fostered by family and friendships and his inquisitiveness into the "range of perceptions" the aesthetic world inspired—was a prime catalyst for Robbins's pursuit of this field throughout his life (1971, 242). More importantly, for Robbins, the various posts he held in art administration, the majority concurrent with his "official" academic (and other) positions, were a means of preserving and enhancing art for the benefit of the citizenry. As already pointed out here, he firmly believed in equalizing opportunity. Yet on a deeper level, he believed that art enriched the spiritual life of the community—that "it was capable of affording unalloyed happiness and enlightenment to . . . hundreds of thousands" (1976b, 187).

The Economist and the Joys of Art Administration

Robbins's introduction to "the material administration of the affairs of . . . museums and galleries began with the Courtauld Institute" (1971,

244) when, during the interwar period, he put his name forward for and received an appointment as the University of London's representative to the institute's management committee. Robbins negotiated this universe well, proving his skill as a mediator early on by resolving a dispute between the institute and one of its founders.[18] Following Sam Courtauld's death, Robbins took over as chairman of the management committee; it was a position he held for the duration of his career by yearly election. He came to count his affiliation with the institute and the associations he derived thereof "among the most illuminating" of his years in the arts (246).

The combination of Robbins's service at the Courtauld and his work in wartime administration for the government contributed to his appointment by the chancellor to the Committee on the Export of Works of Art, Etc. in 1950. The committee reflected governmental (and Robbins's own) concern with the large outflow of paintings, manuscripts, and other antiquities, a mark of World War II and the decline of empire.[19] The committee was charged with examining the system of export controls established in wartime that had gradually come to encompass works of art. It united Robbins with his "war-time leader," Lord Waverley (the committee chairman), whom he deemed a tour de force. Though Waverley had no background in the arts, Robbins (1971, 248) admired his belief that "there exists an art which, properly mastered, should enable a man of good general education to cope with administrative problems of whatever nature." No doubt this maxim reassured Robbins, who himself was dedicated to cultural advancement, though he lacked formal training in the arts. Because of the opportunity to join forces again with Waverley and "the absorbing intellectual interest and national importance" of the committee's assignment, it was for Robbins a "memorable experience" (247).

Robbins's aptitude for art administration was well recognized by the

18. Lord Lee of Fareham, who founded the institute with Sam Courtauld and Sir Robert Witt, had been stalwart in his belief that his bequest of a major collection of paintings would not be handled appropriately, and implied that he might amend his will. Robbins drew on familial connections to appease the dying patron—in his capacity as president of the National Farmers' Union, his father had known Lord Lee as minister of agriculture. Robbins (1971, 244–45) explained his father had said, "If Lord Lee gives you a promise he keeps it. . . . Its repetition worked wonders with Lord Lee"; "thereafter," he recounted, "the going was easy."

19. By far the largest purchaser was the United States (Committee on the Export of Works of Art, Etc. 1952, 9), not in the least because of the favorable tax laws (as described above).

early 1950s. He was asked to become a trustee of the National Gallery in 1952, and he became a trustee of the Tate Gallery in 1953. In 1954, he was appointed by the chancellor to the Committee to Consider a New Queen's Hall (a performance center that had been destroyed in the war), and he became a director of the Royal Opera House, Covent Garden, in 1955.[20] As a lover of the arts, his work for these organizations was among the most satisfying of his career. He recalled of his long tenure at Covent Garden, "to have access to its daily business and *to be obliged as a matter of the duties of a Director* to be a frequent witness of performances was a privilege I had never expected" (1971, 264).

The Economist and the Economics of Art Administration

If Robbins found his experience in art administration to be personally satisfying, as a social scientist he also found the problems associated with it to be challenging and engaging, and he saw them in economic terms.[21] For example, in his analysis of Covent Garden, Robbins saw that once excellence was achieved and crowds were at their maximum, it was not possible for a national performance house to raise its productivity as in manufacturing. Yet as national wage levels rose with productivity, so did the salaries of the house's staff, further increasing deficits and the need for subsidies (265–66).

While Robbins devoted time to publications at the Tate and the National Gallery, dealt with questions of accommodation at the Courtauld, and for a period was chair of the ballet committee at Covent Garden, finance was his main focus at these institutions. Many of the arts reports to which he was signatory explored economic issues and made "economic" recommendations. They reveal a tension, also present in his academic writings, between respect for the free market on the one hand and a notion that special exception should be made for the arts on the other. While Robbins praised the National Gallery, where he was able to conduct operations "more or less, with the freedom of private

20. His dates of service are as follows: National Gallery, 1953–74 (during many of those years he was chairman); Tate Gallery, 1953–59 and 1962–67; Royal Opera House, Covent Garden, 1955–81 (O'Brien 1988, 17).

21. Sir Claus Moser (personal communication 1998), who was chairman of the board at Covent Garden during Robbins's tenure there as head of the finance committee, noted, "Robbins did not act like an economist [at Covent Garden]. But when economic issues came up, we listened more to him than to others. Because of the training of his mind as a social scientist he brought to bear his skills."

enterprise" (251), he did not believe the gallery should be bound by private enterprise's obligation to generate revenue—as evidenced by his staunch support for free entrance to national collections (1976b, 177).

As chairman of the Committee to Consider a New Queen's Hall, Robbins signed a report declaring that demand was insufficient "to establish the economic prospects of a larger Queen's Hall" (Committee to Consider a New Queen's Hall 1955, 11).[22] He and his colleagues objected to the faulty economic arguments upon which a decision to build a larger replacement for the bombed building—on its original site—were based (10). Further, they objected to the view that it was possible for consumer prices to rise to more than twice the 1938 level, without a commensurate rise in the price of admission tickets, which might offset the cost of operating a larger hall. "We find it difficult to believe that, whereas the prices of other amenities have been advanced substantially with no detriment to receipts, the demand for concert tickets should remain so insecurely poised that the slightest readjustment to take account of rises in costs would cause a diminution in aggregate taking" (13). There was further concern for preserving the incentives of the free market lest the cost of building subsidies prove exorbitant to the public (13). Therefore, private building and finance were elevated above public construction (17). In the discussion, the element of economic choice—disposal of scarce means that have alternative uses—came into play. There was recognition that expending funds on a new Queen's Hall would draw off audiences, performances, and funds from other halls in existence and that this depletion could only be offset by a net addition in numbers, which the committee found unlikely to occur. If a central feature of Robbins's economics was neutrality between ends, arts administration, as an outpost of political economy, was not subject to these same constraints.

Accordingly, Robbins's committee weighed in with a judgment on desirable ends: "Until there is more solid evidence of a volume of addi-

22. Indeed, Robbins was but one of a four-person committee. It can be assumed, however, that Robbins's role as chairman was pivotal and decisive. As regards the report of the Waverley Committee to be examined in this section, though Robbins was not chairman, all recommendations were unanimous save one point to which Professor V. H. Gailbraith dissented (Committee on the Export of Works of Art, Etc. 1952, 61). Robbins's endorsement of the findings of the committee can be found in his autobiography (1971, 248–55) and in his essays on art (1963 and 1976b). In fact, Robbins had become chairman of the Reviewing Committee on the Export of Works of Art in 1954, which carried forward the principles of the Waverley Committee.

tional demand which will provide substantial financial support for such a hall and not be a mere subtraction from demand for the use of existing halls there is not strong ground for affording such a project a high priority in the long list of desirable objects of immediate Government expenditure" (17). This verdict was based on "musical grounds and in the interests of the general cultural life of the community" (20). It was acknowledged that the arts could not be held to purely commercial standards: "Many of the witnesses who have appeared before us, when asked to help us make some estimate of the present plan, have tended to reproach us with seeking to decide the question on purely commercial lines. We should therefore like to state that none of us has any such intention" (12). The Waverley Committee also acknowledged the danger of manipulating market forces, but it concluded that the arts were eligible for special dispensation.

The Waverley Committee report did not hide the many drawbacks of export control. First, control inhibited the growth of the domestic art market. Foreign buyers came to favor other markets as they did not wish to expend precious resources in making purchasing decisions that might be refused by government authorities. Prior to controls, witnesses detailed, London was the center of the international art market bringing important works to both the private and public eye. A free market had also provided the intangible benefit of supporting "the body of knowledge upon which a due appreciation of art depends" (Committee on the Export of Works of Art, Etc. 1952, 16). Second, control demanded public expenditure, since its administration was costly. Third, control led to fraud and evasion: for instance, items were frequently undervalued to thwart the system because an export license was only required for articles valued at £100 or more (Reviewing Committee on the Export of Works of Art 1954, 3). Fourth, control was unfair to sellers—either intentionally or otherwise, refusal of an export license frequently resulted in a lower price for the seller and the purchaser (often a national or regional museum). Fifth, control had not been particularly successful in preserving national treasures (Committee on the Export of Works of Art, Etc. 1952, 18). Finally, control was seen as a refusal to accept the cyclical nature of economic growth. Americans, as the predominant buyers, were only attempting to build collections in the twentieth century as Great Britain had done in the eighteenth and nineteenth centuries. Yet even with all these flaws, the Waverley Committee determined that some sort of control was "the only feasible method of reconciling the needs of the collections with the financial and economic necessities of the times" (54).

The machinery of controls was necessary for bringing important cases of national treasures, otherwise lost to the nation forever, to notice. Though controls, it was said, were best applied to a small number of objects of high importance, control became less effective the larger the scope of items included in the scheme (19). Accordingly, the Waverley Committee advocated that the threshold for an export license be raised to £1000 for most items (33). Robbins and his colleagues were careful to specify tests and conditions for determining whether an item was a national treasure and should therefore be refused an export license. Among these was the question, Is the object "so closely associated with our history and national life that its departure would be a misfortune?" (62). The committee also stipulated that if a reviewing committee determined that an item should only be sold domestically, the seller was entitled to a fair, international price (Robbins 1971, 249). Owners of art, it was argued, should not be penalized simply because they had invested in an aesthetic good as opposed to a financial one (such as corporate stock), which was fully exchangeable.

The best option, the Waverley Committee determined (and Robbins echoed in his later writing), was the public purchase of artistic works of national significance:

> It follows from our recommendations that the extent to which national treasures can be safeguarded, while at the same time doing justice to their owners, depends mainly on the provision of additional funds. More money is needed, both to secure national treasures before they reach the export market, and to make possible a reasonable offer to purchase if it is thought that the export should be prevented. If the community is unwilling to pay it must resign itself to the loss.
>
> Nevertheless we cannot emphasise too strongly our view that, if the Government are not prepared to find the necessary money—an amount insignificant by comparison with its expenditure on other things—the consequences will be deplorable. Posterity will be deprived of treasures we think it vital to retain. (Committee on the Export of Works of Art, Etc. 1952, 25)

Robbins, on his own, went further in his assessment of the proper ends of public funds. Commenting on the "beggarly rise" of public funding for the national collections from £10,000 to £12,500 after the

Waverley Committee report, he imputed: "It is difficult not to feel some contempt for this state of mind at a time when, largely for political motives buttressed by bogus economic apologia, something in the neighbourhood of 40 million per annum was being spent in subsidizing the production of domestic pig meat—to say nothing of other agricultural subsidies running into hundreds of millions of pounds" (1971, 254).[23] Robbins wasn't worried if his proposals for increased government support and the provision of tax incentives for donations to the arts proved unpopular.[24] He was a man of strong convictions, whether those convictions related to economics or to art—or to the melding of the two.

Assessing the Economist and His Work in Art Administration

Asked to identify Robbins's legacy to the arts, his friend and colleague Sir Claus Moser (personal communication 1998) stated, "it was his passion, his knowledge, and his interest. It was also the rational way that he approached every issue—whether economic or artistic. He could always be counted on to make a good, wise, and unbiased contribution." It was further in his ability, according to Moser, to "become" the organization with which he was involved. At the door to the National Gallery or the Courtauld or the Tate, Robbins did not as much remove one hat as he did overlay it with another. If Robbins the economist was a theorist, Robbins the political economist was a practitioner. Given this distinction he could—and did—pursue his work in the arts with aplomb. Because of his deep-seated belief in its rectitude, Robbins was not afraid to challenge position. He made pilgrimages to a succession of chancellors to beseech them for an arts-friendly tax policy.

As noted, Robbins (1963, 70) laid the blame for underfunding of the arts at the feet of government ministers. "Noblesse oblige: it is the duty

23. Robbins was convinced that "perpetual dripping wears away a stone." Eventually an arts-inclined Chancellor of the Exchequer raised the grant sum from £12,500 to £100,000. At the time of his autobiography, the figure stood at £480,000 (1971, 255). Yet prices in the art market had also risen steadily (1976b, 181–82).

24. The proposal to purchase a site for the extension of the National Gallery, which Robbins championed, met with strong condemnation, though it was ultimately approved by the government of the day (1971, 252). His son, Richard Robbins (personal communication 1998), recalled his father's jubilant exclamation, "We've done it!" on the day it was clear that the site would not fall into private hands.

of their exalted position to give a lead in matters of this sort; and there is every reason to believe, that if once they could screw themselves up to making what ought to be, for them privately, a pleasurable recommendation, then so far from making themselves unpopular, they would win almost universal applause." In fact, Robbins suggested a government that makes decisions detrimental to the arts would lose popular support, and this was among the arguments he offered against the institution of museum and gallery entrance fees.[25] Robbins had no greater tolerance for shortsightedness or infighting within the art world. He likened run-ins there to those within the academy. He had the feeling that vendettas were "more frequently to be found in artistic and academic circles than in the ordinary business of life" (1971, 262). And "one of the most evil men" Robbins encountered in his career was a Tate figure whom he dismissed as "an utter scoundrel" (263).[26]

If Robbins was unflinching in the honesty of his assessments, he was also inclined to be fair. In a controversy that had raged for more than forty years, over which gallery—the Dublin Municipal Gallery or the National Gallery—was entitled to the Lane Collection of French pictures, Robbins in the late 1950s, carrying forward his aptitude for mediation, assembled a workable agreement to share possession.[27] He believed the deal might do something to "hasten the time when the many misunderstandings and grievances between our two peoples will at last be left to rest in the peace of forgotten, or forgiven, history" (1971, 257). Here then was art administration as positive foreign policy.

25. Entrance fees were also to be discouraged because their administration would be so costly as to offset any sums likely to be gained.

26. The figure in question was one Le Roux Smith Le Roux, who in 1954 launched an apparently underhanded attempt to unseat then Tate director, John Rothenstein (see 1971, 262–63). Despite any unfavorable characters, Robbins indicated he had also "gained many friendships" at the Tate (261).

27. Sir Hugh Lane had specified in his will that his collection should go to the National Gallery, but an unwitnessed codicil suggested that he had later changed his mind in favor of the Dublin Municipal Gallery. The Dublin Municipal Gallery had been offered and declined a compromise when the dispute began after World War I. Some within the National Gallery, therefore, felt Dublin had missed its chance and that the pictures were Great Britain's rightful property. Robbins (1971, 256–57), however, belonged to another group that believed "an offer is an offer if it has not been definitely cancelled and that therefore, although it was decidedly inconvenient that our Irish friends had taken so long to bring themselves to contemplate any compromise, yet now that they had done so, it was our duty to deal with them, however much it might hurt."

The weight and seriousness that characterized Robbins's work administering the arts were underpinned by a deep personal connection. He was "a very rational man, but he was also a very emotional man" (Moser personal communication 1998).[28] For Robbins, art was a kind of religion; it was his resource to that "which we do not understand," a gateway to the "universal harmonies" (R. Robbins personal communication 1998).[29] Not surprisingly then, Robbins (1963, 61) considered the National Gallery "not just a storehouse of dead panels and canvases: it is rather a temple of vital influences perpetually enlarging our capacities for vision and delight." Given its cultural and spiritual import, the gallery could not be left to the whims of laissez-faire doctrine. As a caretaker of the temple, Robbins argued, "I just do not believe that the state has never played a positive and beneficial role in relation to the arts; and I see no reasonable argument to suggest that this is necessarily so, or that there are general principles . . . in the conception of a free society which would lead us to believe that it should be so" (54). There was a measure of civic and national pride implicit in Robbins's (1971, 253) declaration that the state had a responsibility to ensure his (its) temple was "absolutely hors concours as the greatest generally representative collection of Western art among the galleries of the world." Robbins, a nonpartisan "cross-bencher," plied his influence as both a respected economist and arts "official" in an attempt to secure that result, whether in the acquisition of several pictures including Cézanne's *Bathers* or in the "triumphant" cleaning and restoration of great works such as Titian's *Bacchus and Ariadne* (260).[30] While his work in the arts indeed satisfied his individual passions, it also satisfied his humanitarian desire to ensure their accessibility to present and future generations. If there was a link with other work Robbins did

28. Moser (personal communication 1998) recalled a trip to the Hermitage when Robbins saw a particular Rembrandt for the first time and was moved to tears (see also Moser 1984 and O'Brien 1988, 21). His son, Richard Robbins (personal communication 1998), remembered a similar trip to the Duomo in Florence, whereupon seeing a Michaelangelo sculpture he was similarly affected: "Though he had seen it before, it didn't mean he couldn't be moved a second time." Once after listening to a piece by Bach, Robbins remarked, "This is what makes human life worth living."

29. Though raised in a Strict Baptist family, Robbins, as an adult, considered himself to be agnostic (Robbins 1971, chap. 1).

30. Robbins made direct appeals to philanthropists such as Walter Annenberg to make purchases on behalf of the National Gallery. At one auction, J. Paul Getty was apparently notified that he should stop bidding for a particular piece as Lord Robbins wanted it for the National Gallery (R. Robbins personal communication 1998).

beyond the pale of economics, as in the realm of higher education, it was in his fervent belief that all people should have a chance to be all that they might—that they should be given the opportunity to better their minds through education and their souls through art.[31]

Conclusion

The economist in the modern era is often pictured as the bull in the china shop, taking his cold, unfeeling benefit-cost analysis here, there, and everywhere—politics, law, marriage, procreation—in a seemingly endless quest to provide "the" explanation for individual behavior in these various arenas or to increase the efficiency with which the world operates, or both. It is rather ironic that some of the responsibility for this can be laid, indirectly at least, at the feet of Robbins, whose pronouncements regarding the application of economic reasoning to the analysis of those facets of life where choices are made under scarcity eventually gave rise to the extensions of the economic paradigm to virtually all areas of individual and social life. The irony here arises from the fact that Robbins was apparently extremely reticent to apply economic analysis to art in the sort of ruthless way that others have applied it to various "noneconomic" areas, including art.

William Baumol's work on the economics of the performing arts is fairly emblematic of the hard-headed, detached economic approach.[32] At the other end of the spectrum, we could undoubtedly find art-loving economists who fail to make any connection between these two areas.[33] Somewhere between these two extremes we find Robbins. Although Ruth Towse (1997, xiii) has argued that Robbins "did write on the economics of the arts, but his heart occasionally overrode his head when he did so," this is too strong an assessment; Robbins was not writing on "the economics of the arts" but, rather, on the *political economy* of the arts—an area where the efforts and insights of heart and head are nec-

31. On the education front, see Robbins's speech in the House of Lords, in Hansard 1963–64 (11 December 1963).

32. See, for example, Baumol and Bowen 1966 and the numerous essays by Baumol—who, it should be noted, is both an economist and a sculptor and has taught both subjects at Princeton—reprinted in Towse 1997. Interestingly, although Robbins was Baumol's mentor and dear friend, he did not have any significant influence on Baumol's work in this area.

33. Towse (1997, xiii) has (perhaps somewhat inaccurately) put Keynes in this category, describing him as "a classic example of an art-loving economist who failed to make any connection between the two; he never questioned the need for subsidy to the arts and, as the first Chairman of the Arts Council in England, set about seeking ever greater amounts of it."

essarily and appropriately intermingled. In Robbins's hands, the provision of and support for the arts are not something to be worked out according to the dictates of optimality theory. Rather, a fairly clear line appears to be drawn between the aesthetic and the more overtly commercial—between emotion and sentiment on the one hand and crude utility on the other.

Robbins's work on the political economy of the arts is just one of innumerable illustrations of the role that selective perception, sentiment, and valuation play in economic policy analysis. This is neither good nor bad—just a fact of life. And, to his credit, Robbins was very up front about his biases in this regard and eschewed any temptation to cloak his positions in the garb of "economic science." He simply saw the arts as providing substantial net benefits to society as a whole, even if perhaps not in the same proportion as they did to him personally:

> To watch Fonteyn or Seymour dance the love and despair of Juliet or to arrive at that magic moment in *Fidelio* when the cannon quartet takes over and the impossible and indeed absurd plot becomes more intense than real life—or to sit alone in the National Gallery with the great masterpieces on a summer evening when the people have gone home, or to stroll around among them with my son Richard [an artist] who, in my later years, has so often given me what I used, in my younger days, to get from his Uncle Clive, namely contact with and understanding of the creative artistic process—I count such experiences among my greatest privileges. I have had other sources of happiness, love and friendship, speculative thought, writing and teaching; but, in the world of contemplation, I ask no better heaven than these. (1971, 267)

References

Baumol, William J., and William G. Bowen. 1966. *Performing Arts—The Economic Dilemma: A Study of Problems Common to Theater, Opera, Music, and Dance*. New York: Twentieth Century Fund.

Bell, Clive. 1928. *Art*. London: Chatto & Windus.

Coase, Ronald H. (with E. W. Barrett). 1968. *Educational TV: Who Should Pay?* Washington, D.C.: American Enterprise Institute.

Committee to Consider a New Queen's Hall. 1955. *Report of the Committee to Consider a New Queen's Hall*. London: Her Majesty's Stationery Office.

Committee on the Export of Works of Art, Etc. 1952. *The Export of Works of Art, Etc*. London: Her Majesty's Stationery Office.

Fry, Roger. 1921. *Vision and Design*. New York: Bentano's.
Hansard. 1963–64. The Parliamentary Debates, Fifth Series. Vol. 253. House of Lords Official Report, First Volume of Session 1963–64.
———. 1966–67. The Parliamentary Debates, Fifth Series. Vol. 282. House of Lords Official Report, Ninth Volume of Session 1966–67.
Moggridge, Donald E. 1992. *Maynard Keynes: An Economist's Biography*. London: Routledge.
Moser, Claus. 1984. Untitled. In *Tributes in Memory of Lord Robbins*. London: London School of Economics.
O'Brien, D. P. 1988. *Lionel Robbins*. London: Macmillan.
Peacock, Alan T. 1976. Welfare Economics and Public Subsidies to the Arts. In *The Economics of the Arts*, edited by Mark Blaug. Boulder, Colo.: Westview Press. Originally published in *Manchester School of Economics and Social Studies* (December 1969): 323–35.
Reviewing Committee on the Export of Works of Art. 1954. *Report of the Reviewing Committee on the Export of Works of Art, 1953–54*. London: Her Majesty's Stationery Office.
Robbins, Lionel. 1931. Economic Notes on Some Arguments for Protection. *Economica* 11 (February): 45–62.
———. [1935] 1946. *An Essay on the Nature and Significance of Economic Science*. 2d ed. London: Macmillan.
———. 1955. Notes on Public Finance. *Lloyds Bank Review*, n.s., 38 (October): 1–18.
———. 1963. Art and the State. In *Politics and Economics: Papers in Political Economy*, by Lord Robbins. London: Macmillan.
———. 1966. *The University in the Modern World and Other Papers on Higher Education*. London: Macmillan.
———. 1971. *Autobiography of an Economist*. London: Macmillan.
———. 1976a. *Political Economy, Past and Present: A Review of Leading Theories of Economic Policy*. New York: Columbia University Press.
———. 1976b. Unsettled Questions in the Political Economy of the Arts. In *The Economics of the Arts*, edited by Mark Blaug. Boulder, Colo.: Westview Press. Originally published in *Three Banks Review* (September 1971): 3–19.
———. 1981. Economics and Political Economy. *American Economic Review* 71 (May): 1–10.
———. 1998. *A History of Economic Thought: The LSE Lectures*. Edited by Steven G. Medema and Warren J. Samuels. Princeton, N.J.: Princeton University Press.
Skidelsky, Robert. 1986. *John Maynard Keynes: Hopes Betrayed, 1883–1920*. New York: Viking.
Smith, Adam. [1776] 1937. *An Inquiry into the Nature and Causes of the Wealth of Nations*. New York: Modern Library.
Stamp, Josiah. 1929. Æsthetics as an Economic Factor. In *Some Economic Factors in Modern Life*, by Josiah Stamp. London: P. S. King & Sons.
Towse, Ruth. 1997. *Baumol's Cost Disease: The Arts and Other Victims*. Aldershot, England: Edward Elgar.

Economy, Architecture, and Politics: Colonialist and Cold War Hotels

Annabel Wharton

In this essay I look at hotels in Athens, Cairo, and Istanbul to trace a correlation between architectural effects and economic processes. Two moments are unequally considered: the late nineteenth century is offered as a foil to the mid-twentieth. By the end of the nineteenth century, the "grand tour" of the European Enlightenment had been replaced by less elite, more popular voyaging practices.[1] The traveler became a tourist. A broader section of the bourgeoisie engaged in a pursuit of the experience of cultural difference. The expansion of the colonialist empires of England, France, and Germany provided a new level of security for the Western middle-class excursionist. The development of transcontinental train lines and passenger steamships promoted a constant increase in the radius of adventure. Organizers of group travel, most famously Thomas Cook, encouraged the expansion of both the audience and territory of tourism (Brendon 1991). Increasingly, the eastern Mediterranean became an object of touristic desire. To meet

I am very grateful to the Graham Foundation, which supported this project with a major research grant. I am also indebted to the Trent Foundation and to the Research Council of Duke University for additional travel funds. Hilton International Corporation has been extremely supportive of my work. I want particularly to thank Kathleen Baird, director of the Hilton archives at the Conrad Hilton College of Hotel Management, University of Houston, who greatly facilitated my work in the archives; Kenneth J. Sailor, director of architecture and interior design, Hilton International; Curt Strand, president emeritus of Hilton International; Frank Bemiss, long-time director of technical services for Hilton International; Charles Bell, formerly executive vice-president of Hilton International; Val Lehr, president of the engineering firm Lehr Associates; and Charles H. Warner, of WBTL Architects.

1. For a critical discussion of the Grand Tour in relation to tourism, see Böröcz 1996, esp. chap. 2. See also Turner and Ash 1976, esp. 51–59.

the needs of the European bourgeois traveler, European-style bourgeois accommodation was produced where none had previously existed.

Colonialist Hotels

Some grand hotels were constructed by Western travel agents, like Thomas Cook, or by consortia with interests in the expanding transportation system. The Pera Palas in Istanbul was built in 1892 and was managed by the Compagnie Internationale des Wagon-lits et des Grands Express Européens (Saint Phalle 1991, 181–83). Others were owned by expatriates. In Cairo Samuel Shepheard converted the Palace of Alfi Bay, given him by Abbas I Pasha, into a hotel in 1841 (Bird 1957). A few were established by nationals. The Grande Bretagne in Athens was converted from a mansion to a hotel in 1874 by Stathis Lampsa. Lampsa, a gifted cook, had been sent to Paris by his employer, George I, king of the Hellenes, to further his culinary education. He invested the wealth and knowledge that he accrued as a successful chef in Paris in the Grande Bretagne with a partner, Savvas Kendros (Frischauer 1965, 35–54; 1997).

All three hotels were located in the most modern, most elite, most Europeanized sites in their respective cities. The Pera Palas was, as its name suggests, set in Pera, a European suburb located across the Golden Horn from the ancient Byzantine and Ottoman city of Istanbul (fig. 1). From the second half of the nineteenth century through the 1970s, the elite and the modern marked Pera and its northern extensions.[2] The hotel was found just off the lower end of the Grande Rue de Pera, *the* shopping street of Istanbul, in the neighborhood of Western embassies. Around the corner was the U.S. consulate, formerly the Palazzo Corpi, the first American diplomatic property in Europe. Similarly, Shepheard's Hotel was sited in the western, Europeanized extension of medieval Cairo. This new Cairo had been developed by Isma'il Pasha, the grandson of Muhammad 'Ali, to the west and north of the old city, absorbing the space added to the city by the significant shift to the east of the Nile's flow. Isma'il Pasha's model was Haussmann's Paris, which he visited during the Exposition Universelle of 1867 (Abu-

2. For a detailed discussion of the history and politics of the development of Galata, Pera, and the suburbs north of the Golden Horn with bibliography, see Rosenthal 1980; for the architectural expression of this development, see Çelik 1986, 31–49.

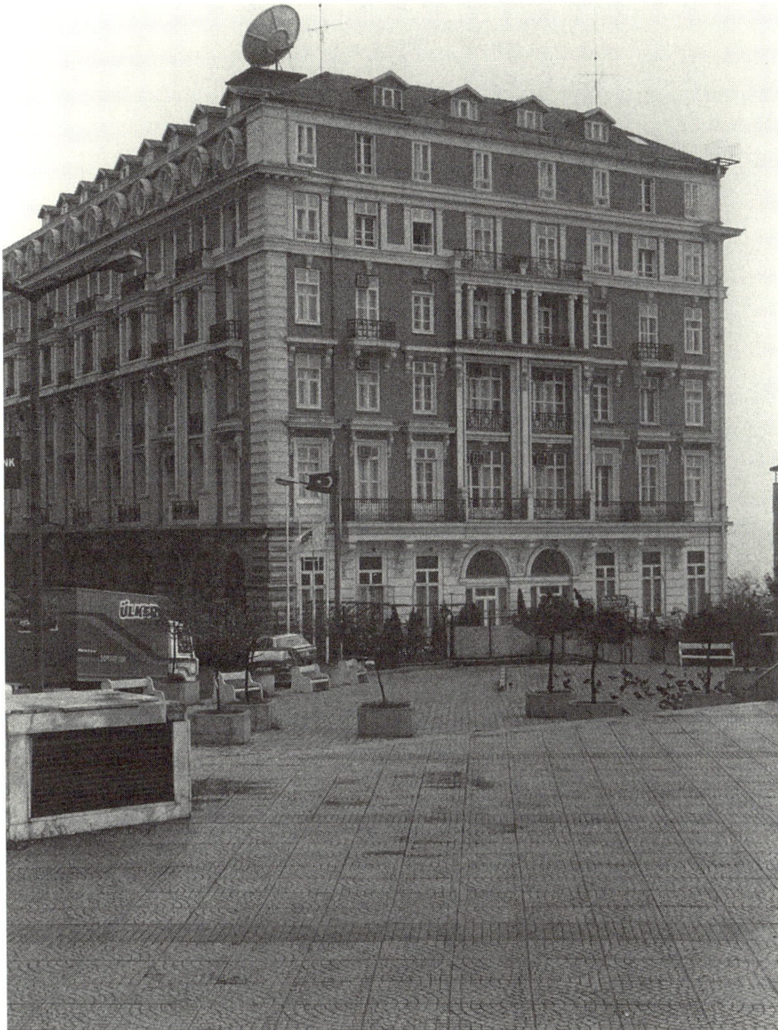

Figure 1 Istanbul, Pera Palas Hotel, terrace facade. Photograph by author.

Lughod 1971, 104). The hotel opened directly to the Street of the Camels, the "Egyptian Champs Elysées." The city of Athens, like the national government of Greece, was reconstituted according to German designs after the successful conclusion of the Greeks' War for Independence.[3] The Grande Bretagne was located centrally, on Constitution Square, across the street from the Royal Palace.

All three buildings were designed by European architects in an eclectic neoclassical style vaguely on the model of Renaissance palazzi. The Grande Bretagne was constructed as a mansion in 1842 for a wealthy Greek by the Danish architect Theophile Hansen. It was a handsome block of three floors with projecting bays framing the restrained double-arcade of its facade. A grand lobby opened directly into the elaborate ballroom at the hotel's core. After its conversion into a hotel in 1874, it offered eighty beds and two baths. The Pera Palas was a taller, more Baroque version of the same building type built by the French architect Alexander Vallaury. A small but sumptuous lobby prefaced an exotically treated, multistory Oriental Hall at the hotel's center. The most privileged of the guestrooms opened into its gallery. Behind the Oriental Hall was a dining room with a view of the street life of Mesrutiyet Cadessi; to its right a bar and tearoom opened in the summer to a marble terrace above the same busy boulevard. Reception was a tiny desk located down three steps in the corner of the entrance hall. By the turn of the century, Shepheard's, too, had been remodeled as an Italianate block. It had an interior courtyard with a central fountain and palm trees.[4] The hotel's ballroom was ornately Louis XVI.[5] In

3. An excellent monographic treatment of the city is Papageorgious-Venetas 1994. Also, Bastéa 1994, 111–24.

4. After its opening in 1841, Shepheard's was frequently rebuilt and remodeled. It was reconstructed in 1891 and enlarged in 1899, 1904, 1909, and 1927. After its destruction in 1952, it was relocated, and in 1957 it was rebuilt as a modern hotel. Nina Nelson's *Shepheard's Hotel* (1960) is typical of the hotel-history genre. It is a celebratory inventory of the famous people who stayed in the hotel and the executives who ran it. It is not a critical assessment of the hotel's architecture or the site's history. Her description of the structure is limited: "It was to be in the Italian style of the period with a covering of thick stucco. Once again the hotel emerged in the form of a rectangle enclosing a courtyard with fountains and palms, and what was to become the famous terrace replaced the balcony. . . . The main ground-floor passage looked like a picture gallery for it was hung with delightful paintings of Egypt by such eminent artists as Lamplough, Linton and Talbot together with etchings, lithographs and drawings of state occasions at Shepheard's. When the building was completed it ranked as one of the most elaborate hotels of the day" (57).

5. The ballroom was remodeled in a Pharaonic style in the 1930s by the French architect Jean Riboult (Nelson 1960, 143).

addition to luxurious carpets and fine furnishings, a collection of paintings of Egypt by English artists adorned its walls. Guarding the entranceway were sphinxes brought from the Temple of Serapis at Memphis. The unscenic squalor behind the hotel's garden was hidden by a sixty-foot-high latticework screen. A raised terrace in the front of Shepheard's staged the popular Azbakiyyah Gardens as exotic theater for the hotel's guests. A nineteenth-century traveler's description gives some sense of both what was present and what was absent in the view of the city:

> In front of the Hotel . . . was to be seen the old Ezbekieh [Azbakiyyah], planned and planted by Mehemet Ali, the primitive Hyde Park of Cairo, with its gigantic trees and thick shrubbery, with Arab Cafés and cafés chantants at intervals, filled nightly with Egyptians of every rank and race . . . chattering like a flock of magpies. . . . There you saw men of all shades of color, different types of race, and varieties of costume; the half-naked Fellah or peasant, the stark-naked Santon or saint, the richly clad Turk, the Arnaut soldier, a walking arsenal, the coal black Nubian, the coffee-colored Abyssinian, the copper-colored Arab and the straight-laced European. All mingled and fused together, conversing together in a perfect Babel of every known dialect of Eastern and Western tongues. The absence of all women, save of the lowest class, rendered the scene still more unique and remarkable. The guests at Shepheard's had thus an "Arabian Nights Entertainment": improvised for them always without care and without cost, in this Egyptian Champs Elysées.[6]

The authentically exotic—most particularly the variously colored and potentially uncovered male body, made more alien by the absence of women—was readily available, close enough to hear, smell, and touch, as well as see. For Edwin de Leon and other tourists, the hotel offered the security and comfort of Europe. It also provided immediate, haptic access to the Other.

The desperate economies of the two world wars and the depression seriously tarnished the glitz of these hotels. Nevertheless, that they retained their social and political importance is indicated even by the abuse they sustained. With the fall of Athens to the Nazis in 1941, the Grande Bretagne was commandeered as Wehrmacht headquarters.

6. De Leon (1890, 159–62), describing Shepheard's as it was in the 1850s.

Shepheard's was one of the principal targets of the anti-British riots of 16 January 1952, which precipitated the end of colonial rule in Egypt. It was burned to the ground. The hotel's destruction suggests how closely it was identified with colonialist power.[7]

Postcolonialist Hotels

New hotel construction had virtually ceased with the beginning of European hostilities of World War I. The depression and World War II further diminished the business of leisure travel. With the exception of the United States, the world of the late 1940s and early 1950s was deeply impoverished. The insecurities bred by the end of colonialism and the advent of the Cold War discouraged tourism through mid-century. The first significant hotel-building initiative in Europe and the Middle East after World War II was undertaken by Hilton International, a division of Conrad Hilton's Hilton Hotel Corporation. Hilton traveled to Europe in 1949 to reconnoiter; by 1950, negotiations were well under way for hotels in Greece, Italy, and Turkey. Conrad Hilton's project was to create a demand, rather than meet one. As Hilton ([1957] 1987, 233) reveals in his autobiography, the plan was promoted not by travel statistics, but by the U.S. government: "Both the State Department and the Department of Commerce suggested that the Hilton organization could make a substantial contribution to the government program of Foreign Aid by establishing American-operated hotels in important world cities. These hotels could stimulate trade and travel, bringing American dollars into the economies of the countries needing help. Besides, and this pleased me especially, they felt that such hotels would create international good will."

The new Hiltons in Istanbul, Cairo, and Athens were unprecedented. They were dominant in their siting, scale, and whiteness and extraordinary in their modernity. Like the grand hotels of the nineteenth century, the Hiltons occupied the most prestigious sites in the city. But in contrast to their predecessors, the status and meaning of the neighborhood often proceeded from the hotel's construction. The location of the Nile Hilton was Qasr al-Nil (Fortress or Palace on the Nile), where it replaced the British barracks of the occupation force. Before it became the locus from which tourists planned their forays into Egypt, it had

7. The new Shepheard's of 1957 never reassumed the social mantle of the old Shepheard's.

functioned as the center of military control. As the site from which itineraries began, the Nile Hilton is the first building mentioned in the *Blue Guide Egypt*. The Istanbul Hilton occupied the upper quadrant of Democracy Park, a five-minute walk from Taksim Square, at the upper end of İstiklal Cadessi, the old Grande Rue de Pera (fig. 2). The Hilton contributed to the shift north of the new corporate and banking center of Istanbul. Airline offices clustered around Hiltons like pigeons around tourists in Venice's Piazza San Marco. The Athens Hilton was provided a dramatic site opposite the Acropolis. Its construction, along with that of the slightly later building of Walter Gropius's enormous new U.S. Embassy, redefined the status of the neighborhood. Property taxes soared.

Instead of fitting into an assemblage of deluxe structures as had the earlier grand hotels, the Hilton represented a dramatic intervention in the landscape. Each of these hotels was the highest building in its respective city at the time of its construction. Just as significantly, each visually subordinated urban landscapes of moderately scaled, classically textured buildings with the shock of their modernity. Their immense fabrics were rendered in the austere clarity of rectilinear geometries. The Istanbul Hilton, designed by the well-known second-generation modern master Gordan Bunshaft, exemplifies the cool abstraction of these buildings.[8] It was a heroically scaled white slab constructed of reinforced concrete, with a regular grid of balconies and lifted off the ground by slender white pilotis. Like a monumental minimalist sculpture, the Istanbul Hilton was an elite modernist object.

These Hiltons defined America for both foreign and local observers. Even for those who did not enter the hotel, its grounds embodied an American utopia. The buildings were framed as the American suburb, complete with the suburbs' fetishized lawns and shrubbery, swimming pools, and tennis courts. The pool particularly, with its colorful cabanas and interesting bodies, became a source of pleasure for those who swam—and for those who looked. Local elites who did not stay at the Hilton also experienced its modernity and Americanism, but from the inside. The Nile Hilton was *the* place to celebrate a wedding until the mid-1970s. Even more commonly, the soda fountain, with its cheese-

8. For Bunshaft, see Krinsky 1988. Another well-known corporate architect, Welton Becket, did the Nile Hilton. The Athens Hilton was built by Greek architects Prokopios Vassiliades, E. M. Vourekas, and Spyros Staikos in close consultation with the American firm Warner Burns, on the model of the Istanbul and Nile Hiltons.

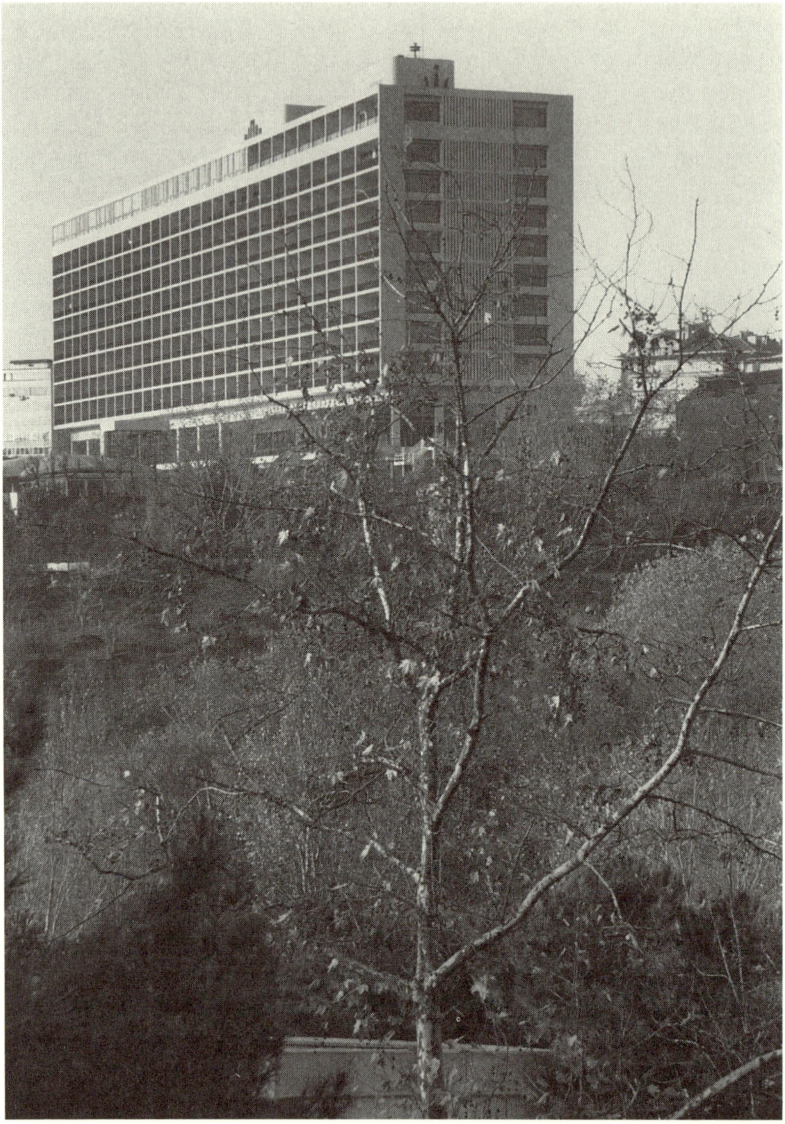

Figure 2 Istanbul, Istanbul Hilton, general view from the east, showing the building after the 1965 addition. The original building was twenty bays wide; the nine-bay addition supplement was included in Bunshaft's original plans. Photograph by author.

burgers and milkshakes, and the hotel's telecommunications center were sought out by those who wished for a taste of American efficiency. The rewards of American capitalism were brilliantly exhibited even to the outsider.

The obvious signages of America—the swimming pool and the cheeseburger—were sustained by a deeper structure of value embodied in the Hilton. The economic principles of corporate America determined the architectural program of Hilton International and were therefore manifest in its forms.

At a microeconomic level, the contract for the Istanbul Hilton stunningly exemplified the economic interests of corporate America. It is a breathtaking example of entrepreneurial capitalism. Hilton International received a third of the hotel's gross profits with no capital investment. The site, which was selected by Hilton, was provided by the owner. The architect, also selected by Hilton, was paid by the owner. The building, which had to conform to Hilton's specifications, was designed, constructed, furnished, and maintained at the sole expense of the owner. And the owner—the Turkish Republic Pension Fund in the case of the Istanbul Hilton—was part of the national government. Governments were also owners of the Nile Hilton and initially of the Athens Hilton, as well as Hiltons elsewhere, including those in Puerto Rico, Havana, and Berlin. The state owner had access, in principle, to unlimited funds. Hilton could and did demand the highest quality construction, cutting-edge technology, and immaculate furnishing independent of cost considerations. Hilton was prepared to work closely with the owner on the building's financing. The host countries were all impoverished, and they all suffered an egregious balance of payments. Hard currency with which to pay for equipment and supplies for the hotel bought from American companies was in very short supply. In the case of the Istanbul Hilton, the problem was solved by the U.S. State Department. Two of the necessary $7 million for the project were supplied by Marshall Plan funds ("Bricks without Straw" 1959, 42–43). The Hilton project was in this case subsidized by the American taxpayer.

The owners of the Istanbul, Athens, and Cairo Hiltons accepted seemingly lopsided terms from the corporation because Hilton International offered a highly desirable product. Especially after the gala opening of the Istanbul Hilton in 1955—an occasion attended by movie stars and other celebrities, as well as by diplomats and businessmen—a Hilton hotel came to be as important to the status of a newly independent country as a national airline. But the structures that were produced by these contractual arrangements were very good. By imposing the highest standards on the owners of these buildings, their quality was assured. As a result, the Hiltons of Istanbul, Athens, and Cairo remain among the finest hotels in their respective cities. Where local political pressures or the owner's own interests resisted such contractual arrangements, as in Berlin, the resulting structure was less distinguished and often ultimately less profitable.

Aesthetics of Commoditization

The micropolitics and microeconomics of the Hilton contracts affected the hotel building most fundamentally by determining its quality. The broader reach of politics and economy—what might be named ideology—also acted on their form and determined their interpretation.[9] America as entrepeneurial capital was reified in the Hiltons' modernity. The modern aesthetics of clarity so perfectly embodied in the Hilton arise from an attention to function. The rationality of the Hiltons lay in their remarkably effective commoditization of space.[10] The International Hiltons were part of a popular American hotel tradition, distinct from that of the conventional European grand hotel.[11] The American hotel, like the Ford motorcar or the Kodak Brownie camera, made its profit by providing with great efficiency what a large middle-class public desired. Democratization of space increased its return. Hilton

9. Here *ideology* does not refer to rigidly held, extremist political views, as it does in the *Washington Times*. I use the word to refer to habits of thought that naturalize idiosyncratic social practice and mask the structures of authority which those social practices empower. This formulation depends on Karl Marx and Frederick Engels (1986) in the chapter on Feuerbach in their book *The German Ideology*. See also Kavanagh 1989, 306–20; Williams 1977, 55–71; Eagleton 1991. For an accessible discussion of theory, ideology, and politics, see Foucault and Deleuze 1990, 9–16.

10. By *commoditization* I mean the conversion of site, object, or process into a vendable good. The texts most commonly cited in discussions of commoditization are Marx [1867] 1967, 35–83, and Mauss 1954. For commoditization and the art market, see Wood 1996, 257–80.

11. The distinction between the traditions of the American and European hotel seems obvious to me, although it has not been teased out in the literature as far as I know. For still the best introduction to the hotel as architectural genre, see Pevsner 1976, 169–92. See also the classic Williamson 1930.

imported to postwar Europe and the Middle East an American concept of a hotel. This concept combined the American urban hotel, like the Statlers, which were designed for salesmen and other business travelers, with the giant American resort hotel, which met the needs of a massive number of middle-class vacationers. Hiltons sold beds abroad in the American way, in unprecedented numbers. Guestrooms were identical, each with appointments that complemented the hotel's high-tech exterior: private bathrooms and balconies, direct-dial telephones, reliable international telecommunications, ice water tapped into the rooms. Interior space was remodeled as efficient and modern, though marked as elite by the use of the highest quality materials and artworks. The generous public areas of the traditional hotel were reconceived as profit-producing. Luxurious lobbies and lounges were complemented by bars and shops. These elite shopping courts offered locally produced luxury items—leathers, jewelry, and carpets—as well as expensive imported goods. The arcade provided tourists protection from the ordeal of experiencing the local market. At the same time, it afforded access to those cultural artifacts which would later, after their return home, furnish proof of their alien encounter. The tourist might thus be saved from the disorienting experience of the Oriental bazaar and the disempowering trial of haggling—though at considerable cost. The soda fountain exemplifies another aspect of this shift. Old hotels had offered expensive food expensively; the Hilton also offered cheap food expensively as pop cuisine.

The Hilton's commoditization of space extended to gaze. The siting of the Hiltons and their plans were determined by the distant view that their guestrooms and their rooftop restaurants were meant to frame. And this was the view that the Hilton sold, beginning with advertisements. A typical advertisement (November 1978) for the Athens Hilton displayed the Acropolis and announced: "THE MOST FAMOUS VIEW IN HISTORY!" In its announcement of the Cairo Hilton, the *Hotel Monthly* ("Nile Hilton Opens in Cairo" 1959, 40) exclaims that, "From nearly any floor in the hotel guests have a panoramic view to the west that includes the Great Pyramids." In Istanbul, it was the view down to Dolmabahçe Camii, across the generous sweep of the Bosphorus to Asia.

The extraordinarily effective commoditization of the Hilton was not solely concerned with monetary profit. It was also about politics. The carefully framed views from the Hilton only appear to be innocent. The Athens Hilton so dominated the view of the Parthenon that, according to Vincent Scully (1963, 102), famous architectural historian and critic, it represented an act of vandalism: "If one takes a position in the Parthenon where Pheidias' ivory and gold statue of Athena once stood, it will be seen that the temple, once orientated directly toward its appropriate sunrise over the mountain, is now oriented toward the sun and the Hilton—whose egg-crate facade leers up on axis between the two central columns. . . . The effect may most accurately be described as obscene." Scully is incensed that the Hilton vied with the Parthenon in the representation of the apogee of democratic culture.

The Nile Hilton focused on the pyramids. It turned its back on the medieval, Oriental city to face a safer, more remote Ancient Egypt. The hotel looks toward the Egypt that the West traditionally constructed as the birthplace of Western civilization. This was the same Egypt that was promoted by *Life* magazine's "Epics of Man" series in the mid-1950s (Barnett 1956a, 1956b); by Helen Gardner's (1959) popular textbook, *Art through the Ages* (in which there are twenty-four pages devoted to Ancient Egypt and three to Islamic Egypt); and by the official Egyptian tourist bureau. The old city was too deeply implicated in Arab nationalism.

Even the idyllic view of the Bosphorus from the Istanbul Hilton could be seen as political. In his address at the gala opening of the hotel, Conrad Hilton ([1957] 1987, 264) names the ideological significance of the hotel's location:

> The Istanbul Hilton stands thirty miles from the Iron Curtain. . . . Here, with the Iron Curtain veritably before our eyes, we found a people who had fought the Russians for the past three hundred years and were entirely unafraid of them. . . . Standing before the assembled guests at the opening ceremonies, I felt this "City of the Golden Horn" was a tremendous place to plant a little bit of America. Here was the site that had known the Persian hordes, become Constantine's capital, seen the invading Crusaders, been the center of the old Ottoman Empire, and where in 1923 Mustafa Kemal Ataturk had fostered a young Republic. "Each of our hotels," I said, "is a 'little America,' not as a symbol of bristling power, but as a friendly center where men of many nations and of good will may speak the language of peace."

In a brief announcement of the ground breaking of the Hilton in the *New York Times* (4 November 1951, II 17:8), the threat of the Soviet

Union was accorded an even greater proximity. Here the Istanbul Hilton was "within ten miles of the Russian border." The claim of geographic immediacy is dramatic; it is also fictional. No part of the former Soviet Union is found within three hundred miles of Istanbul. The remapping of power by Conrad Hilton and the *New York Times* is an indication of the territorial dimension of the Red Scare in the United States in the 1950s. But the importance of the hotel's nearness to the Soviet Union had to do not only with the view it provided of the "Iron Curtain" but also with the antithesis of this perspective. If Russia was "veritably before our eyes," it followed that the Hilton, the representation of America, was veritably before the Soviets' eyes.

Thus for both those on the inside and those on the outside, the Hilton functioned as a metonym of American capital. Conrad Hilton ([1957] 1987, 264) articulated this in his autobiography: "Let me say right here, that we operate hotels abroad for the same reason we operate them in this country—to make money for our stockholders. . . . However, we feel that if we really believe in what we are all saying about liberty, about Communism, about happiness, that we, as a nation, must exercise our great strength and power for good against evil."

Just as the grand hotels were shaped by European colonialism, Hiltons gave material form to an early stage of the globalization of capital. They were architectural expressions of the internationalism of commoditization. They were not a functional reaction to the revival of familiar touristic practices; they were, rather, an evocation of a new leisure industry. The Hiltons were constructed not, as in the nineteenth century, to meet an established need, but to create one. They suggest that this pressure was not produced simply by the desire for profit, but from a remarkable political commitment to the system that promoted profit-making.

Hilton's project depended on his hotels' effective representation of modernity. These buildings prominently and publicly inscribed the cities in which they were built with a monumental sign of an anticommunist America. At the same time, they promised local elites, as well as foreign visitors, participation in an affluent postcolonial Western economy. The peace that Conrad Hilton envisioned was that of globalized capitalism. And, indeed, Hilton was an early contributor to the globalization of the present. The Istanbul Hilton is credited with the 60 percent rise in tourism to Turkey that occurred in the year of its opening. By the 1980s, tourism had become the world's largest nonfood industry, outstripping oil production (Böröcz 1996, 3). The early Hilton International hotels exemplify the economic and political construction of architectural spectacle. I hope that my analysis of the Hilton will contribute to a broader awareness of the spatial economies of the architectures of globalization. From EuroDisney to Las Vegas, the leisure migration industry continuously refines the architectures of commoditization that manipulate us for their profit and our pleasure.

References

Abu-Lughod, Janet L. 1971. *Cairo: 1001 Years of the City Victorious.* Princeton, N.J.: Princeton University Press.

Barnett, Lincoln. 1956a. Egypt the Oldest Nation. *Life* 41 (1 October): 78–98.

———. 1956b. Egypt's Eras of Splendor. *Life* 41 (26 November): 106–17.

Bastéa, Eleni. 1994. Athens. In *Streets: Critical Perspectives on Public Space*, edited by Zeynep Çelik, Diane Favro, and Richard Ingersoll. Berkeley: University of California Press.

Bird, Michael. 1957. *Samuel Shepheard of Cairo.* London: Michael Joseph.

Böröcz, József. 1996. *Leisure Migration: A Sociological Study on Tourism.* Oxford: Pergamon.

Brendon, Piers. 1991. *Thomas Cook: 150 Years of Popular Tourism.* London: Secker & Warburg.

Bricks without Straw. 1959. *Forbes* 83 (15 February): 42–43.

Çelik, Zeynep. 1986. *The Remaking of Istanbul: Portrait of an Ottoman City in the Nineteenth Century.* Seattle: University of Washington Press.

de Leon, Edwin. 1890. *Thirty Years of My Life on Three Continents.* London: Ward & Downey.

Eagleton, Terry. 1991. *Ideology: An Introduction.* London: Verso.

Foucault, Michel, and Gilles Deleuze. 1990. Intellectuals and Power. In *Discourses: Conversations in Postmodern Art and Culture*, edited by Russell Ferguson, William Olander, Marcia Tucker, and Karen Fiss. New York and Cambridge, Mass.: New Museum of Contemporary Art and MIT Press.

Frischauer, Willi. 1965. *An Hotel Is Like a Woman: The Grand Hotels of Europe.* London: Leslie Frewin.

———. 1997. *Hotel Grande Bretagne, Athens.* Athens: A. Georgiadis.

Gardner, Helen. 1959. *Art through the Ages.* New York: Harcourt-Brace.

Hilton advertisement (November 1978).

Hilton, Conrad N. [1957] 1987. *Be My Guest.* Englewood Cliffs, N.J.: Prentice Hall.

Kavanagh, James H. 1989. Ideology. In *Critical Terms for Literary Study*, edited by Frank Lentricchia and Thomas McLaughlin. Chicago: University of Chicago Press.

Krinsky, Carol Herselle. 1988. *Gordon Bunshaft of Skidmore, Owings and Merrill.* New York: Architectural History Foundation.

Marx, Karl. [1867] 1967. Commodities. In *Capital*, edited by Frederick Engels. New York: International Publishers.
Marx, Karl, and Frederick Engels. 1986. *The German Ideology*. Edited by C. J. Arthur. New York: International Publishers.
Mauss, Marcel. 1954. *The Gift: Forms and Functions of Exchange in Archaic Societies*. Translated by Ian Cunnison and with an introduction by E. E. Evans-Pritchard. Glencoe, Ill.: Free Press.
Nelson, Nina. 1960. *Shepheard's Hotel*. New York: Macmillan.
New York Times, 4 November 1951, II 17:8.
Nile Hilton Opens in Cairo. 1959. *The Hotel Monthly* 67.793 (April): 40.
Papageorgious-Venetas, Alexander. 1994. *Athens: The Ancient Heritage and the Historic Cityscape in a Modern Metropolis*. Archaeological Society at Athens Library, 140. Athens: Archaeological Society at Athens.
Pevsner, Nikolaus. 1976. *A History of Building Types*. Bollingen Series 35-19. Princeton, N.J.: Princeton University Press.
Rosenthal, Stephen T. 1980. *The Politics of Dependency: Urban Reform in Istanbul*. Westport, Conn.: Greenwood.
Saint Phalle, Nathalie de. 1991. *Hôtels Littéraires: Voyage Autour de la Terre*. Paris: Quai Voltaire.
Scully, Vincent. 1963. The Athens Hilton: A Study in Vandalism. *Architectural Forum* 119 (July): 100–103.
Turner, Louis, and John Ash. 1976. *The Golden Hordes: International Tourism and the Pleasure Periphery*. New York: St. Martin's.
Williams, Raymond. 1977. Ideology. In *Marxism and Literature*, by Raymond Williams. New York: Oxford University Press.
Williamson, Jefferson. 1930. *The American Hotel: An Anecdotal History*. New York: Knopf.
Wood, Paul. 1996. Commodity. In *Critical Terms for Art History*, edited by Robert S. Nelson and Richard Shiff. Chicago: University of Chicago Press.

Part 3

The Business of Art

The Economics of Art in Early Modern Times: Some Humanist and Scholastic Approaches

Toon Van Houdt

According to Renaissance humanists, man distinguished himself from brute animals by his intellectual abilities and the power to speak. Following the lead of ancient philosophers and rhetoricians such as Cicero and Quintilian, the humanists considered reason and speech, *ratio* and *oratio*, to be the essential marks of humanity (Jacopin and Lagrée 1996, 25–28). This one-sided focus on the humanizing force of speech helps explain why most humanists had disappointingly little to say about the visual arts, especially about painting and sculpture. Humanists defined themselves primarily as men of letters; they regarded artists as manual workers, who sold the products of their craft in shops. Even though this attitude was significantly modified in the course of the sixteenth and seventeenth centuries with the emergence of the learned artist, the gap that separated humanists from architects, painters, and sculptors usually remained vast. Many humanists simply proved unable to understand, let alone to discuss, such typical features of art as color, light, and perspective (Cast 1988, 414–15; Hope and McGrath 1996, 168–69). This is not to say that they neglected the world of art altogether. While few scholars endeavored to establish the proper rules for painting and sculpting, some of them did reflect on the social position of the artist and the economic aspects of his craft. These reflections were laid down in various treatises on politics (*politica*) and husbandry (*oeco-*

This article was written during a visiting fellowship at the Swedish Collegium for Advanced Study in the Social Sciences (SCASSS). I thank Neil De Marchi, Katlijne Van der Stighelen, Marcus de Schepper, and the anonymous referee for their valuable comments and suggestions. Unless otherwise cited, all translations from the Latin are mine.

nomica), which together with ethics (*ethica*) constituted the traditional branches of practical philosophy (cf. Kraye 1988, 303–6).

In the following pages, I discuss the economic analysis of art as it was developed by humanists and theologians in the southern Netherlands in the first half of the seventeenth century. To do this, I concentrate mainly, though not exclusively, on the writings of Justus Lipsius (1564–1606) and Nicolaus Vernulaeus (1583–1649), both of whom were humanist professors at the University of Louvain; along with Carolus Scribani (1561–1629) and Laurentius Beyerlinck (1578–1627), who were prolific writers from Antwerp; and Leonardus Lessius (1554–1623), a late Scholastic theologian who worked at the Jesuit college in Louvain. Close connections tie these authors together. Scribani was a former pupil of Lessius, who in turn was a personal friend of Lipsius. Beyerlinck and Vernulaeus had both studied under Lipsius and promoted his political and moral views. Both Beyerlinck and Vernulaeus were, however, well acquainted with late Scholastic thought, in general, and with Lessius's economic and ethical ideas, in particular. Moreover, all the authors maintained close contacts with Archduke Albert and Archduchess Isabella, the sovereign rulers of the southern Netherlands from 1598 until 1621, as well as with other members of the House of Hapsburg. Last but not least, most of the authors enjoyed strong connections with Antwerp, by far the most important economic and artistic center of the country.[1] It is interesting to note in this respect that Lipsius was a dear friend of the Antwerp artist Otto van Veen (Otho Vaenius) (Morford 1996, 238), whereas Scribani was on excellent terms with Peter Paul Rubens and Anthony Van Dyck (Timmermans 1998, 204); Beyerlinck, for his part, was a prominent member of the *Violieren*, the chamber of rhetoric that formed part of the well-known Antwerp guild of artists called *Saint Lucas* (Timmermans 1998, 186).

It is striking how little effort has been made to date to examine the works of later humanists and theologians in order to present in a comprehensive manner what they have to say about the economic aspects of the world of art. From my exposition I hope it will become clear that, while the above-mentioned authors did not devise an "economics of art" in the proper sense of the word, they did succeed, nonetheless, in constructing an intellectual framework that enabled them to address

1. For further biographical details, see the following works: Brouwers 1961 (Scribani); IJsewijn 1987 (Beyerlinck); Depuydt 1991 (Vernulaeus); Morford 1991 (Lipsius); and Van Houdt 1992 (Lessius).

issues that were particularly relevant to the art trade. To be more precise, they treated at some length such divergent problems as the social status and economic position of the artist, the valuation of art objects, and the consumption of art. Their observations and viewpoints deserve some attention, if only for the fact that they explicitly aimed to model the economic activity of artists, as well as of other craftsmen, according to the moral economy they proposed in their writings.

When discussing late Scholastic and humanist viewpoints on economics and art, we cannot avoid addressing three important issues. The first is whether the ideas put forward by the authors coincided with the self-perception of early modern artists. The second is whether the authors succeeded in having their ideas on economics and art accepted by the artists themselves and were thus able to realize the moral economy they had in mind. Certainly, any attempt to answer these first two thorny questions in sufficient detail would far exceed the limits of this article,[2] so before we try to tackle them, it might be prudent to concentrate on the third, closely related problem that is perhaps somewhat easier to answer: Was the intellectual framework constructed by the aforementioned authors rich and subtle enough to take into account all relevant economic and social aspects of the world of art as it flourished in Antwerp in the first half of the seventeenth century? To put it more poignantly: Was there a gap between theory and practice, and, if so, how large was it? As we shall see, there is ample reason to believe that the authors failed to grasp some of the complexities that surrounded the production, distribution, and consumption of art in Antwerp—the artistic center they were most familiar with.

Social Status and Economic Position of the Artist

In 1610, the Jesuit scholar Carolus Scribani authored a highly rhetorical portrayal of Antwerp and its inhabitants, which was entitled, plainly, *Antverpia*. Following the lead of Lodovico Guicciardini (1521–89), who gave Antwerp pride of place in his *Descrittione di tutti i Paesi Bassi* first issued in 1567, Scribani devotes much attention to the various social groupings in the city and their professional occupations. After

2. An interesting attempt to connect the practices and attitudes of early modern artists with contemporary theoretical views on the production, valuation, and uses of art is offered by De Marchi and Van Miegroet 1994.

a brief description of the local nobility and the numerous merchants active in the city, Scribani concentrates on the various crafts practiced in Antwerp. Most of the technical arts (*artes mechanicae*) are mentioned only in passing as Scribani (1610, 31–55) prefers to highlight only those technical arts that can be deemed "liberal," such as painting, sculpting, engraving, printing, architecture, and engineering. The scope of Scribani's work is admittedly rather one-sided. Far from providing any thoroughgoing economic or social analysis, the author limits himself to a boastful, albeit slightly tedious, account of famous painters, sculptors, architects, and others.[3] This approach clearly suffices to prove one of the central theses of the book: that Antwerp has produced more outstanding artists in the course of one hundred years than the entire world has seen in the course of the past centuries (33).

Despite its blatant limitations, Scribani's treatise is interesting for at least two reasons. For one, the author correctly stresses the overall importance of Antwerp as a leading center in the production of luxury items at the end of the sixteenth and the beginning of the seventeenth centuries. At the same time, he awakens our attention to the fact that works of art were first and foremost regarded as consumer goods produced for a relatively small, albeit wealthy, clientele, both in the Netherlands and abroad—a clientele that wanted and could afford to indulge in conspicuous consumption. Paintings, sculptures, and engravings were collected, along with precious stones, tapestries, sumptuous books, and even exotic animals; then they were stored in lavishly decorated houses and palaces (Thieme 1959, 10–12; Burke 1993; Jardine 1996, 3–34, 377–424). In examining humanist and Scholastic views developed at the beginning of the seventeenth century on the economic aspects of art, it is important to bear in mind that, more often than not, this "economics of art" formed only a small part of a more encompassing analysis of the production, valuation, and consumption of luxury goods.

Scribani's treatise is interesting for yet another reason. It clearly betrays the ambivalent attitude many humanists and theologians—men of letters—had about the visual arts. On the one hand, painters, sculptors, and engravers were regarded as craftsmen; insofar as they

3. While doing so, Scribani followed a tradition that was well established in the Italian Renaissance and ultimately went back to the Roman author Pliny the Elder, who, in his *Natural History*, offered an extensive series of anecdotal stories about famous painters and sculptors. See Hope and McGrath 1996, 168–69; Welch 1997, 125–26.

executed manual labor, they belonged to the same category of people as weavers and shoemakers. On the other hand, it was admitted that their trade involved a much higher degree of intellectual activity. As a consequence, their profession was considered more "liberal." Although strictly speaking these professions belonged to the crafts, they came very close to joining the narrow circle of the liberal arts that traditionally comprised grammar, dialectics, rhetoric, music, arithmetic, geometry, and astronomy.

This ambivalent attitude is most clearly demonstrated in Vernulaeus's treatise on politics, which was first published in 1623 and reissued several times in the course of the seventeenth century. In this work, a handbook aimed at educating future statesmen and civil servants, Vernulaeus offers an astonishingly simple tripartite model of society, consisting of noblemen, the military, and ordinary people (*plebei*). The third class, ordinary people, is further divided according to the profession exercised by the *plebei*. Following the lead of such ancient authors as Cicero and Pliny the Elder, Vernulaeus ([1623] 1647, 231) wholeheartedly attributes the first rank to farmers. In his view, agriculture lies at the root of all other professions and arts: without agriculture, the entire society would simply collapse, as its members would lack the necessary products to feed themselves.

It is interesting to note that Vernulaeus's praise of agriculture does not lead to any condemnation or depreciation of commerce. According to him, commercial activity actually contributes to the strength of cities and states alike: "Business is, so to speak, the life and blood of innumerable cities and provinces. It ensures that there is always plenty of money available, the very nerve of war and peace" (232). Finally, Vernulaeus considers the various crafts that are practiced. A simple criterion is proposed to rank them: the more liberal the art that is executed, the more worthy of esteem the craftsman is (237). As a consequence, printers, painters, goldsmiths, architects, and sculptors are placed high above ordinary craftsmen, although they do not reach the highest level attained by humanists such as Vernulaeus himself—men of letters who exercise the most liberal of arts and, by doing so, seem justified to claim an even higher status in society than magistrates and civil servants (311).

It is altogether clear that the age-old dichotomy between mind and body—between intellectual pursuit and manual labor—determined Vernulaeus's attitude toward the visual arts. Since artistic activity implied a combination of physical and intellectual effort, artists were considered to occupy a middle position between craftsmen and men of letters.[4] Interestingly enough, the same dichotomy is hinted at in a letter sent by Peter Paul Rubens to Sir Dudley Carleton on 12 May 1618. Far from being a prince, he wrote, he had to work with his hands to earn a living: "In effetto io non son Principe *sed qui manducat laborem manuum suarum*" (quoted in Rooses and Ruelens 1898, 149). There is, of course, irony in Rubens's avowal: it was part of a rhetorical strategy aimed at lowering the price of Carleton's collections of antiquities that he eagerly wanted to acquire. Furthermore, by admitting his mechanical occupations in a Latin phrase that amply demonstrated his thorough, liberal education, he adroitly, if only implicitly, undermined the distinction between manual labor and intellectual pursuit to which he referred in his letter (cf. Muller 1989, 56).

In his monumental encyclopedia *Magnum theatrum vitae humanae*, Laurentius Beyerlinck tackles the same issue from a slightly different angle: he takes the Aristotelian doctrine of causes as the basis for his classification of the various technical arts. What distinguishes painting from more vulgar arts is its efficient cause (*causa efficiens*). Indeed, the accomplishment of a painting depends first and foremost on the mind: just as in poetry, the difference between a good and a bad painting depends on judgment (*ingenium*) and genius (*genius*) (Beyerlinck [1631] 1656, 6.P.340E–F).[5] In another passage, Beyerlinck approaches the intellectual nature of artistic activity from again another angle: drawing a comparison between pharmacology and painting, he subsumes both occupations under the more liberal arts because of their close association with medicine and mathematics, respectively (6.P.353E). Certainly, both comparisons (painting with poetry, and painting with mathematics) were strikingly unoriginal: they had long been stock issues in Renaissance debates about the posi-

4. Vernulaeus's position proves to be very similar to the one taken by ancient thinkers such as Seneca, Galen, and others who tried to overcome the all-too-rigid duality between liberal and vulgar arts by introducing a third category comprising occupations that were neither completely illiberal nor perfectly liberal. See Whitney 1990, 43–50; van den Hoven 1996, 94–101.

5. For a thoroughgoing analysis of the various connotations that the notion *ingenium* bore in humanist writings on art, see especially Baxandall 1971, 15–17. For the intimate relationship between *ingenium* and *genius* in Rubens's theory of art, see Muller 1982, 231–32; 1989, 9–10.

tion of the visual arts (Blunt 1962, 49–53, 84; Hulse 1990; Welch 1997, 125–26).

Although the mind was acknowledged as the main efficient cause of the visual arts, there was no denying that artistic pursuits involved quite substantial manual labor as well. This is exactly why Beyerlinck and Vernulaeus did not hesitate to define them as crafts. In his treatise on husbandry, or household economics (*Institutio Oeconomica*), Vernulaeus tried to specify the economic nature of handicraft. Contrary to farmers, who cultivated land and raised cattle, he said, craftsmen used artificial ways to acquire goods. This did not mean their occupation was "unnatural" in the sense that it ran counter to a natural way of earning a living; rather, their occupation was a useful way of supplementing the natural life. Craftsmen applied tools invented by man to transform raw material into a finished product that was not found as such in nature. In so doing, craftsmen contributed to satisfying human needs and wants that could not be realized in nature as it was (Vernulaeus [1626] 1649, 83). However, craftsmanship was to be considered unnatural in yet another, more Aristotelian, sense of the word: Craftsmen did not use things for the purpose nature had given them, but, rather, to sell them at a profit. Thus, a shoemaker did not produce shoes in order to wear them but to sell them at a profit and thereby make a living (83).[6]

The use of the term *profit* (*lucrum*) in Vernulaeus's treatise on husbandry is slightly ambiguous. This ambiguity seems to be symptomatic of the problems he faced when trying to define the economic position of craftsmen more accurately. Vernulaeus presents craftsmen primarily as workers who are entitled to receiving a just compensation for their work. To be more precise, craftsmen are said to belong to the large group of "wage laborers" (*mercenarii*): they hire themselves out for a specific period of time and meanwhile practice their art (87). Appealing to a biblical quotation, Vernulaeus briefly expresses the basic principle of the late Scholastic theory of just wage, as it was developed by, among many others, Leonardus Lessius (1605, 2.24.4) in his treatise on

6. The distinction between the primary (or natural) and secondary (or unnatural) use of goods goes back to Aristotle and played a dominant role in ancient and medieval discussions about money-dealing (the so-called *ars campsoria*) and reception of interest or usury (*usura*): the use of money as a commodity or as a means to gain profit was long believed to conflict with the primary or natural function of money as a medium of exchange. See, for example, Schefold 1989, 40. For the use of the notion "unnatural" (*para physin*) in ancient discussions regarding the technical arts, see further van den Hoven 1996, 78, 86, 88.

justice and right: "Dignus mercenarius mercede sua" (The worker is worthy of his reward) (St. Luke 10:7). Considered from this angle, the profit a craftsman seeks to make (*lucrum*) amounts to the wage that is due him (*merces*). Interestingly, Vernulaeus subsumes "wage labor" (*vita mercenaria*) under the broader category of "life ruled by money" (*vita nummularia*). The latter is defined as "that way of living that seeks profit [*lucrum*] from exchange through coined money [*nummum*] and which is aimed at making money and acquiring riches [*pecuniam ac divitias*] by the selling and buying of goods" (Vernulaeus [1626] 1649, 83). This definition comes very close to the late Scholastic concept of business or commerce (*negotiatio*). Strictly speaking, business consisted of buying a good in order to resell it at a higher price without having changed it so as to realize a profit (Lessius 1605, 2.21.1.4). Clearly, this definition excludes craftsmen altogether. However, a somewhat different approach could be adopted: It enabled late Scholastic and humanist authors, at least in principle, to define craftsmen in general and artists in particular as businessmen (*negotiatores*). In his treatise *On Justice and Right*, first issued in 1597, Lessius's friend and colleague Ludovicus Molina ([1597] 1615, 2.339.2; see also Gómez Camacho 1977, 433–34) stated that "there is a certain kind of buying and selling which consists of buying a good in order to resell it after having transformed it by one's industry." This kind of buying and selling is called *business*, in the broad sense of the word.

The blurring of the categories of craftsmen and businessmen had serious repercussions for the perception of the art profession. Henceforth, artists such as painters and sculptors could be said to produce objects that they tried to sell at a particular price in order to make a profit, just as merchants tried to realize a profit by purchasing goods and reselling them at a higher price at another point in time or place. Admittedly, commercial activity itself was long since considered a kind of labor that entitled the merchant to receive just compensation (Gómez Camacho 1977, 439–41; Langholm 1998, 132). As a corollary, business profit could easily be interpreted in terms of reward or wage. However, most late Scholastic theologians took quite a different position and stated that business profits ultimately depended on the fluctuating circumstances of the market. Far from receiving a fixed reward that covered all his efforts, expenses, and risks, a merchant was actually obliged to operate on the market where he could suffer a loss or realize a profit. Of course, this depended on his good fortune but, above all, on his prudent assessment of the prevailing market conditions (Langholm 1998, 126–28; Van Houdt in press). The same could be said to apply to artists since, like merchants, they were forced to hone their diligence (*diligentia*) and industry (*industria*) so as to perceive and anticipate the conditions on the "art market" as adequately as possible. As a result, painters, sculptors, and engravers ceased to be viewed as mere craftsmen and were, instead, regarded as entrepreneurs.

It can be argued that this viewpoint was fully in line with the changing nature of the art profession itself. As early as the fifteenth century, Italian artists occasionally produced works other than those directly commissioned by a particular client. These works were offered for sale to a wider public, consisting of wealthy and educated people. Thus, these artists tried to secure their economic position and increase their income (Blunt 1962, 56; Baxandall 1988, 1; Welch 1997, 103). In the course of the sixteenth and early seventeenth centuries, a more fully developed art trade gradually came into being. It was practiced by merchants who specialized in the buying and selling of luxury commodities, but also by artists who sought to combine the production of works of art with art-dealing proper (Thieme 1959, 16–17, 23–24). By the beginning of the seventeenth century, the artist-businessman had become a well-known figure on the Antwerp scene. Just as professional art dealers like Matthijs Musson and Willem Forchoudt (both of whom started their career as painters), artist-businessmen like David Teniers the Younger and Cornelis de Vos were eager to grasp new occasions for making money by carefully exploring the market for consumer goods and taking advantage of changes in taste and preference (Floerke [1905] 1972, 87–90; Denucé 1929, 9–14; 1949; Thurn 1994, 28–34, 41–53; Timmermans 1998, 197–98).

Valuation of Works of Art

The changing nature of the art profession and the accompanying redefinition of the artist's economic position and social status were intimately connected to broader shifts in early modern society. There is reason to believe that the emergence of a strong bourgeois class furthered the professionalization of artists, as well as of architects, doctors, and lawyers, and greatly enhanced their respectability. It could be argued that the emergence of a specific art market closely attached to the commercial and financial center of Antwerp played a crucial role in the growth of professional self-consciousness among Antwerp painters (Filipczak 1987, 2–6, 21; cf. Ewing 1990, 580–81). When examining the world of art, humanists and theologians neglected this broader framework altogether; they simply lacked the analytical tools to take into account macrohistorical changes. Nevertheless, it is quite clear that the new definition of the artist led humanists and theologians to espouse new ideas about the valuation of art objects.

When the artist is considered to be a craftsman, the product of his trade will be assessed in terms of the labor invested and the expenses made. These factors were often taken into account by Renaissance artists when they concluded a contract with a client who commissioned a particular work of art (for relevant examples, see Baxandall 1988, 8–9, 16–17; Jardine 1996, 22–23), and late Scholastic authors such as Lessius (1605, 2.21.2.8) generally recognized these factors as relevant elements in the determination of the just price of goods. However, the valuation of art objects was much more complicated, for the factors needed to be defined more precisely. Late Scholastic authors usually omitted to do so, as they focused their attention on the licit or illicit nature of contracts in general rather than on the occupations of specific social and economic groups. Thus, they thoroughly discussed the problem of moneylending and interest-taking, but refrained from giving a detailed account of the harmful activities of pawnbrokers. By the same token, they established a general theory of just pricing in lengthy chapters devoted to buying and selling, but they rarely applied this theory to the valuation of the products of a particular craft such as painting or sculpting.

There is at least one notable exception to the rule, however. As early as the late fifteenth century, the Dominican friar St. Antoninus (1389–1459) gave a detailed economic and ethical analysis of the various professions that were practiced in his home town of Florence. In his monumental *Summa theologica*, which was first issued in 1477 and was reprinted time and again well into the eighteenth century, he attempted to specify the relevant factors in the valuation of art objects. According to St. Antoninus, the expenses incurred by the artist largely depended on the materials he was required to use in the production of a work; thus, the abundant use of precious pigments (such as ultramarine blue and gold) caused the price of a commissioned work to rise. St. Antoninus revised the concept of labor as well: what was relevant was not so much the physical effort exerted by the artist, but, rather, the use of his skill. In general, then, a craftsman who succeeded in delivering a better product deserved a better price. Hence, a great master might demand a higher price for his painting than an unskilled man, even though they were depicting the very same object (Antoninus [1477] 1741, 3.8.4.308B; cf. Baxandall 1988, 23; Rothbard 1995, 87).[7]

St. Antoninus's *Summa theologica* enabled late Scholastic authors to apply the price-determining factors "labor, expenses, and risks" to the assessment of art objects. It is perhaps worthwhile to note, in this respect, that St. Antoninus was frequently consulted and quoted by late Scholastic theologians such as Lessius (Theiner 1970, 75–76; Langholm 1984, 25) and that his *Summa* was available in monastic libraries throughout the Low Countries in the seventeenth century (Van Houdt 1999). However, St. Antoninus's economic and ethical analysis of art was too limited to be wholly satisfactory because the author too narrowly defined the activity of artists in terms of craftsmanship alone. Contrary to his late Scholastic successors, he did not pay any attention to the commercial or "entrepreneurial" aspects of the art profession. It is altogether clear, then, that the blurring of the categories of craftsmen and businessmen compelled late Scholastic theologians to devise a more elaborate theory of value in which certain other elements also played a decisive role.

Apart from labor, expenses, and risks, which all pertain to the producer/seller, Leonardus Lessius (1605, 2.21.2.8) distinguishes three other categories of factors that have to be taken into account when assessing the price of a commodity. First, there are circumstances related to the commodity itself: the scarcity or abundance of goods, along with the need for them and their usefulness (*necessitas et utilitas*). Second, there are conditions that pertain to the buyers rather than to the sellers: the price of a good will vary according to the number of buyers present and the amount of money available. Third, the particular mode of selling a good affects the price; thus, a commodity will be valued higher when it is sold at another's request than will a good that is spontaneously offered for sale by the producer/seller.[8]

Of course, a question remains: Exactly *how* were these factors to be

7. For the overall importance of the dichotomy between quality of material and quality of skill in Renaissance art, see Baxandall 1988, 15–17.

8. The same elements recur in the works of other late Scholastic authors such as Ludovicus Molina and Juan de Lugo. See, for example, Weber 1959, 100–104, and Grice-Hutchinson 1993, 134.

taken into consideration? It was relatively easy to solve this problem as far as victuals such as bread and beer were concerned. In this case, the just price was established through a common estimation (*communis aestimatio*) of the relevant factors by all those who participated in the market. If necessary, this process of establishing a just price on the market could be replaced by the civil authorities fixing a price, as regularly happened in periods of shortage (Lessius 1605, 2.21.2.9). On the basis of this account, some scholars have contended that Lessius understood perfectly the functioning of the market and was strongly in favor of a free-market system, although he accepted state intervention in certain, limited cases (De Roover 1969, 15; Beutels 1987, 24, 69–70). Yet this contention overlooks the crucial point that, according to Lessius, there is no fundamental difference between the two procedures described, since, in both cases, the price established will be firmly based on a preliminary consideration of all relevant circumstances. In other words, the just price is not simply a price established *by* the market as the automatic result of the interplay of demand and supply, but rather a price that is established *on* the market by individual participants who act as responsible moral subjects (see Van Houdt 1998b, 27–28).

Whether the price of a commodity is fixed by the government or established by a common estimation of market participants, it is, at any rate, based on a prudent judgment (*iudicium prudens*). It is important to keep this central idea in mind when we try to understand Lessius's views on the valuation of goods that are "unique" or "nearly unique" and that are not priced by the government or by market participants. What Lessius (1605, 2.21.3) is referring to are consumer items such as rare jewels, exotic animals, and old paintings. The association of old paintings with jewels and exotic animals is telling and seems to sustain Jardine's (1996) claim that, in early modern times, works of art were considered to be luxury commodities. Lessius clearly defines the category of luxury items in *absolute* terms: they comprise specific objects that can be identified as such. Luxury items are superfluous in that they are not necessary to sustain life. No matter how essential a luxury good may be to sustain one's status in society, it should nonetheless be considered superfluous rather than necessary (Lessius 1605, 2.12.12; see also Brants 1912).

Interestingly, Lessius refers only to *old* paintings, thus suggesting that there was a market for new works of art, the price of which could be established through a common estimation by all buyers and sellers together. In fact, such an art market appears to have functioned in Antwerp in the sixteenth and seventeenth centuries. As early as 1540, the upper gallery of the new Antwerp Bourse was made available for the buying and selling of art objects (Floerke [1905] 1972, 9; Thieme 1959, 29–30; Thurn 1994, 44). The painters' *Pand*, as it was called, was the first permanent art market in Europe, and it quickly replaced the older Our Lady's *Pand* that had been built and operated by the church. Although the painters' *Pand* may have served as a site where visitors could commission artists whose exhibited works appealed most to them, it functioned primarily as a marketplace for the buying and selling of ready-made art (Ewing 1990, 576–80). There is reason to believe that Lessius would have analyzed the functioning of this art trade along the same lines as the working of the financial market that took place on the ground level—in terms of prudent judgment and a common estimate, that is.

However, another institutional context for trading art existed at Antwerp—namely, the public auctions that took place at the weekly Friday Market (Thieme 1959, 27–29). The public auction was a mode of selling that occupied a special position in the late Scholastic doctrine of the just price, as it was not governed by the principles of prudent judgment and common estimate. According to Lessius (1605, 2.21.4.35), the price of commodities that are offered for sale at an auction is by definition uncertain; it ultimately depends on good or bad luck. When buyers are plentiful and enthusiastic, prices will easily rise. When they are scarce and frigid, prices will remain low. No matter what the price of a good will be, it has to be considered a just price, since "the just price of such a marketplace is the price that one is able to charge without any fraud through that mode of selling."

In examining the valuation of (nearly) unique commodities, Lessius does not consider either common estimation or public auction as a viable means of determining the price. In fact, he abstracts from any institutional context: two individuals meet each other or correspond with each other and try to come to an agreement. This situation is adequately illustrated by the negotiations between Rubens and Carleton in spring 1618. Carleton proposed to exchange a precious collection of antiquities for a number of original paintings entirely executed by the master himself. The negotiations started on 17 March 1618 and were not concluded until 1 June. In the correspondence that resulted from the negotiations, Rubens occasionally refers to concepts that seem to be reminiscent of late Scholastic economic thought. In a letter dated 12 May 1618, he lets Carleton know that he has scrupulously assessed the value of his own paintings; in fact, he has deliberately underestimated them so that their price falls well below the just price: "Non ecçedono il giusto suo prezzo nella tassa" (quoted in Rooses and Ruelens 1898, 149). However, Rubens is perfectly willing to have his works assessed by another expert: "Mi rimetterei sempre del prezzo al arbitrio di ogni persona intelligente" (149). However brief and casual these remarks may be, they nonetheless clearly suggest that, according to Rubens, the price of (nearly) unique objects should not depend on a process of free bargaining between buyer and seller but, rather, should correspond to the just price—a price that is to be established by an experienced person, an expert.

This position comes remarkably close to the views expressed by Lessius on the valuation of luxury items.[9] In *dubitatio* 3 of chapter 21 of his treatise on justice and right, Lessius questions whether a seller is allowed to fix the price of luxury commodities freely, if not arbitrarily. Two legal maxims stemming from Roman law seemed to support this thesis. The first maxim states that everyone is the moderator and arbiter of his own goods: "Quisque in rebus suis est moderator et arbiter." The second maxim holds that a good is worth what it can be sold for: "Res valet quanti vendi potest." As Odd Langholm (1982), in a seminal article, has convincingly demonstrated, medieval theologians and canonists refused to accept the idea of contractual freedom that was implied in these two legal maxims. Late Scholastic authors simply followed in their footsteps and drastically reduced the impact of the legal maxims by adding that a good is worth what it can be sold for on the explicit condition that the limits of a just estimation are respected. While most Scholastic theologians limited this conclusion to the buying and selling of necessary goods such as victuals (275–77), Lessius (1605, 2.21.3.19) went one step further and extended its application to luxury goods. According to Lessius, *any* good has to be sold at a just price. If it is not fixed by the government or by a common estimation on the marketplace, then it should be established otherwise.

Lessius states that the just price must depend on the judgment of an

9. It is interesting to note in this respect that Rubens was familiar with Lessius's treatise. He devised the frontispiece that was added to the fourth Plantinian edition of *De iustitia et iure,* issued in 1617. Moreover, he owned several copies of the work, as can be deduced from the inventory of his personal library. See Arents in press.

experienced person—possibly, but not necessarily, the seller himself. Insofar as his judgment is based on a careful assessment of all relevant factors or circumstances, it is to be considered a prudent one, and, insofar as his judgment is prudent, the price that is established has to be regarded as fair since the just price always depends on a prudent judgment of all relevant factors, no matter how this judgment is realized in actual practice. Lessius (1605, 2.21.3.16) briefly summarizes his position as follows: "A good is worth a certain price, not because it pleases the seller to sell the good at that price, but rather because it is assessed as being worth that price on grounds of the judgment of prudent men who have taken everything into due consideration. As a consequence, a seller cannot sell his good at the price he likes."

Lessius's position did not win general approval among late Scholastic theologians. It was criticized by, among others, the famous casuists Emmanuel Sa (1530–96) ([1595] 1623) and Antoninus Diana (1585–1663) (1635), whose works were widely spread and frequently used in the southern Netherlands in the course of the seventeenth century (Van Houdt 1999). Diana (1635) begins his discussion by drawing a clear distinction between necessary goods such as grain, wine, and clothes and luxury goods such as paintings and exotic birds. In the first case, the seller has to comply with the just price determined by the government or by a common estimation on the marketplace. If he or she were given the freedom to bargain, he or she would be in a position to exploit the economic need of the buyer—a situation that was deemed unacceptable by all late Scholastic authors (Langholm 1982, 270–75, 280–82). However, the risk that a process of free bargaining will lead to the exploitation of a buyer who happens to be in a weaker position does not occur in the latter case, since the transaction is strictly limited to luxury commodities, which a buyer wants to purchase for his or her own amusement or splendor rather than to fulfill basic economic needs.

According to Diana, then, there is room for contractual freedom where luxury items are concerned. The seller is allowed to determine the price of a good freely and may try to gain from the transaction as high a profit as possible. In Diana's (1635, 56.119; cf. Sa [1595] 1623, s.v. *Venditio*, 14) opinion, this does not run counter to the principle of the just price, for "in such cases the just price is determined solely by the estimation of the buyer who considers the good to be worth so much, as he thinks it pertains to the splendor of his noble position and his wealth to pay such a high price." There is no reason to believe that a buyer is forced by necessity when he or she accepts to pay the price demanded by the seller for the luxury item he or she wants to purchase. Even though the buyer pays a sum that far exceeds the limits of the just price that would have been established by an experienced person on grounds of a careful consideration of all relevant circumstances, he or she is nonetheless supposed to act of his or her own free will. The sum paid above the just price is to be considered a free donation (Diana 1635, 56.119).

The clash of opinion between Lessius and Diana should not be exaggerated. Both authors do agree that a seller is by no means allowed to exploit the needs and wants of the buyer. This was a principle of utmost importance in Scholastic economic thought and constituted the latter part of what Langholm has called the double rule of just pricing. According to this rule, a seller has the right to indemnify him- or herself against the loss he or she suffers by selling a good but is not allowed to profit from the buyer's specific needs by driving up the price (Langholm 1984, 46–48; 1992, 232–34). The first part of the double rule was explicitly invoked by Lessius to uphold a standpoint that allowed him, at least to a certain extent, to bridge the gap separating him from his opponents. While strongly rejecting the idea of contractual freedom in setting the price for luxury commodities, he nonetheless granted the seller the right to take into consideration his or her personal attachment to a commodity he or she owned but which the buyer sought to acquire. When a person is particularly fond of an object, then it represents for him or her an additional value that is subjective but no less real. When selling his or her good, the seller is allowed to include in the price the surplus value he or she loses by parting from it. According to Lessius, this is just a typical case of "damage incurred" (*damnum emergens*), a generally accepted extrinsic title that is covered by the first part of the so-called double rule of just pricing (Lessius 1605, 2.21.3.17, 2.21.4.26).

The argumentation developed by Diana invites us to consider yet another interesting point in the valuation of art objects in early modern times. As already stated here, Diana distinguishes two different aspects, or levels, in the acquisition of luxury items such as jewels and paintings. Indeed, the relationship between seller and buyer is conceived of as a combination of exchange and gift giving. When a rich person decides to pay a large sum for a (nearly unique) painting, she or he enters into a purchase agreement that is ruled by the principle of equality which is, in turn, the cornerstone of commutative justice or, to put it another way, justice in exchange. Insofar as the sum paid exceeds the just price, however, the buyer is assumed to offer such as a "free gift." As late Scholastic authors are well aware, gift giving is not based on equality, but on reciprocity. It usually takes place within a context of friendship or kinship and presupposes such varying attitudes as mutual benevolence, liberality, and gratitude (Lessius 1605, 2.17.1.3, 2.20.18.2).[10] It is not hard to see that the combination of exchange and gift giving can lead to remarkable variations in the valuation of commodities.

Some of these variations are briefly hinted at by Lessius, in his discussion of both purchase agreements (*emptio venditio*) and employment contracts (*locatio conductio*). In chapter 21 of book 2 of his treatise *De iustitia et iure*, which is entirely devoted to buying and selling, Lessius discusses a situation in which a purchaser has paid more than the commodity is worth and is accordingly believed to have made a free gift. In Lessius's (2.21.4.37) opinion, this supposition is only valid if it can be proven that no fraud or necessity intervened and that the contracting parties were bound by ties of friendship or kinship. In chapter 24, Lessius (2.24.4.24) expresses his viewpoints regarding the just remuneration of wage labor. According to him, it is perfectly imaginable that a craftsman receives a lower wage because he gains some other, more immaterial advantages, such as honor and reputation. These advantages form, as it were, an integral part of the wage: "Sunt veluti pars stipendii." Phrased in modern economic terms, they constitute a psychic income that cannot be neglected (Rothbard 1995, 123). It is only fair to add that Lessius did not apply his viewpoints on the interaction between exchange and gift giving explicitly to the art trade. It is quite obvious, however, that this interaction played a particularly dom-

10. To my knowledge, no serious attempt has been made thus far to provide an encompassing study of late Scholastic views on gift giving (*donatio/liberalitas*) in its relationship to commercial exchange (*commutatio*). However, Langholm (1998, 102–4) does refer briefly to the problem of gifts in connection with a regular economic contract and points out that, according to John Duns Scotus and some other Scholastic authors, a "gift" could function as a means to close the gap between different estimates of just value made by two contractual parties. The interaction of exchange and gift giving confronted late Scholastic theologians with serious problems, not only when they tried to assess the just price of (luxury) commodities but also when they sought to examine the licit or illicit (i.e., usurious or nonusurious) nature of loans in which the lender took a surplus above the principle lent. The difficulty lay in the fact that it was hard to determine what the true intention of the contractual parties was, especially when no explicit agreement on the surplus paid was made. For a discussion of these problems, which are intimately connected to the broader issue of "mental usury," see Van Houdt 1995, 345–50, 355–58, 371–74.

inant role in the world of art—a world governed by honor and reputation as much as by money; a world that rested on personal ties of patronage as much as on contractual exchange. As a corollary, it was a world in which gift giving—whether in a material or an immaterial form—frequently interfered with the financial transaction that took place between an artist and his client.[11] In the third and last part of this article, I shift attention from the production and evaluation of art objects to the consumption thereof to gain a better understanding of early-seventeenth-century Scholastic and humanist views on the system of patronage and maecenatism.

Consumption of Art

Not surprisingly, the Scholastic and humanist discussion of the consumption of art centers around the Aristotelian-Thomistic notion of *magnificentia*. Magnificence is a special virtue that allows one to realize truly great deeds or things. When magnificence is directed toward material goods, it is intimately connected to conspicuous consumption; indeed, the person concerned with magnificence sets free huge sums of money to be spent on eye-catching buildings, lavish decorations, splendid paintings and sculptures, and so on.[12] As a virtue, magnificence occupies a middle position between *parvificentia*, which is typical of a person who aspires to accomplish great things but is too narrow-minded to invest a sufficiently large amount of money in them, and *banausia*, which denotes the inappropriate use of riches for small things or, in a somewhat broader and slightly different sense of the word, the indecent display of luxury and splendor.

From a semantic point of view, it is quite telling that in his *Summa theologiae,* St. Thomas Aquinas (1942, II.II.135.2) labeled this vice *consumption* (*consumptio*). (For the ambivalence inherent in the term *consumption,* see further Porter 1993, 70.) Not unlike the Greek word

11. For some striking examples of the way gift giving and mercenary payment could be inextricably interwoven in early modern times, see Jardine 1996, 419–20, and Welch 1997, 121–23. In his commercial dealings with Carleton in spring 1618, Rubens not infrequently invoked the principle of friendship: eager to win Carleton's highly esteemed favor, the painter promised to do more than he was contractually obliged to (see, e.g., Rooses and Ruelens 1898, 162, 170).

12. However, see Burke 1993, 149: "We should avoid identifying conspicuous consumption with magnificence. In a particular social context, simplicity may be the best way of making oneself conspicuous."

banausia, the Latin term *consumptio* refers to fire burning in an oven and consuming everything that is thrown into it. Clearly *parvificentia* and *avaritia* have a lot in common. Both vices imply a tenacious attachment to riches, an unwillingness to part with acquired wealth so as to spend it on magnificent projects (Lessius 1605, 3.2.4.35–36; Beyerlinck [1631] 1656, 5.M.182).

Neither Lessius nor Beyerlinck applied the concept of magnificence to a specific class or group in society. It can be inferred from Vernulaeus's treatises on politics and husbandry, however, that magnificence was considered to be a prerogative of noblemen. Vernulaeus ([1623] 1647, 214–15) devotes an entire chapter of his political handbook to the noble way of living, paying particular attention to housing and urging noblemen to build large and lavishly decorated houses in the city rather than to inhabit a castle somewhere in the countryside. In so doing, he says, they will contribute not only to the splendor of the city but also to its economic prosperity: for one thing, the number of citizens will increase; more important, the conspicuous consumption that nobles owe to their position in society will be fueled by imitating and emulating each other's behavior. As a result, the various crafts will thrive and flourish.[13]

The discussion of the consumption of luxury items takes on a different slant in Vernulaeus's treatise on household economics. Drawing a clear distinction between the private and public sphere and adopting a more outspokenly moralizing tone, he strongly encourages princes to show grandeur and at the same time advises private persons to limit their consumption of luxury goods. This is not to say that private persons should refrain from purchasing art objects altogether. Admittedly, in describing the ideal home, Vernulaeus (90–91) appears to attach greater value to utility than to ornamentation. To his mind, a house should be useful and practically designed; no single part of it should be empty or left unused. At the same time, however, the design should leave sufficient room for embellishment. In his opinion, a considerate housefather (*paterfamilias*) will see to it that his house does not lack beauty and, thus, he will accordingly spend a good deal of money on decoration. Yet he will avoid at all costs any vile imitation of princely

13. It is interesting to note that Vernulaeus's argumentation is somewhat reminiscent of the observation made by the famous political thinker Giovanni Botero in his treatise *Grandezza delle città*, first published in 1589, that living in close proximity in cities caused the Italian nobility to be more prone to competitive display than they had been previously (cited in Burke 1993, 157).

magnificence and will not plunge himself into debt for the sake of embellishment. In short, the ancient ideal of mediocrity should prevail. Following the lead of classical authors such as Horace and Cicero, Vernulaeus concludes that in private buildings mediocrity is always praiseworthy: "In privatis aedificiis laudata semper mediocritas est."[14]

Vernulaeus's rather narrow interpretation of the virtue of magnificence is perfectly in line with the neo-Stoic ethics that were actively promoted by Justus Lipsius and his humanist friends in Louvain and Antwerp. While the neo-Stoics allowed themselves to lead a comfortable life, they eagerly sought to avoid ostentatious luxury (Morford 1991, 191–92). At least in theory. For there is no denying that conspicuous consumption played a crucial role in the persistent attempts made by the Antwerp *haute bourgeoisie*—including those members who sympathized with, or overtly adhered to, neo-Stoicism—to affirm their status and associate themselves more closely with an aristocratic way of living. Combined with his rigid division of society in three separate classes and his insistence on the inviolable privileges of the nobility, Vernulaeus's outspokenly moral position helps explain to a considerable extent why he remained blind to the important social function which the consumption of art fulfilled, not only for influential aldermen such as Nicolaas Rockox but also for affluent merchants such as Cornelis van der Geest *and* successful producers of art such as Peter Paul Rubens (Held 1957; Briels 1980; Timmermans 1998, 148–201).

The neo-Stoic philosophy that flourished in the southern Netherlands at the end of the sixteenth and the beginning of the seventeenth centuries also led to a reconceptualization of the virtue of magnificence—or, to be more precise, to a shift of emphasis from magnificence to magnanimity (*magnanimitas* or *magnitudo animi*). As both Lessius (1605, 3.2.4.31) and Beyerlinck ([1631] 1656, 5.M.182C) pointed out, these virtues were closely linked. Whereas magnificence is primarily aimed at achieving greatness in external things, however, magnanimity is more directed toward greatness in moral action. According to Lipsius, magnanimity rather than magnificence was to be regarded as the

14. It should be added that Vernulaeus has little or nothing to say about magnificence displayed by a private person who donates huge sums of money toward public buildings and monuments, which was a widespread practice in early modern times. Similarly, he devotes no attention to the interaction between private sponsorship, on the one hand, and ecclesiastical institutions and religious orders, on the other, in financing expensive building and decoration projects. For the latter, see Timmermans 1998, 201–13.

hallmark of princes. The concept of magnanimity was developed by Aristotle in his *Nicomachean Ethics* and remodeled by such ancient Stoic philosophers as Chrysippus, Panaetius, and Posidonius (Gauthier 1951, 55–118, 119–76). Lipsius ([1605] 1606) developed his own views on magnanimity in some detail in his handbook *Monita et exempla politica,* which he published in 1605 as a complement to his *Politicorum sive civilis doctrinae libri VI*, first issued in 1589. In the *Monita*, a modernized version of the traditional mirror of princes, Lipsius describes in detail all the moral qualities a prince should possess. Among these virtues, magnanimity, or noblemindedness, holds a central place. A truly virtuous prince sets out to realize lofty and honest goals, thus gaining ever more glory for centuries to come, for "just as the sun is weak at dawn, but steadily rises and becomes clear, so does fame stemming from virtue and merits expand and grow together with immortal time itself" (276). Although a prince's good name depends entirely on his own virtue, it can and should be actively fostered and propagated by humanists and artists alike. It was their specific task to commemorate the virtuous life and deeds of a praiseworthy prince and to ensure that his name would live on for centuries to come. Creating an enduring monument for the prince, either in words or in images, they transformed his life and conduct into an exemplary model that was to be imitated, in the first place, by other rulers and aristocrats, and by future generations of people, more generally (Van Houdt 1998a, 416–17, 426–29).

This message lay at the basis of the numerous panegyrics that were written by Lipsius's disciples in honor of Archduke Albert for his joyous entry in the Netherlands in 1598 and the funeral orations composed on his death and burial in 1621. Joining hands with various artists, Lipsius's disciples contributed to the multimedia spectacles that were created at the time by delivering highly eulogistic orations. In their speeches in honor of the archduke, humanists like Vernulaeus and Beyerlinck stressed the intimate and age-old relationship between epideictic oratory and the visual arts. Following the lead of Cicero and Quintilian, they endeavored to depict an image in words, an image that would encourage the spectators/listeners to follow the example of the ancient Romans Quintus Fabius and Publius Scipio who reportedly felt themselves inflamed to demonstrate their merits when looking at the image of their ancestors (Papy and Van Houdt 1998, 322–23; cf. Austin 1944; MacCormack 1976, 46; MacGowan 1985, 56, 268 n. 21).

In short, humanists and artists were asked to play a political role in society. At the same time, this role was a profoundly moral one: according to Lipsius and his disciples ([1602] 1613, 3.83; cf. Morford 1996, 235–38; Hope and McGrath 1996, 179), humanists and artists alike should have the common pursuit of making society and its citizens better by presenting ideal models of conduct. To play this crucial role, however, humanists and artists had to be actively supported by the princes; hence, Lipsius's plea for an active cultural policy. The rulers had to assume their responsiblity in turn and promote the liberal arts as vigorously as possible. It was not enough that the rulers guaranteed peace, order, and prosperity in general, although these were to be considered necessary conditions for the flourishing of the liberal arts (Van Houdt 1998a, 418–23). Princes had to go one step further: they had to commission specific works and support individual scholars and artists since it was altogether clear that rulers, on the one hand, and humanists and artists, on the other, were mutually interdependent. Rulers had to rely on humanists and artists for the immortal fame they sought to acquire by having their memorable deeds and splendid virtues recorded and represented. Conversely, humanist orators and poets, as well as painters and sculptors, depended to a large degree on the rulers' willingness to support letters and arts in order to make a living and, in turn, immortalize their own names as authors and artists. In other words, the relationship between ruler and artist was defined in terms of courtly patronage—an institution based on the reciprocal exchange of goods and services between two unequal parties engaged in a relationship that is explicitly aimed at mutual benefit and which, therefore, can aptly be described as a form of "useful friendship," or *amicitia utilis* (Van Houdt 1998a, 425). This model of courtly patronage could easily be extended to include the support offered by other rich and powerful persons. It comes as no surprise, then, to see that in praising such an important patron of arts as the Antwerp burgomaster Nicolaas Rockox, humanist authors reiterated crucial elements of the above-sketched model. By supporting the sciences and the arts, Rockox had proved to serve the common good (the *salus publica*) and had gained immortal fame at the same time (Briels 1980, 149–50; Timmermans 1998, 194–95).

Stressing the quintessentially moral function of the liberal arts and creating a rationale for courtly patronage, humanists like Lipsius found a solid justification for their own activities, as well as for those of the artists. Despite their one-sided focus on the merits of language and speech, then, humanists living and working in the southern Netherlands at the beginning of the seventeenth century succeeded in establishing a broad-enough basis for understanding and appreciating the work of artists. Not unlike humanists, artists were seen as privileged custodians of fame who deserved to be protected and supported by wealthy, powerful, and educated patrons. Not unlike humanists, artists were expected to serve the common good and to aspire to lofty moral goals. This moral dimension gave a deeper meaning to the age-old comparison between painting and poetry as it was expressed in the famous dictum *ut pictura poesis*, a simile that went back to the ancient poet Horace and which was repeated time and again in the course of the Italian Renaissance, not the least by artists eager to dissociate themselves entirely from craftsmen by showing that theirs was as noble an art as that of the poets (Blunt 1962, 52–54; Welch 1997, 126–27; cf. Hulse 1990, esp. 157–58). Furthermore, humanists confirmed the assimilation of painting with the narrow circle of the liberal arts, which, already in ancient times, were defined as those arts that aim at virtuousness (van den Hoven 1996, 90–91; Morford 1996, 237). It comes as no surprise, then, to see that the complete integration of the visual arts and the humanist disciplines was occasionally acknowledged by some early-seventeenth-century scholars working in the Low Countries. This was notably the case with the ecclesiastical author Philippus Rovenius (1575–1651), who, not unlike Vernulaeus, attempted to define the various classes in society and examine their respective roles and duties.[15] Contrary to Vernulaeus, however, Rovenius clearly separated painters from craftsmen and subsumed them under the group of people who practiced the liberal arts (Rovenius [1638] 1668, 2.39.487–88). In Rovenius's work, then, the emancipation of the early modern artist was fully accepted and expressed without the slightest trace of hesitation.

Some Partial Conclusions

In the preceding pages, I have attempted to reconstruct the views on economics and art as they were laid down in the works of early-seventeenth-century scholars such as Scribani, Vernulaeus, Beyerlinck, Lessius, and Lipsius. Despite their common political, social, and intellectual backgrounds, these scholars adopted quite divergent approaches to

15. For a detailed biographical account of Rovenius, a former pupil of Lessius, see Visser 1966.

examine the world of art and reached markedly different conclusions regarding its economic features. Vernulaeus and Beyerlinck focused primarily on the social status and economic position of the artist, confining his economic role strictly to practicing a handicraft. Concentrating his attention on contracts rather than on professions, Lessius nonetheless managed to address issues that were of particular relevance to the valuation of art objects. More in general, he suggested a framework that made it possible—at least in principle—to take into account such crucial economic aspects as the functioning of the art market and the entrepreneurial activity of artists and art dealers alike. All the authors reviewed devoted some attention to the consumption of art, and most of them tackled the issue from a strictly Aristotelian-Thomistic point of view by applying the concept of magnificence. This quite traditional approach was abandoned by Lipsius, who developed a blueprint for virtuous princely conduct that allowed him and his successors to highlight the mutual interdependence of rulers and artists and to stress the striking similarities between humanist and artistic pursuits in a world that was thoroughly dominated by courtly patronage.

The ideas put forward by Lipsius and his pupils were by no means novel. The painting as a moral *exemplum*, the artist as a learned figure, and the importance of the patron were all issues that had already been discussed at length by other humanists in the course of the sixteenth century (Cast 1988, 434–38). However, Lipsius and his followers succeeded in adapting this quite traditional humanist message to the political, social, and cultural conditions of their age. As a consequence, their writings proved to be extremely successful. They were read by intellectuals and civil servants all over Europe. There is no reason to assume that their ideas did not catch on among those contemporary painters and sculptors who consciously defined and modeled themselves as learned artists. Yet even Lipsius's views were limited and failed to grasp the rich variety and dazzling complexity of the world of art as it flourished at the beginning of the seventeenth century.

While a painter such as Rubens may have felt attracted to Lipsius's neo-Stoic philosophy (cf. Morford 1991), at the same time, such a philosophy failed to offer more than a far-too-rigid and rudimentary grid with which to grasp the many, often contradictory, facets of his life and work as an artist. Although he was an extremely skilled and scholarly painter, Rubens was simultaneously the director of a large studio and, as such, the head of a remarkably successful commercial enterprise. Rubens was a bourgeois city merchant and liked to present himself as such, but he also desired to be—and managed to transform himself into—a country nobleman. He produced works of art that were commissioned by princes and dynasts all over Europe, and he combined his artistic and diplomatic skills in the service of the House of Hapsburg, to which he was particularly attached. Yet, throughout his lifetime, he consciously avoided getting too deeply entangled in the webs of courtly patronage. Although he was appointed painter to the archducal court in 1609, he was allowed to live in Antwerp and thus gained free access to the patronage of the upper bourgeoisie (Muller 1989; Alpers 1995, 28–34, 50–52).

Applied to an artistic giant like Rubens, the economics of art developed by early-seventeenth-century humanists and theologians inevitably strike us as bleak and reductionistic. Confronted with the many-sided aspects of Rubens's life and work, humanists and theologians had no choice but to give up their somewhat meager economic analysis and launch a hypertrophic eulogy instead. Following the lead of Scribani, the prolific Antwerp writer Laurentius Beyerlinck offered his readers a long list of artists who had worked in the Netherlands and contributed to the glory and luster of the country. The list is concluded with a brief but vigorous praise of contemporary artists living in Antwerp, among whom Rubens is given pride of place:

> It is not unjustified to claim that Antwerp—and only Antwerp—is the true theater of the royal art of painting in Europe. It is here that Peter Paul Rubens is now bearing the torch, so to speak; born to shine over the entire world by the fame of his erudition and talent and the greatness and artistry of his works, he is loved by the noble and humble alike. He is no small ornament to this country of ours. (Beyerlinck [1631] 1656, 6.P.346D)

This is all Beyerlinck has to say about Rubens. It apparently sufficed for his purposes, which were far removed from those of a modern art critic and even further removed from those of an economist of art.

References

Alpers, Svetlana. 1995. *The Making of Rubens*. New Haven, Conn.: Yale University Press.

Antoninus [Saint Antonine of Florence]. [1477] 1741. *Summa theologica*. Verona: P. Ballerinus.

Aquinas, St. Thomas. 1942. *Summa theologiae*, Tomus tertius complectens *Secundam Secundae*. Ottawa: Studium Generale O. Pr.

Arents, Prosper. In press. De bibliotheek van P. P. Rubens. *De Gulden Passer* 78.

Austin, R. G. 1944. Quintilian on Painting and Statuary. *Classical Quarterly* 38:17–26.

Baxandall, Michael. 1971. *Giotto and the Orators: Humanist Observers of Painting in Italy and the Discovery of Pictorial Composition, 1350–1450*. Oxford: Clarendon.

———. 1988. *Painting and Experience in Fifteenth Century Italy: A Primer in the Social History of Pictorial Style*. 2d ed. Oxford: Oxford University Press.

Beutels, Robert. 1987. *Leonardus Lessius (1554–1623): Portret van een Zuidnederlandse laat-scholastieke econoom—Een bio-bibliografisch essay*. Wommelgem: Den Gulden Engel.

Beyerlinck, Laurentius. [1631] 1656. *Magnum theatrum vitae humanae*. Lyon: Ioannes Antonius Huguetan—Marcus Antonius Ravaud.

Blunt, Anthony. 1962. *Artistic Theory in Italy, 1450–1600*. Oxford: Oxford University Press.

Brants, Victor. 1912. Un fragment inédit de L. Lessius De Eleemosyna (1593). *Analectes pour servir à l'histoire ecclésiastique de Belgique* 13:73–89, 302–17.

Briels, J. 1980. Amator Pictoriae Artis: De Antwerpse kunsthandelaar Peeter Stevens (1590–1668) en zijn Constkamer. *Jaarboek van het Koninklijk Museum voor Schone Kunsten Antwerpen*, 139–226.

Brouwers, Louis. 1961. *Carolus Scribani S. J. 1561–1629: Een groot man van de Contra-Reformatie in de Nederlanden*. Antwerp: Ruusbroecgenootschap.

Burke, Peter. 1993. *Res et verba*: Conspicuous Consumption in the Early Modern World. In *Consumption and the World of Goods*, edited by John Brewer and Roy Porter. London: Routledge.

Cast, David. 1988. Humanism and Art. In *Renaissance Humanism: Foundations, Forms, and Legacy*, vol. 3., edited by Albert Rabil Jr. Philadelphia: University of Pennsylvania Press.

De Marchi, Neil, and Hans J. Van Miegroet. 1994. Art, Value, and Market Practices in the Netherlands in the Seventeenth Century. *Art Bulletin* 76.3:451–64.

Denucé, Jan. 1929. *Kunstuitvoer in de 17de eeuw te Antwerpen: de firma Forchoudt*. Antwerp: De Sikkel.

———. 1949. *Na Peter Pauwel Rubens: Documenten uit den kunsthandel te Antwerpen in de XVIIe eeuw van Matthijs Musson*. Antwerp: De Sikkel.

Depuydt, Joost. 1991. Nicolaus Vernulaeus (1583–1649): Een bio-bibliografische studie. Unpublished licentiate thesis, University of Leuven.

De Roover, Raymond. 1969. Leonardus Lessius als economist: De economische leerstellingen van de latere scholastiek in de Zuidelijke Nederlanden. *Mededelingen van de Koninklijke Vlaamse Academie voor Wetenschappen, Letteren en Schone Kunsten van België, Klasse der Letteren* 31.1.

Diana, Antoninus. 1635. *Resolutiones morales*. Mons: Franciscus Waudraeus.

Ewing, Dan. 1990. Marketing Art in Antwerp, 1460–1560: Our Lady's *Pand*. *Art Bulletin* 72:558–84.

Filipczak, Z. Z. 1987. *Picturing Art in Antwerp, 1550–1700*. Princeton, N.J.: Princeton University Press.

Floerke, Hans. [1905] 1972. *Studien zur Niederländischen Kunst- und Kulturgeschichte: Die Formen des Kunsthandels, das Atelier, und die Sammler in den Niederlanden von 15.–18. Jahrhundert*. Soest: Davavo.

Gauthier, René-Antoine. 1951. *Magnanimité: L'idéal de la grandeur dans la philosophie païenne et dans la théologie chrétienne*. Paris: Vrin.

Gómez Camacho, Francisco. 1977. Valoración moral de los "negocios" segun Luís de Molina. *Revista española de Teología* 37:431–45.

Grice-Hutchinson, Marjorie. 1993. The Concept of the Market in Spanish Economic Thought before 1800. In *Economic Thought in Spain: Selected Essays of Marjorie Grice-Hutchinson*, edited by L. S. Moss and C. K. Ryan. Aldershot, England: Edward Elgar.

Guicciardini, Lodovico. 1567. *Descrittione di tutti i Paesi Bassi*. Antwerp: Guglielmo Silvio.

Held, Julius S. 1957. Artis pictoriae amator: An Antwerp Art Patron and His Collection. *Gazette des Beaux-Arts* 6.50:53–84.

Hope, Charles, and Elizabeth McGrath. 1996. Artists and Humanists. In *The Cambridge Companion to Renaissance Humanism*, edited by Jill Kraye. Cambridge: Cambridge University Press.

Hulse, Clark. 1990. *The Rule of Art: Literature and Painting in the Renaissance*. Chicago: University of Chicago Press.

IJsewijn, Jozef. 1987. Laurentius Beyerlinck. *Nationaal Biografisch Woordenboek van België* 12:59–67.

Jacopin, Paul, and Jacqueline Lagrée. 1996. *Erasme: Humanisme et langage*. Paris: Presses Universitaires de France.

Jardine, Lisa. 1996. *Wordly Goods*. London: Macmillan.

Kraye, Jill. 1988. Moral Philosophy. In *The Cambridge History of Renaissance Philosophy*, edited by C. B. Schmitt, Q. Skinner, E. Kessler, and J. Kraye. Cambridge: Cambridge University Press.

Langholm, Odd. 1982. Economic Freedom in Scholastic Thought. *HOPE* 14.2:260–83.

———. 1984. *The Aristotelian Analysis of Usury*. Bergen: Universitets forlaget.

———. 1992. *Economics in the Medieval Schools: Wealth, Exchange, Value, Money, and Usury according to the Paris Theological Tradition, 1200–1350*.

Leiden: E. J. Brill.
———. 1998. *The Legacy of Scholasticism in Economic Thought: Antecedents of Choice and Power*. Cambridge: Cambridge University Press.
Lessius, Leonardus. 1605. *De iustitia et iure ceterisque virtutibus cardinalibus*. Louvain: Joannes Masius.
Lipsius, Justus. 1589. *Politicorum sive civilis doctrinae libri VI*. Leiden.
———. [1602] 1613. Epistolarum selectarum centuriae III ad Belgas. In *Justi Lipsi opera*, vol. 1. Lyons: Hubertus Cardon.
———. [1605] 1606. *Monita et exempla politica libri duo, qui virtutes et vitia Principum spectant*. Antwerp: Joannes Moretus.
MacCormack, Sabine. 1976. Latin Prose Panegyrics: Tradition and Discontinuity in the Later Roman Empire. *Revue des Etudes Augustiniennes* 22:29–77.
MacGowan, Margaret M. 1985. *Ideal Forms in the Age of Ronsard*. Berkeley: University of California Press.
Molina, Ludovicus. [1597] 1615. *De iustitia et iure tomi sex . . . emendati et indicibus aucti*. Antwerp: J. Verdussen.
Morford, Mark. 1991. *Stoics and Neostoics: Rubens and the Circle of Lipsius*. Princeton, N.J.: Princeton University Press.
———. 1996. L'influence de Juste Lipse sur les arts. In *Juste Lipse (1547–1606) en son temps: Actes du colloque de Strasbourg, 1994*, edited by Christian Mouchel. Paris: Honoré Champion Editeur.
Muller, Jeffrey M. 1982. Rubens's Theory and Practice of the Imitation of Art. *Art Bulletin* 64:229–47.
———. 1989. *Rubens: The Artist as Collector*. Princeton, N.J.: Princeton University Press.
Papy, Jan, and Toon Van Houdt. 1998. The Image of Archduke Albert in Seventeenth-Century Funeral Literature. In *Albert and Isabella, 1598–1621: Essays*, edited by Werner Thomas and Luc Duerloo. Turnhout: Brepols.
Porter, Roy. 1993. Consumption: Disease of the Consumer Society? In *Consumption and the World of Goods*, edited by John Brewer and Roy Porter. London: Routledge.
Rooses, Max, and C. Ruelens. 1898. *Correspondance de Rubens et documents épistolaires concernant sa vie et ses oeuvres, tom. 2 (1609–25 juillet 1622)*. Anvers: Jos. Maes.
Rothbard, Murray N. 1995. *Economic Thought before Adam Smith: An Austrian Perspective on the History of Economic Thought*. Vol. 1. Cheltenham, England: Edward Elgar.
Rovenius, Philippus. [1638] 1668. *Reipublicae Christianae libri duo*. Antwerp: Arnoldus a Brakel.
Sa, Emmanuel. [1595] 1623. *Aphorismi confessariorum*. Douai: Balthasar Bellerus.
Schefold, Bertram. 1989. Platon und Aristoteles. In *Klassiker des ökonomischen Denkens*, edited by J. Starbatty. Munich: Beck.
Scribani, Carolus. 1610. *Antverpia*. Antwerp: Joannes Moretus.

Theiner, Johann. 1970. *Die Entwicklung der Moraltheologie zur eigenständigen Disziplin*. Regensburg: Friedrich Pustet.

Thieme, Gisela. 1959. *Der Kunsthandel in den Niederländen im siebzehnten Jahrhundert*. Cologne: Verlag der Löwe.

Thurn, Hans Peter. 1994. *Der Kunsthändler: Wandlungen eines Berufes*. Munich: Hirmer.

Timmermans, Bert. 1998. Een elite in het zeventiende-eeuwse Antwerpen: Het milieu van de wethouders (1585–1699) en de stedelijke samenleving in een periode van transformatie. Unpublished licentiate thesis, University of Leuven.

van den Hoven, Birgit. 1996. *Work in Ancient and Medieval Thought: Ancient Philosophers, Medieval Monks, and Theologians and Their Concept of Work, Occupations, and Technology*. Amsterdam: J. C. Gieben.

Van Houdt, Toon. 1992. Leonardus Lessius. *Nationaal Biografisch Woordenboek van België* 14:416–24.

———. 1995. Leonardus Lessius over lening, intrest en woeker: "De iustitia et iure," lib. 2, cap. 20. Editie, vertaling en studie. Ph.D. diss., University of Leuven.

———. 1998a. Justus Lipsius and the Archdukes Albert and Isabella. *Bulletin de l'Institut historique belge de Rome* 68:405–32.

———. 1998b. Lack of Money: A Re-Appraisal of Lessius' Contribution to the Scholastic Analysis of Money-Lending and Interest-Taking. *European Journal of the History of Economic Thought* 5.1:1–35.

———. 1999. Les ouvrages scolastiques et casuistiques dans la bibliothèque de l'abbaye de Saint-Hubert: Un premier sondage. In *Le catalogue de la bibliothèque de Saint-Hubert en Ardenne (1665): Vie intellectuelle et religieuse d'une communauté bénédictine au XVIIe siècle*, edited by L. Knapen. Leuven: Faculteit Godgeleerdheid.

———. In press. *Just Pricing and Profit Making in Late Scholastic Economic Thought*. In *Studia in honorem Josephi IJsewijn*, edited by D. Sacré and G. Tournoy. Leuven: Leuven University Press.

Vernulaeus, Nicolaus. [1623] 1647. *Institutionum politicarum libri IV*. Louvain: Joannes Vryenborch.

———. [1626] 1649. *Institutionum oeconomicarum libri II*. Louvain: Joannes Vryenborch.

Visser, Jan. 1966. *Rovenius und seine Werke: Beitrag zur Geschichte der nordniederländischen katholischen Frömmigheit in der 1. Hälfte des 17. Jahrhunderts*. Assen: Van Gorcum.

Weber, Wilhelm. 1959. *Wirtschaftsethik am Vorabend des Liberalismus: Höhepunkt und Abschluss der scholastischen Wirtschaftsbetrachtung durch Ludwig Molina S.J. (1535–1600)*. Münster: Aschendorffsche Verlagsbuchhandlung.

Welch, Evelyn. 1997. *Art and Society in Italy, 1350–1500*. Oxford: Oxford University Press.

Whitney, E. 1990. *Paradise Restored: The Mechanical Arts from Antiquity through the Thirteenth Century*. Philadelphia: American Philosophical Society.

Liberalitas, *Magnificentia*, Splendor: The Classic Origins of Italian Renaissance Lifestyles

Guido Guerzoni

The origins of this essay, as often happens in life, are to be found in a chance occurrence. I was asked to take part in the *HOPE* conference called "Economists and Art, Historically Considered." It was originally suggested that my contribution should be on the economic status of artworks and luxury goods in the sixteenth century, in the hope of responding to the question posed at the beginning of a book by Richard Goldthwaite (1995, 7): "Why were so many art works produced in Italy during the Renaissance?"

As I focused on the ideological and cultural origins of this phenomenon, I found myself pushed by the sources toward destinations that were ever more distant historically. These sources impelled me irresistibly toward the comparison of two seemingly innocuous terms, *liberalitas* and *magnificentia*. Although these terms had attracted the attention of specialists in ancient history (Blanchet 1904; Berve 1926; Borsanyi 1938; Barbieri 1958; Kloft 1970; Manning 1985; Wesch-Klein 1990; Forbis 1993), as well as art and architecture historians (Fraser-Jenkins 1970; Gundersheimer 1972; Pacciani 1980; Green 1990; Spilner 1993; Ambrose 1995), they had not aroused similar interest in eco-

I am grateful to Marco Bianchini, Marco Cattini, and Marzio Achille Romani, who supervised the research for this report. Massimo Amato, Claudio Angelozzi, Stefano Baia Curioni, Marina Bianchi, Toon Van Houdt, Marcia Pointon, Gino Zaccaria, and one anonymous referee provided helpful comments on previous versions. James Butler helped me work on the English style, and Aldo Coletto provided magnificent bibliographic information. I am also grateful to Neil De Marchi, who gave me helpful comments, as well as the pleasant opportunity to present the paper at the Duke conference.

nomic and economic thought historians (with the exception of Bianchini 1984; Goldthwaite 1995; Todeschini 1992). In an attempt to fill this gap, I decided to dedicate this study to the history of these two moral virtues. Knowledge of them is of great importance for perceiving the issue of Renaissance luxury and splendor in a new light and for understanding the remote and ideological origins of court-aristocratic behavioral models and consumption patterns.

Prologue: Ancient Virtues or Modern Vices?

In sketching a picture of an Italian gentleman at the end of the sixteenth century, Torquato Alessandri (1609, 89) defined in precise terms the prerequisites necessary for someone to be legitimately and honorably accorded that title: "The maintenance of a large, well-furnished house always open to guests, with many horses in the stables, and servants in the house; always dressed in rich and diverse silk cloths, wearing around the neck a magnificent chain of gold and large diamond rings on the fingers, large golden buttons, an embroidered and perfumed collar, wonderful jewels in the hair, golden sequins in the bag, without forgetting to prepare a huge feast every day with thanks to God."[1] This description was neither polemical nor mocking, nor did it have a heavily moralistic tone. It merely represented, with timely precision, the lifestyle of a great part of the Italian elites,[2] marked by the maintenance of honorably *liberale* (liberal) conduct.

Liberalità (liberality) is really the initial term of our discussion. The goods described by Alessandri, like those listed by Sabba da Castiglione in his famous *Ricordo circa gli ornamenti della Casa* (an essay in da Castiglione 1558), are not manifestations of reprehensible *ostentatio* (ostentation). They are the pledge of the ancient lineage to main-

1. All translations unless otherwise noted are mine. "Tenete casa grande aperta, e ben adobbata, con cavalli in stalla, e servitori e serve, & andate sempre mai di ricchi e varij drappi setili vestito, e portate in ornamento del vostro collo magnifiche catene d'oro, e delle nerbute dita smaltati anelli da diamanti in punta finissimi, e grossissimi incastrati, e d'altre varie gioie inestimabili accompagnati, con bottoni grossi, e massicci d'oro á i profumati, e ricamati colletti, non che superbi gioielli, á tutta perfettione lavorati, á i vostri fini capelli, e patacche d'oro con impronti d'imprese, e piastre d'argento, e zecchini d'oro in borsa, e che del continuo fare una tavola, una mensa dico, ricca d'ogni grazia d'Iddio."

2. The term *elites* here means both the laity and clergy. This is because most of the high clergy came from the ranks of the nobility (at least until late in the 1500s), and they retained throughout the fifteenth and sixteenth centuries a consumption lifestyle that was identical to that of the aristocratic laity.

tain unspoiled their own honor, and the endowment by means of which aspiring nobles could ratify the marriage with the much yearned for "blue blood." These cases involved neither wholly luxurious consumption and voluptuous expenditure nor superfluous goods and capricious waste: "Luxury is any expenditure which exceeds necessities," but the "concept is clearly relative, and its content could be grasped only if is known what is 'necessary'" (Sombart [1913] 1988, 97). And because "beyond affluence there are different degrees of richness considered as legitimate, luxury is defined as only what is beyond this admitted limit: the whole issue lies in the nature of the border between what is right and what is excessive" (Pouillon 1978, 585).

Thus, in some social contexts, the purchase and possession of mirrors and musical instruments, statues and antiques, medals and cameos, pictures and engravings, jewels and crystals, figurines and bronzes, stuccoes and intaglios, tapestries and rugs, silverware and pottery, ornate and valuable furniture, and weapons and books was a response to a categorical imperative. It was behavior marked by the daily liberal employment of wealth that could show real nobility of spirit irrefutably, more than could be done through not always adamantine genealogies. This was because in the sixteenth century meaning, liberality "lying between the two extremes of avarice and prodigality" was properly "a moral virtue, which moderates our feelings with regard to the desire and greed for money. By money we mean any kind of substance or thing which could be measured by the price of money: and this virtue is exercised by dispensing money usefully, where, when, and to whom it is needed" (Antoniano [1584] 1821, 2:39–40).[3]

Liberality is therefore a private virtue that assumed the form of a secular charity whose innate redistributive propensity could be used to set right the errors of fortune, ennobling "fortune" so that it could be conveniently shared with worthy persons, because "rich and powerful men, when they present their wealth to those who are worthy, through liberality, do not want to enrich them, but simply reward them for services and honors received" (Della Casa [1571] 1970,

3. "La liberalità posta nel mezzo tra i due estremi, che sono l'illiberalità, ossia l'avarizia, e la prodigalità . . . è una virtù morale, la quale è la moderatrice degli affetti nostri circa il desiderio, e circa la cupidigia del denaro; e per il denaro si intende ogni sorta di sostanza, o di cosa, che col prezzo del denaro si misura, col qual mezzo principalmente questa virtù si esercita dispensando il denaro utilmente, dove, e quando, ed a chi si conviene."

183).[4] So "he will be liberal who will spend his wealth in support of his household, friends, relatives, and of literary and virtuous men; and finally in support of those who, through no fault, but through the blind stroke of Fortune, have fallen into disgrace and poverty. The liberal man has not to do all these actions out of a vain wish for honours and ostentation, but out of mere virtue and charity" (Piccolomini 1552, 105v–106r).[5] Aristocratic wealth had to escape, then, from the accumulating temptations of *avaritia* (avarice) in order to preserve its real equalizing vocation, which was perennially unbalanced in favor of a giving dimension, since "liberality shows itself better in giving than in receiving" (103v–104r),[6] and "this virtue lies more in giving, than in receiving, because this action is much more difficult, praised, and meritorious" (Antoniano [1584] 1821, 2:39–40).[7]

The liberal use of wealth is not an end in itself but is the means that guarantees the final equity of the allocative process: "Liberality is a moral virtue which is exercised by dispensing money usefully, where, when, and to whom it is needed" (2:39–40)[8] and "the liberal man lies between these two extreme vices of avarice and prodigality. He does not dissipate his wealth, or give presents to the unworthy. He shares with upright judgment his income with others, according to the time, place, and quality of people" (Piccolomini 1552, 105v).[9]

This was an instrument that was used with conscience. Spending and giving were two things that were owed to the house, rather than being whims. Their purpose was to do justice to the sufferings caused by a

4. "I potenti e ricchi, quando a coloro i quali meritevoli ne sono usando della liberalità donano delle loro ricchezze, non si persuadono operare in essi beneficio alcuno, ma sì premiargli de'servigi e dell'onore da loro ricevuto."

5. "Liberal sarà quello, che le spenderà [his wealth] per lo sostenimento della casa sua, de gli amici, de parenti, de le persone virtuose et litterate; e finalmente in sussidio di coloro, che non per colpa loro, ma per colpa della fortuna, saranno fuor de i lor meriti, in miseria e povertà pervenuti. Et tutte queste operationi, debba fare il liberale, non per desio d'honore, non per fasto, o per qual si voglia altro così fatto interesse, ma solamente per mera virtù et carità."

6. "La liberalità più nel ben donare, che nel ben ricevere, palese si manifesta."

7. "Maggiormente questa virtù consista nel dare, piutosto che nel ricevere, come opera di molto maggiore difficoltà, più lodata, e più meritoria."

8. "La liberalitá è una virtú morale, che si esercita dispensando il denaro utilmente, dove, e quando, ed a chi si conviene."

9. "Tra' questi due vitij dell'Avaritia, e della Prodigalità, risiede il Liberale: il qual non dissipando il suo patrimonio, e donando a' chi non conviensi, ma' con retto giuditio, secondo il tempo, il luogho, la qualità de le persone, e simili altre avvertenze, donando fa' altrui parte de le sue rendite."

destiny that was blind to the merits of individuals. In this way it legitimized the inequalities of the social hierarchy. No sin was worse than avarice, which was perceived not as a crime against humanity but as a grave blow to the honor of the class and the prestige of peers, a lack of duty to the rank that legitimized preeminence by virtue of this superior ability to judge, recognize, and reward the merits of subordinates, "sharing his income with others." Not only were spending and giving not morally reprehensible, the contrary was true. Someone who did not meet this caste obligation revealed baseness of spirit. Such a person is one "who, while spending, feels great displeasure, as happens to the illiberal or the miser" (Assandri 1616, 298).[10]

Knowing how to spend and to give thus became incontrovertible proofs of a person's value and his capacity to recognize the value of others because "there is another kind of liberality, which is fake, when somebody is sumptuous when he must be the most miserly, when he spends where he must not spend and gives to someone unworthy of the gift: avarice should not be cured by prodigality, that is to say by excessive spending, without order, without method, without measure" (Fabrini 1547, 81v).[11]

"Spending with measure, order, and method"; "giving money usefully where, when, and to whom it was needed"; "giving according to the time, the place, and the quality of people"—all were different, but equally significant, ways of removing the moral element from the notion of luxury and superfluity and of linking the quality of people to the quality of the things around them. There was no good that could not find its natural worth corresponding to the social order; there was no need that could not be legitimately proved by someone. However, as the lower orders drew closer, appropriating to themselves the goods previously owned by higher groups, so did the elites innovate, refine, and increase the value of their goods in an attempt to reestablish correct social distances. But this citation game, in which goods immediately signaled recognizability, could only be based on a constant raising of the bid. None of the actors in the comedy of life could refuse to play. If one did not want to lose reputation or risk the scorn of one's equals, if one did not want to prejudice one's ambitions, or if

10. "Spendendo sentiressimo dispiacere, come succede nell'illiberale, o Avaro."

11. "È una altra sorte di liberalitá, che è falsa, che è quando uno è suntuoso, dove bisogna essere avarissimo, cioè quando egli spende, dove non debbe, e dona á chi non lo merita . . . che l'avaritia . . . non si medichi co la prodigalitá, cioè co lo smisurato spendere, senza ordine, senza modo, e senza misura."

one simply wanted to maintain social position, it was necessary to own specific goods.

To reestablish the proper social distances, Giovan Battista Pigna (1561, 35–36) could underline that "close to liberality" there was "magnificence, which is in great things."[12] By contrast, Alessandro Piccolomini (1552, 106r–107r) confirmed:

> Close to the virtue of liberality, there is that splendid virtue which is called magnificence, and even though magnificence is in some way similar to liberality, it is nevertheless different from it in many ways. These two virtues are similar, because each of them is related to the use of wealth, but in this aspect they differ: Liberality concerns every action which, with regard to the use of money, could be performed in everyday life, such as gifts and payments, alms, and household expenses. Magnificence, however, takes place only in those expenditures which happen rarely, for important reasons and special occasions. Only someone who makes great things while spending could be properly called "magnific." This happens mostly if he spends on public occasions, special commissions or honors of the Republic, such as appointments of magistrates, receptions of emperors, kings, and princes, gifts for the most distinguished lords, great embassies, building of temples, porticoes, and theaters, display of public festivals and comedies, and other occasions when the honor and dignity of the State needs to be defended. In the same way, this virtue could show itself on private occasions, which happen seldom, such as weddings, parties, banquets, receptions of distinguished guests, expenditures on town and country residences, domestic ornaments and furnishings, and other similar things where one can see sumptuousness and grandness. In magnificent actions, three aspects should be considered: who spends, how much is spent, and the matter of spending. But considering how much is spent, it is obvious that the expenses should be proportional to the quality of who spends. In fact, the way of spending of an emperor, a prince, and so on is different to that of other ranks and conditions of human beings. The same expense that will be magnificent for a private gentleman will not be so for a prince.[13]

12. "Accanto alla liberalità secondo la naturale inclinatione communemente compagna dell'affabilità et mansuetudine" there was "la magnificienza che è in cose grandi."

13. "Appresso alla virtù della liberalità, segue quella splendidissima virtù, che magnificienza si chiama; la quale quantunque in qualche parte alla liberalità si assomigli; nondimeno

The exclusivity of this virtue was also shown in all its clarity in a dialogue of Sigismondo Sigismondi (1604, 23), when considering the question of whether "those who are always spending on banquets, houses, gifts, weddings, and other similar things, thus consuming thousands of coins, even though they will never receive such signs from anybody, are guilty of a vicious action?" He replied:

> If these expenditures were proportionate to the strength and degree of those making them, they were not only not vicious but were proof of a great virtue known as magnificence, this virtue consisting in the undertaking of great expenditures, carried out as a great man would carry them out. Whoever did not meet these obligations would have shown meanness, or more accurately, cowardice of soul, which consists in not spending perfectly in proportion to the occasion and need. There is no virtue more suitable to a great man than liberality and magnificence, but magnificence is the greater of the two, because liberality can also be exercised by a poor man.[14]

---

in molte parti è differente da quella. Simili sono queste due virtù, in quanto ciascheduna di loro, intorno alle ricchezze consiste; ma in questo differiscano poi, che la liberalità si stende á tutte le operationi, che accascar possano tutto'l giorno, intorno al dispor delle ricchezze, come sono donationi, remunerationi, operationi caritative, spese per il sostenimento della famiglia . . . ; dove, che la magnificienza si considera intorno á quelle spese solamente; le quali di rado, per qualche cosa importante, et di gran momento si sogliano fare, tal che Magnifico si può dire colui, che spendendo fa cose grandi; et massimamente per occorrentie publiche, et ricevuti incarchi, o degnità nella Republica; come sariano accettationi di Magistrati, accoglimenti d'Imperatori, Rè, Prencipi, et simili; donationi et presenti, che a singularissimi Signori far si debbino, Ambascerie, edification di Tempii, di Portici, di Teatri; apparati di publiche feste, o Comedie; et simili altre occorrentie, donde l'honore, e 'l decoro della Republica s'appartenga di conservare. Può parimente accascar questa istessa virtù della Magnificienza, in alcune occorrentie private, che di rado avvengano; come sariano nozze, conviti, accoglienze di forestieri importanti, edificii, così nella Città, come ancor nelle Ville, ornamenti di casa, et altri apparati simili a questi; dove sontuosità e grandezza veder si possa. Nelle quali magnifiche operationi, a tre cose rispetto si debba havere; a colui che spende, a quel che si spende, et finalmente alla cosa istessa nella qual si spende. Però che quanto a quel che spende, fa di mestieri, che le spese siano proportionate alla qualità di colui che le fa. Conciosia, che altrimenti s'appartien di spendere ad un imperatore, altrimenti ad un Principe, et cosi de gli altri gradi, et stati de gli uomini di mano in mano. Di maniera, che una medesima spesa ad un privato gentil'huomo sarà Magnifica, che ad un Principe non già."

14. "Quelli che spendono continuamente in banchettare, in alloggi, in occasioni di nozze, et altre spese simili consumando a migliaia il denaio senza che essi ricevano mai da altri simili dimostrationi fanno un'operatione vitiosa? . . . Questo se è conforme alle forze, et al grado di chi lo fa, non solo non è vitio; ma virtù grande chiamata magnificenza, la quale consiste appunto nelle spese grandi, e fatte da huomo grande. Chi colpevolmente non vi si prestasse darebbe nella parvicenza, o, per dir meglio, viltà di animo, la quale consiste in non spendere

It is in the last line that the theoretical justification for the exponential growth in pomp, luxury, and noble grandness can be found: "Liberality can also be exercised by a poor man." So if liberality remains a private virtue that is forced to measure itself against a simple "luxurious" dimension, magnificence was becoming a public duty aimed at safeguarding the dignity of the whole State rather than the honor of the individual.

We should not be surprised by the presence of a real spur to these expenditures: "The munificent cannot refuse or avoid the occasions of doing great things, and when the occasion arrives, has to seek to perform them to the maximum for the sake of his own dignity and the dignity of those for whom it is done" (Piccolomini 1552, 107v–108r).[15] This resulted in the overturning of the classical axioms regarding *emulatio* (emulation). The imitative, and to an ever greater extent the emulative, processes were censured and punished in the larger classes insofar as they led to social confusion: "The artisan now wishes to be the equal of the citizen, the citizen the equal of the gentleman, the gentleman the equal of the noble, and the noble the equal of the prince, and these are intolerable things beyond reason and measure which displease God and lead to a thousand sins" (Antoniano [1584] 1821, 29).[16] This censure and punishment was not applied to aristocratic magnificence, which was not simply condoned but was encouraged: "The munificent should make every effort so that his works cannot be easily imitated, and should always seek to outdo what has already been done by others on similar occasions. His country houses must be magnificent and splendid, the gardens sumptuous, the town house grand and splendid and furnished in accordance with his degree and something over" (Piccolomini 1552, 107v–108r).[17] In this way, the largesse by which the

perfettamente conforme all'occasione, et al bisogno. Infatti non vi è virtù che più convenga ad un Padrone, massime grande, quanto la liberalità et la magnificenza: ma principalmente la Magnificenza, come propria di esso, che la liberalità può anco essercitarsi dal povero."

15. "Al Magnifico dunque appartiensi di non recusare, ó fuggir l'occasioni d'havere á far opere grandi; et occorrendo, con ogni ingegno vegga di farle tali, che siano degne di lui, che le fa, et di coloro per chi si fanno."

16. "L'artigiano voglia uguagliarsi al cittadino, il cittadino al gentiluomo, il gentiluomo al titolato, e questi al principe: queste sono cose troppo fuori d'ogni ragione e misura, ed intollerabile, che dispiacciono a Dio e che conducono a mille peccati."

17. "Il Magnifico sempre ha da por cura, che le opere sue siano tali, che difficilmente siano imitabili, cercando sempre d'avanzar gli altri, che per simili occasioni hanno operato. Le Ville sue siano magnifiche, et splendide, i giardini sontuosi, la casa nella Cittá, sia con grandezza, et splendidezza edificata; et dentro secondo il suo grado, et qualche cosa piu, per ogni parte apparata, et adorna."

elite squandered its wealth was not subjected to any ethical criticism, but was encouraged, praised, and promoted so that it became an absolute social imperative, as pointed out by Giulio Cesare Capaccio (1620, 162): "I do not want princes to combine fame with the poverty of Epaminonda, of Aristide, or of Lissandro, or that they want the glory of Focione, of Fabricio, of Curio and Publicola, because that time is passed. It is necessary now that they are rich and that they use their wealth with Magnanimity."[18]

Neverthless, the references to "because that time is passed" confirm that these were not wholly new concepts but ideas that were again coming forth from ancient times. If Seneca ([65–54 B.C.] 1950) had argued in *De Beneficiis* that liberality was the sure and proven sign of nobility, "the same Aristotle has said that nothing gives somebody more glory than generosity, rather than nobility. Because he is noble who relies on the glory of his ancestors, and he is liberal who honors the virtue of his ancestors. So that all liberal men are noble, but not all noble men are liberal, while some noble men are so distant from the virtue of their ancestors, that, despite their nobility, they are becoming incredibly abject and vile" (Capaccio 1620, 273).[19]

In the face of the significance of this testimony, we could stop here, satisfied that we have identified the ideological origin of ostentatious Renaissance consumption. However, the references to Seneca, Aristotle, and other ancient authors should put us on the alert. Were the words just quoted an original fruit of Renaissance thinking, or were they a genuine, even if freely plundered, inheritance of classical thought?

The Origins of the Issue: Liberality and Magnificence in Aristotelian Thought

The "original fruit" evolved from the Greek *exordia,* when the two virtues that are the subject here were called ἐλευθεριότης (*liberalitas-liberalità*-liberality) and μεγἄλοπρέπεια (*magnificentia-magnificenza-*

18. "Non voglio che i Principi aggiungano alla fama la povertà di Epaminonda, di Aristide, o di Lissandro, o che vogliano la gloria di Focione, di Fabricio, di Curio e Publicola, perché passò quel tempo. Ed é ora necessario che siano ricchi e che delle ricchezze con magnanimità si servano."

19. "L'istesso [Aristotle] poi há pur detto, che maggior gloria ad alcuno non attribuisce la generositá, che la nobiltá; per che nobile è colui, che alla sola gloria de i suoi maggiori si appoggia: e generoso, chi per la virtú de i suoi maggiori si comenda, dal che nasce, che tutti i generosi sono nobili, ma non tutti i nobili sono generosi, mentre alcuni cosi van degenerando dalla virtù de i loro maggiori, che si fanno nella nobiltá abiettissimi, e vili."

magnificence). ἐλευθεριότης, which can be translated as the condition-sentiment-action of a free man/not slave, derives from the noun form of the adjective ἐλευθέριος (proper for a man who is free; literally, liberal), linked to the adjective ἐλεύθερος (*liber-libero*-free) and to the noun ἐλευθερία (*libertas-libertà*-liberty), which signified liberty, independence, and the condition of not being a servant or slave.

By contrast μεγᾰλοπρέπεια comes from the fusion of the prefix μεγᾰλο (*μέγασ-magnus-grande*-great), in this case closely tied to the idea of μέγεθοσ (*magnitudo-grandezza*-magnitude) and the verb πρέπω. This verb has a double significance, since it can be translated as "to stand out, to be noted, to be distinguished, to signal, to emerge," as well as "to be convenient, proper, decorous": τό πρέπον was translated into Latin as *decorum* (the same meaning in English), in confirmation of the strong social tones of this "convenience" (see Labowsky 1934; Pohlenz 1935). Both terms are already mentioned in some Platonic dialogues (see Stein 1963), in the *Politeia* (Plato [365–357 B.C.] 1995, 402: πρίν ἂν τὰ τῆς σωφροσύνης εἴδη καὶ ἀνδρείας καὶ ἐλευθεριότητος καὶ μεγᾰλοπρεπείας; and 486: Ἦι οὖν ὑπάρχει διανοίας μεγᾰλοπρέπεια), where they represent two, albeit separate, noble characteristics of the mind of a free-born man, and in *Theaetetus* (Plato [392–369 B.C.] 1985, 144: πρὸς τὴν τῶν χρημάτων ἐλευθεριότητα), where ἐλευθεριότης is specifically associated with the liberal use of wealth. There are similar, sporadic mentions in the *Eudemian Ethics,* attributed to Aristotle ([335 B.C.] 1983, 5–10), where both appear in a long list of moral virtues.

One has to wait until book 4 of the *Nicomachean Ethics* because Aristotle ([335 B.C.] 1993) offers a systematic treatment of the two terms. Aristotle defines ἐλευθεριότης as the golden mean with regard to material goods (4.1: δοκεῖ δὴ εἶναι ἡ περὶ χρήματα μεσότης). The liberal man is praised for his equilibrium in giving and receiving material goods, with more praise being awarded for giving (4.1: ἀλλὰ περὶ δόσιν χρεμάτων καὶ λῆψιν, μᾶλλον δ' ἐν τῇ δόσει). Importantly, the dominion of "material goods" includes all the things whose value could be measured by money (4.1: χρήματα δὲ λέγομεν πάντα ὅσων ἡ ἀξία νομίσματι μετρεῖται).

Liberality lies between the two opposite vices of prodigality (ἀσωτία-*prodigalitas-prodigalità*-prodigality) and avarice (ἀνελευθερία-*avaritia-avarizia*-avarice), which are positions of excess and defect with regard to material goods. The virtue of the liberal man remains in disequilibrium on the "offer" front, however, in the ability to give, to give to others; it is more liberal to give to those to whom one should give than to receive from those from whom one should receive, or not to receive from where nothing should be taken (4.1: διὸ μᾶλλόν ἐστι τοῦ ἐλευθερίου τὸ διδόναι οἷς δεῖ ἢ λαμβάνειν ὅθεν δεῖ καὶ μὴ λαμβάνειν ὅθεν οὐ δεῖ). The liberal man does not give at random, however, but in a correct way. His objective is the moral beauty of his action and respect for the conditions that make for correct giving, distributing the correct amount with pleasure, at the correct time, to those who genuinely deserve such attention. This is an action not linked to the absolute size of monetary resources and, by extension, to the social position of the giver. Liberality is calculated according to individual wealth, as it does not rest on the absolute amount of things given but in the spiritual disposition of the giver, and it is this disposition that makes the liberal man give in proportion to his wealth (4.2: κατὰ τὴν οὐσίαν δ᾽ ἡ ἐλευθεριότης λέγεται· οὐ γὰρ ἐν τῷ πλήθει τῶν διδομένων τὸ ἐλευθέριον, ἀλλ᾽ ἐν τῇ τοῦ διδόντος ἕξει, αὕτη δὲ κατὰ τὴν οὐσίαν δίδωσιν). For this reason, although Aristotle mentions that it is a common opinion that those who have inherited rather than acquired wealth are the most liberal, as they have never experienced straitened circumstances (4.2: ἐλευθεριώτεροι δὲ εἶναι δοκοῦσιν οι μὴ κτησάμενοι ἀλλὰ παραλαβόντες τὴν οὐσίαν), it is not easy for a liberal person to become rich, as he is not inclined either to take or to hold, but to give, he values his material goods only so far as they make giving possible. The most worthy therefore tend to be the least rich.

At this point, having specified the characteristics of liberality, Aristotle focuses on two extreme vices. Prodigality and avarice are excesses and defects in the two expressions of liberality, giving and taking (4.3: ὑπερβολαὶ καὶ ἐλλείψεις εἰσὶν ἡ ἀσωτία καὶ ἡ ἀνελευθερία, καὶ ἐν δυσίν, ἐν δόσει καὶ λήψει). Prodigality is first perceived as a self-destructive form of indulgence (the prodigal destroys himself with his own hands, by depriving himself of the necessary means for survival). The main fault of the prodigal is his incapacity to give the right amount with pleasure, considering correctly how much, to whom, and when to give. However, a wise guide can transform the prodigal into a liberal man since the prodigal possesses the traits of the liberal man. The prodigal gives and does not take, but he does not do as he should, neither does he do it in the correct way (4.3: ἔχει γὰρ τὰ τοῦ ἐλευθερίου· καὶ γὰρ δίδωσι καὶ οὐ λαμβάνει, οὐδέτερον δ' ὡς δεῖ οὐδ' εὖ). This explains why prodigality is considered better than avarice (4.3: οὐ μικρῷ βελτίων εἶναι τοῦ ἀνελευθέρουού). Furthermore, and this is an idea destined to have long-lasting consequences in the history of Western elites, only private citizens can exhaust their wealth rapidly in giving, and thus be considered prodigals (4.3: ταχέως γὰρ ἐπιλείπει ἡ οὐσία τοὺς ἰδιώτας διδόντας, οἵπερ καὶ δοκοῦσιν ἄσωτοι εἶναι). For this reason tyrants could not be called prodigals, because it would not be easy for them to use up their resources in giving or spending (4.2: τὸ γὰρ πλῆτος τῆς κτήσεως οὐ δοκεῖ ῥᾴδιον εἶναι ταῖς δόσεσι καὶ ταῖς δαπάναις ὑπερβάλλειν). Avarice is an incurable vice that is much more widespread than prodigality, since most men prefer to accumulate wealth rather than distribute it. Avarice can have a double origin: the defect in giving characteristic of misers and of stingy, mean people (4.3: ψειδωλοὶ,γλίσχροι, κίμβικες) is the excess of taking. It is typical of those who greedily seek as much as possible for themselves, as happens in the case of usurers, bawds, gamblers, and pirates. Just for these reasons, avarice is said to be the opposite of liberality (4.3: εἰκότως δὲ τῇ ἐλευθεριότητι ἀνελευθερία ἐναντίον λέγεται), and is considered a worse evil than prodigality.

There then follows the chapter on magnificence. μεγᾰλοπρέπεια is also a virtue connected with material goods (4.4: δοκεῖ γὰρ καὶ αὐτὴ περὶ χρήματά τισ ἀρετὴ εἶναι). It is differentiated from liberality by the fact that it does not extend to all the actions related to material goods, but only to distribution or consumption and expenditure, and in this respect magnificence exceeds liberality in grandness (4.4: οὐχ ὥσπερ δ' ἡ ἐλευθεριότης διατείνει περὶ πάσας τὰς ἐν χρήμασι πράξεις, ἀλλὰ περὶ τὰς δαπανηρὰς μόνον· ἐν τούτοις δ' ὑπερέχει τῆς ἐλευθεριότητος μεγέθει). As its name indicates, magnificence consists of large and suitable expenditure (4.4: ἐν μεγέθει πρέπονσα δαπάνη ἐστίν), carried out with style and pleasure, whose ultimate aim is moral beauty. If its suitability is relative to the spender, and to the circumstance and object of the expenditure, its grandness must be absolute. The magnific is always liberal, but the liberal is not always magnific (4.4: ὁ μὲν γὰρ μεγαλοπρεπὴς ἐλευθέριος, ὁ δ' ἐλενθέριος οὐδὲν μᾶλλον μεγαλοπρεπής).

The extreme vices are also given for this case. Magnificence is the golden mean between the excess of vulgarity and absence of taste

(Βαναυσία καὶ ἀπειροκαλία) and the defect of paltriness and meanness (μικροπρέπεια). The vulgar person spends in a mistaken way, basing a display on pomp for occasions not worthy of it. It is not aimed at moral beauty but at the display of wealth to arouse admiration. The paltry person has the opposite defect; he seeks to save on everything, continuously complaining about expenses and ruining the final result. The magnific man is therefore similar to a wise man, because he can see what is suitable and spend great amounts in proportion. His works will therefore be like his expenditure, large and appropriate. The work must be worthy of the expenditure, and the expenditure worthy of the work, or greater than it (4.4: ὥστε τὸ μὲν ἔργον τῆσ δαπάνης ἄξιον δεῖ εἶναι, τὴν δὲ δαμάνην τοῦ ἔργου, ἢ καὶ ὑπερβάλλειν). Further, and this is a step of great importance, the magnific man will spend with pleasure and with style, because to keep a detailed account of expenditure is niggardly (4.4: ἡ γὰρ ἀκριβογία μικροπρεπές). In later passages, Aristotle lists the areas in which magnificence can show itself, beginning obviously with religion (offers, gifts, sacrifices, buildings), in order to speak in favor of expenditure in the public interest (4.4: καὶ ὅσα πρὸς τὸ κοινὸν): theatrical spectacles, banquets, equipping fleets, and so on. In these cases, expenditure is made in relation to whoever is carrying it out, thus showing who the person is and what his resources are. For this reason a poor man can never be magnific, because he does not have the resources with which to make great expenditure in the appropriate way (4.5: διὸ πένης μὲν οὐκ ἂν εἴη μεγαλοπρεπής· οὐ γὰρ ἔστιν ἀφ' ὧν πολλὰ δαπανήσει πρεπόντως). Thus, suitable magnificence is only possible for men of high birth, illustrious men, and those in possession of similar resources, because they had acquired by their own efforts, inherited them from ancestors, or have social connections, these conditions having greatness and fame (4.5: πρέπει δὲ καὶ οἷς τοιαῦτα προϋπάρχει δι' αὑτῶν ἢ τῶν προγόνων ἢ ὧν αὐτοῖς μέτεστιν, καὶ τοῖς ἐνδόξοις καὶ ὅσα τοιαῦτα· πάντα γὰρ ταῦτα μέγεθος ἔχει καὶ ἀξίομα).

Aristotle includes among the great private expenses all those that happen once, such as marriage ceremonies, expenses that involve the city and people of high rank, the accommodation of foreign guests, and gifts received and exchanged. The reason for including these is the public nature of these private expenses. The magnific man does not spend for himself, but for the common good (4.5: οὐ γάρ εἰς ἑαυτὸν δαπανηρὸς ὁ μεγαλοπρεπὴς ἀλλ' εἰς τὰ κοινά). Aristotle suggests that it is just this representative function that implies the magnific man should build a house suitable to his wealth, because a house is a kind of ornament, and a man of this kind should spend on durable things since these are the most beautiful (4.5: μεγαλοπρεποῦς δὲ καὶ οἶκον κατασκευάσασθαι πρεπόντως τῷ πλούτῳ [κόσμος γάρ τις καὶ οὗτος], καὶ περὶ ταῦτα μᾶλλον δαμανᾶν ὅσα πολυχρόνια τῶν ἔργων [κάλλιστα γὰρ ταῦτα]).

I think the reader will forgive the length of these remarks, considering the importance of the passages quoted. This is a philosophy that theorizes authoritatively about the social lawfulness of aristocratic consumption and elegantly removes the issue of luxury from the province of morality. When talking about liberality, Aristotle uses such terms as *giving* and *distributing*, and when he speaks about magnificence he voluntarily uses *expenditure*, and thus manages to sanction the cultural imperative of patterns of consumption that were usually associated with immorality. We are therefore dealing with a theory of needs and consumption which has crossed the threshold of primary needs. While this theory has not been of particular interest for the scholars involved in ancient *oeconomica* (see on this matter Krüger 1964; Brunner 1970; Bianchini 1976, 1985; Frigo 1985a, 1985b; Lambertini 1985; Natali 1985; Todeschini 1994), one sees in this thought the intellectual bases of twenty-five centuries of consumption patterns that were not conspicuous or flaunted, but burdened by the weight of inevitable social obligation. The references to the moral beauty of some forms of expenditure and the punctilious listing of the conditions that guarantee its correctness; the careful analysis of the social profile of the liberal and magnific man; the fundamental distinction between private luxury and expenses of "public representation" (see also Ampolo 1984, with its rich bibliography); the designation of the common good as the ultimate aim of the magnific's actions (Büsing 1995); the incidental meaning, rich in historical significance, by which niggardly account keeping was seen as genuinely miserly (4.4: ἡ γὰρ ἀκριβολογία μικροπρεπές); the calculated repetition of the grandness, beauty, and permanence that works should possess, all entered silently into the genetic inheritance of European elites, profoundly influencing their mentality. In light of these observations, it is curious how historians have focused so much attention on anthropological research like that of Marcel Mauss, Karl

Polanyi, and Bronislaw Malinowsky, who identified the cultural origins of these behaviors in distant and exotic cultures, when the reality is that their origins were visibly and profoundly rooted in Greek thought, the authentic foundation of Western and European culture.

The Labored Reception in the Latin World

The Latin world, for a long time immersed in its bucolic environment, did not consider the problem of the most virtuous way of using wealth, the Ciceronian precepts remaining in force: "Roman people hate private luxury, Roman people like public magnificence" (Cicero [63 B.C.] 1994b, 36.76).[20] The term *public magnificence* referred above all to public works (whose poverty caused the hilarity of neighboring populations and, more seriously, of subject peoples as well) and to the ceremonies celebrating military victories. I do not think that it was by chance that the use of this term spread throughout the period of the Punic Wars (see Pietilä-Castrén 1987), when the Roman Senate approved the *Oppia* and *Orchia* laws in 215 B.C., which were intended to limit *luxuria privata* (private luxury) (further details in Sauerwein 1970; Miles 1987; Hunt 1996, 19–20).

However, reflections on this issue were the undesired but secondary effects of the process of Hellenization of Roman society that occurred in the second century B.C., after the conquest of Hellenistic kingdoms: "The beauty of Greek cities, the splendor of the country, and the power of the monarchy, the traditions of Athenian culture, the philosophical schools, rational philosophy, and also the mystical cults for the satisfaction of the most individual religious needs, and on the other hand an old religion that had been designed for a population of farmers indissolubly linked to the political sphere, the solid links of the old patriarchal families, a simple and almost unchanged lifestyle, a poor culture, without letters or images" (Zanker 1989, 3–4).

This was neither a peaceful nor a generous comparison, as shown in the title of a brilliant work by Jacob Isager (1993): "The Hellenization of Rome: Luxuria or Liberalitas?" While the most conservative wing of Roman society was trying to defend *mores maiorum* (the ancestors' morals) from the incursion of Greek *luxuriae,* making use of the same arguments employed by ancient Greeks for dealing with the advance of

20. "Odit populus Romanus privatam luxuriam, publicam magnificentia diligit."

Eastern luxury (see Mills 1984; Braund 1994), the most active fringes of the Roman intelligentsia wanted to adopt a liberal and magnific lifestyle. There was thus an almost schizophrenic dissociation between the behaviors to be pursued in moments of *negotium* (activity) and *otium* (leisure), as a result of the enforced temperance of public behaviors in opposition to private behaviors (Clarke 1991; Gazda 1991). The debate was an interesting one, particularly in the late republican period, when *liberalitas* (liberality) gradually lost the links with *libertas* (liberty) as a term identifying a condition, sentiment, or action of the free man (see Stylow 1972; Manning 1985, 82 n. 7), a semantic function delegated to *ingenuitas*, to take on meanings which, while they expressed a specific type of relations with wealth, became more political as they were removed from the Greek context. During the second and first centuries B.C., *liberalitas* signified a balanced and virtuous relation with wealth in an almost wholly private context (Wesch-Klein 1990). Along with *beneficentia* (beneficence), it was a valid instrument for expressing *benignitas* (benignity, good spirit), with the great difference that *beneficentia* referred to works and actions, and *liberalitas* to the wise use of money and the correct granting of *beneficia* (benefit).[21]

Nevertheless, from the dictatorship of Sulla onward, *liberalitas* was increasingly associated with the self-interested employment of private wealth and power.[22] It thus included actions not present in the Greek world, where they were considered prerogatives of the magnific: public distribution of food and money (*congiaria* and *donativa*), public games, gladiatorial spectacles, ruinous banquets, and grandiose buildings,[23]

21. This distinction clearly results from Cicero [44 B.C.] 1992, *De Officiis* 2.52.15: "Deinceps de beneficentia ac de liberalitate dicendum est, cuius est ratio duplex: nam aut opera benigne fit indigentibus aut pecunia."

22. In theory, the action of the genuinely liberal man should be characterized by the absence of any form of personal interest, as a pure act of altruism, as emphasized in other passages by Seneca [65–54 B.C.] 1950 (*De Beneficiis* 5.9.2: "Itaque nec liberalis est qui sibi donat") and Cicero [44 B.C.] 1965, (*Laelius* 30–31: "Benefici liberalesque sumus, non ut exigamus gratiam, neque enim beneficium faeneramur sed natura propensi ad liberalitatem sumus").

23. Running through the list of the meanings attributed to the term *liberalitas* in the epigraphic and numismatic sources compiled by Barbieri 1958, 875–85, we found the following among the emperors' liberalities: *donativa, institutiones alimentariae*, land grants, remissions of debts, restitutions of goods from state treasury to individuals, nominations to political positions, games, and privileges to provinces and cities. Among those granted to individuals were public money distributions, aid to food administration offices, plays, games and spectacles, banquets and food distribution, public works such as amphitheaters, arches,

whose main purpose was the speedy construction of political credit that could be easily spent in the turbulent Roman political arena. This phenomenon explains why authorities like Quintiliano argued that the *prodigus* (the prodigal man) was *liberalis* (liberal) and that *luxuria* (luxury) was not a vice but an expression of *liberalitas* (Manning 1985, 78). This inverted the association that saw *lussuria* (luxury) as always accompanied by *avaritia* (avarice) and *ambitio* (ambition) (see Fischer 1983; Slob 1986; Forbis 1993, 489, nn. 32–33). The term *liberalitas* was thus used as a euphemistic description of the obvious forms of corruption and typical actions of the euergetism (gift giving) which the *populares* politicians easily practiced. It thus became increasingly difficult to distinguish the limits that separated *liberalitas* from the terms identifying large-scale corruption, *ambitus* and *largitio*,[24] and the word came more often to have a meaning linked exclusively to politics and patronage (see Blanchet 1904; Berve 1926, cols. 82–84; Borsanyi 1938, 41; Hellegouarc'h 1963, 219; Veyne 1984, 377; Manning 1985, 77–78). These transformations were clear in Cicero (see Heuer 1941), who dedicated some pages to liberality in the first and second book of *De Officiis* [44 B.C.] 1992. In addition to the previously mentioned distinction between beneficence and liberality, and the relative opposition between works and money, Cicero's emphasis on the beneficiaries of liberality is striking ("Videndum est igitur, ut ea liberalitate utamur, quae prosit amicis, noceat nemini" [1.14.42]; "vulgaris liberalitas referenda est ad illum Enni finem: Nihilo minus ipsi lucet"; and "facultas sit, qua in nostros simus liberales" [1.16.52]). His remarks on the aims of liberal actions are also noteworthy (2.18.63: "Danda igitur opera est ut iis beneficiis quam plurimos adficiamus, quorum memoria liberis posterisque prodatur, ut iis ingratis esse non liceat"). In emphasizing the role of *amici* (friends) and of *nostros* (clients), the receivers of attention from the liberal man, and the importance of the fact that the memory of the gift should remain in the minds of sons and grandsons so they were not ungrateful, Cicero

---

basilicas, libraries, fora, slaughterhouses, walls, porticoes, statues, temples, theaters, and spas and baths.

24. This concept is clearly expressed by Cicero [55 B.C.] 1994a, *De Oratore* 2.105, where he affirms that "nam et de pecuniis repetundis, quae maximae sunt, neganda fere sunt omnia, et de ambitu raro illud datur, ut possis liberalitatem et benignitatem ab ambitu ac largitione seiungere."

admitted the client nature of Latin liberality, which had been absent from the Greek context, and he sanctioned the unreality of the inverse hierarchical sequence *patriae, propinquis, adfinibus, amicis* that had been proposed by Livy ([59 B.C.] 1967, Ep. 9.30). This admission was also the result of the need for caution: if the first two (liberality should not damage anyone and it should not be greater than anyone's wealth) follow the Aristotelian passage faithfully, the reference to giving according to worth is therefore new. As well as analyzing the character of the beneficiary (4.45: "in quo et mores eius erunt spectandi"), it emphasized the importance of the attitude of spirit toward the benefactor, his personal and professional relationships, and favors performed by him in the past (1.14.45: "et animus erga nos et communitas ac societas vitae et ad nostras utilitates officia ante collata"). The abandonment of the anonymous position in which Greek liberality manifested itself appeared in the list of actions that were considered genuinely liberal: freeing pirates' prisoners, paying friends' debts, paying their children's dowries, helping them find money or increasing their wealth (Cicero [44 B.C.] 1992, 2.15.55).[25] There still remained a doubt about what happened when a liberal man had many friends, or as happened to the magistrates *aediles*,[26] faced the institutional obligation of personally providing for such expenditure (public games, gladiatorial spectacles, public works). How was it possible to retain liberal conduct without falling into the temptation of *largitio*, of *profusio*, given the Roman aversion to private forms of magnificence, as in Cicero's harsh criticisms of passages in Teofrasto's lost treatise *On Wealth*, where there is lavish praise for the magnificence of popular

25. "Liberali autem, qui suis facultatibus aut captos a praedonibus redimunt aut aes alienum suscipiunt amicorum aut in filiarum collocatione adiuvant aut opitulantur vel in re quaerenda vel augenda."

26. This was a magistracy with an extensive range of duties, including city police and food distribution, water network management, market and slaughterhouse supervision, and the organization of public spectacles. The holders of this function, which became an obligatory step in the Roman *cursus honorum*, due to the budget constraints of this office, spent a lot of their own funds, above all in public games and spectacles. For many reasons these "public services" performed by private individuals are reminiscent of Greek λειτουργίαι, public duties which the Greek and Hellenistic *poleis* entrusted to particularly rich private citizens, who could afford the expenses involved. The λειτουργίαι could be extraordinary—as the τριηραρχία (equipping a military fleet) or the φιλαρχία (equipping a body of cavalry)—or ordinary, assigned on a yearly basis, such as the χορηγία (paying for a chorus), the γυμνασιαρχία (maintenance of a gymnasium, and l'εστίασις (banquet given to the members of the same tribe).

spectacles, valuing the capacity of wealth to meet these expenses (2.16.56)?[27]

Not being able to place these actions in the public field exclusively, Cicero condemned avarice and praised lasting initiative, from which there was a lasting memory, considering as prodigal most of the actions that Aristotle had categorized as private magnificence (2.15.55).[28] At the same time, Cicero expressed his aversion for public expenditure of limited usefulness and came out in favor of walls, arsenals, ports, and aqueducts and against theaters, porticoes, and new temples (2.17.60).[29] The ambiguity of this position derived from the impossibility of using the term *magnificentia* for identifying private actions, and the growing competition from the term *munificentia*, which, according to Kloft (1970, 47, n. 4), appeared at the end of Caesar's period (65 B.C.) (see also Forbis 1993, 486 n. 17). It was used to identify the grandness of certain architectural initiatives and public games offered by him. Slightly forcing the interpretative line but still respecting the difference of degree, I have discovered some similarities with the previous tripartite division of *benignitas*-benignity (goodwill)–*beneficentia*-beneficence (expressed through actions and works)–*liberalitas*-liberality (through the wise use of money and the granting of *beneficia*-benefit). These virtues, in the highest forms of social expression,[30] generate the analogous sequence *magnanimitas* (magnanimity)–*magnificentia* (magnificence)–*munificentia* (munificence). *Magnanimitas*, the grandness of spirit, comes directly from Aristotlelian μεγαλοψυχία (Knoche 1935; Gauthier 1951). It showed itself through the great works of *magnificus* (magnificent) or through the enormous donations in money of *munificus/munificent*. Since *magnificentia* remained exclusively a state characteristic, honor was awarded to *munificentia*, which, conforming to the

27. "Itaque miror, quid in mentem venerit Theophrasto in eo libro, quem de divittis scripsit, in quo multa praeclare, illud absurde: est enim multus in laudanda magnificentia et apparitione popularium munerum taliumque sumptuum facultatem fructum divitiarum putat."

28. "Omnino duo sunt genera largorum, quorum alteri prodigi, alteri liberales: prodigi, qui epulis et viscerationibus et gladiatorum muneribus ludorum venationumque apparatu pecunias profundunt in eas res, quarum memoriam aut brevem aut nullam omnino sint relicturi."

29. "Atque etiam illae impensae meliores, muri, navalia, portus, aquarum ductus omniaque, quae ad usum rei publicae pertinent. . . . Theatra, porticus, nova templa verecundius reprehendo."

30. Between *liberalitas* and *munificentia* there seems to exist only differences in grade; in fact, if the liberalitas does not have particular social connotations, the *munificentia* is an aristocratic, princely, or regal virtue, as can be seen in Forbis 1993, 486; Johnston 1985; and Mrozek 1984.

Greek equivalent of μεγαλοδωρία, meant to make very large gifts (*munus-facere*), to spend enormous sums of money (Forbis 1993, 486 nn. 16–17).

It was the advent of the Principate that cleared the field of every potential misunderstanding: the term *liberalitas* fell into disgrace, as a result of the embarassing etymological parallel with a *libertas* (liberty) that had already definitively been lost and as a result of the use to which the term had been put in the turbulent period that preceded the accession of Augustus. Only in the first century A.D. did it reappear in the Roman political vocabulary, even if by then it had become an almost exclusively imperial virtue and action (Kloft 1970, 1987; Dopico-Cainzos 1993). This term was used to identify specific forms of euergetism of immediate political value, without signifying differences from the synonymous *congiarium*,[31] as results from the interpretations of many twentieth-century Latinists.[32]

But as liberality declined, *magnificentia publica* was on the increase, since Augustus gave it new style and significance. In fact, in his project to restore the ancient values that had been betrayed, he conducted a merciless war against private luxury (see Kloft 1996), specifically against building luxury (detailed descripted by Romano 1994), but at the same time he counterproposed a great campaign of architectural improvement.[33] This plan, while it focused on collective needs with the construction of aqueducts, fountains, drains, markets and slaughterhouses, and parks and public gardens, was above all directed at reli-

31. The *congiaria* were distributions of food and/or money, given to the entire Roman plebs. They were similar to the *donativa* given to victorious soldiers or campaign veterans. Originally, the *congiaria* were distributions of food, as the etymological origin of the term *congius* shows, it was a standard cubic unit of measurement of 3.25 liters, used for wine and cereals. Later, more or less since Caesar's *congiaria in denarios*, they became distributions of silver and bronze coins. For more, see Corbier 1997; Millar 1991.

32. The cases of Barbieri 1958 and Blanchet 1904, for example. Barbieri, following the interpretations of Strack and Van Berchem in the 1930s, stops at a very precise chronological reconstruction of the Roman imperial *liberalitates*, from Caesar to Galerio Massimiano, strongly convinced that "liberalitas or congiarium: there is no difference between the two words, as can be seen from the coins used from the beginning of the II century A.D." (839). Berve 1926, on the other hand, argues at cols.84–86 that the *liberalitates* were donations and expenses based on the private princely wealth, the *patrimonium*, while the *congiaria* were a burden on the state treasury, the *fiscus*.

33. On the character of Augustus's *magnificentia publica*, see Zanker 1989, 146–50, and Hesberg 1992.

gious buildings, giving to the term that religious nuance, which led to the fifteenth-century rediscovery.

The aversion to private magnificence derived from the troubled reception of the Hellenistic models, which become widespread at first through the Roman generals who returned triumphant from the Eastern campaigns, marveling at the *sumptus* (sumptuousness) (literally, "the great expense"), the *pompa* (pomp), and the *apparati* (arrays) of the defeated Eastern kings. In this ostentatiousness of power, the Roman senators of the third and second century B.C. saw not only clear denials of republican virtues but also the insidious fragmentation that resulted from the spread of personality cults. This fragmentation ran counter to that "anonymous" spirit of service that ought to permeate the souls of the military leaders engaged in conquest. And, bearing in mind first-century B.C. Roman history, it cannot be denied that such fears were founded, since it was in the military world itself, which was so sensitive to Hellenistic pomp, that the tendencies to the cult of the individual developed, which became flagrant in the dramatic period just prior to the advent of Augustus.

From the Medieval Debate to the Fifteenth-Century Renaissance

The fall of the Roman Empire did not stop the debate about the liberal and magnificent usage of wealth, thanks to the numerous interventions of the church hierarchy. Patristic literature devoted ample space to these arguments, setting in action an interesting Christianization process of the Greek and Latin lexicals. However, if reflections about magnificence remained stuck on the theological level, the pronouncements on liberality were very different (see Todeschini 1992, 200–215, and 1994, 123, 193–94). *Liberality* was used as a synonym for *eleemosyna-largitio/largitas*,[34] as in the opening passage of Thomas Aquinas's ([1266–73] 1949) *Summa Theologica*: "And, with another name, liberalitas is called largitas."[35] The two words *largitio/liberalitas* included in their semantic field the lexical of *misericordia* (mercy) and

34. While in the patristic literature the terms *largitas* and *largitio* were used without difference, it should be mentioned that in the Latin world they had two well distinct meanings: *largitas* indicates a generic act of generosity, while *largitio* identifies large-scale corruption.

35. "Et alio nomine liberalitas largitas nominatur."

of *caritas* (charity) (see Pétré 1931, 1948), the definition being given as "both a general Christian attitude toward the neighbor (at a theological-moral level of significance) and a multitude of charitable practices, that is, public and private forms of management of socially approved wealth (at an administrative level of significance)" (Todeschini 1994, 123). In this sense, if liberality governed the set of lemma defining the equal charitable distribution of wealth and superfluous goods, as appears to be the case in the passages of Augustine and Ambrosius,[36] as well as those of authors such as Guillame Pérault (1190–1255),[37] avarice headed the awful vices threatening the cohesion of the Christian community and its solidarity: Isidoro of Seville (ca. 560–636) compared it to a fluorescent leprosy (Isidoro of Seville 1601, 469); Hincmaro of Rheims (ca. 806–882) made a scrupulous list of all the reasons for avoiding it (Hincmaro of Rheims 1879, 867); and Bernardus Claraevallensis (1090–1153) mentioned it in his invective against the luxury of bishops and clerics (Claraevallensis 1851, 1:658).

A decisive stimulus for renewing discussion of the issue came from the rediscovery of Aristotelian texts in the thirteenth century, specifically with the appearance of the first translation into Latin of the *Nichomachean Ethics* in 1247. This coincided with a period of profound transformation, due to socioeconomic changes that altered the previous equilibrium and resulted in new ranks and forces that wanted to have their voices heard. Thus, alongside the intransigent positions of the mendicant orders, deeply influenced by the reflections of the Franciscans and Dominicans about poverty as the rule of life, there were the more conciliatory attitudes of the authors who had been deeply affected by Aristotelian thought: Brunetto Latini (ca. 1220–1294), Thomas Aquinas (ca. 1226–1274), and Romanus Aegidius (ca. 1246–1316).

Of the three, the least interesting contribution was perhaps that of the first, who limited his work to a succinct but precise paraphrase of the *Nichomachean Ethics*, introducing only a few elements clearly

36. For instance, for Ambrosius ([386 B.C.] 1977, 244, quoted in Todeschini 1992, 219), liberality, placed between the two extremes of *inhumanum* and *prodigum*, consists in "giving abundantly to pilgrims, not superfluous but suitable things, not superabundant but convenient to human nature (largire peregrinis, non superflua sed competentia, non redundantia sed congrua humanitati)."

37. Still in the thirteenth century, Guillame Pérault ([1236–48] 1595, 306) considered as synonymous *liberalitas, misericordia*, and *largitas* (liberality, mercy, and largesse), reinforcing the Christianity of his interpretation with numerous *exempla* quoted from the Old and New Testaments and the four Gospels.

inspired by Christianity. Thus Latini ([1270] 1869, 37) reduced *magnanimitas* (*magnanimità*-magnanimity) to a virtue concerned with the employment of economic means (Gauthier 1951, 55–176, quoted in Greaves 1964; Van Houdt, this volume): "Liberality, magnificence and magnanimity are similar, since all of them regard the receiving and giving of money."[38] This implied an evident straining of Greek and Latin interpretations, justified by the effort to "operationalize" the religious significance of the concept. If it was true that "he is magnanimous who is suited to the greatest works, and who rejoices and enjoys in doing great things," it was clear that "the real magnanimity is only in the greatest things, that is to say in the actions in which man serves God the glorious" (37).[39]

Much more significant is the contribution of Aquinas whose *Summa* devoted ample space to the treatment of the triad *liberality, magnificence, magnanimity*. His analysis faithfully follows Aristotle, from whom he differed in the sporadic placing of Latin and pre-Christian quotations. As far as liberality is concerned, he said, the most important observations involve the following fine distinction: "Magnificence regards also the use of wealth, but according to some special reason, that is, when wealth in used in the achievement of some great work. So magnificence is in some way additional with respect to liberality" (Aquinas [1266–73] 1949, IIa, IIIae, quaestio 117, ar 3, ra 1).[40] It also contains significant emphasis on the propaedeutics of the exercise of this virtue, that is, the acquisition and administration of wealth: "so liberality does not regard only the use of money, but also preparing and preserving money for a suitable use" (IIa, IIIae, quaestio 117, ar 3, ra 2).[41] These references were already present in the Greek text but were given more space in the Aquinas treatment, which was concerned to discipline possible excesses of a virtue which already had a socially undifferentiated profile. Every good Christian, whether rich or poor,

38. "La liberalitade e la magnificenza e la magnanimitade hanno comunitade tra loro, però che tutte sono in ricevere e in dare pecunia."

39. "Magnanimo è colui che è acconcio a grandissimi fatti, e rallegrasi, e gode di far gran cose," and "la vera magnanimitade si è solamente nelle cose grandissime, cioè nelle cose per le quali l'uomo serve a Domenedio glorioso."

40. "Ad magnificentiam etiam pertinet uti divitiis secundum quandam specialem rationem, idest secundum quod assumuntur in alicuius magni operis expletionem, unde et magnificentia quammodo se habet ex additione ad liberalitatem."

41. "Sic etiam ad liberalitatem pertinet non solum uti pecunia, sed etiam preparare et conservare ad idoneum usum."

could be liberal, but "the use of money regards the liberal man in one way, and the magnific man in another way; in fact it concerns the liberal man by a regular affection for the money" (IIa, IIIae, quaestio 134, ar 3, co).[42] This course was different from that followed in the introduction of a double moral and offered in the name of God to absolve the guilt of the magnificent: "Magnificence regards the intention of making some great work; and in order to ensure that some great work was conveniently carried out, proportionate expenditures are required; in fact the great works cannot be made without great expenditures. So magnificence concerns making great expenditures in something that was made conveniently great" (IIa, IIIae, quaestio 134, ar 3, co).[43] It remained an insurmountable limit, however, consisting of the limit where one had to tender the magnificence of Aquinas. While not ignoring the importance of works of collective interest (like when is made something which interests all the citizens),[44] he attributed eminently religious connotations to this virtue: "In fact no aim of human works is greater than honoring God, and for this reason magnificence principally makes great works in order to honor God" (IIa, IIIae, quaestio 134, ar 3, ra 2).[45]

The work of the most brilliant of the followers of Aquinas was much more influential. Romanus Aegidius's *De regimine principum*, which was finished between 1277 and 1279 and popularized in 1288, provoked open revolution. While he did not abandon the original Aristotle passages as far as the relations between liberality and magnificence were concerned, Romanus Aegidius argued first that "for kings and princes it could not in any way be possible to be prodigal, and that for them it is particularly detestable to be greedy and really suitable to be liberal" (18).[46] He insisted on the fact that "since kings and princes have a lot of properties and wealth, they should give bigger recom-

42. "Quod usus pecuniae aliter pertinet ad liberalem, et aliter ad magnificum. Ad liberalem enim pertinet secundum quod procedit ex ordinato affectu circa pecunias."

43. "Ad magnificentiam pertinet intendere ad aliquod magnum opus faciendum, ad hoc autem quod aliquod magnum opus convenienter fiat, requiruntur proportionati sumptus, non enim possunt magna opera fieri nisi cum magnis expensis. Unde ad magnificentiam pertinet magnos sumptus facere ad hoc quod magnum convenienter fiat."

44. "Sicut cum facit aliquid ad quod tota civitas studet."

45. "Nullus autem finis humanorum operum est adeo magnus sicut honor dei, et ideo magnificentia praecipue magnum opus facit in ordine ad honorem dei."

46. "Quod reges et principes quodammodo impossibile est esse prodigos et quod maxime detestabile esse eos esse avaros et quod potissime decet liberales esse."

penses and they should spend with more pleasure and promptness" (20),[47] above all in works that did not coincide with the traditional religious sphere: "Having honorable houses, making convenient weddings, equipping admirable armies" (20).[48]

In such a way, Aegidius managed to praise the lay spirit of magnificence, thus constructing an excellent moral alibi for princes who wanted to mark themselves out with the penitential Christian tutelage. It is not surprising that his work profoundly influenced the thought of later authors and that his *De regimine principum* had a large following (see Frigo 1985b, 22–28, 51–53), shown by the success of the writings of Fra Paolino Minorita ([1330] 1868, book 3, *De regimine gentis*), Conrad von Megenberg ([1353] 1973–77, book 2, *De regimine curie principum temporalioum*), and Vincenzo di Beauvais (Vincentius [1250–52] 1938). These works contributed decisively to the definition of the sumptuous lifestyle of princes, which, already absolved from stringent moral obligations, attracted the attention of the princes of the church, and papal intervention, this being intended to limit the scandalous waste of cardinal banquets, as in the *Dat vivendi normam* of 1316 issued by Giovanni XXII and the *Ad honorem* promulgated in 1357 by Innocenzo VI (see Zacour 1975), as well as the texts of Conrad von Megenberg ([1353] 1973–77, book 3, *De dominbus divinis*), who proposed models of virtuous management of the ecclesiastical courts and households. In the meantime, however, the debate moved from the abstract focus of the Scholastic disputations to the more concrete decisions of municipal and feudal councils: the term *magnificence* appeared in Florentine documents from the second half of the fifteenth century onward, and earlier still in the Milan area.[49] As Louis Green (1990, 98) has perceptively noted, in his work on the relations between the Dominican Galvano Fiamma and the Duke of Milan, Azzone Visconti, the reopening of the debate about magnificence "was due to a late medieval Aristotelian response to a new political phenomenon, the North Italian regional or territorial." Fiamma, in the fifteenth chapter (*De magnificentia edificio-*

47. "Quanto igitur reges et principes magis habundant facultatibus et divitiis, magis decet eos ampliores retributiones facere et magis delectabiliter et prompte expendere."

48. "Habendo habitationes honorabiles, faciendo nupcias decentes, exercendo militias admirabiles."

49. Green (1990, 98 n. 3) found this term quoted in some letters written in 1356–57, while Spilner (1993, 455) found it in the document with which in 1371 the Signoria and Councils of Florence approved a plan to construct an addition to Palazzo Vecchio.

rum) of his *Opusculum de rebus gestis ab Azone, Luchino et Johanne Vicecomitibus* (in Green 1990), examined the traditional passages of Aristotle, showing the need to give magnificence an essentially architectonic expression, in line with the strongly religious intonation of Thomas Aquinas.[50] However, Fiamma also suggested that the prince should have "a magnificent habitation" as "an appropriate place of residence for a multitude of officials."[51] This was a revolutionary passage in many respects because of its curious proto-functionalism. It hypothesized the birth of that magnificently laid courtly space that had captured the attention of kings and architects for centuries. It not only celebrated the glory of the prince, but also the dignity of the state by ensuring that its faithful officers had a suitable space for the daily exercise of their functions. It was already evident that the expression of fifteenth-century magnificence was predominantly architectonic and, above all, secular rather than religious. It was also evident that it was suitable as a means for satisfying the self-celebratory needs of the emerging ranks because it symbolically described the new relations of forces established in both the free communes and seignories.

Confirmation was provided by the lively debate in Florence. It was not by chance that this occurred during the Albizzi period (see Pacciani 1980, esp. chap. 1) and that it was stimulated by the works of Leonardo Bruni, who translated and commented on the *Nicomachean Ethics* in the 1420s. Between 1420 and 1421 (Frigo 1985b, 28–29), he translated and commented on the *Economics pseudo-Aristotelian*. His work had a rapid effect: Buonaccorso da Montemagno, in his *De Nobilitate* of 1429, which was focused on the Roman republic, makes one of his speakers assert that "a useful additional aspect to nobility of blood was constituted by wealth, by which the noble man was able to exercise liberality" (quoted in Donati 1988, 10).[52] Meanwhile Leon Battista Alberti ([1432–34] 1969, 258) argued that "unnecessary expenditures are liked if they are made with some reason, while they do not hurt if they are not made. And such kind of unnecessary expenditures consists in painting the loggia, buying silverware, being magnificent with pomp, with

50. See Green 1990, 101: "*The honourable expenses which a magnificent prince should defray pertain to God*—honorabiles sumptus, quos debet facere princeps magnificus, sunt circa Deum."

51. See Green 1990, 101: "Habitatio magnifica, conveniens habitatio pro moltitudine ministrorum."

52. "Un utile accessorio della nobiltà di sangue era costituito dalle ricchezze, mediante le quali il nobile era in grado di esercitare la liberalità."

clothing, with liberality. Expenditures made in order to delight in pleasures and polite entertainment are unnecessary, but not without some reason."[53]

This new lay concept of liberality and magnificence testified to the different attitude of many thinkers in regard to wealth. Although it was not yet considered the source of virtue and the guarantee of nobility, it was no longer condemned a priori, as had happened in the first years of the fifteenth century in the violent sermons of Bernardino of Siena and Antonino of Florence. This change is most clearly seen in the works of the 1430s and 1450s of the many Italian authors such as Mattia Palmieri ([1439] 1843), Poggio Bracciolini ([1538] 1964), Giovanni Caldiera (see King 1975), Leon Battista Alberti ([1452] 1966), and Antonio Ivani ([1470] 1825). There was a real proliferation of moral philosophy texts focused on moral and social virtues, and these always dealt with liberality, magnificence, and magnanimity (King 1975, 547–53).

Moreover, emphasis in the second half of the fifteenth century was put on the social profile of magnificence, oriented in a broader sense. If in 1443 Francesco Filelfo ([1443] 1537), talking about *magnidecentia* (his translation of Aristotelian μεγἄλοπρέπεια-magnificence), stated that it was simply a virtue of the rich, a few years later Sabatino degli Arienti and Giovanni Pontano considered it a typical aristocratic virtue.

The *De triumphis religionis* of Sabatino degli Arienti (see Johannes Sabadinus Argenteus 1496) is a typical apologetic text (see Gundersheimer 1972), and it was inspired by the close relationship with the Florentine milieu[54] and by the princely biographies written in those years by Pier Candido Decembrio (1399–1477) and Vespasiano di Bisticci (1421–1498), who described widely the magnificent architectural works promoted by their lords. In *De triumphis religionis* Sabatino praised Ercole I Este's magnificence, which "consists in things sumptuous, great and sublime, and its name resounds largesse and grandness

53. "Le spese non necessarie con qualche ragione fatte piacciono, non fatte non nuociono. E sono queste come dipignere la loggia, comperare gli arienti, volersi magnificare con pompa, con vestire, con liberalità. Sono anche poco necessarie, ma non senza qualche ragione, le spese fatte per asseguire piaceri, sollazzi civili."

54. The manuscript of Sabadino degli Arienti shows some analogies with the contents of the *In magnificentiae Cosmi Medicei Florentini detractores*, written by Timoteo Maffei between 1454 and 1456 and deeply analyzed by Fraser-Jenkins 1970. For further details on the relationships between Florence and Ferrara, see Kent 1977, 313–14.

in expending gold and silver in eminent, high, and divine works that are suitable for the magnificent man" (Argenteus 1496, 34r).[55] Nevertheless, the most intriguing part of the manuscript is not where it magnifies the architectural works of the famous duke of Ferrara, but that it included in the domain of the virtuous an ample set of activities and consumptions which had been previously neglected. Sabatino celebrated lavish banquets and sumptuous hospitality, rich greetings and magnificent weddings, elaborate comedies and great jousts and tournaments, great hunts and splendid funerals. Thus, every action or aristocratic consumption could be morally justified by the desire to pursue full magnificence.

Even more audacious was Giovanni Pontano (1518), who, while remaining loyal to the most traditional Aristotelian-Thomist interpretations concerning liberality and magnificence (118v),[56] clearly marked the differences between liberality and beneficence by recurring to the Latin conceptions (97r–117v and 124r–137r). He hypothesized a revolutionary concept: that of "*splendor*-splendor, which shines in domestic decoration, in bodily ornaments, in house furniture, and in many other different things" (136r–140v).[57] If until then, the magnificence remained limited to durable works and exceptional occasions, splendor included all daily or common objects: "vases, textiles, beds, paintings, ivory seats, crystal vases, gems, etc." (136r–140v).[58] For the splendid man there were no longer superfluous goods, but only splendid objects!

Nevertheless, these transformations were not provoked just by lay desiderata, but were above all requested by the even more sumptuous papal and cardinal courts (see Byatt 1983), which needed an ideological justification for their immoral lifestyle. The striking contrast between the statements of Paolo Cortesio is not random. While in the *Sentenze* (1504) he maintained very conservative positions, stressing the eminently religious nature of liberality ("we define liberality as the virtue that helps in order to render ourselves well-deserving for many peo-

55. "La magnificentia in cose sumptuose grande et sublime consiste: come il nome di epsa suona largheza et amplitudine in expendere auro et argento in cose eminente alte et dive a la convenientia del magnifico."

56. "Beneficence is close to liberality . . . nevertheless this is remarkable, that liberality helps only with money, beneficence only with actions." (Liberalitati finitima est beneficentia . . . , tamen hoc interest, quod illa pecunia tantum adiuvat, haec opera.)

57. "At splendor, quod in ornamentis domesticis, in cultu corporis, in supellectile, in apparatum rerum diversarum praelucet."

58. "Vasa, textilia, lectos, tabulae pictae, eburnae sellae, vascula e cristallo, gemmas, etc."

ple") and following the most traditional thesis regarding magnificence ("instead we want magnificence to come from that spiritual strength which finishes off great works, done with the most suitable expenditures") (1504, liber tertium, distinctio octava),[59] in the *De Cardinalatu* (1510, especially 55–58; see also Priscianese 1543) he stated defiantly that cardinals, being princes (even if princes of the church) could not be accused of being wasteful, since they could spend in the same way and to the same degree as lay princes.

Concluding Reflections on the Sixteenth-Century Debate

Reading again the passages from the sixteenth-century treatise authors on liberality and magnificence that were examined in the second section, we should understand the importance of two phenomena. We can now answer the question posed at the end of the second section: "Were the sixteenth-century passages about liberality, splendor, and magnificence an original fruit of Renaissance thinking, or were they a genuine inheritance of classical thought?" The answer is that, in this debate as well, the significance of the hereditary component was greater than the new, innovative component. It is now about time that the French and Anglo-Saxon students of the seventeenth- to eighteenth-century luxury debate realized the opportunity and the need to study these authors, themes, and texts more deeply, since the sixteenth- and seventeenth-century Italian discussion had such a large European following, which is worth further research and study.

It should be realized, however, that in the sixteenth century, alongside very faithful Aristotelian-Thomist arguments, there were parallel interpretations that attributed new meanings to these virtues. These were the result of an evident hermeneutic strain, as can be seen by comparing the rigorous Aristotelian-Thomist manner of Cesare Capaccio with the less involved positions assumed by Gerolamo Muzio. According to Capaccio (1620, 273), "Aristotle himself has said that nothing gives somebody more glory than generosity, rather than nobility. Because he is noble who relies on the glory of his ancestors, and he is liberal who honors the

59. "Liberalitatem definimus ut ea sit ad bene de multis promerendum opitulatrix virtus. . . . Magnificentiam autem volumus ex eadem fortitudine nasci quae sit magnorum operum confectrix cum decentia sumptuum collocandorum."

virtue of his ancestors. So that all liberal men are noble, but not all noble men are liberal."[60] Muzio (1575, 9), in contrast, argued that "liberality is a proper virtue of the aristocrat, and scholars state that tenacity and avarice are the sure signs of an ignoble and villainous spirit."[61] Comparison should also be made with the devious sixteenth-century reeditions of fifteenth-century treatises, which often put forward risky views (i.e., Massaciucoli 1561).

The predominantly political and social nature of this debate remains clear. It was a new modification of the social profile of this virtue in a decisively elitist sense. The bourgeois liberality that could be exercised by anyone in the fifteenth century who had the quality of dignity now became an exclusively noble prerogative, while the aristocratic magnificence of the sixteenth century became a heroic princely attribute. In both cases the ideological foundations of noble and patrician behavioral models had to be reinforced in the vain and desperate attempt to inhibit the phenomenon of social emulation. Emulation, during the process of gradual closure of social ranks and the crystallization of hierarchies, characterized the dynamics of Italian society in the early sixteenth century. The climate of effervescent social mobility in the fifteenth century, with its sudden rises and falls of fortune, gave way to an atmosphere of silent consolidation, where the question of the origin and nature of nobility could not be ignored (see Donati 1988, 128–50). In this regard, the role of wealth and its possible uses was becoming a determinant, as a source and mark of social distinction, and the problematic definition of the criteria of identification of, inclusion in, and exclusion from the elite was pursued by an equally articulated process of closure of the subordinate social orders. So the real dangers did not arise from the mass consumption of luxury or artistic goods, which had already been definitively demoralized (Berry 1994, 101–8), but from efforts to increase this consumption to levels beyond the capacity of social states: "Household is eroded by games, useless banquets, by the desire to exceed the number of servants, to compete with the richest and vainest persons in clothing and parties, in feeding dogs

60. "L'istesso [Aristotle] poi há pur detto, che maggior gloria ad alcuno non attribuisce la generositá, che la nobiltá; per che nobile è colui, che alla sola gloria de i suoi maggiori si appoggia: e generoso, chi per la virtú de i suoi maggiori si comenda, dal che nasce, che tutti i generosi sono nobili, ma non tutti i nobili sono generosi."

61. "La liberalitá è propria virtú dei nobili; & dicono i Dottori che la tenacitá et la avaritia è vero indicio di animo ignobile & villano."

and horses, and many other superfluous things beyond the decency of one's own social state" (Antoniano [1584] 1821, 2:2.107.27).[62]

In this regard, the scandalized references to the fact that "I omit to mention furnishings, since they have reached such excessive luxury, that those which are displayed in country houses today outdo in value those which our forebears, even the most noble and richest citizens, used in the capital cities only a few years ago" (2:2.107.27),[63] seem to express more the supine attachment to a topos from classical rhetoric (the unreachable virtues of "the ancients," the irredeemable corruption of "the moderns") than a sincere expression of a sense of moral outrage. The actual scandal was therefore not that somebody owned such goods but that "nearly everyone" owned them—that the passion for works of art and archaeological goods, for instance, had become a mass phenomenon. The distance between the atmosphere of austere admiration evoked by Titian's portrait of the famous antiquarian Jacopo da Strada and the derision expressed by authors who were quick to understand the comic side of this mass enthusiasm cannot be ignored. Giuseppe Orologgi (1562, 124–25), for example, mocked "those at Rome whom everybody calls antiquarians. They state that they are able to recognize any kind of ancient object and that they know everything about them. They say the most thievish and scurrilous things in the world. This kind of man used often to play strange jokes on 'modern men,' and they repeatedly say what is more convenient for them, finding ears which are always willing to believe everything that they want to say."[64] Silvio Antoniano ([1584] 1821, 2:2.107.27), on the other hand, derided "those who devote themselves body and soul to collecting antique statues, which has been described with good reason by others as fanaticism"[65] and

62. "Mettono in disordine le cose domestiche i giuochi, i conviti superflui, il voler eccedere nel numero de'servitori, il fare a gare con i piú ricchi, e con i piú vani nel vestire, nel festeggiare, ed in nutrire cavalli, cani, e tante altre simili superfluitá fuori dalla decenza del proprio stato."

63. "Tralascio parlare delle suppellettili, che sono giunte a tanto eccessivo lusso, che quelle che oggidí si usano nelle ville, oltrepassano assai in valore quelle che i nostri maggiori, anche de' piú nobili, e benestanti cittadini, adoperavano, non sono giá molti anni, nelle cittá capitali."

64. "Vi sono di quelli in Roma chiamati antiquari da ogn'uno; che . . . dicono le piú ladre e manigolde cose del mondo; . . . questa maniera d'huomini sogliono far il piú delle volte si strani scherzi ai moderni . . . e dicono e ridicono come loro torna meglio; trovando le orecchie altrui ben disposte a dar credenza a tutto quel, che vien loro in animo di dire."

"those who desire pictures from famous painters, or those who want jewels and similar things, which are bought at high price, moreover by those who have this kind of appetite, despite the fact that when needed only very small sums are received for them."[66]

The heart of the question and the origin of the widespread social fears did not lie in the possession of certain goods but in the fact that some people tried to copy through them the consumption style of the elite. It was thus popular emulation and not luxury that was the real enemy, as could be evinced from analysis of the development of sumptuary laws.[67] Emulation threatened the social peace by stimulating the unhealthy ambitions for social elevation of the humblest classes, and, more seriously still, it embarrassed the aristocratic families who could not go on raising the ante in the unending game of social prestige, as Annibale Romei (1591, 259) pointed out in one of his discourses: "It happens that those who are equal to others in terms of nobility but inferior in terms of wealth, being unable to bear the pomp and the arrogance of the richest in their lifestyle, clothing, and other external matters, crushed by the richest and discontented with their

65. "Altri che fanno, come essi dicono, studio di raccogliere, statue antiche, che altri con piú ragione chiamano fanatismo."

66. "Altri vogliono quadri di pittori insigni; altri gioje, e cose simili, che si comperano, massime dagli appetitosi, a caro prezzo; e che poi nei bisogni non se ne ricava che una tenuissima somma."

67. Just for this reason the traditional butts of the fourteenth- and fifteenth-century sumptuary laws—feminine vanity, aristocratic arrogance, and the risks of impoverishing the community (see on this aspect Hughes 1983; Muzzarelli 1996)—were replaced in the sixteenth century by an impregnable mobile target: social emulation. This trend started early in the formulation of the "Prammatica o sia Regolamento sopra il sontuoso vestire degli Huomini e Donne e sopra le larghe spese de i convitti, e funerali," which came from Savoy on 17 June 1430. This regulation laid down in the greatest detail the clothing rules for members of the Savoy household, and those of the "barons, vavasors, doctors and knights 'not in arms,' noble doctors, squires, doctors of law, those with legal and medical licenses, treasurers, magistrates, citizens and bourgeoisie living on their own incomes, those with factories or trading activities outside their own area, other senior members of the bourgeoisie, merchants, artisans, farmers and their employees, and all the women of these classes" (Levi-Pisetzky 1964, 2:471–72). This measure was the basis for a radical change in the sumptuary law itself, which from the second half of the 1400s onward did not single out luxury good consumption as such, as much as it punished the attempts of lower classes to assume forms of social identity that were not really theirs by the possession and showing off of goods and symbols which reflected a higher social status. It is not surprising, then, that in the course of the 1500s the sumptuary laws took on an increasingly classist character, skating elegantly over the limits imposed on nobles, knights, aliens, aristocrats, and their respective wives and reaching levels of unprecedented ferocity vis-à-vis the "unforgivable affectations" of servants, workers, traders, and so on.

own condition, would easily seek to make the prince fall and install a republic."[68]

Nor was the bewildering policy of product differentiation enough to stop the mounting tide of collective emulation that already existed in the second half of the sixteenth century by adopting the goods most suitable for satisfying the growing needs of social distinction of each social class: a good example is the discussion by Cardinal Gabriele Paleotti ([1582] 1960, 919) of the subjects who had to be painted to satisfy the needs of various publics (painters, men of letters, ecclesiastics, and "the third kind of persons, who should necessarily be satisfied: the idiots—who are the majority of the population—for whom sacred pictures were introduced").[69] Other examples are Giovanni Paolo Lomazzo's (1585) wonderful book 7,[70] and the equally surprising book 3 of Giovanni Battista Armenini (1586) devoted to the "distinction and convenience of paintings according to the places and the qualities of persons," in which a good painter has to consider carefully the needs of "persons for whom work is performed, as these works vary a great deal in their use and quality, in the same way that the customs, professions, and nobility of patrons vary."[71]

Anxiety about reestablishing and maintaining correct social distances concerned not only relations between the noble and patrician ranks and the bourgeoisie but also relations between the different ranks of the aristocracy: "So it happens that human beings are by nature so vain and ambitious, that the plebeians compete in their manner of dress

68. "Conciosia che quelli, che di nobiltá eguali e di ricchezze alli altri inferiori si trovano, non potendo tolerar il fasto e la superbia di piú ricchi nell'essere, nel vestire, e nelle altre apparenze esteriori, soprafatti da quelli, poco contenti dal lor stato, cercarebbero facilmente mutatione di stato nella Repubblica."

69. "La terza sorte di persone, a chi necessariamente si ha da soddisfare, sono gl'idioti, che è la maggior parte del popolo, per servizio de'quali principalmente furono introdotte le pitture sacre."

70. In book 7 are listed (in chap. 21) the pictures to be used in sepulchres, cemeteries, underground churches, and other melancholy places; (in chap. 22) those used in important religious buildings; (in chap. 23) those used in large rooms (meeting-rooms and audience chambers); (in chap. 24) those used in palaces and princely residences; (in chap. 25) those used in fountains, gardens, and rooms for pleasure; (in chap. 26) those used in schools and colleges; and (in chap. 27) those used in taverns and similar places.

71. "Della distinzione e convenienza delle pitture secondo i luoghi e la qualitá delle persone; con che ragione elle si fanno fra sé diverse e con quali avertimenti e giudicio si deve governare il pittore intorno ad esse. . . . persone per cui si fanno le opere, poichè tali opere per uso e qualità variano molto, così come variano molto per costumi, professione e nobiltà gli stessi committenti."

to be taken for nobles, the nobles for princes, and they put all their energies into improving only their external appearance and do not worry about living in their houses like beggars as long as they can seem rich in the city squares" (Romei 1591, 259).[72] A double objective has therefore to be pursued: to justify from the theoretical point of view the strained consumption of the aristocrats, the only limits to which were their excessive affectation[73] and ridiculous ostentation,[74] and to note the simultaneous difference between simply liberal lifestyles and lifestyles marked by the attainment of heroic magnificence. This was because the idea that had taken root was that "there is no virtue more suitable to a great man than liberality and magnificence, but magnificence is the greater of the two, because liberality can also be exercised by a poor man" (Sigismondi 1604, 23).[75] Further, "the way of spending of an emperor, a prince, and so on is different to that of other ranks and conditions of human beings. The same expense that will be magnificent for a private gentleman, will not be for a prince" (Piccolomini 1552, 5.5.107r).[76]

It is therefore clear that there was an interpretative distance separating the positions of the late fifteenth and early sixteenth centuries on the issue of magnificence from those of the late sixteenth and early seventeenth centuries. At first, this virtue was contained in the genetic inher-

72. "Conciosia che gli huomini, di natura siano tanto vani & ambitiosi, che i plebei a gara col vestir di parer nobili; & i nobili di parer Principi si sforzano: ne ponendo il lor studio in altro che ad una certa apparenza esteriore, non si curano di vedersi in casa mendichi pur che in piazza paiano ricchi."

73. See, for instance, Antoniano [1584] 1821, 1:2.93.382: "The good father should not accept his young son to have his face painted, his ears pierced, and his hair curled. The young son has not to appear in public as an affected female, full of scent and lasciviousness, dressed with pomp." (Non peró soffra il buon padre in alcun modo che il giovanetto . . . sia dipinto sul volto, o abbia forate le orecchia, ed inanellati i capelli, sicché appara in publico come una vezzosa femminetta, pieno di odori, e di lascivia, vestito pomposamente."

74. See in Gracian [1583] 1693, the *maximes* dedicated to ostentation, nn. 85, 106, 123, 127, 203; in particular n. 277, pp. 319–20, *L'Homme d'ostentation*, where "toutes le fois que l'ostentation s'est faite à contretems, elle a mal réussi, rien ne soufre moins l'afectation, que l'ostentation échaüe, parce qu'elle aproche sort de la vanité, et que celle-ci est tres-sujete au mê pris. Elle a besain d'un grand temperament paur ne pas donner dans le vulgaire." (Spelling errors—for example, "contretems" for "contretemps"—are in original.)

75. "Infatti non vi è virtù che più convenga ad un Padrone, massime grande, quanto la liberalità et la magnificenza: ma principalmente la Magnificenza, come propria di esso, che la liberalità può anco essercitarsi dal povero."

76. "Conciosia, che altrimenti s'appartien di spendere ad un imperatore, altrimenti ad un Principe, et cosi de gli altri gradi, et stati de gli uomini di mano in mano. Di maniera, che una medesima spesa ad un privato gentil'huomo sarà Magnifica, che ad un Principe non già."

itance of every good prince, since "the good and wise prince will be very fair, sober, temperate, strong, and learned, full of liberality, magnificence, religion, and clemency" (Castiglione [1528] 1981, 389),[77] but it remained a virtue that the rich, as well as princes, could practice, regardless of the quality of their blood. A century later, being noble was not enough; it was necessary to be a prince, a hero. The parallel development of the figure of the hero was not extraneous to this process (see Botteri 1986). The nobleman was to the hero as liberality was to magnificence. It is not by chance that Francesco India (1591, 61–62), in his dialogue on heroic virtues, posed the question, "If this heroic virtue could exist in a man of any grade and condition, and if it could not exist in every kind of person, in which kind of men could it be found?"[78] His answer:

> Peripatetics believe that this heroic virtue could be found only in men of high birth, who had grown up with illustrious forces and resources, whose actions are very splendid. So Peripatetics say that the heroic virtue is splendor and excellence in the pursuit of the aim of life. Such greatness is a matter of illustrious resources and conditions, and so the Peripatetics do not want magnificence to be attributed to anybody. So it happens that those who are called and celebrated as heroes have illustrious origin and lineage, and according to the opinion of these Peripatetics, this heroic virtue shines particularly in the man raised to the grade of prince, who is a common and clear example to nations. This is a sublime and illustrious position, in which all things shine with majesty.[79]

77. "Il principe bono e savio sarà giustissimo, continentissimo, temperatissimo, fortissimo e sapientissimo, pien di liberalità, magnificenzia, religione e clementia."

78. "La virtù Heroica può aver loco in qual si voglia grado, e conditione di huomo, et se non in ogni stato di persona, in qual maniera di huomini può ritrovarsi."

79. "È opinione de Peripatetici che questa virtù Heroica solamente si possa conoscere ne gli huomini splendidamente nati, et nodriti, muniti di forze, e di stromenti illustri, le cui attioni sono molto più splendide, perciò che essi dicono, che la virtù Heroica è splendore, e eccellenza per conseguire il fine della presente vita, onde à quella grandezza è di mistiero di stromenti, e conditioni illustri, e perciò meno vogliono che la magnificienza a tutti si possa attribuire, e di qui aviene che quelli che sono chiamati, e celebrati Heroi, hanno la loro origine, et il ceppo loro illustre, e risplende questa Heroica virtù secondo l'opinione di questi (i peripatetici) particolarmente nell'huomo al grado di Principe innalzato, il quale è commune, et chiaro essempio de popoli, in cui come in sublime, et illustre seggio, tutte le cose con maestà risplendono."

This argument shows very clearly that magnificence was not only a virtue attributable to any nobleman, but that it remained a heroically princely prerogative.

Calculation or Instinct?

It would be erroneous, unjust, and historically incorrect, however, to argue that aristocratic liberality, splendor, and magnificence were pursued in an atmosphere characterized by improvisation, caprice, indulgence, or failure to remember economic reality. On the contrary, the elite knew it had to sustain it at any cost if it did not want to lose a reputation based on the ability to honor obligations imposed by its social rank.

The Italian elites were perfectly aware of the political nature of the expenditures and of the differences between the healthy economics of country life and the inescapable exorbitance of urban life (see De Guevara 1602, 6.47–56), since "spending is an accident inseparable from court life" (Sigismondi 1604, 4.26).[80] They knew as well that in a phase of great economic and social crises, however, it was not easy to preserve their liberality, splendor, and magnificence without seriously compromising their finances and their own dynastic future.

These anxieties explain the efforts made to limit as far as possible the areas of action of liberality: "The sincerely liberal man takes care of his property, and he does not give it away indiscriminately and without judgment, in order to use it where is necessary in those times and places, and with those persons which the honest and proper circumstances of the virtue require" (Antoniano [1584] 1821, 2:2.92.39–41).[81] These same anxieties also explain a more important point—the assumption of new theoretical positions that partially repudiated the Aristotelian and Thomist arguments, censuring excesses of aristocratic magnificence and recommending a more sober conduct to lay and ecclesiastic princes who should be more attentive to the state of their finances. Machiavelli's scandalous "invitations" to parsimony derived from the tensions of realpolitik and the need for stable and ample financial resources: "If somebody wants to preserve among men the fame of being liberal, it is necessary

80. "Lo spendere è un accidente inseparabile dalla Corte."

81. "L'uomo veramente liberale ha cura della roba sua, e non la dispensa indifferentemente, e senza senno, per servirsene poi dove è necessario in quei tempi e luoghi, e con quelle persone, che l'onesto, e le debite circostanze della virtù lo richiedono."

not to omit any quality of sumptuousness; in this way a prince will always squander in similar works all his wealth. Thus, he will be obliged, if he wants to preserve the fame of being liberal, to burden people heavily and to impose the highest taxes, and to do all those things which can be done in order to raise money. This will make him odious to his subjects, and nobody will esteem him" (Machiavelli [1532] 1960, 16.66).[82] His argument was that a prince with sufficient money "can defend himself from whoever wages war on him as well as he can perform exploits without burdening people. Thus, he will be liberal with those from whom he will not take away anything, who are innumerable, while he will be miserly with those to whom he will not give anything, who are a few"(16.67).[83]

This is very different from the domestic tone that dominates one of the two dialogues of Nicoló Franco (1542, 5.78v), published first in 1539, "in which the author introduces an avaricious servant, who reprimands his lord for his liberality, by teaching him the art of managing his court and by showing him all the ways of saving and making money."[84] This text had an enormous publishing success and anticipates many arguments destined to enjoy wide credit in the late sixteenth and in the seventeenth centuries. During this period, in the effort to contain the most destructive consequences of baroque liberality and

82. "A volersi mantenere infra li uomini il nome del liberale, è necessario non lasciare indrieto alcuna qualità di suntuosità; talmente che sempre, uno principe così fatto consumerà in simili opere tutte le sue facultà; e sarà necessitato alla fine, se si vorrà mantenere il nome del liberale, gravare e' populi estraordinariamente, et essere fiscale, e fare tutte quelle cose che si possono fare per avere denari. Il che comincerà a farlo odioso con sudditi, e poco stimare da nessuno."

83. "Un principe . . . veggendo che con la sua parsimonia le sue entrate li bastano, può defendersi da chi li fa guerra, può fare imprese senza gravare e' populi; talmente che viene ad usare liberalità a tutti quelli a chi non toglie, che sono infiniti, e miseria a tutti coloro a chi non dà, che sono pochi."

84. The servant reprimands his lord, asking: "Where are the accounts? I promise you that whoever spent, kept the money. I can assure you that whoever managed, earned a lot. Why is it not possible to see any accounts regarding the kitchen, the pantry, the stable, the wardrobe? Dear Lord, I am sure that for every capon you eat, the sauce costs the same as the capon. You do not wear any jacket made of satin, which had not been accounted for as golden cloth. . . . In which court did it ever happen, except in this one, that the servants eat the same bread which is distributed on the the lord's own table? You have to do in your household, as is done in all the other courts: you have to give your servants unleavened, badly cooked black bread, as happens in every other court." (Dove sono i conti? Io vi prometto; che chi ha speso, ha preso. Io vi so dire; che chi ha ministrato ha ben guadagnato. Che conto non ci saria da vedere, e di sala e di dispensa, e di stalla, e di guardarobba? Deh padrone, io vi so intendere; che non mangiate mai capone, che non ve ne costi la salsa, ne mai vestite giubbone di raso,

magnificence, there were two influences at work. The first of these were pressures from the new Counter-Reformed Church (see Fragnito 1991), which was anxious to limit the most evident waste and ready to propose defensive arguments like those of Peregrini (1634, 6.174): "However the moderation of the prince could be considered not as a proof of avarice, but as a demonstration of prudence."[85] There were also pressures in the calls to parsimony in the beautiful, but neglected, discipline of court *oeconomica*.[86] These texts abandoned their original philosophical vocations and were offered increasingly as useful, even indispensable, tools for managing aristocratic households and princely courts.

One should not think that this literary production was without effect. Alongside the development of treatises, the number of accounting controls increased, as well as auditing, and examination of invoice and price congruity. When studying the accounting records of the great Renaissance courts, one has a strong impression of the almost obsessive effort to reach total order and exact measure (see Fantoni 1985, 1994; Guerzoni 1995, 1998a, 1998b, 1998c; Guerzoni and Romani 1997). There was no good that was not measurable and measured, valuable and valued, as each good, including the most trivial, measured and reflected the position occupied by its owner or consumer in the social order. The qualities of both things and men were inseparable, the undeniable evidence of reciprocal value. It was thus necessary to guarantee a perfect correspondence between the rank of the men and the rank of the goods and service in their competence—food and clothing, weapons and jewels, horses and gifts, hospitality and recreation had all to be exactly measured for the smallest hierarchical shade, and no expenditure could

---

che non vi sia posto per tela d'oro. . . . In quale Corte si vidde mai, eccetto in questa, che la famiglia mangi di quel pane istesso; che si pone ne la tavola del patrone? Si dee fare ne la vostra casa, come si fa per tutto. Si dee dare a vostri servi del pan nero, mal impastato, e peggio cotto, come s'usa per ogni corte."

85. "Però la strettezza del Principe può haver titolo non tanto d'avaritia, quanto di prudenza."

86. More than to the well-known texts of classical *oeconomica* (Assandri 1616, Di Gozze 1589, Lantieri 1560, Menochio 1626, Razzi 1568, Settala 1626, Tasso 1583, Tommasi 1580), I refer to the manuals devoted to the management of the courts: Adami 1657, Canonhiero 1609, Caporali 1590, Castori 1622, Ducci 1601, Evitascandolo 1598, Fabrini 1547, Frachetta 1599, Frigerio 1579, Fusoritto 1593, Liberati 1658, Peregrini 1634, Refuge 1621, Sigismondi 1604, Timotei 1614, Vizani 1609. These texts have been analyzed in Guerzoni 1996, in particular chapters 2 and 3.

escape this imperative. In this regard, to guarantee the perfect matching of the quality of men and the quality of things, very satisfying and high levels of product differentiation were attained through the use of every imaginable criterion of hierarchy: cloth hierarchies were involved in the design of a coat (velvet versus damask versus satin), as well as hierarchies of color (light colors versus dark colors), cut (French versus Venetian), accessories (lining, buttons, trimming, plumes, and so on), and the smallest details (from stitches to perfumes). In nearly every noble house there were documents such as the *ordinari*—registers in which the criteria of assignation of the goods appropriate to their members were established. Thus, at the d'Este courts the *ordinari del vino* laid down week by week the names of those who could receive the allowances of four different qualities of wine (*da signore*, *da tinello*, *da famiglia fresco e buido*); the *ordinari del pane* laid down the assignation of eight types of bread (*pane intiero da signore di primo e secondo fiore*, *pan taia*, *roseffo*, *frescho*, *da famiglia*, *da cani*, *biscotto*); the *ordinari del pesce* regulated who could eat the most second-rate and the highest quality fish (only the duke or duchess and other princes of the blood *familiae* regularly ate seafish and shellfish, sturgeon, and freshwater crayfish); that of *grassa* regulated the distribution of olive oil, salted meat, cheese, candles, and grain); the *ordinari del legnaro* guaranteed the just division of wood for fireplaces; and the *ordinari* of the *guardaroba* and of the *drapperia* regulated the assignation of footwear, sheets, pillows, bedding, and mattresses of different qualities and established the kinds of pictures, tapestries, basins, and sculptures that should decorate the rooms of different types of guest. Nor were less accurate records kept of gifts made, of goods "munificently" bestowed on guests, of the maintenance costs of horses in the ducal stables (the *ordinari delle biave*), of falcons (*ordinari de la falconaria*), and of hunting dogs (*ordinari de canataria*): the great Princes of the d'Este house laid down in the smallest detail the daily quantities of millet to be given to the birds in the aviary at the palace of Belfiore and provided that every hunting dog should be given "1 tiera di pan taia de onze 20," while guard dogs should receive "1 tiera de onze tranta l'una di pane negro." The eleven tabby cats at Belvedere consumed "1 tiera de pan negro," and the daily maintenance of two leopards cost "4 denari 10 marchesini" each (Messisbugo [1540] 1984, 100–101).

Perhaps this paradoxical "paltriness" and highly bourgeois attention to detail was the secret of the success of the much acclaimed liberality, splendor, and magnificence of the Italian Renaissance. It seems to be more the result of a conscientious, effective, and rational calculation than an unconscious or ostentatious consumer impulse. Considering this evidence, it is worthwhile to reconsider the question of aristocratic and ecclesiastical consumption of artistic and luxury goods. Again nowadays, most economic history is convinced that the consumer frenzies of the vain and empty Italian elites of the seventeenth and eighteenth centuries alone provoked the dramatic, sudden collapse of both the economy and Italian society. I hope that this first evidence will encourage a calmer reconsideration, aimed at long last at serious and well-documented historical investigation.

References

Adami, Antonio. 1657. *Il novitiato del Maestro di Casa*. Rome: Tommaso Coligni.

Aegidius, Romanus. [1277–79] 1491. *De regimine principum*. Rome: Stefano Planck.

Alberti, Leon Battista. [1432–34] 1969. *I libri della famiglia*. Edited by Ruggero Romano and Alberto Tenenti Alberti. Turin: Einaudi.

———. [1452] 1966. *De re aedificatoria*. Edited by Giovanni Orlandi and Paolo Portoghesi. Milan: Il Polifilo.

Alessandri, Torquato. 1609. *Il cavalier compito*. Viterbo: Girolamo Discepolo.

Ambrose, Cole Alison. 1995. *Virtue and Magnificence: Art of the Italian Renaissance Courts*. New York: Harry N. Abrams Hall.

Ambrosius. [386 B.C.] 1977. *De Officis*. In *Opere*, vol. 13. Milan: Biblioteca Ambrosiana.

Ampolo, Carmine. 1984. Il lusso nelle società arcaiche: Note preliminari sulla posizione del problema. *OPUS* 3:469–76.

Antoniano, Silvio. [1584] 1821. *Dell'educazione cristiana e politica de'figliuoli libri tre*. 2 vols. Milan: Antonio Pogliani.

Aquinas, Thomas. [1266–73] 1949. *Summa Theologica*. Florence: Salani.

Argenteus, Johannes Sabadinus. 1496. *De triumphis religionis*. Rome: Biblioteca Apostolica Vaticana, Fondo Rossiano, n.176.

Aristotle. [335 B.C.] 1983. *Etica Eudemia*. Rome: Laterza.

———. [335 B.C.] 1993. *Etica Nicomachea*. Rome: Laterza.

Armenini, Giovanni Battista. 1586. *De' veri precetti della pittura, libri III*. Ravenna: Francesco Tebaldini.

Assandri, Giovan Battista. 1616. *Della economica ovvero disciplina domestica di G.B.A.* Cremona: Belpiero.

Barbieri, Guido. 1958. Liberalitas. In *Dizionario Epigrafico di Antichità Romane*, edited by Ettore Di Ruggero. Vol. 4, parts 27–28:838–85. Rome: Istituto Italiano per la Storia Antica.

Berry, Christopher. 1994. *The Idea of Luxury: A Conceptual and Historical Inves-*

tigation. Cambridge: Cambridge University Press.
Berve, Helmut. 1926. Liberalitas, die freie, edel, großzügige Denkungsart und das entsprechende Verhalten gegenüber den Mitmenschen. In *Paulys Realencyclopädie der classischen Altertumwissenschaft, neue Bearbeitung*. Vol. 13.1, cols. 82–93. Stuttgart: Fünfundzwanzigster Halbband.
Bianchini, Marco. 1976. Elementi di economia nel pensiero politico di Cicerone. *Nuova Rivista Storica* 60:1–21.
———. 1984. La riflessione economica nell'Italia secentesca. *Cheiron* 3:31–50.
———. 1985. L'"economica" romana come espressione della crisi della repubblica. *Cheiron* 4:31–44.
Blanchet, Adrien. 1904. Liberalitas. In *Dictionnaire des antiquités Grecques et Romaines*. Vol. 13. Paris: Hachette.
Borsanyi, Karl. 1938. L'Histoire de l'idée de liberalitas. *Egyetemes Philologiai Koezloeny* 26:39–42.
Botteri, Santa M. 1986. Per un discorso sull'eroe moderno. Quattro schede e una premessa. *Cheiron* 6:9–24.
Bracciolini, Poggio. [1538] 1964. *Opera Omnia*. Edited by Riccardo Fubini. Turin: Bottega d'Erasmo.
Braund, David. 1994. The Luxuries of Athenian Democracy. *Greece and Rome* 41.1:41–48.
Brunner, Otto. 1970. La "casa come complesso" e l'antica "economica europea." In *Per una nuova storia costituzionale e sociale*, edited by Paolo Schiera. Milan: Vita e Pensiero.
Büsing, Hermann. 1995. Großbauten und Prunkbautem im Klassischen Athen. In *Affirmation und Kritik: Zur politischen Funktion von Kunst und Literatur im Altertum*, edited by Gerhard Binder and Effe Bernd. Trier: Wissenschaftlicher Verlag Trier.
Byatt, Lucinda. 1983. "Una suprema magnificenza": Niccolò Ridolfi, a Florentine Cardinal in Sixteenth-Century Rome. Ph.D. diss., European Institute, Florence.
Canonhiero, Andrea. 1609. *Il perfetto Cortegiano, et dell'uffizio del Prencipe verso'l Cortegiano*. Rome: Bartolomeo Zannetti.
Capaccio, Giulio Cesare. 1620. *Il Principe del signore Giulio Cesare Capaccio*. Venice: Barezzo Barezzi.
Caporali, Cesare. 1590. *Dialogo sopra la corte*. Ferrara: Benedetto Mamarello.
Castiglione, Baldassarre. [1528] 1981. *Il libro del cortegiano*. Edited by Amedeo Quondam. Milan: Garzanti.
Castori, Bernardino. 1622. *Institutione civile et Christiana per uno, che desideri vivere tanto in corte, quanto altrove honoratamente, e christianamente*. Rome: Alessandro Zannetti.
Cicero. [44 B.C.] 1965. *Laelius*. Bologna: Zanichelli.
———. [44 B.C.] 1992. *De Officiis*. Milan: Rizzoli.
———. [55 B.C.] 1994a. *De Oratore*. Milan: Rizzoli.
———. [63 B.C.] 1994b. *Pro Murena*. Milan: Fabbri.
Claraevallensis, Bernardus. 1851. *Sancti Bernardi abbatis primi clarae-vallensis*

opera omnia. Milan: Giacomo Gnocchi.

Clarke, John R. 1991. *The Houses of Roman Italy, 100 B.C.–A.D. 250: Ritual, Space, and Decoration*. Berkeley: University of California Press.

Corbier, Mireille. 1997. Congiarium. In *Der Neue Pauly: Enzyklopädie der Antike*. Stuttgart & Weimar: Verlag J. B. Metzler.

Cortesio, Paolo. 1504. *Quattruor libri sentiarum per Paulum Cortesium Protonotarium Apostolicum*. Rome: Eucharius Silber alias Franck Calchographus.

———. 1510. *De Cardinalatu*. Castro Cortesio: Symeon Nicolai Nardi.

da Castiglione, Sabba. 1558. *Ricordi overo ammaestramenti di monsignor Sabba Castiglione cavalier gierosolimitano*. Venice: Comin da Trino di Monferrato.

De Guevara, Antonio. 1602. *Il dispregio della corte e lode della villa del reverendissimo Monsignore: Antonio di Guevara, Vescovo di Mondogneto*. Brescia: La Compagnia Bresciana.

Della Casa, Giovanni. [1571] 1970. Trattato degli uffici comuni tra gli amici superiori e inferiori. In vol. 1 of *Prose di G. Della Casa e altri trattatisti cinquecenteschi del comportamento*, edited by Arnaldo Di Benedetto. Turin: Utet.

Di Gozze, Niccolò V. 1589. *Governo della famiglia*.Venice: Aldo.

Donati, Claudio. 1988. *L'idea di nobiltá in Italia, secoli XIV–XVIII*. Rome: Laterza.

Dopico-Cainzos, Maria D. 1993. Liberalitas y aeternitas principis en Plinio el Joven. *Ktema* 18:227–43.

Ducci, Lorenzo. 1601. *Arte aulica di Lorenzo Ducci*. Ferrara: Vittorio Baldini.

Evitascandolo, Cesare. 1598. *Dialogo del maestro di casa*. Rome: Giovanni Martinelli.

Fabrini, Giovanni. 1547. *Il sacro regno el Gran Patritio de'l vero reggimento, e de la vera felicitá de' l Principe, e beatitudine umana*. Venice: Comin de Trino.

Fantoni, Marcello. 1985. Feticci di prestigio, il dono alla corte medicea. In *Rituale, Cerimoniale, Etichetta*, edited by Sergio Bertelli and Giuliano Crifò. Milan: Bompiani.

———. 1994. *La corte del Granduca: Forma e simboli del potere mediceo tra cinque e seicento*. Rome: Bulzoni.

Filelfo, Francesco. [1443] 1537. *Convivia Mediolanensia*. Cologne: Gymnicus.

Fischer, Siegfried. 1983. Avaritia, Luxuria und Ambitio in der Satire II 3 des Horaz. *Philologus* 127:72–79.

Forbis, Elizabeth P. 1993. Liberalitas and Largitio: Terms for Private Munificence in Italian Honorary Inscriptions. *Athenaeum* 81.2:483–98.

Frachetta, Gerolamo. 1599. *Il Prencipe di Girolamo Frachetta*. Venice: Giovanni Battista Ciotti.

Fragnito, Gigliola. 1991. La trattatistica cinque e seicentesca sulla corte cardinalizia. *Annali dell'Istituto storico italo-germanico in Trento* 18:135–85.

Franco, Nicoló. 1542. *Dialogi piacevoli di M. Nicolo Franco*. Venice: Gabriel Giolito Ferrari.

Fra Paolino, Minorita. [1330] 1868. *De regimine rectoris*. Edited by Adolfo Mussafia. Florence: Tendler.

Fraser-Jenkins, Anthony D. 1970. Cosimo de' Medici's Patronage of Architecture and the Theory of Magnificence. *Journal of the Warburg and Courtauld Institutes* 33:162–70.

Frigerio, Bartolomeo. 1579. *L'economo prudente di Bartolomeo Frigerio di Ferrara.* Rome: Lodovico Grignani.

Frigo, Daniela. 1985a. Governo della casa, nobiltà e "repubblica": l'"economica" in Italia tra Cinque e Settecento. *Cheiron* 4:75–94.

———. 1985b. *Il padre di famiglia: Governo della casa e governo civile nella tradizione dell'Economica tra Cinque e Seicento.* Rome: Bulzoni.

Fusoritto, Narni da. 1593. *Il maestro di Casa di Cesare Pandini.* Venice: Giovanni Varisco.

Gauthier, René-Antoine. 1951. *Magnanimité: L'Idéal de la grandeur dans la philosophie païenne et dans la théologie chrétienne.* Paris: Vrin.

Gazda, Elaine K., ed. 1991. *Roman Art in the Private Sphere: New Perspectives on the Architecture and Decor of the Domus, Villa, Insula.* Ann Arbor: University of Michigan Press.

Goldthwaite, Richard. 1995. *Ricchezza e domanda nel mercato dell'arte in Italia del Trecento al Seicento.* La cultura materiale e le origini del consumismo. Translated by Maria Colombo. Milan: Unicopli.

Gracian, Baltasar. [1583] 1693. *L'Homme de Cour de Baltasar Gracian.* Lyon: François Barbier.

Greaves, Margaret. 1964. *The Blazon of Honour: A Study in Renaissance Magnanimity.* New York: Methuen.

Green, Louis. 1990. Galvano Fiamma, Azzone Visconti, and the Revival of the Classical Theory of Magnificence. *Journal of the Warburg and Courtauld Institutes* 53:98–113.

Guerzoni, Guido. 1995. La corte gonzaghesca in età moderna: Struttura, ordini e funzioni. In *I Gonzaga: Monete, arte, storia*, edited by Silvana Balbi-DeCaro . Milan: Electa.

———. 1996. La corte estense dal 1471 al 1559: Aspetti economici e sociali. Ph.D. diss., University Luigi Bocconi, Milan.

———. 1998a. Angustia ducis, divitiae principum: Patrimoni e imprese estensi tra Quattro e Cinquecento. In *Tra rendita e investimenti: Formazione e gestione dei grandi patrimoni in età moderna e contemporanea*, edited by Igina Lo Pane. Bari: Cacucci.

———. 1998b. The Courts of Este in the First Half of the XVIth Century: Socioeconomic aspects. In *The Court as an Economic Institution*, edited by Maurice Aymard and Marzio Achille Romani. Paris: Editions de la Maison des Sciences des Hommes.

———. 1998c. The Demand for Art of Italian Renaissance Court: The Case of Este (1471–1560). In *Markets for Art, 1400–1800*, edited by Michael North and David Ormrod. Proceedings of the Twelfth International Economic History Congress. Madrid: Secretario de Publicaciones, Universidad de Sevilla.

Guerzoni, Guido, and Marzio Achille Romani. 1997. Looking for a Model: The

Court as an Economic Institution. The Cases of Gonzaga, d'Este, and Farnese from the Fifteenth Century to the Seventeenth Century. Paper presented at the conference on "Beyond Elias? Court Society: The Center as Symbol and Locus of Power," University of California at Los Angeles, 2–3 May.

Gundersheimer, Werner. 1972. *Art and Life at the Court of Ercole I d'Este: The "De Triumphis religionis" of Giovanni Sabadino degli Arienti.* Geneva: Travaux d'Humanisme et Renaissance.

Hellegouarc'h, Joseph. 1963. *Le vocabulaire Latin des relations et des parties politiques sous la République.* Paris: Belles Lettres.

Hesberg, Henner von. 1992. Publica Magnificentia: Eine antikklassizistiche Intention der frühen augusteischen Baukunst. *Jahrbuch des Deutschen Archäologischen Instituts* 107:125–47.

Heuer, Karl H. 1941. Comitas, facilitas, liberalitas: Studien zur gesellschaftlichen Kultur der ciceronischen Zeit. Diss. Phil. und Naturwiss., Münster University.

Hincmaro of Rheims. 1879. Opuscola varia, caput II, De fuga Avaritiae. In *Patrologiae cursus completis, Tomus CXXV, Hincmari Rhemensis Archiepiscopi tomus prior.* Paris: Garnier.

Hughes, Owen Diane. 1983. Sumptuary Laws and Social Relations in Renaissance Italy. In *Disputes and Settlements: Law and Human Relations in the West*, edited by John Bossy. Cambridge: Cambridge University Press.

Hunt, Alan. 1996. *Governance of the Consuming Passions: A History of Sumptuary Law.* New York: St. Martin's.

India, Francesco. 1591. *L'Heroe overo della virtù heroica.* Verona: Gerolamo Discepolo.

Isager, Jacob. 1993. The Hellenization of Rome: Luxuria or Liberalitas? In *Aspects of Hellenism in Italy: Towards a Cultural Unity?* edited by Bilde Pia Guldager, Inge Nielsen, and Marjatta Nielsen. Copenhagen: Museum Tusculanum.

Isidoro of Seville. 1601. *Sancti Isidori Hispaniensis episcopi opera omnia quae existant.* Paris: Michele Sonnium.

Ivani, Antonio. [1470] 1825. *Del governo della famiglia civile.* Edited by Antonio Bertoloni. Bologna: Marsigli.

Johnston, David. 1985. Munificence and Municipia: Bequests to Towns in Classical Roman Law. *Journal of Roman Studies* 75:105–25.

Kent, Francis W. 1977. "Più superba di quella de Lorenzo": Courtly and Family Interest in the Building of Filippo Strozzi's Palace. *Renaissance Quarterly* 30:311–23.

King, Margaret L. 1975. Personal, Domestic, and Republican Values in the Moral Philosophy of Giovanni Caldiera. *Renaissance Quarterly* 28:535–74.

Kloft, Hans. 1970. Liberalitas Principis: Herkunft und Bedeutung. Studien zur Prinzipatsideologie. Diss. Phil., Universität Köln.

———. 1987. Freigebigkeit und Finanzen: Der soziale und finanzielle Aspekt der augusteischen Liberalitas. In *Saeculum Augustum I: Herrschaft und Gesellschaft*, edited by Gerhard Binder. Darmstadt: Wissenschaftliche Buchgesellschaft.

———. 1996. Überlegungen zum Luxus in der frühen römischen Kaiserzeit. In *Energeia: Studies on Ancient History and Epigraphy Presented to H. W. Pleket,* edited by Johan Strubbe, Rolf Tybout, and Hendrik Simon Versnel. Amsterdam: Gieben.

Knoche, Ursula. 1935. Magnitudo animi: Untersuchungen zur Entstehung und Entwicklung eines römischen Wertgedankes. *Philologus* 27.3:34–54.

Krüger, Sabine. 1964. Zum Verständnis der Oeconomica Jorrads von Megenberg. *Deutsches Archiv* 20:475–561.

Labowsky, Lotte. 1934. Der Begriff des Prèpon in der Ethik des Panaitios. Diss. Phil., Leipzig University.

Lambertini, Roberto. 1985. Per una storia dell'oeconomica tra alto e basso Medioevo. *Cheiron* 4:46–74.

Lantieri, Giacomo. 1560. *Della economica*. Venice: Valgrisi.

Latini, Brunetto. [1270] 1869. *Il tesoro di Brunetto Latini volgarizzato da Bono Giamboni*. Venice: Coi Tipi del Gondoliere.

Levi-Pisetzky, Rosita. 1964. *Storia del costume in Italia*. 2 vols. Milan: Istituto Editoriale Italiano.

Liberati, Francesco. 1658. *Il perfetto maestro di casa*. Rome: Angelo Bernabò dal Verme.

Livy. [59 B.C.] 1967. *Epistole*. Milan: Fabbri.

Lomazzo, Giovanni Paolo. 1585. *Trattato della pittura, scultura e architettura*. Milan: Paolo Gottardo Ponzio e Pietro Tini.

Machiavelli, Niccolò. [1532] 1960. *Il principe*. Edited by Sergio Bertelli. Milan: Feltrinelli.

Manning, Charles E. 1985. Liberalitas—The Decline and Rehabilitation of a Virtue. *Greece and Rome*, 2d ser. 32.1:73–83.

Massaciucoli, Gaspare. 1561. *Dui trattati di Messer Giovanni Pontano de la liberalità e beneficienza*. Lucca: Busdrago.

Megenberg, Conrad von. [1353] 1973–77. *Werke: Ökonomik*. Edited by Sabine Krüger. Stuttgart: MGH Staatsschriften des späteren Mittelalter III, 5/1.

Menochio, Giovanni Stefano. 1626. *Istitutionis oeconomicae ex sacris litteris depromptae libri duo*. Lyon: Rovillio.

Messisbugo, Cristoforo. [1540] 1984. *Compendio per l'anno 1540*. Edited by Luigi Chiappini. Ferrara: Sate.

Miles, Devi. 1987. Forbidden Pleasures: Sumptuary Laws and the Ideology of Moral Decline in Ancient Rome. Ph.D. diss., London University.

Millar, Fergus. 1991. Les congiaires à Rome et la monnaie. In *Nourrir la plèbe*, edited by Adalberto Giovannini. Basel-Kassel: Reinhardt Verlag.

Mills, Arianne. 1984. Greek Clothing Regulations: Sacred or Prophane? *Zeitschrift für Papyrologie und Epigraphik* 57:255–65.

Mrozek, Stanislaw. 1984. Munificentia Privata in Bauwesen und Lebensmittelverteilungen in Italien während des Prinzipates. *Zeitschrift für Papyrologie und Epigraphik* 57:233–40.

Muzio, Gerolamo. 1575. *Il gentilhuomo del Mutio Iustopolitano*. Venice: Luigi Valvassori e Giovanni Domenico Micheli.

Muzzarelli, Giuseppina. 1996. *Gli inganni delle apparenze: Disciplina di vesti e ornamenti alla fine del Medioevo*. Turin: Scriptorum.

Natali, Carlo. 1985. Alle origini della "economica" antica. *Cheiron* 4:9–30.

Orologgi, Giuseppe.1562. *L'inganno*. Venice: Gabriele Giolito Ferrari.

Pacciani, Riccardo.1980. *Brunelleschi e la magnificenza*. Florence: Centro Di.

Paleotti, Gabriele. [1582] 1960. *Discorso intorno alle immagini sacre e profane*. In vol. 3 of *Scritti d'arte del Cinquecento*, edited by Paola Barocchi. Milan: Riccardo Ricciardi.

Palmieri, Matteo. [1439] 1843. *Della vita civile*. Milan: Pirotta.

Pérault, Guillame. [1236–48] 1595. *Virtutum vitiorumque exempla ex utriusque legis promptuario decerpta*. Lyon: Gulielmum Rovillium.

Peregrini, Matteo. 1634. *Della pratica comune a principi e servitori loro libri cinque*. Viterbo: Diotallevi.

Pétré, Helene. 1931. Misericordia: Histoire du mot et de l'idée du paganisme au christianisme. *Revue des études latines* 12:376–89.

———. 1948. *Caritas: Étude sur le vocabulaire latin de la charité chrétienne*. Louvain: Spicilegium Sacrum Lovaniense.

Piccolomini, Alessandro. 1552. *De la institutione di tutta la vita de l'homo nato nobile e in cittá libera*. Venice: Giovanni Maria Bonelli.

Pietilä-Castrén, Leena. 1987. *Magnificentia publica: The Victory Monuments of the Roman Generals in the Era of the Punic Wars*. Helsinki: Societas Scientiarum Fennica.

Pigna, Giovanni Battista. 1561. *Gli heroici di Giovan Battista Pigna*. Venice: Gabriele Giolito Ferrari.

Plato. [392–369 B.C.] 1985. *Theaetetus*. Milan: Mursia.

———. [365–357 B.C.] 1995. *Politeia*. Rome: Laterza.

Pohlenz, Max. 1935. *Tó Prèpon: Ein Beitrag zur Geschichte des griechischen Geistes*. Göttingen: Gesellschaft der Wissenschaften zu Göttingen.

Pontano, Giovanni Gioviano. 1518. *Ioannis Ioviani Pontani opera omnia soluta oratione composita*. Venice: Aldo.

Pouillon, François. 1978. Lusso. In vol. 8 of *Enciclopedia Einaudi*. Turin: Einaudi.

Priscianese, Francesco. 1543. *Del governo della Corte d'un signore in Roma*. Rome: Francesco Priscianese.

Razzi, Silvano. 1568. *Della economica cristiana e civile i primi due libri*. Florence: Sermantelli.

Refuge, Eustache. 1621. *Trattato della Corte del Signor di Refuge*. Venice: Ciotti.

Romano, Elisa. 1994. Dal De Officiis a Vitruvio, da Vitruvio a Orazio: Il dibattito sul lusso edilizio. In *Le projet de Vitruve: Objet, destinataires et réception du De Architectura*. Paris: De Boccard—L'Erma di Bretschneider.

Romei, Annibale. 1591. *Discorsi del conte Annibale Romei Gentil'huomo Ferrarese*. Pavia: Andrea Viani.

Sauerwein, Ingo. 1970. Die leges sumptuarie als römischen Maßnahme gegen Sittenverfall. Diss. Phil., University of Hamburg.

Seneca. [65–54 B.C.] 1950. *De Beneficiis*. Los Angeles: University of California Press.

Settala, Ludovico. 1626. *De ratione istituendae et gubernandae familiae*. Milan: Bidelli.

Sigismondi, Sigismondo. 1604. *Prattica cortigiana, morale et economica nella quale si discorre minutamente de' Ministri, che servono in Corte d'un Cardinale*. Ferrara: Vittorio Baldini.

Slob, Ewoud. 1986. *Luxuria: Regelgeving en maatregelen van censoren ten tijde van de Romeinse Republiek*. Zutphen: De Walburg Press.

Sombart, Werner. [1913] 1988. *Lusso e capitalismo*. Translated by Mauro Protti. Milan: Unicopli.

Spilner, Paula. 1993. Giovanni di Lupo Ghini and a Magnificent New Addition to the Palazzo Vecchio, Florence. *Journal of the Society of Architectural Historians* 52:453–65.

Stein, Rudolf. 1963. Megaloprepreia bei Platon. Diss. Phil., University of Bonn.

Stylow, Arnim. 1972. Libertas und Liberalitas: Untersuchungen zur innenpolitischen Propaganda der Römer. Diss. Phil., University of Munich.

Tasso, Torquato. 1583. *Il padre di famiglia*. Venezia: Aldo.

Timotei, Michele. 1614. *Il cortegiano, nel quale si tratta di tutti li offitii della corte, offitiali, et ministri de prencipi*. Rome: Giacomo Mascardi.

Todeschini, Giacomo. 1992. Quantum valet? Alle origini di un'economia della povertà. *Bullettino dell'Istituto storico italiano per il Medioevo* 98:173–234.

———. 1994. *Il prezzo della salvezza: Lessici medievali del pensiero economico*. Florence: La Nuova Italia Scientifica.

Tommasi, Francesco. 1580. *Reggimento del padre di famiglia*. Florence: Marescotti.

Veyne, Paul. 1984. *Il pane e il circo. Sociologia storica e pluralismo politico*. Translated by Annamaria Sanfelice di Monforte. Bologna: Il Mulino.

Vincentius, Bellovacensis. [1250–52] 1938. *De eruditione filiorum nobilium*. Edited by Steiner Arpad. Cambridge: Medieval Academy of America.

Vizani, Pompeo. 1609. *Breve trattato del governo famigliare*. Bologna: Rossi.

Wesch-Klein, Gabriele. 1990. *Liberalitas in Rem Publicam: Private Aufwendungen zugusten von Gemeinden in römischen Afrika bis 284 n. Chr.* Bonn: Habelt.

Zacour, Norman P. 1975. Papal Regulation of Cardinals' Households in the Fourteenth Century. *Speculum* 50:434–55.

Zanker, Paul. 1989. *Augusto e il potere delle immagini*. Translated by Flavio Cuniberto. Turin: Einaudi.

Ingenuity, Preference, and the Pricing of Pictures: The Smith-Reynolds Connection

Neil De Marchi and Hans J. Van Miegroet

There were substantive connections between the moral philosopher Adam Smith (1723–90) and the painter Sir Joshua Reynolds (1723–92). These had to do, in a general way, with an expectation of novelty, a relish for change, a fascination with the manipulation of nature, and experimentation of a thousand sorts—all widespread in the latter part of the eighteenth century. Those very features were noted, by one of its rediscoverers, as accompaniments of the so-called consumer revolution of the early modern period (see Plumb 1982). But for Smith and Reynolds this made up the background only. Their interests intersected because of a common preoccupation with and pleasure in something more specific: ingenuity, the successful composing of apparently unconnected elements and notions into new products and systems of ideas.

In fact, Smith and Reynolds held the same view of ingenuity, and this is the first of two connections between them that we will explore. Smith's emphasis was on ingenuity as the action of bringing into view hidden or at least unexpected causal connections, whether in natural philosophy, the arts, or engineering. Reynolds's interest, we might assume,

We are grateful to Marina Bianchi, Tony Brewer, Craufurd Goodwin, Marcia Pointon, and Donald Winch for discussions and for careful and critical readings of drafts. Very special thanks go to Marcia Pointon; she waded through numerous, often greatly altered, versions, each time patiently offering reactions and suggestions, and she also supplied us with a steady stream of references. Useful suggestions were received at presentations at the University of Amsterdam, November 1997, and at the conference "Luxury and the Marketplace in Eighteenth Century Europe," Warwick, 6–8 July 1998.

would be less philosophic, but in his advice to students of the Royal Academy he urged them to take seriously the *facture* of paintings—their "get-up," or manner, of manufacture—and to think in terms of cause-effect relations, which govern everything from composition to the properties of materials.

The second connection has to do with pricing. In *The Wealth of Nations* Smith ([1776] 1981) outlined how price is formed in the case of rare objects, which includes unique (or near-unique) objects such as certain sorts of paintings. The factors he identified were strength of desire and means to pay. Under the primary influence of these two factors, he argued, price might deviate considerably from materials costs or from materials plus labor, where labor time is costed at the conventional wage rate. This opened up an intriguing possibility. Unique or "limited-edition" objects might be crafted deliberately to seduce the senses, thereby enhancing desire, and price, while time to completion and labor costs are kept to a minimum. Without theorizing about price, Reynolds aimed to achieve precisely these results. He was the premier portraitist of his day, and his artistic practices are exactly what we would expect of a craftsman bent on enhancing his personal reward by finding ways to minimize time while contriving desirable surface effects. Those effects in his pictures often were fleeting, suggesting that the integrity and durability of his product were not Reynolds's chief concern. His physically unstable products therefore parallel in an intriguing way the fragility that skeptical contemporaries ascribed to prices driven by fashion or "fancy"—that is, prices not anchored in costs.

That Reynolds and Smith shared certain ideas should not surprise us. At the height of their fame, the two men moved in interlocking circles in London. Friends such as Edward Gibbon, Edmund Burke, and Sir Joseph Banks were held in common. Moreover, both devoted a good deal of thought to the imitative arts. In particular they asked, What is the relation between imitation (copying) and creativity; and, Why do we take pleasure in imitation? In 1775 Reynolds was able to welcome Smith into the club he had founded eleven years earlier to provide his friend Samuel Johnson with a suitable forum. Reynolds had had contact with Smith's ideas even earlier: his first publication, a letter to the *Idler* in September 1759, drew on elements of Smith's thinking on the contingency of tastes found in *The Theory of Moral Sentiments*. And this appreciation of Smith on matters touching on the imitative arts continued. At a meeting in 1782 of the Johnson Literary Club (*the* Club), Smith spoke on why we derive pleasure from imitation, and afterwards Reynolds expressed his complete agreement with the reasoning (Hilles 1952, 174).

But the two connections we stress were not of this direct influence and physical contact variety. The second is not even a case of shared ideas, for it is most unlikely that Reynolds had studied Smith's analysis of pricing. Moreover, there were other instances of a similarly indirect sort, such as the fact that both were fascinated by the way seventeenth-century Netherlandish paintings were made. This suggests that something additional was at work. A likely candidate for this "something additional" has been indicated already: both men had a driving interest in ingenuity, which each pursued in different ways though against the same background of widespread fascination with and delight in ingenious contrivance. We aim to show here this mutual, compelling interest.

In the concluding section, however, we will argue that what both Smith and Reynolds analyzed, and Reynolds applied, was only proximately ingenuity. Viewed from a distance, what they were examining is what it takes to sustain consumer interest in buying, along with the preconditions for effective emulation (competitiveness). Those preconditions were an understanding of pleasure and preferences, of materials, and of design. The connections we stress between the two men are, in fact, threads in a larger, more elaborate mesh which, however, remains unseen as long as we think of Smith principally as the first theorist of resource allocation and growth and Reynolds as the premier portraitist of his age and a political advocate for the arts. We aim to show them also as theorists of processes of desiring and of making, of the why and the how of goods, both of which are logically prior to—in the sense that they give point to—their other achievements.

As Smith himself outlined the logical order of thinking in these matters, before we consider "the most proper method" of obtaining our physical needs and conveniences, we must define opulence or plenty. Prior to this, we must consider "what are the natural wants and demands of mankind" (*LJ* A, 333–34; *LJ* B, 487).[1] By "demands," Smith at once

1. In referring to Smith's works, rather than using dates of publication, which can be confusing, we shall use the now common abbreviations of titles in the Glasgow edition of the *Works and Correspondence of Adam Smith: WN* for *The Wealth of Nations*, *LJ* A, B, or ED for *The Lectures on Jurisprudence* (A for student notes from the 1762–63 session and B for those from the 1763–64 session; ED for an early draft of *The Wealth of Nations*), *EPS* for *Essays on Philosophical Subjects*, and *TMS* for *The Theory of Moral Sentiments.*

explained, should be understood all the refinements we insist on effecting to things naturally available to us. Preferences are created on the basis of these artificial refinements, however inessential ("frivolous") they may be. The link with opulence is that the whole panoply of the arts of mankind has been invented to gratify these preferences of ours (*LJ* A, 336–37; *LJ* B, 488, 507; cf. *TMS*, 183). Reynolds put this last, crucial point more succinctly, though only for the imitative arts: the rules of our art must be shaped by the impressions we observe it makes on its audience (Hilles 1952, 133; said originally in an admiring comment on Shakespeare).

In discussing invention, artifice, and ingenuity, we find ourselves also having to address luxury. This is because, while new goods of every sort proliferated from the middle of the seventeenth century onward, few if any of these were necessities, while many—an increasing number, as the evidence on patents suggests—were the result of design and invention. Reynolds's portraits, made principally of and for the rich and famous, also sold at prices that made them luxury items. Yet both *ingenuity* and *luxury* are problem terms: ingenuity because it has at times been mixed with the notion of genius as something inexplicable, a gift, which is a notion far removed from the Reynolds-Smith conception; luxury because up to the mid–eighteenth century it formed part of a moral discourse. The "luxury debate" as such, however, was neither a main concern of Smith's nor, it seems safe to say, uppermost in the minds of Reynolds or his sitters.[2] To appreciate what our two protagonists had to say, we need to clarify the newness of their conceptions in both areas.

Luxury and Ingenuity: Smith

Bernard de Mandeville and Nicholas Barbon had made great play with the notion that true necessities are very few, so that virtually everything we buy must be considered a luxury. This ignored the fact that those very few things may have accounted for four-fifths or more of the

2. This is not to deny that Smith's ethics was implicitly shaped by his desire to respond to Mandeville, or that Mandeville himself was directly involved in "debating" Shaftesbury. But by the mid-1760s, as Smith turned to the serious preparation of *The Wealth of Nations*, the focus of his attention had so shifted that it is unhelpful to think of his mature work as being part of the so-called luxury debate. For a convincing recent exploration of Mandeville's influence on Smith, see Van Ngo 1998.

expenditure of many families. Outside the context of the luxury debate, we need a notion of luxury that ties it more closely to means.

Smith is more helpful here. He seems to have regarded wantonness and caprice as the marks of true luxury spending, in this way directing us to means as well as to motive and to wealth levels as well as to types of goods as such. For it is only the very wealthy who *can* indulge their whims whenever they wish, a simple point that Smith underscored by using wealth and greatness (or power) interchangeably and regularly pairing both with such phrases as "wanton luxury," "more extravagant luxury," "luxury and caprice," and "frivolous desires" (*WN*, 23, 74; *TMS*, 182–84). Though he observed that workers received more than enough to cover bare necessaries (*WN*, 22, 91), there can be no suggestion that he equated their modest comforts and "conveniencies" with luxury in the above sense.

Smith did have reservations about the kind of character developed by those who devoted themselves to caprice; nevertheless, for the most part his concern was to discover categories that would facilitate intertemporal and between-country comparisons of well-being. He defined opulence as ease of accomodation, the condition that goods are readily available and cheap, or "comeatible" (*LJ* A, 343; cf. *LJ* ED, 567). It follows, if our suggestion is correct, that luxury goods are those which are *not* easily come at by the bulk of the population. Or, in terms of how price is formed, luxuries are goods that are rare and whose price is not determined by the mass of consumers but, instead, by the relatively few people of means. This certainly accords with the (brief) analysis he gives of how the prices of necessaries and of luxuries are determined (*WN*, 73–74). But Smith's definition of luxuries according to the conjunction of motive *and* means also has the advantage that it can accommodate actual changes in spending patterns due, for example, to income increases, or to shifts in distribution that favor the bottom 90 percent, or to alterations in relative or absolute prices.

For Smith, as we have stated already, ingenuity had to do with intuiting ways to link by causes effects that seem remote from one another. The appearance of remoteness means that there are no obvious connections. The ingenious inventor, then, is one who forges those connections via many small links whose eventual chainlike character strikes the outside observer as "strange and wonderful"—precisely because it is more or less unexpected. That, indeed, is the impression received by the viewer of ordinary workshop processes: "When we enter the work-houses of the most common artizans; such as dyers, brewers, distillers we observe a number of appearances, which present themselves in an order that seems to us very strange and wonderful" (*EPS*, 44). Smith makes exactly the same point not just of such processing activities but of what he calls "ingenious . . . machines." The "condensing engine" or "fire engine" was one such (*EPS*, 139; *LJ* ED, 570). Smith lauds the one who first formed "the idea of producing so great an effect by a power in nature which had never before been thought of" (*LJ* ED, 570). Possibly, Smith had in mind Newcomen's atmospheric pumps, which made use of the condensation of steam introduced into a cylinder.[3] In these pumps, the combination of steam pressure raised and vacuum upon condensation depressed a piston. Attached to the piston was a beam, linked at its other end to a rod, which rose as the piston was depressed, and which could thus be used to draw water out of a shaft (Curti 1990, 358). Smith also regarded the plow, windmills, and watermills as ingenious machines (*WN*, 19, editorial note 15 and references there cited).

Finally, Smith applied the by now familiar notion of "connect[ing] together disjointed appearances" to systems of natural philosophy (in his essay on the history of astronomy, *EPS*, 61). Such systems, he even allowed, "*in many respects resemble machines*" (66; emphasis added). He also applied this view to paintings, as we shall see next. In every instance, whatever the particular field, we stand amazed at cause-effect relations that we ourselves never would have thought existed.

In the context of painting, nonetheless, ingenuity took on special connotations, which were elaborated by Smith in an essay on the imitative arts (in *EPS*). In painting, he says, what pleases us is not the imitation's resemblance to the original—it is not deception that counts—but the ingenuity involved in bridging the gap between two very different spheres: that of objects and that of their representations (*EPS*, 185). The painter captures the world of solid objects and of depth on a

3. Smith may also have had his Glasgow colleague James Watt in mind. Watt encountered one of Newcomen's engines, owned by the University of Glasgow, when, in 1763, it came to him for repair. Watt made certain modifications to the design, including a better seal to the piston chamber and a separate condenser, patenting his more efficient "single-action" steam engine in 1769. Further improvements followed. Watt applied steam to both upward and downward strokes of the piston, and he converted the rectilinear action of piston and beam into rotary motion, eliminating intermittency in the movement. The improved engines were thereby rendered suitable for adaptation to driving machinery and thus for use in manufacturing (Curti 1990, 358–60; figure 5 here shows the design).

flat surface, where we are offered the appearance of solidity and depth via the contrivances of light and shadow, color, and perspective construction. In turn, our pleasure varies inversely with the greatness of the disparity between object and image that is overcome and with the "awkwardness of the instruments" available (182). The result, when well done, gives rise to wonder. But that is mainly a reaction of the uninformed. Greater mental satisfaction requires that we move beyond wonder to admiration, by coming to understand "the way and manner in which . . . [such works] are produced" (185). Fortunately, ingenious works "carry as it were, their own explication along with them, and demonstrate, even to the eye" how they are made. By following the maker's explication—the chain of small links connecting original with imitation—we replace "the pleasing wonder of ignorance" with the "still more pleasing satisfaction of science" (185). All this, recall, is said of paintings, "Dutch" in particular, not of systems of natural philosophy, though the terminology and the message are interchangeable.

Smith's notion of ingenuity was closely related to his concept of specialization and its consequence, division of labor. Many inventions and ingenious improvements, he thought, were the product of workmen whose attention was focused quite narrowly on a single link in the chain (*WN*, 20–21). But for many, too, we must rely on specialist "philosophers" or "meer m[e]n of speculation . . . people whose trade it is not to do anything but to observe every thing, and who are upon that account capable of combining together the powers of the most opposite and distant objects" (*LJ* ED, 570; cf. *WN*, 21–22 and editorial note 23, listing nine sorts of specialist thinker). Moreover, inventions and improvements invariably are in some measure the "successive discoveries of time and experience" (*WN*, 21, editorial note 20). Smith's point is that it is focus, which comes with specialization, plus on-the-job experience and understanding that give rise to inventiveness. (Too much specialization, of course, has just the opposite effect, as he recognized: *WN*, 781–72; *LJ* B, 539–49.) There is not a hint in Smith of ingenuity's being a product of inspiration, of the operation of some external force. "Genius," as one of his hearers recorded at a lecture he delivered during the 1963–64 session at Glasgow University, "is more the effect of the division of labour than the latter is of it" (*LJ* B, 493; cf. *WN*, 28, 65).

Reynolds on Ingenuity and Facture

As we might expect, Reynolds's view of ingenuity emerges in the context of discussions of artistic genius. Our source for his views is the discourses that he delivered between 1769 and 1790 as the first president of the Royal Academy, on the occasion of the annual prize-giving for students. The academy was meant to embody the claim that painting is primarily intellectual, one of the liberal arts.[4] Notwithstanding, Reynolds defended the view that "genius" is no "phantom of inspiration." Instead, inventiveness arises from imitation—copying—usually deemed one of the purely mechanical aspects of the painter's craft.

All three elements of Smith's view are to be found in what Reynolds said: that a great deal of inventiveness can be traced to specialization; that time and experience also play a role; and that ingenuity, after all, consists in identifying and freshly applying relations of a cause-effect sort.

Thus, for Reynolds, copying meant not slavish replication but selective borrowing. For example, if the excellence of a work consists "in its general effect," then it is sufficient to capture only "the machinery and general management" of the original (*Discourses*, 30).[5] The good copyist always has such a "determinate object" in view (29). In the right sort of copying, in short, there is necessarily a considerable mental component, and the labor is *focused*.

Furthermore, it is not just "well-directed labour" (35), but "a reiterated experience" (45) that is required to turn copying into well-contrived art. Reynolds describes the evolution of painting in terms of an accretion of best-practice techniques, or "rules." At first, each of these is just one artist's "invariable principle for himself to work by," but such rules, through improvements wrought by others over time, may become established practice. If rules only stated how nature might be captured in accurate representations (hence how to produce decep-

4. Reynolds certainly hoped that the Royal Academy would be a vehicle for promoting good taste and civic virtue in the sense of Shaftesbury; and even for moving toward consensus on what might constitute a national style, goals clarified by Barrell (1986). His views on ingenuity and facture, however, have not been treated as important to an understanding of British visual culture. We aim to restore these to the list of his concerns and contributions.

5. There are several modern editions of Reynolds's *Discourses*, of which perhaps the best known is that first issued by Robert R. Wark in 1959. Here we use the 1997 updated version of that edition, referring in the text simply to *Discourses*. Wark's edition includes Blake's marginalia and Hazlitt's essays on the *Discourses*, but not Reynolds's three *Idler* letters, which, however, are appended to the Penguin edition (1992), edited by Pat Rogers.

tion), they would indeed be part of the mechanical. The fact is, however, that rules come to govern more and more of art, which anyway is far more than "the power of merely drawing the likeness of any object" (96; cf. 42). Among the elements of painting that Reynolds lists as rule-governed are "the beauty of form, the expression of the passions, the art of composition, even the power of giving a general air of grandeur to a work" (97).

On this view, ingenuity is represented as acquired capabilities, the acquisition coming through emulation and experimentation. But true capability consists in going beyond just "admiring and relishing" the work of others—Smith's wonder of ignorance. At the very least it requires that "we . . . enter into the principles on which the work is wrought," into "the contrivance of the composition" (101)—Smith's admiration of science. That is, we must come to understand the means-ends connections relevant to achieving any particular result. The rules then emerge as a sort of shorthand statement of these causal chains: "Even works of Genius, like every other effect, as they must have their cause, must likewise have their rules; it cannot be by chance, that excellencies are produced with any constancy or any certainty" (97–98). Painting in this respect is no different from science. Reynolds noted of science that it eschews tricks and mechanical habits, and also guesswork. Instead, "by a profound knowledge of ends and means, [it] discovers the shortest and surest way to its own purpose" (194).

We can approach ingenuity from a slightly different direction by pressing Reynolds on this matter of principled practice. In notes made in preparation for his final discourse, he defined genius as the ability to produce at will what he called "those refined excellences" (as distinct from "the common ro[u]tine of practice") (Hilles 1936, 244). But how exactly is this facility acquired? We get a precise answer by combining some passages from the *Discourses* with his own methods of discovery.

To learn the ways of producing any desired effect with constancy, we must be familiar with the discoveries made by others: "We *learn* to invent; as by reading the thoughts of others we learn to think" (*Discourses*, 98; emphasis added; cf. 99). Moreover, we learn better from works of art themselves than from precepts (102). Reynolds rubbed down, in whole or in part (or is reported to have done so) originals he owned by Parmigianino, Watteau, Rubens, and Titian (Talley 1986, 56–57). That was one way to learn the manner of build-up practiced by others. Another was observation. Reynolds undertook a journey to the

Low Countries in 1781 principally to view paintings by those he admired and works by whom, in some cases, he already owned: Rubens, Rembrandt, and Lievens, for example (Postle 1995, 123, and 327 n. 3). As he described the motive for the trip, "the business . . . is to explain how those works are built" (Mount 1996, 150). On that occasion, however, he trusted to "close inspection, and minute examination" (*Discourses*, 30), as if following Smith in the conviction that superior paintings "carry as it were, their own explication along with them, and demonstrate, even to the eye, the way and manner in which they are produced" (*EPS*, 185).

So, learning from existing works of art meant taking them apart, physically if necessary, but in any event with an experimenter's scrutiny: we must experiment with them as we do with the thoughts we encounter by reading. The knowledge thus gained is of the Baconian sort. Bacon ([1620] 1944, paragraphs 82, 100, 105–6) had hoped that his analytical way of investigating nature would quite replace the school logic and mere "vague and arbitrary experience." When Reynolds literally deconstructed some works by his chosen masters, and dissected others with a trained eye, in order to rise above chance outcomes, he was doing exactly as Bacon had enjoined (paragraph 124, where Bacon insists on the need for "dissecting and anatomizing the world").[6]

6. Reynolds as experimenter is an unfamiliar figure. It is also true that he may have taken to reading Bacon only quite late in his career: the only known quotations he records among notes on his reading appear to have been intended for use in his twelfth discourse, delivered in 1784 (Hilles 1936, 130, 214). Two citations of Bacon in the third discourse were not in the original text but appear first in the published version of 1797 (108 n. 3). Even then it is not clear that Reynolds knew *The New Organon* or *The Advancement of Learning*. But if he did not, he nonetheless practiced Baconian induction for years without the advantage of having read the master's own accounts of the procedure. Reynolds was an intuitive Baconian, borrowing his science as he did his art theory from others and layering it like glazes over a core of self-engendered experimental practice. His chief creditor in the knowledge of what Bacon was about, and the language of the new science, could easily have been his friend Johnson, whom Gibbon called Reynolds's "oracle." Johnson has been studied chiefly as a literary figure, but his grasp of the new science was extraordinary even by the polymathic standards of the time. He wrote biographies of the Baconian and Newtonian physician-experimenters Sydenham, Rusych, and Boerhaave; he prepared notices of newly published scientific works; and he sought the company of serious men of science (Schwartz 1971). Dr. Kippis recorded that he "once heard Dr. Johnson speak in the Society of Arts and Manufactures, upon a subject relative to mechanics, with a propriety, perspicuity, and energy, which excited general admiration" (Hudson and Luckhurst 1954, 29). Johnson turned to Bacon for many of the terms of natural philosophy in his *Dictionary*, reading his works on natural philosophy for the purpose. At one time he even planned a life of Bacon and an edition of his English works

It is through such experimentation that discoveries gradually evolve into rules of practice. This explains, as well, why Reynolds spent so much time in his discourses on practice, for, once he had acknowledged that more and more aspects of painting are subject to rules, it also became important to him that students hear about technique, talk of the grand style and the sublime notwithstanding. In the eleventh of his discourses, he even invoked Vasari in support of this endeavor. Vasari, he acknowledged, was not well disposed toward the Venetians in general, yet he "every where" commends their manner of making (*modo di fare*: *Discourses*, 195). "Modo di fare," or facture, however, cannot be understood by shortcuts, and so we are back with "science," "selection," and the knowledge of "fixed principles" (196). In practice, this came down to something like the following:

> The sagacious imitator does not content himself with merely remarking what distinguishes the different manner or genius of each master; he enters into the contrivance in the composition, how the masses of lights are disposed, the means by which the effect is produced, how artfully some parts are lost in the ground, others boldly relieved, and how all these are mutually altered and interchanged according to the reason and scheme of the work. He admires not the harmony of colouring alone, but examines by what artifice one colour is a foil to its neighbour. He looks closely into the tints, examines of what colours they are composed, till he has formed clear and distinct ideas, and has learnt to see in what harmony and good colouring consists. (102)

The language here is intended to elevate the understanding of facture above the knowledge possessed by the connoisseur, which typically was based only on a comparison of styles. The passage is also an appropriate pendant to Reynolds's talk about science. It occurs in the sixth discourse, but by "the contrivance" and "artifice" here Reynolds clearly means just what he subsequently comprehended under "il modo di

---

(Rogers 1996, 21). But his vocabulary reflects his grasp of science whether or not there is an explicit debt acknowledged to Bacon or other writers on scientific matters (see Harp 1986, *Dictionary* entries on Artificial Arguments, Experience, Matter, Reality, Reason, Theory, Truth). Richard Schwartz (1971) sheds a great deal of light on Johnson's scientific interests; he also makes a case for a Baconian reading of Johnson's *Journey to the Western Islands of Scotland* and identifies the scientific content and allusions in what are generally treated as his purely literary writings.

fare" of the Venetians. Both ways of putting the point presuppose selective emulation, experimentation, a grasp of how desired effects can be reliably produced.

We will return to ingenuity considered as a source of pleasure, but first it is worth stressing that Reynolds's and Smith's views on ingenuity were not the common ones. The prevailing view was that genius is inspiration; only recently had Edward Young reiterated this view, in his *Conjectures on Original Composition* ([1759] 1966). Robert Dossie, who published an account of the premiums awarded during its first thirteen years by the London Society for the Encouragement of the Arts, Manufactures, and Commerce, inadvertently conveyed well what the Young view implied.[7] Reflecting on the record of premiums awarded for the spinning of linen, cotton, and woolen yarns, Dossie (1768, 94–95) mentioned that the society had for a time rewarded "the greatest quantity . . . spun in one year in work houses"; such awards, however, had been discontinued when it was realized that they rewarded "labour and industry only, without novelty, invention, or improvement." Dossie caught the Young concept of genius well, but from Smith's point of view, and Reynolds's, the two aspects were not so readily to be separated. For them, inventiveness was an outcome of embedded craft: of on-the-job learning, of time (experience), and of an experimental habit.

Pleasure, and the Pricing of Luxuries

We have touched on a connection between ingenuity and pleasure already, in outlining Smith's views on what pleases us about the imitation of painting. But Smith also developed this connection more fully in his lectures on jurisprudence, in a section on the qualities of objects that we find pleasurable and which therefore shape our preferences. He treated form or figure, rarity, and color, as well as "imitation," and said things remarkably similar to the so-called new experimental aesthetics that developed around the work of the psychobiologist D. E. Berlyne in the 1960s and 1970s (Berlyne 1960, 1974). Berlyne confirmed experimentally what nineteenth-century researcher Wilhelm Wundt (1832–1920) had discovered: pleasure, measured by a hedonic index, rises with added stimulus, but reaches a maximum and declines if the stim-

7. Dossie was the friend of Johnson, who "assisted" his election to membership (Hudson and Luckhurst 1954, 29).

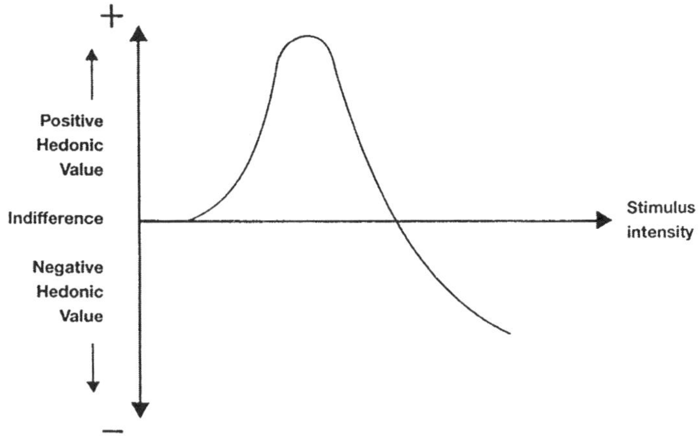

Figure 1 Wundt-like figure from Berlyne 1960, 201. Compare with figure in Wundt 1874, 431–35.

ulus is made very intense (figure 1). Berlyne studied the effect of "arousal potential" along two-valued dimensions such as familiarity-novelty and simplicity-complexity, with comparable results.[8] The similarity of such complex dimensions to Smith's "uniformity mixd at the same time with a certain degree of variety" (*LJ* A, 335) or its Hutcheson-Hartley variant, "uniformity amidst variety" (Hutcheson [1725] 1965, 86, 89; cf. Hartley [1749] 1996, 103) is evident.

Berlyne's results also capture what Smith (and Reynolds) seems to have had in mind. Smith noted that, while we enjoy splendid color and figures that are not uniform, we may have too much of brilliance and of complexity ("variety") of form (*LJ* A, 336; *LJ* B, 488). Independently, Reynolds insisted that too much regularity (repetition) fatigues us (Mount 1996, 126) and that we need the relief of variety (Hilles 1952, 133; cf. *Discourses*, 208). But he also noted that "the mind can bear with pleasure but a small portion of novelty at a time" (*Discourses*, 146) and raised the possibility that "detail of particulars" and perfection of finish in a painting can be carried too far, obscuring or destroying the "general effect" or impression and decreasing satisfaction (192–93, 201; Mount 1996, 14–15, 124–26).[9] Smith again clearly considered

8. We owe our awareness of Berlyne's work to Marina Bianchi (1998, esp. 2, 73).
9. This was said in particular of the painter Adriaen van der Werff (1659–1722).

increasing rarity a cause of pleasure to those who wish for the distinction of possessing something others cannot afford (*LJ* B, 488; cf. *WN*, 190), though it is unclear whether the hedonic curve in this case has a declining range. As to imitation, his fourth quality, since he contrasted unfavorably the "sorry carpet which now lies before me" with those represented in Dutch paintings, presumably shoddy replications also decrease pleasure (*EPS*, 178–79). But his attention cannot have been fixed on replication; for, as was explained earlier in this essay, true imitation involves overcoming the disparity between one sphere and another. Our pleasure, recall, is said to increase with the "distance" between these spheres and with the difficulty of the achievement of bridging it. It is true, however, that replication, by mechanical means, can belittle the greatness of the initial imitative effort and also that we may be so taken with ingenious contrivances that we allow ourselves to become weighed down with them, physically and mentally (*TMS*, 180–83). In these ways, then, the imitative process can also go awry and diminish pleasure.

We will say no more here about Smith's analysis of pleasure and the grounds of preference, except to note that Reynolds intuitively understood the issue Smith was addressing and the importance of staying on the positively sloped portion of the Wundt curve (*Discourses*, 208; cf. Hilles 1952, 133). Instead, we move to discuss Smith's views on the pricing of rare objects (luxuries). This returns us to the second connection with Reynolds mentioned at the outset. The link here, recall, is that, although Reynolds wrote nothing about pricing, and probably did not know Smith's analysis, he nonetheless applied exactly Smith's notions in his own business, which was principally the making and marketing of portraits.[10] We shall see how in a moment.

Smith, once again in the lectures on jurisprudence, though also in summary fashion in *The Wealth of Nations*, examined the pricing of goods whose demanders "cannot be supplied with the quantity which they want" (*WN*, 73). Unique or near-unique goods, such as certain sorts of paintings, are a limiting case, though Smith did not use that language. His focus was more on how price is formed when competition among suppliers does not come into play so as to force price to conform to costs of reproduction, conventionally measured. Thus, strictly

10. Sara Zablotney, in her contribution to this volume, draws attention to other ways in which Reynolds applied commonsense economic notions.

limited supply here means simply that reproducibility is not a factor in determining price (*LJ* B, 496; cf. *LJ* A, 357).[11]

If not costs, what does determine price in such instances? Smith stressed "means" and "wanton luxury," caprice and fancy. Thus, take a single object, and suppose it to be the only one available at this time and place, while there are two buyers of means. The buyers, Smith supposes, have the same desire for the object, but their means are different. Price, then, as in an auction, will settle at the highest bid, which will be made by the buyer of greater means (*LJ* A, 358).

This is very different from necessaries, in the competition for which the relatively few buyers of means will be altogether swamped by a mass of buyers of limited means. In the price-determining process, the few of means will become anonymous, of no particular account (*LJ* A, 358; *LJ* B, 496). Smith implicitly assumes that reproduction is possible in the case of necessaries. Price in this case will settle at the lowest amount offered consistent with some supplier covering costs and making the conventional rate of return (*WN*, 74). The (relatively) few buyers of means enjoy a sort of rent here since they do not have to engage in a bidding war with others of their kind; but, again, Smith does not speak of this.

The upshot of this analysis is that, in the case of goods in strictly limited supply, fancy and means drive a wedge between costs (reproduction costs, always conventionally measured) and price. A maker of near-unique objects, according to Smith's scenario, could seduce buyers by appealing to their fancy, caprice, or vanity and, assuming the means were available, drive up price. And a really determined maker could extract a larger share of the already-heightened price by, at the same time, shortening his own labor time.

11. Reproducibility was Smith's normal focus, and it undergirds his notion of "natural" price. This focus does not serve him well, however, when it comes to pricing rare objects that are made, not found—for the makers of such objects should reckon their labor costs *not* at the conventional wage rate, but at whatever they can extract for talent of their particular sort. Thus, properly speaking, the price of rare objects is fully accounted for in terms of materials costs plus labor time valued *not* at some notional average wage, but at the unique rate applicable to each maker. Strictly, then, there is no such thing as a wedge between price and costs of the sort that Smith wants to see in the case of near-unique objects: See *LJ* B, 496, where we read, "The market price of [such] goods is regulated by quite other circumstances [than minimal necessary supply costs: cf. 494–95]. When a buyer comes to the market, he never asks of the seller what expenses he has been at in producing them." We are grateful to William Grampp for pressing us to clarify this point.

Reynolds's Seductive Effects

This is precisely what Reynolds did. He sought to discover techniques for producing entrancing visual effects in his portraits and other works. Broadly speaking, effect could mean one of two sorts of things: first, an appeal to the imagination or conception of the viewer—"The great end of art is to strike the imagination" (*Discourses*, 59); second, what was variously referred to as force, expression, "fullness of effect" (41, 43, 160). Whereas the former qualities' appeal when successful would give "mental pleasure" (57), the latter qualities were intended to "warm the heart of the spectator" (41).

There is thus a whole range of things comprehended under effect. At one end of the spectrum stood creativity: on the one hand, design or composition and, on the other, "fancy"—the deliberate introduction of the heroic or the mythological into portraits, for example, by which they were transformed into means for promoting virtue and vehicles for the imagination. Certainly, Reynolds intended and was appreciated for these qualities. Mrs. Papandiek recalled that, in contrast to Gainsborough ("renowned for his effects of colouring"), Reynolds's great strength was "in the drawing and general arrangement of his figures" (Broughton 1887, 115).[12] A reviewer for the *Morning Chronicle* of 27 April 1774, commenting on Reynolds's *Three Ladies Adorning a Term of Hymen*, stressed both aspects of creativity. Here, the reviewer wrote, we are presented with more than mere portraiture, the picture has besides "an elegant design and fancy" (cited by Pointon 1997, 67). Gainsborough's own often-quoted remark on Reynolds picked up on his creative agility in the most sweeping sense: "Damn him, how various he is!" (67).

At the other end we encounter Reynolds's fascination with the contrivance of dazzling, purely visual effects—those neither requiring nor inviting reflection, but which stopped viewers in their tracks. Immediate impression, he was aware, made the difference between whether a visitor to a gallery "will stop, or pass along" (*Discourses*, 61). The notes Reynolds made on his journey to the Low Countries are full of praise for sensual effect, so much so that it seems to stand even higher in his estimation than mental appeal. Allowance must be made here for the common presumption, which he and Smith also shared, that

12. Marcia Pointon generously supplied us with this and the two following references.

Netherlandish paintings were mainly good for giving pleasure to the eye. But Reynolds also stated of these pictures that "whilst they are before you scarce any price appears too great," and he translated this into action, trying to buy several available paintings at substantial sums (see Mount 1996, 107, 109, 209–12).

We wish to emphasize this second class of effects—those that dazzle the eye and warm the heart. It seems natural to think of science and rules as relating to design and composition, but recall that Reynolds insisted that they govern equally expression and grandeur of effect. Visual impact is as much the result of ingenuity as is proportion or perspective, only the contrivance is directed to impressing the spectator rather than engaging the mind. As Reynolds wrote appreciatively of Shakespeare, in the words we paraphrased earlier, the rules of his art were formed in response to "the impressions that he observed were made on the audience" (Hilles 1952, 133).

Reynolds's notes during his journey to the Low Countries show clearly what he had in mind. There he employed the language of "force and brilliancy" (Mount 1996, 10; cf. 19), of "brilliant effect" (31), and of "eloquence, which bears down everything before it"(18). But these expressions were mixed freely with references to experimentation (21, note g) and "contrivance" (32), to "the power of execution" and "the Artifice of painting" in Netherlandish works (107). Reynolds even said, of Rubens's *Virgin and Child with Saints* (Augustinian Church, Antwerp), that it is "a vast machine conducted with the greatest science" (55, note g). Moreover, he wrote of the masses of light and shade in Rubens's altarpiece in the Church of the Unshod Carmelites (Brussels) that they were "*conducted* with the greatest judgement" (13; our emphasis), an allusion to order and control, echoing an account he had given already in his eighth discourse. "Fullness of effect," he there explained, has a great deal to do with the *management* of light and shadow: it "is produced by melting and losing the shadows in a ground still darker than those shadows" (*Discourses*, 160–61).

Both the immediacy of Reynolds's effects and his ordering of light and shadow in particular were much appreciated by viewers. Sylas Neville, on viewing Jervais's glass painting of Reynolds's design for the *Nativity* for the west window of the chapel at New College, Oxford, noted that "the effects of light and shade are beautifully managed" (Postle 1995, 183), while the artist Fuselli, viewing Reynolds's *Death of Dido*, was struck by "the powerful masses of chiar'oscuro" (189). The

London Courant of 7 May 1781, meanwhile, also reporting on the *Dido*, compared Reynolds favorably with Benjamin West: Reynolds "expresses what . . . [West] is not capable of conceiving, and those expressions are visible *instantaneously and without reflection*" (192; our emphasis).

Against this background, we can now summarize Reynolds's practices—his attempts to create striking sensual effects while keeping time to completion down, or what we choose to interpret as an application of the wedge identified by Smith between price and costs in the case of goods in strictly limited supply. The combined pursuit of ever new surface effects, under a self-imposed time constraint, stretched the limits of established practice. It was not possible for Reynolds to create his seductive effects in short space yet guarantee that the product would endure. Here is a short list of his radical measures and their associated negative consequences for physical integrity:

1. Reynolds was able to get his time-to-completion of a head down to a day, if the sitter so desired, though this was not often the case (Talley 1986, 60). Traditional practice in oil portraiture nonetheless called for weeks or even months (Hilles 1929, 56; Talley 1986, 67).[13] To finish in a day required the use of fast-drying glazes and varnishes.[14] Adding siccatives, or applying varnish layers too quickly, however, or standing a portrait before the fire to hasten drying (for an instance of which see Talley 1986, 64), would have caused fine surface cracks (craquelure); these are present in many of his surviving works, and could have appeared

13. The Dutch painter Adriaen van der Werff, whom Reynolds singled out for criticism for the evenness of his surfaces (at the expense of relief and the differentiation of light and shadow), not infrequently took three months of spaced work to complete a painting with a single figure (see Mount 1996, 124–26; Gaertgens 1987, 442–46). The same is true of his pupil Henrik van Limborch (1681–1759): see Jansen 1997, 31, 35 (illustrations 4 and 8, pages from the painter's day-book). For various portraits he took between six days (for a "small" piece) and eighteen, spread over periods of from two to five months. Some of these portraits involved drapery which Van Limborch may have done himself, thus not simply heads; but the practice of not rushing to a finish is very clear, by contrast with Reynolds's practice.

14. Talley (1986, 62)—basing himself on Reynolds's student Northcote's *Life*, on Reynolds's own technical memoranda, and on later artists' guesses—suggests *megilp,* or mastic dissolved in turpentine then mixed with linseed oil boiled over lead to make it dry faster, and gum tragacanth mixed with water (to avoid the slower-drying oil altogether). There has been relatively little published technical analysis of surviving paintings by Reynolds, so we depend for the moment on the artist's own notes and inferences by others. But Reynolds's method with driers cannot have differed greatly from what is listed above: cf. White and Kirby 1994, 67–71.

within Reynolds's lifetime (on "early crackle" see Marijnissen 1985, 115).

2. In order to produce softness of appearance, Reynolds would rub painted layers with wax. He also used wax emulsions (e.g., wax and copal varnish, wax and Venice turpentine, or wax and mastic) to make a more malleable medium. Such emulsions might also contain water, either if egg is involved or if the pigments used were kept under water once ground, something often done with lead white, for example, to prevent inhalation of the dust (Wetering 1997, 239). However, unless any water involved is acid-free, the mixtures are apt to disintegrate and will fail to adhere well to the support. These are problems which, to judge from anecdotal evidence, also overcame some of Reynolds's canvases (Talley 1986, 55–56, quoting Northcote; 63, citing Beechey; and 64, reporting a complaint of Sir George Beaumont).[15]
3. Deep cracking, and loss of paint, can also result from using thick masses of white to create creamy impasto highlights in the manner of Rembrandt, if varnish is applied before the paint is dry and, especially, if the varnish is applied over wax (which juxtaposes layers, the one containing agents which accelerate and the other agents which retard drying: Marijnissen 1985, 115).[16] Loss of paint from one of these causes appears to have occurred with the design of the *Nativity*. Reynolds's friend Mason watched him rushing to finish this work in time for the Royal Academy exhibition of 1779, "laying loads of color and varnish upon it, at the same time prognosticating to myself that it would never stand the test of time" (Postle 1995, 173, quoting Cotton). The work was

15. Wax can be mixed with a variety of agents, including water and egg, but also gelatin, casein, and cherry-gum tempera. Adding water and egg to the paint has the advantage that the resulting mixture can be more easily worked and brushstrokes retain their shape after the brush is lifted (Wetering 1997, 239). The tradition of using wax emulsions is ancient. As *cera colla* they were used even by Byzantine painters, while early Italian painters used wax mixed with two parts glue-water as an intermediate varnish (Doerner [1940] 1960, 227–28). This produces a soft, enamel-like effect. Reynolds is said to have preferred to dissolve his wax with Venice turpentine (larch resin), which has the advantage that it can be done cold; it also dries efficiently. Not all Reynolds's paintings containing wax have worn badly: one in good condition is *Portrait of George IV when Prince of Wales* (Wetering 1997, 228 and 308 n. 2, reporting chemical analysis of the medium).

16. Recent analysis suggests that Reynolds was mistaken if he believed that Rembrandt's impasto highlights involved wax (Wetering 1997, 229 and table A).

bought by the Duke of Rutland for the enormous sum of £1200, but it lost paint while being carried to his seat, Belvoir Castle, in 1784 (Hilles 1929, 111). Reynolds offered to make repairs, and may have done so, but in 1796 his assistant Marchi was also engaged in restoration work on the picture, "infusing a preparation of paste through the cracks" (Postle 1995, 175).

4. Reynolds favored organic pigments such as cochineal carmine. This allowed him to produce subtle flesh tints in his glazes; but these pigments are light-sensitive and faded within his lifetime, famously in the case of *Anne, Countess of Albemarle* (figure 2; National Gallery, London; Saunders and Kirby 1994, 79–80), though also in many other instances.[17]
5. Finally, he liked to use asphaltum as an underlayer, for its lustrous brown-black color and the depth it helped give to a work. But asphaltum never dries, so adding glazes or varnish overlayers creates brittle surfaces over an unstable underlying layer, and movement in the base tends to tear apart the upper parts of the painting and leave deep fissures. An example, with repair work resembling that to a road after a severe winter, is apparent in the upper part of Reynolds's *Lord Heathfield* (National Gallery, London). The self-portrait shown in figure 3 is another striking instance.

Numerous questions arise out of Reynolds's radical disregard for established practice: Was he being irrational? Was he alone in doing this? Since buyers knew about the risk of effects turning out to be fleeting, how are we to explain his continued ability to sell, and at ever higher prices? Was Reynolds perhaps using his fleeting effects as an ironic comment on the values of connoisseurs or the lives of his sitters? Only the briefest of answers is possible here.

Irrationality would imply that Reynolds hurt his business by producing works of suspect integrity and probably short life. But in the aggregate his business didn't suffer,[18] which means that durability was a sep-

17. John Byng, Lord Torrington, viewed "some faded pictures by Sir Joshua Reynolds—of no value to anyone" at Grimesthorpe in 1789 (Postle 1995, 184). Two other instances of fading are mentioned by Talley (1986, 65, 67: *James, 17th earl of Erroll*, and *Robert, 4th earl of Holderness*).

18. His prices were at least 20 percent ahead of those of various rivals—including Gainsborough, Romney, and Lawrence—at all stages of his career, and he seems never to have lacked for sitters. For Reynolds's prices, see Talley 1986, 58; for those of rivals, see Pointon 1984.

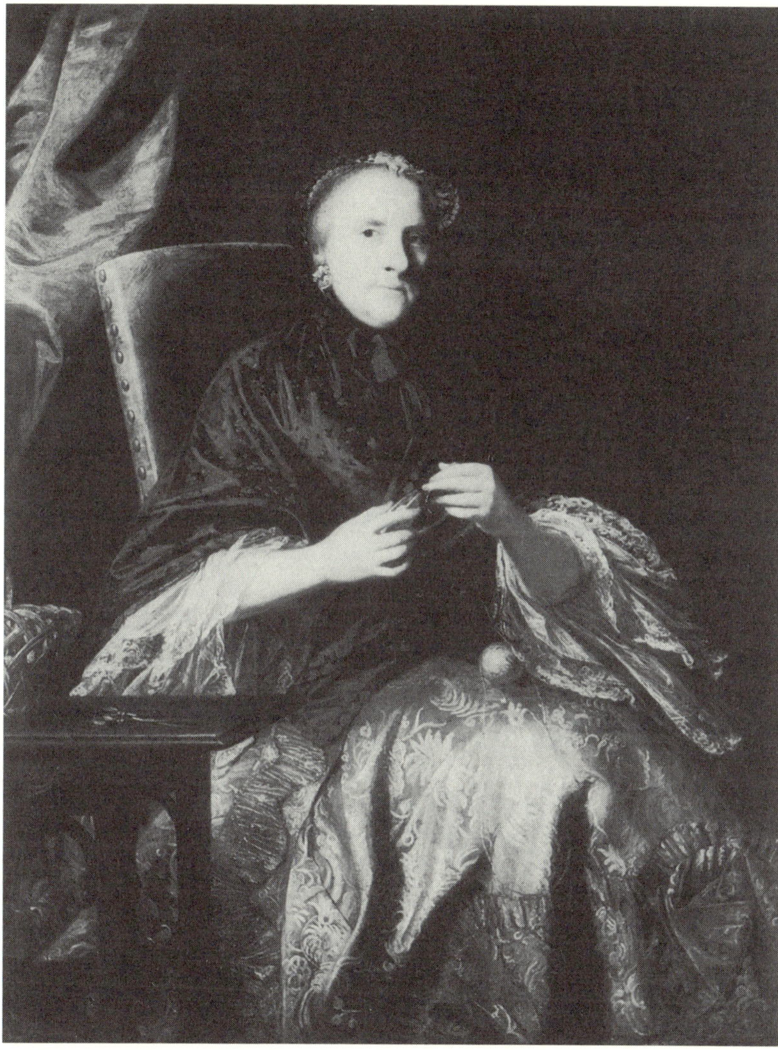

Figure 2 Sir Joshua Reynolds, *Anne, Countess of Albemarle*. National Gallery, London.

The facial pallor of this subject does not show up so strikingly in a black-and-white photograph, but the total absence of tonality betrays the loss of the lake flesh tones.

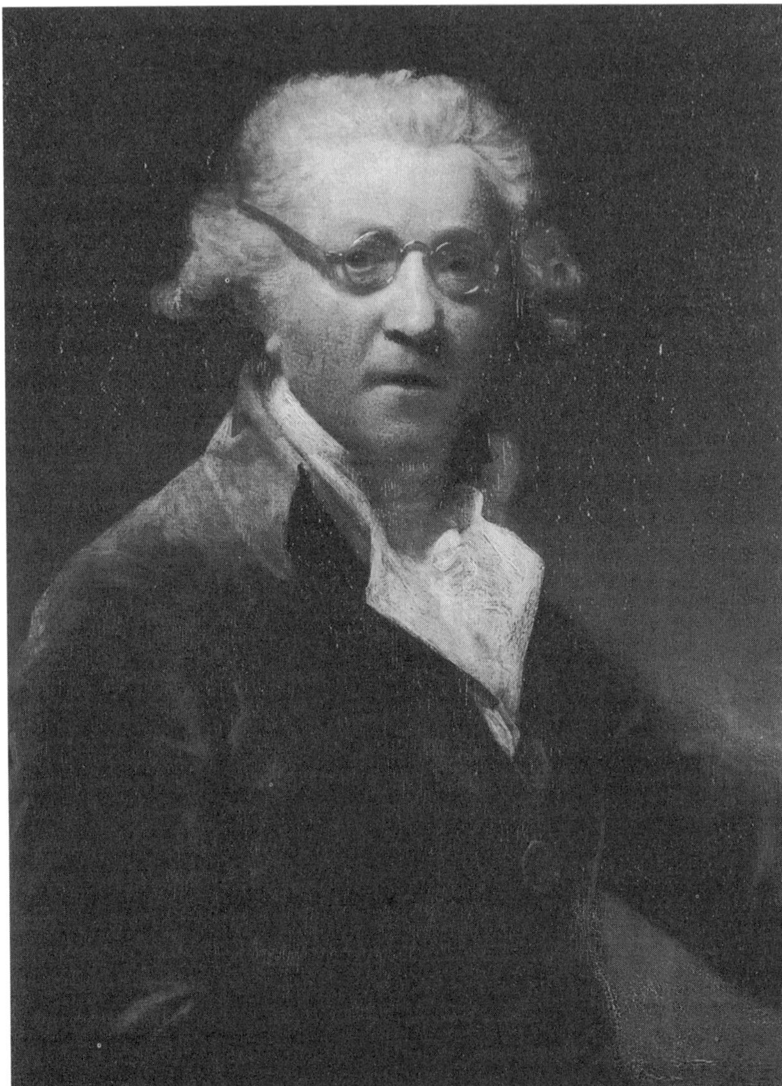

Figure 3 Sir Joshua Reynolds, *Self-portrait*. The Royal Collection. Copyright © Her Majesty Queen Elizabeth II.

This direct photograph minimizes what would be startling in a raking shot, but the damage is still apparent.

arate issue—for him and for the average buyer—from success in creating pleasing effects. Nor was he alone in experimenting to the point of threatening his own products: Opie (1761–1807), and Phillips (1708–47), among contemporaries, and Turner shortly afterward, did the same.[19] Even if only 10 or 20 percent of Reynolds's pictures cracked badly, lost paint, or faded, however, would-be buyers were necessarily entering into a wager when purchasing a picture by him. As Sir George Beaumont answered a couple reluctant to have their daughter painted by Reynolds because his pictures were known to fade: "No matter, take the chance." But Beaumont added: "Even a faded picture from Reynolds will be the finest thing you can have" (Talley 1986, 55). This last presumably was a reference to Reynolds's other acknowledged qualities: design and composition (even if often borrowed), imagination (fancy), variety, and individuality—Reynolds refused to employ accepted formulae for poses, and he sought to capture spontaneous attitudes struck by sitters, by which means a doubly individual product could be made (61–62).

Of the possibility that Reynolds was being ironic, the following can be said. Many of his portraits and fancy pictures were idealizing images, portraying his sitters as virtuous, beautiful, heroic, wise, steadfast, and so on. But these were often matched in prints and in the press by satirical depictions emphasizing better-known sides of their behavior (Donald 1986). It may have been Reynolds's way of declaiming about folly, fashion, vanity, and duplicity in the class to which his patrons belonged to portray the finer virtues in a medium that would prove literally decadent. Or was the joke actually on those who insisted on seeing quality and durability as one?

These are just speculations, and in any event the answer may be simpler: Reynolds was careful to have engravings made of a great many of his portrait pictures before he let them out of his studio. A good engraving would do justice to his management of masses of light and shadow. Most engravings after his pictures, moreover, were done using the tonal mezzotint technique, which is worked from dark to light and was therefore well suited to his sfumato outlines, his subtle shading and chiaroscuro, and the softness of surface he tried all too hard to achieve with glazes and wax in his paintings (see, for example, figure 4).

19. We thank Marcia Pointon for this information about Opie and Phillips. On Turner, see Townsend 1996.

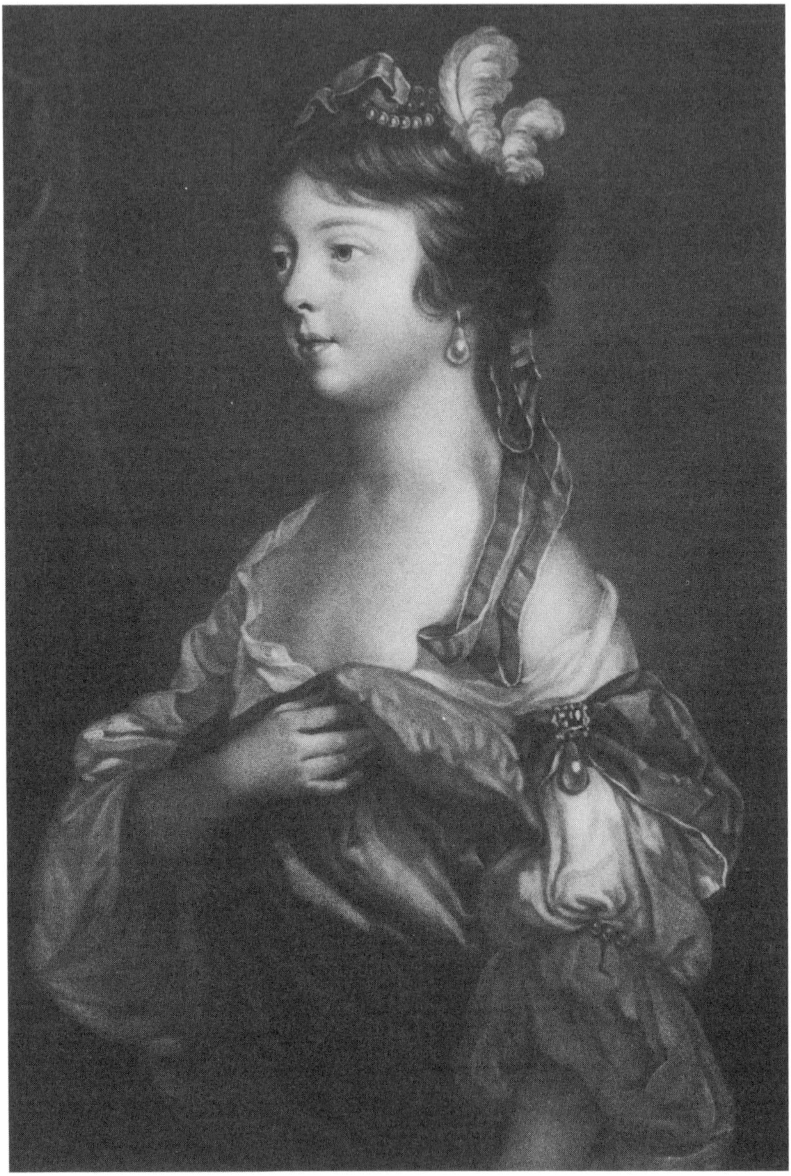

Figure 4 James McArdell after Reynolds, *Lady Charlotte Fitzwilliam.* The British Museum.

This print is thought to be the earliest mezzotint after a Reynolds painting.

Reynolds is supposed to have remarked of his early favorite mezzotint engraver, James McArdell: "By this man I shall be immortalized" (Wax 1990, 42, quoting Goodwin; cf. Lambert 1987, 76)—perhaps in itself a sad reflection on the durability anticipated of the paintings from which the engravings were made.

But that comment also reveals Reynolds's sharp economic intuition. Not only did he employ the notion of efficiency, as we have seen ("science . . . discovers the shortest and surest way to its own purpose": *Discourses*, 194), but also he spoke of exchange and of capital, though without using the terms themselves, with the facility of a familiar (e.g., 99, 105, 107). His dealings with the engraver-printer-entrepreneur John Boydell, moreover, show that this was not accidental. Reluctant to contribute a painting to Boydell's Shakespeare Gallery, Reynolds used as argument that his opportunity cost of diverting time away from portraiture might well make the contribution too expensive for Boydell (Hilles 1952, 181–84; cf. Zablotney, this volume). He also understood independently of Smith the argument used by the latter to account for the high prices commanded by diamonds and other gems—namely, their singularity and the distinction this conferred on an owner (*LJ* A, 336; cf. *LJ* B, 488). For the inverse of this is a piece of reasoning Reynolds heard from the curator of the Elector's Gallery in Dusseldorf and clearly appreciated—namely, that multiple copies of an original painting, which will pass for the original, must depreciate its value (Mount 1996, 112). Finally, but most pertinent here, Reynolds's dickering with Boydell (about due recompense for a work he ultimately contributed to the latter's illustrated Shakespeare project) has him arguing in effect that the true value of a painting made to be engraved is equal to the returns expected from subsequent print sales (Hilles 1952, 181–84). These are examples of a rich economic understanding, which suggest that the links between ingenuity and efficiency implied by Smith's analysis of division of labor, and the basis for pricing rare goods—unique services, in Reynolds's case—must have been almost self-evident to an astute practitioner with a personal economic interest.

Conclusion

We have maintained four propositions. First, that Smith held ingenuity in goods to be a source of pleasure. Second, that his notion of ingenuity, shared by Reynolds, involved uncovering hidden means-ends relations. It is in the wonder and especially the admiration felt at seeing these connections displayed and explained that our pleasure resides. Third, that fancy and means can drive a wedge between price and cost in the case of goods (and services) in limited supply. In showing this, Smith was in fact rationalizing the inclinations of makers such as Reynolds to enhance the visual appeal of their near-unique products, and thus their price, while minimizing time to completion—a double challenge to ingenuity. Fourth, that inventiveness is a matter of specialization and application; it is an acquisition not a gift. This uncommon notion of genius, too, was something held by both Smith and Reynolds.

We have argued as well that circumstances, plus their shared fascination with ingenuity, make at least some of the connections observed between Reynolds and Smith entirely natural. But what, after all, do those connections signify? Are they mere historical curiosities, or do they point to things of larger importance? We think the latter and will take the space here to show why.

One such pointer is contained in Smith's conviction that preferences are actively formed. Recall that he discussed color, figure, rarity, and imitation as qualities that give us pleasure and thus become "the foundation of . . . preferenc[e]s" (*LJ* A, 336; cf. *LJ* B, 488). At the same time, if it is true, as Mandeville insisted, that we have a "violent Fondness to change, and greater Eagerness after Novelties" ([1732] 1924, 1:178), then we face a challenge. How can we supply ourselves with novelty while avoiding the negative-sloping portions of the Wundt curve? How can we avoid the negative pleasure produced by too much brightness; too great a complexity of form; the loss of distinction as our possessions become reproducible, hence common; and the displeasure felt at multiplied imitations, lacking all real ingenuity, such as Smith's own "sorry carpet"?[20] A partial answer is to try to move onto new product curves before the decreasing-pleasure portions of old ones are reached. But this requires the avoidance of exhausting embellishments and of imitations that lower quality and overall delight. The implication is that novelty of the right sort and degree can be engineered—contrived.

20. One of the premiums given by the Society of Arts was for an imitation of "the Turky" [*sic*]. It is not true that all Oriental carpets were "Turkish," but this was a commonly used designation. The fact that Smith compared the sorry specimen on his study floor with those in Dutch paintings, which were most often referred to as Turkish, suggests that his may have been a poor domestic imitation of a Turkish carpet.

At this point, ingenuity takes on an enhanced significance. But so it had to. In the seventeenth century, novelties from the Far East and the Americas were available for the taking; many of these were curiosities of nature. By the late eighteenth century, however, the novelty horizon had been moved outward, and men and women had to seek pleasure in deliberate artifice—in contrivances ingeniously wrought. There was a growing delight in and, at several levels, an urgently felt need for artifice: to stimulate the senses afresh, though without forcing them; to sustain the march of scientific understanding; to emulate (and supplant) the foreigner's best inventions.

Evidence of a felt need, and of selective creative responses to it, is in the premiums offered by the Dublin Society for Promoting Husbandry and other useful arts from 1740, by the London Society of Arts from 1754, and by the Edinburgh Select Society from 1755. Many of the prizes were offered for imitations of existing goods of foreign origin. The surge in patents granted for imitations in the final decades of the century points in the same direction.[21]

The strength of delight is reflected in such phenomena as the attendance at the jeweler and toy maker James Cox's museum (1772–75), where clocks could be seen encased in the most elaborate and improbable jeweled automata. In her essay in this volume, Marcia Pointon notes that Cox's display, though extraordinary in itself, was also part of a shift in the second half of the century, from earlier "one-off displays" to "organized collections" (425). There were large numbers of these, "promoted as places of visual pleasure, wonder and curiosity, learning, nationalism, and commerce." The appeal of novelty is also reflected in the apparently well-founded fears of Matthew Boulton that his new designs would be pirated at once if he did not control public access to his own display rooms (Baker 1995, 124). There is evidence, too, of a growing awareness of and pleasure in ingenuity among consumers in the fact that advertisers began inserting terms like "new-invented" in their promotions, a striking instance of which is Packwood's advertisements for his razor strops (McKendrick 1982, 152–53).

As the examples of Josiah Wedgwood and of James Watt also attest, the newly ingenious product was more and more a result of careful

21. Maxine Berg (1999) has surveyed patents on "core consumer industries" from 1697 to 1825 and, with specific reference to imitations, observes a generally increased rate in those granted for imitations in the final decades of the eighteenth century.

experimentation and of a conscious application of scientific thinking and the geometrical imagination. Wedgwood preserved the record of innumerable trials with clays, glazes, and firing conditions spanning many years (Forty 1986, chap. 2; Young 1995, catalogue entries B 13 and B 46 and entries on Black Basalt [pp. 29, 32], Jasper [37–38], and the Pyrometer [42–43]). Watt exemplifies more the conceptual approach. After devising his "double-action" engine, in which steam was applied to a piston in a cylinder on both the up and the down strokes, he worked on ways of effectively transmitting all the additional power thus made available to the beam. The mechanism he conceived and eventually employed was an application of the draftsman's pantograph—"an articulated parallelogram" as he described it (Curti 1990, 360; visible at top left in figure 5).

But with these specific emphases, we are back with Reynolds and Smith. In their grasp of the importance of ingenuity, Reynolds and Smith were representative of their age, but they were also unusually perspicacious representatives, on the one hand articulating the connections between novelty and pleasure, while on the other insisting, in word and, in Reynolds's case, in practice, on the importance to *successful* invention of an understanding of materials, science, and design.

Because of the constraint of something like the Wundt curve, success also required that the novelty appeal to consumers without overwhelming them with complexity and decorative flourishes. Reynolds showed a clear grasp of both facture and the requirements behind appeal. Thus he understood the importance of variety (Hilles 1952, 133; *Discourses*, 208), and his inventive range, which so astonished Gainsborough, was very consciously directed toward satisfying the desire of his clients for something different, just as his surface effects were contrived to seduce their senses. Moreover, though he was a less careful experimenter than Wedgwood, and he placed no great emphasis on perspective or on a knowledge of anatomy (Hilles 1936, 235–36), these must not be misinterpreted to suggest that he undervalued the proper role of experimentation or the science of his art. It was simply that elements and techniques must not take precedence over the main object, which was to convey effectively to a viewer "the idea of an whole" (235–36; *Discourses*, 198). But toward the end of keeping the "whole" in view, Reynolds insisted on habits of sketching and designing (Hilles 1936, 214). In practice this meant "*contriving* various methods," "*trying* different effect[s]"—for composition, for light and shade, even, we must

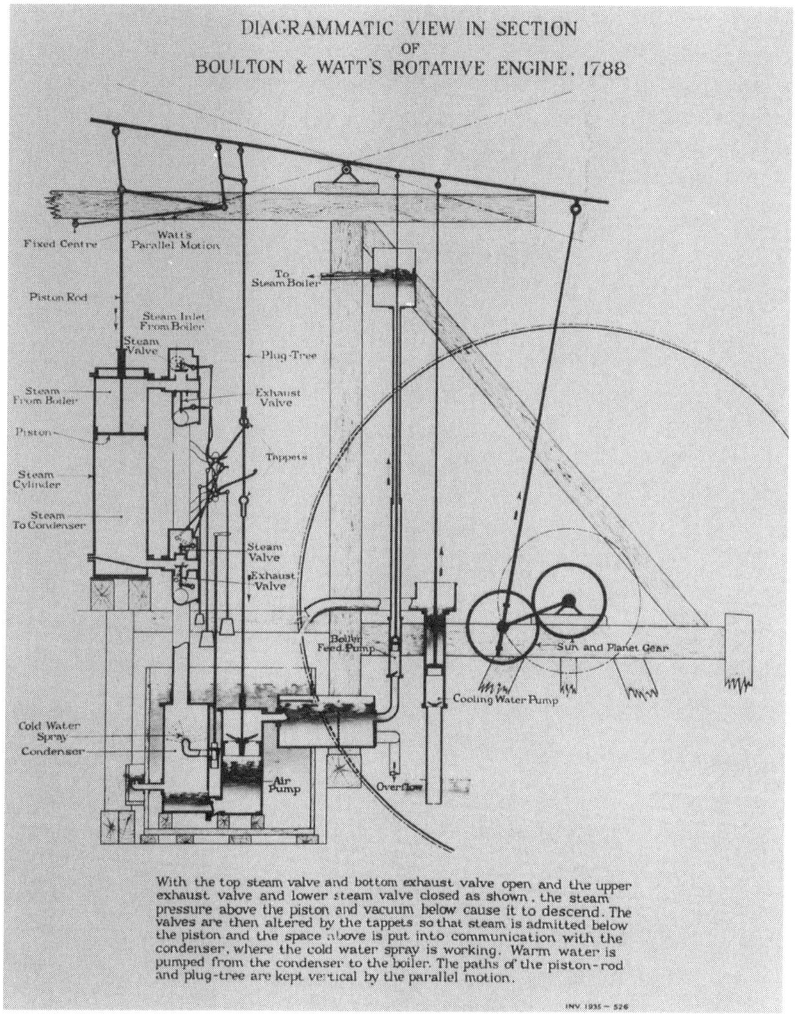

Figure 5 Watt design for rotative steam engine. The Science Museum/ Science and Society Picture Library, London.

assume, for the general form and attitude of figures (197–99; our emphases). Or, as he put it in notes on the method of the celebrated masters, once they had arrived at a conception of a subject, "they first made a Variety of Sketches [of it]" and only then a finished drawing of the whole (217). What might seem like mere striving after novelty or effect, with casual attention to detail and method, is in fact the opposite. Novelty for its own sake is condemned, as were shortcuts and the appearance of facility unrelated to labor and practice. What Reynolds stressed was care in design, ceaseless experimentation, and, as we have seen throughout, a knowledge of causes and effects.

The significant difference with Wedgwood is that Reynolds was not in the business of industrial replication but of creating relatively unique "wholes." Focusing on the whole meant for him that a part could be sacrificed or that, in any particular picture, rules could be applied with some freedom (for illustrative comment, see *Discourses*, 160–62). For unique ways of creating the desired effect might always be judged appropriate to a particular subject-treatment combination. Uniqueness also implied that studio memoranda could be cryptic, as Reynolds's were—mere reminders of the technique and materials applied in a particular instance; they differed from the meticulous notes kept by Wedgwood as part of his striving after consistency.

Smith, like Reynolds, appreciated the importance of variety and novelty (*LJ* B, 488; *TMS*, 199), and, as we know, he was particularly taken with novelties that were ingenious. He even suggested that the Impartial Spectator "distinguishes with such admiration the condition of the rich and great" because of "the numberless artificial and ingenious contrivances" they possess, whether or not these actually serve the end of "conveniency" (*TMS*, 182).[22] Consistently with this perspective, however, we find Smith also insisting that novelty must be "connected": "Connected variety, in which each new appearance seems to be introduced by what went before it, and in which all the adjoining parts seem to have some natural relation to one another, is more agreeable than a disjointed and disorderly assemblage of unconnected objects" (199–200). This was at one with his view that successful innovation typically is a simplifying move, rather than a pleasure-reducing shift toward greater complexity (*EPS*, 196–97). But connectedness was also a summary expression for his basic insight about ingenuity—that it consists in chains of small links, which together compellingly show some previously unsuspected connection between effects.

22. In an interesting inversion of this, Henry Fielding in *The Adventures of Joseph Andrews* ([1742] 1961, 198) decries admiration for the mere possessor, when we should be admiring "the builder, the workman, the painter, the lace-maker, the tailor, and the rest, by whose ingenuity . . . [the possessions] are produced." We are grateful to Marina Bianchi for this reference.

Our account of the intersections of interest and conviction between Reynolds and Smith exemplifies this same perspective. The connections spring most obviously from their mutual fascination with ingenuity. But they saw ingenuity itself as crucial to the conquest of boredom, and the giving of pleasure, and thus to *successful* industrial design and import replacement, in a late-eighteenth-century Britain that was swamped with products from every quarter. Both saw clearly that embellishment as such is no guarantee that a novelty will please. The only fortuitous element in our account is that it was a concern with the imitative arts that brought our two protagonists together. Yet even this is not wholly fortuitous. Broadly similar stories could be told using other pairs—for instance, Smith and James Watt and Reynolds and Wedgwood. And there are numerous others as well. In any of these micro-narratives, details of connections would emerge whose significance is that they exemplify the larger concerns we have identified here: how to sustain the pleasure of novelty; how to turn a knowledge of materials, of relations of a cause-effect sort, and of design, to the service of ingenuity and thereby—closing the circle—to pleasure.

References

Bacon, Francis. [1620] 1944. *Novum Organum; or True Suggestions for the Interpretation of Nature*. Edited by James Edward Creighton. New York: Wiley.

Baker, Malcolm. 1995. A Rage for Exhibitions: The Display and Viewing of Wedgwood's Frog Service. In *The Genius of Wedgwood*, edited by Hilary Young. London: Victoria & Albert Museum.

Barrell, John. 1986. *The Political Theory of Painting from Reynolds to Hazlitt*. New Haven, Conn.: Yale University Press.

Berg, Maxine. 1999. New Commodities, Luxuries, and Their Consumers in Eighteenth-Century England. In *Consumers and Luxury: Consumer Culture in Europe, 1650–1850,* edited by Maxine Berg and Helen Clifford. Manchester: Manchester University Press.

Berlyne, D. E. 1960. *Conflict, Arousal, and Curiosity*. New York: McGraw-Hill.

———, ed. 1974. *Studies in the New Experimental Aesthetics: Steps toward an Objective Psychology of Aesthetic Appreciation*. Washington, D.C.: Hemisphere.

Bianchi, Marina. 1998. *The Active Consumer: Novelty and Surprise in Consumer Choice*. London: Routledge.

Broughton, V. D., ed. 1887. *Court and Private Life in the Time of Queen Charlotte*. London: R. Bentley.

Curti, Orazio. 1990. Steam Pumps and Machines. In *History of Industrial Design*. Vol. 1, *1750–1850: The Age of the Industrial Revolution*, edited by Carlo Pirovano. Milan: Electa.

Doerner, M. [1940] 1960. *The Materials of the Artist and Their Use in Painting, with Notes on the Techniques of the Old Masters.* 6th ed. New York: Harcourt, Brace.

Donald, Diana. 1986. "Characters and Caricatures": The Satirical View. In *Reynolds,* edited by Nicholas Penny. New York: Abrams.

Dossie, Robert. 1768. *Memoirs of Agriculture, and Other Oeconomical Arts.* London: J. Nourse.

Fielding, Henry. [1742] 1961. *The Adventures of Joseph Andrews.* Edited by Martin C. Battestin. Boston: Houghton Mifflin.

Forty, Adrian. 1986. *Objects of Desire.* New York: Pantheon.

Gaertgens, Barbara. 1987. *Adriaen Van Der Werff, 1659–1722.* Munich: Deutscher Kunstverlag.

Harp, Richard L. 1986. *Dr. Johnson's Critical Vocabulary: A Selection from His Dictionary.* Lanham, Md.: University Press of America.

Hartley, David. [1749] 1996. *Observations on Man.* Excerpted in *The Sublime: A Reader in British Eighteenth-Century Aesthetic Theory,* edited by Andrew Ashfield and Peter de Bolla. Cambridge: Cambridge University Press.

Hilles, Frederick Whiley, ed. 1929. *Letters of Sir Joshua Reynolds.* Cambridge: Cambridge University Press.

———. 1936. *The Literary Career of Sir Joshua Reynolds.* New York: Macmillan.

———. 1952. *Portraits by Sir Joshua Reynolds: Character Sketches . . . together with Other Manuscripts of Reynolds Discovered among the Boswell Papers.* Yale editions of the Private Papers of James Boswell. New York: McGraw-Hill.

Hudson, Derek, and Kenneth W. Luckhurst. 1954. *The Royal Society of Arts, 1754–1954.* London: John Murray.

Hutcheson, Francis. [1725] 1965. *An Inquiry into the Original of Our Ideas of Beauty and Virtue.* Reprinted (in part) in *Aesthetic Theories: Studies in the Philosophy of Art,* edited by Karl Aschenbrenner and Arnold Isenberg. Englewood Cliffs, N.J.: Prentice Hall.

Jansen, Guido M. C. 1997. De *Notitie der dagelijxe schilderoeffening* van Henrik van Limborch (1681–1759). *Bulletin van het Rijksmuseum* 45:27–67.

Lambert, Susan. 1987. *The Image Multiplied: Five Centuries of Printed Reproductions of Paintings and Drawings.* London: Trefoil.

Mandeville, Bernard. [1732] 1924. *The Fable of the Bees.* Edited by J. B. Kaye. Vol. 1. Oxford: Clarendon.

Marijnissen, R. H. 1985. *Paintings: Genuine, Fraud, Fake: Modern Methods of Examining Paintings.* Brussels: Elsevier.

McKendrick, Neil. 1982. George Packwood and the Commercialization of Shaving: The Art of Eighteenth-Century Advertising or "The Way to Get Money and Be Happy." In McKendrick, Brewer, and Plumb 1982.

McKendrick, Neil, John Brewer, and J. H. Plumb. 1982. *The Birth of a Consumer Society: The Commercialization of Eighteenth-Century England.* London: Europa.

Mount, Harry, ed. 1996. *Sir Joshua Reynolds: A Journey to Flanders and Holland.* Cambridge: Cambridge University Press.

Plumb, J. H. 1982. The Acceptance of Modernity. In McKendrick, Brewer, and Plumb 1982.

Pointon, Marcia. 1984. Portrait-Painting as a Business Enterprise in London in the 1780s. *Art History* 7:187–205.

———. 1997. *Strategies for Showing: Women, Possession, and Representation in English Visual Culture, 1665–1800.* Oxford: Oxford University Press.

Postle, Martin. 1995. *Sir Joshua Reynolds: The Subject Pictures.* Cambridge: Cambridge University Press.

Rogers, Pat, ed. 1992. *Sir Joshua Reynolds: Discourses.* London: Penguin.

———. 1996. *The Samuel Johnson Encyclopaedia.* Westport, Conn.: Greenwood.

Saunders, David, and Jo Kirby. 1994. Light-Induced Colour Changes in Red and Yellow Lake Pigments. *National Gallery Technical Bulletin* 15:79–97.

Schwartz, Richard B. 1971. *Samuel Johnson and the New Science.* Madison: University of Wisconsin Press.

Smith, Adam. [1759] 1982. *The Theory of Moral Sentiments* [*TMS*]. Vol. 1 of the Glasgow edition of the *Works and Correspondence of Adam Smith*, edited by D. D. Raphael and A. L. Macfie. Indianapolis: Liberty Press.

———. [1776] 1981. *An Inquiry into the Nature and Causes of the Wealth of Nations* [*WN*]. Vol. 2 of the Glasgow edition. Edited by R. H. Campbell and A. S. Skinner, general editors, and W. B. Todd, textual editor. Indianapolis: Liberty Press.

———. 1982a. *Essays on Philosophical Subjects* [*EPS*]. Vol. 3 of the Glasgow edition. Edited by W. P. D. Wightman. Indianapolis: Liberty Press.

———. 1982b. *Lectures on Jurisprudence* [*LJ*]. Vol. 4 of the Glasgow edition. Edited by R. L. Meek, D. D. Raphael, and P. G. Stein. Indianapolis: Liberty Press.

Talley, M. Kirby, Jr. 1986. "All Good Pictures Crack": Sir Joshua Reynolds's Practice and Studio. In *Reynolds*, edited by Nicholas Penny. New York: Abrams.

Townsend, Joyce. 1996. *Turner's Painting Techniques.* 2d ed. London: Tate.

Van Ngo, Minh. 1998. The Subtlety and Versatility of Smith's Ethics. Mimeo, Duke University.

Wark, Robert R., ed. [1959] 1997. *Sir Joshua Reynolds: Discourses on Art.* New Haven, Conn.: Yale University Press, for the Paul Mellon Centre for Studies in British Art.

Wax, Carol. 1990. *The Mezzotint: History and Technique.* London: Thames & Hudson.

Wetering, Ernst van der. 1997. *Rembrandt: The Painter at Work.* Amsterdam: Amsterdam University Press.

White, Raymond, and Jo Kirby. 1994. Rembrandt and His Circle: Seventeenth-

Century Dutch Paint Media Re-examined. *National Gallery Technical Bulletin* 15:64–77.

Wundt, Wilhelm. 1874. *Grundzüge der Physiologischen Psychologie*. Leipzig: Engelman.

Young, Edward. [1759] 1966. *Conjectures on Original Composition*. Leeds: Scolar Press.

Young, Hilary, ed. 1995. *The Genius of Wedgwood*. London: Victoria and Albert Museum.

Production and Reproduction: Commerce in Images in Late-Eighteenth-Century London

Sara Zablotney

It has long been common to analyze the creation and sale of art as a response to the creative genius of producers. Accounts are now becoming available of the commercial side of an artist's life. But even these tend not to examine the underlying economic forces behind artists' decisions. Artists themselves are presented as actors isolated from market forces, responding to impulses far removed from the laws of supply and demand for the creation of their oeuvre. In fact, producers of art since the early modern period—painters, engravers, and printers—have often led sophisticated economic lives, and it is not surprising that the application of economic principles can help explain why certain kinds of paintings or prints were produced and the reasons economic actors paid or received the prices they did. I wish to make such an application to the art market in late-eighteenth-century London. In the relationships between printing entrepreneurs such as John Boydell and certain painters are found such classic economic concepts as opportunity costs, present value calculations of the value of a capital investment, and negotiations over rent. The men and women involved in these relationships used economic language, and their actions accorded with their intuitive understandings of the consequences of economically motivated behavior.

Throughout the eighteenth century English fine and popular arts were well patronized and of high quality. Demand for paintings and engravings was extremely strong and expanded as the century progressed. In compiling various probate records from the first half of the century, Lorna Weatherill (1996, 76) estimated that by 1725 at least 41 percent of Londoners and about 37 percent of all English families owned at least one image.[1] There is no evidence to suggest that the percentage of families owning visual images decreased later in the century; in fact, Stana Nenadic (1997, 207) states that "the middle and later eighteenth century witnessed a mania for print collecting throughout Britain." There was a steady creation of paintings as well, but the demand was limited due to their relatively high price (for some prices, see the following discussion).

The demand for fine art was largely satisfied by reproductive prints of ancient and modern paintings, many of which were imported from France and Holland (Clayton 1997, 122). However, due to both the increase of high-quality prints produced in Britain and the war on the continent at mid-century, England, during the latter half of the eighteenth century, went from being a net importer of prints to being a net exporter (Gray 1937, 12). The producers of engravings relied on painters and picture-dealers to supply them with their basic input beyond skill, paper, and ink. They paid these agents sums above the ordinary auction prices paid for paintings. This raises the questions that form the main focus here.

An entrepreneur could amass a considerable fortune by selling prints of popular paintings. Various engravers turned to printselling, importing, exporting, and distributing the works of others and thereby increased their revenues (Clayton 1997, 112). For instance, John Boydell, who eventually became an alderman and later lord mayor of London, founded his business on profits from the publication of prints taken from Richard Wilson's *Niobe* and Benjamin West's *Death of General Wolfe*. He had begun his career as an apprentice engraver, and until 1750 he made his living by selling his own landscape engravings. He began dealing in others' works by purchasing old plates and publishing new runs. The publication of *Niobe* and *The Death of General Wolfe* established him as a speculative publisher who specialized in wholesaling and distributing others' works (Clayton 1997, 115).

Boydell published *Niobe* in 1762 in a run of 8,000 impressions that were sold for 5 shillings each. He grossed 2,000 pounds from this paint-

1. Although I generally mean "fine art reproductive prints" when I refer to prints or engravings, Weatherill's data refer to anything from a popular broadsheet bought from a peddler to a fine oil painting. In this context I am merely pointing out a trend, not trying to establish a definite relationship. I am indebted to Marcia Pointon for pointing out this possible inconsistency.

ing "at a time when Wilson was hardly able to sell his work." His largest single expenditure was a 150-guinea payment (157 pounds 10 shillings) to William Wollett to execute the engraving, an "unheard of price" for the time (Clayton 1997, 188). In this instance Boydell held claim to only a one-third share in the profits over a fifteen-year period, but he still grossed in excess of 15,000 pounds from the sales. Assuming that he made 1,000 pounds per year from such prints, even such a high payment as 500 pounds for the underlying painting still represented profits of over 2,000 percent at the prevailing rate of interest, 4 percent (Homer 1977, 158 chart 5).[2] At a time when one could acquire a Guercino for 80 pounds and when some masterworks cost as little as 10 pounds (Graves 1918), this represented a substantial amount of money. It is even more substantial when one realizes that it was the distributor of copies, not the creator of the original image, who made the bulk of the profits.

Profits from printselling were possible because prints were in high demand and were sold across a wide socioeconomic spectrum. Ranging in price from 1 or 2 shillings for a single mezzotint portrait to 40 pounds for an original Rembrandt line engraving sold at auction (Nenadic 1997, 206), prints were collected by the aristocracy and the middle class alike. Indeed, some contemporary moralists condemned the widespread popularity of prints as a sign of the "universal luxury of the times" (Clayton 1997, 129). The exhibitions of the Royal Academy drew large crowds composed of people who could not afford to buy many paintings; they could, however, afford the prints (181). Thus it is not surprising that painters and printsellers hoped to tap into this desire by publishing engravings.

The printmaker's problem was to acquire the rights to reproduce suitable works. The copyright law of 1767 bestowed copyright on the owner of the plate, no matter who had designed or engraved it, for twenty-eight years (198). Although portraitists and their subjects might commission engravings of their paintings for sale as a kind of advertisement for themselves, they retained ownership of the image and

2. My calculation assumes a stream of payments of £1,000 over fifteen years and no expectation of inflation. The rate of interest in 1764 is estimated at 4 percent in Sidney Homer's 1963 work *A History of Interest Rates*. Thus, the present value in 1764 of the £15,000 received by Boydell is £11,563. This represents a 2,312.6 percent profit for the printer, who paid £500 for the original painting.

reaped most of the benefits from the sale of the engraving.[3] Reynolds, for example, like many other portrait painters of his time, compiled a portfolio of his previous works and of the works of others to display to potential customers. His student and assistant James Northcote ([1819] 1971, 83), noted that Reynolds "kept a port-folio in his painting-room, containing every print that had then been taken from his portraits; so that those who came to sit, had this collection to look over, and if they fixed on any particular attitude, in preference, he would repeat it precisely in point of drapery and position; as this much facilitated the business, and was sure to please the sitter's fancy."

If a printer, like John Boydell, wished to profit from printing fine reproductions, he had either to own an original plate of an already existing engraving, to enter into an arrangement with the owner of the painting to take the engraving, to buy the painting for the same purpose, or to commission a painting specifically for engraving and painting. Painters were far less likely to produce the kind of subject picture and historical works that made popular fine-art prints because the marginal revenue on a portrait was much greater than for a subject painting to most painters. However, because of the expected return on engravings of subject paintings, publishers were prepared to pay painters and connoisseurs large sums of money, either for the rights to engrave a painting or for the painting itself.

Because of the slow nature of the work of engraving, legal contracts were necessary. Publishers often offered collections of works on subscription so that patrons paid for a volume of related prints in installments as the prints were produced, ensuring both a continuous stream of funds for the publisher and a less risky investment for the buyer. Furthermore, printers entered into arrangements with engravers in order to ensure the production of plates. There has survived a contract between Boydell and an artist named James Heath for the engraving of John Singleton Copely's painting *The Death of Major Peirson*, which shows the economic problems presented by the drawn-out nature of the process of engraving. Boydell promised to pay Heath 300 pounds per annum until the engraving was produced, and in fact did so. Boydell

3. Paintings and engravings tended to advertise each other. On the one hand, a painting could be exhibited to advertise the sale of a print; on the other hand, a print might be made by an artist, sold to his friends to prove its worth, then the plate sold to a distributor like Boydell. Thus in some sense, a successful engraving could be seen as adding value to a painting; in other circumstances it might work in the reverse fashion.

had commissioned the original painting for 800 pounds in 1784; the engraving was published twelve years later, in 1796 (Griffiths 1992, 184–85). This illustrates the moral hazard problem. The contract specified no outer time limit. Heath was to have as much time as he needed to complete the engraving. Although the painting was quite large and would be expected to take some amount of time, the fact that Heath was paid on a per annum basis reduced his incentive to complete the picture speedily. The fact that Boydell could afford to pay 300 pounds shows the profitability of the business. The implication here, though, is that well-thought-out contracts were necessary for successful business. In fact, it was Boydell's nephew Josiah, not Boydell himself, who arranged this agreement. Such an open-ended contract was never entered into again by the Boydells.

Contracts also exist for obtaining the use of paintings to serve in producing plates. These, too, show a painting's enormous value to the producer of prints. According to notes Sir Thomas Lawrence made in his copy of the catalog to John Julius Angerstein's picture collection in 1823, Boydell paid Angerstein 500 pounds for the *loan* of Hogarth's entire *Marriage à la Mode* in order to take engravings. These payments were purely for the use of the paintings as inputs since Boydell never became the owner of the paintings. However, considering the expected returns from a profitable engraving, the payments for the pictures appear minuscule. The present value of Boydell's earnings at 4 percent interest in 1776, assuming equal 1,000-pound payments over fifteen years, as with the *Niobe*, would have been 11,563 pounds.

When Boydell commissioned paintings, he treated them exactly like capital stock. Typically they were used for various engravings and collections, then sooner or later they were auctioned off. For instance, in 1771, Boydell held a "housecleaning" sale of his stock, including pictures, plates, and models (Friedman 1976, 46). Thus, the paintings had both a value as capital, generating a stream of payments through the rights to an engraving, and a "face value" or "scrap value," which the owner of the painting could redeem after having used it in his production process.

Boydell's *Shakespeare Gallery* provides another excellent example of how producers of prints commissioned paintings as productive inputs. In this case, Boydell paid the producers sums above their normal fees to acquire the paintings for use in his *Illustrated Shakespeare*. Boydell's volume of Shakespeare was to present the text of the plays with illustrations engraved after paintings by England's best artists. It was to cost approximately 100 guineas[4] by subscription (Farington, quoted in Friedman 1976, 63). In the end, the payment scheme (along with the disruptions caused by the French Revolution) proved the downfall of the gallery, but both the structure for payment and the prices Boydell offered to painters to create pictures for the gallery show how Boydell saw his expenditures on paintings as expenditures on capital stock. To own the *Shakespeare Gallery* volumes (there were eventually nine), one committed to a down payment of 2 guineas, followed by a payment of 5 guineas per installment (there were eighteen issues) (Friedman 1976, 67). This put the cost of the volume at about 90 guineas, an enormous sum, although the payments would be spread out over time. Payments to artists were also spread out over time. Over the twelve years of the gallery's existence, Boydell paid painters and engravers a total of 42,972 pounds (244).

Although many "forgettable" painters contributed to Boydell's *Gallery*, such well-known painters as James Barry, Johann Fuseli, Gavin Hamilton, William Hamilton, Julius Caesar Ibbetson, Angelica Kauffmann, James Northcote, John Opie, Sir Joshua Reynolds, George Romney, and Benjamin West produced works for him. Boydell paid large amounts for their original paintings. For instance, Reynolds was paid 525 pounds for a scene from *Henry VI* (Friedman 1976), over twice his full-length portrait fee of 200 pounds at that time (Pointon 1984, 200); and he was paid 1,000 pounds, five times his fee for a full-length portrait, for his picture from *Macbeth*. Similarly, Romney was paid 195 pounds for two of his pictures and 525 for a third (Friedman 1976); his quarter-length portrait price was 20 pounds in 1781 (Reynolds received over 50 pounds for the same dimensions) (Pointon 1984, 200). Northcote received fees ranging from 105 to 315 pounds for his work—a far cry from his usual portrait price of 16 guineas (Friedman 1976).

Boydell clearly spent the amount of money that he did on the commissioning of paintings for use in the production of his illustrations because of the profits he expected to generate. When the paintings were sold at auction twenty years later, buyers valued them far below what Boydell had originally paid for them. The paintings sold mostly for less than half their original price. For instance, the painting for which Northcote was paid 315 pounds sold at Christie's for only 113 pounds.

4. A pound contained 20 shillings; a guinea, 21 shillings.

But it fared better than Romney's painting of a scene from *The Tempest,* for which he was paid 525 pounds but which sold for only 53 pounds (Freidman 1976). However, these prices may be viewed as if they were the "scrap value" of the investment. According to his prior experiences with popular prints, Boydell could expect these engravings to lead to a series of payments over time whose present value far outweighed the initial large investment in the painting.

In proof that these payments were not so out of the ordinary, Boydell was not alone among producers of engravings who paid such commissions. Thomas Macklin paid similar fees for pictures to be engraved for his *Bible.* He paid 1,150 pounds to Reynolds for three paintings, 350 pounds per painting to Gainsborough, 100 pounds to William Hamilton, and 400 pounds to Benjamin West (Reitlinger 1961, 72). These were large sums for a single picture, considering that it was possible to buy history paintings by well-known ancient and modern artists at auction for as little as 25 pounds (Graves 1918). Other engravers—such as John Raphael Smith, Valentine Green, and Sir Robert Strange, for example—became large-scale publishers. Like Boydell, they owed their success to employing the best paintings by the best painters as their original input (Clayton 1997, 210).

Why did publishers of prints pay so much for original paintings? The answer has been given already. Painters of portraits could earn substantial sums in that line, and any other employment was an opportunity cost that had to be more than compensated. In addition, painters were likely to know something of the printers' profits and could be expected to claim a portion of the profit stream up front. Both issues emerge very clearly in Boydell's negotiations with Sir Joshua Reynolds over the painting from *Macbeth.* Reynolds asked 1,500 pounds for the production of the picture and claimed that in so valuing it, he was actually selling his time at a loss. Boydell did not agree to this asking price, though he had given a 500-pound down payment and had told Sir Joshua that he was to have more should he demand it (Hilles 1952, 179). Reynolds also planned to tell Boydell that "it is supposed that Mr. Boydell will acquire a considerable fortune by his patronage of the arts, and as he acknowledged that the living painters have been his coadjutors, it seems but reasonable that they should have a share in the profit" (183).

Reynolds was here thinking to exercise his monopoly power. Nevertheless, painters were not immune to competition. There is evidence that Boydell calculated the relative worth of various paintings based on the profitability of that artist's previous works translated into prints. For instance, Reynolds could command high prices because of the immense popularity of his paintings and prints, as could Benjamin West—witness the success of works like the *Niobe* and *The Death of General Wolfe*. Other painters, with no track record or an inferior one, did not get paid as well. For instance, Joseph Wright of Derby, who painted two pictures for Boydell, wrote the alderman in 1789 to complain about the prices he was being quoted: 315 pounds and 126 pounds, respectively. He argued that "you gave Sir Joshua 500gs for his picture, and a very considerable fee besides; also, you gave Mr. West 500gs for his picture, and yet you were paving the way to offer me a much less sum. Is not my picture as large as Mr. West's? Has it not equal, nay, more work in it? Is it not as highly finished? And has not the public spoken well of it?" (quoted in Friedman 1976, 108). Boydell replied that not only was Mr. Wright's painting not of the first consequence, but it also was difficult to engrave (109). In addition, engravings from Wright's history paintings had not brought in as large sums as those from the other painters he had mentioned; therefore, it is natural that Boydell would pay him less since the expected return was less.

Another possible reason for the prices offered is that in some ways the production of commissioned engravings is a case of bilateral monopoly. To this extent, the prices paid represent a fight over rent. Boydell and other publishers held a large degree of monopsony power over the buying of paintings directly commissioned for use in engravings, although Reynolds and other painters held monopoly power over the production and sale of their own work. Buyers (printers) wanted to minimize their factor costs and maximize the amount of revenue created per use of each factor. Therefore, they wanted to buy the paintings at the lowest possible price. The seller (the painter) wanted to maximize the total amount of revenue per painting less his costs per painting that he would receive from the buyer. Therefore, he wished to set his price as high as possible for as few paintings as possible, thus minimizing his costs and maximizing his profits. When the product was a commissioned painting for a specific publication like the *Shakespeare Gallery*, the printers and the painters had to buy and sell from each other. This created a situation in which each tried to maximize his share of the economic rent.

There is no unique solution in such cases. When a monopolist faces a monopsonist, the outcome and final price is decided by bargaining or arbitration or both. This is what happened in the case of the paintings created for the *Shakespeare Gallery*. There were no set prices for each painting produced for the book. Each painter negotiated his price on a per-painting basis with the printer, operating on information each had of the expected profits of the scheme. As Reynolds made clear, he expected the *Shakespeare Gallery* to earn substantial profit for Boydell. In quoting his extraordinarily high price, over seven times his normal portrait fee of 200 pounds, Reynolds was taking into account the expected surplus Boydell would realize from the painting's reproduction and sale. As the only person qualified to produce an authentic "Reynolds," the painter thought himself perfectly justified in trying to capture as much of this surplus as possible. Boydell, by contrast, trying to preserve as much of the surplus for himself as possible, wanted to pay Reynolds a much smaller price. In accordance with modern theory, the final price paid was somewhere in between each man's preferred outcome.

The economic relationships that existed among producers of fine art in late-eighteenth-century London are easily understood using modern economic analysis. On the one hand, entrepreneurs like John Boydell, who produced and distributed fine reproductive prints, depended on artists for their basic inputs. Paintings were valuable not only as art objects but also as inputs in the creation of prints. A clever distributor could make a great deal of money if he could correctly predict the tastes of the market and acquire the necessary paintings and plates. On the other hand, painters and engravers wanted to receive as much of the benefit from the reproduction of their work as possible. To a certain extent, a successful print added value to a painting. Beyond this, however, painters and engravers wanted to share in the profits from the sale of the prints. The many interesting contracts that were drawn up between the two parties show both the extent of the potential awards and the conflicting interests involved.

References

Clayton, Timothy. 1997. *The English Print: 1688–1802*. New Haven, Conn.: Yale University Press.

Friedman, Winifred H. 1976. *Boydell's Shakespeare Gallery*. New York: Garland.

Graves, Algernon. 1918. *Art Sales from Early in the Eighteenth Century to Early in the Twentieth Century (Mostly Old Master and Early English Pictures)*. 3 vols. London: Chiswick Press.

Gray, Basil. 1937. *The English Print*. London: Adam & Charles Black.
Griffiths, Antony. 1992. Two Contracts for British Prints. *Print Quarterly* 9.2 (June): 184–87.
Hilles, Frederick W. 1952. *Portraits by Sir Joshua Reynolds: Character Sketches of Oliver Goldsmith, Samuel Johnson, and David Garrick, together with Other Manuscripts of Reynolds Discovered among the Boswell Papers and Now First Published*. New York: McGraw-Hill.
Homer, Sidney. 1977. *A History of Interest Rates*. 2d ed. New Brunswick, N.J.: Rutgers University Press.
Nenadic, Stana. 1997. Print Collecting and Popular Culture in Eighteenth-Century Scotland. *History* 82.266 (April): 203–22.
Northcote, James. [1819] 1971. *Life of Sir Joshua Reynolds*. Vol. 1 of 2. London: Cornmarket Press.
Pointon, Marcia. 1984. Portrait Painting as a Business Enterprise in London in the 1780s. *Art History* 7.2 (June): 187–201.
Reitlinger, Gerald. 1961. *The Economics of Taste: The Rise and Fall of Picture Prices 1760–1960*. Vol. 1 of 3. London: Barrie and Rockliff.
Weatherill, Lorna. 1996. *Consumer Behaviour and Material Culture in Britain 1660–1760*. 2d ed. London: Routledge.

Dealer in Magic: James Cox's Jewelry Museum and the Economics of Luxurious Spectacle in Late-Eighteenth-Century London

Marcia Pointon

So when great Cox, at his mechanic call,
Bids orient pearls from golden dragons fall,
Each little dragonet, with brazen grin,
Gapes for the precious prize, and gulps it in.
Yet when we peep behind the magic scene,
One master-wheel directs the whole machine:
The self-same pearls, in nice gradation, all
Around one common centre, rise and fall:
Thus may our state-museum long surprise;
And what is sunk by votes in bribes arise;
Till mocked and jaded with the puppet-play,
Old England's genius turns with scorn away.
—William Mason, "Epistle to Dr. Shebbeare," in P. Toynbee, *Satirical Poems Published Anonymously* . . .

The linking of the words *industry* and *heritage* appears to belong unmistakably to our own era of global tourism, media as manufacture, museology, and so-called indirect earnings. Jules Lubbock (1995, 134) has argued that Adam Smith's prescience as an economic theorist hits a problem with the arts owing to his insistence "that productive labour was only that which resulted in some permanent object 'which lasts for some time.'" The spectacle I examine in this essay comprised objects

I would like to thank the following people who have generously helped me in researching James Cox: Helen Clifford, Steve Conner, Sarah Kane, Julia Lambert, Clare Le Corbeiller, and Lucy Peltz. I would also like to thank Neil De Marchi for making me think about economics. This essay is part of a full-length study of Cox and jeweled automata in eighteenth-century London.

that were transitional (stylistically and materially) in a display that had all the hallmarks of ephemerality and brilliance that characterize the language of economic debate in late-eighteenth-century England, which was, perhaps, more multifaceted than Lubbock has assumed. The issue of ingenuity that Neil De Marchi and Hans Van Miegroet (this volume) identify as a major element in arguments about economic and aesthetic effect is here examined as part of a microhistory of a particular, and short-lived, manifestation of the arts in London at the moment of publication of Smith's most celebrated work. It is important perhaps to state at the outset that although "heritage" implies permanence, visual culture then as now is largely ephemeral. I suggest that the museum Cox established in the 1770s illuminates an eighteenth-century arts industry located in London, the nature of which needs to be better understood if we are adequately to understand the concept of an alliance between heritage and commerce for the benefit of the nation in which much current economic and cultural discourse is grounded. I therefore initially propose a geneology for the notion of *heritage industry* and then examine how an entrepreneurial craftsman working in the 1760s–80s situated his own product at the interstices of commerce and the arts.

Museum history is usually told as a series of moves in the nineteenth century that transformed the princely collection into a public gallery. In the process, what had been private capital was translated into transcendent worth. England invested heavily in works of art that would nurture its populace free of charge. The indignation in the late 1980s at the campaign by the Saatchis' advertising firm to promote the Victoria and Albert Museum as an Ace Caff (colloquial for fancy cafe) with quite a nice museum attached stemmed from the fact that the jingle ruptured that concept of a neutral space protected from the market that our Victorian ancestors had so successfully promoted. To a Londoner of the 1770s, the implied connection between art and economic interest would have been taken for granted; admission charges were the rule at every show from the Royal Academy to Rackstrow's Museum in Fleet Street, where you could see "a large collection of curiosities preserved in spirits, among which are miscarriages, from the size of a pin's head, to a perfect state."[1] Early one-off displays were succeeded in the second

1. For a contemporary debate on admission charges at the Royal Academy and the distribution of profits, see Pye [1845] 1970. An advertisement for Rackstrow's Museum dated 1783 is in the Guildhall Library, London (*A Collection of Various Extracts* n.d.).

half of the eighteenth century by organized collections, of which there were a very large number; these were promoted as spaces of visual pleasure, wonder and curiosity, learning, nationalism, and commerce (Altick 1978).[2] Value for money and ephemerality of effect were by no means incompatible with worth, and novelty imparted particular quality to any display. London abounded in museums, but for a period from 1772 to 1776 all other exhibitions were eclipsed by Cox's Museum or, the Museum as it was widely termed.[3]

James Cox was a jeweler and toy maker who, from the mid-1760s, produced luxury articles for trade with the Far East (Harcourt-Smith 1933; Chapuis and Droz 1949, 109–14); public interest in the exotic artifacts produced for export is evinced as early as 1766 when the *Gentleman's Magazine* (1766, 36:586) published a description of two curious clocks made by English artists, with moving figures, set with diamonds and rubies, intended as a present from the East India Company to the Emperor of China. The chronology for the Museum has been much disputed. What seems certain is that the opening, planned for spring 1771, was delayed until February 1772. However, Cox had been exhibiting automata since at least 1769, when he put on show, prior to export, a chronoscope ornamented with bulls, storks, dolphins, dragons, and elephants with moving trunks (*Description of a Most Magnificent Piece* 1769). Moreover, while much has been made of the short-lived nature of the Museum (Cox's application to sell the contents in a lottery was passed as a bill in Parliament in May 1773), it is equally evident, first, that there was nothing unusual about museums enjoying a relatively short life span and, second, that Cox continued to exhibit his jeweled automata throughout the run-up to the lottery draw, which took place only on 20 May 1775, and even after it.[4] The sale of Cox's

2. See also Exhibitions of Mechanical Ingenuity, scrapbook assembled by Peckham and now in the British Libraray (1269/h38) upon which Altick draws heavily, and the Guildhall Library, which includes sections on museums and waxworks.

3. See, for example, notice advertising publication of *A Collection of Various Extracts . . .*, the Bodleian Library, Lotteries iv, f. 20.

4. Dorothy Richardson recorded in her journal visiting Cox's Museum and buying a catalog on 14 July 1775 (Dorothy Richardson's Tours, MS, John Rylands University Library of Manchester, Eng.Ms. 1124, f. 170. The writer's library has not been located). Richardson, an antiquarian, is punctilious about the accuracy of the information she records so it is extremely unlikely she is referring here to Weeks's Museum, which succeeded Cox's Museum and displayed some of Cox's pieces.

automata spawned a number of other shows that continued well into the nineteenth century; particularly noteworthy are the show opened by John Joseph Merlin (who had worked for Cox) (French 1985, 13) and Weeks's Museum in Tichborne Street, valued at £400,000 in 1819 when its contents were still described as "prepared for the Chinese market" (Rush 1845, 35; Altick 1978, chap. 25).

Cox's Museum immediately attracted visitors, including James Boswell, who went on Johnson's advice (Boswell 1960, 99). While Fanny Burney's ([1778] 1968, 76–77) Evelina thought Cox's Museum "very astonishing, and very superb," it nonetheless afforded her little pleasure "for it is mere show, though a wonderful one." As the visitors, including the vulgar francophile Madame Duval and the equally obnoxious and xenophobic Captain, engage in a vigorous debate about utility ("will you tell me the use of all this? for I'm not enough of a conjurer to find out"), their attention is attracted by a pineapple "which suddenly opening, discovered a nest of birds, who immediately began to sing" (76–77; see also *Divine Predictions of Daniel and St. John* 1774; this must surely be a spoof). If Burney used Cox's Museum to point up the debate between ingenuity and utility, William Mason in his "Epistle to Dr. Shebbeare" (quoted at the opening of my essay; Toynbee 1928, 112) turns the Museum into a model of corrupt centralized government, a "puppet-play" against which "Old England's genius turns with scorn away." Walpole (1955, 325) admired these verses as immortal and thought that they were far more brilliant and would last much longer than the Museum they described. If Cox's Museum was opened in reaction to a commercial crisis, it is clear that it struck a chord with educated citizens and readily became a seductive metaphor and a compelling stage for debating the troublesome issues of political and economic stability.

Cox's specialty, as I have indicated, was large and elaborate clocks incorporating gold surface detail and ornamented with genuine and paste jewels which he successfully exported to China and India (Pagani 1993, 1995; Le Corbeiller 1960, 1970).[5] The chariot, pushed by a Chinese man, with a seated woman and a clock, made by Cox, and now in the Metropolitan Museum, New York (1982.60.137) (figure 1) contains

5. The most comprehensive account of the trade with China to which Cox was a contributory is in Pagani 1993. There is no equivalent study for India, but a considerable amount of useful information on Anglo-Indian trade in this period is in Jaffer 1995.

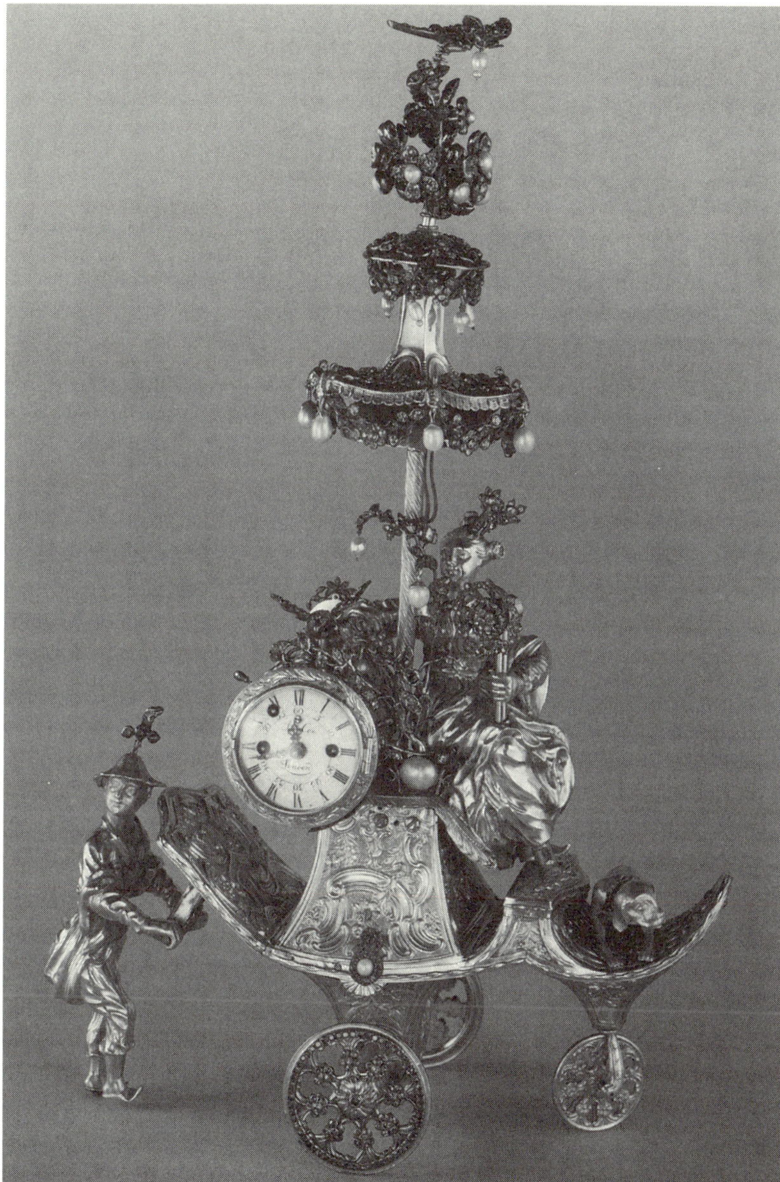

Figure 1 James Cox, automaton in the form of a chariot pushed by a Chinese attendant and set with a clock: gold, brilliants, and paste jewels, 25.4 cm high. The Metropolitan Museum of Art, New York. The Jack and Belle Linsky Collection (1982.60.137).

gold over a base and real pearls as well as glass stones. The larger automata clocks of the type made by Cox, one of which was sold in 1996 by Aspreys, seem to consist entirely of paste jewels. Cox himself claims in his various descriptions that he uses real jewels, and that is certainly borne out by the sums raised when they were sold. The diamond earrings that formed the pièce de résistance of the lottery (figure 2) were evidently authentic, and Cox (*Descriptive Inventory* 1773) offered to buy them back from the winner for £5,000, stating that "the drops were several years matching, even at a time when the diamonds of Golconda poured in upon us more abundantly than they ever did, or probably ever will again." The diamonds, Cox states, are "incomparably fellowed, as if cut from one divided stone; they are of the first, and purest crystaline water, of the finest form, the nicest proportion, and the most beautiful lustre."

Little is known of Cox's exports to India, but something of the complexity of his business can be gleaned from an announcement of 19 April 1774 in which Cox tells his creditors that his attorneys in Calcutta have succeeded in getting payment from a number of creditors to the tune of £20,000, which, once his debts in Bengal have been paid, will permit him to discharge some of his debts at home (JJC Lotteries iv, f. 25). The moment that is of interest for this essay occurred in 1772 when Cox was apparently unable to sell a valuable consignment overseas. Le Corbeiller (1970, 352) identifies the opening of the Museum with a report in *St. James's Chronicle* (27–29 August 1772) of a shipment of English toys that had been refused in China and had returned. Cox, however, claimed that he had fitted up the Museum to allow the public the opportunity of seeing his pieces "before they are consigned abroad" ("An Account of Mr. Cox's Intended Exhibition" 1772). He decided to hire a domed room in Spring Gardens; carpet it throughout, including the stairs; decorate it with emblematic paintings representing the Liberal Arts "in chiaroscuro" by "a celebrated artist"; centrally heat it, and situate there his jeweled automata concealed under crimson curtains which were raised on mechanically operated pulleys at the moment of display. Portraits of George III and Queen Charlotte were commissioned from the first-rank artist, Johann Zoffany, an entry ticket (figure 3) was designed by Biaggio Rebecca and engraved by Francesco Bartolozzi, both of whom signed it (*Descriptive Cata-*

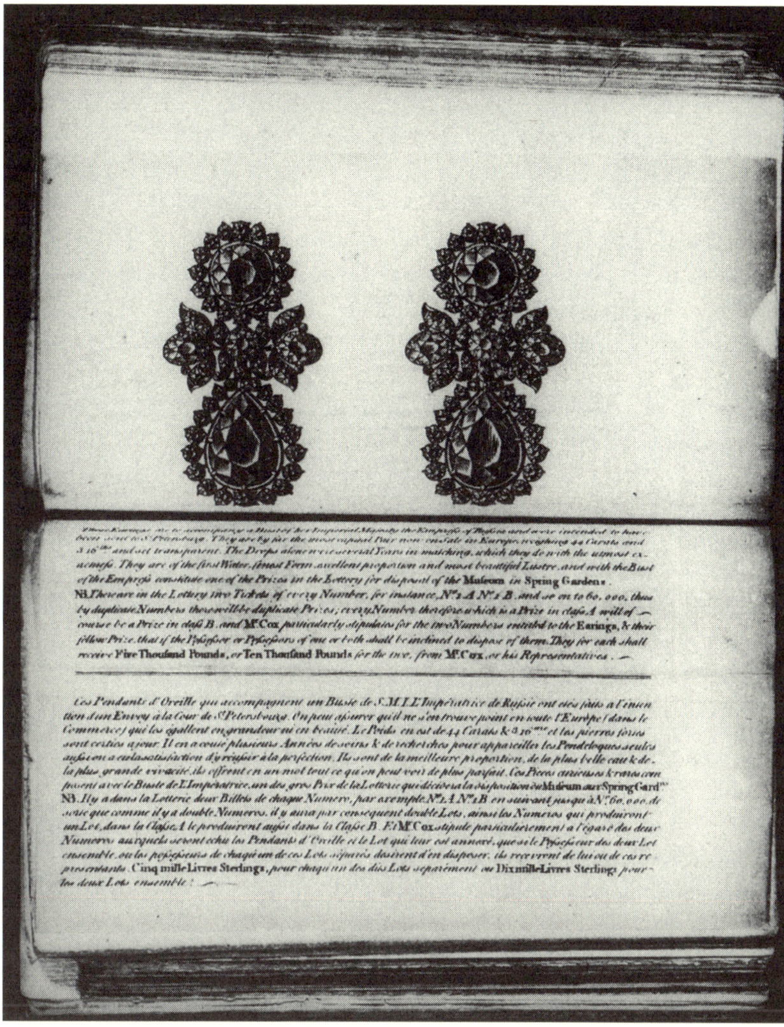

Figure 2 Engraved frontispiece to *A Descriptive Inventory . . .*, 1774, showing brilliant diamonds offered as prize in James Cox's lottery of his museum. Reprinted by permission of the British Library (T.447 [4]) (anonymous).

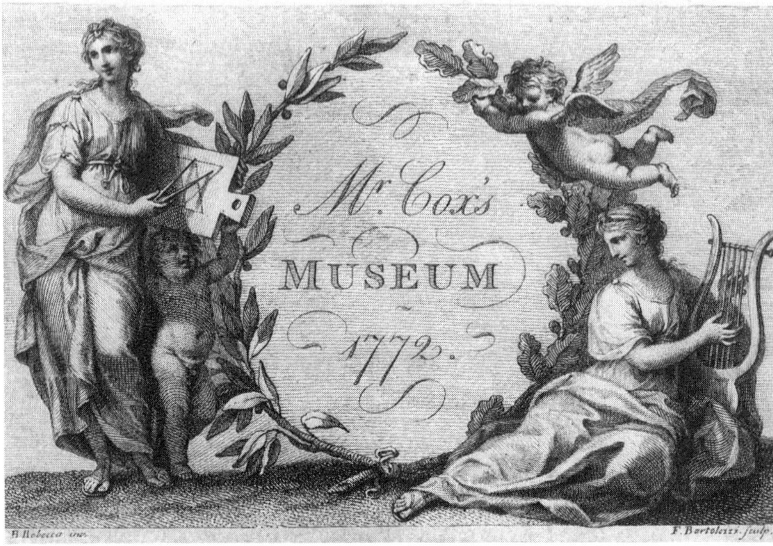

Figure 3 Francesco Bartolozzi after Biaggio Rebecca, trade card for Mr. Cox's museum, 1772, John Johnson Collection, Bodleian Library, Oxford, Lotteries iv.

logue 1772).[6] By hiring rooms that had been regularly used for the exhibition of paintings (the Society of Artists exhibited there) and by publishing a series of descriptive catalogs including one with a grand frontispiece dedicated to George III,[7] and a French translation,[8] Cox insisted on occupying the high cultural ground. The best-known sur-

6. Cox had placed an annoucement in the press in June 1771 declaring his intention to open the Museum and apologizing for the delay which, it is alleged, is due partly to the Incorporated Society of Artists' occupation of the rooms for their exhibition, and partly to delay in delivery of Zoffany's portraits "on ovals of copper, half length, size of life" (JJC Lotteries iv, f. 16).

7. This is mentioned in an unattributed newscutting ("in quarto upon a large royal gilt paper" as presented to their majesties with a portrait of the king engraved by Sherwin) in JJC Lotteries iv, f. 25.

8. This is announced in 1772 (cutting in JJC Lotteries iv, f. 18), but there is no edition in French in the British Library, though the frontispiece to *A Descriptive Inventory* . . . (1774) carries a French translation. Cox mentioned the French a great deal in his public communications and saw them both as commercial competitors and as potential visitors. He was arguably matching Boydell's double-language usage in the letterpress of prints. The "Frenchness" of Cox's Museum is an issue also in the discussion recorded in *Evelina* (Burney [1778] 1968).

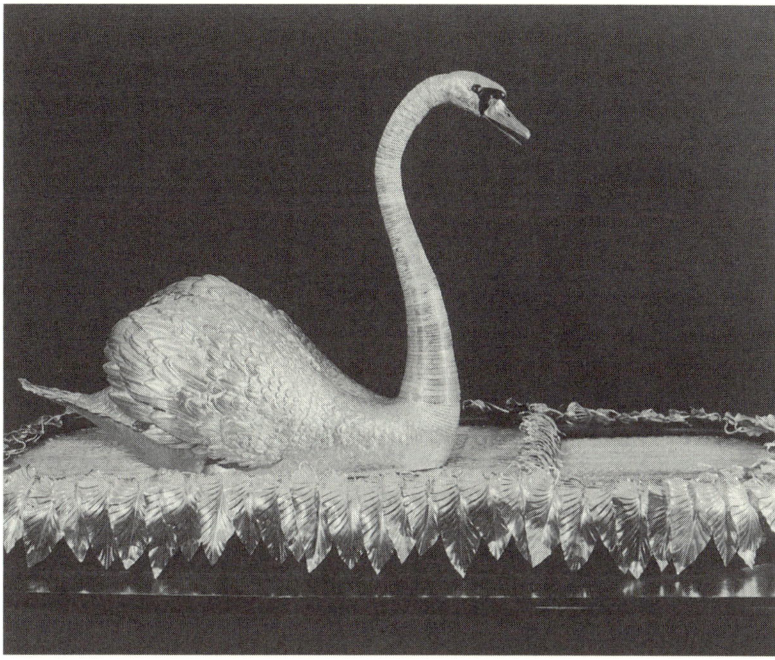

Figure 4 James Cox, life size silver swan automaton, 1773. The Bowes Museum, Barnard Castle, County Durham.

vival of Cox's Museum is the silver swan (figure 4), now in the Bowes Museum at Barnard Castle, which, albeit without its original stand, remains in good working order and performs daily at 3:00 P.M., when visitors can see it raise its elegant neck, turn its head, and (implausibly) pick up small fishes from the rotating glass rods that simulate flowing water.[9]

The Museum was illuminated by candles in candelabra and girandoles suspended from dragons' mouths, and Cox engaged "proper persons to exhibit and explain to foreigners and natives what each piece performs both of mechanism and music" (Newscutting 7 June 1772, JJC Lotteries iv, f. 18). Admission was half a guinea, which, according

9. An excellent account of the subsequent history of this piece, its popular appeal, and its museum status is in Kane 1996–97. A technical account is given in Camerer Cuss 1965. There is also a peacock attributed to Cox which belonged to the Empress Catherine of Russia and is now in the Hermitage Museum, St. Petersburg.

to a letter (probably written by Cox himself) in the *Public Ledger* (17 March 1772) was the same as entry to the Pantheon, to Fischer's benefit concerts,[10] and "to hear Signiora [*sic*] Sirmen sing" (*Collection of Various Extracts* n.d.). Nonetheless, Cox reduced the admission price by half at certain hours in July 1772 (*Collection of Various Extracts* n.d.) and, at the same time, made special arrangements to open at 8:00 P.M. for people going to masked balls at Haymarket (Newscutting JJC Lotteries iv, f. 20), and offered a select exhibition at 9:00 P.M. "by desire of Noble families and Persons of Distinction" (*St. James's Chronicle* 27–29 August 1772). Cox's Museum has been treated somewhat dismissively by scholars.[11] Although it did not survive the century, the Museum's celebrity, as well as its owner's disposition as a disseminator of advertising copy, generated a large amount of documentation. Within the context of eighteenth-century commerce and letters where "puffs" abound, hyperbolic declarations of the kind Cox indulged in were par for the course, and we should appreciate the possibilities opened up by this rich archive for an understanding of the cultural and economic dynamic of a characteristically commercial museum.

To sum up so far, we can draw a number of general conclusions. First, people expected to pay for museums and charges were graduated to allow for different audiences; like Wedgwood (McKendrick, Brewer, and Plumb 1982; Baker 1995), Cox deliberately offered a product considered to be expensive and was evidently targeting a cosmopolitan audience. One of the eulogistic press articles (from a Lover of Merit, and Well-wisher to Trade and Commerce) claiming to have "seen most of the foreign cabinets and splendid apartments of different Princes in Europe" found that none could compare with the Museum (Letter to the *London Evening Post* 29 February 1772, repr. in *Collection of Various Extracts* n.d.). If we assume this originated with Cox, it would be an interesting indication of his determination to situate his Museum in the great courtly Kunstkammer tradition, while transforming an elite art form into a demotic spectacle, open to all who could pay for their

10. Fischer was Thomas Gainsborough's son-in-law; see *Gainsborough and His Musical Friends* 1977.

11. French, Le Corbeiller, and Pagani all seem driven by a notion of craftsmanship that is independent of the market and which is concerned chiefly to establish great geniuses; they are thus somewhat negative toward Cox's venture.

entertainment. Second, the kinds of categories into which historians have seen fit to organize cultural material from this period have privileged painting over those visual media that had the greatest impact on metropolitan audiences. The exhibitions of the Royal Society of Arts, the Royal Academy, and the Incorporated Society of Artists should, therefore, be recontextualized; Cox takes pains to situate his Museum as one further manifestation of "the gradual encreased [*sic*] of taste and elegance, within these last twenty years, in this metropolis" (ibid.).

Third, the kind of careful and planned exploitation of the commercial potential of visual curiosity—a term associated in the eighteenth century with the quest for totality, as compared with the cult of the amateur that was identified with the theme of laudable desire (Pomian 1990, 53–64; Benedict 1990)—that was an ingredient of Wedgwood's and Boydell's success was found in the display of other kinds of goods; commerce, trade, and the Museum are demonstrably overlapping in ways that should make us rethink current orthodoxies about the relationship between nineteenth-century department stores and exhibitions as originary moments, as argued by recent writers (Richards 1991; Bennett 1995). Museums capitalized on actualities: Cox turned his unsalable cargo into a Museum: Wedgwood exhibited the Frog Service prior to delivering it to Empress Catherine (Baker) and thereby helped to offset the huge deficit incurred by the manufacture of such a labor-intensive production, just as Reynolds made sure he exhibited *The Infant Hercules*, commissioned by the Empress, at the Royal Academy in 1788 (cat. no. 167) before having it shipped to St. Petersburg (Penny 1986, cat. no. 140).[12] Boydell similarly cashed in on the fashion for Shakespeariana following the tercentenary celebrations when he cre-

12. For example, at "the elegant exhibition adjoining Somerset House, in the Strand (consisting of Automaton Figures which move in a great variety of descriptions, by clockwork, with the Diamond Beetle . . . [and] some of the most beautiful and striking Pencil and Chalk Drawings . . . by Mr. Lawrence [i.e., Thomas Lawrence] (1788)" (Whitley 1928, 2:104); at Mrs. Palin's Wax Work of "the Grand Canoverian Cabinet," including George IV, the Emperor of Russia, and "a most beautiful representation of the late Princess Charlotte and her Infant lying in state" (suggesting a date of 1817), Temple Bar, Fleet Street, admission 1 shilling, children six pence; at the Royal Wax Work, 67 Fleet Street with HM George IV, Napoleon in death, and some fine cabinets of French and Roman busts; and at the Waterloo Exhibition, 1 St. James's Street, Pall Mall, 1815, including clothes, swords, equipages, Empress Maria Louisa's wardrobe, knapsacks, and collections of caricatures published in Paris since Napoleon's abdication (JJC Waxworks, III).

ated his potentially lucrative Shakespeare Gallery (Pape and Burwick 1996).[13]

Fourth, in these museums, manufacture was foregrounded; these are the forerunners of the Musée d'Arts et de Metiers founded in Paris in the 1790s and the Victoria and Albert Museum initiated in 1851. Thus, for example, Cox's chronoscope (defined by the *Oxford English Dictionary* as "an instrument for observing and measuring time") was raised on an ornamented pedestal on casters "of a peculiar construction, not affected by the weight they support" that permitted the level to be corrected. The whole thing included four bulls supporting a table; dolphins, dragons, and storks; mathematical instruments to reveal when it was elevated to a perfect level; and an elephant with a moving trunk and a tartar guiding the elephant from a gallery on its back. It also incorporated a seven-day clock. Moreover, the mechanism for the clock was "so contrived, that the motion and running of the wheels, which is extremely curious, may be seen through the transparency of the dial." The *Description of a Most Magnificent Piece* (1769) makes a point of drawing attention to features of construction. Thus, we are told that "the various holes to introduce the keys for winding up the clock-work, music part, and mechanism, are all hid by ornaments formed for that purpose: other ornaments are also contrived to shift the tunes, make the music play for a short time or perpetual: likewise to make the elephant go round or move his trunk at pleasure." This is precisely the kind of beauty in contrivance and ingenuity, pleasure in facility, about which Adam Smith ([1759] 1976) wrote in his *Theory of Moral Sentiments* and which lies at the heart of the analysis of De Marchi and Van Miegroet in this volume.

At Cox's Museum, visitors were invited not only to marvel at the illusionism of swans gliding over water and pagodas rising of their own volition but also to meditate on the costs involved in the production of these automata and on the contribution of such curious inventions to the national economy. In the case of the chronoscope, for instance, we are told that "besides the great weight of gold employed in various parts . . . there are near one hundred thousand stones set in ornaments

13. Shakespeare also featured in Cox's Museum: The *Descriptive Inventory* of 1774 lists as "piece the twenty-ninth," a musical chime on top of which is an octagon temple standing on a quadrangular ground, at the corners of which are four gilt pineapples. "The dome of the Temple is blue and gold, terminating with a gilt vase; within the temple is a moving procession of the various characters of Shakespeare's Jubilee."

and embellishments of it, including diamonds, rubies, emerald, precious stones, and pearls"; Cox also refers to "stones of a ruby colour" (*Description of a Most Magnificent Piece* 1769). Economic value is therefore tied to visual effect that is part authentic and part illusion. The commercial worth of each individual object (its export value) generated problems of conservation and maintenance, but it was this notion of visible value that was a key element in what was being marketed and consumed. In the same spirit, Adam Smith, who was in London from 1773 through 1777 (Ross 1995, chap. 15), lays great stress on "the appearance of expence" when discussing the imitative arts: "As the idea of expence seems often to embellish, so that of cheapness seems as frequently to tarnish the lustre even of very agreeable objects" (Smith 1980, 182–83). Accordingly, Cox tells his prospective audiences of the "very different circumstances that distinguish this from every other exhibition . . . the prodigious charge at which this entertainment has been prepared . . . the necessity, from the nature of the undertaking, of admitting but a limited number of spectators at one time, and the expensive attendance requisite on each exhibition" (*Public Advertiser*, 9 March 1772, repr. in *Collection of Various Extracts* n.d.; repeated as a postscript to *Descriptive Catalogue of the Several . . . Pieces* 1772).

All this demonstrates what it means to move from the water- and air-driven mechanisms of the sixteenth century, and the aristocratic cabinets of the seventeenth, to the highly refined mechanical repertoire of the eighteenth century (see Benhamou 1987), and from that academic milieu to the public exhibition. In 1621, for example, we know that Rudolf II's Kunstkammer in Prague comprised a long table "covered with globes, clocks, mechanical devices, caskets, mirrors, musical instruments . . . , silver vases with flowers of coloured silver" and a mechanized device "in the form of a peacock, which walked, turned around and fanned its tail of real feathers" (Bukovinská 1997, 203). The interest in imitating nature reached its apogee with M. Vaucanson, whose artificial duck could be seen "eating, drinking, macerating the Food, and voiding Excrements; pluming her Wings, picking her Feathers, and performing several operations in Imitation of a living Duck" in London in 1742, along with his marvelous flute player (*Account of the Mechanism of an Automaton* 1742, title). Cox's Museum united Vaucanson's animation with the German tradition for *artificialiae* associated with the Augsburg goldsmiths and was exemplified by the spectacular work of the Dinglinger family (von Watzdorf 1962). The objects col-

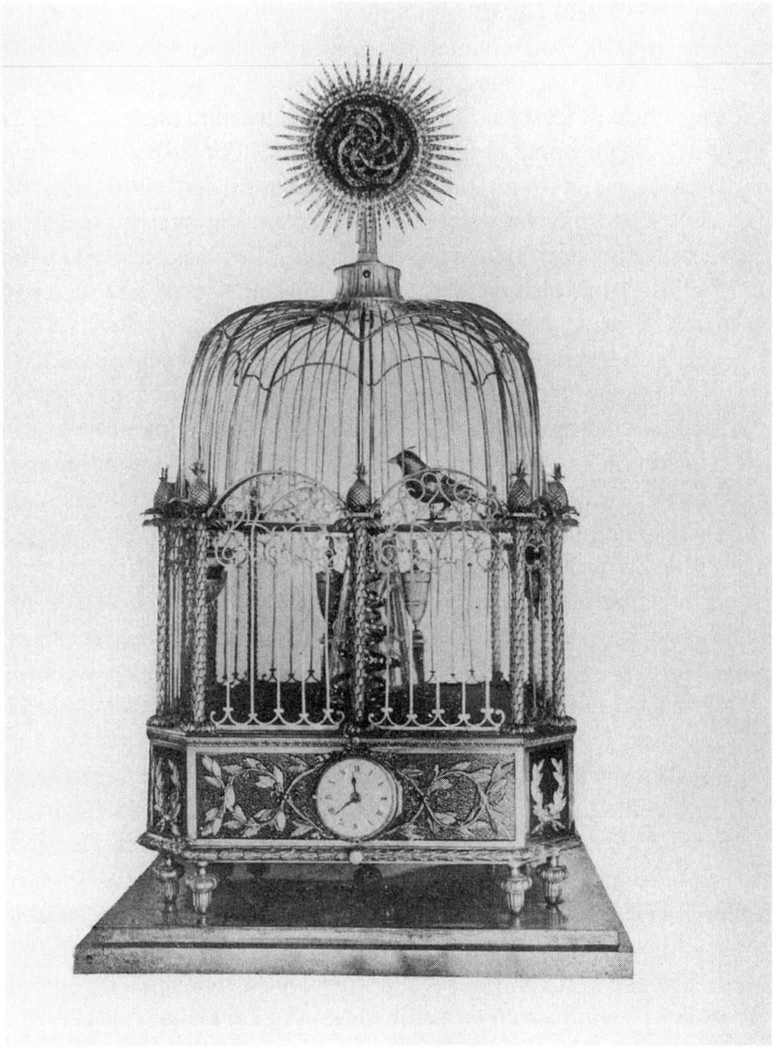

Figure 5 James Cox, mechanical bronze gilt automaton clock, c. 85 cm high, Imperial Museum, Peking, Harcourt-Smith, plate XVI. Reprinted by permission of the British Library (7802.pp.10).

lected in the Grünes Gewölb in Dresden are distinguished for their precious materials and their miniaturization as well as for their potential for movement.[14] Cox, on the other hand, created very large pieces in which movement was at least as important as craftsmanship (figure 5). He had no hesitation in combining precious and semiprecious stones with glass—thus exemplifying the notion found in Adam Smith's work that the value of an artifact resides in the contrivance rather than in the cost of the materials used (De Marchi and Van Miegroet, this volume)—and strove to control audience response through sound and a variety of theatrical devices.

Vaucanson insists that he is less interested in public applause than in the recognition of the august members of the Académie Royale that his extraordinary automata are "raised on the solid Principles of Mechanicks," which he had taken from them (*Account of the Mechanism of an Automaton* 1742, 3). The work of Vaucanson and other French *méchaniciens* continued to appear in London. In May 1766, for example, the "Sieur Comus having performed many surprising feats by means of an artificial mermaid" went on to show an artificial swan. The *Gentleman's Magazine* (1766, 36:207) gave a graphic account of this and supplied a fold-out plate that may well be the source for Cox's silver swan that first appears in *A Descriptive Inventory* of 1773 and was probably made, therefore, late in 1772 when Cox was enhancing his Museum. Cox follows Vaucanson's example in producing a very detailed and carefully modulated prose description of each piece and how it works, a description in marked contrast to the hyperbole of the press reactions. But Cox is distinctly interested in public applause, and he presents his work within a complex economic discourse; with Cox, the uniqueness and exclusivity of the Kunstkammer and the technical demonstration of Enlightenment savants are transformed into a commercially oriented spectacle, which time and again invokes the capacity of discourse to engender a popular cultural memory and to provide a common point of reference (figure 6). Thus, when Sheridan's *Rivals* was first performed in London in 1775, the entire audience would have understood that when Sir Anthony Absolute spoke of a lady "as ugly as I choose . . . [whose] one eye shall roll like the bull's in Cox's Museum" (Apperson

14. Cox's work is more similar to the ornamented jeweled clocks made by J. H. Köhler of Dresden, examples of which can be seen in the Semper Galerie.

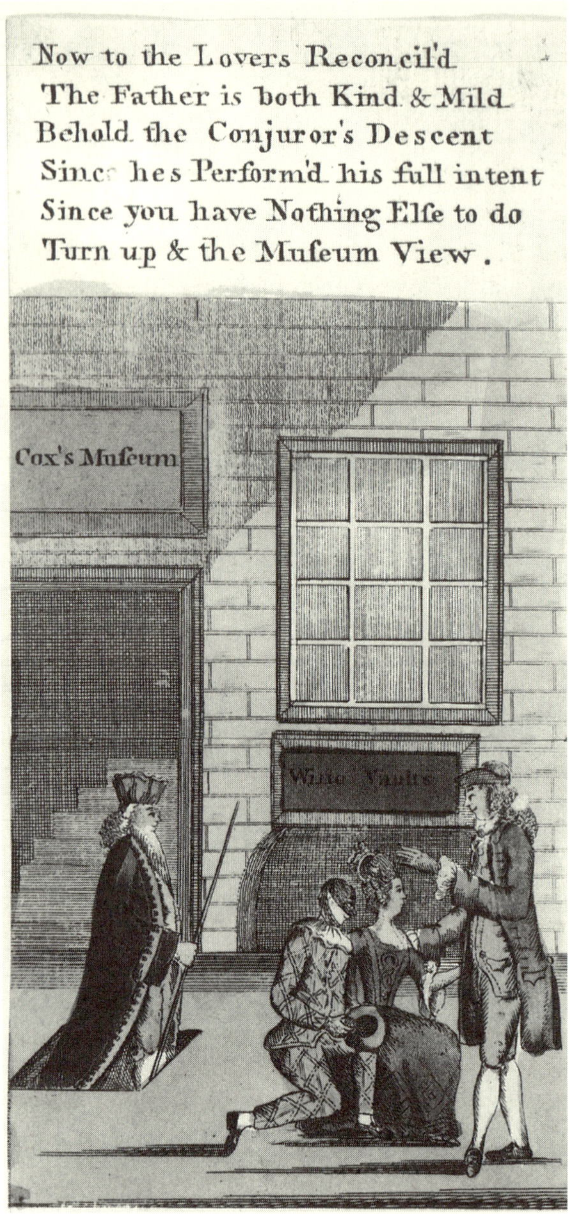

Figure 6 Engraved theatrical illustration featuring James Cox's museum, c. 1773. John Johnson Collection, Bodleian Library, Oxford, Lotteries iv (anonymous).

1899, 276), he was referring to Cox's "richly caparaisoned bulls" (*Descriptive Inventory* 1774, no. 9).

Historians value longevity of craftsmen and companies: it makes provenances easier to establish, and lineages via the apprenticeship system enable the charting of stylistic change. It is not surprising, however, that Cox's flamboyant, high-risk activities in the jewelery trade, culminating in his bankruptcy in 1778 (*Gentleman's Magazine* 1778, 48:552) have been greeted with some distaste. I wish to propose that, quite apart from the interest of the objects he displayed, the discourses surrounding Cox's Museum provide a unique resource for examining art in relation to economics. I shall focus on labor and Orientalism. First the question of labor. In the press Cox repeatedly claimed to have brought employment to a large number of workers in various trades. "While forming this splendid assemblage of mechanical rarities," he says of himself, "he has found means to make the labour and industry of so great a number of the most ingenious artists concur to its perfection. The painter, the Goldsmith, the Jeweller, the Lapidary, the Sculptor, the Watchmaker; in short almost all the liberal arts have found employ in it" (*Collection of Various Extracts* n.d.).

Cox was never a member of the goldsmith's guild and did not use a personal mark; it is therefore virtually certain that he subcontracted (Le Corbeiller 1970, 356). As Helen Clifford (1998) remarks, he was, perhaps, the nearest London equivalent to a *marchand mercier*. Accordingly, it may have been with justification that he claimed to have "given bread to many hundreds of our most eminent workmen in the jewellery business" (Letter from Candour to the *Public Ledger* 17 March 1772, repr. in *Collection of Various Extracts* n.d.). The most bombastic statement occurs in a letter from Mercartor to the *Public Ledger* on 11 April 1772 (repr. in *Collection of Various Extracts* n.d.). Here Cox offers himself as an example of the ingenious manufacturer who contributes to the greatness of the nation by extending its foreign commerce: "Whether I view it in a commercial light, or merely as works of art; whether I consider the magnitude and expence [*sic*] of the undertaking, or the spirit and genius of the proprietor, I am filled with pleasure and admiration," declares Mercartor. By uniting the West's mechanical skill with the imagination of the "Asiatics," continues the correspondent, Cox has "absolutely struck out a new and important field of commerce, beneficial to himself and his country." I will return to the question of the Asiatic imagination shortly. For the moment, let us notice how this argument develops, for Cox's chief merit, it is proposed, is not his abilities as an artist or a merchant, but his foresight in exporting "the superfluities we received from other countries, worked up by our artisans." This is probably a reference to the import of escapement mechanisms for Cox's automata from Jaquet-Droz and Leschot in Neuchâtel (Le Corbeiller 1970, 355–56; Chapuis and Jaquet 1956, chap. 6). This assertion makes possible the claim that Cox "exports, in short, the *labour* of our people": "The Emperor of China support(s) some hundreds of mechanicks in the parish of St. Brides; the Nabob of the Carnatic, and our friend Shujah Dowla, have considerably improved several branches of art among us; they do at this moment give bread to many of our industrious tradesmen; and even our dreaded neighbours, the Marrattoes, this dealer in magic [James Cox] has more than once laid under contribution" (Letter from Mercartor to the *Public Ledger* 11 April 1772, repr. in *Collection of Various Extracts* n.d.).

Claiming that Cox sells his wares from the Gulf of Persia to the remotest areas of China, and northward among the Tartar nations "who have received from his performances the first idea of the excellence of European art," the writer continues: "The inhabitants of the Eastern world want neither our food nor our clothing, and they do not relish our luxuries; but their productions have always been eagerly sought by us, and therefore the wealth of Europe has for a long succession of ages, rolled to that quarter, and centred there. We see at length a channel opened by which we may bring back a part of ourselves: a channel more flattering than even the supply of necessaries would be, because more unlimitted [*sic*]." The nation would, asserts the writer, be much better off if, instead of "having our mercantile coffee houses filled with men who prey on the ignorance and credulity of others, we should see them striving to emulate each other in profiting by the labour of our people, and the extension of our manufactures." Though Cox's profits have been "much larger than fall to the lot of many," we are told, he has not built palaces or given in to fashionable dissipations. Rather, he "contents himself with giving ease to the indigent mechanic, and with bringing the ingenious from obscurity." Cox here presents himself, in contrast to financial speculators who sit around in coffeehouses, as a proponent of enlightened mercantilism, concerned about the nation's balance of payments, and engaging in arguments familiar from Thomas Mun's *England's Treasure by Forraign Trade* (1664) and developed in book 4 of Smith's *Wealth of Nations*.

It is difficult, of course, to establish Cox's investment, his turnover, or his payroll and even more difficult to discover the overall value of the export trade with which he was concerned. In 1793 Lord Macartney calculated that the collection of English clocks and watches, many by English makers, kept by the Chinese emperors at Jehol was worth £2 million (Macartney 1962, 261, quoted in Pagani 1993, 147). The diamond earrings that, along with a bust of the empress of Russia by Nollekens, were a lottery prize in 1774 when Cox tried to dispose of the Museum and recoup his losses (see figure 2), were valued at £5,000, while the total prize money was calculated at £197,500.[15] Some comparison of these costs can be made if we note that, for example, in 1772 the jeweler Charles Belliard charged Sir John Delaval £70 10s. for 154 small rose diamonds and £21 for setting them into three bows.[16] What cannot be in doubt is that Cox was dealing in very large investments. In 1774 he announced to his creditors that he had succeeded in paying off £20,000 of debts and that the capital sum of over £60,000 remained. That these sums had been raised in India as a result of payment by several princes for large purchases from Cox in 1771 and 1772 is valuable evidence, not only of the sums involved but also of Cox's mercantile activities on that continent.[17]

Cox's claim to have employed many hundreds is probably an exaggeration, though he must have been instrumental in bringing employment to a very large range of people: clerks, attendants, textile and glass manufacturers, and printers, as well as individuals employed in all the different branches of goldsmithing and jewelry. It is striking, first, that Cox conceptualized the labor force in terms of Adam Smith's economic model for productive labor, asserting that he reinvested cap-

15. Nollekens returned from Rome in December 1770 and seems to have accepted commissions for decorative objects; Cox had allegedly made the peacock clock, which was bought by the Empress Catherine and is now in the Hermitage. John Kenworthy Brown is of the view that the Nollekens bust (which would most probably have been in plaster rather than marble and would have been based on an existing portrait) was made as a bonus for whoever purchased the clock. There is a reference to the bust in J. T. Smith's list of Nollekens's busts. I am grateful to John Kenworthy Brown for this information (personal communication 22 March 1996). Details of the insurance costs and the prize money are given in JJC Lotteries, ff. 9 and 10, and in the *Descriptive Inventory* of 1774, vii–x.

16. Invoice dated 19 January 1772, paid 18 March 1772, Delaval MS. Northumberland County Record Office, 2DE/31/10/20(b).

17. Le Corbeiller (1970, 355) has established that John Henry Cox is first cited in East India Company records as a private merchant in Canton in 1781.

ital in labor and, second, that he insists on the utility of his exhibition of arts. Indeed, Cox asserts, in his 1774 *Descriptive Inventory*, that the arts "furnish employment for thousands" and "keep immense sums at home, which the oppulent would otherwise send abroad for works of splendour or ingenuity; and they even bring in immense sums from other kingdoms." Therefore, Cox declares, the arts should "be weighed in the scale of utility, as well as in the balance of ornament," a theme taken up, as we have seen, in the visit to the Museum described in Burney's *Evelina*. In short, states Cox, "to philosophize and rail against the arts, as luxuries, is to lay a general axe to the root of all Art and Science," for, he continues predictably, "the luxuries of the rich are the chief forces of employment for the poor, and the revenues of the State are collected in a great measure from the luxuries of the whole community" (iv). Thus Cox, inflecting the case for luxury familiar from Mandeville, points out that "it has . . . been repeatedly observ'd of Mr. Cox's labours, that though they are wonders of ingenuity and splendour, they were nevertheless of no real *use*"; on the contrary, "surely they were of great utility, if they brought half a million into the kingdom" (vi).

The second area I wish to explore is that of Orientalism. It is generally agreed that the artifacts that made up Cox's Museum had been intended for the Eastern market. The 1772 *Descriptive Catalogue of Several Pieces* describes one of its exhibits, a chronoscope, as fellow to a similarly "stupendous piece sent in 1769 on board the Triton Indiaman to Canton and now in the palace of the Emperor of China." The latter is clearly the chronoscope "of a peculiar construction" and covered in ornaments that I have already described and that was exhibited on its own in 1769 (*Description of a Most Magnificent Piece* 1769). As the chronoscope exhibited in 1772—remaining in the Museum throughout, though changing its place from number one to number forty-six (*Descriptive Inventory* 1774, 36, 46th piece)—was stated to be signed and inscribed with the date 1772, it seems likely not to have been a "fellow" of that which was exported but a replica produced for exhibition later. Despite the difficulty of establishing whether any of the pieces in Cox's Museum were actually made for export rather than for display in London, it is well established that there were problems for European manufacturers caused by the glut of "sing songs" being exported to China in the 1760s (Chapuis and Droz 1949, 110–14; Le Corbeiller

1970, 355; Pagani 1993, 208).[18] What interests me is how Cox turned this to account. Financially his gamble failed, but his Museum had to be packaged, and I suggest it is to that packaging that we should turn our attention. By contrast with a view of Cox's enterprise as an opportunistic endeavor by a somewhat unprincipled showman to make the best of an economic downturn, my concern is to suggest how explanations based on economic determinants might be enhanced--nuanced or inflected—by recognition of the significant interpretative and shaping role of language. In displaying his artifacts, many of which were evidently made expressly for the Museum,[19] Cox was self-consciously selling an idea of the "other." Of course, goods from the East were nothing new in eighteenth-century England, nor was the notion of China as a foil to discussions about England's economy. It is interesting to note that Adam Smith ([1776] 1976 I (viii): 24–26; (ix): 15) raises the question of why, given its natural advantage, China has stagnated in income per head instead of having grown. The notion of China as a foil to the energy of Western commerce was a trope that long remained effective; Dickens exploits it in 1851 when writing about the Great Exhibition of 1851 (356–60).

The objects that Cox sought to export to the Far East were part of a trade in luxury goods that had developed in the wake of Jesuit missions from the late sixteenth century and diplomatic visits with their accompanying elaborate gift rituals. Especially favored were clocks and watches, not for telling the time, but as status symbols (Pagani 1993, 13–18, 156, 351). The artifacts made by Cox were dominated by the motifs of Chinoiserie—in other words, they reproduced Western stereotypes of Chinese cultural identity—pagodas, mandarins, chiming bells, and dragons. For the Chinese consumer, however, as Pagani points out, these artifacts were attractive because they appeared representative of European taste. Clocks made in China were different. Cox's gambits to attract visitors to his Museum characteristically stage some of the

18. Pagani (1993) indicates that Geneva was proving more successful in exporting automata than London (208) and also that Jaquet-Droz was exporting to James Cox and Son's outlet in Canton from 1783 (215).

19. The 1773 *Descriptive Inventory* contained thirty-six new items out of a total of fifty-six pieces, including the swan and a Vaucanson-like flute player; it has generally been assumed, therefore, that Cox made these specially for the Museum, if not for the lottery. The 1774 edition is identical to the 1773 edition and appears to be a reprinting by the same publisher rather than a new edition.

rhetorical maneuvers that exemplify Orientalist discourse. On the one hand, we are invited to view a national art that will unsettle the popular view that the French are superior in taste and design—and consequently benefit the balance of trade. On the other, Cox offers the public in 1772 a glimpse of specimens such as those that now adorn the palaces of the king of Delhi and the princes of the Decan "before they are consigned abroad" (Account of Mr. Cox's Intended Exhibition, *British Magazine* January 1772, repr. in *Collection of Various Extracts* n.d.).[20] Cox's advertisement proposes that the Museum provides an opportunity for considering "the difference between the European and Asiatic tastes." Collapsing into one synthetic notion of the exotic "other" the Chinese and Indian markets in which he trades, Cox claims that his work unites "the exquisite Mechanism of the West" with Asiatic conceptions that are "warmer," less restrained, and less correct than ours (Letter from Mercartor to the *Public Ledger* 11 April 1772, repr. in *Collection of Various Extracts* n.d.).

The question of whether Cox's articles were on their way to China or to India; whether they had been dispatched, failed to sell, and been returned; or whether they were made specifically to be shown in London as a capital means of raising cash is, ultimately, not the point.[21] What is historically and textually significant about Cox's Museum as an episode in eighteenth-century English economic and cultural history is the way in which it constructs an environment that vividly produces a walkabout experience of the Oriental (what one text calls "fairyland")[22] framed within a nationalist economic discourse and re-presented in relays of discursive explanation and justification across the whole

20. As he later added pieces to the Museum, he may actually have intended the advertised items for export.

21. Harcourt-Smith (1933, introduction) states that Cox's exhibits had been delivered to China and returned. This may be unreliable since he also dates an automaton clock (no. xvi) to 1783, five years after Cox's bankruptcy (though the signature could possibly be that of his son). Phillips on 5 July 1808, following Cox's death, sold a collection that it advertised as "Valuable Mechanical Museum, Jewels, &c. from China" (cutting, JJC Lotteries iv, f. 28); in his advertisement for the lottery of his Museum, Cox stated that he intended to give "a constant edge to public curiosity" by gradually making sales to the Eastern markets, so that "the pieces thus sold will amply pay for the introduction of new articles" (JJC Lotteries iv, f. 8); Le Corbeiller (1970, 352) cites a report in the *St. James's Chronicle* in 1772 to the effect that a shipment of English toys and jewelry had been refused at China and turned back.

22. "Enclos'd is your passport, take Bell in your hand, / And feast on the wonders of this FAIRYLAND!" (Verses to a Lady, enclosing a Ticket for Cox's Museum, *Public Ledger* 3 March 1772, repr. in *Collection of Various Extracts* n.d.).

range of the London press. The sumptuously ornamental automata stand not only for the idea of the bottomless wealth of the East, which the commercial successes of the East India Company might be expected to continue to tap, but also for the brilliant technological skill of English jewelers or, as Cox prefers to call himself, artists. The uncertainties hanging over the chronology (are they on their way as exports? or have they been returned?) are necessary elements in the construction of an environment redolent of travel, alien visual experience, and what these things traditionally generated—that is, curiosity and awe. Cox's decision to join the period fashion for lotteries appears to have been governed at an economic level by necessity. But it was also, I suggest, an appropriate cultural culmination to his enterprise. His need to recoup his losses was not the only thing at stake. As Adam Smith ([1776] 1976, x; [1759] 1976, 27) declared: "The world neither ever saw, nor ever will see, a perfectly fair lottery; or one in which the whole gain compensated for the whole loss; because the undertaker could make nothing by it. In the state lotteries the tickets are really not worth the price paid by the original subscribers, and yet commonly sell for twenty, thirty, and sometimes forty per cent advance." Also to be taken into account is the ingenuity devoted to disposing of a display that exploited notions of the fluidity and instability of money and of cultural identity. It is not an accident that the purchasers of lottery tickets are described as "adventurers"; they, too, were participating in an economic expansionism which, like the activities of the East India Company, were mediated at home through a practice of cultural representation.

The summation of Cox's Museum was not the rhinoceros standing on a rock of gold stone supporting an onyx and gold cabinet or the temple of agate with triumphal chariots moving on a rich gallery supported by palm trees. It was a pair of portraits of the reigning monarch, George III, and his consort, Queen Charlotte, commissioned from Zoffany and placed "between the sophas" at the upper end of the room.[23] It is to this aspect of the Museum that I will, in conclusion, turn. The portraits were

23. Described as oval on copper, half length, size of life, the production of these portraits caused the delay in opening the Museum in June 1771 (JJC Lotteries iv, f. 16). The description is taken from the *Descriptive Catalogue* of 1772. In fact, the portraits measure roughly 78 x 65 cm and are now in the royal collection. Webster (1976; nos. 68 and 69) points out that the Cox portraits were based on the full-length portraits produced by Zoffany in 1771 but that the relative informality of those portraits was abandoned for robes of state.

plac'd in frames of metal finely wrought and richly gilt, from whence issue numberless rays forming a glory or irradiation like beams of the sun, in various reflected colours of light, some of which, when in motion, appear like liquid fire extending on every side.

Suspended from above by genii over each picture are imperial resplendant crowns embellish'd with jewels and pearls, placed under a canopy of crimson velvet border'd, fring'd, and tassel'd with gold and adorn'd with pearls, upon the cieling [*sic*] of which, and in front is a glory formed of glass and gold; laurels and palms of gold also decorate the picture of the king, as lillies and roses do that of the Queen, and are most exquisitely wrought from nature, and richly gilt.

Before the portraits upon a Throne of gold thirty-two feet in circumference of six steps, stand two rich and finely adorn'd altars of silver, border'd and embellish'd with gold; on the front of one within a wreath of oak is the cypher of His Majesty in letters of gold; upon the other, within a wreath of myrtle, the cypher of Her Majesty, finely executed. Upon the altars, form'd in high relief, various attributes and emblems are plac'd, distinguishing one as the altar of peace, the other of concord; beneath the throne is a band of mechanical musick, playing upon kettle drums, trumpets and other instruments, various fine pieces, compos'd by Mr. Smith, concluding with God Save the King; at the foot of the Throne on each side are pillars of silver, in richness, elegance and design corresponding with the altar, and upon them two elegant vases filled with flowers of jewellers work, copied from nature; containing musical machines and mechanical motions, by which the flowers unfold, and insects move like life: at the back of the Throne are plac'd four other most elegant vases, two of them pearl and gold, and two of jaspar, decorated with figures, flowers, animals, and other ornaments, each containing beautiful bouquets of flowers of jewellery, and in the center flower of each, a curious time piece; the whole together is the most distinguished display of art and elegance which the fancy of the proprietor could form. (*Descriptive Catalogue* 1772, 18–19)[24]

It is, perhaps, not surprising to find royal portraits as part of the Museum since Cox, like other contemporary entrepreneurs, was keen

24. The use of vases is interesting in light of the hugely popular production of vases by Wedgwood.

for royal patronage.[25] At the same time, the presence of portraits framed by mechanical inventions was a means of pointing up Cox's insistence that his endeavors be understood as not just equal in value to what was on the walls of the Royal Academy but as actually surpassing it. The presence of royal portraits by a leading artist who had been elected to the Royal Academy in 1769 and who was much favored by the royal family provided the most spectacular demonstration of Cox's conviction that his Museum should be accorded the same status as the Royal Academy and the Royal Society of Arts. Reynolds was by no means the royal family's preferred artist; the German-born Johann Zoffany offered a much less flamboyant, showy, painterly style of portraiture than either Reynolds or Gainsborough. All the more spectacular, then, that with music and automata, Cox could apparently bring to life the mimetic but immobile art of portraiture in ways unimaginable in the studios of fashionable portrait painters. George III was a well-known collector of mechanical instruments, and the Queen, a great lover of jewelry (Pointon 1997, 1998), regularly spent sums at London's toy merchants (see entries in the royal accounts, British Library Add. MS. 17870, 24 vols.). So the appeal to royal patronage of this prelude to the era of the Eidophusikon and ultimately of the *son et lumière*, if finally not very productive, was well founded. Perhaps it may seem ironic that Cox has represented the least absolutist of the Hanoverians in this baroque format, with "brilliant rays of glory" emanating from their images. But these portraits were by no means participating in the culture of similitude that was the medium of the up-and-coming portraitists of the day. Rather, this was an iconic and symbolic representation in which portraits stand for the royal presence in a traditional manner going back centuries.

The insertion of portraits of royalty into an environment full of clocks is also significant; it is clear that all the timepieces in their jeweled surrounds were not there to enable people to tell the time. Clocks and watches have a widespread currency in the seventeenth and eigh-

25. A report (presumably by Cox) in the *British Magazine*, January 1772, yokes "the noble protection already granted by his majesty to the royal academicians" to the success of Bolton and Fothergill in attracting to themselves some of the expenditure on French luxury goods made by English consumers; in a letter to the *London Evening Post* 29 February 1772, Cox refers again to the proof of the monarch's taste for arts and science (all reprinted in *Collection of Various Extracts* n.d.). Princess Amelia is reported to have visited the Museum on 14 March 1772 (cutting, JJC Lotteries iv, f. 17).

teenth centuries as metaphors for the machinery of power and government; we might mention here not only Adam Smith's celebrated example of the acquisition of an expensive watch by someone whose interest lies not in punctuality but in the perfection of the machine (Smith [1759] 1976, 1:455) but also Paley's comparison of God to a watch (Paley [1802] 1821, iv). Kings and princes in the early modern period were also recommended to be "not merely like the hands of a clock within the machinery of government but rather the balance spring / that gives the other gears time to turn / since therein lies the art of rule" (Bredekamp 1995, quoting Diego de Saavedra Fajardo, *Idea de un príncipe político christiano*, Munich 1640). By introducing royal portraits as the climax to an experience centered on an elaborate display of jeweled automata containing timepieces, it is implied that George III and Queen Charlotte, models of good government, are the ultimate jewels in the Treasure House. If in the seventeenth century God was the referent for the curiosities of the realms of *naturalis* and *artificialia* that filled the Kunstkammer, in Cox's Museum it is free trade supported by what its proprietor (advertisement, repr. in *Collection of Various Extracts* n.d.) describes as "an enlightened lover of the Arts and Sciences . . . a generous patron to those efforts they produce . . . [one who in] adorning his capital . . . render[s] it, what is very capable of becoming, the ATHENS OF EUROPE."

References

Pamphlets Connected with James Cox's Museum and Ephemera

An Account of Mr. Cox's Intended Exhibition at Spring Gardens. *British Magazine* January 1772; reprinted in *A Collection of Various Extracts* . . . London: J. Bell, no date; sporadic pagination. (Guildhall Library, London, PAM 6546.)

An Account of the Mechanism of an Automaton, or Image playing on the German-Flute: *as it was presented in a* Memoire, *to the Gentlemen of the Royal-Academy of Sciences at Paris,* by *M. Vaucanson*, Inventor and Maker of the Said Machine. *together with A Description of an artificial Duck. . . . Translated by J. T. Desaguliers, LLD, FRS, Chaplain to His Royal Highness the Prince of Wales*. London: T. Parker, 1742.

A Collection of Various Extracts, in Prose and Verse, from the London Publications, Relative to the Museum, in Spring Gardens; Containing Many Favourable Testimonies and Judicious Observations, of that Superb and Singular Display of Art. London: J. Bell, no date; sporadic pagination. (Guildhall Library, London, PAM 6546.)

A Description of a Most Magnificent Piece of Mechanism and Art. London, 1769.

(BL 8766.c.19.)

A Descriptive Catalogue of the Several Superb and Magnificent Pieces of Jewellery exhibited in Mr. Cox's Museum, at Spring Gardens, Charing Cross. London, 1772. (BL T.306 (5) and BL 8766.bb.24.)

A Descriptive Catalogue of the Several Superb and Magnificent Pieces of Mechanism and Jewellery exhibited in the Museum, at Spring Gardens, Charing-Cross. London, 1773. (BL 1651/149.)

A Descriptive Inventory of the Several Exquisite and Magnificent Pieces of Mechanism and Jewellery, comprised in the Schedule annexed to an Act of Parliament made in the Thirteenth Year of His Present Majesty, George the Third; for enabling Mr. James Cox, to dispose of his Museum by way of Lottery. London: H. Hart for Mr. Cox, 1773. (BL T 1208 (i).)

A Descriptive Inventory of the Several Exquisite and Magnificent Pieces of Mechanism and Jewellery, comprised in the Schedule annexed to an Act of Parliament made in the Thirteenth Year of His Present Majesty, George the Third; for enabling Mr. James Cox, to dispose of his Museum by way of Lottery. London: H. Hart for Mr. Cox, 1774. (BL T.447 (4).)

The Divine Predictions of Daniel and St. John Demonstrated, in a Symbolical Theological Dissertation on Cox's Museum, Dedicated to the Bishop of Gloucester. London: J. Wheble, 1774. (BL 3186.h.8.)

Books and Journals

Altick, R. 1978. *The Shows of London*. Cambridge: Harvard University Press.

Apperson, G. L. 1899. Some Old London Museums and Collections: James Cox's Museum. *Antiquary* 35:276–79.

Baker, M. 1995. A Rage for Exhibitions. In *The Genius of Wedgwood,* edited by H. Young. London: Victoria and Albert Museum.

Benedict, B. 1990. The "Curious Attitude" in Eighteenth-Century Britain: Observing and Owning. *Eighteenth-Century Life* 14 (November): 58–97.

Benhamou, R. 1987. From *Curiosité* to *Utilité*: The Automaton in Eighteenth-Century France. *Studies in Eighteenth-Century Culture* 17:91–105.

Bennett, T. 1995. *The Birth of the Museum: History, Theory, Politics*. London: Routledge.

Boswell, J. 1960. *The Yale Edition of the Private Papers of James Boswell.* Edited by W. K. Wimsatt Jr. and F. A. Pottle. London: Heinemann.

Bredekamp, H. 1995. *The Lure of Antiquity and the Cult of the Machine: The Kunstkammer and the Evolution of Nature, Art, and Technology*. Translated by A. Brown. Princeton, N.J.: Markus Weiner.

Bukovinská, B. 1997. The Kunstkammer of Rudolf II: Where It Was and What It Looked Like. In *Rudolf II and Prague: The Court and the City*, edited by E. Fucíkova. Prague: Prague Castle Administration; London: Thames & Hudson.

Burney, Fanny. [1778] 1968. *Evelina, or the History of a Young Lady's Entrance into the World*. Edited by E. A. Bloom. London: Oxford University Press.

Camerer Cuss, T. P. 1965. The Silver Swan. *Antiquarian Horology* 11.4 (June):

330–34.

Chapuis, A., and E. Droz. 1949. *Les Automates: Figures artificielles d'hommes et d'animaux. Histoire et technique*. Neuchâtel: Griffon.

Chapuis, A., and E. Jaquet. 1956. *The History of the Self-Winding Watch 1770–1931*. Translated by R. Savaré Grandvoinet. Neuchâtel: Griffon; New York: Central Books.

Clifford, H. 1998. Entry on James Cox. Draft for *New Dictionary of National Biography.*

Dickens, Charles. 1851. The Great Exhibition and the Little One. *Household Words* 3.5 (July): 356–60.

French, A. 1985. *John Joseph Merlin: The Ingenious Mechanick*. London: Iveagh Bequest, Kenwood House, GLC.

Gainsborough and His Musical Friends. 1977. London: Iveagh Bequest, Kenwood House, GLC.

Gentleman's Magazine. 1766. 36 (May), (December).

———. 1778. 48 (November).

Harcourt-Smith, S. 1933. *A Catalogue of the Various Clocks, Watches, Automata, and other Miscellaneous Objects of European Workmanship . . . in the Palace Museum and the Wu Ying Tien, Peiping*. Beijing: Palace Museum.

Jaffer, A. K. 1995. Furniture in British India 1750–1830. Ph.D. diss., Victoria and Albert Museum, London, and the Royal College of Art.

John Johnson Collection, Bodliean Library, Oxford University. Various archives. [JJC]

Kane, S. 1996–97. The Silver Swan: The Biography of a "Curiosity." *Things* 5 (winter): 39–57.

Le Corbeiller, C. 1960. James Cox and His Curious Toys. *Metropolitan Museum of Art Bulletin* June: 318–20.

———. 1970. James Cox: A Biographical Review. *Burlington Magazine* 112: 351–58.

Lubbock, J. 1995. *The Tyranny of Taste: The Politics of Architecture and Design in Britain 1550–1960*. New Haven, Conn.: Yale University Press.

Macartney, G. 1962. *An Embassy to China: Being the Journal Kept by Lord Macartney during His Embassy to the Emperor Ch'ien-lung 1793–1794*. Edited by J. L. Cranmer-Byng. London: Longman.

McKendrick, N., J. Brewer, and J. H. Plumb. 1982. *The Birth of a Consumer Society: The Commercialisation of Eighteenth-Century England*. London: Europa.

Pagani, C. 1993. "Eastern Magnificence and European Ingenuity": Clocks and Automata of Later Imperial China. Ph.D. diss., University of Toronto.

———. 1995. The Clocks of James Cox: Chinoiserie and the Clock Trade with China in the Late Eighteenth Century. *Apollo* 141 (January): 15–21.

Paley, W. [1802] 1821. *Natural Theology*. In *The Works of William Paley DD . . . in Five Volumes*. London: F. C. & J. Rivington.

Pape, W., and F. Burwick, eds. 1996. *The Boydell Shakespeare Gallery.* Bottrop: Peter Pomp.

Penny, N., ed. 1986. *Reynolds*. London: Royal Academy of Arts and Weidenfeld & Nicolson.

Pointon, M. 1997. Intriguing Jewellery: Royal Bodies and Luxurious Consumption. *Textual Practice* 11.3 (winter): 494–516.

———. 1998. Jewellery, Intrigue, and Economics: Court Culture and Display in England and France in the 1780s. In *Markets for Art in Europe, 1400–1800*, edited by M. North. Aldershot, England; Brookfield, Vt.: Ashgate.

Pomian, C. 1990. *Collectors and Curiosities: Paris and Venice, 1500–1800*. Translated by E. Wiles-Portier. Cambridge: Polity.

Pye, J. [1845] 1970. *Patronage of British Art*. London: Cornmarket.

Richards, T. 1991. *The Commodity Culture of Victorian England*. London: Verso.

Ross, I. S. 1995. *The Life of Adam Smith*. Oxford: Clarendon.

Rush, R. 1845. *A Residence at the Court of London*. 2nd series. Vol. 1. London: Richard Bentley.

Smith, Adam. [1776] 1976. *An Inquiry into the Nature and Causes of the Wealth of Nations*. Edited by W. B. Todd. Oxford: Clarendon.

———. [1759] 1976. *The Theory of Moral Sentiments*. Edited by D. D. Raphael and A. L. Macfie. Oxford: Clarendon.

———. 1980. Of the Imitative Arts. In *Adam Smith, Essays on Philosophical Subjects*, edited by W. P. D. Wightman and J. C. Bryce. Oxford: Clarendon.

St. James's Chronicle, no. 1000.

Toynbee, P., ed. 1928. *Satirical Poems Published Anonymously by W. Mason with Notes by Horace Walpole*. Oxford: Oxford University Press.

von Watzdorf, E. 1962. *Johann Melchior Dinglinger: Der Goldschmied des deutschen Barock*. Berlin: Gebr. Mann Verlag.

Walpole, Horace. 1955. *The Yale Edition of Horace Walpole's Correspondence*. Edited by W. S. Lewis. New Haven, Conn.: Yale University Press.

Webster, M. 1976. *Johan Zoffany 1733–1810*. London: National Portrait Gallery.

Whitley, W. 1928. *Artists and Their Friends in England 1700–1799*. 2 vols. London: Chatto.

"Seeing Is Believing": Otto Neurath, Graphic Art, and the Social Order

Robert J. Leonard

> The principle of visualization . . . , based on the ISOTYPE method, . . . shows connexions between facts instead of discussing them. Impressive visual aids do not merely act as illustrations or as eye-bait. . . . they are part of the explanations themselves.
>
> —Otto Neurath, *Modern Man in the Making*

> Visual education leads to internationalisation much more than word education does. . . . Visual education is related to the extension of intellectual democracy within single communities and within mankind, it is an element of international social planning and engineering.
>
> —Otto Neurath, "Visual Education: Humanisation versus Popularisation"

> Altering our scientific language is cohesive with altering our social and private life. There is no exterritoriality [*sic*] for sociologists, or for other scientists, and this is not always sufficiently acknowledged. Sociologists . . . also argue, decide, and act like other human beings within their scientific field. Imagine sailors who, far out at sea, transform the shape of their clumsy vessel from a more circular to a more fishlike one. They make use of some drifting timber, besides the timber of the old structure, to modify the skeleton and the hull of their vessel. But they cannot put the ship in dock in order to start from scratch. During their work they stay on the old structure and deal with heavy gales and thundering waves. In transforming their ship they take care that

For comments on an earlier draft, I am grateful to an anonymous referee, as well as to participants at both the Art and Economics conference on which this volume is based and the European Conference on the History of Economics, Antwerp, April 1998. For research assistance, I am grateful to graduate students Paolo Longato and Jérôme Thiollier. The research for this essay was supported by grants from the Canadian Social Science and Humanities Research Council and Quebec's Fonds pour la Création et la Recherche.

> dangerous leakages do not occur. A new ship grows out of the old one, step by step—and while they are still building, the sailors may already be thinking of a new structure, and they will not always agree with one another. The whole business will go on in a way we cannot even anticipate today. That is our fate.
>
> —Otto Neurath, "Foundations of the Social Sciences"

This essay is about Otto Neurath (1882–1945), teacher, socialist, founding member of the Vienna Circle, and tireless advocate of economic planning. He is of particular interest for any discussion of the links between art and economics for the simple reason that, in a unique manner, he managed to essentially *meld* the two. I do not mean that he was interested in the economic analysis of artistic work or that he had an eye for economic or commercial themes in the history of art. Rather, beginning after World War I and ending with his death in 1945, Neurath seized on a particular kind of art—modern German graphic art of the interwar period—and made it an integral element of both his politics and his theoretical analysis of the socioeconomic order. He appropriated what he saw as a modern, clear, and therefore politically congenial, art form and used it to develop a "view"—literally—of economic organization.

In particular, graphic art allowed Neurath to portray the economy as a collection of visible, tangible, and potentially manipulable objects, rather than as the manifestation of invisible, intangible, and less controllable beliefs and desires. This was cohesive with Neurath's dismissal of orthodox, neoclassical economic theory, whose utilitarian basis he regarded as metaphysical and whose focus on monetary calculation he saw as no more than an outdated inheritance from premodern times. His recourse to art, therefore, was an integral part of what separated him from his opponents. To Friedrich Hayek, in particular, who learned to see the economy as a complexly structured mechanism, coordinating the beliefs and desires of dispersed, and differently informed, individuals, Neurath's focus on the visible, the concrete, was "naive" and, of course, politically dangerous. While Hayek turned to the mind to ground the market social structure in the invisible characteristics of a relatively fixed human nature, Neurath turned to visual language as a way to avoid addressing the role of the mind, or the "mental," in social theory. His appropriation of visual art was part of a bid to give plasticity to the socioeconomic order—to portray it as highly malleable, and ultimately dependent on social debate and political action rather than on impersonal market forces. Graphic art helped Neurath suggest that the social structure, like the sailors' ship, might be built in many possible ways.

Background

Neurath received a doctorate from the school of philosophy at Berlin's Friedrich-Wilhelms-Universität, with a dissertation on ancient concepts of commerce and agriculture, supervised by Eduard Meyer and Gustav Schmoller (see Cartwright et al. 1996, the various autobiographical and biographical essays in "Memories of Otto Neurath" in M. Neurath 1973, 1–80, and other references therein). He then became a teacher of economics and history at the Neue Wiener Handelsakademie, publishing a reader on economics from Plato to Marx, as well as an economic textbook (Neurath and Schapire-Neurath 1910; Neurath 1910). Around 1912, he became involved in discussions with his brother-in-law, mathematician Hans Hahn, and with Rudolf Carnap, Herbert Feigl, and others in what was known as the "early" Vienna Circle. In 1912–13 he spent time in the Balkan states studying the economic effects of war, where he drew early conclusions about the nature and efficacy of wartime planning and control of the economy. He emphasized that, during war, profit considerations were given lower priority than economic production and efficiency and barter reemerged, indicating the non-necessity of monetary exchange. "He had a concrete vision of the complete organisation of a state at war, starting with centralisation of bread production via an expansion of the storehouse system up to the standardisation of railway wagons" (Cartwright et al. 1996, 18). War, for Neurath, was the "midwife" for the planned economy-in-kind.

He was drafted during the war and became head of the General War and Army Economics section attached to the War Ministry and then director of the Museum of War Economy in Leipzig. Here, aided by fellow socialist Wolfgang Schumann, who was editor of the cultural journal *Kunstwart und Kulturwart*, he organized exhibitions of statistical tables and models designed to show the mechanism of the economy in conditions of war. This marked the beginning of his activities in visual education (see M. Neurath 1973), and he was decorated for this work at the war's end. In 1919, he was involved in the movement for socialization in Saxony and Bavaria, giving lectures to miners in Southern Saxony and then setting up the central planning administration for the "soviet republic" that was proclaimed by the Bavarian Communists, Socialists, and anarchists led by Kurt Eisner. Here Neurath developed his ideas on economic planning—on the feasibility of organizing the central administration of raw materials, to be distributed to associations of factories, mines, and cooperatives of craftsmen and farmers. A central bank would control credit in what would essentially be a moneyless economy, based on wages in kind and barter. In writing on planning, he was following in a well-established tradition, with the models of Ballod and Popper-Lynkeus having being discussed for years. The latter, for example, was known for his proposal of a minimum living wage for the whole population, with a form of conscription to be used to create a "food army" in which citizens would serve for a short period, working for society. Other variants were developed by both Otto Bauer, of the Viennese Social Democrats, who emphasized legislative reform and only the very gradual socialization of businesses, and German Communist Karl Korsch, who favored more radical means, including immediate widespread socialization and the use of force. With the Bavarian movement crushed by the "white forces," Neurath found himself in jail, but he was soon released through the intervention of the Austrian government, with testimony in his defense from others, including Max Weber and Bauer. Their arguments portrayed Neurath as an economic technician, concerned primarily with the logistical aspects of economic organization and naively deluded about the separation of economics and politics. In fact, although often criticized for his views on economics, he was anything but politically unaware.[1]

Being-in-the-World with Neurath

Neurath's scientific and philosophical writings reflected his radical politics. For him, science, philosophy, politics, and art were all interwoven. His aim was the creation of a new modern form of life: a collectivist transformation of the social order, predicated on, among other things, the unification of science (from physics to economics) and a new attitude to art in which clarity would be achieved by dispelling with pre-

1. It was these writings by Neurath, Bauer, and other advocates of planning that helped provoke the refutation by liberal Ludwig von Mises (1935), which gave rise to the protracted socialist calculation debate (see Chaloupek 1990; Lavoie 1985).

modern ornament. Neurath saw the unification of science as a necessary condition for social progress. The dispersal of metaphysics and the advancement of the "scientific view of the world" were both necessary for the development of undisputed knowledge, which, in turn, paved the way for social transformation. If theology and metaphysics had served to console and fragment the workers, true science would alert and unify them: the collectivization of scientific work was seen as concomitant with political collectivization. Thus in a 1928 essay on "Personal Life and Class Struggle," Neurath wrote: "A scientific attitude is spreading, even among the less educated, whereas the less scientific attitude of the theological and philosophical era was often held by the most highly educated people of their time. . . . Today nobody wants to do without science . . . [and] investigation can show that scientific thinking is safeguarded best by the proletariat which can use it to best advantage. . . . Scientific attitude and solidarity go together. Whoever joins the proletariat can say with justification that he joins love and reason" ([1928] 1973, 252). And on the role of scientific knowledge in effecting social transformation, he was quite explicit: "[The] better the proletariat *grasps the social engineering relations of our order* and surveys its own chances, the more successfully it can fight. . . . For the proletarian front the technique of the struggle and the interests of propaganda coincide with high esteem for science and the overcoming of metaphysics" (296–97; emphasis added). As we shall see, it was precisely here, in helping the proletariat "grasp the social engineering relations" of the economy, that visual art had a role to play.

This comingling of philosophy and politics is evident in the Vienna Circle's 1929 manifesto, "The Scientific Conception of the World," where Neurath equates the new scientific outlook with the advancement of a new form of life and suggests that there existed unity in this respect among Circle members:

> [Our] attitudes towards questions of life also showed a noteworthy agreement. . . . For these attitudes are more closely related to the scientific world-conception than it might at first glance appear from a purely theoretical point of view. For instance, endeavours toward a new organization of economic and social relations, toward a unification of mankind, toward a reform of school and education, all show an inner link with scientific world-conception; it appears that these endeavours are welcomed and regarded with sympathy by the

members of the Circle, some of whom indeed actively further them. ([1929] 1973, 304–5)[2]

The manifesto also reflected Neurath's particular interests in the prominence it gave to the social sciences, demanding their "purification" along the lines of that achieved in physics. Concepts such as the "folk spirit" were to be abandoned in favor of an empiricist, antimetaphysical science, whose object was simply "people, things and their arrangement" (315). The emergence of such a science was linked to both the displacement of metaphysical ideas by the increased mechanization and modernization of production and discontent among the proletariat: "So it is that in many countries the masses now reject these doctrines much more consciously than ever before, and along with their socialist attitudes tend to lean towards a down-to-earth empiricist view . . . [and] look forward with hope to the course of events to come" (317).

In his own writings on the subject, Neurath describes in greater detail what constitutes valid political economy in an age in which metaphysics has been abandoned (see [1928], [1930], [1931b], and [1931c] all in Neurath 1973; [1935] 1987; [1939–40] 1983; 1944). He named his proposal "Physicalist Sociology":

> [This is] the application of the latest successes of the scientific conception of the world with its physicalism, and its resultant analysis, to sociological inquiries. The analysis of the pursuit of science, as given by Carnap, Frank, Russell, Schlick, Wittgenstein and others, partly following Mach, can also be applied to the sociological field. Here it is not the length of possible deductions or the subtlety of analysis that are essential, but rather that one should note above all which concepts and statements can be considered as part of genuine science and which not. . . . Naturally such an analysis cannot be

2. It was with statements like this that Schlick, the liberal reformer but not radical socialist, was in greatest disagreement. Neurath and Schlick, one contemporary noted, stood on opposite ends of the political spectrum: "Neurath represented the extreme left in the Vienna Circle. . . . At the extreme right . . . stood Schlick. These two men were opposites not only in their thinking but also in their personalities. Schlick, the soft-spoken tall man, supposed to be of aristocratic parentage, lived in the style of the grand bourgeoisie . . . loved to travel, gave musical parties and dinners in the style of cultured rich people of the bourgeois era; Neurath, the consciously non-bourgeois revolutionary, disregarded the petit-bourgeois forms in home and dress (mostly bareheaded, he sometimes wore a cap to show his solidarity with the working class), interested as he was in a novel way of life" (Heinrich Neider, quoted in M. Neurath 1973, 47–48). Schlick's antiradicalism was shared by Karl Menger, another associate of the Circle (see Leonard 1998).

> made from without; it requires concrete analysis of reality on the fundamental basis of the sharpened conceptual tools now at our disposal. ([1931b] 1973, 413)

In his pamphlet "Empirical Sociology," Neurath ([1931b] 1973) surveys the history of economics quite extensively, highlighting and rejecting all traces of metaphysics and developing his own framework, "sociology on a materialist basis." This was a neo-Marxist sociology, employing only such concepts as are ultimately reducible to spatiotemporal terms and pointing inexorably toward central planning. Recourse to nonphysicalist concepts was to give way to the use of a strict behaviorism, in which humans were to be studied as one might study a colony of ants. One considered the economic geography of the group, their physical surroundings—what Neurath termed the "life terrain"—and then examined the living standards secured by different forms of socioeconomic arrangement, different "social orders." The dependence on the concept of utility was to be overcome by considering *physical* bundles of consumption and their associated standards of life, the latter being easily compared, according to Neurath:

> Living standard is the central concept of all circumstances that condition . . . a man's mode of behavior, his sorrows and joys. Shelter, food, clothing, health, books, theatres, friendly human surroundings, all this belongs to the standard of living. . . . The living standard is the condition of the behavior we call a style and attitude of life. We speak of a lower living standard if a man's attitude is generally depressed by such a living standard. This of course presupposes that we can arrange attitudes in a sequence, that we may venture to speak of a man having a more or less happy expression, or even dare to compare the modes of behavior of two men along these lines. . . . It is in any case quite legitimate to speak of the living standards of individual men. Within certain bounds one can confidently say that the living standard in one case is worse than in another. (401)[3]

The emphasis on the material, the physical, was tied to Neurath's rejection of the link between money values and living standards. In his "What Is Meant by a Rational Economic Theory?" ([1935] 1987) and

3. Neurath continues: "If in one case a man sits hungry and crying in a dirty, little hole, and in another the same man has a friendly smile and eats happily in a bright villa, we should say that in the first case, the living standard is less favourable than in the second" (401).

his 1944 essay "Foundations of the Social Sciences," he rejects the "idol of monetary calculation." The use of money as a medium of exchange and the tendency to evaluate goods in monetary terms, he claims, is merely a convention. It is a habit, a tradition, grounded socially and not by any fixed feature of human nature, as was shown by the existence of barter economies in the past. We were no more tied to the monetary economy than we were to the premodern taboo on the inclusion of the thirteenth floor in the elevator, which is the example employed by Neurath (see also 1939, 131). For Neurath, the task of a progressive sociology, which is taken to include economics, is first the clarification and then the transformation of the social order: "The theory of social structure is essential for any social engineer, which means anyone who participates as collaborator in the planned organization of all social formations. Prediction of the coming social structure and of the functioning of a given social structure is then at the center of a planned way of life" ([1931b] 1973, 403).

The prelude to such planning, and a constitutive part of his physicalist sociology, was the clarification/illustration of the social order and its (physical) living standards: the "people, things and their arrangement," cited above. And this is where Neurath's museum came in: his economic sociology and his educational museum exhibitions were intermeshed parts of the new form of life he was advancing. The economics he rejected was that which featured metaphysical statements—statements that generated arguments "with strongly emotional colouring"; "whereas in physical matters this colouring has mostly become imperceptible, in sociology it often stands out clearly" (325). A physicalist sociology would privilege clarity, would be without such coloring. Such clarity would be aided through the development of a visual language, the mobilization of the right kind of art toward the right political ends, giving the people "information which is easily remembered": "Such simple, careful symbolic representation is educationally superior to expressionistic play with strong effective colours, to sentimental naturalism, and also to the jokes of caricature" ([1931a] 1973, 215).

Shaping the Social Order: Neurath's Pictorial Politics

In the early 1920s, when he returned to Vienna from Bavaria, Neurath became involved in the work of the city's socialist government. This was Red Vienna, the "third way" between Bolshevism and parliamentary reformism, which emphasized education and the transformation of culture in preparation for the future, poorly specified, revolution. A socialist enclave in a larger conservative Austria, Red Vienna survived from 1920 until the crackdown by the Christian Social Dollfuss national government in 1934. Among the core members of the Vienna Circle, Neurath, Hans Hahn, physicist Philipp Frank (brother of the architect Josef), and Rudolf Carnap were committed Socialists, and they were close to the ruling intelligentsia of the Social Democrats, which included Otto Bauer and Friedrich Adler.

Neurath became general secretary of the Research Institute for Social Economy (Forschungsinstitut für Gemeinwirtschaft), and in 1921 he helped establish the Cooperative Housing and Allotment Association. Here, he engaged several well-known architects, including Adolf Loos, Josef Frank, and Josef Hoffman, to design projects for improved social living. For example, Neurath himself apparently preferred simple terraced housing with connecting gardens and a communal kitchen. The plans and models for these villages were exhibited at what became the Museum for Housing and Urban Development in Vienna, at Parkring 12. Throughout the 1920s, Neurath was very involved in this architectural work, collaborating with members of the Bauhaus in Germany and lecturing there. Like Walter Gropius, Neurath embraced architecture's "shift away from the mystical and toward the streamlined and industrial" (Galison 1990, 715), seeing in it the possibility for a new form of life, based on philosophical clarity, respect for science, and the development of fellow-feeling.

The Housing Museum gave way in 1925 to the Social and Economic Museum of Vienna (SEMV), run by Neurath. This was directed toward a Viennese working class, little inclined to self-education through reading. It was part of the *Bildungspolitik* program of the city's Social Democratic municipal government, and Neurath's efforts were funded by the city, the Viennese Chamber of Workers and Employees, and several large social insurance institutions. Using the "Vienna Method" of pictorial statistics, this center exhibited educational material to the Viennese population, largely involving statistics on social and economic change. The museum had three departments: Labor and Organization, Culture and Life, and Housing and Urban Development. The information was expressly tailored to accommodate an uneducated audience, the use of pictorial symbols intending to overcome literacy and educational barriers and thus stimulate the interest of poor, uneducated Viennese who might otherwise have never set foot inside a museum. During the course of the 1920s, Neurath was able to involve a number of graphic artists in the work of the Museum for Housing and Urban Development and then the SEMV. These included W. J. H. B. Sandberg and Peter Alma, both of whom were Dutch; one Bruno Zuckermann; and the German Gerd Arntz. I have been able to trace some of the work of Alma and Arntz, although they are notable in their absence from the main references in art history and, as far as I can see, in their relative obscurity among historians of art (see Breuille 1991; also Sandberg 1929 and 1931, both of which are cited in Faludi 1996).[4]

Working both in paint and with woodcuts, Peter Alma studied at The Hague in 1904–6.[5] He spent time in Paris close to the circle around Fernand Léger and Diego Rivera, and was one of several Dutch artists in Paris at the time, including Conrad Kickert, Piet Mondrian, and Lodewijk Schelfhout. He had exhibitions in 1912–13 at the Moderne Kunstkring in Amsterdam, the Sonderbund Ausstellung in Cologne, and the Salon des Indépendants in Paris. He was apparently influenced by Mondrian and, in particular, Van der Leck. From 1915 onward, he refined a style that involved the use of primary colors, flat surfaces, and simple forms, with compositions generally based on the horizontal and vertical and lacking depth. He visited the Soviet Union in 1921, making contact with the Russian Constructivists and Suprematists, including Kandinsky, Lissitsky, Tatlin, and Malevitch, and, on returning, encountered another artist *engagé*, the German Gerd Arntz, to whom he would remain close for the next few decades. Reflecting his politics, Alma's work are critical, whether of soul-destroying unemployment or the brutishness of manual labor (see figures 1, 2, and 3). Alma worked for a while in Vienna for Neurath, in the mid-1920s it seems, and published some pamphlets in Dutch dealing with the use of graphic art in the construction of pictorial statistics (see Alma 1930, 1932).

4. I might also mention that my attention was initially drawn to Neurath's use of art not by any of the now-extensive literature on Neurath, but by the remark made by Viennese contemporary Karl Menger concerning the aesthetic (as distinct from political) satisfaction he derived from the graphic work of Alma, Arntz, and Frans Masereel. The Belgian Masereel's interwar novels in woodcuts were marvelous flights of imagination in a period marked by misery. See, for example, his *Le Soleil*, *Mon livre d'heures*, and *Histoire sans paroles*. To the empiricist Neurath, however, Masereel's romantic flights of the imagination and Freudian explorations of unfulfilled desires were all too metaphysical for comfort.

5. Alma was born in Sumatra in 1886 and died in Amsterdam in 1969.

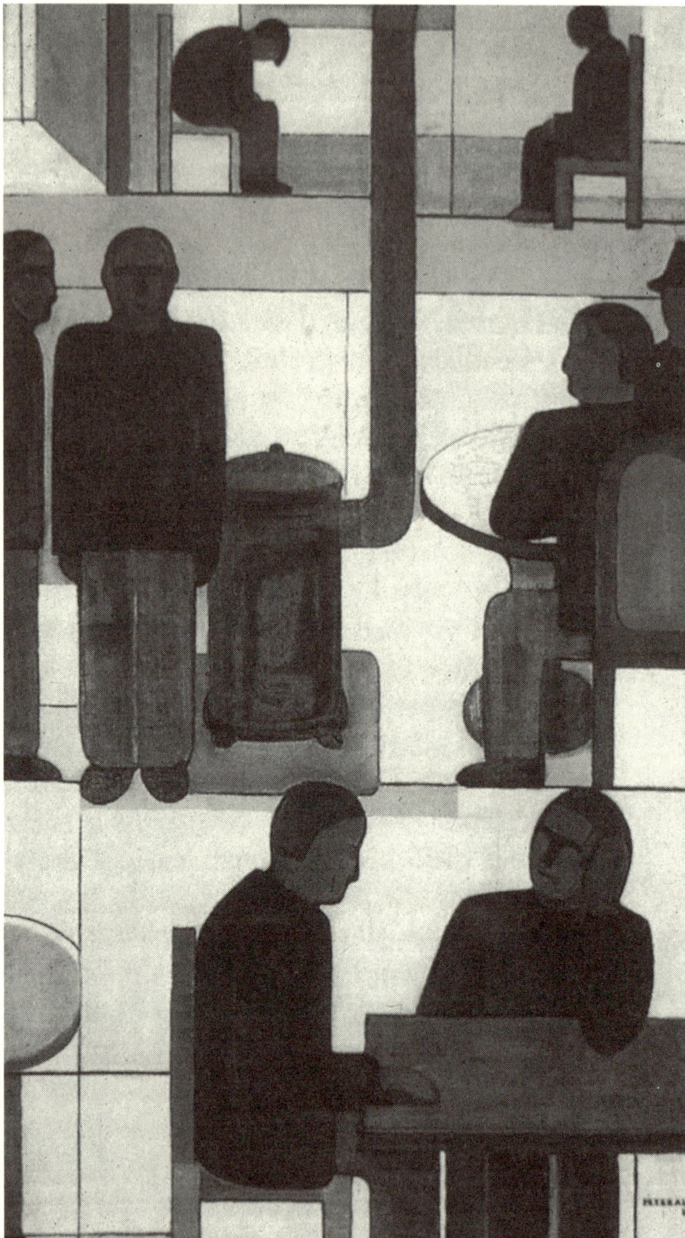

Figure 1 Peter Alma, *Unemployed in a Waiting Room*, 1929. From Breuille 1991, 27.

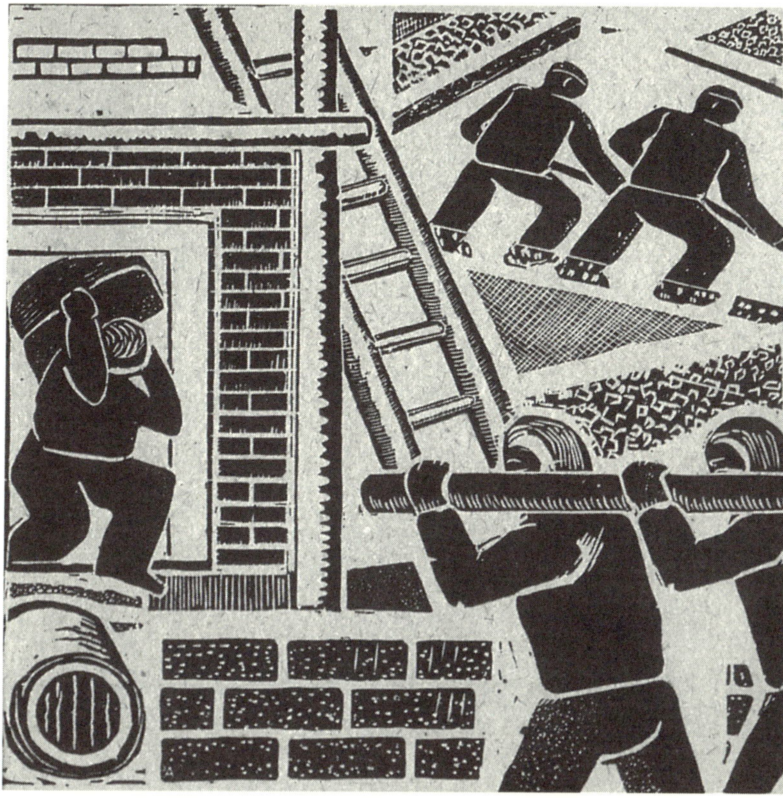

Figure 2 *Builders*, woodcut, c. 1923. From Sandberg and Jaffé 1961, illustration 199.

Similar social and political themes were explored by Gerd Arntz, who studied in Düsseldorf and was associated with a group of artists, "Stupid," in Cologne in 1920. From 1922, Arntz specialized in lino- and woodcuts and exhibited at many German centers throughout the decade. He became known for his woodcuts, with their simple illustrations in the style of Expressionist engraving, with a geometrical touch inspired by Russian Constructivism (see figure 4). Later, the influence of Alma became evident in more rounded, almost "cartoonish," figures. Like Alma, the element of political critique is key, with class conflict a recurring theme. It was in 1926 in Düsseldorf, at the GESOLEI exhibition (for health, social insurance, and gymnastics),

a. b.

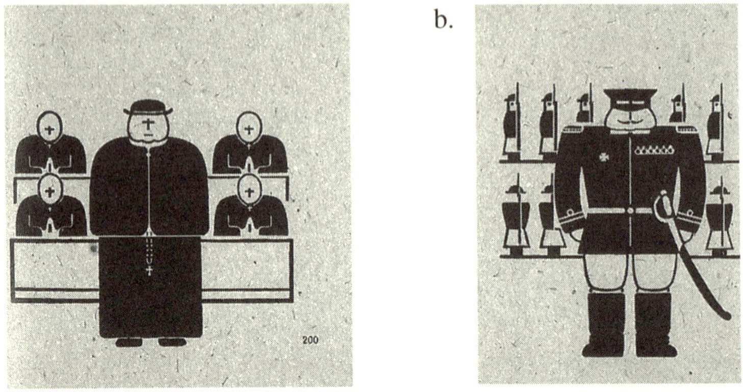

Figure 3 Peter Alma, (a) *Priest*, woodcut, c. 1929, and (b) *General*, woodcut, c. 1929. From Sandberg and Jaffé 1961, illustrations 200 and 201.

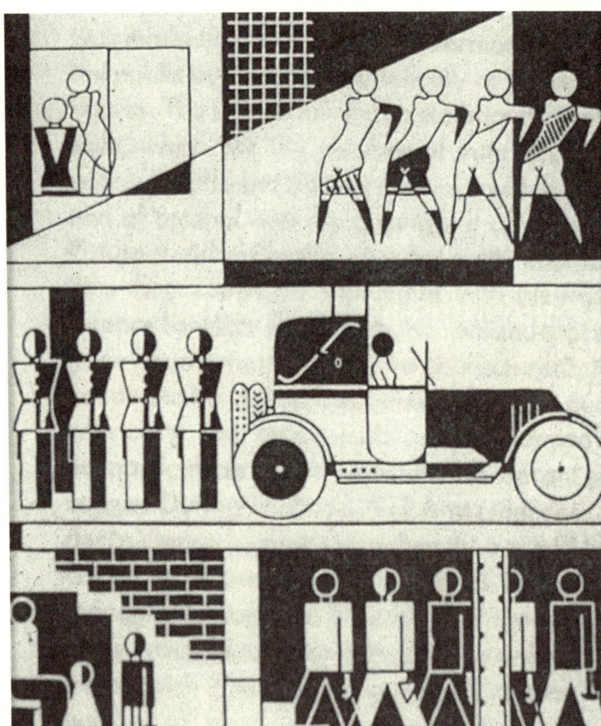

Figure 4 Gerd Arntz, *The Social Order*, woodcut, 1926. From Arntz and Broos, 1979, 10.

that Arntz was discovered by Neurath and inducted into the operations of the SEMV.[6]

With the SEMV, Neurath intended to deliberately subvert the traditional conception of the "museum," stripping it of its traditional mystique, elitism, and historical "weight" and turning it into a reproducible, demystified, collective, modern site. Just as the capacities of the book as an instrument of education/propaganda had been revolutionized by the development of printing techniques, so, too, said Neurath, should the museum cease to strive for uniqueness and become reproducible and uniform. The museum, in his view, was a crucial locus involving social conflict, authority, and discipline:

> And why must the poor visitor to a museum of natural history look at hundreds of birds, even though he can perhaps hardly distinguish the differences, just because some particular ornithologist considers it necessary? . . . What significant questions are answered by such exhibits? . . . Isn't it curious: we are constantly told that we are living in the age of technology, and yet when we enter a modern museum of natural history, there is no sign of it. . . . A huge whale hangs in the middle of the hall; but we do not learn . . . how the skin is transformed into shoes, or the fat into soap that finds its way to the dressing room of a beautiful woman. Nor do we learn how many whales are caught per annum . . . [or] what countries are predominantly engaged in whaling. . . . Human fortunes are connected with this exhibit—starving seamen, hungry families of fishermen in the north of Norway. And so, everything leads to men and society.
>
> *How to organize human life socially—that is the great question which people are asking today with ever greater insistence. The social museum is the museum for our time. And this is its twofold task: to show social processes, and to bring all the facts of life into some recognisable relation with social processes.* ([1933] 1973, 219–20; emphasis added)

6. Neurath's second wife, Marie, recalls: "What [Otto] needed was a designer who had the same tendency towards clear expression that he had. This is how he found Gerd Arntz, his star designer. . . . [In Düsseldorf] he looked around in art exhibitions . . . and saw some wood cuttings by Gerd Arntz. He discovered where he lived and asked him: 'How much do you cost?' . . . For a year or two [Arntz] contributed by sending us designs to Vienna, but then he joined us about 1928" (M. Neurath 1973, 60).

For Neurath, the modern museum was to be democratic—accessible to everybody. It should have branches located in areas convenient to the larger population and with opening hours tailored to suit the pattern of the working week. There were to be no "trustees," Neurath regarding this as a form of feudal holdover, and the general atmosphere was to be light and open rather than weighty and oppressive. The information conveyed was to be simple, clear, and accessible to the uneducated, entertaining where possible, without being trivial. Throughout, the museum was to be a site where visualization would play a role in social transformation: "Modern man is conditioned by the cinema and a wealth of illustrations. He gets much of his knowledge during leisure hours in the most pleasing way through his eyes. If one wants to spread social knowledge, one should use means similar to modern advertisements" (Neurath [1925] 1973, 214). This point is made repeatedly in his writings:

> Besides being more international, visual education from the beginning enforces a more human approach than education through words. It can only deal with things which are within the grasp of everyone's understanding. . . . It would be childish to think of educational means as something isolated from social organisation. . . . With visual aids, one could create something that is common to all, we could educate children in various countries . . . in a way which gives them the feeling of having knowledge in common for human brotherhood. Because I believe that visual aids have this peculiarity, I wish to promote visual education, as an element of human brotherhood. (Neurath [1945] 1973, 248)

Neurath's means of spreading social(ized) knowledge were the pictorial statistics of the "Vienna Method," later coined ISOTYPE (International System of Typographic Education).[7] On the face of it, the principles used in the design of educational statistics were simple. If such pictures were to be pedagogically effective, said Neurath: "At first glance one should be able to distinguish everything important, at second glance some important facts are added, and at third glance, one takes note of some details. If one notices something new the fourth time

7. The Greek etymology of *iso* also conveyed the idea of sameness, the repeated use of the same symbols.

one looks, then the image is insufficient" (Neurath 1991, 1, quoted in Jansen 1996, 147).

The most important of the museum's informative graphic art came from the chisel of Arntz, Neurath's chief designer from 1928, who spoke about the differences between a creative painting or woodcut and a pictorial statistic. The latter, he said, "has different elements and different laws than painting, since the proportions are given through the reality of the quantity of things, and a harmonization is not possible on the surface of the chart, if the content is to be shown with all its contrasts" (Arntz 1930, 30, quoted in Jansen 1996, 151) (e.g., contrast a statistic with his "Social Order"). The basic principle was that one symbol meant a given number—for example, 1 million soldiers—and larger and smaller quantities were represented by, respectively, more and less symbols.[8] Conveying quantitative information by symbols was deemed superior to doing it by the more common geometric means of curves and areas: "Not only that symbols of men and trees are friendlier to look at. If you saw a row of black coffins and a row of red babies, you would be able to remember, even after a long time, that this chart was about deaths and births. But the red curve and the black curve could have meant births and deaths as well as the production of wine and shoepolish" (Neurath 1991, 1, quoted in Jansen 1996, 152). The symbols used also often conveyed information about the emotional state of the person represented. Thus, Arntz's linotype of the unemployed man, reminiscent of the figures in Alma's portrayal of the *chômeurs*, shows him slouched and despondent, in contrast with the alert and upright employed workers in other symbols (see figures 1 and 5).[9] Attention was paid to the portrayal of light and space, so that, for example, in the representation of infant mortality rates, the interiors of

8. Multiplying the number of symbols made the comparison of quantities easier than did increasing areas: "That a square has twice the surface size as any other can only be computed, but not recognized by eye. However, two squares aligned with each other can immediately be compared with such an isolated square in terms of quantity" (Neurath 1991, 388, quoted in Jansen 1996, 151).

9. Skopec (1996, 160) points out how this wealth of detail was made possible by the classical form of representation involved and was considerably greater than that obtainable in today's digital media: "Contrary to the wishes of many artists, designers' and developers' presentation standards are being established through CD-ROM, computer games and on-line applications, e.g. 640 x 480 pixels, which falls short of the quality required for differentiated visualisation. And even if there is hope for (much) higher resolution in the future, it will never provide scope for such varied differentiation in the representation of symbols as is achieved with ISOTYPE visual presentations."

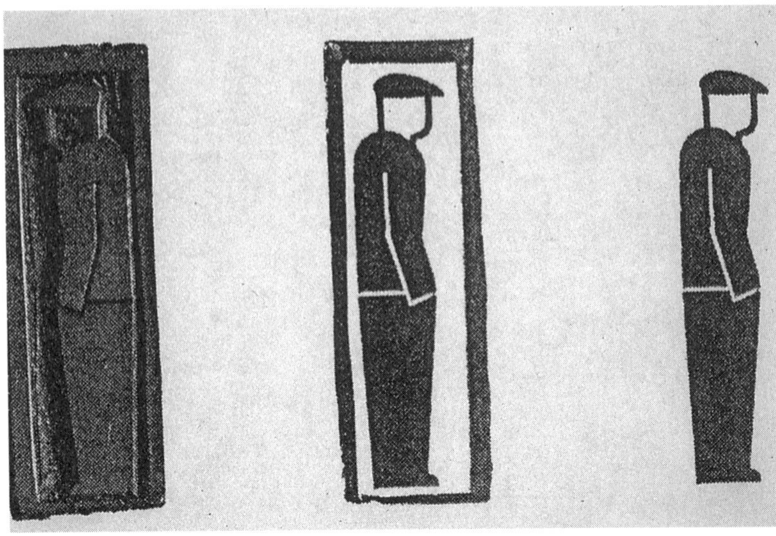

Figure 5 Gerd Arntz, linocut and impression of the symbol "unemployed." From Arntz and Broos 1979, 12.

wealthy homes were brighter and more spacious than those of the homes of poor children (see figure 6).

The pictorial graphics divided up the picture plane in a systematic manner. When necessary, changes in time were represented along the vertical dimension, and changes in quantity along the horizontal, a principle maintained throughout (see figure 7). Often, an illustration was included in the graphic to enliven the whole or reinforce a particular point (see figure 8). Sometimes, colors were used to make distinctions between, say, social and national groups (see figure 9), and when only black and white were used, differences were portrayed by, for example, different headgear or dress.

In keeping with Neurath's physicalist view of the economy, there is absolutely no mention in these statistics of money, costs, or value indices of any kind. The purpose of the symbols was to enable comparison, by an imaginary, possibly uneducated observer, of different social orders and different economic arrangements. What mattered, for Neurath, were the material conditions of life, the living standard (*Lebenslage*), as represented by housing, nutrition, clothing, working hours, and less obvious measures such as the prevalence of suicide and

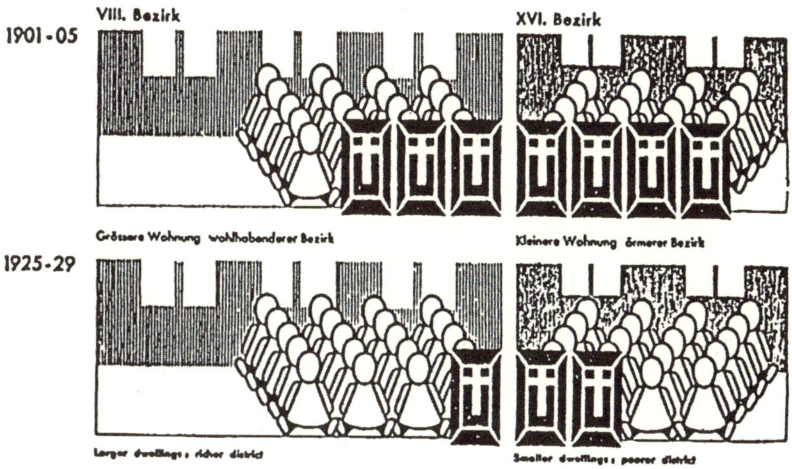

Figure 6 Infant mortality and social position in Vienna. From Neurath [1933] 1973, 221.

the availability of radio sets. To Neurath, it was these measures, more than any monetary measure, which were indicative of a society's well-being (*Lebensstimmung*). Steadfastly resorting to visual and architectural metaphors, Neurath created what he called economic and social "silhouettes," brief collections of statistics relating to physicalist features of the economy, with never any attempt to reduce them to a single index (see figure 10). Elsewhere, illustrations of how war reduced seasonal variation in coal production or how the market led to destruction of coffee stocks for purposes of price maintenance bore an implicit critique of the market system and were intended to promote the need for planning (see figures 7 and 11).

The displays of the Social and Economic Museum, therefore, were an integral part of Neurath's political economy. They substituted for conventional economic statistics and avoided all questions of money value. They were intended to promote a new, socialist sensibility, to prepare the workers of Vienna for the upcoming revolution. They supported, and were supported by, Neurath's rejection of utility theory and the monetary economy. As art, they were flat images, deliberately lacking perspective. As economics, they were part of Neurath's attempt to stay at the surface and to focus on the physical, avoiding the speculative realms of utility theory and the role of the mind.

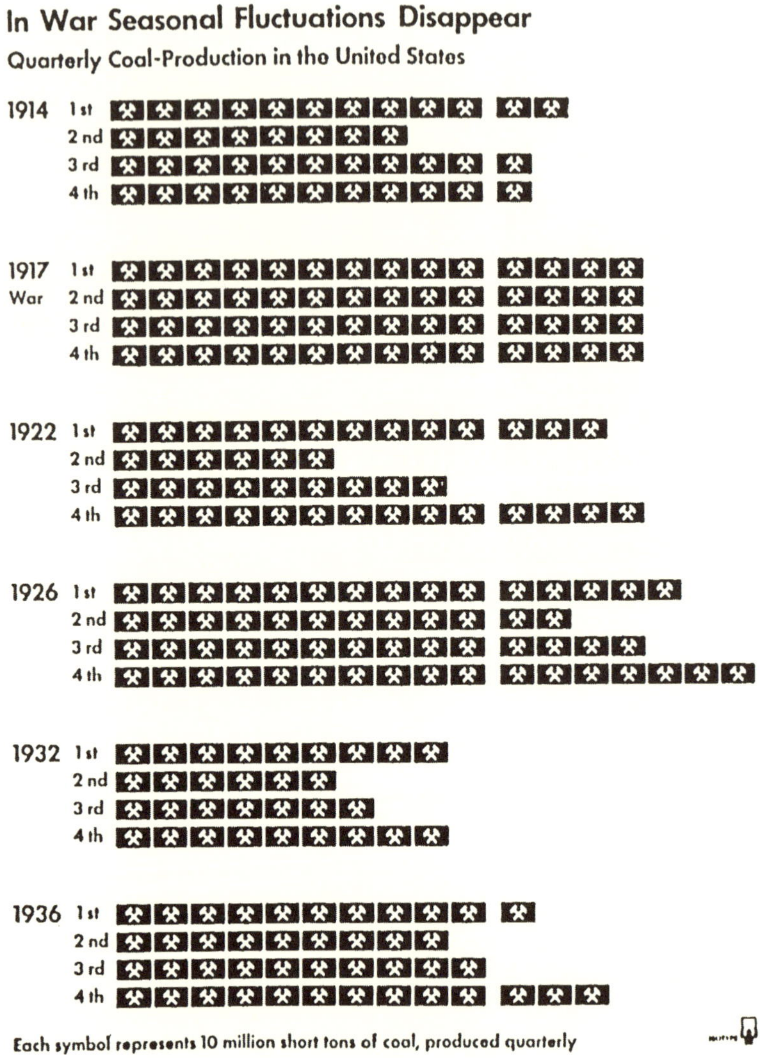

Figure 7 In war seasonal fluctuations disappear. From Neurath 1939, 87.

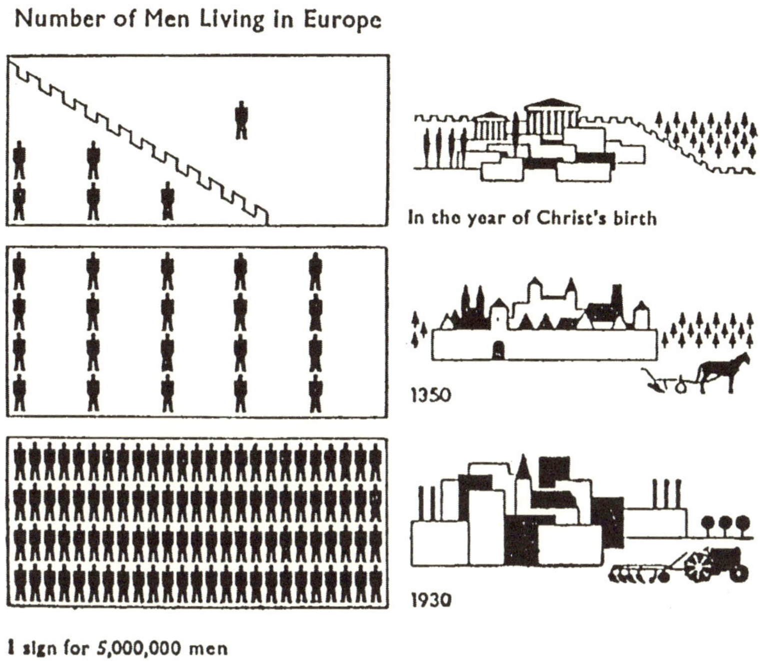

Figure 8 Number of men living in Europe. From O. Neurath 1973, 245.

In his impassioned 1944 monograph "Foundations of the Social Sciences," Neurath once again addressed the interrelations between the two areas, making clear how the use of art was an integral part of social science. As an empiricist, he wanted to eliminate all unempiricist expressions such as *mind*, *concept*, *mental*, *essence*, and, especially, terms appealing to transcendent or absolute qualities, such as *justice*, *truth*, and *falsity*. Terms such as these, he said, did not appear in physicalist language. Empiricist social scientists would limit themselves to phrases, basic observation-statements, which could be translated and recognized in all languages: "The old man lived in this stone building" or "Many trees have been found there." His pictorial images were intended to be visual statements of such a kind.

Again and again, however, Neurath repeats that the social scientists cannot be expected to start out tabula rasa. They will always, inevitably,

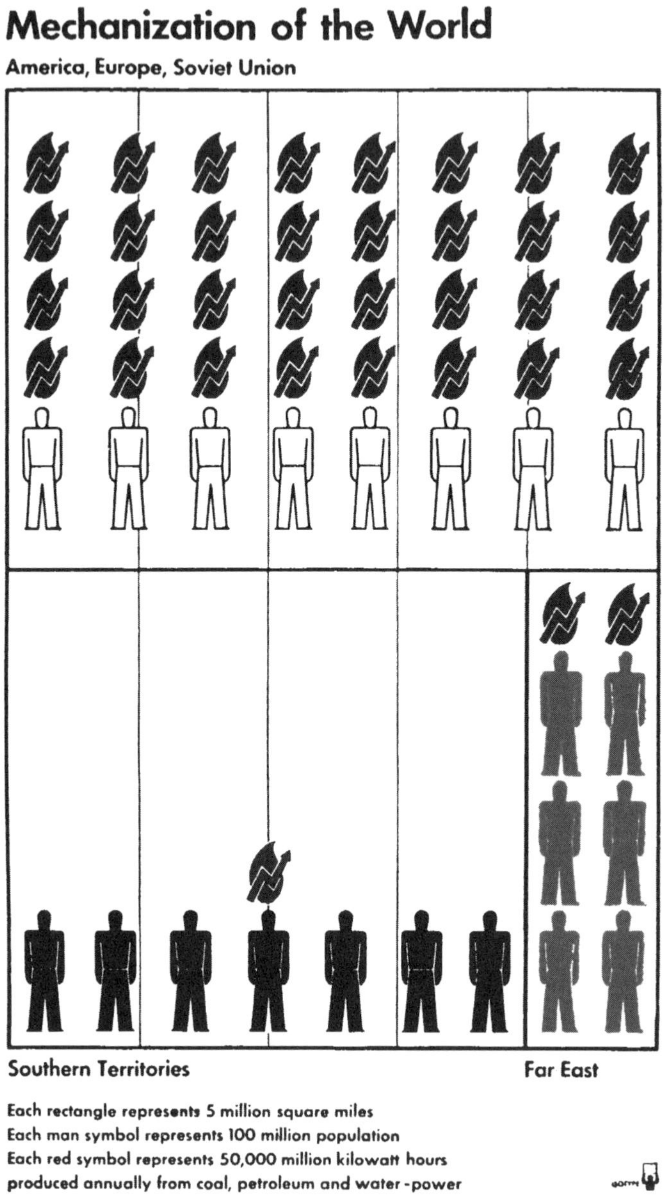

Figure 9 Mechanization of the world. From Neurath 1939, 48.

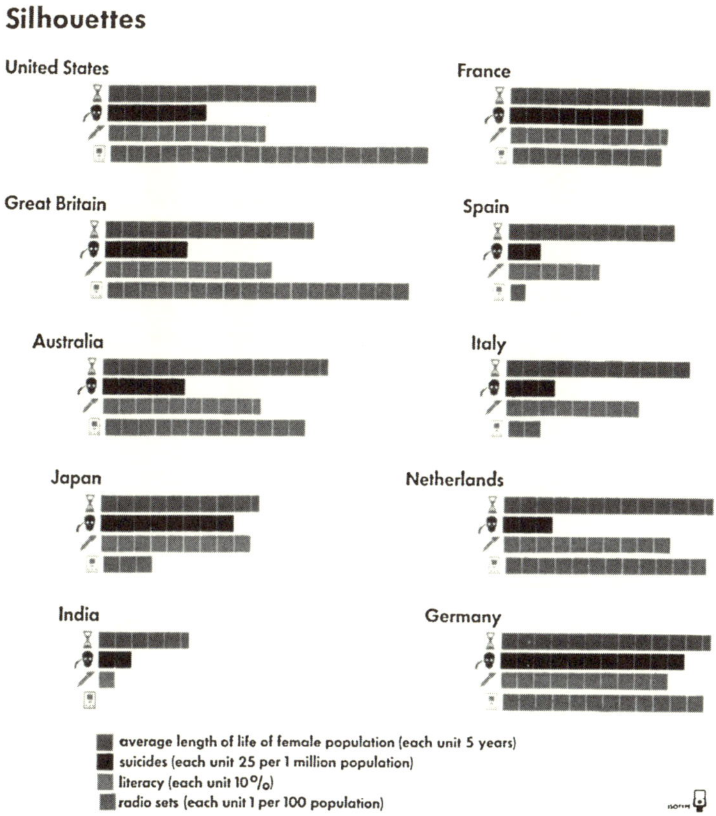

Figure 10 Silhouettes. From Neurath 1939, 61.

have to use terms that are vaguely defined. What was important was to develop an empiricist attitude, to assay sentences made by means of observation-statements. The most one could hope for in social science, epistemologically, was to have systems of basic statements that were coherent yet ungrounded in any "reality": the ship would always be afloat. In the social sciences, in particular, plurality and multiplicity are the order of the day. Neurath (1944, 13) thus remained at arm's length from Pareto and the discourse of optimization: "I suggest being suspicious wherever a writer tells us of an 'optimum,' except in cases in which a well-defined calculatory situation enables us to speak of an 'optimum.' It is just in the social sciences that we meet this tendency to speak often of an 'optimum.' This tendency is perhaps connected

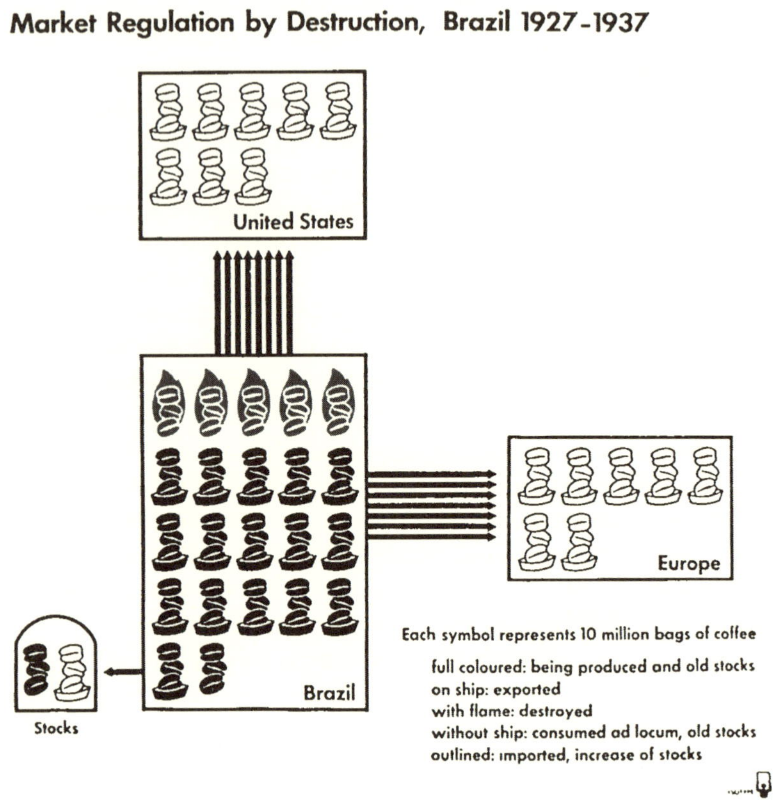

Figure 11 Market regulation by destruction, Brazil, 1927–37. From Neurath 1939, 77.

with a certain tendency to comprehensive determinism as Laplace formulated it in a very 'absolute' way." On the contrary, social scientists required a certain vagueness and even fuzziness, for only then could they cover the history of arts, the history of technology, the history of religion, and the history of church organization—that is, social life in all its richness.

Arguing that society had great freedom in choosing among its possible "futures," Neurath implicitly takes us back to some of the visual displays examined here and to their role as sources of social transformation. Social "silhouettes" allow one to compare different social situations without speaking in terms of a single indicator, whether that be utility, happiness, or the value of output. Multidimensional comparisons of this kind, he insists, are meaningful to anthropologists who study tribes without money. They are a way of transcending the local, contextual concern with money reckoning, of saying something with meaning for "mankind." He takes us to back to the Brazilian coffee: "Let us start with the statement that the traditional market society leads to the intentional destruction of milk, coffee, wheat, etc. in periods of hunger and starvation. It is plausible that there are people who imagine some new type of society in which no such destruction could take place. Discussion on rich and poor, on standards of living and similar items, arise" (36). And even though it is scientifically impossible to measure happiness or to make interpersonal comparisons, social engineers can provide descriptive (visual) statements on the happiness of individuals or of groups. They can provide silhouettes, the discussion of which may be of great importance to those making decisions that affect the social order and, thus, happiness. Neurath thus leaves us with a world in which there is neither formula, recipe, nor clear-cut prescription. There is only openness and indeterminacy, but therefore enormous scope for political decision. Neurath leaves us with a vision of society, the political economy, as a ship, afloat, yet capable, one might say, of choosing a course, using visual beacons as guide.

Coda

There was a certain poetry in Neurath's ultimately fleeing Holland and the Nazis on a boat. In February 1934, when Dollfuss sent in the troops against the Viennese Social Democrats, Neurath was in Moscow, on a contract with the Soviet regime's ISOSTAT Institute to help in their development of visual education. His offices in Vienna were searched; some of his material was confiscated and destroyed; and his colleague, and later wife, Marie Reidemeister, warned him against returning to Austria. He fled to Holland. There he was joined by Arntz, and they continued their activities at the Mundaneum Institute in The Hague. The highpoint of their efforts was the 1939 publication of the very successful visual collection *Modern Man in the Making*. In May 1940, when the Nazis invaded Holland, Neurath and Reidemeister fled, with nothing but the clothes they were wearing, from Rotterdam harbor, on an overcrowded lifeboat. When the fuel ran out, they floated until they were picked up by a British destroyer. As enemy aliens they were interned on the Isle of Man and released only in early 1941, with the intervention of philosopher Susan Stebbing. With her help, and the help of G. D. H. Cole and others, the irrepressible Neuraths set up shop again, at Oxford, working on visual statistics, films, and documentaries. He died in December 1945.

References

Alma, Peter. 1930. Beeldstastiek en sociologische grafiek. *Wendlingen* 11:1–18.

———. 1932. Beeldsatistiek. *De 8 en opbouw* 3:189–90.

Arntz, Gerd. 1930. Bewegung in Kunst und Statistik. *A bis Z* (May 8): 30.

Arntz, Gerd, and Kees Broos. 1979. *Symbolen voor onderwijs en statistiek, 1928–1965* [Symbols for education and statistics, 1928–1965]. The Hague: Mart. Spruijt.

Breuille, Jean-Philippe, ed. 1991. *L'Art du XXe siècle: Dictionnaire de peinture et de sculpture*. Paris: Larousse.

Cartwright, Nancy, Jordi Cat, Lola Fleck, and Thomas E. Uebel. 1996. *Otto Neurath: Philosophy between Science and Politics*. Cambridge: Cambridge University Press.

Chaloupek, Gunther. 1990. The Austrian Debate on Economic Calculation in a Socialist Society. *HOPE* 22.4:659–75.

Faludi, Andreas. 1996. Otto Neurath and Planning Theory. In *Encyclopedia and Utopia: The Life and Work of Otto Neurath (1882–1945)*, edited by Elisabeth Nemeth and Friedrich Stadler. Dordrecht: Kluwer.

Galison, P. 1990. Aufbau/Bauhaus: Logical Positivism and Architectural Modernism. *Critical Inquiry* 16 (summer): 709–52.

Hayek, Friedrich, ed. 1935. *Collectivist Economic Planning: Critical Studies on the Possibilities of Socialism*. London: Routledge.

Jansen, Angela. 1996. Isotype and Infographics. In *Encyclopedia and Utopia: The Life and Work of Otto Neurath (1882–1945),* edited by Elisabeth Nemeth and Friedrich Stadler. Dordrecht: Kluwer.

Lavoie, Don. 1985. *Rivalry and Central Planning*. Cambridge: Cambridge University Press.

Leonard, Robert. 1998. Ethics and the Excluded Middle: Karl Menger and Social Science in Interwar Vienna. *Isis* 89.1:1–26.

McGuiness, Brian, ed. 1987. *Unified Science*. Vienna Circle Collection, vol. 19. Dordrecht: Reidel.

Mises, Ludwig von. 1935. Economic Calculation in the Socialist Commonwealth. In *Collectivist Economic Planning: Critical Studies on the Possibilities of Socialism*, edited by Friedrich Hayek. London: Routledge.

Nemeth, Elisabeth, and Friedrich Stadler, eds. 1996. *Encyclopedia and Utopia: The Life and Work of Otto Neurath (1882–1945)*. Vienna Circle Institute Yearbook.

Dordrecht: Kluwer

Neurath, Marie. 1973. 26 September 1924 and After [biographical note on Otto Neurath]. In *Empiricism and Sociology*, by Otto Neurath, edited by Marie Neurath and Robert S. Cohen. Dordrecht: Reidel.

Neurath, Otto. 1910. *Lehrbuch der Volkswirtschaftslehre*. Vienna: Hölder.

———. [1920] 1973. Experiences of Socialization in Bavaria [from a lecture given in 1920 to the Sociological Society of Vienna]. Reprinted in Neurath 1973.

———. [1925] 1973. Gesellschafts- und Wirtschaftsmuseum in Wien. *Österreichische Gemiende-Zeitung* 2.16. Translated as "The Social and Economic Museum in Vienna," in Neurath 1973.

———. [1928] 1973. *Lebensgestaltung und Klassenkampf*. Berlin: E. Laub. Partially translated as "Personal Life and Class Struggle," in Neurath 1973.

———. [1929] 1973. *Wissenschaftliche Weltauffassung: Der Wiener Kreis*. Unsigned; preface signed by Hans Hahn, Otto Neurath, and Rudolf Carnap. Vienna: Artur Wolf. Translated as "The Scientific Conception of the World: The Vienna Circle," in Neurath 1973.

———. [1930] 1983. Wege der wissenschaftlichen Weltauffassung. *Erkenntnis* 2.4:106–25. Translated as "Ways of the Scientific World-Conception," in Neurath 1983.

———. [1931a] 1973. Bildhafte Pädagogil im Gesellschafts- und Wirtschaftsmuseum in Wien. *Museumkunde*, n.s. 3, 3:125–29. Translated as "Visual Education and the Social and Economic Museum in Vienna," in Neurath 1973.

———. [1931b] 1973. Empirische Soziologie: Der wissenschaftliche Gehalt der Geschichte und Nationalökonomie. *Schriften zur wissenschaftlichen Weltauffassung*. Vol. 5. Vienna: Julius Springer. Translated as "Empirical Sociology: The Scientific Content of History and Political Economy," in Neurath 1973.

———. [1931c] 1983. Soziologie im Physikalismus. *Erkenntnis* 2.5–6:393–431. Translated as "Sociology in the Framework of Physicalism," in Neurath 1983.

———. [1933] 1973. Museums of the Future. *Survey Graphic* 22.9:458–63. Reprinted in Neurath 1973.

———. [1935] 1987. Was bedeutet rationale Wirtschaftsbetrachtung? In *Zur Enzyklopaedie der Einheitswissenschaft*, vol. 4, edited by Otto Neurath. Vienna: Gerold & Co. Translated as "What Is Meant by a Rational Economic Theory?" In McGuiness 1987.

———. [1937] 1973. A New Language from Visual Education. *Survey Graphic* 24.1:25–28. Reprinted in Neurath 1973.

———. [1938] 1987. Die neue Enzyklopaedie. In *Zur Enzyklopaedie der Einheitswissenschaft*, vol. 6, edited by Otto Neurath. The Hague: Van Stockum & Zoon. Translated as "The New Encyclopedia," in McGuiness 1987.

———. 1939. *Modern Man in the Making*. New York: Knopf.

———. [1939–40] 1983. The Social Sciences and Unified Science. *Journal of Unified Science (Erkenntnis)* 9:244–48. Reprinted in Neurath 1983.

———. 1944. Foundations of the Social Sciences. In vol. 2 of *International Encyclopedia of Unified Science*. Chicago: University of Chicago Press.

———. [1945] 1973. Visual Education: Humanisation versus Popularisation. Excerpt from unfinished 1945 manuscript, *Empiricism and Sociology*, edited by M. Neurath and R. Cohen, in Neurath 1973.

———. 1973. *Empiricism and Sociology*. Edited by Marie Neurath and Robert S. Cohen. Vienna Circle Collection, vol. 1. Dordrecht: Reidel.

———. 1983. *Philosophical Papers, 1913–1946*. Edited by Robert S. Cohen and Marie Neurath. Vienna Circle Collection, vol. 16. Dordrecht: Reidel.

———. 1991. *Gesammelte bildpädagogische Schriften*. Vienna: Hölder-Pichler-Tempsky.

Neurath, Otto, and A. Schapire-Neurath. 1910. *Lesebuch der Volkswritschaftslehre*. Leipzig: Klinkhart; 2d ed., Leipzig: Glöckner, 1913.

Neurath, Paul. 1996. Otto Neurath (1882–1945)—Life and Work. In *Encyclopedia and Utopia: The Life and Work of Otto Neurath (1882–1945)*, edited by Elisabeth Nemeth and Friedrich Stadler. Dordrecht: Kluwer.

Sandberg, W. J. H. B. 1929. *Het verleden in Egyptische reliëfs: Het heden in statistisch beeld*. Amsterdam.

———. 1931. *Aardrijskundige platen*. Rotterdam: Nijgh & Van Ditmaar.

Sandberg, W. J. H. B., and H. I. C. Jaffé. 1961. *Les Pionniers de notre temps au Stedelijk Museum*. Paris: Editions des Deux Mondes.

Skopec, David. 1996. The Changing Media of Visual Statistics. In *Encyclopedia and Utopia: The Life and Work of Otto Neurath (1882–1945)*, edited by Elisabeth Nemeth and Friedrich Stadler. Dordrecht: Kluwer.

Contributors

Márcia L. Balisciano holds a doctorate in economic history from the London School of Economics. Her research focuses on American economic planning between 1930 and 1950. She currently serves as an adviser to the American Chamber of Commerce in the United Kingdom and is director of the Benjamin Franklin House in London.

William J. Barber is the Andrews Professor of Economics Emeritus at Wesleyan University. He authored *Designs within Disorder: Franklin D. Roosevelt, the Economists, and the Shaping of the American Economy* (1996) and served as the general editor of *The Works of Irving Fisher*, 14 volumes (1997).

Neil De Marchi teaches economics at Duke University; studies consumption, pleasure, and preferences, especially in relation to art, in the seventeenth and eighteenth centuries; and is engaged in a team project to map the evolution of institutions linked to the marketing of paintings during the period 1450 to 1840.

Bertil Fridén has worked on rural industry and the history of political economy. He is presently researching architectural-economic imagination in the Swedish building industry in the twentieth century, at Chalmers University of Technology. He is the head of the Qvarnarp Preservation Centre.

Craufurd D. W. Goodwin is James B. Duke Professor of Economics at Duke University and editor of *HOPE*. He is interested in the relationship between the history of economic thought and the history of art. A recent book by him is *Art and the Market: Roger Fry on Commerce in Art*.

Guido Guerzoni is assistant professor of economic history at Bocconi University in Milan, where he also teaches cultural economics. His research interests include the social and economic history of the Italian Renaissance, the history of collectable goods markets, the history of play, and the economics of art.

Robert J. Leonard is a professor of economics at the University of Quebec at Montreal. He works on the history of twentieth-century economics and its intersection with the histories of science and mathematics. His book, *From Red Vienna to Santa Monica: Von Neumann, Morgenstern, and Social Science, 1925–1960*, is scheduled for publication in 2000 by Cambridge University Press.

Harro Maas is a lecturer in the history and methodology of economics at the economics department of the University of Amsterdam. His main research interest is the development of the industrial mind in nineteenth-century political economy.

Ernest Mathijs is currently finishing a dissertation on frames of reference in contemporary criticism and interpretation. He is a researcher at the Center Leo Apostel of the Free University of Brussels and teaches media ethics at the Erasmus Hogeschool Brussels.

Steven G. Medema is professor of economics at the University of Colorado at Denver. His research interests include law and economics and the economic role of government in the history of economic thought. His most recent books are *Economics and the Law: From Posner to Post Modernism* (with Nicholas Mercuro) and *Lionel Robbins, A History of Economic Thought: The LSE Lectures*, which he edited with Warren J. Samuels.

Bert Mosselmans studied economics and philosophy and recently presented his doctoral dissertation on the economic thought of William Stanley Jevons and its relation to his ethics, logic, and aesthetics. He is an assistant professor of economics in the Department of Business Studies and Public Administration at the Hogeschool Gent and a researcher at the Free University of Brussels.

Zarinés Negrón graduated from Duke University in May 1999 with a bachelor of science degree in economics. She credits her interest and involvement in economics and art (and hence to the 1999 *HOPE* conference) to the Bloomsbury Group and their views of art, production, and psychology. She is currently working in international economic development at the Center for Institutional Reform and the Informal Sector in College Park, Maryland.

Marcia Pointon is Pilkington Professor of History of Art, and Research and Graduate Dean at the University of Manchester. Her most recent books are *Hanging the Head: Portraiture and Social Formation in Eighteenth-Century England* (Yale University Press 1993) and *Strategies for Showing: Women, Possession, and Representation in English Visual Culture 1665–1800* (Oxford University Press 1997), which won the book prize awarded by the Society for Research in the History of Early Modern Women. She is currently working on the display culture of jewels and jewelry in early modern Europe.

Dr. Helen Rees is a part-time lecturer in the School of Art History and Archaeology at the University of Manchester, a visual arts consultant, and a freelance curator of art exhibitions.

Toon Van Houdt is an associate professor of classical studies at the Catholic University of Leuven, Belgium. His scholarly research focuses primarily on the history of economic and ethical thought in early modern Europe. He recently published a facsimile edition, together with a summary in German, of Lessius's "De iustitia et iure" in the Klassiker der Nationalökonomie series.

Hans J. Van Miegroet is an associate professor of art history at Duke University.

Annabel Wharton received her Ph.D. from the Courtauld Institute, University of London. As professor of art history at Duke University she teaches and publishes in the fields of Byzantine art and late antique urbanism. At present she is completing, with the support of a Graham Foundation Grant, a book on Hilton hotels, the Cold War, and the commoditization of space.

Michael V. White is senior lecturer in the economics department at Monash University in Clayton, Australia. His published work has principally been concerned with the political economy of W. S. Jevons.

Sara Zablotney graduated in May 1999 with a bachelor of arts degree in economics and history from Duke University, where she studied under Craufurd Goodwin and Neil De Marchi. She is currently a first-year law student at New York University.

Index